The
Helm Information
Literary Sources
& Documents
Series

General Editor

Graham Clarke

THE
AMERICAN
CIVIL WAR

LITERARY SOURCES
&
DOCUMENTS

1. Abraham Lincoln, 27th February 1860,
Photograph by Mathew Brady.

THE AMERICAN CIVIL WAR

LITERARY SOURCES & DOCUMENTS

Edited and with an Introduction by
Jon Roper

Volume I
Black and White

HELM INFORMATION

Selection and editorial matter
© 2000 Helm Information Ltd
The Banks,
Mountfield,
near Robertsbridge,
East Sussex TN32 5JY,
U.K.

ISBN 1-873403-12-7

A CIP catalogue record for this book
is available from the British Library.

Frontispiece: Abraham Lincoln, 27th February 1860.

Printed on neutral-sized ('acid-free') paper and
bound by MPG Books Ltd., Bodmin, Cornwall

072501-33000 D 2/3

Contents

VOLUME I
Black and White

I. Introduction: Contextualising Slavery

II. Nat Turner's Revolt

III. The Abolitionist Mission

IV. The Rights of the States

V. Stepping to Secession: 1856–1861

VI. Schism

VII. John Brown's Raid at Harper's Ferry: 1859

VIII. The House Divides

IX. Union and Confederacy: 1861

VOLUME II
Blue and Gray

XII. 1863: Gettysburg

XIII. 1864: The Wilderness Campaign to Sherman's March

XIV. 1865: Appomattox

XV. The Assassination of Abraham Lincoln

VOLUME III
Shadows and Shades

XVI. The End of the Confederacy

XVII. Heard Around the World

XVIII. Literary Reactions

XIX. Memoirs

List of Illustrations

Volume I

Volume II

Volume III

Volume I:
Black and White

General Editor's Preface

Literary Sources & Documents is, as its title suggests, a series concerned with offering the reader a substantial and wide-ranging body of significant source material in relation to a specific theme, period, event, or movement of cultural and historical importance. In so doing, these sources make accessible a mass of often disparate material invariably scattered over a wide series of disciplines or simply unavailable in many library collections. Each set is thus a research tool—offering an overview of its subject whilst allowing close reading of original and important texts basic to a needful sense of the subject in both its specific and general contexts.

Although each title in the *Literary Sources & Documents Series* follows this essential aim, the approach and structure of each set differs according to its subject. All, however, are characterized by the range and *bulk* of material included as a way of entering areas of often baffling complexity and plurality. They do not claim to be exhaustive, but they are representative of the material offered, just as, in their individual contents and structures, they allow the reader to find a series of individual paths through a plethora of material to be consulted.

Each 'source' and 'document' has its own brief introduction which places it in context, further adding to a distinct editorial apparatus which underscores each set as a research tool. A substantial introduction(s) offers a critical overview of the subject, while bibliographies, chronologies and illustrations extend the perspectives and further guide the reader to the critical and other material beyond the immediate scope of the volumes.

Thus it is hoped that each set will offer a range of responses and a variety of texts—opening up the subject in as many ways as possible and revealing the connections between texts, writers and periods as well as allowing the reader to establish patterns of response and new connections through access to a substantial and diverse body of material.

As the series develops, so the sets will extend and relate to each other—offering a widening field of reference and range of relevant material: a significant fund of sources and documents which, in their relative significance, underline E. M. Forster's dictum to 'only connect'—as much in the historical and cultural sense, as in one's own reading and research.

Graham Clarke
General Editor
University of Kent at Canterbury

Introduction

"The war is not even over before it is transformed into a hundred thousand printed pages and set before the tired palates of the history hungry as the latest delicacy."

Friedrich Nietzsche[1]

I

So it is with America's Civil War. It defines nineteenth-century American history. The first half of that century is a prelude to the main event, building to a crescendo that culminated in the secession crisis, and the inexorable steps towards conflict. The war is both catalyst and catharsis. It punctuates the historical experience of democracy in America. Before it happened, the creation of the United States as a democratic republic was an experiment. Afterwards it could be presented as the fulfilment of a providential destiny. In 1776, in writing the Declaration of Independence (see Document 1), Thomas Jefferson accepted the ideal of equality as a self-evident truth, and suggested that among an individual's "certain unalienable rights" were "Life, Liberty and the pursuit of Happiness". Before the war, such political ideas and moral principles were conditional: while slavery existed, it made America's experience of democracy provisional. National political life would become haunted by the question: how could a democratic community tolerate this most illiberal of institutions in its Southern States? Slaves were by status unequal and by definition unfree. The war was fought in part to resolve that dilemma. Reconstruction demonstrated, however, that changing habits of the mind still proved far more difficult than amending the Constitution itself. So the legacy of the controversies which led to war rumbled on after it. The South's surrender did not end the matter: racism remained the fundamental fault-line that defined the contours of the American polity. All this suggests that to understand the war means to engage mentally with the protean forces which led to its outbreak, which sustained both North and South through four years of conflict, and which continued to impact upon American politics, culture and society in its aftermath. The documents in this collection thus contextualise the war. They focus on the events, the debates and the arguments which conspired to create the circumstance of war; they chart the course of the conflict; and they provide insights into how the war was interpreted in its aftermath—how Americans and others made sense of what had occurred.

In many ways, it is a familiar story. The narrative has been told and re-told. As

Nietzsche's comment implies, the Civil War, in common with other wars, has been transmuted into an historical battleground of critical analysis and revisionist argument. In seeking perspectives on the war these documents juxtapose the expected with the less well known in an attempt to bring together in one collection not simply those texts most often sought and cited, but also others which illuminate the subject and the sub-text of the war itself. It follows that the three volumes are arranged in roughly chronological order, beginning with documents which set the scene.

The first volume, *Black and White*, establishes the basis of the argument between North and South, between slave-holders and Abolitionists, between those to whom state sovereignty was non-negotiable, and those who looked to the federal government to define the limits of law and liberty within the United States. Volume two, *Blue and Gray*, is a study of the American Republic in time of war, as North and South struggle through force of arms to resolve those issues which had led to political, cultural and social division. The third volume, *Shadows and Shades*, examines some critical moments during and in the aftermath of the conflict, looking at contemporary documents and also memoirs written in a more tranquil age. It examines, too, the path of reconstruction, not simply in its political aspect, but also in terms of the South's re-invention of its experience as "the Lost Cause". For as the war was mediated through popular culture as well as through history, then image became everything: indeed the retrieval of objectivity in such a contested and turbulent past might have proved an increasingly difficult task.

In re-constructing the narrative which contextualises these documents, then, it is possible to draw upon a multiplicity of different sources and interpretations. To bring some organisational coherence to the subject, however, this introduction follows broadly the path taken by James McPherson in his comprehensive and accessible work, *Battle Cry of Freedom*.[2] At the same time, it attempts to use the documents as vignettes which illuminate aspects of the complex and multi-faceted debates, arguments and events which eventually conspired to cause the Civil War.

If the Declaration of Independence became the lodestar of those who willed the end of slavery, so the federal Constitution (Document 2) is a key text in any understanding of the political arguments that dominated the ante-bellum period. The bitter national debate, which became more and more vituperative as political consensus broke down in the years before the outbreak of the Civil War, focussed upon interpretations of this Constitution, influenced by differing views on the issue of slavery. The Philadelphia Convention in 1787 created a multi-layered system of government, a framework which had to prove flexible enough to accommodate different visions of the nature of the federal design. The Constitution had been ratified with difficulty. Suspicions remained. As Marcus Cunliffe has suggested:

> the 1787 Constitution mapped out a broad division of jurisdictions, allotting primary powers to the federal government in areas like foreign policy. But the frontier between national and state power was unavoidably indistinct.[3]

The early years of the Republic were marked by controversies over the interpretation of the document. What was permissible, and what went against the spirit of the Founder's intentions? Should a broad-brush approach permit the Federal Government to act as the creative political and economic motor of the Republic? Or should a concern for the detail of the document influence the relationship between the federal centre and its satellite states? When the controversy arose over whether to charter a national bank, George Washington, as president, decided to support Alexander Hamilton's idea of a broad constructionist approach, rather than Thomas Jefferson's more restricted vision of adherence solely to powers enumerated in the Constitution. But that was not an end to the matter. It merely served to draw attention to the fact that political argument would continue on the borders drawn between state sovereignty and federal power. And this would become the context for the debate over slavery.

The Constitution was not colour-blind. In fact, in dealing with the question of apportionment—how many representatives each state should elect to congress, and how many votes each state should have in the presidential electoral college—the Philadelphia Convention had had to confront the issue of slavery head on. In *Federalist 54* (Document 3) the compromise which corrupted the Constitution was rationalised and explained. Southern States were to be effectively over-represented in the Federal Government by a factor of three-fifths, because they could count their slave populations for the purpose of calculating apportionment. This was right because

> the federal Constitution . . . decides with great propriety on the case of our slaves, when it views them in the mixed character of persons and of property. This is in fact their true character.

And yet, it was an argument that was difficult to sustain. For, later, *Federalist 54* suggests that the way forward is for

> the case of the slaves be considered, as it is in truth, a peculiar one. Let the compromising expedient of the Constitution be mutually adopted, which regards them as inhabitants, but as debased by servitude below the equal level of free inhabitants; which regards the *slave* as divested of two-fifths of the *man*.

Circumlocutions avoided enshrining the word "slave" in the document, but this, in effect, was the Constitution's "smoking gun". And as Abolitionists took up the cause, it became self-evident that this clause which privileged the Southern States would not be re-written without a fight.

The foremost architects of American independence and nationalism—Thomas Jefferson, who wrote the Declaration of Independence, George Washington who won the revolutionary war against Britain's imperial power, and James Madison, whose subtlety of political thought influenced the design of the federal Constitution—all came from Virginia: a slave state. In his will, Washington freed his slaves; in his life, Jefferson was at least humane in his treatment of his, so too was Madison. Indeed, one of his slaves, Paul Jennings, thought that

> Mr. Madison . . . was one of the best men that ever lived. I never saw him in a passion, and never knew him to strike a slave, although he had over one hundred; neither would he allow an overseer to do it.[4]

This, then is a portrait of the slave-owner as paternalist: but not all were as enlightened as Washington, Jefferson or Madison.

So these members of the Virginian élite, each of whom would serve as president of the United States, thus tolerated slavery, excused it, and rationalised it: whatever their ultimate views on the "peculiar institution", they accepted that it was part of their culture, and left it to the future to resolve the antagonisms it caused. And yet, views on slavery would be shaped by contemporary attitudes towards racial difference. Thus Jefferson, in his *Notes on the State of Virginia* (Document 4) was prepared to argue in favour of his "suspicion" that "the blacks . . . are inferior to the whites in the endowments of body an"d mind", and this represented "a powerful obstacle to the emancipation of these people". This form of casuistry can be understood only as a product of the intellectual climate of the times. But it is an example of the way in which the issue of race contextualises the problem of slavery: what might have happened after emancipation had the slaves been white?

In 1776, Jefferson had asserted that "all men are born equal" and that among other unalienable rights, they shared the right to liberty. To deny then explicitly that such sentiments applied to slaves involved an intellectual sleight of hand. Yet acceptance of the institution of slavery was necessary, at some level, to cajole the Southern States into accepting the advantages of joining a federal republic. The debates which then arose over the technicalities of constitutional interpretation nevertheless could not detract attention from the more emotive, and ultimately more compelling arguments over the morality of the South's "peculiar institution". To those who pressed for the abolition of both slavery and the slave trade in the early years of the republic, the case could be presented as a statement of principle. Thus, Jonathan Edwards, a pastor who shared an illustrious name, (his namesake had indeed inspired America's "Great Awakening" in the eighteenth century) delivered a sermon in 1791 (Document 5). Was slavery justified by racism?

> Their colour indeed is different from ours. But does this give us a right to enslave them? . . . if a black complexion subject a nation or an individual to slavery, where shall slavery begin? Or where shall it end?

It was a direct challenge to those who owned slaves. Furthermore,

> it is a principle, the truth of which hath in this country been generally if not universally acknowleged, ever since the commencment of the late war, that all men are born equally free. If this is true, the Africans are by nature equally entitled to freedom as we are; and therefore we have no more right to enslave, or to afford aid to enslave them, than they have to do the same to us.

Edwards proceeded then to demolish arguments for slavery which rested on Biblical interpretation, and made his case against the practice rest on the sound foundation of Christian conscience. In those terms he was right.

His sermon contributed to the growing sentiment within another Protestant revivalist movement—the Second Great Awakening—which was influential, particularly in the North, during the early part of the nineteenth century. Slavery became a natural target for evangelists who saw the need for moral and cultural reformation. As McPherson points out, for them

> the most heinous social sin was slavery. All people were equal in God's sight; the souls of black folks were as valuable as those of whites; for one of God's children to enslave another was a violation of the Higher Law, even if it was sanctioned by the Constitution.[5]

But that was still the point. The Constitution itself incorporated a compromise which effectively undercut the argument that slaves were worthy of equal respect and had equal rights under its laws. For slave-holders, moreover, there was no contest in an argument that invited a choice between conscience and Constitution.

Preservation of the Union became the issue which more than any other tested the political ingenuity of a generation of the nation's leaders. In 1820, North and South again compromised over the issue of slavery. In the controversy surrounding the admission of Missouri to the Union, Congress, in an agreement engineered by Henry Clay, fixed the boundary which was to divide slave states and free-soil states. The Missouri Compromise effectively created a border between two sections of the United States. South of a line of latitude slavery was allowed; north of that line, it was prohibited. But the politics of the compass point only went so far: the question which remained unresolved, was what would happen when the nation expanded to the west? For the moment, however, the South had preserved its position within the Union. And it too had God on its side.

In 1822, Baptists in South Carolina held a convention at which the Biblical justification for slave ownership was articulated as a riposte to the views of those like Jonathan Edwards who had argued the case against from an equally principled Christian perspective. As Richard Furman put it (Document 6):

> the right of holding slaves is clearly established by the Holy Scriptures, both by precept and example. . . . In proving this subject justifiable by Scriptural authority, its morality is also proved; for the divine Law never sanctions immoral actions.

The mistake of those who opposed the "peculiar institution" was to conflate slavery and cruelty, thus finding a just cause for moral outrage. Furman, instead, presented slavery as, on the whole, a beneficent welfare system in which the master looked after his property, and reciprocal obligations of duty and trust characterised the master–slave relationship. Such romanticised portraits, coupled with both Old and New Testament quotations, justified the maintenance of the institution upon which Southern society and culture was based. The Baptists of South Carolina had met to discuss, among other things, the failure of a potential slave rebellion in the State. At that time, there was a self-congratulatory, not to say complacent, attitude towards such an event. Delegates at the Convention were convinced that such an insurrection would have been unsustainable and ill-supported. Furthermore, although

> in some parts of our Union there are Citizens, who favour the idea of general emancipation; yet, were they to see slaves in our Country, in arms, wading through blood and carnage to effect their purpose, they would do what both their duty and interest would require; unite under the government with their fellow citizens at large to suppress the rebellion, and bring the authors of it to condign punishment.

9

The prospects of successful revolts were slim.

During the first fifty years of its existence, the history of the United States of America was punctuated by such polemics on the subject of slavery. The issue became a preoccupation of national and sectional politics, and increasingly defined Southern culture both to itself and to the wider world. While there were those in the South who were and would remain blind to the moral bankruptcy of their "peculiar institution", those from elsewhere, either within the United States or from abroad, observed the steady erosion of the South's democratic credibility. In 1831, Gustave de Beaumont arrived in the United States from France, and travelled extensively around the country, including a tour of the South. He subsequently published a novel, *Marie ou L'Esclavage aux Etats-Unis*, which was inspired by his antipathy towards slavery. And his travelling companion, Alexis de Tocqueville, the foremost and most formidable analyst of *Democracy in America*, was equally trenchant in his criticism.

Tocqueville argued (Document 7) that the South was trying to stem the irresistible tide of contemporary history, which had seen revolutions fought—not least in France—in the name of liberty and equality. Democracy was the way of the future: the South resisted at its peril. Thus, "slavery, now confined to a single tract of the civilized earth, attacked by Christianity as unjust and political economy as prejudicial, and now contrasted with democratic liberty and the intelligence of our age, cannot survive." Moreover, in contrast to the complacency of those Southern Baptists who believed that the possibility of a slave revolt was remote, Tocqueville predicted, "if liberty be refused to the Negroes of the South, they will in the end forcibly seize it for themselves": an assessment borne out by events which occurred during his visit to the United States.

II

In 1831, in Virginia, Nat Turner flouted conventional Southern wisdom. In so doing he turned the spectre of slave rebellion into a real and frightening *cause célèbre*. In Massachusetts, William Lloyd Garrison, who had founded his journal, *The Liberator*, earlier that year to promote the cause of abolition, saw Turner's revolt as justification of his belief that only immediate emancipation could prevent further outbreaks of violence (Document 8). Turner was a portent of things to come: in Old Testament language Garrison argued that unless the South repented the sin of slavery, it would suffer the "vengeance of Heaven". The revolt thus took on an immediate and symbolic significance.

What began as a spontaneous uprising by Turner and a handful of followers, gathered momentum as it spread. Moving among the farms of Southampton County, Turner was joined by over eighty slaves, indiscriminately killing white families until the state militia regained control of the situation. Turner—naturally—was found guilty of the massacre of at least fifty-five people, motivated by, as he confessed, mystical visions and conversations with spirits (Document 9). In one such revelation he had seen "white spirits and black spirits in battle, and the sun was darkened—the thunder rolled in the heavens, and blood flowed in streams". Such apocalyptic language contrasted sharply with the emotive, yet legalistic and patronising judgement of the court. Nat Turner was

> convicted of plotting in cold blood, the indiscriminate destruction of men, of helpless women, and of infant children. The evidence before us leaves not a shadow of doubt, but that your hands were often imbrued in the blood of the innocent; and your own confession tells us that they were stained with the blood of a master, in your own language, "too indulgent".

There is a hint of self-righteousness in that verdict. This slave had been well-treated: what right had he to turn on his master, and rebel against the institution into which he had been born? As the correspondence between the Governors of Virginia and Georgia shows (Document 10), the effects of his actions were to make the South even more suspicious of the activities of Northern Abolitionists, and to persuade states like Virginia to enact more stringent laws in an attempt to control the behaviour of their slaves.

III

Whereas Nat Turner's revolt was an elemental reaction against an institution that itself was maintained upon the twin bases of fear and violence, other individuals, like David Walker, who had escaped north to Boston, became part of that movement which progressively and aggressively kept up a propaganda war against Southern slavery. His was an influential voice, not least because, as a member of the African–American community, his writings were aimed at the slaves themselves. The incendiary impact of such a pamphleteer—like that of Tom Paine at the time of the American revolution—was sufficient for his work to be banned in the South, and for Walker's early death to be surrounded with suspicion of unnatural cause. But his polemical attack on slavery (Document 11) points to a radical consciousness which shows that Abolitionism was not simply the preserve of well-meaning enlightened white liberals. Women too—Angelina Grimké as an outstanding example—understood that slavery threatened not simply the moral fabric of society, but had an impact too upon their own status, notably in the South itself (Document 12). Here, as Hugh Brogan points out,

> white women had to be denied education and political rights, so that no challenge could be made to the supremacy of the white male: one challenge might breed another, and if men once conceded that they had no right to tyrannize over women, what right could they claim to tyrannize over slaves?[6]

Nineteenth-century radicalism would thus embrace not simply the cause of civil rights for African–Americans held in slavery, but also, by extension, the demand for increased political representation and participation for women. It was thus no accident that many leading Abolitionists were women.

Angelina Grimké, like many Abolitionists, came from a Quaker community. And by the 1830s, as the contemporary historian George Bancroft noted,

> there is fast rising in New England a moral Democracy in harmony with Christianity . . . in harmony with the progress of Civilization. Democracy is practical Christianity.[7]

Boston was an important hub of abolitionism, but in 1833, the focus of activity shifted to Philadelphia: symbolically to the city where the Constitution itself had been written. It was there that William Lloyd Garrison founded the American Anti-Slavery society. He and his supporters believed that slavery was illegal: if it was not unconstitutional, then certainly it ran counter to the claims of natural justice. Yet in its *Declaration of Sentiments* (Document 13), the Society was not prepared to call for the use of federal power to over-rule the sovereignty of individual states. Congress could not intervene in the internal affairs of a state. It could act only to suppress the domestic slave trade, where its jurisdiction could presumably hold sway under the Constitution's inter-state commerce clauses. The society, however, did appeal to the other principal document of the nation's founding period in order to make its case:

> with entire confidence in the overruling justice of God, we plant ourselves upon the Declaration of our Independence and the truths of Divine Revelation, as upon the everlasting Rock.

Seven years later, the society had over a quarter of a million members.

For Abolitionists the price of liberty indeed became eternal vigilance. They were always on the lookout for issues, events, circumstances which might be exploited to dramatise the iniquities and anomalies that would inevitably arise as long as the nation remained half-slave and half-free. The courts were a potentially creative theatre for the debate over slavery to be joined, and the incident of the Spanish ship, *Amistad*, taken over by its "cargo" of African slaves and subsequently captured by the United States Navy, became significant, not least because it allowed John Quincy Adams, the former president, to argue the case before the Supreme Court. Justice Joseph Story, who was, like Adams, from Massachussetts, and was himself a former member of Congress before his appointment to the Supreme Court in 1811, set the Africans free on appeal (Document 14). Story, who was also on the law faculty at Harvard, was a notable constitutional scholar: in 1833 he published his *Commentaries on the Constitution of the U.S.* Yet such was the emotive power of the *Amistad* case that arid constitutional wrangling was less important than the fact that Story's decision created the ingredients for a fable that could be re-told: one hundred and fifty years later it became a defining metaphor through which Hollywood—in Steven Spielberg's movie—would imaginatively recall a step on the long journey towards freedom and the achievement of civil rights.

Despite such successes as the *Amistad* decision, the institution of slavery was so woven into the fabric of Southern society, that it was impossible there to achieve progress towards liberty through the courts. The only option open to a slave wishing to escape from slavery was to escape from the South. Those who were successful became important symbols for the abolitionist cause, none more than Frederick

Douglass. Through his public speaking, and through the publication of his autobiography, Douglass was able to use his experience of the "peculiar institution" as a way of exposing its impact on those who suffered under it. His personal testimony appeared as a powerful authentication of abolitionist arguments (Document 15). As Wendell Phillips wrote in his introduction to Douglass's narrative:

> in reading your life, no one can say that we have unfairly picked out some rare specimens of cruelty. We know that the bitter drops, which even you have drained from the cup, are no incidental aggravations, no individual ills, but such as mingle always and necessarily in the lot of every slave. They are the essential ingredients, not the occasional results, of the system.

Frederick Douglass's memoirs were vital to the abolitionist effort to keep the issue of Southern slavery in the forefront of Northern political and social debate and discussion.

To win freedom, Douglass became a fugitive from Southern law. But what happened if a slave who made no attempt at escape was transported across a state line where different legal provisions existed? Defining and redefining the relationship between master and slave, and the nature of that relationship in slave-holding states and in free states, was a matter of legal debate and argument. To take but one example from 1845: in Ohio, Salmon Chase, who was later to become Chief Justice of the Supreme Court, pursued an issue of racial justice through the courts. He lost, but his supporters were prepared to count it as a victory that his advocacy changed a judge's mind, setting a precedent for the future, even if the case in which this occurred was decided still against the interests of a slave (Document 16).

Samuel Watson, a slave in transit through Ohio, a free state, was temporarily separated from his master. Had he thus technically become free? In order to reclaim his "property", his master had to allow his slave a day in court. Although Chase could not gain Watson's freedom, in his summary of his decision the judge made a significant concession, admitting that

> the relation of master and slave is strictly territorial. If the master take his slave beyond the influence of the laws which create the relation, it fails—there is nothing to support it, and they stand as man to man.

Chase had argued this very point in court in 1837. Now he would hear,

> the principle which, when you first asserted it, was pronounced a mere chimera of fanaticism, proclaimed in the adjudication of the case of Watson, as the established law of the State,

even though in that case it proved insufficient to gain freedom for a slave. Yet Abolitionists found encouragement from small victories which might set large precedents for future legal battles. Changing hearts and minds was a tortuous process, but they were convinced that they maintained the moral high-ground. As Chase himself put it:

> I maintain that the Declaration of Independence and the Constitution of the United

States, are the expressions of the anti-slavery sentiment of an anti-slavery people.

If that was right, then the weight of constitutional authority would ultimately side against those who maintained faith in the "peculiar institution".

And yet, as if in riposte to Chase and his abolitionist friends, in 1850 the United States Congress passed the Fugitive Slave Law, a successor to the act of 1793 (under which the case of Watson had been heard). The new law marked a turning point in the coming crisis of the Civil War. It required that escaped slaves be returned into slavery, even if they had managed to find their way to free soil, and was part of the complex negotiations which took place as the United States expanded westwards. The genius of the federal system was that it allowed new territories to be organized as states, which might then join the Federal Union. But with the creation of each new state, Americans had to confront the dilemma at the heart of their constitution. Would they permit the extension of slavery? It was a critical decision. The balance of forces in the Federal Senate was a fine one: there slave states and free-soil states counter-balanced one another, voting as notionally equal blocks. The compromise which persisted for some time was to admit states in pairs—one slave, one free—to maintain this equilibrium. But the nature of such an agreement was merely to postpone confrontation rather than to tackle the broader issues which the existence of slavery would repeatedly force the nation to consider.

In 1850 the threat to the republic occurred again as the result of potential territorial expansion: this time the proposed admission to the Union of California and New Mexico as free-soil states. By this time, politicians were accustomed to tortuous negotiation through such difficulties: the architect of agreement once more was Henry Clay. Yet whereas the Missouri Compromise had lasted for thirty years, now the settlement would hold for a little over a decade. As James McPherson observes, the 1850 Compromise

> was not really a compromise in which all parties conceded part of what they wanted, but a series of separately enacted measures each of which became law with a majority of congressmen from one section voting against a majority of those from another.

It indeed "averted a grave crisis. But hindsight makes clear that it only postponed the trauma."[8]

From the perspective of the South, Congressional endorsement of the Fugitive Slave Law was a rare instance when the Federal Government appeared to act in its interests. It appeared as a set-back for the anti-slavery movement—how, for example, would Frederick Douglass have managed under such circumstances? And yet it led to such moral outrage among some Abolitionists that it inspired one, Harriet Beecher Stowe to write *Uncle Tom's Cabin*. This was without doubt the single most effective piece of abolitionist propaganda produced during the ante-bellum period. As McPherson remarks, Stowe "aimed the novel at the evangelical conscience of the North. And she hit her mark."[9] And even Southerners could not ignore it: there was high demand for copies of *Uncle Tom's Cabin* there, despite attempts to ban it. Within a year it had sold 300,000 copies in the United States, and it would became an international best seller as well: revealing an image of the "peculiar institution" to a world-wide readership.

To win support, Abolitionists needed to represent slavery as a battle between good and evil, a dramatic narrative being played out in a section of the United States, where every slave-owner was a tyrant, every slave a victim, and all were brutalised by an institution that remained at odds with the values of Christianity, democracy, civilisation and social justice. It was a story which had to be told in stark terms: indeed the arguments were black and white. This, then, was the climate of opinion which produced *Uncle Tom's Cabin*. It was brilliant advocacy through literature. As Harriet Beecher Stowe wrote (Document 17):

> the object of these sketches is to awaken sympathy and feeling for the African race, as they exist among us; to show their wrongs and sorrows, under a system so necessarily cruel and unjust as to defeat and do away with the good effects of all that can be attempted for them, by their best friends, under it.

The Fugitive Slave Law was the catalyst for the work. In her "concluding remarks" to the book, Stowe admitted that, after that legislation, when she heard "Christian and humane people" debating whether they had a duty to return fugitives to slavery or to follow their more enlightened consciences, she concluded that such

> Christians cannot know what slavery is; if they did, such a question could never be open for discussion. And from this arose a desire to exhibit it in a *living dramatic reality*.

The power and influence of the book represented an unprecedented achievement: *Uncle Tom's Cabin* presented an image of slavery which became established in popular imagination so forcefully that those who tried to defend the South's "peculiar institution" could not dislodge it.

IV

For the first half of the nineteenth century, therefore, the South tried to preserve its political position within the United States: demanding that outsiders did not interfere in its social, economic and cultural traditions, and that the federal whole respected its right to be different: to hold slaves. It might have managed in that attempt, had it not been faced with the dynamic of expansionism, for the other drama of contemporary American history lies in the winning of the West. Would slavery too expand, or would it be encircled? If free-soil states outnumbered slave states, the South's influence in federal politics would be increasingly eroded: and it could ignore the moral argument against the "peculiar institution" only as long as it retained the power within the Federal Government to resist any attempts to intervene in its internal politics. So the issue of states' rights—belief in the absolute autonomy of individual states in areas where the Federal Government threatened to expand its authority—became the fulcrum on which the South's constitutional defence of slavery turned. Equally, Northerners were prepared to concede the argument up to the point where the South threatened secession, in the hope of preserving the Union. Thus it was that politicians from both sides sought compromise, even though their efforts became more and more strained as time went by.

When James Madison died in 1836, the freedom of one of his slaves, Paul Jennings, was bought by Daniel Webster for $120. Jennings paid off his debt by working for Webster for a wage of $8 a month. In that same year, Webster ran for the presidency as one of three Whig party candidates, but was supported only by Massachussetts, the state which he represented in the Federal Senate. The universe of federal politics was powerful but small—a world in which a Northerner who aspired to the executive might make a gesture of help to the slave of a Southerner, and a former president himself. Throughout his twenty-five years in the Senate, moreover, Webster was struggling with Madison's legacy: a Constitution under which states' rights clashed with Federal authority, never so directly as over the issue of slavery.

In the debates over the 1850 Compromise, Webster made an important speech—on March 7th—in which he argued against the idea of Southern secession yet attempted to rally Northern support in favour of a stricter law to deal with the issue of fugitive slaves. He began with a sentiment that became famous: "I wish to speak to-day, not as a Massachussetts man, nor as a Northern man but as an American". And he continued with the equally well-known plea: "I speak to-day for the preservation of the Union. Hear me for my cause".[10] For Webster, strengthening the law dealing with fugitive slaves was a concession that was worth while to keep the South in the Union. Four months later he became secretary of state in Millard Fillmore's administration, with responsibility for enforcing the Fugitive Slave Act. His speech and his actions led anti-slavers, who had previously supported him, to break with him, and the Whig party also became irretrievably divided. Yet for Webster, the preservation of Madison's vision: a federal republic of the United States, was his over-riding philosophical commitment and political goal.

He had said as much twenty years before. When the South, outraged by the Tariff Act of 1828, threatened Federal authority with the doctrine of nullification, (proposed by John Calhoun as a substitute for full-scale Southern secession), Webster had intervened in the debate (Document 18). His concern was not about slavery. Rather it revolved around where the South's stand would take it in defiance of the Federal Government.

> When my eyes shall be turned to behold for the last time the sun in heaven, may I not see him shining on the broken and dishonored fragments of a once glorious Union; on states dissevered, discordant, belligerent; on a land rent with civil feuds, or drenched, it may be, in fraternal blood!

Webster died in 1852, missing his apocalyptic vision by ten years. He remained of that generation that tried to make sense of an increasingly untenable political situation and who thus lived through repeated crisis and compromise as the South stubbornly asserted the doctrine of states' rights in the face of Federal measures it saw as calculated to undermine its economy, and thus its social order.

A major problem for the South was that its aggressive defence of an agrarian economy sustained by slavery clashed with the North's equally energetic attempts to industrialise. Domestic industries benefited from protective tariffs against overseas competition, but if that led to economic warfare, then the South, which relied on the export of a primary product—cotton—for its wealth, would be disproportionately at risk. Such economic sectionalism fuelled regional conflict. In the controversy over the introduction of tariffs, therefore, it was the Southern states, not least South Carolina, which took the lead in questioning the power of the Federal Government to enact such legislation. In November 1832, and ignoring the arguments of those who, like Daniel Webster, saw where the confrontation might end, South Carolina adopted an Ordinance of Nullification, challenging the legitimacy of the tariff and by implication of Federal laws in general. In response, Andrew Jackson issued a Presidential Proclamation to the people of the state (Document 19).

"If this doctrine had been established at an earlier day, the Union would have been dissolved in its infancy." Jackson was right in seeing that to concede the principle of nullification woul0d be to make Federal authority rest upon the whim of a capricious minority:

> you must perceive that the crisis your conduct presents at this day would recur whenever any law of the United States displeased any of the States, and that we should soon cease to be a nation.

Southerners in Congress had threatened nullification in an attempt to make the federal government reduce the burden of the tariff. South Carolina's action went further. For Jackson, it amounted to treason. He expressed his "determination to execute the laws, to preserve the Union by all constitutional means, to arrest, if possible, by moderate measures the necessity of a recourse to force". But the Union came first: as the crisis continued, he also threatened to collect forcibly the duties owed to the federal government from South Carolina, and to arrest and hang the nullification leaders, gaining authority from Congress in support of such violence in the so-called "Force Act" passed in 1833. With the United States on the brink of such civil war, Henry Clay—again—negotiated the compromise on the tariff issue which brought about a gradual reduction in the rates demanded by the federal government. Yet South Carolina's defiance demonstrated that the vigorous assertion of states' rights against Federal authority, or conversely the determination of the national government to assert its power against the perceived interests of certain states, did not simply end in constitutional deadlock. It threatened war.

When Jackson was first elected in 1828, his vice-president was from South Carolina: John Calhoun. He was the product of that particular and peculiar cultural and social environment of the ante-bellum South and, as a politician and political theorist, he became the foremost advocate for the preservation of the southern way of life within the Union. He provided intellectual respectability for sectional priorities in works of political theory such as his *Disquisition on Government* and the *Discourse on the Constitution and Government of the United States* (both published posthumously). Calhoun's great contribution to the southern cause lay not only in his writing, but also in his speeches: having broken with Jackson over the tariff issue, he resigned the vice-presidency and, apart from another brief spell in the executive branch of government, for the remainder of his life he spoke for the South as a representative of his home state in the Federal Senate.

In 1849, on the eve of the crisis that was to be triggered by western expansion, Calhoun drafted the "Address of the Southern Delegates in Congress to their Constituents", signed by representatives from twelve states (Document 20). Here, the history of Southern grievances as to how the region had been treated within the Union were rehearsed. The South thus "had no cause to complain prior to the year 1819" but the trouble had started with the controversy over the admission of Missouri to the Union. If the Missouri Compromise had clearly defined which states were, at that time, by virtue of their geography, slave-holding and which were free-soil, it had also clearly defined a hope for fugitive slaves that by escaping north they might become free. As anti-slavery sentiment grew in the North, the impact of the Fugitive Slave Law as a measure whereby Southerners might protect their "property" had been diluted. "Systematic agitation" by Abolitionists from about 1835 had been aimed to undermine further that which Southerners regarded as their "domestic institution". Now, the prospect of western expansion threatened the South once more. If territories in the west were established as free-soil, then Southerners could not take their slaves with them if they emigrated there. And yet, the Address argued, Southern states, as equal partners in the enterprise of Union, had equal rights in deciding on the governance of such territories: indeed Southern troops had been prominent in the war with Mexico that had led to the opening up of the west for American expansionism.

With its "peculiar institution" under attack, its position within the Union under threat, and little prospect that things would improve, the only option was for the South to unite in resistance to what it saw as a sustained and co-ordinated attack on its way of life. By mid-century, then, as the Address makes clear, North and South had emerged as two distinct sections of the country, at loggerheads over the issue of slavery, and with the South feeling increasingly embittered, oppressed and at the same time vulnerable: believing that it would be forced to abandon slavery if it was to stay within the Union. Through united action it might continue to press its case. Indeed, during 1849, there was a call for a convention of slave-holding states "to devise and adopt some mode of resistance to northern aggression".[11] But as it increasingly defined itself as separate but equal within the Union, so battle-lines were effectively being drawn for the time when its position as part of the United States became ultimately untenable.

V

In private, Calhoun had given up. In February 1850, he confessed that the South "cannot with safety remain in the Union . . . and there is little or no prospect of any change for the better."[12] But in his last formal speech to the United States Senate, during the 1850 Compromise debate, he argued once more—eloquently—for the Southern cause (Document 21). As McPherson writes,

> three days before Webster's speech, the dying Calhoun gave his valedictory to the nation. Too weak to speak for himself, the gaunt Carolinian sat wrapped in flannels while James Mason of Virginia read his speech to the Senate. Calhoun's prophecies of doom were reflected in the piercing eyes that stared from deep sockets within the shroud.[13]

It is a compelling vignette which becomes an allegory for the United States as it began stepping towards the secession crisis: the final stage of the long journey into civil war.

The fundamental problem remained. If the American Republic was based upon principles of equality and the individual's right to liberty, how could it tolerate slavery as an institution in its Southern States? Abolitionists continued to press their case. While Americans might celebrate Jefferson's achievement in writing the Declaration of Independence, as Frederick Douglass rightly pointed out in 1852, "What to the Slave is the Fourth of July?" (Document 22) It was a date that had no meaning. "This Fourth of July is *yours*, not *mine*. *You* may rejoice, *I* must mourn." While slavery endured, the Declaration appeared to those who suffered under it as tantalising rhetoric. Independence Day was a festival of exclusion—while some could participate in the annual ritual which reminded them of their achievement, for others the "sounds of rejoicing are empty and heartless . . . your shouts of liberty and equality, hollow mockery." Whatever the constitutional compromises of the period, it was a self-evident truth that the continued existence of slavery within the United States was causing increasing political tension.

The 1850 Compromise proved to be an empty edifice built on quicksand. The decade between the passage of the Fugitive Slave Law and the election of Abraham Lincoln as President was thus marked by an accelerating and increasingly desperate search for ways in which slavery might be accommodated within the United States. In the end, it was futile. While the drama was played out in the realm of high politics and oratory, the reality that drove North and South to war was marked by successive critical events. Of these, the controversy over the Kansas–Nebraska act was such that it appeared almost as a rehearsal for Civil War, with pro-slave and anti-slave forces confronting each other directly. In order to pass the measure through Congress, its sponsor, Stephen Douglas, conceded to Southern demands that the principles of the 1850 Compromise would apply to these new territories, which might lead theoretically to the extension of slavery. It was a political gamble which seemed a safe enough bet. Douglas was hopeful that circumstances of geography and climate, coupled with a popular majority against slavery among the settlers there which was likely to be augmented as a result of population movements, would mean that in practical terms the area would remain free soil.

Such was the suspicion of Southern motives, however, that others remain unconvinced. Salmon Chase, then representing Ohio in the Senate, drafted a manifesto endorsed by fellow congressional Abolitionists, and published in *The New*

19

York Times on January 24, 1854 (Document 23). It described the Nebraska bill as

> part and parcel of an atrocious plot to exclude from a vast unoccupied region immigrants from the Old World and free labourers from our own States, and convert it into a dreary despotism, inhabited by masters and slaves.

Like the Fugitive Slave Law, this was a measure that polarised, and which benefited the anti-slavery cause. Horace Greeley, who had coined the famous slogan: "Go west, young man," to encourage the migration across the continent, and who at the time was editor of the *New York Tribune*, claimed, as McPherson observes, that "the bill created more Abolitionists in two months than William Lloyd Garrison and Wendell Phillips had created in twenty years."[14] His newspaper also commented critically on the proposed legislation (Document 24).

For the *New York Tribune* the only way for slavery to survive was through expansion. Slavery

> loves aggression, for when it ceases to be aggressive it stagnates and decays. It is the leper of modern civilization, but a leper whom no cry of 'unclean' will keep from intrusion into uninfected company.

Congress was "plotting the surrender to Slavery of the free territory west of the Mississippi". Douglas's bill in effect repealed the Missouri Compromise which had previously strictly delimited the extent of slave territory. To the *New York Tribune*, such a concession played into Southern hands even if the outcome would ultimately destroy the very institution it wished to preserve: "Slavery is imperious, encroaching, truculent, belligerent. Its own conduct will thus ultimately generate an explosive force that must blow it to atoms." It was a prescient comment: for even after the Kansas–Nebraska Act was passed, the controversy continued.

Kansas was a rehearsal for the main event. In 1855, a pro-slavery legislature was elected after immigrants from neighbouring Missouri settled in the territory. Meeting in Lecompton, it adopted Missouri's civil and criminal code, with additional provisions which made it a crime to deny anyone the right to hold slaves, and instituting the death penalty for anyone helping slaves to liberty. The free-soil advocates then seceded from the government and at a convention in Topeka framed their own constitution. Conflict broke out.

Among those who fought was John Brown, later to journey to his epiphany at Harper's Ferry. In May 1856, he and seven others, including four sons from among his twenty children, murdered five pro-slavery settlers they had taken from their homes. Three months later, Brown and forty others were attacked by ten times the number of pro-slavers from Missouri in a battle in which two hundred lost their lives. "Bleeding Kansas" was where the fight over the issue of slavery erupted into unrestrained violence. As Benjamin Thomas put it in his biography of Abraham Lincoln, "tinder for a civil war was ready for the match in Kansas."[15] It was only in 1861 that Kansas—as a free state—was finally admitted to what was then left of the Union.

While Kansas was erupting into conflict, the discontent felt in the North over the enactment of the Fugitive Slave Law simmered on. As Harriet Beecher Stowe had seen so clearly, here was an act of Congress that created a dilemma: whether to obey the Federal Government or the dictates of a Christian conscience. For Henry David Thoreau, there was no contest. His transcendentalist philosophy would lead him to defy the Federal Government, and in an act of passive resistance spend a night in prison rather than support that government's policies over slavery and the Mexican war. His account of the experience—the *Essay on Civil Disobedience*—would influence a later generation of reformers—among them Mahatma Ghandi, and Martin Luther King. On Independence Day 1854, he delivered an address to an anti-slavery convention in Massachussetts, which stands as a counterpoint to Frederick Douglass's oration two years earlier (Document 25). Indeed, as Horace Greeley commented in an editorial in the *New York Tribune*, Thoreau's

> remarks have a racy piquancy and telling point which none but a man thoroughly in earnest and regardless of self in his fidelity to a deep conviction ever fully attains. The humor here so signally evinced is born of pathos—it is the lightning which reveals to hearers and readers the speaker's profound abhorrence of the sacrifice or subordination of one human being to the pleasure or convenience of another.[16]

Thoreau's deep suspicion of government, coupled with his conviction that morality should define the course of public policy, led him to support the abolitionist cause.

"Will mankind never learn that policy is not morality—that it never secures any moral right, but considers merely what is expedient?" Thoreau's rhetorical question led him to the conclusion that "what is wanted is men, not of policy but of probity—who recognize a higher law than the Constitution, or the decision of the majority." But such individuals were rare in contemporary public life. The Compromise of 1850 had privileged expediency over morality, and the frustration of those who opposed slavery was self-evident. At the same meeting, William Lloyd Garrison set fire to a copy of the Constitution.

The United States seemed to be held together not so much through compromise but rather as the result of a series of corrupt bargains between politicians from both North and South: as pragmatists and realists they may have believed that the survival of the Union took political precedence over the abolition of slavery. But for those opposed to the "peculiar institution", this demonstrated a moral cowardice that called into question the worth of America's "great experiment" in republican government itself. Walt Whitman, "the poet of American democracy", who had been among the first to promote the idea of the "democratic faith", arguing that "we must be constantly pressing onward—every year throwing the doors wider and wider—and carrying our experiment of democratic freedom to the very verge of the limit",[17] was also among those for whom the 1850s was a decade of disillusionment. In 1856, he wrote "The Eighteenth Presidency" (Document 26), described by Ralph Gabriel as "one of the bitterest diatribes against the practices of realistic democracy to be found in the literature of American politics".[18]

As the 1856 presidential election campaign was under way, Whitman interpreted his contemporary political world. Political offices, including the presidency itself were thus "bought, sold, electioneered for, prostituted, and filled with prostitutes". The ordinary people of America, in whom he had invested his democratic faith, were "credulous, generous, deferential" in permitting such leaders to take charge. It was an inherently unstable situation.

> On all sides tyrants tremble, crowns are unsteady, the human race restive, on the watch for some better era, some divine war. No man knows what will happen next, but all who know that some such things are to happen as mark the greatest moral convulsions of the earth. Who shall play the hand for America in these tremendous games?

It seems a remarkably prescient question.

James Buchanan, the last president of the ante-bellum era, took office holding few cards. He entered the White House, "convinced that I owe my election to the inherent love for the Constitution and the Union which still animates the hearts of the American people", and in his inaugural address (Document 27) asked for "their powerful support in sustaining all just measures calculated to perpetuate these". Yet his constant search for compromise would satisfy few and alienate more. As his quest to maintain the integrity of the Union increasingly seemed at odds with the temper of the times, Buchanan himself would be blamed by his contemporaries for the descent into a war which he worked hard to avoid. During his administration, Abolitionists and secessionists turned away from any search for common ground.

Yet were the North and South so different? There were some who were prepared to argue both were equally reliant upon forms of slavery: the South at least had the courage to admit its fault. In an attempt to counter the impact made upon popular opinion by such works as *Uncle Tom's Cabin*, Southern writers mounted a defence of slavery. George Fitzhugh offered a paternalistic defence of the "peculiar institution", arguing in, for example, *Cannibals All!* (Document 28) that at least on their plantations slaves were an asset to be preserved and protected, whereas elsewhere America's capitalist economy ruthlessly exploited its workers—free blacks and poor whites—in the relentless pursuit of profit.

> We are all, North and South, engaged in the White Slave Trade, and he who succeeds best is esteemed most respectable. It is far more cruel than the Black Slave Trade, because it exacts more of its slaves, and neither protects nor governs them. . . .No wonder men should prefer white slavery . . . since it is more profitable, and is free from all the cares and labors of black slave-holding.

Fitzhugh's portrait of contented Southern slaves, watched over by humane owners, and contrasted with the wretched conditions that existed in the sweatshops that were Northern factories is so much rhetorical exaggeration. His was an attempt to justify an essentially racist argument by shifting the grounds of debate to the issue of economic class. If his criticisms of capitalism were accepted, that did not imply that his defence of slavery was valid. It remained a clever polemic that rested on intellectual legerdemain.

VI

Slavery and racism were inextricably intertwined. When the Chief Justice of the Supreme Court, Roger Taney, (incidentally the first Roman Catholic to serve in this position), delivered his opinion in *Dred Scott v. Sanford* on March 6 1867—two days after Buchanan's inaugural address—it was apparent that his legal judgment was influenced by a belief that blacks were inherently inferior to whites, or at least that they had no rights worthy of respect (Document 29). As such, the Declaration of Independence and the Constitution were documents written by one race which defined for them and them alone the ideals and the terms of their social and political community. Slaves were property: "articles of merchandise." Dred Scott was a slave who could not escape his condition, wherever he was taken, whatever happened to his master, and despite any claims to the contrary. As James McPherson points out, as a Southerner Taney "had long wanted to write" this opinion. Although he had freed his own slaves, "the main theme of his twenty-eight year tenure on the Court was the defense of slavery." In his view, "southern life and values . . . seemed organically linked to the peculiar institution and unpreservable without it."[19] The Dred Scott decision may have indeed moved the United States a step closer to the war. Unlike the Union, however, Taney would survive the secession crisis, continuing as Chief Justice until his death in 1864, when Abraham Lincoln would nominate as his successor Salmon Chase.

From 1847 to 1849, Lincoln had been a member of the Federal House of Representatives, representing Illinois' Seventh Congressional District, but had then "retired" from politics to practise law. Five years later, as the State Senator, Stephen Douglas, managed the Kansas–Nebraska bill through Congress, Lincoln was sufficiently concerned to return to the arena. As his biographer, Benjamin Thomas puts it, "He will stand forth hereafter as a political analyst and debater of surpassing power." The issue on which the Kansas–Nebraska controversy turned—the extension of slavery—became, for Lincoln, one of moral concern. Moreover,

> the impact of a moral challenge, purging Lincoln of narrow partisanship and unsure purpose, is about to transform an honest, capable, but essentially self-centered small-town politician of self-developed but largely unsuspected talents into a statesman who will grow to world dimensions.[20]

It was inevitable, then, that Lincoln would choose to comment on the Dred Scott decision. On June 26, 1857, he spoke in Springfield, Illinois, in reply to an earlier address by Stephen Douglas, in which the Senator had attempted to justify both his policy on Kansas and Taney's opinion in the case (Document 30). Lincoln argued that "both the Chief Justice and the Senator" were guilty of misrepresenting "the plain unmistakable language of the Declaration". Jefferson and the founding fathers:

> meant to set up a standard maxim for free society, which should be familiar to all, and revered by all; constantly looked to, constantly labored for, and even though never perfectly attained, constantly approximated, and thereby constantly spreading and deepening its influence and augmenting the happiness and value of life to all people of all colors everywhere.

Lincoln's Declaration of Independence was inclusive, not exclusive, tolerant of racial differences and colour-blind.

The following year, 1858, Lincoln challenged Douglas for his seat in the federal Senate. As part of the campaign, the candidates confronted each other directly seven times in debates which McPherson believes are deservedly the most famous in American history. They matched two powerful logicians and hard-hitting speakers, one of them nationally pre-eminent and the other little known outside his region. . . . The stakes were higher than a senatorial election, higher even than the looming presidential contest of 1860, for the theme of the debates was nothing less than the future of slavery and the Union.

Throughout the summer, in towns all over Illinois, Lincoln and Douglas covered much the same ground. "Tariffs, banks, internal improvements, corruption, and other staples of American politics received not a word in these debates—the sole topic was slavery."[21]

If there had ever been a dialogue on the issue, the Lincoln–Douglas debates show that it was breaking down (Documents 31–33). Those who believed in the principles of states' rights and self-determination—and who thereby condoned the "peculiar institution"—could not convince those who thought that slavery was a travesty of political and democratic morality, that there was a case to answer. Douglas summed up the chasm that separated the two sides. Thus Lincoln

> says that he looks forward to a time when slavery shall be abolished everywhere. I look forward to a time when each state shall be allowed to do as it pleases. . . . I care more for the great principle of self-government, the right of the people to rule, than I do for all the negroes in Christendom. I would not endanger the perpetuity of this Union, I would not blot out the great inalienable rights of the white men for all the negroes that ever existed.[22]

It was a matter of right versus rights.

For Benjamin Thomas "the debates made Lincoln a national figure and put the Presidency within his reach."[23] Although he lost the election to Douglas, the incumbent, the campaign in many ways was a dress rehearsal for what was to come: Lincoln and Douglas would be the main protagonists of the 1860 presidential contest. Before the campaign, Lincoln was little known outside Illinois. After it his profile was dramatically enhanced, but he still seemed an outsider compared to other nationally-known Republican politicians. Salmon Chase from Ohio and William Seward from New York—both elected to the Federal Senate—would be canvassed as potential presidential candidates in 1860. In then end, then, Lincoln would carry less political baggage than the others—he had made fewer enemies within the Republican party than his rivals. He might appear indeed as Whitman's "Redeemer President": an "heroic, shrewd, fully-informed, healthy-bodied, middle-aged, beard-faced American" who would "come down from the West across the Alleghanies, and walk into the Presidency". His time was approaching.

By the time of the Lincoln–Douglas debates, therefore, it was increasingly evident that the issue of slavery in its Southern States, and its potential expansion elsewhere, would break the Union apart. In the same electoral season of 1858, William Seward, who would become Lincoln's wartime Secretary of State, refuted the Southern belief—popularised by Fitzhugh—that "labor in every society, by whomsoever performed, is necessarily unintellectual, grovelling, and base" (Document 34). Slavery, he argued, demeaned its victims whereas those paid for their work were on a path to self-improvement and the achievement of social status. So instead of being mirror images of exploitation, slavery and free-labour were two systems of social organization so opposed to one another that an "irrepressible conflict" between them meant that ultimately one would prevail over the other.

VII

John Brown was a man with a mission. Involved in some of the bloodiest incidents of the confrontation in "Bleeding Kansas", his objective became to end slavery in the South through creating the conditions for the enslaved themselves to revolt against the "peculiar institution". As McPherson observes, "Like the Old Testament warriors he admired and resembled, he yearned to carry the war into Babylon."[24] Or, to use another analogy, Brown's ideas seem curiously similar to those which would inspire the Cuban revolution a century later. He planned a guerrilla campaign from a stronghold in the mountains: encouraging the oppressed to join in the effort to overthrow the corrupt regime under which they suffered. While John Brown was no Fidel Castro, in his martyrdom he became an icon of his age: like Che Guevara in Bolivia he found his apotheosis in his doomed effort to ferment an armed struggle in the cause of revolutionary freedom.

His was an insane plan. The guerrilla campaign would need weapons. The federal armoury at Harper's Ferry in Virginia had plenty of them. So if Brown—with only a token band of helpers, including three of his sons—seized the armoury, he might, in that one dramatic gesture, give the oxygen of publicity to his mission, and be able to supply his slave recruits with the means to attack their enemy. The problem with the scheme was that Harper's Ferry was impossible to defend against any co-ordinated counter-attack which would inevitably come from federal forces. Those who had warning of the project—including Frederick Douglass—saw that it was not even a calculated risk: it was suicidal. And yet, Brown appeared to sense that whatever happened, his action would be one of historic significance. Indeed, as McPherson points out:

> it was almost as if he knew that failure with its ensuing martyrdom would do more to achieve his ultimate goal than any 'success' could have done. In any event, that was how matters turned out.[25]

His madness was touched with genius.

On October 16th 1859, Brown and eighteen accomplices captured the armoury complex at Harper's Ferry. They then waited for slaves to revolt. But not one joined the cause voluntarily. The mass uprising failed to materialise. The following day, Brown's force was attacked by local residents, who were subsequently re-inforced by the Virginia and Maryland State militias. He was forced to retreat to the fire-engine house, where the eventual dénoument of the raid took place. Federal troops from Washington D.C., placed under the command of Robert E. Lee, arrived on the evening of October 18, and soon after dawn the following day, they stormed the building.

Israel Green, who was in charge of the detachment of marines who battered down the door of the engine-house, later provided an important eye-witness account of what happened (Document 35). Entering the building, he was recognised by one of the hostages taken in the raid, Colonel Lewis Washington (a great grandnephew of the nation's first president). Washington pointed out John Brown, whom Green struck and stunned with his dress sword. His wounds were superficial: "immediately after the fight, Brown was carried out of the engine-house, and recovered consciousness while lying on the ground in front." The following day, he was handed over to the civil authorities. The incident at Harper's Ferry was over: but its implications, for both North and South, continued to reverberate as the ordeal of the Union continued.

Abolitionists seized upon John Brown's raid as another opportunity to promote their uncompromising call to end slavery. Lydia Mary Child, whose early popularity as a writer had been compromised after she published her *Appeal for that Class of Americans Called Africans* (1833), had continued to work for the anti-slavery cause, editing, with her husband, the *National Anti-Slavery Standard*. Now she embarked upon a correspondence with the Governor of Virginia, Henry Wise, published in Greeley's *New York Tribune* along with her letter to John Brown, his reply, and her acerbic exchange of views with Mrs Mason, whose husband chaired the Senate committee which investigated the raid (Document 36).

Mrs Child asked Governor Wise if she could minister to Brown in prison, a request which brought a broadly conciliatory reply—Wise would be impressed by his captive's bearing and demeanour both during and after his trial. Yet he could not resist then rising to the abolitionist bait. His letter referred to the prisoner as "one who whetted knives of butchery for our mothers, sisters, daughters and babes". Such a sentiment allowed Lydia Child to write again, this time antagonistically, pointing out that "because slaveholders so recklessly sowed the wind in Kansas, they reaped the whirlwind at Harper's Ferry". Once again, the spirit and the tone of the correspondence demonstrated both the tenacity with which Abolitionists adhered to their cause, and the ever-widening gulf that separated them from Southerners who remained committed to the preservation of slavery.

Most Abolitionists were advocates of non-violence. John Brown's raid forced them into an anxious re-appraisal of that conviction. Initially, as McPherson points out, the "Northern response was a kind of baffled reproach."[26] Even William Lloyd Garrison appeared to distance himself from the action: the raid had been "a misguided, wild and apparently insane . . . effort."[27] But then "opinions soon changed into a perception of Brown as a martyr to a noble cause".[28] In the event, it was Henry David Thoreau, the apostle of non-violent civil disobedience, who became one of Brown's foremost apologists. In a speech he gave less than two weeks after the raid (Document 37), Thoreau was critical of Garrison and other editors: "I read all the newspapers I could get within a week after this event, and I do not remember in them a single expression of sympathy for these men" who had risked all by their actions at Harper's Ferry.

For Thoreau, however, Brown had "a spark of divinity in him". Speaking over a month before the prisoner was executed, but realising the inevitable verdict that would end his trial, Thoreau predicted his apotheosis: "Some eighteen hundred years ago Christ was crucified; this morning, perchance, Captain Brown was hung. These are two ends of a chain which is not without its links. He is not Old Brown any longer, he is an Angel of Light." Brown, then, was rapidly transformed from a violent, insane, reckless maverick into a potential redeemer whose glorious failure nevertheless gave Abolitionists an heroic martyr for their cause.

In his reply to Mrs Child's offer to visit him in prison, John Brown himself had seemed less concerned with the wider and enduring impact of his actions than with the domestic security of his remaining family. He asked her not to come, but instead to contribute a small sum of money towards their welfare. In his last speech before the court that tried him (Document 38), however, he appeared conscious of the drama of the historical moment:

> Now, if it is deemed necessary that I should forfeit my life for the furtherance of the ends of justice, and mingle my blood further with the blood of my children and with the blood of millions in this slave country whose rights are disregarded by wicked, cruel and unjust enactments,—I submit; so let it be done!

Thoreau would have agreed with that sentiment. Another sympathiser from Massachussetts, the clergyman Theodore Parker judged that Brown's words made him "not only a martyr . . . but also a *saint*".[29] Abraham Lincoln, however, was prosaic, but perhaps more prescient in his reaction. On a speaking tour in Kansas at the time of Brown's execution, he reminded those in his audience who supported slavery that if the South tried to destroy the Union, "it will be our duty to deal with you as old John Brown has been dealt with."[30]

The raid on Harper's Ferry gained Brown not only national notoriety and renown but international fame as well. Victor Hugo, then in exile (he had left when Louis Napoleon had declared himself Emperor of France, and in 1859 rejected the offer of amnesty that would have allowed him to return) was one who ensured yet more publicity for the case. In his letter to *The London News* (Document 39), Hugo argued that to allow Brown's execution would be to offend against America's democratic values, its sense of justice and spirit of morality: if it took place the world would witness "the assassination of Emancipation by Liberty". Indeed, "Let America know it, and ponder on it well—there is something more terrible than Cain slaying Abel: It is Washington slaying Spartacus!" International concern could not overturn the verdict. Even though, as Emerson would suggest in his eulogy for Brown (Document 40), "All people, in proportion to their sensibility and self-respect, sympathize with him," the harsh reality of the contemporary, precarious, political accommodation between North and South meant clemency was neither sought nor given. So on the day Hugo wrote his letter,

> John Brown went to the gallows in Charles Town, Virginia, seated imperturbably on his coffin and remarking as he gazed at the blue haze softening the outline of the mountains: "This *is* a beautiful country".[31]

His had been a remarkable odyssey: his soul would indeed go marching on.

VIII

"His ambition was a little engine that never quit."[32] Following his electoral defeat in Illinois in 1858, Abraham Lincoln appeared, skilfully and patiently, to be backing towards the limelight: positioning himself for the presidential election campaign of 1860. In February that year, following his speaking tour of Kansas, he travelled to New York, where he had been invited to give a lecture at the Reverend Henry Ward Beecher's church in Brooklyn. In the event, he delivered his address at the Cooper Institute before an audience of fifteen hundred (Document 41). His speech would subsequently become part of his campaign literature. He ended with an impassioned plea:

> neither let us be slandered from our duty by false accusations against us, nor frightened from it by menaces of destruction to the Government nor of dungeons to ourselves. Let us have faith that right makes might, and in that faith let us to the end dare to do our duty as we understand it.

And yet, despite enhancing his national reputation with this address, Lincoln's hopes seem pious in relation to contemporary events. For as a prelude to the break-up of the Union, the election year was marked by the collapse of the existing federal party system, riven by sectional rivalry (Document 42). The Republicans remained the most cohesive political force. They nominated Lincoln as their presidential candidate at their convention in Chicago. The Republican Platform was, for McPherson "one of the most effective documents of its kind in American history".[33] It held "in abhorrence all schemes for Disunion, come from whatever source they may". To threaten secession was "an avowal of contemplated treason, which it is the imperative duty of an indignant People sternly to rebuke and forever silence".

In contrast, the Democrats, meeting first in Charleston, South Carolina, split into Northern and Southern factions. The former reconvened in Baltimore to nominate Stephen Douglas as their candidate. Its platform admitted "differences of opinion exist in the Democratic party" on the issue of whether slavery should be extended to the territories, but, in an effort to circumvent the controversy, proposed to "abide by the decisions of the Supreme Court of the United States on the questions of Constitutional law". The anti-Douglas Southerners, who had again walked out of the convention in Baltimore, adopted their own candidate, John Breckenridge—then vice-president—and constructed a platform which affirmed the right of all citizens of the United States "to settle with their property" in new territories, any one of which might then enter the Union "whether its Constitution prohibits or recognizes the institution of Slavery". For them there could be no further compromise.

Meanwhile, the conservative phoenix of the Whig party, from the ashes of which the Republicans had been formed, re-invented itself as the Constitutional Union party, with John Bell of Tennessee—himself a slave-holder—as its candidate. Its platform was a "pious resolution"[34] which pledged them "to maintain, protect and defend, separately and unitedly", the "great principles of public liberty and national safety" symbolised by the Constitution, the Union and the laws which governed the nation.

The 1860 election thus became two more or less self-contained contests. Lincoln tackled Douglas in the North, and Breckenridge faced Bell in the South. Lincoln won. He did not receive a single vote in ten Southern States (where the Republicans did not even appear on the ballot). In the five other slave states, he won 4% of the popular vote. But he could afford to lose the South and still win enough electoral college votes to become president. Southern states could recall Calhoun's words: they were indeed "a fixed and hopeless minority".[35] The Fugitive Slave Law, the Kansas–Nebraska Act, the Dred Scott decision, John Brown's actions at Harper's Ferry and finally Lincoln's election itself thus become part of the historical context which provided a backdrop to the crisis of secession. If each is considered as a skirmish prior to the main event—the war itself—this is not to argue that, had they not occurred, the "irrepressible conflict" might have been avoided. There is a sense of resignation—a realisation that the Union had failed—which hangs over the United States at mid-century. It is reflected in contemporary rhetoric, and acts as a counterpoint to the theme of compromise. For the South, what other way could the dilemma of slavery be resolved if not by secession? For the North, what other way could the Union be preserved if not by war?

If it was Lincoln's election that triggered the secession crisis, it was South Carolina that played the opening gambit in the end-game. Its legislature called a convention to discuss secession, and on December 20, 1859 it unanimously adopted an ordinance that dissolved its political and constitutional ties with the United States. Even as it did so, the Federal Senate was still searching for a solution that would avoid such an action. John Crittenden from Kentucky, in the spirit of Henry Clay, proposed a compromise in the form of a series of amendments to the Constitution (Document 43). These would have guaranteed the continuation of slavery in those states where it existed, and in the District of Columbia. The domestic slave trade would have been protected, and slave-holders compensated for the loss of runaway slaves. The line of latitude defining the Missouri Compromise should be extended to the Pacific Ocean, and slavery permitted south of it. Such amendments could not be overturned by future amendments: the South's position within the Union, complete with its "peculiar institution" would be constitutionally enshrined. The Republicans—and notably Lincoln as president-elect—could not support such proposals: effectively a capitulation to slavery for the sake of preserving the Union. The Crittenden Compromise came to nothing.

So South Carolina "resumed her separate and equal place among nations" (Document 44). Crittenden's plan would not have prevented Lincoln taking office, and this, more than anything else, symbolised for Southern States their impotence within the Union. According to the declaration with which South Carolina justified secession,

> a geographical line has been drawn across the Union, and all the States north of that line have united in the election of a man to the high office of President of the United States, whose opinions and purposes are hostile to slavery. . . . all hope of remedy is rendered vain, by the fact that public opinion at the North has invested a great political

error with the sanctions of a more erroneous religious belief.

Could South Carolina thus be allowed simply to leave the United States? For Greeley's *New York Tribune*, "If the Cotton States become satisfied they can do better out of the Union than in it, we insist on letting them go." In the same editorial, written just after Lincoln's election, and less than two weeks before South Carolina acted, Greeley observed that ,"We hope never to live in a republic whereof one section is pinned to the residue by bayonets."[36] There was, moreover, the belief that this was a temporary schism. As Oliver Wendell Holmes, whose son—and namesake—would serve and be wounded in the Civil War,[37] put it (Document 45): "Go, then, our rash sister! Afar and aloof,— / Run wild in the sunshine away from our roof, / But when your heart aches and your feet have grown sore, / Remember the pathway that leads to our door".

Less than three weeks after South Carolina quit the Union, however, others did the same. Mississippi, Florida and Alabama left on successive days, beginning on January 9th, 1861. On January 19th, Georgia left, followed, a week later, by Louisiana. Texas voted to leave on February 1st, provided that a popular vote, held on February 23rd, endorsed the decision. It did. Texas seceded on March 2nd, the last of the seven states to do so prior to Lincoln assuming the presidency. In this rapid transitional phase, as the Union disintegrated and the Confederacy was established, Southerners argued that their action was constitutional and that they should not be subject to any coercion as a result of it. Jefferson Davis, in his farewell address to the Senate (Document 46), made the point that there was an important distinction between nullification and secession. A state which refused to obey a federal law might reasonably expect to be forced into line. But in states which had seceded, no federal law applied. Davis expressed the hope that "peaceable relations" might be maintained between his state, Mississippi, and the Union "though we must part". The right of secession flowed from a belief in the sovereignty of each state as an autonomous entity that might choose either to join or to leave the Federal Republic, according to its interests. It was by no means a declaration of war.

IX

On February 4th 1861, the seven states that had seceded—including Texas, whose action was at that time still conditional upon the result of the popular referendum—met in Montgomery, Alabama. For McPherson, "it was significant that only seven slave states were represented . . . the main goal of compromise maneuvers was to keep the other eight from going out."[38] There was a strong sense of unionism in these states of the upper South, and the Republican gamble was that as long as they stayed committed to the ideal of the United States, those which had seceded would gradually drift back to join them. It was, however, a precarious political situation. If the North appeared to threaten the states which had seceded, these remaining Southern states might well prefer to show sectional solidarity at the expense of loyalty to the Union. So, in the run-up to his inauguration, "Lincoln made it his objective to maintain the national authority while avoiding any rash or provocative action."[39] In Washington, there were further attempts at compromise. The Washington "peace convention", sponsored by the Virginia state legislature, coincided with the Confederate convention in Alabama. After three weeks of discussion, it proposed a modified form of the Crittenden Compromise (Document 47), and it suffered a similar fate.

Meanwhile, on February 9th, the Confederate convention had unanimously endorsed Jefferson Davis as the provisional President of its new government until elections were held in the following November (the timing of them was a provision copied from the 1787 Constitution). As McPherson observes,

> austere, able, experienced in government as a senator and former secretary of war, a Democrat and a secessionist but no fire-eater, Davis was the ideal candidate. . . . His sense of duty—and destiny—bid him accept.[40]

In his inaugural address (Document 48), he hinted at the future enlargement of the new Confederation through the admission of the remaining slave states, and at the same time suggested that the separation from the North was irrevocable and permanent:

> with a Constitution differing only from that of our fathers in so far as it is explanatory of their well-known intent, freed from the sectional conflicts which have interfered with the pursuit of the general welfare it is not unreasonable to expect that the States from which we have recently parted may seek to unite their fortunes with ours under the government which we have instituted. . . . but beyond this, . . . a reunion with the States from which we have separated is neither practicable nor desirable.

If the battle-lines were being drawn, there was still some doubt as to which states would end up on whose side.

On March 4th 1861, therefore, Abraham Lincoln took office as the United States disintegrated, but before North and South had taken any irrevocable steps towards war. In his inaugural address (Document 49), however, he made it clear that secession was illegal: "no state upon its own mere motion can lawfully get out of the Union . . . resolves and ordinances to that effect are legally void." So for the new President, the United States remained a constitutional given, and secession a legal fiction. Moreover, the Southern States were not being coerced by a Northern moral majority on the issue of slavery. There had been no law passed compelling abolition of the "peculiar institution": the South could not claim that it had been deprived of any constitutional rights. Lincoln argued indeed that "the central idea of secession is the essence of anarchy." Finally, the new President appealed to Southern patriotism in an attempt to bring about reconciliation and an end to the secession crisis:

> I am loath to close. We are not enemies, but friends. We must not be enemies. Though passion may be strained, it must not break our bonds of affection. The mystic chords of memory, stretching from every battle-field, and patriot grave, to every living heart and hearthstone, all over this broad land, will yet swell the chorus of the Union, when again touched, as surely they will be, by the better angels of our nature.

The Confederacy ignored him.

Its provisional constitution had been unanimously adopted at the convention in Montgomery. A week after Lincoln's inauguration, this was presented for formal ratification as the Constitution of the Confederate States of America (Document 50). It was virtually identical to the one it would replace: the source of the South's quarrel with the North had been about constitutional interpretation rather than with the principles of the document itself. Where it parted company with the 1787 original was—self-evidently—in its provisions which strengthened the institution of slavery, and in its weakening of executive power: the president was limited to one six-year term in office. If it was merely a nuanced imitation of Madison's design, however, it still had a similar significance. It created a nation, another federal republic, contiguous with the older version, and on what was now its southern border. As the contemporary account by Felix De Fontaine, which first appeared in the *New York Herald,* makes clear (Document 51), the Confederacy bore

> all the marks of a well developed, well digested plan of government—a government now as independent as were the old thirteen States after the Fourth of July, 1776, and possessing what our ancestors of that date did not fully have—the wealth, ability and power to meet almost any contingency that may arise. Meanwhile, judging from the disposition of republicans in Congress and throughout the country, the ball thus set in motion will not stop. The States already united will undoubtedly remain so, and form the nucleus around which will gather others. The new Union will grow in strength as it grows in age.

The South's hope remained Lincoln's fear.

Yet if the Confederate Constitution purported to be, in all but name and fine print, a mirror image of its counterpart of 1787, its animating principles were very different. As Alexander Stephens, who became Vice-President under Davis, explained in his "Cornerstone Speech" of 21st March 1861 (Document 52), the new government was built upon a segregationist—racist—philosophy. The Constitution of the United States had "rested upon the assumption of the equality of races. This was an error. It was a sandy foundation, and the government built upon it fell when the 'storm came and the wind blew'."

The Confederacy was based upon

> exactly the opposite idea; its foundations are laid, its corner-stone rests upon the great truth, that the negro is not equal to the white man; that slavery—subordination to the superior race—is his natural and normal condition.

However complex the arguments had been, however convoluted the compromises, however earnest the attempts to preserve the Union, here, at last, was revealed the extent and the depth of the chasm which separated the South from the remainder of the United States. The language of racial supremacy and exclusion ultimately could not co-exist with the rhetoric of equality and a natural right to liberty.

On April 12th, Confederate forces began a bombardment of Fort Sumter, which had remained a Union outpost in South Carolina. Two days later, the federal forces capitulated: the Confederates gained possession of the Fort without loss of life on either side. What in retrospect appeared a fairly innocuous way to start a war gained its significance through the symbolism which both Confederates and Unionists attached to the event. As McPherson points out it "confronted the upper South with a crisis of decision".[41] Which side would the remaining slave states join? In many of these states, pro-secession sentiment was fuelled by the Confederacy's success at Fort Sumter. And Lincoln's immediate response then tipped the balance (Document 53). On April 15th, he issued a proclamation calling on the States to raise a 75,000 strong militia, appealing

> to all loyal citizens to favor, facilitate, and aid this effort to maintain the honor, the integrity, and the existence of our National Union and the perpetuity of popular government and to redress wrongs already long enough endured.

Two days later, Virginia seceded (subject to the endorsement of a popular referendum to be held the following month).

Lincoln then announced a federal blockade of ports in the original seven States of the Confederacy, subsequently extending this to Virginia and North Carolina even before they had formally joined the Southern cause, but after pre-emptive strikes had been made against federal property in those states. At the end of April, he suspended the writ of *habeas corpus* in certain areas of Maryland. On May 3rd, he increased the size of the regular army and navy: the North began mobilising for war. A week later, *habeas corpus* was suspended in Union fortresses in Florida, and "all dangerous or suspected persons" were to be removed from their vicinity. During the same month Arkansas, North Carolina and Tennessee seceded, and in due course, Missouri and Kentucky would also be admitted to the Confederacy.

At the end of April, the Confederate Constitution was ratified. In his message to the Confederate Congress to mark the event (Document 54), Jefferson Davis referred to Lincoln's proclamation of the 15th as a "declaration of war". He was convinced—accurately as it turned out—that

> the whole of the slave-holding States of the late Union will respond to the call of honor and affection, and by uniting their fortunes with ours promote our common interests and secure our common safety.

And having reviewed the state of military readiness in the South, he remained confident that it was prepared for a forthcoming conflict.

Virginia was the most powerful state to defy the Union. During the critical month of April , the *Staunton Spectator*, a Whig newspaper, reflected its changing political mood: from pro-unionism to support for secession (Document 55). And the state's decision to leave the Union was of undeniable significance to the South's cause. Thus, for McPherson,

> Virginia brought crucial resources to the Confederacy. Her population was the South's largest. Her industrial capacity was nearly as great as that of the seven original Confederate states combined. . . . Virginia's heritage from the generation of Washington, Jefferson, and Madison gave her immense prestige that was expected to attract the rest of the upper South to the Confederacy.[42]

It would be at Manassas, in Virginia, that the fighting would begin in earnest.

On July 4th 1861, Lincoln sent a message to the Federal Congress in which he reviewed the events of the secession crisis (Document 56). He suggested that "the course taken in Virginia was the most remarkable, perhaps the most important." The convention that had been called to consider secession had contained a majority of pro-unionists. It was meeting when Fort Sumter fell.

> Almost immediately . . . many members of that majority went over to the original disunion minority. . . . The people of Virginia have thus allowed this giant insurrection to make its nest within her borders, and this Government has no choice but to deal with it where it finds it.

Lincoln concluded his message with characteristic eloquence:

> And having thus chosen our course, without guile and with pure purpose, let us renew our trust in God, and go forward without fear and with manly hearts.

Eighty-five years to the day after its Declaration of Independence, Thomas Jefferson's home state, Virginia, was poised to become a principal theatre in America's Civil War.

Notes

1. Friedrich Nietzsche, 'On the Uses and Disadvantages of History for Life', in R. Schacht, ed., *Nietzsche: Selections*, (New York, 1993) p. 60.

2. James McPherson, *Battle Cry of Freedom*, (Harmondsworth, 1990).

3. Marcus Cunliffe, 'American Thought' in Dennis Welland, ed., *The United States—A Companion to American Studies*, (London, 1977) p. 534.

4. Paul Jennings, *A Colored Man's Reminiscences of James Madison*, (New York, 1865).

5. McPherson, *Battle Cry of Freedom*, p. 8.

6. Hugh Brogan, *The Pelican History of the United States of America*, (Harmondsworth, 1986) p. 294.

7. Quoted in Avery Craven, *Civil War in the Making*, (Baton Rouge, 1959) p. 22.

8. McPherson, *Battle Cry of Freedom*, p. 71.

9. *Ibid.* p. 89.

10. Daniel Webster, 'Address to the Senate', 7 March, 1850, *Congressional Globe* (Washingon D.C., 1850) 31st Congress, 1st session.

11. Quoted in McPherson, *Battle Cry of Freedom*, p. 69.

12. Quoted *ibid.* p. 69.

13. McPherson, *Battle Cry of Freedom*, p. 72.

14. Quoted in James McPherson, *Ordeal by Fire*, (New York, 1982) p. 89.

15. Benjamin Thomas, *Abraham Lincoln*, (New York, 1968) p. 162.

16. Horace Greeley, *New York Tribune*, August 2, 1854.

17. Quoted in Alan Grimes, *American Political Thought*, (New York, 1955) p. 195.

18. Ralph Gabriel, *The Course of American Democratic Thought*, (New York, 1956) p. 129.

19. McPherson, *Battle Cry of Freedom*, p. 173.

20. Thomas, *Abraham Lincoln*, p. 143.

21. McPherson, *Battle Cry of Freedom*, p. 182.

22. Douglas made this remark during the final debate between the candidates at Alton. See Paul Angle, *Created Equal?* (Chicago, 1958) p. 400.

23. Thomas, *Abraham Lincoln*, p. 192.

24. McPherson, *Battle Cry of Freedom*, p. 202.

25. *Ibid.* pp. 205–6.

26. *Ibid.* p. 208.

27. William Lloyd Garrison, *The Liberator*, October 21, 1859.

28. McPherson, *Battle Cry of Freedom*, p. 208.

29. Quoted *ibid.* p. 209.

30. Quoted in Thomas, *Abraham Lincoln*, p. 200.

31. *Ibid.* p. 199.
32. Quoted in Stephen Ambrose, *Nixon: The Education of a Politician 1913–1962*, (New York, 1987) p. 71. As Ambrose comments, "The statement fits Nixon as well."
33. McPherson, *Battle Cry of Freedom*, p. 220.
34. *Ibid.* p. 221.
35. Quoted in Richard Hofstadter, *The American Political Tradition*, (New York, 1948) p. 77.
36. Horace Greeley, *New York Tribune*, November 9, 1860.
37. Oliver Wendell Holmes Jr would later be appointed to the Supreme Court by Theodore Roosevelt, and would serve on it for thirty years, until his retirement in 1932.
38. McPherson, *Battle Cry of Freedom*, p. 254.
39. Thomas, *Abraham Lincoln*, p. 231.
40. McPherson, *Battle Cry of Freedom*, p. 259.
41. *Ibid.* p. 276.
42. *Ibid.* p. 280.

Chronology
1776–1930

All entries in **bold type** denote writers/documents included in these volumes.

1776   **Declaration of Independence** from Britain, 4th July. Adam Smith, *The Wealth of Nations*

1777   The Stars and Stripes (13 of each) adopted as American flag.

1779   Thomas Jefferson, 'Bill for Establishing Religious Freedom in Virginia'.

1780   American Academy of Sciences founded in Boston.

1782   Crèvecoeur, *Letters from an American Farmer*; **Thomas Jefferson, *Notes on the State of Virginia.***

1783   Treat of Versailles ends war and Britain recognizes independence of the 13 colonies.

1786   Virginia enacts the separation of church and state.

1787   **Federal Constitution** agreed at Philadelphia and ratified by South Carolina, Delaware, Pennsylvania and New Jersey. The dollar adopted as official currency.

1788   Georgia, Connecticut, Massachusetts, Maryland, New Hampshire, Virginia and New York ratify the Constitution and are admitted. **Alexander Hamilton, James Madison and John Jay, *The Federalist,* no. LIV;** Immanual Kant, *Critique of Pure Reason*

1789   French Revolution begins: the Storming of the Bastille. First meeting of US Congress. George Washington elected first President of the United States and Washington, D.C. founded as the capital. North Carolina admitted.

1790   Edmund Burke, *Reflections on the Revolution in France*; Immanuel Kant, *Critique of Judgement.*

1791   Vermont admitted. **Jonathan Edwards, 'The injustice and impolicy of the slave trade, and of the slavery of the Africans . . .';** William Bartram, *Travels Through North and South Carolina*; Tom Paine, *The Rights of Man*; Mozart, *The Magic Flute.*

1792   The Republic proclaimed in France. Kentucky admitted. Mary

Wollstonecraft, *A Vindication of the Rights of Women.*

1793 George Washington starts 2nd term as President. Louis XVI guillotined.

1794 Tom Paine, *The Age of Reason.* First abolition of slavery in French colonies. Timothy Dwight, *Greenfield Hill.* First turnpike road: Philadelphia–Lancaster Turnpike.

1795 Presbyterians, Methodists and Baptists lead religious revivals in Kentucky and Tennessee. Napoleon appointed Commander-in-Chief of French armies.

1796 Tennessee admitted. John Adams elected President (1797–1801). Napoleon's Italian Campaigns. Death of Catherine the Great of Russia.

1798 Napoleon Campaigns in Egypt; Battle of the Nile, Horatio Nelson defeats French. Napoleon's Egyptian sojourn ends.

1800 Thomas Jefferson elected President (1801–1809). New York City population is 60,000. Boston population is 20,000.

1802 Britain signs Treaty of Amiens with Napoleon Bonaparte. Napoleonic wars briefly halt.

1803 Ohio admitted. US purchases Louisiana from the French. Britain declares war on Napoleon again.

1804 Napoleon crowns himself Emperor.

1804-6 Lewis and Clark expedition across US.

1805 October 21: Battle of Trafalgar, Napoleon defeated. December 2: Battle of Austerlitz, Napoleon victorious. Napoleon king of Italy.

1807 Slavery abolished in Britain (still legal in numerous colonies). Beethoven's *Fifth Symphony.*

1808 James Madison elected President (1809–17). Importation of slaves in the US forbidden. Peninsula Campaign begins under Arthur Wellesley, Duke of Wellington, against Napoleon. Goethe, *Faust* (part one).

1810 Birth of Chopin.

1811 Jane Austen, *Sense and Sensibility.*

1812 Napoleon's Russian Campaign ends in the retreat from Moscow.

1812-14 The War of 1812 between Britain and the US.

1813 Births of Wagner, Verdi and Kirkegaard. Jane Austen, *Pride and Prejudice.*

1814 The Battle of Washington. British capture American capital and burn it in retaliation for American burning of York, now Toronto. Napoleon surrenders to Allies; exiled to Elba. Jane Austen, *Mansfield Park.*

1815 Napoleon defeated at the Battle of Waterloo and banished to St. Helena.

1816 Indiana admitted. James Monroe elected President (1817–1825). Gioacchino Antonio Rossini, *The Barber of Seville*; Jane Austen, *Emma*.

1817 Mississippi admitted. First treaty with Native Americans regarding their relocation to lands west of the Mississippi River. Death of Jane Austen. David Ricardo, *On the Principles of Political Economy*.

1818 Illinois admitted. Jane Austen, *Northanger Abbey* and *Persuasion* (published posthumously); Mary Shelley, *Frankenstein*. Birth of Karl Marx.

1819 Alabama admitted. Spain cedes Florida. 'Peterloo' Massacre. Schopenhauer, *The World As Will and Representation*.

1820 Maine admitted. 'The Missouri Compromise': slavery banned north of 36° 30' in territories of Louisiana Purchase. Death of George III.

1821 Missouri admitted. Mexico gains independence. Births of Dostoevsky, Flaubert and Baudelaire. Death of Napoleon. Greece rebels against Turkey. Thomas De Quincey, *Confessions of an English Opium Eater*.

1822 **Richard Furman, 'Exposition of the Views of the Baptists, Relative to the Coloured Population in the United States'.**

1823 James Fenimore Cooper, *The Pioneers*. Monroe doctrine extends US protection to Spanish–American republics. Beethoven, *Ninth Symphony*.

1826 James Fenimore Cooper, *The Last of the Mohicans*.

1827 John James Audubon begins to publish *Birds of North America*. Cooper's *The Prairie*. Death of Beethoven.

1828 First publication of Webster's *Dictionary*. Birth of Tolstoy.

1829 Catholic Emancipation in Great Britain.

1829–30 **David Walker, *Appeal in Four Articles, Together with a Preamble, to the Coloured Citizens of the World***

1830 **Daniel Webser, 'Webster's Great Reply to Hayne ...'.** July Revolution in Paris. Death of George IV. Greek independence recognized. Stendhal, *Red and Black*.

1831 **Thomas R. Gray, *The Confessions of Nat Turner, the Leader of the late Insurrection in Southampton, Va. as fully and voluntarily made to Thomas R. Gray;* John Floyd, letter to Governor James Hamilton, Jr; William Lloyd Garrison, editorial from *The Liberator*.** Goethe, *Faust* (part 2).

1832 Black Hawk Indian War. Captain Bonneville's expedition to the Rockies. **Angelina Grimké, *An Appeal to the Women of the Nominally Free States;* Andrew Jackson, 'Proclamation to the People of South**

Carolina']. Great Reform Bill, Great Britain.

1832–33 US Nullification Crisis.

1833 **Declaration of the Anti-Slavery Convention,** *Abolitionist:* American Anti-Slavery Society founded. Slavery abolished in the British Empire. Chicago is a village of some 350 people (1836–4,000; 1848–20,000).

1834 Indian territory constituted. Balzac, *Pere Goriot*

1835 Texas declares its independence from Mexico. **Alexis de Tocqueville,** ***Democracy in America;*** Washington Irving's *Tour on the Prairies.*

1835–38 Cherokees forced into Oklahoma territory from Georgia.

1836 Texas wins independence. Battle of the Alamo. Arkansas admitted. Ralph Waldo Emerson, *Nature*. Fort Dallas built.

1837 Michigan admitted. Theodore Weld, 'Letter to Sarah and Angelina Grimké'; *Address to the Citizens of the United States of America on the Subject of Slavery from the Yearly Meeting of the Religious Society of Friends.* Nathaniel Hawthorne, *Twice-Told Tales*. Telegraph developed in USA; Morse code invented. Accession of Queen Victoria.

1837–38 Schism in the Presbyterian church, in part over slavery.

1838 Charles Dickens, *Oliver Twist.*

1839–42 First Opium War in China; British gain Hong Kong.

1840 Edgar Allan Poe, 'The Man of the Crowd'

1841 First publication of New York *Herald Tribune*. Dallas founded. **Justice Joseph Story, Opinion in the** ***Amistad*** **Case.** First emigrant group of settlers to follow the Oregon Trail. Whig William Harrison becomes President; dies within weeks, succeeded by Democrat Tyler.

1842 Northeastern boundary between U.S. and Canada agreed in Treaty of Washington.

1844 Murder of the Mormon Prophet, Joseph Smith and his brother in the gaol at Nauvoo, Illinois. Methodist schism, largely over slavery. Birth of Nietzsche.

1845 Formation of the Southern Baptist Convention after differences with Northerners about the role of slave-owners and missionary work. Florida and Texas admitted. Congress adopts joint resolution for annexation of Texas. James Polk inaugurated as President. **Frederick Douglass,** ***Narrative of the Life of Frederick Douglass, an American Slave; The Address and Reply on the Presentation of a Testimonial to S. P. Chase, by the Colored People of Cincinnati [. . .]';*** Edgar Allan Poe, *Tales of Mystery and Imagination.*

1846   Irish Potato Famines force mass emigration, especially to the USA. Iowa admitted. The Oregon Treaty extends the Canadian–US boundary west from the Great Lakes along the 49° Parallel. Mormon migration west led by Brigham Young. Republic of California proclaimed

1846–48 The Mexican War.

1847   Battle of Buena Vista. Taylor defeats Santa Anna.

1848   Abolition of slavery in French West Indies. Seneca Falls convention inaugurates organised movement for women's rights. Louis Napoleon obtains power in France following revolution. Wisconsin admitted. Karl Marx and Friederich Engels, *Communist Manifesto*.

1849   **John C. Calhoun, 'The Address of the Southern Delegates in Congress to their Constituents'.** Fort Worth founded as an army post. Brigham Young settles in Salt Lake City which becomes the centre for the Mormons. California Goldrush. Zachary Taylor inaugurated President. Henry David Thoreau, 'Civil Disobedience'; Charles Dickens, *David Copperfield*.

1850   **John C. Calhoun, 'Speech on the Slavery Question';** Lucretia Mott, *Discourse on Women*. California admitted. Nathaniel Hawthorne, *The Scarlet Letter*. Millard Fillmore becomes President following Taylor's death.

1851   Herman Melville, *Moby-Dick*. Harriet Beecher Stowe, *Uncle Tom's Cabin*. *New York Times* first published. Great Exhibition at Crystal Palace, Great Britain.

1852   **Harriet Beecher Stowe, *Uncle Tom's Cabin;* Frederick Douglass, 'What to the Slave is the Fourth of July?'**

1853   The Crimean War begins. Franklin Pierce inaugurated President. Charles Dickens, *Bleak House*; Herman Melville, 'Bartleby, The Scrivener'.

1854   **'Slavery Extension: The Nebraska Bill in Congress' in The *New York Times;* Three Editorials from The *New York Tribune;* Henry David Thoreau, 'Slavery in Massachusetts'.** US Republican party founded. Henry Thoreau, *Walden*. US forces Japan to end isolation by the Treaty of Kanagawa.

1855   Walt Whitman, *Leaves of Grass* (1st edition).

1856   Crimean War ends. Charles Sumner beaten by Preston Brooks. **Walt Whitman, 'The Eighteenth Presidency!';** 'Crossing Brooklyn Ferry'.

1857   James Buchanan inaugurated as President. Free-state legislature elected in Kansas in October; Pro-slavery Lecompton constitution adopted. **James Buchanan, 'Inaugural Address' [4th March]; Justice Roger Taney, 'Opinion of the Supreme Court in the Dred Scott Case'; Abraham**

Lincoln, 'Speech on Dred Scott decision'; George Fitzhugh, *Cannibals All! Or Slaves Without Masters;* Flaubert, *Madam Bovary.*

1857–58 Religious revivals across the country.

1858 Abraham Lincoln, 'Speech at Springfield'[16 June]; Stephen Douglas, 'Speech at Springfield' [17 July], Abraham Lincoln, 'Speech at Springfield' [17 July]; William H. Seward, 'Speech in Rochester' [28 Oct.]. Denver established. Minnesota admitted.

1859 John Brown's raid on Harper's Ferry [18 Oct.]. Lydia Mary Child & Others, Correspondence on John Brown and Slavery [26 Oct.– ; Henry David Thoreau, 'A Plea for Captain John Brown' [30 Oct.]; Charles Mackay, *Life and Liberty in America.* Oil wells in America first discovered. Pullman luxury railway coaches. Oregon admitted. Charles Darwin, *The Origin of Species*; John Stuart Mill, *On Liberty*

1860 Outbreak of the American Civil War following secession of Southern states. Kansas admitted. Abraham Lincoln, 'Address at Cooper Institute' [27 Feb.]; Presidential Election Party Platforms, *Tribune Almanac;* Abraham Lincoln elected US President. Crittenden Compromise, *Congressional Globe,* [18th Dec.]. *Declaration of the Immediate Causes which Induce and Justify the Session of South Carolina from the Federal Union:* South Carolina and other states secede from Union. Abraham Lincoln, 'Proclamation of a National Fast Day'. Unification of Italy.

1861 Telegraph line across the USA completed. F. G. De Fontaine, *American Abolitionism, From 1787 to 1861.* Walt Whitman, '1861', *Drum-Taps;* Belle Boyd, from *Belle Boyd in Camp and Prison.*

21 January	Jefferson Davis, 'Farewell Speech to US Senate'.
February	Washington Peace Conference Proposals.
18 February	Jefferson Davis, 'Inaugural Address as Provisional President of the Confederate States'.
4 March	Abraham Lincoln, 'First Inaugural Address'.
11 March	Ratification of Constitution of the Confederate States of America which had been adopted on 8th February.
21 March	Alexander Stephens, 'Cornerstone Speech'.
25 March	Oliver Wendell Holmes, 'Brother Jonathan's Lament for Sister Caroline'.
26 March–15 April	Mary Chesnut, from *A Diary from Dixie.*
2 April	'Policy of the Border States', *Staunton Spectator.*
12–14 April	Siege of Fort Sumter. Major Robert Anderson, Reports on the Siege on Fort Sumter
15 April	Proclamation by Abraham Lincoln.

16 April	'The Fruits of Secession Agitation', *Staunton Spectator.*
19 April	**Proclamation by Abraham Lincoln**
23 April	'Resolution to form Regiment of Volunteers' and 'Glorious "Old Augusta"', *Staunton Spectator*
27 April	**Proclamation by Abraham Lincoln**
29 April	**Jefferson Davis, 'Message on Constitutional Ratification'**
30 April	'Action of the Town Council'; 'How Virginia was United' and 'Correspondence', *Staunton Spectator.*
3 May	**Proclamation by Abraham Lincoln**
10 May	**Proclamation by Abraham Lincoln.** Union victory at Camp Jackson, MO, under Lyon
1 June	Union victory at Fairfax Courthouse, VA, under Thompkins
3 June	Union victory at Philippi, WV, under Rosecrans
10 June	Confederate victory at Big Bethel, VA, under Magruder
4 July	**Abraham Lincoln, 'Message to Congress'**
11 July	Union victory at Rich Mountain, WV, under Rosecrans
13 July	Union victory at Carrick's Ford, WV, under McClellan
13 July–2 Sept.	**Mary Chesnut, from *A Diary from Dixie.***
21 July	Confederate victory at **Battle of 1st Manassas (Bull Run)** under Beauregard: **Brig.-Gen. Irvin McDowell and Gen. P. G. T. Beauregard, Reports; Walt Whitman, 'The Battle of Bull Run'**
26 July	Confederate victory at Fort Fillmore, NM, under Baylor
10 August	Confederate victory at Camp Jackson, MO, under McCulloch
12 August 1861–17 March 1862	**Surgeon Charles S. Tripler, Operations of the Medical Department of the Army of the Potomac**
10 September	Confederate victory at Carnifex Ferry, WV, under Floyd
10–15 September	Union victory at Cheat Mountain, WV, under Reynolds
20 September	Confederate victory at Lexington, KY, under Price
8–9 October	Union victory at Santa Rose Island, FL, under Brown
12 October	Confederate victory in naval engagement between *Manassas* and *Richmond* under Stevenson
21 October	Confederate victory at Balls Bluff, VA, under Evans and a Union victory in naval engagement at Port Royal Sound, SC, under DuPont
7 November	Confederate victory at Belmont, MO, under Polk
7 December	**'The Confederate Flag', *Richmond Dispatch***
25 December	**Karl Marx, 'Progress of Feeling in England'**
1861–1868	***The Rebellion Record***

1862 Abraham Lincoln, 'Meditation on the Divine Will'. Walt Whitman, letters to Nathaniel Bloom and John. F. S. Gray. **Rose O'Neal Greenhow, from *My Imprisonment and the First Year of Abolition Rule at Washington.*** Sioux war in Minnesota.

10 January	Confederate victory under Marshall at Middle Creek, KY
19 January	Union victory under Thomas at Mill Springs, KY
1 February	**Karl Marx, 'English Public Opinion'**
6 February	Union victory under Grant at Ft Henry, TN
14–16 February	Union victory under Grant at Ft Donelson, TN
8 February	Union victory at Roanoke Island, NC, under Burnside
February	**Julia Ward Howe, 'The Battle Hymn of the Republic'; Charles Sumner, 'Relations of the Seceded States'; John Stuart Mill, 'The Contest in America'**
5–8 March	Union victory under Curtis at Pea Ridge, AR
8–9 March	**Hampton Roads Battles: Union Navy Official Records; Report of Flag Officer Franklin Buchanan**
13–14 March	Union victory under Pope at New Madrid, TN
14 March	Union victory at New Bern, NC, under Burnside
23 March	Union victory at Kernstown, VA, under Banks
5 April–4 May	Union victory under McClellan at Yorktown, VA
6–7 April	**Battle of Shiloh: Reports of Maj.-Gen. Ulysses S. Grant and Gen. P. G. T. Beauregard; General George McClellan, Letter to Abraham Lincoln on the conduct of the war**
24 April	Confederate and Union victories in naval engagements involving *Governor Moore* and *Varuna*; *Pensacola* and *Governor Moore*
25 April	Union victory under Farragut in naval engagment, New Orleans, LA
30 April–30 May	Union victory under Halleck at Corinth, MS
4–5 May	Union victory under McClellan at Williamsburg, VA
8 May	Confederate victory under Jackson at McDowell, VA
14 May	Union victory under Grant at Jackson, MS
16–17 May	Confederate victory under Marshall at Princeton, WV
23 May	Confederate victory under Jackson at Front Royal, VA
24 May	Confederate victory under Jackson at Newton, VA
25 May	Confederate victory under Jackson at Winchester, VA
27 May	Union victory under Porter at Hanover Court House, VA
30 May	Union victory under Kimball at Front Royal, VA
31 May–1 June	Union victory under McClellan at Fair Oaks and Seven Pines, VA
29 June	Union victory under McClellan at Savage's Station and Allen's Farm, VA
30 June	Confederate victory under Lee at White Oak Swamp, VA; Union victory under Sykes at Turkey Bridge, VA
1 July	Union victories under McClellan at Malvern Hill, VA, and under Sheridan at Booneville, MS
5 August	Union victory under Williams at Baton Rouge, LA

6 August	Union victory under Porter in naval engagement involving *Essex* and *Arkansas*
7 August	**Battle of 2nd Manassas (Bull Run): Reports of Maj.-Gen. Irvin McDowell and Gen. Robert E. Lee.**
9 August	Confederate victory under Jackson at Cedar Mountain, VA
23 August	Confederate victory under Stuart at Catlett's Stations, VA
28-29 August	Confederate victory under Lee at Groveton, VA
29-30 August	Confederate victory under Kirby Smith at Richmond, KY
30 August	Confederate victory under Lee at **Second Battle of Bull Run (2nd Manassas): Reports of Maj.-Gen. Irvin McDowell and Gen. Robert E. Lee**
1 September	Confederate victory under Lee at Chantilly, VA
12-15 September	Confederate victory under Jackson at Harpers Ferry, VA
14 & 17 September	**Battles of South Mountain, VA and Antietam, MD: Reports of Maj.-Gen. George McClellan, Maj.-Gen. Ambrose E. Burnside, and Col. Joseph Walker**
14-17 September	Confederate victory under Bragg at Munfordville, KY
19 September	Confederate victory under Lee at Blackford's Ford, VA
19-20 September	Union victory under Rosecrans at Iuka, MO
3-4 October	Union victory under Rosecrans at Corinth, MO
5 October	Union victory under Ord at Big Hatchie River
8 October	Union victory under Buell at Perryville, KY
12 October	**William Ewart Gladstone, Speech at Newcastle** (England); Confederate victory under Stuart at Monocacy, MD
22 October	Union victory under Blunt at Old Fort Wayne, AR
13 November	Union victory under Grant at Holly Springs, MS
28 November	Confederate victory under Marmadue at Cane Hill, AR
7 December	Union victory under Blunt at Prairie Grove, AR
13 December	Confederate victory under Lee at **Battle of Fredericksburg: Reports of Maj.-Gen. Ambrose E. Burnside and Gen. Robert E. Lee.**
18 December	Confederate victory under Forrest at Lexington, TN
19 December	Union victory under Sullivan at Jackson, TN
20 December	Confederate victory under Van Dorn at Holly Springs, MS
21 December	**Giuseppi Garibaldi, Letter to Abraham Lincoln**
27-29 December	Confederate victory under Smith at Chicksaw Bluffs, MS
30 Dec-3 Jan	Union victory under Rosecrans at Murfreesboro, TN
31 December	Union victory under Dunham at Parker Cross Roads, TN

1863 West Virginia admitted. Walt Whitman, letter to Thomas Jefferson. Polish rebellion.

1 January	**Abraham Lincoln, The Emancipation Proclamation** (abolishes slavery in areas in rebellion)
29 January	Union victory under Conner at Bear River, ID

11 January	Union victory under McClernand at Ft Hindman; Confederate *Alabama* beats *Hatteras* in naval engagement
31 January	Confederate *Palmetto State* beats *Mercedita* Confederate *Chicora* beats *Keystone State* in naval engagements
6–7 February	Confederate victory under Lomax at Barnett's Ford, VA
4 March	Confederate victory under Van Dorn at Spring Hill, TN
17 March	Union victory under Stuart at Kelly's Ford, VA
26 March	**John Bright, Speech at St. James's Hall** (England)
11 April–4 May	Union victory under Peck at Suffolk, VA
12–14 April	Confederate victory under Taylor at Irish Bend and Fort Bisland, LA
17 April–2 May	Union victory under Grierson, on Grierson's Raid
1 May	Union victory under Grant at Port Gibson, MS
1–4 May	Confederate victory under Lee at Chancellorsville, VA
3–4 May	Union victory under Segdwick at Salem CHurch, VA
10 May	**Virginia Military Institute, 'The Death of "Stonewall" Jackson'**
12 May	Confederate victory under Gregg at Raymond, MS
14 May	Union victory under Grant at Jackson, MS
16 May	Union victory under Grant at Champion's Hill, MS
27 May–9 July	Union victory under Banks at Port Hudson, LA
9 June	Union victory under Pleasonton at Brandy Station, VA
13 June	Confederate victory under Rhodes at Berryville, VA
13–15 June	Confederate victory under Ewell at Winchester, VA
14 June	Confederate victory under Jenkins at Martinsburg, WV
17 June	Confederate victories under Munford at Aldie, VA and under Stuart at Middleburg, VA; the Union *Kearsage* beats *Alabama* in naval engagement
19 June	Union victory under Gregg at Middleburg, VA
20 June	Confederate victory under Ewell at Greencastle, PA
27 June	Confederate victory under Hampton at Fairfax Court House, VA and the Confederate *Archer* beats *Caleb Cushing* in naval engagement
29 June	Confederate victory under Stuart at Westminster, MD
30 June	Union victories under Kilpatrick at Hanover, PA and under Ewen at Sporting Hill, PA
1–3 July	Union victory under Meade at the **Battle of Gettysburg: Reports of Maj.-Gen. George G. Meade, Gen. Robert E. Lee, Lieut.-Gen. James Longstreet, Brig.-Gen. George Armstrong Custer**
4 July	Union victories under Grant at Vicksburg, MS and under Prentiss at Helena, AK
5 July	Confederate victory under Morgan at Bardstown, KY
10 & 18 July	Confederate victory under Taliaferro at Fort Wagner, SC

19 July	Union victory under Hobson at Buffington Island, OH
24 July	Confederate victory under Hill at Battle Mountain, VA
1–3 August	Confederate victory under Stuart at Rappahannock Station, VA
8 September	Confederate victory under Dowling at Sabine Pass, TX and in naval engagement under Beauregard at Fort Sumter, SC
19–20 September	Confederate victory under Bragg at Chickamauga, TN
6 October	Confederate victory under Quantrill at Baxter Springs, KN
10 October	Union victory under Burnside at Blue Springs, TN
14 October	Confederate victory under Lee at Bristoe Station, VA and Union victory under Owen at Catlett's Station, VA
19 October	Confederate victory under Stuart at Buckland Mills, VA
28 October	Union victory under Grant at Wauhatchie, TN
7 November	Union victory under Meade at Rappahannock Bridge and Kelly's Ford, VA
16 November	Union victory under Hantraft at Campbell's Station, TN
19 November	**Abraham Lincoln, Address at the Dedication of Gettysburg National Cemetery**
23–25 November	Union victory under Grant at Chattanooga, TN
27–29 November	Union victory under Banks at Fort Esperanza, TX
29 November	Union victory under Benjamin at Fort Sanders, TN

1864   Nevada admitted.

6 January	Union forces under Carson fight and defeat Navajo Indians at Cañon de Chelly, NM
16 February	Confederate *Hunley* under Dixon beats *Housatonic* in naval engagement
20 February	Confederate victories under Finegan at Olustree, FL and under Forrest at West Point, MS
22–27 February	Confederate victory under Johnston at Dalton, GA
28–4 March	Confederate victory under Lee at Richmond, VA
12 March	'The Historicus Letter', *The New York Herald*
8 April	Confederate victory under Taylor at Sabine Cross Roads, LA
9 April	Union victory under Banks at Pleasant Hill, LA
9–13 April	Union victory under Steele at Prairie D'Ane, AR
12 April	Confederate victory under Forrest at Fort Pillow, TN
17–20 April	Confederate victory under Hoke, Plymouth, NC
19 April	Confederate *Albemarle* under Cooke beats *Miami* and *Southfield* in naval engagement
25 April	Confederate victory under Fagan at Mark's Mill, AR
30 April	Confederate victory under Smith at Jenkins' Ferry, AR
May–June	**The Wilderness Campaign: Reports of Maj.-Gen. Ambrose E. Burnside and Lieut.-Gen. James Longstreet; Mary**

	Chesnut from *A Diary from Dixie*. Sherman begins his 'March through Georgia'.
1–8 May	Union victory under Banks at Alexandria, LA
5–11 May	Union victory under Sherman at Rocky Face Ridge, GA
4–16 May	Confederate victory under Beauregard, at Drewry's Bluff, VA
5–7 May	Confederate victory under Lee at Wilderness, VA
5–9 May	Confederate victory under Stuart at Todd's Tavern, VA
9 May	Confederate victory under Beauregard at Ware Bottom Church, VA
11 May	Union victory under Sheridan at Yellow Tavern, VA
13–16 May	Union victory under Sherman at Resaca, GA
14–16 May	Union victory under Banks at Avoyelles Prairie, LA
15 May	Confederate victory under Breckinridge at New Market, VA
18 May	Confederate victory under Taylor at Bayou De Glaize, LA
20 May	Union victory under Butler at Ware Bottom Church, VA
23–27 May	Confederate victory under Lee at North Anna River, VA
28–31 May	Confederate victory under Lee at Totopotomy Creek, VA
28 May	Union victory under Gregg at Haw's Shop, VA
31 May–12 June	Confederate victory under Lee at Cold Harbor, VA
5 June	Union victory under Hunter at Piedmont, VA
9 June	Confederate victory under Wise at Petersburg, VA
10 June	Confederate victory under Forrest at Brice's Cross Roads, MS
11 June	Confederate victory under Morgan at Cynthiana, KY
11–12 June	Confederate victory under Hampton at Trevilian Station, VA
15–18 June	Confederate victory under Beauregard at Petersburg, VA
17–18 June	Confederate victory under Early at Lynchburg, VA
19 June	Union *Kearsage* under Winslow beats *Alabama* in naval engagement
22–23 June	Confederate victory under Lee at Weldon Railroad, VA
27 June	Confederate victory under Johnston at Kenesaw Mountain, GA
2 July	**The Wade-Davis Bill**
5–17 July	Union victory under Sherman at Chattahooche River, GA
9 July	Confederate victory under Early at Monocacy, MD
12 July	Union victory under Wright at For Stevens, MD
13–15 July	Union victory under Smith at Tupelo, MS
14 July	Confederate victory under Heath at Falling Waters, VA
20 July	Union victories under Averell at Stephenson's Depot, VA and under Sherman at Peachtree Creek, GA
22 July	Union victory under McPherson at Atlanta, GA
23–24 July	Confederate victory under Early at Kernstown, VA
27–29 July	Confederate victory under Lee at Deep Bottom Run, VA
28 July	Union victory under Sherman at Ezra Church, GA
3–23 August	Union victory under Granger at Forts Gaines, Morgan and

	Powell, AL
5 August	Union forces under Farragut win naval engagement in Mobile Bay, AL
5–6 August	Confederate victory under Hood at Utoy Creek, GA
7 August	Union victory under Averell at Moorefield, WV
17 August	**Abraham Lincoln, letter to Charles D. Robinson**
13–20 August	Confederate victory under Lee at Deep Bottom Run, VA
14–16 August	Union victory under Laiboldt at Dalton, GA
18–21 August	Union victory under Grant at Globe Tavern, VA
19 August	Confederate victory under Jackson at Jonesboro, GA
25 August	Confederate victory under Lee at Reams' Station, VA; Union forces under Carson fight and defeat Navajo Indians at Sacramento Mountain, NM
31 August	Confederate victory under Rhodes at Martinsburg, WV
2–6 September	Confederate victory under Hood at Lovejoy, GA
September	**Sherman takes Atlanta in Georgia and orders expulsion of inhabitants: William T. Sherman & Others, Correspondence.**
16 September	Confederate victory under Hampton at Coggin's Point, VA
19 September	Union victory under Sheridan at Winchester, VA
22 September	Union victory under Sheridan at Fishers Hill, VA
28–30 September	Confederate victory under Lee at New Market Heights, VA
30 Sept–2 Oct	Union victory under Grant at Poplar Springs Church, VA
4 October	Union *Wachusset* under Collins beats *Florida* in naval engagement
5 October	Union victory under Tourtelotte at Altoona, GA
7 October	Union victory under Kautz at Darbytown and New Market Roads, VA
9 October	Union victory under Torbert at Tom's Book, VA
13 October	Confederate victory under Lee at Darbytown Road, Va
19 October	Union victory under Sheridan at Cedar Creek, VA
23 October	Union victory under Curtis, at Westport, MO
27 October	Confederate victory under Hill at Hatcher's Run, VA; Union forces under Cushing defeat *Albemarle* in naval engagement
27–28 October	Confederate victory under Lee at Fair Oaks, VA
4–5 November	Confederate victory under Forrest at Johnsonville, TN
16 November	Union victory under Walcutt at Griswoldville, GA
23–25 November	Union victory under Howard at Ball's Ferry, GA
25 November	Comanche Indians defeat Union forces under Carson at Abobe Walls, TX
26 November	Union victory under Sherman at Sandersville, GA
29 November	Union victories under Kilpatrick at Waynesboro, GA and under Schofield at Spring Hill, TN
30 November	Confederate victory under Smith at Honey Hill, SC and

	Union victory under Schofield at Franklin, TN
7 December	Confederate victory under Forrest at Murfreesboro, TN
9 December	Union forces under Chivington defeat Cheyenne and Arapahoe Indians at Sand Creek, CO
13 December	Union victory under Hazen at Fort McAllister, GA
15 December	Confederate victory under Forrest at Murfreesboro, TN
15–16 December	Union victory under Thomas at Nashville, TN
7–11 December	Union victory under Warren at Weldon Railroad, VA
7–27 December	Confederate victory under Lamb at Fort Fisher, NC
December	**Eliza Frances Andrews, [19–24 Dec.] from** *A War-Time Journal of a Georgia Girl 1864–1865*

1865   The ratification of the 13th amendment to the Constitution ends slavery throughout the country. Andrew Jackson elected President. Estimated 15,000,000 buffalo on plains. **Carl Schurz,** *Report to President Johnson*

6–15 January	Union victory under Terry at Fort Fisher, NC
5–7 February	Confederate victory under Mahone at Hatcher's Run, VA
March	**Abraham Lincoln, Second Inaugural Address.**
2 March	Union victory under Custer at Waynesboro, VA
3 March	**The First Freedmen's Bureau Act**
13 March	**Debate in The House of Commons (London) regarding British neutrality**
16 March	Union victory under **Slocum at Averasboro, NC**
19–21 March	Union victory under **Sherman at Bentonville, NC**
21 March–2 May	**Mary Chesnut, from** *A Diary from Dixie*
25 March	Union victory under Hartranfat at Fort Stedman, VA
29 March	Union victory under Grant at Quaker Road, VA
30 March–1 April	Union victory under Grant at Five Forks, VA
1–9 April	Union victory under Canby at Blakely, AL
3 April	Union victory under Custer at Namozine Church, Willicomack Creek, VA
5 April	Union victory under Davies at Amelia Springs
6 April	Union victory under Meade at Saylor's Creek, VA, and Confederate victory under Rosser at High Bridge, VA
7 April	Union victory under Meade at Farmville & High Bridge, VA
9 April	**Union victory under Grant at Battle of Appomatox—Lee surrenders: Lieut.-Gen. Ulysses S. Grant and Gen. Robert E. Lee, correspondence; Lee, Report of Surrender and Last Order to the Army of Northern Virginia; Grant, Recollections of Lee's Surrender**
11 April	**Abraham Lincoln, Last Public Address**
14 April	**William Lloyd Garrison, 'The Governing Passion of My Soul'.** Abraham Lincoln is assassinated: **Brig.-Gen. Henry**

Lawrence Burnett, 'Assassination of President Lincoln and the Trial of the Assassins'; John W. Millington, 'Account of the Chase and Capture of John Wilkes Booth'.

19 April	Dr. Phineas Gurley, 'Faith in God', Sermon at the Funeral of Abraham Lincoln
26 April	Union forces under Sherman accept Johnston's surrender
27 & 29 April	Leading Articles, *The Times.*
10 May	Union forces under Wilson accept surrender of Florida
13 May	Confederate victory under Ford at Palmito Ranch, TX
26 May	Union forces under Canby accept surrender of trans-Mississippi Confederates
29 May	Andrew Johnson, 'Proclamation of Amnesty'
14 June	Howell Cobb, 'Suggestions on Reconstruction'
December	Ku Klux Klan founded in Tennessee.
18 December	Thaddeus Stevens, 'Reconstruction'; The Thirteenth Amendment to the Constitution

1865–67 The Sioux War.

1866	Herman Melville, *Battle-Pieces and Aspects of the War,*
9 April	Congress enacts Civil Rights Act.
May	Race riots in Memphis.
20 June	Joint Committee of Reconstruction, 'The "Forfeited Rights" Plan'
July	Race riots in New Orleans.
16 July	The Second Freedmen's Bureau Act
3 September	Andrew Johnson, Speech in Cleveland
November	Republicans win mid-term Congressional elections.

1867 First Republican reconstruction act. Nebraska admitted. USA purchases Alaska from Russia. House votes to impeach Johnson. British North America becomes Confederation of Canada; British Reform Act. Meiji restoration in Japan. John Esten Cooke, *The Wearing of the Gray; Being Personal Portraits, Scenes and Adventures of the War;*

28 Feb–3 March	Articles of Impeachment
2 March	Tenure of Office Act; First Reconstruction Act
23 March	Andrew Johnson, 'The President's Answer'; Supplementary Reconstruction Act
19 July	Third Reconstruction Act

1868 Fort Laramie Treaty. Johnson acquitted. Fourteenth Amendment added to Constitution. Grant elected President. John Wallace, *Carpet-Bag Rule in Florida; The Great Impeachment and Trial of Andrew Johnson;*

Fourth Reconstruction Act; The Fourteenth Amendment to the Constitution

1869 Public Credit Act. Transcontinental Railway: the Union Pacific and Central Pacific meet at Promontory Summit, Utah. Women in Wyoming win suffrage. Formation of the Knights of Labor. **Louisa May Alcott, 'The Brothers',** *Camp and Fireside Stories*

1870 Chicago population reaches 300,000. John D. Rockefeller forms Standard Oil. First African–American in the Senate. **The Fifteenth Amendment to the Constitution.** Franco-Prussian War. Death of Charles Dickens.

1871 **Second Enforcement Act; Third Enforcement or 'Ku Klux Klan' Act**

1872 Grant re-elected President. **Jubal Early,** *The Campaigns of Gen. Robert E. Lee. An Address by Lieut. General Jubal A. Early, before Washington and Lee University, January 19th, 1872*

1874 Exposure of Tweed Ring. Women's Christian Temperance Union campaigns. Louisa May Alcott, 'Transcendental Wild Oats'.

1875 Civil Rights Act. Whiskey scandal exposed. First edition of **Mary Baker Eddy's** *Science and Health.* Dwight L. Moody returns in triumph from a revivalist tour of Britain and is thereafter the dominant figure in American Protestantism until his death in 1899. **W. T. Sherman,** *Memoirs of General W. T. Sherman, Written by Himself*

1876 Battle of Little Big Horn. Philadelphia World Fair. As a mark of the growth of black denominational and congregational independence the membership of the African Methodist Episcopal Church reaches 200,000. Colorado admitted.

1877 Rutherford B. Hayes inaugurated President after disputed presidential election.

1878 Sojourner Truth, *Narrative of Sojourner Truth*

1879 **Richard Taylor,** *Destruction and Reconstruction: Personal Experiences of the Late War in the United States*

1880 **John Bell Hood,** *Advance and Retreat: Personal Experiences in the United States and Confederate State Armies;* John Bell Hood, *Advance and Retreat: Personal Experiences in the United States and Confederate State Armies.* G. A. Henty, *With Lee in Virginia*

1882 **Walt Whitman, 'Memories of President Lincoln',** *Specimen Days.*

1883 Statue of Liberty presented to New York by France. Mark Twain, *Life on the Mississippi.*

1884 **Frederick Douglass,** *The Life and Times of Frederick Douglass; from 1817–1882*

1885   Twain's *Adventures of Huckleberry Finn*. Fewer than 1,000 buffalo remaining on the plains. Josiah Strong, *Our Country: Its Possible Future and Its Present Crisis*. Walt Whitman, 'Washington Monument, February, 1885'.

1877   Henry James, *The American*. The Desert Land Act

1878   The Timber and Stone Act.

1881   Henry James, *The Portrait of a Lady*; **Jefferson Davis, *The Rise and fall of the Confederate Government***

1885   Publication of **Israel Green, 'The Capture of John Brown'**.

1887   Queen Victoria's Golden Jubilee

1888   Dunlop develops the pneumatic tyre

1889   North and South Dakota, Montana and Washington admitted. Settlers allowed into Oklahoma Indian Territory.

1890   Battle of Wounded Knee. Idaho and Wyoming admitted.

1891   Jacob Riis, *How the Other Half Lives*.

1892   **Walt Whitman, 'Calhoun's Real Monument', *The Complete Prose Works of Walt Whitman***

1893   Stephen Crane, *Maggie: A Girl of the Streets*. Henry Blake Fuller, *The Cliff Dwellers*. James Bryce, *The American Commonwealth*. Julian Ralph, *Our Great West*.

1893   Frederick Jackson Turner's 'The Significance of the Frontier in American History'.

1894   **Dabney Herndon Maury, *Recollections of a Virginian in the Mexican, Indian and Civil Wars*.**

1895   **Stephen Crane, *Red Badge of Courage*.**

1896   First public film show in the USA. Abraham Cahan, *Yekl: A Tale of the New York Ghetto*. First Olympic Games in Athens. **James Longstreet, *From Manassas to Appomattox, Memoirs of the Civil War in America*.**

1899   **J. T. Derry, *Sherman in Georgia***

1900   Escalator invented in USA. Theodore Dreiser, *Sister Carrie*.

1901   Assassination of US President McKinley: Theodore Roosevelt becomes President. **Stephen K. Williams, ed., *Cases Argued and Decided in the Supreme Court of the United States, Lawyer's Edition, Book 41*.** Death of Queen Victoria and accesstion of Edward VII

1903   Mass European emigration to US. Pogroms in Russia. Suffragette movement begins in England

1904   John B. Gordon, *Reminiscences of the Civil War;* Robert E. Lee, Jr., *Recollections and Letters of General Robert E. Lee by his Son, Capt. Robert E. Lee*

1905   First Russian Revolution. Einsteins's Special Theory of Relativity

1906   Walter L Fleming, ed., *Documentary History of Reconstruction*; Thomas Dixon Jr., *The Clansman: An Historical Account of the Ku Klux Klan.* Vitamins discovered

1908   Edward Curtis, 'Glimpses of Hospital Life in War Times'

1909   Ambrose Bierce, 'What I saw of Shiloh', *The Collected Works of Ambrose Bierce.* US supports revolution in Nicaragua

1910   Edward Trenchard, 'The Services and Sacrifices of the Daughters of the Republic during the Rebellion'; Grenville M. Dodge, *The Battle of Atlanta and other Campaign Addresses, etc.* Union of South Africa formed. E. M. Forster, *Howard's End*; Post-Impressionist Exhibition in London

1911   Amundsen reaches South Pole. Rutherford develops nuclear model of the atom

1912   Benson, Berry, 'Sergeant Benson's Story as Written by Himself', *Elmira Prison Camp.* Titanic sinks.

1914   Panama Canal opens. Assassination of Arch-Duke Ferdinand in Sarajevo sparks war

1914–18 First World War

1917   John S. Mosby, *The Memoirs of Col. John S. Mosby.* US enters First World War. Russian Revolution: abdication of Czar Nicholas II

1918   Adams, Henry, *The Education of Henry Adams: An Autobiography.* Armistice 11 November

1922   USSR formed. Mussolini forms government in Italy. James Joyce, *Ulysses*; T. S. Eliot, *The Waste Land*

1924   Death of Lenin. US economy growing fast

1927   Stalin in power in Russia and fall of Trotsky. BBC founded.

1928   Stephen Vincent Benét, 'John Brown's Prayer', *John Brown's Body.* Pencillin discovered. Walt Disney, *Mickey Mouse*

1929   Wall Street crashes.

Admission of the States

South Carolina	May 23, 1787
Delaware	December 7, 1787
Pennsylvania	December 12, 1787
New Jersey	December 18, 1787
Georgia	January 2, 1788
Connecticut	January 9, 1788
Massachusetts	February 6, 1788
Maryland	April 28, 1788
New Hampshire	June 21, 1788
Virginia	June 25, 1788
New York	July 26, 1788
North Carolina	November 21, 1789
Rhode Island	May 29, 1790
Vermont	March 4, 1791
Kentucky	June 1, 1792
Tennessee	June 1, 1796
Ohio	March 1, 1803
Louisiana	April 30, 1812
Indiana	December 11, 1816
Mississippi	December 10, 1817
Illinois	December 3, 1818
Alabama	December 14, 1819
Maine	March 15, 1820
Missouri	August 10, 1821
Arkansas	June 15, 1836
Michigan	January 26, 1837
Florida	March 3, 1845
Texas	December 29, 1845
Iowa	December 28, 1846
Wisconsin	May 29, 1848
California	September 9, 1850
Minnesota	May 11, 1858
Oregon	February 14, 1859
Kansas	January 29, 1861
West Virginia	June 19, 1863
Nevada	October 31, 1864

Nebraska	March 1, 1867
Colorado	August 1, 1876
North Dakota	November 2, 1889
South Dakota	November 2, 1889
Montana	November 8, 1889
Washington	November 11, 1889
Idaho	July 3, 1890
Wyoming	July 10, 1890
Utah	January 4, 1896
Oklahoma	November 16, 1907
New Mexico	January 6, 1912
Arizona	February 14, 1912
Alaska	January 3, 1959
Hawaii	August 21, 1959

The Legal Position of Slavery in 1861

Free Union States (no slavery)

California	Massachusetts	Oregon
Connecticut	Michigan	Pennsylvania
Illinois	New Hampshire	Rhode Island
Indiana	New Jersey	Vermont
Iowa	New York	Wisconsin
Maine	Ohio	[Kansas]

Confederate States (slave states)

Alabama	Louisiana	Tennessee
Arkansas	Mississippi	Texas
Florida	North Carolina	Virginia
Georgia	South Carolina	

Slave States not part of the Confederacy

Delaware	Kentucky	Missouri
	Maryland	

Territories open to Slavery after the Dred Scott Decision, 1857

Colorado	Nebraska	Utah
Dakota	Nevada	Washington
Indian Territory	New Mexico	

Bibliography of Sources & Documents

The Address and Reply on the Presentation of a Testimonial to Salmon P. Chase, by the coloured People of Cincinnati, Cincinnati, 1845. [1.16]

Anti-Slavery Tracts, New York: American Anti-Slavery Society, 1860, No. 1. New Series, Daniel A. P. Murray collection in the Library of Congress. [1.36]

The Constitution of the United States of America, 1787, Washington D.C.: National Archives. [1.2]

The Declaration of Independence, July 4th 1776, Washington D.C: National Archives. [1.1]

Documents Relating to the Death of Stonewall Jackson, Lexington: Virginia Military Institute Archives, 1863. [2.85]

The Great Impeachment and Trial of Andrew Johnson, Philadelphia, 1868. [3.149; 3.157; 3.158; 3.160]

Official Records of the Union and Confederate Armies, 128 vols., Washington, 1880–1901. [1.55]

Official Records of the Union and Confederate Navies in the War of the Rebellion, 30 vols., Washington, 1894-1922. [2.70]

The Rebellion Record, New York: G. P. Putnam, 1861-1868. [3.132]

Records of the Supreme Court of the United States, compiled by Marion M. Johnson, 20 vols., Washington, National Archives, RG 267. [1.14; 1.29]

State of South Carolina, Journal of the Convention of the Peoples of South Carolina, Held in 1860, 1861, and 1862. Together with the Ordinances, Reports, Resolutions, etc., Columbia, S.C.: R. W. Gibbes, Printer to the Convention, 1862. [1.44]

The Statutes at Large of the United States of America, Washington: Government Printing Office, 1867. [3.148; 3.152; 3.154; 3.161; 3.162; 3.163]

The War of the Rebellion: A Compilation of the Official Records of the Union and Confederate Armies, Washington D.C.: Government Printing Office, 1880. [2.57; 2.59; 2.60; 2.65; 2.71; 2.72; 2.74; 2.75; 2.76; 2.77; 2.78; 2.79; 2.81; 2.82; 2.86; 2.87; 2.88; 2.89; 2.94; 2.95; 2.102; 2.103]

Adams, Henry, *The Education of Henry Adams: An Autobiography*, Boston: The Riverside Press, 1918. [3.124]

Alcott, Louisa May, *Camp and Fireside Stories*, Boston: Robert Brothers, 1869. [3.130]

Ambler, Charles H., *Life of John Floyd*, Ralph-Macon College, 1918.

American Anti-slavery Society, *Abolitionist*, I, December 1833, 1.13

Andrews, Elizabeth Francis, *The War-Time Journal of a Georgia Girl, 1864–1865,* New York: D. Appleton & Co., 1908. [2.100]

Baker, George, ed., *The Works of William H. Seward,* Boston: Houghton, Mifflin and Company, 1884, vol. 4, new edition. [1.34]

Bee-Hive, The, 26 March 1863. [3.127]

Benét, Stephen Vincent, *John Brown's Body,* London : William Heinemann Ltd., 1928. [3.138]

Benson, Berry, 'Sergeant Benson's Story as Written by Himself', *Elmira Prison Camp,* ed. Clay W. Holmes, New York and London: G. P. Putnam's Sons, 1912. [3.141]

Bierce, Ambrose, *The Collected Works of Ambrose Bierce,* New York: The Neale Publishing Company, 1909. [3.131]

Blakeman, Noel, ed., *Personal Recollections of the War of the Rebellion,* New York, 1912. [3.139; 3.145]

Boyd, Belle, *Belle Boyd in Camp and Prison,* London: Saunders, Otley & Co., 1865. [2.63]

Bright, John, Speech, *The Bee-Hive,* 28 March 1863. [3.127]

Brooks, Phillips, *The Life and Death of Abraham Lincoln,* Philadelphia: H. B. Ashmead, printer, 1865. [2.113]

Burnett, Henry Lawrence, *Assassination of President Lincoln and the Trial of the Assassins,* New York: Ohio Society of New York, 1906. [2.110]

Cable, George Washington, *John March, Southerner,* New York: George Scribner's Sons, 1894. [3.134]

Calhoun, John C., *The Works of John C. Calhoun,* ed. by Richard K. Crallé, Columbia, S. C: Printed by A. S. Johnston, 1851–56. [1.21; 1.22]

Chesnut, Mary, *A Diary from Dixie,* New York: D. Appleton and Company, 1905 edition. [2.58; 2.64; 2.96]

Cleveland, H., *Alexander H. Stephens, in Public and Private: With Letters and Speeches, before, during, and since the War,* Philadelphia: National Publishing Co., 1866. [1.53]

Congressional Globe, 18th December 1860. [1.43; 3.121; 3.122]

Cooke, John Esten, *Wearing of the Gray: Being Personal Portraits, Scenes and Adventures of the War,* New York: E.B. Treat & Co., 1867. [3.144; 3.173]

Cooper, Thomas, *American Politics from the Beginning to Date,* Boston: Russell & Henderson, 1885 edition. [1.46; 2.73]

Crane, Stephen, *The Red Badge of Courage,* New York: D. Appleton and company, 1895. [3.136]

Curtis, Edward, 'Glimpses of Hospital Life in Wartime,' (1908) in Noel Blakeman ed., *Personal Recollections of the War of the Rebellion,* New York and London: George Putnam's Sons, Ltd., 1912. [3.145]

Davis, Jefferson, *The Rise and Fall of the Confederate Government,* 2 vols., London: Longmans, Green and Co., 1881. [3.117]

Dixon, Thomas, Jr., *The Clansman: An Historical Account of the Ku Klux Klan.* New York: Doubleday, Page and Company, 1906. [3.175]

Dodge, Grenville M.., *The Battle of Atlanta and other Campaign Addresses, etc*, Council Bluffs, Iowa: The Monarch Printing Company, 1910. [3.142]

Douglass, Frederick, *Narrative of the Life of Frederick Douglass, an American Slave, Written by Himself*, Boston: The Anti-Slavery Office, 1845 [1.15];

——, *My Bondage and My Freedom*, 1855 [1.23];

——, *The Life and Times of Frederick Douglass from 1817–1882*, London: Christian Age Office, 1884. [3.146; 3.170]

Early, Jubal, *The Campaigns of Gen. Robert E. Lee. An Address by Lieut. General Jubal A. Early, before Washington and Lee University, January 19th, 1872*, in Baltimore: J. Murphy and Company, 1872. [3.172]

Edwards, Jonathan, 'The injustice and impolicy of the slave trade, and of the slavery of the Africans: illustrated in a sermon preached before the Connecticut society for the promotion of freedom, and for the relief of persons unlawfully holden in bondage, at their annual meeting in New Haven, Sept. 15, 1791', Boston: Wells & Lilly-Court-Street, second edition, 1822. [1.5]

Emerson, Ralph Waldo, *Complete Works*, London: George Routledge and Sons, Ltd, 1903 edition. [1.40]

Evans, C. A., ed., *Confederate Military History: A Library of Confederate States History Written by Distinguished Men of the South*, Atlanta, 1899. [2.99]

Fitzhugh, George, *Cannibals All! Or, Slaves Without Masters*, Cambridge, 1960.

Fleming, Walter, ed., *Documentary History of Reconstruction*, Cleveland: Arthur H. Clarke Company, 1906. [3.116; 3.120; 3.150; 3.151; 3.164; 3.165; 3.166; 3.167; 3.168; 3.176; 3.177]

Floyd, John, from a letter to Governor James Hamilton, Jr., of South Carolina, 19th November 1831, rptd Charles H. Ambler, *Life of John Floyd*, (Randolph-Macon College, Va:, John P. Branch Historical Papers, 1918), vol. V, No. 1. [1.10]

De Fontaine, F. G., *American Abolitionism, from 1787 to 1861. A Compendium of Historical Fact, Embracing legislation in Congress and Agitation Without*, New York: D. Appleton Co., 1861. The pamphlet is in the Daniel A. P. Murray Collection in the Library of Congress. [1.50]

Furman, Richard, 'Exposition of the Views of the Baptists, Relative to the Coloured Population in the United States', 1822, Charleston: A. E. Miller, 1838, second edition. [1.6]

Garibaldi, Giuseppe, Letter to Abraham Lincoln, *Reynolds's Newspaper*, December 21, 1862.

Garrison, William Lloyd, *The Liberator*, September 3, 1831. [1.8]

Gladstone, William Ewart, Speech, *Reynolds's Newspaper*, October 12, 1862.

Gordon, John B., *Reminiscences of the Civil War*, London: Archibald Constable & Co., 1904. [3.118]

Gray, Thomas R., *The Confessions of Nat Turner, the Leader of the late Insurrection in Southampton, Va. As fully and voluntarily made to Thomas R. Gray*, Baltimore: Lucas & Deaver, 1831. [1.9]

Greenhow, Rose O'Neal, *My Imprisonment and the First Year of Abolition Rule in*

Washington, London: Richard Bentley, 1863. [2.62]

Grimké, Angelina, *An Appeal to the Women of the Nominally Free States*, 1832, Boston: Isaac Knapp, second edition 1838. [1.12]

Gurley, Phineas, *Faith in God: Dr. Gurley's Sermon at the Funeral of Abraham Lincoln*, Philadelphia: General Assembly of the Presbyterian Church in the USA, 1940. [2.112]

Hamilton, Alexander, James Madison and John Jay, *The Federalist*, No. LIV, 12th February 1788, reptd New York: E.P. Dutton & Co. Inc., 1911. [1.3]

Hansard, Volume CLXXVII (Third Series), 1865. [3.129]

Henty, G. A., *With Lee in Virginia*, (1880), New York: Hurst and Company, 1900. [3.133]

Holmes, Oliver Wendell, *The Poetical Works of Oliver Wendell Holmes*, Boston: H. O. Houghton & Co., 1908 edition. [1.45]

Hood, John Bell, *Advance and Retreat: Personal Experiences in the United States and Confederate States Armies*, New Orleans: G. T. Beauregard, 1880. [2.80; 2.91]

Howe, Julia Ward, 'The Battle Hymn of the Republic', *Atlantic Monthly*, February 1862. [2.68]

Illinois State Journal, 18 June 1858, [1.31]; 20–21 July, [1.33]

Illinois State Register, 19 July 1858. [1.32]

Jefferson, Thomas, *Notes on the State of Virginia*, 1782, rptd New York: W. W. Norton & Co., 1954. [1.4]

Joint Committee on Reconstruction, Report, Washington: Government Printing Office, 1866. [3.153]

Lee, Robert E., Jr., *Recollections and Letters of General Robert E. Lee by his Son, Capt. Robert E. Lee*, London: Archibald, Constable and Company Ltd., 1904. [3.174]

Letters on American Slavery, Boston: The American Anti-Slavery Society, 1860. [1.39]

Longstreet, James, *From Manassas to Appomattox: Memoirs of the Civil War in America*, Philadelphia: J. B. Lippincott Co., 1896. [2.90; 2.104]

Marx, Karl, 'Progress of Feeling in England', *The New York Daily Tribune*, 25th December 1861; 'English Public Opinion,' *The New York Daily Tribune*, 1st February 1862.

Maury, Dabney Herndon, *Recollections of a Virginian in the Mexican, Indian and Civil Wars*, London: Sampson Low, Marston & Co., 1894. [2.76; 2.84; 3.119]

McPherson, E., *Political History of the United States of America during the Great Rebellion*, Washington D.C.: Philp & Solomons, 1865. [1.47]

Melville, Herman, *Battle-Pieces and Aspects of the War*, New York: Harper and Brothers, 1866. [3.132]

McPherson, E., *Political History of the United States of America During the Great Rebellion*, Washington, 1865.

Mill, John Stuart, 'The Contest in America,' *Fraser's Magazine*, 1862. [3.123]

Moore, Frank, ed., *The Rebellion Record*, 11 vols., New York, 1861–1866. [2.67]

Mosby, John S., *The Memoirs of Colonel John S. Mosby*, ed. Charles Wells Russell,

New York, 1917. [3.143]

The New York Herald, 12 March, 1864. [2.93]

New York Tribune, [Editorials], 'Slavery in the Field', 6th January 1854; 'Slavery Militant', 11th January 1854; 'The Rascals at Washington', 26th January 1854. [1.18]

New York Times, 'Slavery Extension. The Nebraska Bill in Congress. Address to the People', 24th January 1854. [1.24]

North American Review, December 1885, [1.35]

Palmerston, Viscount John Henry Temple, Speech, Hansard, March 13, 1865.

Portland Journal, February 1937. [2.111]

Reynolds's Weekly Newspaper, 12 October 1862. [3.126]

——, 21 December 1862. [3.128]

Richardson, James D., ed., *A Compilation of the Messages and Papers of the Presidents*, New York: Bureau of National Literature, Inc., 1897. [1.20; 1.27; 1.48; 1.52; 1.56; 2.83, 2.101; 3.147; 3.149]

Richmond Dispatch, 7 December 1861. [2.67]

Seward, William H., *The Works of William H. Seward*, ed. by George Baker, Boston, 1884.

Sherman, William T., *The Memoirs of William T. Sherman, Written by Himself*, New York and London: Henry King and Co., 1875. [2.98; 3.140]

Stevens, Thaddeus, Speech, *The Congressional Globe*, Washington, 1862.

Stowe, Harriet Beecher, *Uncle Tom's Cabin*, 1852. [1.17]

Sumner, Charles, Speech, *The Congressional Globe*, Washington, 1865.

Taylor, Richard, *Destruction and Reconstruction: Personal Experiences of the Late War in the United States*, Edinburgh and London: William Blackwood and Sons, 1879. [3.169]

Times, The, April 27th, 1865; April 29th, 1865, [2.114]

Tocqueville, Alexis de, *Democracy in America*, 1835, 2 vols., reptd New York: Alfred A. Knopf, 1980. [1.7]

Trenchard, Edward, 'The Services and Sacrifices of the Daughters of the Republic during the Rebellion', (1910) in Noel Blakeman (ed.), *Personal Recollections of the War of the Rebellion*, New York, 1912. [3.139]

Tribune Almanac, 1861, New York: New York Tribune, 1868, (facsimile), pp. 30–32, 34. [1.43]

Turner, Nat, *The Confession of Nat Turner, the Leader of the Late Insurrection in Southampton, Va. As Made Voluntarily to Thomas R. Gray*, Baltimore, 1831.

Twain, Mark, *The Adventures of Huckleberry Finn*, (1885), New York: Harper and Brothers, 1912. [3.135]

Walker, David, *Appeal in Four Articles; Together with a Preamble, to the Coloured Citizens of the World*, Boston: D. Walker, 1830. [1.11]

Wallace, John, *Carpet-Bag Rule in Florida*, Jacksonville: Da Costa Printing and Publishing House, 1868. [3.155; 3.171]

Webster, Daniel, 'Webster's Great Reply to Hayne Webster's Great Reply to Hayne In which he "Expounds the Constitution," delivered in Senate, January 26,

1830', in Thomas Cooper, *American Politics From The Beginning To Date*, Boston: Mass.: Russell & Henderson, 1885, Book III. [1.19]

Whitman, Walt, *Leaves of Grass*, New York, 1865–66, 1881; 2.115

——, *Drum-Taps*, New York, 1865; [2.66]

——, *The Complete Prose Works of Walt Whitman*, Philadelphia: D. McKay, 1892. [3.137]

Stephen K. Williams, ed., *Cases Argued and Decided in the Supreme Court of the United States, Lawyer's Edition, Book 41'*, Rochester: The Lawyer's Co-operative Publishing Company, 1901. [3.178; 3.179; 3.180]

Young, John Russell, *Around the World With General Grant*, New York, 1879.

Some Modern Editions

Angle, Paul, ed., *Created Equal? The Complete Lincoln–Douglas Debates of 1858*, Chicago: University of Chicago Press, 1958.

Brassler, Roy P., ed., *The Collected Works of Abraham Lincoln*, New Brunswick, N.J.: Rutgers University Press, 1953.

Commager, Henry Steele, ed., *Documents of American History*, New York: Appleton-Century-Crofts, 1968.

Crallé, Richard K., ed., *The Works of John C. Calhoun*, New York: Russell & Russell, 1968

Davis, Jefferson, *The Papers of Jefferson Davis*, ed. by Lynda C. Crist and Mary S. Dix, Baton Rouge, 1992–.

Douglass, Frederick, *My Bondage and My Freedom*, New York: Dover Publications, 1969.

Fitzhugh, George, *Cannibals All! Or, Slaves Without Masters*, Cambridge, MA: Harvard University Press, 1960.

Furness, C., ed. *Walt Whitman's Workshop*, New York: Russell & Russell, 1964.

Glick, Wendell, ed., *The Writings of Henry D. Thoreau*, Princeton: Princeton University Press, 1973

Jefferson, Thomas, *Notes on the State of Virginia*, New York: W. W. Norton & Co., 1954.

Philip Van Doren Stern, ed., *The Life and Writings of Abraham Lincoln*, New York: Random House, 1940.

Stowe, Harriet Beecher, *Uncle Tom's Cabin*, London: J. M. Dent & Sons Ltd, 1961.

de Tocqueville, Alexis, *Democracy in America*, New York: Alfred A. Knopf, 1980.

Whitman, Walt, *The Collected Writings of Walt Whitman*, New York: New York University Press, 1963.

Wilson, Woodrow, *The Papers of Woodrow Wilson*, ed. by Arthur S. Link, 69 vols., Princeton, 1983.

Critical Bibliographies

General Studies

Boatner, Mark, M., *The Civil War Dictionary*, New York, 1959.

Boorstin, Daniel J., *An American Primer*, Chicago:University of Chicago Press,, 1966.

Catton, Bruce, *The Centennial History of the Civil War*, 3 vols., Garden City, 1961–1965.

Cooper, Thomas, *American Politics From The Beginning To Date*, Boston: Mass.: Russell & Henderson, 1885.

Cullen, Jim, *The Civil War in Popular Culture: A Reusable Past*, Washington, 1995.

Farmer, Alan, *The American Civil War: 1861–1865*, London, 1996.

Faust, Patricia L., ed., *Historical Times Illustrated Encyclopedia of the Civil War*, New York, 1986.

Foote, Shelby, *The Civil War: A Narrative*, 3 vols., 1958–1974.

Jones, Virgil Carrington, *The Civil War at Sea*, 3 vols., New York, 1960–1962.

Katcher, *The American Civil War Source Book*, London, 1992

Long, E.B., *The Civil War Day by Day: An Almanac, 1861–1865*, Garden City, 1971.

McPherson, James, *Battle Cry of Freedom: The Civil War Era*, Oxford, 1988.

——, *Ordeal by Fire: The Civil War and Reconstruction*, rev. ed., New York, 1992.

——, *Drawn with the Sword: Reflections on the American Civil War*, Oxford, 1996.

Nevins, Allan, *Ordeal of the Union*, 4 vols., New York, 1947–1971.

Parish, P.J., *The American Civil War*, New York, 1975.

Sewell, R.M., *A House Divided: Sectionalism and Civil War 1848–1865*, Baltimore, 1988.

Ward, Geoffrey C., Ric Burns and Ken Burns, *The Civil War: An Illustrated History of the War Between the States*, London, 1992.

Wilson, Edmund, *Patriotic Gore: Studies in the Literature of the American Civil War*, New York, 1966.

Slavery and Abolitionism

Berlin, Ira, *Slaves without Masters: The Free Negro in the Antebellum South*, New York, 1974.

Blassingame, John W., *The Slave Community: Plantation Life in the Antebellum South*, rev. ed., New York, 1979.

Campbell, Stanley, *The Slave Catchers: Enforcement of the Fugitive Slave Law 1850–*

1860, Chapel Hill, 1970.

Duff, John, & Peter Mitchell, eds, *The Nat Turner Rebellion: The Historical Event and the Modern Controversy*, New York: Harper & Row, 1971.

Elkins, Stanley M., *Slavery: A Problem in American Institutional and Intellectual Life*, 3rd ed., Chicago, 1976.

Escott, Paul D., *Slavery Remembered*, Chapel Hill, 1979.

Filler, Louis, ed., *Slavery in the United States*, New Brunswick, 1998.

Fogel, Robert W. and Stanley L. Engerman, *Time on the Cross: The Economics of Negro Slavery*, Boston, 1974.

Genovese, Eugene D., *The Political Economy of Slavery*, New York, 1965.

——, *Roll, Jordan, Roll: The World the Slaves Made*, New York, 1974.

Gutman, Herbert G., *The Black Family in Slavery and Freedom*, New York, 1976.

Kolchin, Peter, *American Slavery: 1619–1877*, London, 1993.

Morris, Thomas D. *Free Men All: The Personal Liberty Laws of the North 1780–1861*, Baltimore, 1974.

Oakes, James, *The Ruling Race: A History of American Slave-holders*, New York, 1982.

Rose, Willie Lee, *Slavery and Freedom*, New York, 1982.

Sewell, Richard H., *Ballots for Freedom: Antislavery Politics in the United States 1837–1860*, New York, 1976.

Stampp, Kenneth M., *The Peculiar Institution: Slavery in the Antebellum South*, New York, 1956.

Takaki, Ronald T., *A Pro-Slavery Crusade: The Agitation to Re-Open the Slave Trade*, New York, 1971.

Secession and the Origins of the Civil War

Adams, Charles, *When in the Course of Human Events: Arguing the Case for Southern Secession*, Lanham, 2000.

Anbinder, T.G., *Nativism and Slavery: The Northern Know Nothings and the Politics of the 1850s*, Oxford, 1992.

Bateman, Fred and Thomas Weiss, *A Deplorable Scarcity: The Failure of Industrialization in the Slave Economy*, Chapel Hill, 1981.

Borrit, Gabor, ed., *Why the Civil War Came*, Oxford, 1996.

Channing, Steven A., *A Crisis of Fear: Secession in South Carolina*, New York, 1970.

Craven, Avery, *The Coming of the Civil War*, rev. ed., Chicago, 1957.

——, *The Growth of Southern Nationalism 1848–1861*, Baton Rouge, 1953.

Dumond, Dwight L., *The Secession Movement 1860–1861*, New York, 1931.

Fehrenbacher, D. E., *The Dred Scott Case: Its Significance in American Law and Politics*, Oxford, 1978.

Finkleman, P., *His Soul Goes Marching On: Responses to John Brown and the Harper's Ferry Raid*, Charlottesville, 1995.

Fite, Emerson D., *The Presidential Campaign of 1860*, New York, 1911.

Foner, Eric, *Free Soil, Free Labor, Free Men: The Ideology of the Republican Party before the Civil War*, New York, 1970.

Garfinkle, Norton ed., *Lincoln and the Coming of the Civil War*, Boston, 1959.

Hamilton, Holman, *Prologue to Conflict: The Crisis and Compromise of 1850*, Lexington, 1964.

Holt, Michael F., *The Political Crisis of the 1850s*, New York, 1978.

McCardell, John, *The Idea of a Southern Nation: Southern Nationalists and Southern Nationalism, 1830–1860*, New York, 1979.

Milton, George Fort, *The Eve of Conflict: Stephen A. Douglas and the Needless War*, Boston, 1934.

Potter, David M., *Lincoln and His Party in the Secession Crisis*, rev. ed., New Haven, 1962.

—, *The Impending Crisis 1846–61*, New York, 1976.

Pressly, Thomas J., *Americans Interpret Their Civil War*, Princeton, 1954.

Rawley, James A. *Race and Politics: "Bleeding Kansas" and the Coming of the Civil War*, Philadelphia, 1969.

Reid, Brian Holden, *The Origins of the American Civil War*, London, 1996.

Reynolds, Donald E., *Editors Make War: Southern Newspapers in the Secession Crisis*, Nashville, 1970.

Rozwenc, Edwin C., *The Causes of the American Civil War*, 2nd ed., Lexington, 1972.

—, *Slavery as a Cause of the Civil War*, 2nd ed., Boston, 1963.

Russell, Robert Royal, *Economic Aspects of Southern Sectionalism, 1840–1861*, Urbana, 1923.

Stampp, Kenneth, *And the War Came: The North in the Secession Crisis, 1860–1861*, Baton Rouge, 1950.

—, *America in 1857*, Oxford, 1990.

—, ed., *The Causes of the Civil War*, 3rd ed., New York, 1991.

Trefousse, Hans, L., *The Causes of the Civil War: Institutional Failure or Human Blunder?* Hinsdale, 1971.

Wender, Herbert, *Southern Commercial Conventions 1837–1859*, Baltimore, 1930.

Wooster, Ralph, *The Secession Conventions of the South*, Princeton, 1962.

The Confederacy

Alexander, Thomas B. and Richard E. Beringer, *The Anatomy of the Confederate Congress*, Nashville, 1972.

Ash, Stephen V., *When the Yankees Came: Conflict and Chaos in the Occupied South, 1861–1865*, Chapel Hill, 1995.

Cleveland, H., *Alexander H. Stephens, in Public and Private*, Philadelphia, 1866.

Connelly, Thomas Lawrence and Archer Jones, *The Politics of Command: Factions and Ideas in Confederate Strategy*, Baton Rouge, 1973.

Coulter, E. Merton, *The Confederate States of America 1861–1865*, Baton Rouge, 1950.

Current, R. N., *The Encyclopedia of the Confederacy*, 4 vols., New York, 1993.

Davis, W. C., *"A Government of Our Own": The Making of the Confederacy*, London, 1994.

Durrell, Wayne K., *War of Another Kind: A Southern Community in the Great Rebellion*, New York, 1990.

Eaton, C., *A History of the Southern Confederacy*, New York, 1954.

Escott, Paul D., *After Secession: Jefferson Davis and the Failure of Southern Nationalism*, Baton Rouge, 1978.

Faust, Drew Gilpen, *The Creation of Confederate Nationalism: Ideology, Identity in the Civil War South*, Baton Rouge, 1988.

——, *Mothers of Invention: Women of the Slaveholding South in the American Civil War*, Chapel Hill, 1996.

Fox-Genovese, Elizabeth, *Within the Plantation Household: Black and White Women of the Old South*, Chapel Hill, 1988.

Gallagher, Gary W. *The Confederate War*, Cambridge, 1999.

Hill, Louise B., *State Socialism in the Confederate States of America*, Charlottes-ville, 1936.

Massey, Mary Elizabeth, *Ersatz in the Confederacy*, Columbia, 1952.

Nelson, Larry E., *Bullets, Bayonets, and Rhetoric: Confederate Policy for the United States Presidential Contest of 1864*, University, 1980.

Owens, Harry P. and James J. Cooke, eds., *The Old South in the Crucible of War*, Jackson, 1983.

Owsley, Frank L., *State Rights in the Confederacy*, Chicago, 1925.

Paludan, Philip S., *Victims: The True History of the Civil War*, Knoxville, 1981.

Patrick, Rembert, *Jefferson Davis and His Cabinet*, Baton Rouge, 1944.

Rable, George C., *Civil Wars: Women and the Crisis of Southern Nationalism*, Urbana, 1989.

——, *The Confederate Republic: A Revolution Against Politics*, Chapel Hill, 1994.

Ramsdell, Charles W. *Behind the Lines in the Southern Confederacy*, Baton Rouge, 1944.

Ringold, May S., *The Role of State Legislatures in the Confederacy*, Athens, 1966.

Schwab, John C., *The Confederate States. . . .A Financial and Industrial History of the South During the Civil War*, New York, 1901.

Simkins, Francis B. and James W. Patton, *The Women of the Confederacy*, Richmond, 1936.

Strode, Hudson, *Jefferson Davis*, 3 vols., New York, 1955–64.

Tatum, Georgia Lee, *Disloyalty in the Confederacy*, New York, 1972.

Todd, Richard C., *Confederate Finance*, Athens, 1954.

Thomas, Emory M., *The Confederacy as a Revolutionary Experience*, Englewood Cliffs, 1971.

——, *The Confederate Nation, 1861–1865*, New York, 1979.

Vandiver, Frank E., *Their Tattered Flags: The Epic of the Confederacy*, New York, 1970.

Wiley, Bell Irvin, *Southern Negroes 1861–1865*, New Haven, 1938.

Wyatt-Brown, Bertram, *Southern Honor: Ethics and Behaviour in the Old South*, New York, 1982.

Yearns, Wilfred B., *The Confederate Congress*, Athens, 1960.

The Union

Andreano, Ralph, *The Economic Impact of the Civil War*, 2nd ed., Cambridge, 1967.

Belz, Herman, *A New Birth of Freedom: The Republican Party and Freedmen's Rights, 1861–1866*, Westport, 1976.

——, *Emancipation and Equal Rights: Politics and Constitutionalism in the Civil War Era*, New York, 1978.

Blied, Benjamin, *Catholics and the Civil War*, Milwaukee, 1945.

Cook, Adrian, *The Armies of the Streets: The New York City Draft Riots of 1863*, Lexington, 1974.

Cox, LaWanda, *Lincoln and Black Freedom: A Study in Presidential Leadership*, Columbia, 1981.

Dell, Christopher, *Lincoln and the War Democrats*, Madison, 1975.

Donald, David H., *Lincoln*, London, 1995.

Fite, Emerson D., *Social and Economic Conditions in the North*, New York, 1910.

Frederickson, George M., *The Inner Civil War: Northern Intellectuals and the Crisis of the Union*, New York, 1965.

Gilchrist, Davis, and W. David Lewis, eds., *Economic Change and the Civil War Era*, Greenville, 1965.

Gray, Wood, *The Hidden War: The Story of the Copperheads*, New York, 1942.

Hammond, Bray, *Sovereignty and an Empty Purse: Banks and Politics in the Civil War*, Princeton, 1970.

Hesseltine, William B., *Lincoln and the War Governors*, New York, 1948.

Kirkland, Edward C., *The Peacemakers of 1864*, New York, 1927.

Klement, Frank L., *The Limits of Dissent: Clement Vallandigham and the Civil War*, Lexington, 1970.

——, *Dark Lanterns, Secret Political Societies, Conspiracies and Treason Trials in the Civil War*, Baton Rouge, 1984.

McPherson, James M., *The Struggle for Equality: Abolitionists and the Negro in the Civil War and Reconstruction*, Princeton, 1964.

——, *The Negro's Civil War*, New York, 1965.

Montgomery, Davis, *Beyond Equality: Labor and the Radical Republicans, 1862–1872*, New York, 1967.

Moorhead, James H., *American Apocalypse: Yankee Protestants and the Civil War*, New Haven, 1978.

Quarles Benjamin, *The Negro in the Civil War*, Boston, 1953.

——, *Lincoln the President: Bull Run to Gettysburg*, New York, 1956.

Riddle, Albert G., *Recollections of War Times: Reminiscences of Men and Events in Washington, 1861–1865*, New York, 1895.

Silbey, Joel, *A Respectable Minority: The Democratic Party in the Civil War Era*, New

York, 1977.

Smith, George W. and Charles Judah, eds., *Life in the North During the Civil War*, Albuquerque, 1966.

Sprague, Dean, *Freedom Under Lincoln*, Boston, 1965.

Stern, Philip Van Doren, *The Life and Writings of Abraham Lincoln*, New York, 1940.

Tap, Bruce, *Over Lincoln's Shoulder: The Committee on the Conduct of the War*, Lawrence, 1998.

Trefousse, Hans L., *The Radical Republicans: Lincoln's Vanguard for Racial Justice*, New York, 1969.

Voegeli, V. Jacque, *Free But Not Equal: The Midwest and the Negro in the Civil War*, Chicago, 1967.

Williams, Harry T., *Lincoln and the Radicals*, Madison, 1941.

Zornow, William F., *Lincoln and the Party Divided*, Norman, 1954.

Military Studies

Adams, George W., *Doctors in Blue: The Medical History of the Union Army in the Civil War*, New York, 1952.

Adams, Michael C. C., *Our Masters the Rebels: A Speculation on Union Military Failure in the East, 1861–1865*, Cambridge, 1978.

Bruce, Robert V., *Lincoln and the Tools of War*, Indianapolis, 1956.

Castel, Albert, *Decision in the West: The Atlanta Campaign of 1864*, Lawrence, 1992.

Catton, Bruce, *Mr. Lincoln's Army*, Garden City, 1951.

——, *Glory Road*, Garden City, 1952.

——, *A Stillness at Appomattox*, Garden City, 1953.

Connelly, Thomas L., *The Marble Man: Robert E. Lee and his Image in American Society*, New York, 1977.

Cunningham, Horace H., *Doctors in Gray: The Confederate Medical Service*, Baton Rouge, 1958.

Fischel, Edwin C., *The Secret War for the Union: The Untold Story of Military Intelligence in the Civil War*, Boston, 1996.

Freeman, Douglas Southall, *Robert E. Lee: A Biography*, 4 vols., New York, 1934–1935.

——, *Lee's Lieutenants: A Study in Command*, 3 vols., New York, 1942–1944.

Fuller, J.F.C., *Grant and Lee: A Study in Personality and Generalship*, London, 1923.

——, *The Generalship of Ulysses S. Grant*, London, 1929.

Furguson, Ernest B., *Chancellorsville 1863: The Souls of the Brave*, New York, 1992.

Glatthaar, Joseph T., *Partners in Command: The Relationships between Leaders in the Civil War*, New York, 1994.

Grimsley, Mark, *The Hard hand of War: Union Military Policy Toward Southern Civilians, 1861–1865*, Cambridge, 1995.

Hart, Basil H. Liddell, *Sherman: Soldier, Realist, American*, New York, 1929.

Hassler, Warren W., Jr., *George B. McClellan: Shield of the Union*, Baton Rouge, 1957.

Henderson, G.F.R., *Stonewall Jackson and the American Civil War*, 2 vols., New York, 1898.

Herbert, Walter H., *Fighting Joe Hooker*, Indianapolis, 1944.

McWhiney, Grady and Perry D. Jamieson, *Attack and Die: Civil War Military Tactics and the Southern Heritage*, University, 1982.

Moore, Albert B., *Conscription and Conflict in the Confederacy*, New York, 1924.

Murdock, Eugene C., *One Million Men: The Civil War Draft in the North*, Madison, 1971.

Nolan, Alan T., *Lee Considered: General Robert E. Lee and Civil War History*, Chapel Hill, 1991.

Perry, Milton F., *Infernal Machines: The Story of Confederate Submarine and Mine Warfare*, Baton Rouge, 1965.

Rowland, Thomas J., *George B. McClellan and Civil War History: In the Shadow of Grant and Sherman*, Kent, 1998.

Sears, Stephen W., *George B. McClellan: The Young Napoleon*, New York, 1988.

——, *To the Gates of Richmond: The Peninsula Campaign*, New York, 1992.

——, *Chancellorsville*, Boston, 1996.

——, *Controversies and Commanders: Dispatches from the Army of the Potomac*, Boston, 1999.

Spear, Lonnie R., *Portals to Hell: Military Prisons of the Civil War*, Mechanicsburg, 1997.

Starr, Stephen Z., *The Union Cavalry in the Civil War*, Baton Rouge, 1981.

Tidwell, William A. and James O. Hall, *Come Retribution: The Confederate Secret Service and the Assassination of Lincoln*, Jackson, 1988.

Turner, George E. *Victory Rode the Rails*, Indianapolis, 1953.

Warner, Erza J., *Generals in Gray*, Baton Rouge, 1959.

——, *Generals in Blue*, Baton Rouge, 1964.

Wiley, B. I., *The Life of Johnny Reb: The Common Soldier of the Confederacy*, Indianapolis, 1943.

——, *The Life of Billy Yank: The Common Soldier of the Union*, Indianapolis, 1952.

Williams, T. Harry, *Lincoln Finds a General: A Military Study of the Civil War*, 5 vols. New York, 1949–59.

The Civil War Abroad

Adams, E. D., *Great Britain and the American Civil War*, 2 vols., London, 1925.

Bourne, Kenneth, *Britain and the Balance of Power in North America, 1815–1908*, London, 1967.

Crook, D. P., *The North, the South and the Powers: !861–1865*, New York, 1974.

——, *American Democracy in English Politics: 1815–1850*, Oxford, 1965.

Crawford, Martin, *The Anglo-American Crisis of the Nineteenth Century: The Times and America, 1850–1862*, Athens, 1987.

Ellison, Mary, *Support for Secession: Lancashire and the American Civil War*, Chicago, 1972.

Ferris, Norman, *The Trent Affair: A Diplomatic Crisis*, Knoxville, 1977.

Foner, Philip S. *British Labor and the American Civil War*, New York, 1981.

Hernon, Joseph M., *Celts, Catholics and Copperheads: Ireland Views the American Civil War*, Ohio, 1968.

Hymen, Harold, ed., *Heard Around the World: The Impact of the Civil War Abroad*, New York, 1969.

Jenkins, Brian, *Britain and the War for the Union*, 2 vols., Montreal, 1974 and 1980.

Jones, Howard, *Union in Peril: The Crisis over British Intervention in the American Civil War*, Chapel Hill, 1992.

Jordan, Donaldson and Edwin J. Pratt, *Europe and the American Civil War*, London, 1931.

Lester, Richard, *Confederate Finance and Purchasing in Great Britain*, Charlottesville, 1975.

May, Robert E. ed., *The Union, the Confederacy and the Atlantic Rim*, West Lafayette, 1995.

Merli, Frank J., *Great Britain and the Confederate Navy: 1861–1865*, Bloomington, 1970.

Owsley, Frank Lawrence, *King Cotton Diplomacy: Foreign Relations of the Confederate States of America*, 2nd ed. revised by Harriet Owsley, Chicago, 1959.

Spencer, Warren F., *The United States and France: Civil War Diplomacy*, Philadelphia, 1970.

Van Auken, Sheldon, *The Glittering Illusion: English Sympathy for the Confederacy*, London, 1988.

Warren, Gordon H., *Fountain of Discontent: The Trent Affair and Freedom of the Seas*, Boston, 1981.

Winks, Robin, *Canada and the United States: The Civil War Years*, Baltimore, 1960.

Victory and Reconstruction

Abbot, Martin, *The Freedmen's Bureau in South Carolina, 1865–1872*, Chapel Hill, 1967.

——, *The Republican Party and the South, 1855–1877: The First Southern Strategy*, Chapel Hill, 1986.

Belz, Herman, *Reconstruction the Union: Theory and Policy during the Civil War*, Ithaca, 1969.

Benedict, Michael, *A compromise of Principle; Congressional Republicans and Reconstruction, 1863–1869*, New York, 1974.

——, *The Impeachment and Trial of Andrew Johnson*, new York, 1973.

Bentley, George R., A History of the Freedman's Bureau, Philadelphia, 1955.

Bogue, Allan G., The Earnest men: Republicans of the Civil War Senate, Ithaca, 1981.

Bradley, Erwin S., The Triumph of Militant Republicanism, Philadelphia, 1964.

Carter, Dan, When the War Was Over: The Failure of Self-Reconstruction in the South, 1865–1867, Baton Rouge, 1985.

Coulter, E. Merton, The South During Reconstruction 1865–1877, Baton Rouge, 1947.

Curry, Richard O., ed., Radicalism, Racism and Party Realignment: The Border States During Reconstruction, Baltimore, 1969.

Dawson, Joseph G., Army Generals and Reconstruction: Louisiana, 1862–1877, Baton Rouge, 1972.

Donald, David, H., The Politics of Reconstruction, 1863–1867, Baton Rouge, 1965.

—, Charles Sumner and the Rights of Man, New York, 1970.

Du Bois, W.E.B., Black Reconstruction in America, New York, 1935.

Dunning, William A., Reconstruction, Political and Economic 1865–1877, New York, 1907.

Foner, Eric, Reconstruction; America's Unfinished Revolution, 1863–1877, New York, 1988.

Gambill, Edward, L., Conservative Ordeal: Northern Democrats and Reconstruction, 1865–1868, Ames, 1981.

Gerteis, Louis S., From Contraband to Freedman: Federal Policy Toward Southern Blacks 1861–1865, Westport, 1973.

Gillette, William, Retreat from Reconstruction 1869–1879, Baton Rouge 1979.

Gutman, Herbert G., The Black Family in Slavery and Freedom 1750–1925, New York, 1976.

Howard, Black Liberation in Kentucky: Emancipation and Freedom, 1862–1884, Lexington, 1983.

Hyman, Harold M., A More Perfect Union: The Impact of the Civil War and Reconstruction Upon the Constitution, New York, 1973.

Jones, Archer, How the North Won: A Military History of the Civil War, Urbana, 1983.

Kaczorowski, Robert, The Politics of Judicial Interpretation: The Federal Courts, Department of Justice and Civil Rights, 1866–1876, New York, 1985.

Litwack, Leon F., Been in the Storm So Long: The Aftermath of Slavery, New York, 1979.

McKitrick, Eric L., Andrew Johnson and Reconstruction, Chicago, 1960.

Mohr, Clarence L., On the Threshold of Freedom: Masters and Slaves in Civil War Georgia. Athens, 1986.

Nieman, Donald G., To Set the Law in Motion: The Freedmen's Bureau and the Legal Rights of Blacks, 1865–1868, Millwood, 1979.

Olsen, Otto H., Reconstruction and Redemption in the South, Baton Rouge, 1980.

Perman, Michael, Reunion Without Compromise: The South and Reconstruction 1865–1868, New York, 1973.

Powell, Lawrence N., *New Masters: Northern Planters during the Civil War and Reconstruction*, New Haven, 1980.

Roark, James L., *Masters Without Slaves: Southern Planters in the Civil War and Reconstruction*, New York, 1977.

Sefton, James E., *The United States Army and Reconstruction 1865–1877*, Baton Rouge, 1967.

Trelease, Allen W., *White Terror: The Ku Klux Klan Conspiracy and Southern Reconstruction*, New York, 1971.

Wiley, Bell Irvin, *The Road to Appomattox*, Memphis, 1956

Wood, Forrest G., *Black Scare: The Racist Response to Emancipation and Reconstruction*, Berkeley, 1968.

I. Introduction: Contextualising Slavery

⊹1⊹

The Declaration of Independence

Jefferson's spare and elegant prose in the Declaration of Independence (July 4th, 1776) expressed the moral high-ground taken by the colonies in their dispute with George III. The values he enshrined at the core of the nascent American Republic: equality and a commitment to the natural rights of life, liberty and the pursuit of happiness, would provide the context for the debate over the place of slavery within the United States. The Declaration thus became part of the political controversy that would end in civil war.

In Congress,
July 4, 1776.

The unanimous Declaration of the thirteen
united States of America,

When in the Course of human events, it becomes necessary for one people to dissolve the political bands which have connected them with another, and to assume among the powers of the earth, the separate and equal station to which the Laws of Nature and of Nature's God entitle them, a decent respect to the opinions of mankind requires that they should declare the causes which impel them to the separation.

We hold these truths to be self-evident, that all men are created equal, that they are endowed by their Creator with certain unalienable Rights, that among these are Life, Liberty and the pursuit of Happiness.—That to secure these rights, Governments are instituted among Men, deriving their just powers from the consent of the governed,—That whenever any Form of Government becomes destructive of these ends, it is the Right of the People to alter or to abolish it, and to institute new Government, laying its foundation on such principles and organizing its powers in such form, as to them shall seem most likely to effect their Safety and Happiness. Prudence, indeed, will dictate that Governments long established should not be changed for light and transient causes; and accordingly all experience hath

Source: *The Declaration of Independence,* July 4th 1776,
Washington D.C: National Archives

shewn, that mankind are more disposed to suffer, while evils are sufferable, than to right themselves by abolishing the forms to which they are accustomed. But when a long train of abuses and usurpations, pursuing invariably the same Object evinces a design to reduce them under absolute Despotism, it is their right, it is their duty, to throw off such Government, and to provide new Guards for their future security.—Such has been the patient sufferance of these Colonies; and such is now the necessity which constrains them to alter their former Systems of Government. The history of the present King of Great Britain is a history of repeated injuries and usurpations, all having in direct object the establishment of an absolute Tyranny over these States. To prove this, let Facts be submitted to a candid world.

He has refused his Assent to Laws, the most wholesome and necessary for the public good.

He has forbidden his Governors to pass Laws of immediate and pressing importance, unless suspended in their operation till his Assent should be obtained; and when so suspended, he has utterly neglected to attend to them.

He has refused to pass other Laws for the accommodation of large districts of people, unless those people would relinquish the right of Representation in the Legislature, a right inestimable to them and formidable to tyrants only.

He has called together legislative bodies at places unusual, uncomfortable, and distant from the depository of their public Records, for the sole purpose of fatiguing them into compliance with his measures.

He has dissolved Representative Houses repeatedly, for opposing with manly firmness his invasions on the rights of the people.

He has refused for a long time, after such dissolutions, to cause others to be elected; whereby the Legislative powers, incapable of Annihilation, have returned to the People at large for their exercise; the State remaining in the mean time exposed to all the dangers of invasion from without, and convulsions within.

He has endeavoured to prevent the population of these States; for that purpose obstructing the Laws for Naturalization of Foreigners; refusing to pass others to encourage their migrations hither, and raising the conditions of new Appropriations of Lands.

He has obstructed the Administration of Justice, by refusing his Assent to Laws for establishing Judiciary powers.

He has made Judges dependent on his Will alone, for the tenure of their offices, and the amount and payment of their salaries.

He has erected a multitude of New Offices, and sent hither swarms of Officers to harrass our people, and eat out their substance.

He has kept among us, in times of peace, Standing Armies without the Consent of our legislatures.

He has affected to render the Military independent of and superior to the Civil power.

He has combined with others to subject us to a jurisdiction foreign to our constitution, and unacknowledged by our laws; giving his Assent to their Acts of pretended Legislation:

For Quartering large bodies of armed troops among us:

For protecting them, by a mock Trial, from punishment for any Murders which they should commit on the Inhabitants of these States:

For cutting off our Trade with all parts of the world:

For imposing Taxes on us without our Consent:

For depriving us in many cases, of the benefits of Trial by Jury:

For transporting us beyond Seas to be tried for pretended offences:

For abolishing the free System of English Laws in a neighbouring Province, establishing therein an Arbitrary government, and enlarging its Boundaries so as to render it at once an example and fit instrument for introducing the same absolute rule into these Colonies:

For taking away our Charters, abolishing our most valuable Laws, and altering fundamentally the Forms of our Governments:

For suspending our own Legislatures, and declaring themselves invested with power to legislate for us in all cases whatsoever.

He has abdicated Government here, by declaring us out of his Protection and waging War against us.

He has plundered our seas, ravaged our Coasts, burnt our towns, and destroyed the lives of our people.
He is at this time transporting large Armies of foreign Mercenaries to compleat the

works of death, desolation and tyranny, already begun with circumstances of Cruelty & perfidy scarcely paralleled in the most barbarous ages, and totally unworthy the Head of a civilized nation.

He has constrained our fellow Citizens taken Captive on the high Seas to bear Arms against their Country, to become the executioners of their friends and Brethren, or to fall themselves by their Hands.

He has excited domestic insurrections amongst us, and has endeavoured to bring on the inhabitants of our frontiers, the merciless Indian Savages, whose known rule of warfare, is an undistinguished destruction of all ages, sexes and conditions.

In every stage of these Oppressions We have Petitioned for Redress in the most humble terms: Our repeated Petitions have been answered only by repeated injury. A Prince whose character is thus marked by every act which may define a Tyrant, is unfit to be the ruler of a free people.

Nor have We been wanting in attentions to our British brethren. We have warned them from time to time of attempts by their legislature to extend an unwarrantable jurisdiction over us. We have reminded them of the circumstances of our emigration and settlement here. We have appealed to their native justice and magnanimity, and we have conjured them by the ties of our common kindred to disavow these usurpations, which, would inevitably interrupt our connections and correspondence. They too have been deaf to the voice of justice and of consanguinity. We must, therefore, acquiesce in the necessity, which denounces our Separation, and hold them, as we hold the rest of mankind, Enemies in War, in Peace Friends.

We, therefore, the Representatives of the united States of America, in General Congress, Assembled, appealing to the Supreme Judge of the world for the rectitude of our intentions, do, in the Name, and by Authority of the good People of these Colonies, solemnly publish and declare, That these United Colonies are, and of Right ought to be Free and Independent States; that they are Absolved from all Allegiance to the British Crown, and that all political connection between them and the State of Great Britain, is and ought to be totally dissolved; and that as Free and Independent States, they have full Power to levy War, conclude Peace, contract Alliances, establish Commerce, and to do all other Acts and Things which Independent States may of right do. And for the support of this Declaration, with a firm reliance on the protection of divine Providence, we mutually pledge to each other our Lives, our Fortunes and our sacred Honor.

[56 Signatories as follows]

Georgia:
Button Gwinnett
Lyman Hall
George Walton

North Carolina:
William Hooper
Joseph Hewes
John Penn

South Carolina:
Edward Rutledge
Thomas Heyward, Jr.
Thomas Lynch, Jr.
Arthur Middleton

Massachusetts:
John Hancock
Samuel Adams
John Adams
Robert Treat Paine
Elbridge Gerry

Maryland:
Samuel Chase
William Paca
Thomas Stone
Charles Carroll of
        Carrollton

Virginia:
George Wythe
Richard Henry Lee
Thomas Jefferson
Benjamin Harrison
Thomas Nelson, Jr.
Francis Lightfoot Lee
Carter Braxton

Pennsylvania:
Robert Morris
Benjamin Rush
Benjamin Franklin
John Morton
George Clymer
James Smith
George Taylor
James Wilson
George Ross

Delaware:
Caesar Rodney
George Read
Thomas McKean

New York:
William Floyd
Philip Livingston
Francis Lewis
Lewis Morris

New Jersey:
Richard Stockton
John Witherspoon
Francis Hopkinson
John Hart
Abraham Clark

New Hampshire:
Josiah Bartlett
William Whipple
Matthew Thornton

Rhode Island:
Stephen Hopkins
William Ellery

Connecticut:
Roger Sherman
Samuel Huntington
William Williams
Oliver Wolcott

❧ 2 ❧

The 1787 Constitution of the United States of America

The Constitution agreed at the Philadelphia Convention of 1787 is the founding document of the United States of America. It ensured the over-representation of slave-holding states in the Congressional House of Representatives and in the Electoral College for the President by allowing slaves to count as three-fifths of a Person in deciding apportionment. Disputes over its interpretation would lie at the heart of the political argument over slavery. At the time, when asked what the Convention had achieved, the venerable Ben Franklin replied: 'a Republic, if you can keep it'. The civil war was to show the prescience of his remark.

The Constitution of the United States

We the people of the United States, in order to form a more perfect Union, establish Justice, insure domestic Tranquility, provide for the common defence, promote the general Welfare, and secure the Blessings of Liberty to ourselves and our Posterity, do ordain and establish this Constitution for the United States of America.

Article I

Section 1.
All legislative Powers herein granted shall be vested in a Congress of the United States, which shall consist of a Senate and House of Representatives.

Section 2.
The House of Representatives shall be composed of Members chosen every second Year by the People of the several States, and the Electors in each State shall have the Qualifications requisite for Electors of the most numerous Branch of the State Legislature.

Source: *The Constitution of the United States of America*, 1787,
Washington D.C.: National Archives.

No Person shall be a Representative who shall not have attained to the Age of twenty five Years, and been seven Years a Citizen of the United States, and who shall not, when elected, be an Inhabitant of that State in which he shall be chosen.

Representatives and direct Taxes shall be apportioned among the several States which may be included within this Union, according to their respective Numbers, which shall be determined by adding to the whole Number of free Persons, including those bound to Service for a Term of Years, and excluding Indians not taxed, three fifths of all other Persons. The actual Enumeration shall be made within three Years after the first Meeting of the Congress of the United States, and within every subsequent Term of ten Years, in such Manner as they shall by Law direct. The Number of Representatives shall not exceed one for every thirty Thousand, but each State shall have at Least one Representative; and until such enumeration shall be made, the State of New Hampshire shall be entitled to chuse three, Massachusetts eight, Rhode-Island and Providence Plantations one, Connecticut five, New-York six, New Jersey four, Pennsylvania eight, DeLaware one, Maryland six, Virginia ten, North Carolina five, South Carolina five, and Georgia three.

When vacancies happen in the Representation from any State, the Executive Authority thereof shall issue Writs of Election to fill such Vacancies.

The House of Representatives shall chuse their Speaker and other Officers; and shall have the sole Power of Impeachment.

Section 3.

The Senate of the United States shall be composed of two Senators from each State, chosen by the Legislature thereof, for six Years; and each Senator shall have one Vote.

Immediately after they shall be assembled in Consequence of the first Election, they shall be divided as equally as may be into three Classes. The seats of the Senators of the first Class shall be vacated at the Expiration of the second Year, of the second Class at the Expiration of the fourth Year, and the third Class at the Expiration of the sixth Year, so that one third may be chosen every second Year; and if Vacancies happen by Resignation, or otherwise, during the Recess of the Legislature of any State, the Executive thereof may make temporary Appointments until the next Meeting of the Legislature, which shall then fill such Vacancies.

No Person shall be a Senator who shall not have attained to the Age of thirty Years, and been nine Years a Citizen of the United States and who shall not, when elected, be an Inhabitant of that State for which he shall be chosen.

The Vice President of the United States shall be President of the Senate, but shall have no Vote, unless they be equally divided.

The Senate shall chuse their other Officers, and also a President pro tempore, in the Absence of the Vice President, or when he shall exercise the Office of President of the United States.

The Senate shall have the sole Power to try all Impeachments. When sitting for that Purpose, they shall be on Oath or Affirmation. When the President of the United States is tried, the Chief Justice shall preside: And no Person shall be convicted without the Concurrence of two thirds of the Members present.

Judgment in Cases of Impeachment shall not extend further than to removal from Office, and disqualification to hold and enjoy any Office of honor, Trust or Profit under the United States: but the Party convicted shall nevertheless be liable and subject to Indictment, Trial, Judgment and Punishment, according to Law.

Section 4.

The Times, Places and Manner of holding Elections for Senators and Representatives, shall be prescribed in each State by the Legislature thereof; but the Congress may at any time by Law make or alter such Regulations, except as to the Places of chusing Senators.

The Congress shall assemble at least once in every Year, and such Meeting shall be on the first Monday in December, unless they shall by Law appoint a different Day.

Section 5.

Each House shall be the Judge of the Elections, Returns and Qualifications of its own Members, and a Majority of each shall constitute a Quorum to do Business; but a smaller Number may adjourn from day to day, and may be authorized to compel the Attendance of absent Members, in such Manner, and under such Penalties as each House may provide.

Each House may determine the Rules of its Proceedings, punish its Members for disorderly Behaviour, and, with the Concurrence of two thirds, expel a Member.

Each House shall keep a Journal of its Proceedings, and from time to time publish the same, excepting such Parts as may in their Judgment require Secrecy; and the Yeas and Nays of the Members of either House on any question shall, at the Desire of one fifth of those Present, be entered on the Journal.

Neither House, during the Session of Congress, shall, without the Consent of the other, adjourn for more than three days, nor to any other Place than that in which the two Houses shall be sitting.

Section 6.

The Senators and Representatives shall receive a Compensation for their Services, to be ascertained by Law, and paid out of the Treasury of the United States. They shall in all Cases, except Treason, Felony and Breach of the Peace, be privileged from Arrest during their Attendance at the Session of their respective Houses, and in going to and returning from the same; and for any Speech or Debate in either House, they shall not be questioned in any other Place.

No Senator or Representative shall, during the Time for which he was elected, be appointed to any civil Office under the Authority of the United States, which shall have been created, or the Emoluments whereof shall have been encreased during such time: and no Person holding any Office under the United States, shall be a Member of either House during his Continuance in Office.

Section 7.

All Bills for raising Revenue shall originate in the House of Representatives; but the Senate may propose or concur with Amendments as on other Bills.

Every Bill which shall have passed the House of Representatives and the Senate, shall, before it become a Law, be presented to the President of the United States; if he approve he shall sign it, but if not he shall return it, with his Objections to that House in which it shall have originated, who shall enter the Objections at large on their Journal, and proceed to reconsider it. If after such Reconsideration two thirds of that House shall agree to pass the Bill, it shall be sent, together with the Objections, to the other House, by which it shall likewise be reconsidered, and if approved by two thirds of that House, it shall become a Law. But in all such Cases the Votes of both Houses shall be determined by Yeas and Nays, and the Names of the Persons voting for and against the Bill shall be entered on the Journal of each House respectively. If any Bill shall not be returned by the President within ten Days (Sundays excepted) after it shall have been presented to him, the Same shall be a Law, in like manner as if he had signed it, unless the Congress by their Adjournment prevent its Return, in which Case it shall not be a Law.

Every Order, Resolution, or Vote to which the Concurrence of the Senate and House of Representatives may be necessary (except on a question of Adjournment) shall be presented to the President of the United States; and before the same shall take Effect, shall be approved by him, or being disapproved by him, shall be repassed by two thirds of the Senate and House of Representatives, according to the Rules and Limitations prescribed in the Case of a Bill.

Section 8.

The Congress shall have Power to lay and collect Taxes, Duties, Imposts and Excises, to pay the Debts and provide for the common Defence and general Welfare of the United States; but all Duties, Imposts and Excises shall be uniform throughout the United States;

To borrow Money on the credit of the United States;

To regulate Commerce with foreign Nations, and among the several States, and with the Indian tribes;

To establish a uniform Rule of Naturalization, and uniform Laws on the subject of Bankruptcies throughout the United States;

To coin Money, regulate the Value thereof, and of foreign Coin, and fix the Standard of Weights and Measures;

To provide for the Punishment of counterfeiting the Securities and current Coin of the United States;

To establish Post Offices and post Roads;

To promote the Progress of Science and useful Arts, by securing for limited Times to Authors and Inventors the exclusive Right to their respective Writings and Discoveries;

To constitute Tribunals inferior to the Supreme Court;

To define and punish Piracies and Felonies committed on the high Seas, and Offences against the Law of Nations;

To declare War, grant Letters of Marque and Reprisal, and make Rules concerning Captures on Land and Water;

To raise and support Armies, but no Appropriation of Money to that Use shall be for a longer Term than two Years;

To provide and maintain a Navy;

To make Rules for the Government and Regulation of the land and naval Forces;

To provide for calling forth the Militia to execute the Laws of the Union, suppress Insurrections and repel Invasions;

To provide for organizing, arming, and disciplining, the Militia, and for governing such Part of them as may be employed in the Service of the United States, reserving to the States respectively, the Appointment of the Officers, and the Authority of training the Militia according to the discipline prescribed by Congress;

To exercise exclusive Legislation in all Cases whatsoever, over such District (not exceeding ten miles square) as may, by Cession of particular States, and the Acceptance of Congress, become the Seat of the Government of the United States, and to exercise like Authority over all Places purchased by the Consent of the Legislature of the State in which the Same shall be, for the Erection of Forts, Magazines, Arsenals, dock-Yards, and other needful Buildings;—And

To make all Laws which shall be necessary and proper for carrying into Execution the foregoing Powers, and all other Powers vested by this Constitution in the Government of the United States, or in any Department or Officer thereof.

Section 9.

The Migration or Importation of such Persons as any of the States now existing shall think proper to admit, shall not be prohibited by the Congress prior to the Year one thousand eight hundred and eight, but a Tax or duty may be imposed on such Importation, not exceeding ten dollars for each Person.

The privilege of the Writ of Habeas Corpus shall not be suspended, unless when in Cases of Rebellion or Invasion the public Safety may require it.

No Bill of Attainder or ex post facto Law shall be passed.

No Capitation, or other direct, Tax shall be laid, unless in Proportion to the Census or enumeration herein before directed to be taken.

No Tax or Duty shall be laid on Articles exported from any State.

No Preference shall be given by any Regulation of Commerce or Revenue to the Ports of one State over those of another: nor shall Vessels bound to, or from, one State, be obliged to enter, clear or pay Duties in another.

No Money shall be drawn from the Treasury, but in Consequence of Appropriations made by Law; and a regular Statement and Account of Receipts and Expenditures of all public Money shall be published from time to time.

No Title of Nobility shall be granted by the United States: and no Person holding any Office of Profit or Trust under them, shall, without the Consent of the Congress, accept of any present, Emolument, Office, or Title, of any kind whatever, from any King, Prince, or foreign State.

Section 10.
No State shall enter into any Treaty, Alliance, or Confederation; grant Letters of Marque and Reprisal; coin Money; emit Bills of Credit; make any Thing but gold and silver Coin a Tender in Payment of Debts; pass any Bill of Attainder, ex post facto Law, or Law impairing the Obligation of Contracts, or grant any Title of Nobility.

No State shall, without the Consent of the Congress, lay any Imposts or Duties on Imports or Exports, except what may be absolutely necessary for executing it's inspection Laws: and the net Produce of all Duties and Imposts, laid by any State on Imports or Exports, shall be for the Use of the Treasury of the United States; and all such Laws shall be subject to the Revision and Controul of the Congress.

No State shall, without the Consent of Congress, lay any Duty of Tonnage, keep Troops, or Ships of War in time of Peace, enter into any Agreement or Compact with another State, or with a foreign Power, or engage in War, unless actually invaded, or in such imminent Danger as will not admit of delay.

Article II

Section 1. The executive Power shall be vested in a President of the United States of America. He shall hold his Office during the Term of four Years, and, together with the Vice President, chosen for the same Term, be elected, as follows:

Each State shall appoint, in such Manner as the Legislature thereof may direct, a Number of Electors, equal to the whole Number of Senators and Representatives to which the State may be entitled in the Congress: but no Senator or Representative, or Person holding an Office of Trust or Profit under the United States, shall be appointed an Elector.

The Electors shall meet in their respective States, and vote by Ballot for two Persons, of whom one at least shall not be an Inhabitant of the same State with themselves. And they shall make a List of all the Persons voted for, and of the Number of Votes for each; which List they shall sign and certify, and transmit sealed to the Seat of the Government of the United States, directed to the President of the Senate. The President of the Senate shall, in the Presence of the Senate and House of Representatives, open all the Certificates, and the Votes shall then be counted. The Person having the greatest Number of Votes shall be the President, if such Number be a Majority of the whole Number of Electors appointed; and if there be more than one who have such Majority, and have an equal Number of Votes, then the House of Representatives shall immediately chuse by Ballot one of them for President; and if no Person have a Majority, then from the five highest on the List the said House shall in like Manner chuse the President. But in chusing the President, the Votes shall be taken by States, the Representation from each State having one Vote; A quorum for this purpose shall consist of a Member or Members from two thirds of the States, and a Majority of all the States shall be necessary to a Choice. In every Case, after the Choice of the President, the Person having the greatest Number of Votes of the Electors shall be the Vice President. But if there should remain two or more who have equal Votes, the Senate shall chuse from them by Ballot the Vice President.

The Congress may determine the Time of chusing the Electors, and the Day on which they shall give their Votes; which Day shall be the same throughout the United States.

No Person except a natural born Citizen, or a Citizen of the United States, at the time of the Adoption of this Constitution, shall be eligible to the Office of President; neither shall any Person be eligible to that Office who shall not have attained to the Age of thirty five Years, and been fourteen Years a Resident within the United States.

In Case of the Removal of the President from Office, or of his Death, Resignation, or Inability to discharge the Powers and Duties of the said Office, the Same shall devolve on the Vice President, and the Congress may by Law provide for the Case of Removal, Death, Resignation or Inability, both of the President and Vice President, declaring what Officer shall then act as President, and such Officer shall act accordingly, until the Disability be removed, or a President shall be elected.

The President shall, at stated Times, receive for his Services, a Compensation, which shall neither be increased nor diminished during the Period for which he shall have been elected, and he shall not receive within that Period any other Emolument from the United States, or any of them.

Before he enter on the Execution of his Office, he shall take the following Oath or Affirmation:—"I do solemnly swear (or affirm) that I will faithfully execute the Office of President of the United States, and will to the best of my Ability, preserve, protect and defend the Constitution of the United States."

Section 2.

The President shall be Commander in Chief of the Army and Navy of the United States, and of the Militia of the several States, when called into the actual Service of the United States; he may require the Opinion, in writing, of the principal Officer in each of the executive Departments, upon any Subject relating to the Duties of their respective Offices, and he shall have Power to grant Reprieves and Pardons for Offences against the United States, except in Cases of Impeachment.

He shall have Power, by and with the Advice and Consent of the Senate, to make Treaties, provided two thirds of the Senators present concur; and he shall nominate, and by and with the Advice and Consent of the Senate, shall appoint Ambassadors, other public Ministers and Consuls, Judges of the supreme Court, and all other Officers of the United States, whose Appointments are not herein otherwise provided for, and which shall be established by Law: but the Congress may by Law vest the Appointment of such inferior Officers, as they think proper, in the President alone, in the Courts of Law, or in the Heads of Departments.

The President shall have Power to fill up all Vacancies that may happen during the Recess of the Senate, by granting Commissions which shall expire at the End of their next Session.

Section 3.

He shall from time to time give to the Congress Information of the State of the Union, and recommend to their Consideration such Measures as he shall judge necessary and expedient; he may, on extraordinary Occasions, convene both Houses, or either of them, and in Case of Disagreement between them, with Respect to the Time of Adjournment, he may adjourn them to such Time as he shall think proper; he shall receive Ambassadors and other public Ministers; he shall take Care that the Laws be faithfully executed, and shall Commission all the Officers of the United States.

Section 4.

The President, Vice President and all civil Officers of the United States, shall be removed from Office on Impeachment for, and Conviction of, Treason, Bribery, or other high Crimes and Misdemeanors.

Article III

Section 1.

The judicial Power of the United States, shall be vested in one supreme Court, and in such inferior Courts as the Congress may from time to time ordain and establish. The Judges, both of the supreme and inferior Courts, shall hold their Offices during good Behaviour, and shall, at stated Times, receive for their Services, a Compensation, which shall not be diminished during their Continuance in Office.

Section 2.

The judicial Power shall extend to all Cases, in Law and Equity, arising under this Constitution, the Laws of the United States, and Treaties made, or which shall be made, under their Authority;—to all Cases affecting Ambassadors, other public Ministers and Consuls;—to all Cases of admiralty and maritime Jurisdiction;—to Controversies to which the United States shall be a Party;—to Controversies between two or more States;—between a State and Citizens of another State;—between Citizens of different States;—between Citizens of the same State claiming Lands under Grants of different States, and between a State, or the Citizens thereof, and foreign States, Citizens or Subjects.

In all Cases affecting Ambassadors, other public Ministers and Consuls, and those in which a State shall be Party, the supreme Court shall have original Jurisdiction. In all the other Cases before mentioned, the supreme Court shall have appellate Jurisdiction, both as to Law and Fact, with such Exceptions, and under such Regulations as the Congress shall make.

The Trial of all Crimes, except in Cases of Impeachment, shall be by Jury; and such Trial shall be held in the State where the said Crimes shall have been committed; but when not committed within any State, the Trial shall be at such Place or Places as the Congress may by Law have directed.

Section 3.

Treason against the United States, shall consist only in levying War against them, or in adhering to their Enemies, giving them Aid and Comfort. No Person shall be convicted of Treason unless on the Testimony of two Witnesses to the same overt Act, or on Confession in open Court.

The Congress shall have Power to declare the Punishment of Treason, but no Attainder of Treason shall work Corruption of Blood, or Forfeiture except during the Life of the Person attainted.

Article IV

Section 1.

Full Faith and Credit shall be given in each State to the public Acts, Records, and judicial Proceedings of every other State. And the Congress may by general Laws prescribe the Manner in which such Acts, Records, and Proceedings shall be proved, and the Effect thereof.

Section 2.

The Citizens of each State shall be entitled to all Privileges and Immunities of Citizens in the several States.

A Person charged in any State with Treason, Felony, or other Crime, who shall flee from Justice, and be found in another State, shall on demand of the executive Authority of the State from which he fled, be delivered up, to be removed to the State having Jurisdiction of the Crime.

No Person held to service or labor in one State, under the Laws thereof, escaping into another, shall, in Consequence of any Law or Regulation therein, be discharged from such Service or Labour, but shall be delivered up on Claim of the Party to whom such Service or Labour may be due.

Section 3.

New States may be admitted by the Congress into this Union; but no new States shall be formed or erected within the Jurisdiction of any other State; nor any State be formed by the Junction of two or more States, or Parts of States, without the Consent of the Legislatures of the States concerned as well as of the Congress.

The Congress shall have Power to dispose of and make all needful Rules and Regulations respecting the Territory or other Property belonging to the United States; and nothing in this Constitution shall be so construed as to Prejudice any Claims of the United States, or of any particular State.

Section 4.

The United States shall guarantee to every State in this Union a Republican Form of Government, and shall protect each of them against Invasion; and on Application of the Legislature, or of the Executive (when the Legislature cannot be convened) against domestic Violence.

Article V

The Congress, whenever two thirds of both Houses shall deem it necessary, shall propose Amendments to this Constitution, or, on the Application of the Legislatures of two thirds of the several States, shall call a Convention for proposing Amendments, which, in either Case, shall be valid to all Intents and Purposes, as Part of this Constitution, when ratified by the Legislatures of three fourths of the several States, or by Conventions in three fourths thereof, as the one or the other Mode of Ratification may be proposed by the Congress; Provided that no Amendment which may be made prior to the Year one thousand eight hundred and eight shall in any Manner affect the first and fourth Clauses in the Ninth Section of the first Article; and that no State, without its Consent, shall be deprived of its equal Suffrage in the Senate.

Article VI

All Debts contracted and Engagements entered into, before the Adoption of this Constitution, shall be as valid against the United States under this Constitution, as under the Confederation.

This Constitution, and the Laws of the United States which shall be made in Pursuance thereof; and all Treaties made, or which shall be made, under the Authority of the United States, shall be the supreme Law of the Land; and the Judges in every State shall be bound thereby, any Thing in the Constitution or Laws of any State to the Contrary notwithstanding.

The Senators and Representatives before mentioned, and the Members of the several State Legislatures, and all executive and judicial Officers, both of the United States and of the several States, shall be bound by Oath or Affirmation, to support this Constitution; but no religious Test shall ever be required as a Qualification to any Office or public Trust under the United States.

Article VII

The Ratification of the Conventions of nine States, shall be sufficient for the Establishment of this Constitution between the States so ratifying the Same.

Attest William Jackson Secretary

Done in Convention by the Unanimous Consent of the States present the Seventeenth Day of September in the Year of our Lord one thousand seven hundred and Eighty seven and of the Independence of the United States of America the Twelfth. In witness whereof We have hereunto subscribed our Names,

G°. Washington—Presid^t.
and deputy from Virginia

Delaware
Geo: Read
Gunning Bedford jun
John Dickinson
Richard Bassett
Jaco: Broom

Maryland
James McHenry
Dan of St. Thos. Jenifer
Danl. Carroll

Virginia
John Blair
James Madison Jr

North Carolina
Wm. Blount
Richd. Dobbs Spaight
Hu Williamson

South Carolina
J. Rutledge
Charles Cotesworth
                    Pinckney
Charles Pinckney
Pierce Butler

Georgia
William Few
Abr Baldwin

New Hampshire
John Langdon
Nicholas Gilman

Massachusetts
Nathaniel Gorham
Rufus King

Connecticut
Wm. Saml. Johnson
Roger Sherman

New York
Alexander Hamilton

New Jersey
Wil: Livingston
David Brearley
Wm. Paterson
Jona: Dayton

Pennsylvania
B. Franklin
Thomas Mifflin
Robt. Morris
Geo. Clymer
Thos. FitzSimons
Jared Ingersoll
James Wilson
Gouv Morris

⊰ 3 ⊱

Federalist Paper 54

ALEXANDER HAMILTON, JAMES MADISON and JOHN JAY

The Federalist papers, written principally by James Madison and Alexander Hamilton, with a contribution also from John Jay, were intended to win over those who were sceptical about the constitutional design agreed in Philadelphia. This paper offers a rationalisation and justification for allowing the Southern states to be over-represented in the Congress and in terms of votes in the presidential electoral college, by permitting them to count slaves as three-fifths of a person in the process of apportionment. This provision, necessary to bring the South into the Union, nevertheless placed the controversial issue of slavery at the heart of the new constitution.

From the *New York Packet*, Tuesday, February 12, 1788

The Federalist. No. LIV
[Hamilton or Madison]

To the People of the State of New York:

The next view which I shall take of the House of Representatives relates to the appointment of its members to the several States, which is to be determined by the same rule with that of direct taxes.

It is not contended that the number of people in each State ought not to be the standard for regulating the proportion of those who are to represent the people of each State. The establishment of the same rule for the appointment of taxes will probably be as little contested; though the rule itself, in this case, is by no means founded on the same principle. In the former case, the rule is understood to refer to the personal rights of the people, with which it has a natural and universal connection. In the latter, it has reference to the proportion of wealth, of which it is

Source: Alexander Hamilton, James Madison and John Jay, *The Federalist*, No. LIV, 12th February 1788, rptd in New York: E. P. Dutton & Co. Inc., 1911 edition.

in no case a precise measure, and in ordinary cases a very unfit one. But notwithstanding the imperfection of the rule as applied to the relative wealth and contributions of the States, it is evidently the least objectionable among the practicable rules, and had too recently obtained the general sanction of America, not to have found a ready preference with the convention.

All this is admitted, it will perhaps be said; but does it follow, from an admission of numbers for the measure of representation, or of slaves combined with free citizens as a ratio of taxation, that slaves ought to be included in the numerical rule of representation? Slaves are considered as property, not as persons. They ought therefore to be comprehended in estimates of taxation which are founded on property, and to be excluded from representation which is regulated by a census of persons. This is the objection, as I understand it, stated in its full force. I shall be equally candid in stating the reasoning which may be offered on the opposite side.

"We subscribe to the doctrine," might one of our Southern brethren observe,

"that representation relates more immediately to persons, and taxation more immediately to property, and we join in the application of this distinction to the case of our slaves. But we must deny the fact that slaves are considered merely as property, and in no respect whatever as persons. The true state of the case is, that they partake of both these qualities: being considered by our laws, in some respects, as persons, and in other respects as property. In being compelled to labour, not for himself, but for a master; in being vendible by one master to another master; and in being subject at all times to capricious will of another,—the slave may appear to be degraded from the human rank, and classed with those irrational animals which fall under the legal denomination of property. In being protected, on the other hand, in his life and in his limbs, against the violence of all others, even the master of his labour and his liberty; and in being punishable himself for all violence committed against others,— the slave is no less evidently regarded by the law as a member of the society, not as a part of the irrational creation; as a moral person, not as a mere article of property. The federal Constitution, therefore, decides with great propriety on the case of our slaves, when it views them in the mixed character of persons and of property. This is in fact their true character. It is the character bestowed on them by the laws under which they live; and it will not be denied that these are the proper criterion; because it is only under the pretext that the laws have transformed the negroes into subjects of property that a place is disputed them in the computation of numbers; and it is admitted, that if the laws were to restore the rights which have been taken away, the negroes could no longer be refused an equal share of representation with the other inhabitants.

This question may be placed in another light. It is agreed on all sides, that numbers are the best scale of wealth and taxation, as they are the only proper scale of representation. Would the convention have been impartial or consistent, if they had rejected the slaves from the list of inhabitants when the shares of representation were to be calculated, and inserted them on the lists when the tariff of contributions was to be adjusted? Could it be reasonably expected that the Southern States would concur in a system which considered their slaves in some degree as men when burdens were to be imposed, but refused to consider them in the same light when advantages were to be conferred? Might not some surprise also be expressed, that those who reproach the Southern States with the barbarous policy of considering as property a part of their human brethren, should themselves contend that the government to which all the States are to be parties, ought to consider this unfortunate race more completely in the unnatural light of property than the very laws of which they complain?

It may be replied, perhaps, that slaves are not included in the estimate of representatives in any of the States possessing them. They neither vote themselves nor increase the votes of their masters. Upon what principle, then, ought they to be taken into the federal estimate of representation? In rejecting them altogether, the Constitution would, in this respect, have followed the very laws which have been appealed to as the proper guide.

This objection is repelled by a single observation. It is a fundamental principle of the proposed Constitution, that as the aggregate number of representatives allotted to the several States is to be determined by a federal rule, founded on the aggregate number of inhabitants, so the right of choosing this allotted number in each State is to be exercised by such part of the inhabitants as the State itself may designate. The qualifications on which the right of suffrage depend are not, perhaps, the same in any two States. In some of the States the difference is very material. In every State, a certain proportion of inhabitants are deprived of this right by the constitution of the State, who will be included in the census by which the federal Constitution apportions the representatives. In this point of view the Southern States might retort the complaint, by insisting that the principle laid down by the convention required that no regard should be had to the policy of particular States towards their own inhabitants; and consequently, that the slaves, as inhabitants, should have ben admitted into the census according to their full number, in like manner with other inhabitants, who, by the policy of other States, are not admitted to all the rights of citizens. A rigorous adherence, however, to this principle, is waived by those who would be gainers by it. All that they ask is that equal moderation be shown on the other side. Let the case of the slaves be considered, as it is in truth, a peculiar one. Let the compromising expedient of the Constitution be mutually adopted, which regards them as inhabitants, but as debased by servitude below the equal level of free inhabitants; which regards the *slave* as divested of two-fifths of the *man*.

After all, may not another ground be taken on which this article of the Constitution will admit of a still more ready defence? We have hitherto proceeded on the idea that representation related to persons only, and not at all to property. But is it a just idea? Government is instituted no less for protection of the property, than of the persons, of individuals. The one as well as the other, therefore, may be considered as represented by those who are charged with the government. Upon this principle it is that in several of the States, and particularly in the State of New York, one branch of the government is intended more especially to be the guardian of property, and is accordingly elected by that part of the society which is most interested in this object of government. In the federal Constitution this policy does not prevail. The rights of property are committed into the same hands with the personal rights. Some attention ought, therefore, to be paid to property in the choice of those hands.

For another reason, the votes allowed in the federal legislature to the people of each State ought to bear some proportion to the comparative wealth of the States. States have not, like individuals, an influence over each other, arising from superior advantages of fortune. If the law allows an opulent citizen but a single vote in the choice of his representative, the respect and consequence which he derives from his fortunate situation very frequently guide the votes of others to the objects of his choice; and through this imperceptible channel the rights of property are conveyed into the public representation. A State possesses no such influence over other States. It is not probable that the richest State in the Confederacy will ever influence the choice of a single representative in any other State. Nor will the representatives of the larger and richer States possess any other advantage in the federal legislature, over the representatives of other States, than what may result from their superior number alone. As far, therefore, as their superior wealth and weight may justly entitle them to any advantage, it ought to be secured to them by a superior share of representation. The new Constitution is, in this respect, materially different from the existing Confederation, as well as from that of the United Netherlands, and other similar confederacies. In each of the latter, the efficacy of the federal resolutions depends on the subsequent and voluntary resolutions of the states composing the union. Hence the states, though possessing an equal vote in the public councils, have an unequal influence, corresponding with the unequal importance of these subsequent and voluntary resolutions. Under the proposed Constitution, the federal acts will take effect without the necessary intervention of the individual States. They will depend merely on the majority of votes in the federal legislature, and consequently each vote, whether proceeding from a larger or smaller State, or a State more or less wealthy or powerful, will have an equal weight and efficacy: in the same manner as the votes individually given in a State legislature, by the representatives of unequal counties or other districts, have each a precise case, it proceeds from the difference in the personal character of the individual representative, rather than from any regard to the extent of the district from which he comes."

Such is the reasoning which an advocate for the Southern interests might employ on this subject; and although it may appear to be a little strained in some points, yet, on the whole, I must confess that it fully reconciles me to the scale of representation which the convention have established.

In one respect, the establishment of a common measure for representation and taxation will have a very salutary effect. As the accuracy of the census to be obtained by the Congress will necessarily depend, in a considerable degree, on the disposition, if not on the co-operation, of the States, it is of great importance that the States should feel as little bias as possible to swell or to reduce the amount of their numbers. Were their share of representation alone to be governed by this rule, they would have an interest in exaggerating their inhabitants. Were the rule to decide their share of taxation alone, a contrary temptation would prevail. By extending the rule to both objects, the States will have opposite interests, which will control and balance each other, and produce the requisite impartiality.

PUBLIUS.

4

Laws

THOMAS JEFFERSON

Jefferson's discussion of slavery in Query XIV, 'Laws', in his *Notes on the State of Virginia*, provides an insight into his thinking on the South's 'peculiar institution'. It is built around a pseudo-scientific discourse on racial differences. Jefferson's argument for the abolition of slavery was based on a conviction that it would be necessary to send the freed slaves back to Africa. His assumptions about racial characteristics led him to doubt if it would be possible ever to achieve racial integration in America.

It will probably be asked, Why not retain and incorporate the blacks into the state, and thus save the expense of supplying, by importation of white settlers, the vacancies they will leave? Deep rooted prejudices entertained by the whites; ten thousand recollections, by the blacks, of the injuries they have sustained; new provocations; the real distinctions which nature has made; and many other circumstances, will divide us into parties, and produce convulsions, which will probably never end but in the extermination of the one or the other race.—To these objections, which are political, may be added others, which are physical and moral. The first difference which strikes us is that of colour. Whether the black of the negro resides in the reticular membrane between the skin and scarf-skin, or in the scarf-skin itself; whether it proceeds from the colour of the blood, the colour of the bile, or from that of some other secretion, the difference is fixed in nature, and is as real as if its seat and cause were better known to us. And is this difference of no importance? Is it not the foundation of a greater or less share of beauty in the two races? Are not the fine mixtures of red and white, the expressions of every passion by greater or less suffusions of colour in the one, preferable to that eternal monotony, which reigns in the countenances, that immovable veil of black which covers all the emotions of the other race? Add to these, flowing hair, a more elegant symmetry of form, their own judgement in favour of the whites, declared by their preference of them, as uniformly as is the preference of the Oran-ootan for the black

Source: Thomas Jefferson, 'Laws', *Notes on the State of Virginia*, 1782, rptd New York: W. W. Norton & Co., 1954.

women over those of his own species. The circumstance of superior beauty, is thought worthy attention in the progagation of our horses, dogs, and other domestic animals; why not in that of man? Besides those of colour, figure, and hair, there are other physical distinctions proving a difference of race. They have less hair on the face and body. They secrete less by the kidnies, and more by the glands of the skin, which gives them a very strong and disagreeable odour. This greater degree of transpiration renders them more tolerant of heat, and less so of cold than the whites. Perhaps too a difference of structure in the pulmonary apparatus, which a late ingenious experimentalist has discovered to be the principal regulator of animal heat, may have disabled them from extricating, in the act of inspiration, so much of that fluid from the outer air, or obliged them in expiration, to part with more of it. They seem to require less sleep. A black after hard labour through the day, will be induced by the slightest amusements to sit up till midnight, or later, though knowing he must be out with the first dawn of the morning. They are at least as brave, and more adventuresome. But this may perhaps proceed from a want of forethought, which prevents their seeing a danger till it be present. When present, they do not go through it with more coolness or steadiness than the whites. They are more ardent after their female: but love seems with them to be more an eager desire, than a tender delicate mixture of sentiment and sensation. Their griefs are transient. Those numberless afflictions, which render it doubtful whether heaven has given life to us in mercy or in wrath, are less felt, and sooner forgotten with them. In general, their existence appears to participate more of sensation than reflection. To this must be ascribed their disposition to sleep when abstracted from their diversions, and unemployed in labour. An animal whose body is at rest, and who does not reflect, must be disposed to sleep of course. Comparing them by their faculties of memory, reason, and imagination, it appears to me that in memory they are equal to the whites; in reason much inferior, as I think one could scarcely be found capable of tracing and comprehending the investigations of Euclid; and that in imagination they are dull, tasteless, and anomalous. It would be unfair to follow them to Africa for this investigation. We will consider them here, on the same stage with the whites, and where the facts are not apocryphal on which a judgment is to be formed. It will be right to make great allowances for the difference of condition, of education, of conversation, of the sphere in which they move. Many millions of them have been brought to, and born in America. Most of them indeed have been confined to tillage, to their own homes, and their own society: yet many have been so situated, they they might have availed themselves of the conversation of their masters; many have been brought up to the handicraft arts, and from that circumstance have always been associated with the whites. Some have been liberally educated, and all have lived in countries where the arts and sciences are cultivated to a considerable degree, and have had before their eyes samples of the best works from abroad. The Indians, with no advantages of this kind, will often carve figures on their pipes not destitute of design and merit. They will crayon out an animal, a plant, or a country, so as to prove the existence of a germ in their minds which only wants cultivation. They astonish you with strokes of the most sublime oratory; such as prove their reason and sentiment strong, their imagination glowing and elevated. But never yet could I find that a black had uttered a thought above the level of plain narration; never saw even an elementary trait of painting or sculpture. In music they are more generally gifted than the whites with accurate ears for tune and time, and they have been found capable of imagining a small catch. Whether they will be equal to the composition of a more extensive run of melody, or of complicated harmony, is yet to be proved. Misery is often the parent of the most affecting touches in poetry.—Among the blacks is misery enough, God knows, but no poetry. Love is the peculiar oestrum of the poet. Their love is ardent, but it kindles the senses only, not the imagination. Religion indeed has produced a Phyllis Whately but it could not produce a poet. The compositions published under her name are below the dignity of criticism. The heroes of the *Dunciad* are to her, as Hercules to the author of that poem. Ignatius Sancho has approached nearer to merit in composition; yet his letters do more honour to the heart than the head. They breathe the purest effusions of friendship and general philanthropy, and show how great a degree of the latter may be compounded with strong religious zeal. He is often happy in the turn of his compliments, and his style is easy and familiar, except when he affects a Shandean fabrication of words. But his imagination is wild and extravagant, escapes incessantly from every restraint of reason and taste, and, in the course of its vagaries, leaves a tract of thought as incoherent and eccentric, as is the course of a meteor through the sky. His subjects should often have led him to a process of sober reasoning: yet we find him always substituting sentiment for demonstration. Upon the whole, though we admit him to the first place among those of his own colour who have presented themselves to the public judgement, yet when we compare him with the writers of the race among whom he lived and particularly with the epistolary class, in which he has taken his own stand, we are compelled to enrol him at the bottom of the column. This criticism supposes the letters published under his name to be genuine, and to have received amendment from no other hand; points which would not be of easy investigation. The improvement of the blacks in body and mind, in the first instance of their mixture with the whites, has been observed by every one, and proves that their inferiority is not the effect merely of their condition of life. We know that among the Romans, about the Augustan age especially, the condition of their slaves was much more deplorable than that of the blacks on the continent of America. The two sexes were confined in separate apartments, because to raise a child cost the master more than to buy one. Cato, for a very restricted indulgence to his slaves in this particular, took from them a certain price. But in this country the slaves multiply as fast as the free inhabitants. Their situation and manners place the commerce between the two sexes almost without restraint.—The same Cato, on a principle of economy, always sold his sick and superannuated slaves. He gives it as a standing precept to a master visiting his farm, to sell his old oxen, old wagons, old tools, old and diseased servants, and every thing else become useless. '*Vendat boves vetulos, plaustrum vetus, ferramenta, vetera, servum senem, servum morborsum, & si quid aliud supersit vendat.*' The American slaves cannot enumerate this among the injuries and insults they receive. It was the common practice to expose in the island Esculapius, in the Tyber, diseased slaves, whose cure was like to become tedious. The Emperor Claudius, by an edict, gave freedom to such of them as should recover, and first declared that if any person chose to kill rather than expose them, it should be deemed homicide. The exposing them is a crime of which no instance has existed with us; and were it to be followed by death, it would be punished capitally. We are told of a certain Vedius Pollio, who, in the presence of Augustus, would have given a slave as food to his fish, for having broken a glass. With the Romans, the regular method of taking the evidence of their slaves was under torture. Here it has been thought better never to resort to their evidence. When a master was murdered, all his slaves, in the same house, or within hearing, were condemned to death. Here punishment falls on the guilty only, and as precise proof is required against him as against a freeman. Yet notwithstanding these and other discouraging circumstances among the Romans, their slaves were often their rarest artists. They excelled too in science, insomuch as to be usually employed as tutors to their masters' children. Epictetus, Terence, and Phaedrus, were slaves. But they were of the race of whites. It is not their condition then, but nature, which has produced the distinction. Whether further observation will or will not verify the conjecture, that nature has been less bountiful to them in the endowments of the head, I believe that in those of the heart she will be found to have done them justice. That disposition to theft with which they have been branded, must be ascribed to their situation, and not to any depravity of the moral sense. The man, in whose favour no laws of property exist, probably feels himself less bound to respect those made in favour of others. When arguing for ourselves, we lay it down as a fundamental, that laws, to be just, must give a reciprocation of right; that, without this, they are mere arbitrary rules of conduct, founded in force, and not in conscience: and it is a problem which I give to the master to solve, whether the religious precepts against the violation of property were not framed for him as well as his slave? And whether the slave may not as justifiably take a little from one, who has taken all from him, as he may slay one who would slay him? That a change in the relations in which a man is placed should change his ideas of moral right or wrong, is neither new, nor peculiar to the colour of the blacks. Homer tells us it was so 2,600 years ago.

> Ἥμισυ, γάρ τ'ἀρετῆς ἀροαίνθται εὐρύρα Ζεὺς
> ἀνέρος, εὖτ' ἄν μιν κατὰ δούλιον ἦμαρ ἕλησιν.
>
> *Jove fix'd it certain, that whatever day*
> *Makes man a slave, takes half his worth away.*

But the slaves of which Homer speaks were whites. Notwithstanding these considerations which must weaken their respect for the laws of property, we find among them numerous instances of the most rigid integrity, and as many as among their better instructed masters, of benevolence, gratitude and unshaken fidelity. The opinion, that they are inferior in the faculties of reason and imagination, must be hazarded with great diffidence. To justify a general conclusion, requires many observations, even where the subject may be submitted to the Anatomical knife, to

Optical classes, to analysis by fire, or by solvents. How much more then where it is a faculty, not a substance, we are examining; where it eludes the research of all the senses; where the conditions of its existence are variously combined; where the effects of those which are present or absent bid defiance to calculation; let me add too, as a circumstance of great tenderness, where our conclusion would degrade a whole race of men from the rank in the scale of beings which their Creator may perhaps have given them. To our reproach it must be said, that though for a century and a half we have had under our eyes the races of black and of red men, they have never yet been viewed by us as subjects of natural history. I advance it therefore as a suspicion only, that the blacks, whether originally a distinct race, or made distinct by time and circumstances, are inferior to the whites in the endowments both of body and mind. It is not against experience to suppose, that different species of the same genus, or varieties of the same species, may possess different qualifications. Will not a lover of natural history then, one who views the gradations in all the races of animals with the eye of philosophy, excuse an effort to keep those in the department of man as distinct as nature has formed them? This unfortunate difference of colour, and perhaps of faculty, is a powerful obstacle to the emancipation of these people. Many of their advocates, while they wish to vindicate the liberty of human nature, are anxious also to preserve its dignity and beauty. Some of these, embarrassed by the question "What further is to be done with them?" join themselves in opposition with those who are actuated by sordid avarice only. Among the Romans emancipation required but one effort. The slave, when made free, might mix with, without staining the blood of his master. But with us a second is necessary, unknown to history. When freed, he is to be removed beyond the reach of mixture.

❧ 5 ❧

The Injustice and Impolicy of the Slave Trade and of the Slavery of the Africans

JONATHAN EDWARDS

Jonathan Edwards, whose illustrious namesake had been a driving force behind the 'Great Awakening' of the eighteenth century, here outlines the case against the slave trade and the institution of slavery itself. The argument, based on a strong sense of moral principle combined with biblical references, clearly demonstrates the religious foundations of the anti-slavery cause, which was to inform the abolitionist movement. The sermon is from a pamphlet in the Daniel A. P. Murray collection held in the Library of Congress.

Matthew VII. 12.
Therefore all things whatsoever you would, that men should to do you, do ye even so to them; for this is the law and the prophets.

This precept of our divine Lord hath always been admired as most excellent; and doubtless with the greatest reason. Yet it needs some explanation. It is not surely to be understood in the most unlimited sense, implying that because a prince expects and wishes for obedience from his subjects, he is obliged to obey them: that because parents wish their children to submit to their government, therefore they are to submit to the government of their children: or that because some men wish that others would concur and assist them to the gratification of their unlawful desires therefore they also are to gratify the unlawful desires of others. But whatever we are conscious, that we should, in an exchange of circumstances, wish, and are

Source: Jonathan Edwards, 'The injustice and impolicy of the slave trade, and of the slavery of the Africans: illustrated in a sermon preached before the Connecticut society for the promotion of freedom, and for the relief of persons unlawfully holden in bondage, at their annual meeting in New Haven, Sept. 15, 1791', Boston: Wells & Lilly-Court-Street, second edition, 1822.

persuaded that we might reasonably wish, that others would do to us; that we are bound to do to them. This is the general rule given us in the text; and a very extensive rule it is, reaching to the whole of our conduct: and is particularly useful to direct our conduct toward inferiors, and those whom we have in our power. I have therefore thought it a proper foundation for the discourse, which by the Society for the promotion of Freedom, and for the Relief of Persons unlawfully holden in Bondage, I have the honour to be appointed to deliver, on the present occasion.

This divine maxim is most properly applicable to the slave-trade, and to the slavery of the Africans. Let us then make the application.

Should we be willing, that the Africans or any other nation should purchase us, our wives and children, transport us into Africa and there sell us into perpetual and absolute slavery? Should we be willing, that they by large bribes and offers of a gainful traffic should entice our neighbours to kidnap and sell us to them, and that they should hold in perpetual and cruel bondage, not only ourselves, but our posterity through all generations? Yet why is it not as right for them to treat us in this manner, as it is for us to treat them in the same manner? Their colour indeed is different from our's. But does this give us a right to enslave them? The nations from Germany to Guinea have complexions of every shade from the fairest white, to a jetty black: and if a black complexion subject a nation or an individual to slavery; where shall slavery begin? or where shall it end? I propose to mention a few reasons against the right of the slave-trade—and then to consider the principal arguments, which I have ever heard urged in favour of it.—What will be said against the slave-trade will generally be equally applicable to slavery itself; and if conclusive against the former, will be equally conclusive against the latter.

As to the slave-trade, I conceive it to be unjust in itself—abominable on account of the cruel manner in which it is conducted—and totally wrong on account of the impolicy of it, or its destructive tendency to the moral and political interests of any country.

I. It is unjust in itself—.It is unjust in the same sense, and for the same reason, as it is, to steal, to rob, or to murder. It is a principle, the truth of which hath in this country been generally, if not universally acknowledged, ever since the commencement of the late war, that all men are born equally free . If this be true, the Africans are by nature equally entitled to freedom as we are; and therefore we have no more right to enslave, or to afford aid to enslave them, than they have to do the same to us. They have the same right to their freedom, which they have to their property or to their lives. Therefore to enslave them is as really and in the same sense wrong, as to steal from them, to rob or to murder them.

There are indeed cases in which men may justly be deprived of their liberty and reduced to slavery; as there are cases in which they may be justly deprived of their lives. But they can justly be deprived of neither, unless they have by their own voluntary conduct forfeited it. Therefore still the right to liberty stands on the same basis with the right to life. And that the Africans have done something whereby they have forfeited their liberty must appear, before we can justly deprive them of it; as it must appear, that they have done something whereby they have forfeited their lives, before we may justly deprive them of these.

II. The slave-trade is wicked and abominable on account of the cruel manner in which it is carried on.

Beside the stealing or kidnapping of men, women and children, in the first instance, and the instigation of others to this abominable practice; the inhuman manner in which they are transported to America, and in which they are treated on their passage and in their subsequent slavery, in such as ought forever to deter every man from acting any part in this business, who has any regard to justice or humanity. They are crowded so closely into the holds and between the decks of vessels, that they have scarcely room to lie down, and sometimes not room to sit up in an erect posture; the men at the same time fastened together with irons by two and two; and all this in the most sultry climate. The consequence of the whole is, that the most dangerous and fatal diseases are soon bred among them, whereby vast numbers of those exported from Africa perish in the voyage: others in dread of that slavery which is before them and in distress and despair from the loss their parents, their children, their husbands, their wives, all their dear connections, and their dear native country itself, starve themselves to death or plunge themselves into the ocean. Those who attempt in the former of those ways to escape from their persecutors, are tortured by live coals applied to their mouths. Those who attempt an escape in the latter and fail, are equally tortured by the most cruel beating, or otherwise as their persecutors please. If any of them make an attempt, as they sometimes do, to recover their liberty, some, and as the circumstances may be, many, are put to immediate death. Others beaten, bruised, cut and mangled in a most inhuman and shocking manner, are in this situation exhibited to the rest, to terrify them from the like attempt in future: and some are delivered up to every species of torment, whether by the application of the whip, or of any other instrument, even of fire itself, as the ingenuity of the ship-master and of his crew is able to suggest or their situation will admit; and these torments are purposely continued for several days, before death is permitted to afford relief to these objects of vengeance.[1]

By these means, according to the common computation, twenty-five thousand, which is a fourth part of those who are exported from Africa, and by the concession of all, twenty thousand, annually perish, before they arrived at the places of their destination in America. But this is by no means the end of the suffering of this unhappy people. Bred up in a country spontaneously yielding the necessaries and conveniences of savage life, they have never been accustomed to labour: of course they are but ill prepared to go through the fatigue and drudgery to which they are doomed in their state of slavery. Therefore partly by this cause, partly by the scantiness and badness of their food, and partly from dejection of spirits, mortification and despair, another twenty-five thousand die in the seasoning, as it is called, i.e. within two years after their arrival in America. This I say is the common computation. Or if we will in particular be as favourable to the trade as in the estimate of the number which perishes on the passage, we may reckon the number which dies in the seasoning to be twenty thousand. So that of the hundred thousand annually exported from Africa to America, fifty thousand, as it is commonly computed, or on the most favourable estimate, forty thousand, die before they are seasoned to the country.

Nor is this all. The cruel sufferings of these pitiable beings are not yet at an end. Thenceforward they have to drag out a miserable life in absolute slavery, entirely at the disposal of their masters, by whom not only every venial fault, every mere inadvertence or mistake, but even real virtues, are liable to be construed into the most atrocious crimes, and punished as such, according to their caprice or rage, while they are intoxicated sometimes with liquor, sometimes with passion. By these masters they are supplied with barely enough to keep them from starving, as the whole expense laid out on a slave for food, clothing and medicine is commonly computed on an average at thirty shillings sterling annually. At the same time they are kept at hard labour from five o'clock in the morning, till nine at night excepting time to eat twice during the day. And they are constantly under the watchful eye of overseers and Negro-drivers more tyrannical and cruel than even their masters themselves. From these drivers, for every imagined, as well as real neglect or want of exertion, they receive the lash, the smack of which is all day long in the ears of those who are on the plantation or in the vicinity; and it is used with such dexterity and severity, as not only to lacerate the skin, but to tear out small portions of the flesh at almost every stroke.

This is the general treatment of the slaves.[2] But many individuals suffer still more severely. Many, many are knocked down; some have their eyes beaten out; some have an arm or a leg broken, or chopt off; and many for a very small or for no crime at all, have been beaten to death merely to gratify the fury of an enraged master or overseer.

Nor ought we on this occasion to overlook the wars among the nations of Africa excited by the trade, or the destruction attendant on those wars. Not to mention the destruction of property, the burning of towns and villages, it hath been determined by reasonable computation, that are annually exported from Africa to the various parts of America, one hundred thousand slaves, as was before observed; that of these, six thousand are captives of war; that in the wars in which these are taken, ten persons of victors and vanquished are killed, to one taken; that therefore the taking of the six thousand captives is attend with the slaughter of sixty thousand of their countrymen. Now does not justice? does not humanity shrink from the idea, that in order to procure [one] slave to gratify our avarice, we should put to death ten human beings? Or that in order to increase our property, and that only in some small degree, we should carry on a trade, or even connive at it, to support which sixty thousand of our own species are slain in war?

These sixty thousand, added to the forty thousand who perish on the passage and in the seasoning, give us an hundred thousand who are annually destroyed by the trade; and the whole advantage gained by this amazing destruction of human lives is sixty thousand slaves. For you will recollect, that the whole number exported from Africa is an hundred thousand; that of these forty thousand die on the passage and in the seasoning, and sixty thousand are destroyed in the wars. Therefore while one hundred and sixty thousand are killed in the wars and are exported from Africa, but sixty thousand are added to the stock of slaves.

Now when we consider all this; when we consider the miseries which this unhappy people suffer in their wars, in their captivity, in their voyage to America, and during a wretched life of cruel slavery: and especially when we consider the annual destruction of an hundred thousand lives in the manner before mentioned; who can hesitate to declare this trade and the consequent slavery to be contrary to every principle of justice and humanity, of the law of nature and of the law of God?

III. This trade and this slavery are utterly wrong on the ground of their impolicy. In a variety of respects they are exceedingly hurtful to the state which tolerates them.

1. They are hurtful, as they deprave the morals of the people.—The incessant and inhuman cruelties practised in the trade and in the subsequent slavery, necessarily tend to harden human heart against the tender feelings of humanity in the masters of vessels, in the sailors, in the factors, in the proprietors of the slaves, in their children, in the overseers, in the slaves themselves, and in all who habitually see those cruelties. Now the eradication or even the diminution of compassion, tenderness and humanity, is certainly a great depravation of heart, and must be followed with correspondent depravity of manners. And measures which lead to such depravity of heart and manners, cannot but be extremely hurtful to the state, and consequently are extremely impolitic.

2. The trade is impolitic as it is so destructive of the lives of seamen. The ingenious Mr. Clarkson hath in a very satisfactory manner made it appear, that in the slave-trade alone Great-Britain loses annually about nineteen hundred seamen; and that this loss is more than double to the loss annually sustained by Great-Britain in all her other trade taken together. And doubtless we lose as many as Great-Britain in proportion to the number of seamen whom we employ in this trade.—Now can it be politic to carry on a trade which is so destructive of that useful part of our citizens, our seamen?

3. African slavery is exceedingly impolitic, as it discourages industry. Nothing is more essential to the political prosperity of any state, than industry in the citizens. But in proportion as slaves are multiplied, every kind of labour becomes ignominious: and in fact, in those of the United States, in which slaves are the most numerous, gentlemen and ladies of any fashion disdain to employ themselves in business, which in other states is consistent with the dignity of the first families and first offices. In a country with Negro slaves, labour belongs to them only, and a white man is despised in proportion as he applies to it.—Now how destructive to industry in all the lowest and middle class of citizens, such a situation and the prevalence of such ideas will be, you can easily conceive. The consequence is, that some will nearly starve, others will betake themselves to the most dishonest practices, to obtain the means of living. As slavery produces indolence in the white

people, so it produces all those vices which are naturally connected with it; such as intemperance lewdness and prodigality. These vices enfeeble both the body and the mind, and unfit men for any vigorous exertions and employments either external or mental. And those who are unfit for such exertions, are already a very degenerate race; degenerate, not only in a moral, but a natural sense. They are contemptible too, and will soon be despised even by their Negroes themselves.

Slavery tends to lewdness not only as it produces indolence, but as it affords abundant opportunity for that wickedness without either the danger and difficulty of an attack on the virtue of a woman of chastity, or the danger of a connection with one of ill fame. And we learn the too frequent influence and effect of such a situation, not only from common fame, but from the multitude of mulattoes in countries where slaves are very numerous.

Slavery has a most direct tendency to haughtiness also, and domineering spirit and conduct in the control of them. A man who has been bred up in domineering over Negroes, can scarcely avoid contracting such a habit of haughtiness and domination, as will express itself in his general treatment of mankind, whether in his private capacity, or in any office civil or military with which he may be vested. Despotism in economics naturally leads to despotism in politics, and domestic slavery in a free government is a perfect solecism in human affairs.

How baneful all these tendencies and effects of slavery must be to the public good, and especially to the public good of such a free country as ours, I need not inform you.

4. In the same proportion as industry and labour are discouraged, is population discouraged and prevented. This is another respect in which slavery is exceedingly impolitic. That population is prevented in proportion as industry is discouraged, is, I conceive, so plain that nothing needs to be said to illustrate it. Mankind in general will enter into matrimony as soon as they possess the means of supporting a family. But the great body of any people have no other way of supporting themselves or a family, than by their own labour. Of course as labour is discouraged, matrimony is discouraged and population is prevented.—But the impolicy of whatever produces these effects will be acknowledged by all. The wealth, strength and glory of a state depend on the number of its virtuous citizens: and a state without citizens is at least as great an absurdity, as a king without subjects.

5. The impolicy of slavery still further appears from this, that it weakens the state, and in proportion to the degree in which it exists, exposes it to become an easy conquest.—The increase of free citizens is an increase of the strength of the state. But not so with regard to the increase of slaves. They not only add nothing to the strength of the state, but actually diminish it in proportion to their number. Every slave is naturally an enemy to the state in which he is holden in slavery, and wants nothing but an opportunity to assist in its overthrow. And an enemy within a state, is much more dangerous than one without it.

These observations concerning the prevention of population and weakening of the state, are supported by facts which have fallen within our own observation. That the southern states, in which slaves are so numerous are in no measure so populous, according to the extent of territory, as the northern, is a fact of universal notoriety: and that during the late war, the southern states found themselves greatly weakened by their slaves, and therefore were so easily overrun by the British army, is equally notorious.

From the view we have now taken of this subject, we scruple not to infer, that to carry on the slave-trade and to introduce slaves into our country, is not only to be guilty of injustice, robbery and cruelty toward our fellow-men; but it is to injure ourselves and our country; and therefore it is altogether unjustifiable, wicked and abominable.

Having thus considered the injustice and ruinous tendency of the slave-trade, I proceed to attend to the principal arguments urged in favour of it.

1. It is said, that the Africans are the posterity of Ham, the son of Noah; that Canaan one of Ham's sons, was cursed by Noah to be a servant of servants; that by Canaan we are to understand Ham's posterity in general; that as his posterity are devoted by God to slavery, we have a right to enslave them.—This is the argument: to which I answer:

It is indeed generally thought that Ham peopled Africa; but that the curse on Canaan extended to all the posterity of Ham is a mere imagination. The only reason given for it is, that Canaan was only one of Ham's sons; and that it seems reasonable, that the curse of Ham's conduct should fall on all his posterity, if on any. But this argument is insufficient. We might as clearly argue, that the judgments denounced on the house of David, on account of his sin in the matter of Uriah, must equally fall on all his posterity. Yet we know, that many of them lived and died in great posterity. So in every case in which judgments are predicted concerning any nation or family.

It is allowed in this argument, that the curse was to fall on the posterity of Ham, and not immediately on Ham himself; If otherwise, it is nothing to the purpose of the slave-trade, or of any slaves now in existence. It being allowed then, that this curse was to fall on Ham's posterity, he who had a right to curse the whole of that posterity, had the same right to curse a part of it only, and the posterity of Canaan equally as any other part; and a curse on Ham's posterity in the line of Canaan was as real a curse on Ham himself, as a curse on all his posterity would have been.

Therefore we have no ground to believe, that this curse respected any others, than the posterity of Canaan, who lived in the land of Canaan, which is well known to be remote from Africa. We have a particular account, that all the sons of Canaan settled in the land of Canaan; as may be seen in *Gen.* X: 15-20.

> And Canaan begat Sidon his first born, and Heth, and the Jebusite, and the Emorite, and the Girgasite, and the Hivite, and the Arkite, and the Sinite, and the Arvadite, and the Zemorite, and the Hamathite: and afterward were the families of the Canaanites spread abroad. And the border of the Canaanites was from Sidon, as thou goest to Gerar, unto Gaza; as thou goest unto Sodom and Gomorrah, Admah, and Zeboim, even unto Lashah.

—Nor have we account that any of their posterity except the Carthaginians afterward removed to any part of Africa: and none will pretend that these peopled Africa in general; especially considering, that they were subdued, destroyed and so far extirpated by the Romans.

This curse then of the posterity of Canaan, had no reference to the inhabitants of Guinea, or of Africa in general; but was fulfilled partly in Joshua's time, in the reduction and servitude of the Canaanites, and especially of the Gibeonites; partly by what the Phenicians suffered from the Chaldeans, Persians and Greeks; and finally by what the Carthagenians suffered from the Romans.

Therefore this curse gives us no right to enslave the Africans, as we do by the slave-trade, because it has no respect to the Africans whom we enslave. Nor if it had respected them, would it have given any such right; because it was not an institution of slavery, but a mere prophecy of it. And from this prophecy we have no more ground to infer the right of slavery, than we have from the prophecy of the destruction of Jerusalem by Nebuchadnezzar, or by the Romans, to infer their right respectively to destroy it in the manner they did; or from other prophecies to infer the right of Judas to betray his master, or of the Jews to crucify him.

2. The right of slavery is inferred from the instance of Abraham, who had servants born in his house and bought with his money.—But it is by no means certain, that these were slaves, as our Negroes are. If they were, it is unaccountable, that he went out at the head of an army of them to fight his enemies. No West-India planter would easily be induced to venture himself in such a situation. It is far more probable, that similar to some of the vassals under the feudal constitution, the servants of Abraham were only in a good measure dependent on him, and protected by him. But if they were to all intents and purposes slaves, Abraham's holding of them will no more prove the right of slavery, than his going in to Hagar, will prove it right for any man to indulge in criminal intercourse with his domestic.

3. From the divine permission given the Israelites to buy servants of the nations round about them, it is argued, that we have a right to buy the Africans and hold them in slavery. See *Leviticus* XXV: 44–47.

> Both thy bondmen and thy bondmaids, which thou shalt have, shall be of the heathen that are round about you; of them shall ye buy bondmen and bondmaids. Moreover, of the children of the strangers that do sojourn among you, of them shall ye buy, and of their families, that are with you, which they begat in your land; and they shall be your possession. And ye shall take them as an inheritance for your children after you, to inherit them for a possession; they shall be your bondmen for ever: but over your brethren the children of Israel ye shall not rule one over another with rigour.

But if this be at all to the purpose, it is a permission to every nation under heaven to buy slaves of the nations round about them; to us, to buy of our Indian neighbours; to them, to buy of us; to the French, to buy of the English, and to the English to buy of the French; and so through the world. If then this argument be valid, every man has an entire right to engage in this trade, and to buy and sell any other man of another nation, and any other man of another nation has an entire right to buy and sell him. Thus according to this construction, we have in *Lev.* XXV:

107

43, an institution of an universal slave-trade, by which every man may not only become a merchant, but may rightfully become the merchandise itself of this trade, and may be bought and sold like a beast.—Now this consequence will be given up as absurd, and therefore also the construction of scripture from which it follows, must be given up. Yet it is presumed, that there is no avoiding that construction or the absurdity flowing from it, but by admitting, that this permission to the Israelites to buy slaves has no respect to us, but was in the same manner peculiar to them, as the permission and command to subdue, destroy and extirpate the whole Canaanitish nation; and therefore no more gives countenance to African slavery, than the command to extirpate the Canaanites, gives countenance to the extirpation of any nation in these days, by an universal slaughter of men and women, young men and maidens, infants and sucklings.

4. It is further pleaded, that there were slaves in the time of the apostles; that they did not forbid the holding of those slaves, but gave directions to servants, doubtless referring to the servants of that day, to obey their masters, and count them worthy of all honour

To this the answer is, that the apostles teach the genteral duties of servants who are righteously in the state of servitude, as many are or may be, by hire, by indenture, and by judgment of a civil court. But they do not say, whether the servants in general of that day were justly holden in slavery or not. In like manner they lay down the general rules of obedience to civil magistrates, without deciding concerning the characters of the magistrates of the Roman empire in the reign of Nero. And as the apostle Paul requires masters to give their servants that which is just and equal, (*Colossians* IV: i) so if any were enslaved unjustly, of course he in this text requires of the masters of such, to give them their freedom.—Thus the apostles treat the slavery of that day in the same manner that they treat the civil government; and say nothing more in favour of the former, than they say in favour of the latter.

Besides, this argument from the slavery prevailing in the days of the apostles, if it prove any thing, proves too much, and so confutes itself. It proves, that we may enslave all captives taken in war, of any nation, and in any the most unjust war, such as the wars of the Romans, which were generally undertaken from the motives of ambition or avarice. On the ground of this argument we had a right to enslave the prisoners, whom we, during the late war, took from the British army; and they had the same right to enslave those whom they took from us; and so with respect to all other nations.

5. It is strongly urged, that the Negroes brought from Africa are all captives of war, and therefore are justly bought and holden in slavery.—This is a principal argument always urged by the advocates for slavery; and in a solemn debate on this subject, it hath been strongly insisted on, very lately in the British parliament. Therefore it requires our particular attention.

Captives in a war just on their part, cannot be justly enslaved; nor is this pretended. Therefore the captives who may be justly enslaved, must be taken in a war unjust on their part. But even on the supposition, that captives in such a war may be justly enslaved, it will not follow, that we can justly carry on the slave trade, as it is commonly carried on from the African coast. In this trade any slaves are purchased, who are offered for sale, whether justly or unjustly enslaved. No enquiry is made whether they were captives in any war; much less, whether they were captivated in a war unjust on their part.

By the most authentic accounts, it appears, that the wars in general in Africa are excited by the prospect of gain from the sale of the captives of the war. Therefore those taken by the assailants in such wars, cannot be justly enslaved. Beside these, many are kidnapped by those of neighbouring nations; some by their own neighbours; and some by their kings or his agents; others for debt or some trifling crime are condemned to perpetual slavery—But none of these are justly enslaved. And the traders make no enquiry concerning the mode or occasion of their first enslavement. They buy all that are offered, provided they like them and the price.— So that the plea, that the African slaves are captives in war, is entirely insufficient to justify the slave trade as now carried on.

But this is not all; if it were ever so true, that all the Negroes exported from Africa were captives in war, and that they were taken in a war unjust on their part; still they could not be justly enslaved.—We have no right to enslave a private foe in a state of nature, after he is conquered. Suppose in a state of nature one man rises against another and endeavours to kill him; in this case the person assaulted has no right to kill the assailant, unless it be necessary to preserve his own life. But in wars between nations, one nation may no doubt secure itself against another, by other means than slavery of its captives. If a nation be victorious in the war, it may exact some towns or a district of country, by way of caution; or it may impose a fine to deter from future injuries. If the nation be not victorious, it will do no good to enslave the captives whom it has taken. It will provoke the victors, and foolishly excite vengeance which cannot be repelled.

Or if neither nation be decidedly victorious, to enslave the captives on either side can answer no good purpose, but must at least occasion the enslaving of the citizens of the other nation, who are now, or in future may be in a state of captivity. Such a practice therefore necessarily tends to evil and not good.

Besides; captives in war are generally common soldiers or common citizens; and they are generally ignorant of the true cause or causes of the war, and are by their superiours made to believe, that the war is entirely just on their part. Or if this be not the case, they may by force be compelled to serve in a war which they know to be unjust. In either of these cases they do not deserve to be condemned to perpetual slavery. To inflict perpetual slavery on these private soldiers and citizens is manifestly not to do, as we would wish that men should do to us. If we were taken in a war unjust on our part, we should not think it right to be condemned to perpetual slavery. No more right is it for us to condemn and hold in perpetual slavery others, who are in the same situation.

6. It is argued, that as the Africans in their own country, previously to the purchase of them by the African traders, are captives in war; if they were not bought up by those traders, they would be put to death: that therefore to purchase them and to subject them to slavery instead of death, is an act of mercy not only lawful,

but meritorious.

If the case were indeed so as is now represented, the purchase of the Negroes would be no more meritorious, than the act of a man, who, if we were taken by the Algerines, should purchase us out of that slavery. This would indeed be an act of benevolence, if the purchaser should set us at liberty. But it is no act of benevolence to buy a man out of one state into another no better. Nay, the act of ransoming a man from death gives no right to the ransomer to commit a crime or an act of injustice to the person ransomed. The person ransomed is doubtless obligated according to his ability to satisfy the ransomer for his expence and trouble. Yet the ransomer has no more right to enslave the other, than the man who saves the life of another who was about to be killed by a robber or an assassin, has a right to enslave him.—The liberty of a man for life is a far greater good, than the property paid for a Negro on the African coast. And to deprive a man of an immensely greater good, in order to recover one immensely, is an immense injury and crime.

7. As to the pretence, that to prohibit or lay aside this trade, would be hurtful to our commerce; it is sufficient to ask, whether on the supposition, that it were advantageous to the commerce of Great-Britain to send her ships to these states, and transport us into that perpetual slavery in the West Indies, it would be right that she should go into trade.

8. That to prohibit the slave trade would infringe on the property of those, who have expended large sums to carry on that trade, or of those who wish to purchase the slaves for their plantations, hath also been urged as an argument in favour of the trade.—But the same argument would prove, that if the skins and teeth of the Negroes were as valuable articles of commerce as furs and elephant's teeth, and a merchant were to lay out his property in this commerce, he ought by no means to be obstructed therein.

9. But others will carry on the trade, if we do not.—So others will rob, steal and murder, if we do not.

10. It is said, that some men are intended by nature to be slaves.—If this mean, that the author of nature has given some men a licence, to enslave others; this is denied and proof is demanded. If it mean, that God hath made some of capacities inferior to others, and that the last have a right to enslave the first; this argument will prove, that some of the citizens of every country, have a right to enslave other citizens of the same country; nay, that some have a right to enslave their own brothers and sisters.—But if this argument mean, that God in his providence suffers some men to be enslaved, and that this proves, that from the beginning he intended they should be enslaved, and made them with this intention; the answer is, that in like manner he suffers some men to be murdered, and in this sense, he intended and made them to be murdered. Yet no man in his senses will hence argue the lawfulness of murder.

11. It is further pretended, that no other men, than Negroes, can endure labour in the hot climates of the West Indies and the southern states.—But does this appear to be fact? In all other climates, the labouring people are the most healthy. And I confess I have not yet seen evidence, but that those who have been accustomed to

labour and are inured to those climates, can bear labour there also.—However, taking for granted the fact asserted in this objection, does it follow, that the inhabitants of those countries have a right to enslave the Africans to labour for them? No more surely than from the circumstance, that you are feeble and cannot labour, it follows, that you have a right to enslave your robust neighbour. As in all other cases, the feeble and those who choose not to labour, and yet wish to have their lands cultivated, are necessitated to hire the robust to labour for them; so no reason can be given, why the inhabitants of hot climates should not either perform their own labour, or hire those who can perform it, whether Negroes or others.

If our traders went to the coast of Africa to murder the inhabitants, or to rob them of their property, all would own that such murderous or piratical practices are wicked and abominable. Now it is as really wicked to rob a man of his liberty, as to rob him of his life; and it is much more wicked, than to rob him of his property. All men agree to condemn highway robbery. And the slave-trade is as much a greater wickedness than highway robbery, as liberty is more valuable than property. How strange is it then, that in the same nation highway robbery should be punished with death, and the slave-trade be encouraged by national authority.

We all dread political slavery, or subjection to the arbitrary power of a king or of any man or men not deriving their authority from the people. Yet such a state is inconceivably preferable to the slavery of the Negroes. Suppose that in the late war we had been subdued by Great-Britain; we should have been taxed without our consent. But these taxes would have amounted to but a small part of our property. Whereas the Negroes are deprived of all their property; no part of their earnings is their own; the whole is their masters'.—In a conquered state we should have been at liberty to dispose of ourselves and of our property in most cases, as we should choose. We should have been free to live in this or that town or place; in any part of the country, or to remove out of the country; to apply to this or that business; to labour or not; and excepting a sufficiency for the taxes, to dispose of the fruit of our labour to our own benefit, or that of our children, or of any other person. But the unhappy Negroes in slavery can do none of these things. They must do what they are commanded and as much as they are commanded, on pain of the lash. They must live where they are placed, and must confine themselves to that spot, on pain of death.

So that Great-Britain in her late attempt to enslave America, committed a very small crime indeed in comparison with the crime of those who enslave the Africans.

The arguments which have been urged against the slave-trade, are with little variation applicable to the holding of slaves. He who holds a slave, continues to deprive him of that liberty, which was taken from him on the coast of Africa. And if it were wrong to deprive him of it in the first instance, why not in the second? If this be true, no man hath a better right to retain his Negro in slavery, than he had to take him from his native African shores. And every man who cannot show, that his Negro hath by his voluntary conduct forfeited his liberty, is obligated immediately to manumit him. Undoubtedly we should think so, were we holden in the same slavery in which the Negroes are: And our text required us to do to others, as we would that they should do to us.

To hold a slave, who has a right to his liberty, is not only a real crime, but a very great one. Many good Christians have wondered how Abraham, the father of the faithful, could take Hagar to his bed; and how Sarah, celebrated as an holy woman, could consent to this transaction: Also, how David and Solomon could have so many wives and concubines, and yet be real saints. Let such inquire how it is possible, that our fathers and men now alive, universally reputed pious, should hold Negro slaves, and yet be the subjects of real piety? And whether to reduce a man, who hath the same right to liberty as any other man, to a state of absolute slavery, or to hold him in that state, be not as great a crime as concubinage or fornication. I presume it will not be denied, that to commit theft or robbery every day of a man's life, is as great a sin as to commit fornication in one instance. But to steal a man or to rob him of his liberty is a greater sin, than to steal his property, or to take it by violence. And to hold a man in a state of slavery, who has a right to his liberty, is to be every day guilty of robbing him of his liberty, or of manstealing. The consequence is inevitable, that other things being the same, to hold a Negro slave, unless he have forfeited his liberty, is a greater sin in the sight of God, than concubinage or fornication.

Does this conclusion seem strange to any of you? Let me entreat you to weigh it candidly before you reject it. You will not deny, that liberty is more valuable than property; and that it is a greater sin to deprive a man of his whole liberty during life, than to deprive him of his whole property; or that manstealing is a greater crime than robbery. Nor will you deny, that to hold in slavery a man who was stolen, is substantially the same crime as to steal him. These principles being undeniable, I leave it to yourselves to draw the plain and necessary consequence. And if your consciences shall, in spite of all opposition, tell you, that while you hold your Negroes in slavery, you do wrong, exceedingly wrong; that you do not, as you would that men should do to you; that you commit sin in the sight of God; that you daily violate the plain rights of mankind, and that in a higher degree, than if you committed theft or robbery; let me beseech you not to stifle this conviction, but attend to it and act accordingly; lest you add to your former guilt, that of sinning against the light of truth, and of your own consciences.

To convince yourselves, that your information being the same, to hold a Negro slave is a greater sin than fornication, theft or robbery, you need only bring the matter home to yourselves. I am willing to appeal to your own consciences, whether you would not judge it to be a greater sin for a man to hold you or your child during life in such slavery, as that of the Negroes, than for him to indulge in one instance of licentious conduct or in one instance to steal or rob. Let conscience speak, and I will submit to its decision.

This question seems to be clearly decided by revelation. *Exodus* XXI: 16:

> He that stealeth a man and selleth him, or if he be found in his hand, he shall surely be put to death.

Thus death is, by the divine express declaration, the punishment due to the crime of man-stealing. But death is not the punishment declared by God to be due to fornication theft or robbery in common cases. Therefore we have the divine authority to assert, that manstealing is a greater crime than fornication, theft or robbery. Now to hold in slavery a man who has a right to liberty, is substantially the same crime as to deprive him of his liberty. And to deprive of liberty and reduce to slavery, a man who has a right to liberty, is man-stealing. For it is immaterial whether he be taken and reduced to slavery clandestinely or by open violence. Therefore if the Negroes have a right to liberty, to hold them in slavery is man-stealing, which we have seen is, by God himself, declared to be a greater crime than fornication, theft or robbery.

Perhaps, though this truth be clearly demonstrable both from reason and revelation, you scarcely dare receive it, because it seems to bear hardly on the characters of our pious fathers, who held slaves. But they did it ignorantly and in unbelief of the truth; as Abraham, Jacob, David and Solomon were ignorant, that polygamy or concubinage was wrong. As to domestic slavery our fathers lived in a time of ignorance which God winked at; but now he commandeth all men every where to repent of this wickedness, and to break off this sin by righteousness, and this iniquity by shewing mercy to the poor, if it may be a lengthening out of their tranquillity. You therefore to whom the present blaze of light as to this subject has reached, cannot sin at so cheap a rate as our fathers.

But methinks I hear some say, I have bought my Negro; I have paid a large sum for him; I cannot lose this sum, and therefore I cannot manumit him.—Alas! this is hitting the nail on the head. This brings into view the true cause which makes it so difficult to convince men of what is right in this case—You recollect the story of Amaziah's hiring an hundred thousand men of Israel, for an hundred talents, to assist him against the Edomites; and that when by the word of the Lord, he was forbidden to take those hired men with him to the war, he cried out, "But what shall we do for the hundred talents, which I have given to the army of Israel?" In this case, the answer of God was, "The Lord is able to give thee much more than this."—To apply this to the subject before us, God is able to give thee much more than thou shalt lose by manumitting thy slave.

You may plead, that you use your slave well; you are not cruel to him, but feed and clothe him comfortably. Still every day you rob him of a most valuable and important right. And a highway-man, who robs a man of his money in the most easy and complaisant manner, is still a robber; and murder may be effected in a manner the least cruel and tormenting; still it is murder.

Having now taken that view of our subject, which was proposed, we may in reflection see abundant reason to acquiesce in the institution of this society. If the slave-trade be unjust, and as gross a violation of the rights of mankind, as would be, if the Africans should transport us into perpetual slavery in Africa; to unite our influence against it, is a duty which we owe to mankind, to ourselves and to God too. It is but doing as we would that men should do to us.—Nor is it enough that we have formed the society; we must do the duties of it. The first of these is to put an end to the slave-trade. The second is to relieve those who, contrary to the laws of the country, are holden in bondage. Another is to defend those in their remaining legal and natural rights, who are by law holden in bondage. Another and not the least important object of this society, I conceive to be, to increase and disperse the light of truth with respect to the subject of African slavery, and so prepare the way for its total abolition. For until men in general are convinced of the injustice of the trade and of the slavery itself, comparatively little can be done to effect the most important purposes of the institution.

It is not to be doubted, that the trade is even now carried on from this state. Vessels are from time to time fitted out for the coast of Africa, to transport the Negroes to the West-Indies and other parts. Nor will an end be put to this trade, without vigilance and strenuous exertion on the part of this society, or other friends of humanity, nor without a patient enduring of the opposition and odium of all who are concerned in it, of their friends and of all who are of the opinion that it is justifiable. Among these we are doubtless to reckon some of large property and considerable influence. And if the laws and customs of the country equally allowed of it, many, and perhaps as many as now plead for the right of the African slave-trade, would plead for the right of kidnapping us, the citizens of the United States, and of selling us into perpetual slavery.—If then we dare not incur the displeasure of such men, we may as well dissolve the society, and leave the slave-trade to be carried on, and the Negroes to be kidnapped, and though free in this state, to be sold into perpetual slavery in distant parts, at the pleasure of any man, who wishes to make gain by such abominable practices.

Though we must expect opposition, yet if we be steady and persevering, we need not fear, that we shall fail of success. The advantages, which the cause has already gained, are many and great. Thirty years ago scarcely a man in this country thought either the slave-trade or the slavery of Negroes to be wrong. But now how many and able advocates in private life, in our legislatures, in Congress, have appeared and have openly and irrefragably pleaded the rights of humanity in this as well as other instances? Nay the great body of the people from New-Hampshire to Virginia inclusively, have obtained such light, that in all those states the further importation of slaves is prohibited by law. And in Massachusetts and New-Hampshire, slavery is totally abolished.

Nor is the light concerning this subject confined to America. It hath appeared with great clearness in France, and produced remarkable effects in the National Assembly. It hath also shone in bright beams in Great-Britain. It flashes with splendour in the writings of Clarkson and in the proceedings of several societies formed to abolish the slave-trade. Nor hath it been possible to shut it out of the British parliament. This light is still increasing, and in time will effect a total revolution. And if we judge of the future by the past, within fifty years from this time, it will be as shameful for a man to hold a Negro slave, as to be guilty of common robbery or theft. But it is our duty to remove the obstacles which intercept the rays of this light, that it may reach not only public bodies, but every individual.

And when it shall have obtained a general spread, shall have dispelled all darkness, and slavery shall be no more; it will be an honour to be recorded in history, as a society which was formed, and which exerted itself with vigour and fidelity, to bring about an event so necessary and conducive to the interests of humanity and virtue, to the support of the rights and to the advancement of the happiness of mankind.

Appendix.

Some objections to the doctrine of the preceding sermon, have been mentioned to the author, since the delivery of it. Of these it may be proper to take some notice.

1. The slaves are in a better situation than that in which they were in their own country; especially as they have opportunity to know the Christian religion and to secure the saving blessings of it. Therefore it is not an injury, but a benefit to bring them into this country, even though their importation be accompanied and followed with slavery. It is also said, that the situation of many Negroes under their masters is much better, than it would be, were they free in this country; that they are much better fed and clothed, and are much happier; that therefore to hold them in slavery is so far from a crime, that it is a meritorious act.

With regard to these pleas, it is to be observed, that every man hath a right to judge concerning his own happiness, and to choose the means of obtaining or promoting it; and to deprive him of this right is the very injury of which we complain; it is to enslave him. Because we judge, that the Negroes are more happy in this country, in a state of slavery, than in the enjoyment of liberty in Africa, we have no more right to enslave them and bring them into this country, than we have to enslave any of our neighbours, who we judge would be more happy under their own. Let us make the case our own. Should we believe, that we were justly treated, if the Africans should carry us into perpetual slavery in Africa, on the ground that they judged, that we should be more happy in that state, than in our present situation?

As to the opportunity which the Negroes in this country are said to have, to become acquainted with Christianity; this with respect to many is granted: But what follows from it? it would be ridiculous to pretend, that this is the motive on which they act who import them, or they who buy and hold them in slavery. Or if this were the motive, it would not sanctify either the trade or the slavery. We are not at liberty to do evil, that good may come; to commit a crime more aggravated than theft or robbery, that we may make a proselyte to Christianity. Neither our Lord Jesus Christ, nor any one of his apostles has taught us this mode of propagating the faith.

2. It is said, that the doctrine of the preceding sermon imputes that as a crime to individuals, which is owing to the state of society. This is granted; and what follows? It is owing to the state of society, that our neighbours, the Indians roast their captives: and does it hence follow, that such conduct is not to be imputed to the individual agents as a crime? It is owing to the state of society in Popish countries,

that thousands worship the beast and his image: and is that worship therefore not to be imputed as a crime to those, who render it? Read the Revelation of St. John. The state of society is such, that drunkenness and adultery are very common in some countries; but will it follow, that those vices are innocent in those countries?

3. If I be ever so willing to manumit my slave, I cannot do it without being holden to maintain him, when he shall be sick or shall be old and decrepit. Therefore I have a right to hold him as a slave.—The same argument will prove, that you have a right to enslave your children or your parents: as you are equally holden to maintain them in sickness and in decrepit old age.—The argument implies, that in order to secure the money, which you are afraid the laws of your country will some time or other oblige you to pay; it is right for you to rob a free man of his liberty or be guilty of man-stealing. On the ground of this argument every town or parish obligated by law, to maintain its helpless poor, has a right to sell into perpetual slavery all the people, who may probably or even possibly occasion a public expence.

4. After all, it is not safe to manumit the Negroes: they would cut our throats; they would endanger the peace and government of the state. Or at least they would be so idle, that they would not provide themselves with necessaries: of course they must live by thievery and plundering.

This objection requires a different answer, as it respects the northern, and as it respects the southern states. As it respects the northern, in which slaves are so few, there is not the least foundation to imagine, that they would combine or make insurrection against the government; or that they would attempt to murder their masters. They are much more likely to kill their masters, in order to obtain their liberty, or to revenge the abuse they receive, while it is still continued, than to do it after the abuse hath ceased, and they are restored to their liberty. In this case, they would from a sense of gratitude, or at least from a conviction of the justice of their masters, feel a strong attachment, instead of a murderous disposition.

Nor is there the least danger, but that by a proper vigilance of the selectmen, and by a strict execution of the laws now existing, the Negroes might in a tolerable degree be kept from idleness and pilfering.

All this hath been verified by experiment. In Massachusetts, all the Negroes in the commonwealth were by their new constitution liberated in a day: and none of the ill consequences objected followed either to the commonwealth or to individuals.

With regard to the southern states, the case is different. The negroes in some parts of those states are a great majority of the whole, and therefore the evils objected would, in case of a general manumission at once, be more likely to take place. But in the first place there is no prospect, that the conviction of the truth exhibited in the preceding discourse, will at once, take place in the minds of all the holders of slaves. The utmost that can be expected, is that it will take place gradually in one after another, and that of course the slaves will be gradually manumitted. Therefore the evils of a general manumission at once, are dreaded without reason.

If in any state the slaves should be manumitted in considerable numbers at once, or so that the number of free Negroes should become large; various measures might be concerted to prevent the evils feared. One I beg leave to propose: That overseers of the free Negroes be appointed from among themselves, who shall be empowered to inspect the morals and management of the rest, and report to proper authority, those who are vicious, idle or incapable of managing their own affairs, and that such authority dispose of them under proper masters for a year or other term, as is done, perhaps in all the states, with regard to the poor white people in like manner vicious, idle or incapable of management. Such black overseers would naturally be ambitious to discharge the duties of their office; they would in many respects have much more influence than white men with their countrymen: and other Negroes looking forward to the same honourable distinction, would endeavour to deserve it by their improvement and good conduct.

But after all, this whole objection, if it were ever so entirely founded on truth; if the freed Negroes would probably rise against their masters, or combine against government; rests on the same ground, as the apology of the robber, who murders the man whom he has robbed. Says the robber to himself, I have robbed this man, and now if I let him go he will kill me, or he will complain to authority and I shall be apprehended and hung. I must therefore kill him. There is no other way of safety for me.—The coincidence between this reasoning and that of the objection under consideration, must be manifest to all. And if this reasoning of the robber be inconclusive; if the robber have no right on that ground to kill the man whom he hath robbed; neither have the slave-holders any more right to continue to hold their slaves. If the robber ought to spare the life of the man robbed, take his own chance and esteem himself happy, if he can escape justice; so the slave-holders ought immediately to let their slaves go free, treat them with the utmost kindness, by such treatment endeavour to pacify them with respect to past injuries, and esteem themselves happy, if they can compromise the matter in this manner.[3]

In all countries in which the slaves are a majority of the inhabitants the masters lie in a great measure at the mercy of the slaves, and may most rationally expect sooner or later, to be cut off, or driven out by the slaves, or to be reduced to the same level and to be mingled with them into one common mass. This I think is by ancient and modern events demonstrated to be the natural and necessary course of human affairs. The hewers of wood and drawers of water among the Israelites, the Helots among the Lacedemonians, the slaves among the Romans, the villains and vassals in most of the kingdoms of Europe under the feudal system, have long since mixed with the common mass of the people, and shared the common privileges and honours of their respective countries. And in the French West-Indies the Mulattoes and free Negroes are already become so numerous and powerful a body, as to be allowed by the National Assembly to enjoy the common rights and honours of free men. These facts plainly show, what the whites in the West-Indies and the Southern States are to expect concerning their posterity, that it will infallibly be amalgamated with the slave population or else they must quit the country to the Africans whom they have hitherto holden in bondage.[4]

Notes

1. If any doubt these statements, they are requested to peruse Clarkson's History of the Abolition of the slave trade. This trade is at present carried on in all its horrors.

2. This declaration we are happy to say is not at the present time true; at least as it respects our own country. We can testify to the mildness and humanity of the treatment which the slaves generally experience from the respectable Planters of the South. Instances of cruelty, we doubt not, occur, but we believe receive no countenance from public opinion.

3. Some exceptionable sentences may perhaps be found in this Discourse. We cannot altogether agree with the Reverend Author in this passage. His reasoning will apply in its full force to slave-traders. The present slave-holders stand, we think, upon different ground. We however hope that these will soon be convinced, that it is an immediate and imperious duty, to adopt plans, and proceed with energy in the execution of them, which shall terminate in universal emancipation. Every master of slaves, enlightened on this subject, who does not act, (as far as the regulations of government will permit, and who does not exert his influence to change the law, where it opposes his design,) with reference to the accomplishment of this end, is, we believe, regarded by God as an enemy of the human race. We cannot, we would not, speak with moderation of a principle which would bind down millions of our race, to ignorance and the chains of perpetual servitude.

4. We trust that evils like these will be known only in imagination. But what shall prevent them? Nothing but united and strenuous efforts in the execution of a plan similar to that which has been devised by the American Colonization Society.—Let this Association receive universal support.

⫷⏀6⏀⫸

Exposition of the Views
of the Baptists

RICHARD FURMAN

Richard Furman's forceful defence of slavery from the perspective of the Southern Baptists of South Carolina, communicated to the governor of the state in 1822, demonstrates that both sides of the slavery argument could draw on biblical sources and justifications for their beliefs. The pamphlet is held in the South Carolina Baptist Historical Collection, Furman University.

Rev. Dr. Richard Furman's EXPOSITION
of The Views of the Baptists,
RELATIVE TO THE COLOURED POPULATION
In the United States IN A COMMUNICATION
To the Governor of South-Carolina

Sir,

When I had, lately, the honour of delivering to your Excellency an Address, from the Baptist Convention in this State, requesting that a Day of Public Humiliation and Thanksgiving might be appointed by you, as our Chief Magistrate, to be observed by the Citizens of the State at large, in reference to two important recent events, in which the interposition of Divine Providence has been conspicuous, and in which the interests and feelings of our Citizens have been greatly concerned,— viz: The protection afforded them from the horrors of an intended Insurrection; and the affliction they have suffered from the ravages of a dreadful Hurricane—I took the liberty to suggest, that I had a further communication to make on behalf of the Convention, in which their sentiments would be disclosed respecting the policy of the measure proposed; and on the lawfulness of holding slaves—the subject being considered in a moral and religious point of view.

Source: Richard Furman, 'Exposition of the Views of the Baptists, Relative to the Coloured Population in the United States', 1822, Charleston: A. E. Miller, 1838, second edition.

You were pleased, sir, to signify, that it would be agreeable to you to receive such a communication. And as it is incumbent on me, in faithfulness to the trust reposed in me, to make it, I now take the liberty of laying it before you.

The Political propriety of bringing the intended Insurrection into view by publicly acknowledging its prevention to be an instance of the Divine Goodness, manifested by a providential, gracious interposition, is a subject, which has employed the serious attention of the Convention; and, if they have erred in the judgment they have formed upon it, the error is, at least, not owing to a want of consideration, or of serious concern. They cannot view the subject but as one of great magnitude, and intimately connected with the interests of the whole State. The Divine Interposition has been conspicuous; and our obligations to be thankful are unspeakably great. And, as principles of the wisest and best policy lead nations, as well as individuals, to consider and acknowledge the government of the Deity, to feel their dependency on him and trust in him, to be thankful for his mercies, and to be humbled under his chastening rod; so, not only moral and religious duty, but also a regard to the best interests of the community appear to require of us, on the present occasion, that humiliation and thanksgiving, which are proposed by the Convention in their request. For a sense of the Divine Government has a meliorating influence on the minds of men, restraining them from crime, and disposing them to virtuous action. To those also, who are humbled before the Heavenly Majesty for their sins, and learn to be thankful for his mercies, the Divine Favour is manifested. From them judgments are averted, and on them blessings are bestowed.

The Convention are aware that very respectable Citizens have been averse to the proposal under consideration; the proposal for appointing a Day of Public Thanksgiving for our preservation from the intended Insurrection, on account of the influence it might be supposed to have on the Black Population—by giving publicity to the subject in their view, and by affording them excitements to attempt something further of the same nature. These objections, however, the Convention view as either not substantial, or over-balanced by higher considerations. As to publicity, perhaps no fact is more generally known by the persons referred to; for the knowledge of it has been communicated by almost every channel of information, public and private, even by documents under the stamp of Public Authority; and has extended to every part of the State. But with the knowledge of the conspiracy is united the knowledge of its frustration; and of that, which Devotion and Gratitude should set in a strong light, the merciful interposition of Providence, which produced that frustration. The more rational among that class of men, as well as others, know also, that our preservation from the evil intended by the conspirators, is a subject, which should induce us to render thanksgivings to the Almighty; and it is hoped and believed, that the truly enlightened and religiously disposed among them, of which there appear to be many, are ready to unite in those thanksgivings, from a regard to their own true interests: if therefore it is apprehended, that an undue importance would be given to the subject in their view, by making it the matter of public thanksgiving; that this would induce the designing and wicked to infer our fear and sense of weakness from the fact, and thus induce them to form some other scheme of mischief: Would not our silence, and the omission of an important religious duty, under these circumstances, undergo, at least, as unfavorable a construction, and with more reason?

But the Convention are persuaded, that publicity, rather than secrecy is the true policy to be pursued on this occasion; especially, when the subject is taken into view, in connexion with other truths, of high importance and certainty, which relate to it, and is placed in a just light; the evidence and force of which truths, thousands of this people, when informed, can clearly discern and estimate. It is proper, the Convention conceives, that the Negroes should know, that however numerous they are in some parts of these Southern States, they, yet, are not, even including all descriptions, bond and free, in the United States, but little more than one sixth part of the whole number of inhabitants, estimating that number which it probably now is, at Ten Millions; and the Black and Coloured Population, according to returns made at 1,786,000: That their destitution in respect to arms, and the knowledge of using them, with other disabilities, would render their physical force, were they all united in a common effort, less than a tenth part of that, with which they would have to contend. That there are multitudes of the best informed and truly religious among them, who, from principle, as well as from prudence, would not unite with them, nor fail to disclose their machinations, when it should be in their power to do it: That, however in some parts of our Union there are Citizens, who favour the idea of general emancipation; yet, were they to see slaves in our Country, in arms, wading through blood and carnage to effect their purpose, they would do what both their duty and interest would require; unite under the government with their fellow citizens at large to suppress the rebellion, and bring the authors of it to condign punishment: That it may be expected, in every attempt to raise an insurrection (should other attempts be made) as well as it was in that defeated here, that the prime movers in such a nefarious scheme, will so form their plan, that in case of exigency, they may flee with their plunder and leave their deluded followers to suffer the punishment, which law and justice may inflict: And that therefore, there is reason to conclude, on the most rational and just principles, that whatever partial success might at any time attend such a measure at the onset, yet, in this country, it must finally result in the discomfiture and ruin of the perpetrators; and in many instances pull down on the heads of the innocent as well as the guilty, an undistinguishing ruin.

On the lawfulness of holding slaves, considering it in a moral and religious view, the Convention think it their duty to exhibit their sentiments, on the present occasion, before your Excellency, because they consider their duty to God, the peace of the State, the satisfaction of scrupulous consciences, and the welfare of the slaves themselves, as intimately connected with a right view of the subject. The rather, because certain writers on politics, morals and religion, and some of them highly respectable, have advanced positions, and inculcated sentiments, very unfriendly to the principle and practice of holding slaves; and by some these sentiments have been advanced among us, tending in their nature, directly to disturb the domestic peace of the State, to produce insubordination and rebellion among the slaves, and to infringe the rights of our citizens; and indirectly, to deprive the slaves of religious privileges, by awakening in the minds of their masters a fear, that acquaintance with the Scriptures, and the enjoyment of these privileges would naturally produce the aforementioned effects; because the sentiments in opposition to the holding of slaves have been attributed, by their advocates, to the Holy Scriptures, and to the genius of Christianity. These sentiments, the Convention, on whose behalf I address your Excellency, cannot think just, or well-founded: for the right of holding slaves is clearly established by the Holy Scriptures, both by precept and example. In the Old Testament, the Israelites were directed to purchase their bond-men and bond-maids of the Heathen nations; except they were of the Canaanites, for these were to be destroyed. And it is declared, that the persons purchased were to be their 'bond-men forever;' and an 'inheritance for them and their children.' They were not to go out free in the year of jubilee, as the Hebrews, who had been purchased, were: the line being clearly drawn between them.[1] In example, they are presented to our view as existing in the families of the Hebrews as servants, or slaves, born in the house, or bought with money: so that the children born of slaves are here considered slaves as well as their parents. And to this well known state of things, as to its reason and order, as well as to special privileges, St. Paul appears to refer, when he says, "But I was free born."

In the New-Testament, the Gospel History, or representation of facts, presents us a view correspondent with that, which is furnished by other authentic ancient histories of the state of the world at the commencement of Christianity. The powerful Romans had succeeded, in empire, the polished Greeks; and under both empires, the countries they possessed and governed were full of slaves. Many of these with their masters, were converted to the Christian Faith, and received, together with them into the Christian Church, while it was yet under the ministry of the inspired Apostles. In things purely spiritual, they appear to have enjoyed equal privileges; but their relationship, as masters and slaves, was not dissolved. Their respective duties are strictly enjoined. The masters are not required to emancipate their slaves; but to give them the things that are just and equal, forbearing threatening; and to remember, they also have a master in Heaven. The "servants under the yoke"[2] (bond-servants or slaves) mentioned by Paul to Timothy, as having "believing masters," are not authorized by him to demand of them emancipation, or to employ violent means to obtain it; but are directed to "account their masters worthy of all honour," and "not to despise them, because they were brethren" in religion; "but the rather to do them service, because they were faithful and beloved partakers of the Christian benefit." Similar directions are given by him in other places, and by other Apostles. And it gives great weight to the argument, that in this place, Paul follows his directions concerning servants with a charge to Timothy, as an Evangelist, to teach and exhort men to observe this doctrine.

Had the holding of slaves been a moral evil, it cannot be supposed, that the inspired Apostles, who feared not the faces of men, and were ready to lay down their lives in the cause of their God, would have tolerated it, for a moment, in the Christian Church. If they had done so on a principle of accommodation, in cases where the masters remained heathen, to avoid offences and civil commotion; yet, surely, where both master and servant were Christian, as in the case before us, they would have enforced the law of Christ, and required, that the master should liberate his slave in the first instance. But, instead of this, they let the relationship remain untouched, as being lawful and right, and insist on the relative duties.

In proving this subject justifiable by Scriptural authority, its morality is also proved; for the Divine Law never sanctions immoral actions.

The Christian golden rule, of doing to others, as we would they should do to us, has been urged as an unanswerable argument against holding slaves. But surely this rule is never to be urged against that order of things, which the Divine government has established; nor do our desires become a standard to us, under this rule, unless they have a due regard to justice, propriety and the general good.

A father may very naturally desire, that his son should be obedient to his orders: Is he, therefore, to obey the orders of his son? A man might be pleased to be exonerated from his debts by the generosity of his creditors; or that his rich neighbour should equally divide his property with him; and in certain circumstances might desire these to be done: Would the mere existence of this desire, oblige him to exonerate his debtors, and to make such a division of his property? Consistency and generosity, indeed, might require it of him, if he were in circumstances which would justify the act of generosity; but, otherwise, either action might be considered as the effect of folly and extravagance.

If the holding of slaves is lawful, or according to the Scriptures; then this Scriptural rule can be considered as requiring no more of the master, in respect of justice (whatever it may do in point of generosity) than what he, if a slave, could consistently, wish to be done to himself, while the relationship between master and servant should still be continued.

In this argument, the advocates for emancipation blend the ideas of injustice and cruelty with those, which respect the existence of slavery, and consider them as inseparable. But, surely, they may be separated. A bond-servant may be treated with justice and humanity as a servant; and a master may, in an important sense, be the guardian and even father of his slaves.

They become a part of his family, (the whole, forming under him a little community) and the care of ordering it and providing for its welfare, devolves on him. The children, the aged, the sick, the disabled, and the unruly, as well as those, who are capable of service and orderly, are the objects of his care: The labour of these, is applied to the benefit of those, and to their own support, as well as that of the master. Thus, what is effected, and often at a great public expense, in a free community, by taxes, benevolent institutions, bettering houses, and penitentiaries, lies here on the master, to be performed by him, whatever contingencies may happen; and often occasions much expense, care and trouble, from which the servants are free. Cruelty, is, certainly, inadmissible; but servitude may be consistent with such degrees of happiness as men usually attain in this imperfect state of things.

Some difficulties arise with respect to bringing a man, or class of men, into a

123

state of bondage. For crime, it is generally agreed, a man may be deprived of his liberty. But, may he not be divested of it by his own consent, directly, or indirectly given: And, especially, when this assent, though indirect, is connected with an attempt to take away the liberty, if not the lives of others? The Jewish law favours the former idea: And if the inquiry on the latter be taken in the affirmative, which appears to be reasonable, it will establish a principle, by which it will appear, that the Africans brought to America were, slaves, by their own consent, before they came from their own country, or fell into the hands of white men. Their law of nations, or general usage, having, by common consent the force of law, justified them, while carrying on their petty wars, in killing their prisoners or reducing them to slavery; consequently, in selling them, and these ends they appear to have proposed to themselves; the nation, therefore, or individual, which was overcome, reduced to slavery, and sold would have done the same by the enemy, had victory declared on their, or his side. Consequently, the man made slave in this manner, might be said to be made so by his own consent, and by the indulgence of barbarous principles.

That Christian nations have not done all they might, or should have done, on a principle of Christian benevolence, for the civilization and conversion of the Africans: that much cruelty has been practised in the slave trade, as the benevolent Wilberforce, and others have shown; that much tyranny has been exercised by individuals, as masters over their slaves, and that the religious interests of the latter have been too much neglected by many cannot, will not be denied. But the fullest proof of these facts, will not also prove, that the holding men in subjection, as slaves, is a moral evil, and inconsistent with Christianity. Magistrates, husbands, and fathers, have proved tyrants. This does not prove, that magistracy, the husband's right to govern, and parental authority, are unlawful and wicked. The individual who abuses his authority, and acts with cruelty, must answer for it at the Divine tribunal; and civil authority should interpose to prevent or punish it; but neither civil nor ecclesiastical authority can consistently interfere with the possession and legitimate exercise of a right given by the Divine Law.

If the above representation of the Scriptural doctrine, and the manner of obtaining slaves from Africa is just; and if also purchasing them has been the means of saving human life, which there is great reason to believe it has; then, however the slave trade, in present circumstances, is justly censurable, yet might motives of humanity and even piety have been originally brought into operation in the purchase of slaves, when sold in the circumstances we have described. If, also, by their own confession, which has been made in manifold instances, their condition, when they have come into the hands of humane masters here, has been greatly bettered by the change; if it is, ordinarily, really better, as many assert, than that of thousands of the poorer classes in countries reputed civilized and free; and, if, in addition to all other considerations, the translation from their native country to this has been the means of their mental and religious improvement, and so of obtaining salvation, as many of themselves have joyfully and thankfully confessed— then may the just and humane master, who rules his slaves and provides for them, according to Christian principles, rest satisfied, that he is not, in holding them, chargeable with moral evil, nor with acting, in this respect, contrary to the genius of Christianity.—It appears to be equally clear, that those, who by reasoning on abstract principles, are induced to favour the scheme of general emancipation, and who ascribe their sentiments to Christianity, should be particularly careful, however benevolent their intentions may be, that they do not by a perversion of the Scriptural doctrine, through their wrong views of it, not only invade the domestic and religious peace and rights of our Citizens, on this subject; but, also by an intemperate zeal, prevent indirectly, the religious improvement of the people they design, professedly, to benefit; and, perhaps, become, evidently, the means of producing in our country, scenes of anarchy and blood; and all this in a vain attempt to bring about a state of things, which, if arrived at, would not probably better the state of that people; which is thought, by men of observation, to be generally true of the Negroes in the Northern states, who have been liberated.

To pious minds it has given pain to hear men, respectable for intelligence and morals, sometimes say, that holding slaves is indeed indefensible, but that to us it is necessary, and must be supported. On this principle, mere politicians, unmindful of morals, may act. But surely, in a moral and religious view of the subject, this principle is inadmissible. It cannot be said, that theft, falsehood, adultery and murder, are become necesssary and must be supported. Yet there is reason to believe, that some of honest and pious intentions have found their minds embarrassed if not perverted on this subject, by this plausible but unsound argument. From such embarrassment the view exhibited above affords relief.

The Convention, Sir, are far from thinking that Christianity fails to inspire the minds of its subjects with benevolent and generous sentiments; or that liberty rightly understood, or enjoyed, is a blessing of little moment. The contrary of these positions they maintain. But they also consider benevolence as consulting the truest and best interests of its objects; and view the happiness of liberty as well as of religion, as consisting not in the name or form, but in the reality. While men remain in the chains of ignorance and error, and under the domination of tyrant lusts and passions, they cannot be free. And the more freedom of action they have in this state, they are but the more qualified by it to do injury, both to themselves and others. It is, therefore, firmly believed, that general emancipation to the Negroes in this country, would not, in present circumstances, be for their own happiness, as a body; while it would be extremely injurious to the community at large in various ways: And, if so, then it is not required even by benevolence. But acts of benevolence and generosity must be free and voluntary; no man has a right to compel another to the performance of them. This is a concern, which lies between a man and his God. If a man has obtained slaves by purchase, or inheritance, and the holding of them as such is justifiable by the law of God; why should he be required to liberate them, because it would be a generous action, rather than another on the same principle, to release his debtors, or sell his lands and houses, and distribute the proceeds among the poor? These also would be generous actions: Are they, therefore, obligatory? Or, if obligatory, in certain circumstances, as personal, voluntary acts of piety and benevolence, has any man or body of men, civil or ecclesiastic, a right to require them? Surely those, who are advocates for compulsory, or strenous measures to bring about emancipation, should duly weigh this consideration.

Should, however, a time arrive, when the Africans in our country might be found qualified to enjoy freedom; and, when they might obtain it in a manner consistent with the interest and peace of the community at large, the Convention would be happy in seeing them free: And so they would, in seeing the state of the poor, the ignorant and the oppressed of every description, and of every country meliorated; so that the reputed free might be free indeed, and happy. But there seems to be just reason to conclude that a considerable part of the human race, whether they bear openly the character of slaves or are reputed freemen, will continue in such circumstances, with mere shades of variation, while the world continues. It is evident, that men are sinful creatures, subject to affliction and to death, as the consequences of their nature's pollution and guilt: That they are now in a state of probation; and that God as a Righteous, All-wise Sovereign, not only disposes of them as he pleases, and bestows upon them many unmerited blessings and comforts, but subjects them also to privations, afflictions and trials, with the merciful intention of making all their afflictions, as well as their blessings, work finally for their good; if they embrace his salvation, humble themselves before him, learn righteousness, and submit to his holy will. To have them brought to this happy state is the great object of Christian benevolence, and of Christian piety; for this state is not only connected with the truest happiness, which can be enjoyed at any time, but is introductory to eternal life and blessedness in the future world: And the salvation of men is intimately connected with the glory of their God and Redeemer.

And here I am brought to a part of the general subject, which, I confess to your Excellency, the Convention, from a sense of their duty, as a body of men, to whom important concerns of Religion are confided, have particularly at heart, and wish it may be seriously considered by all our Citizens: This is the religious interests of the Negroes. For though they are slaves, they are also men; and are with ourselves accountable creatures; having immortal souls, and being destined to future eternal reward. Their religious interests claim a regard from their masters of the most serious nature; and it is indispensible. Nor can the community at large, in a right estimate of their duty and happiness, be indifferent on this subject. To the truly benevolent it must be pleasing to know, that a number of masters, as well as ministers and pious individuals, of various Christian denominations among us, do conscientiously regard this duty; but there is a great reason to believe, that it is neglected and disregarded by many.

The Convention are particularly unhappy in considering, that an idea of the Bible's teaching the doctrine of emancipation as necessary, and tending to make servants insubordinate to proper authority, has obtained access to any mind; both on account of its direct influence on those, who admit it; and the fear it excites in others, producing the effects before noticed. But it is hoped, it has been evinced, that the idea is an erroneous one; and, that it will be seen, that the influence of a right acquaintance with that Holy Book tends directly and powerfully, by promoting the fear and love of God, together with just and peaceful sentiments toward men, to produce one of the best securities to the public, for the internal and domestic peace of the State.

It is also a pleasing consideration, tending to confirm these sentiments, that in the late projected scheme for producing an insurrection among us, there were very few of those who were, as members attached to regular Churches, (even within the sphere of its operations) who appear to have taken a part in the wicked plot, or indeed to whom it was made known; of some Churches it does not appear, that there were any. It is true, that a considerable number of those who were found guilty and executed, laid claim to a religious character; yet several of these were grossly immoral, and, in general, they were members of an irregular body, which called itself the African Church, and had intimate connection and intercourse with a similar body of men in a Northern City, among whom the supposed right to emancipation is strenuously advocated.

The result of this inquiry and reasoning, on the subject of slavery, brings us, sir, if I mistake not, very regularly to the following conclusions:—That the holding of slaves is justifiable by the doctrine and example contained in Holy writ; and is; therefore consistent with Christian uprightness, both in sentiment and conduct. That all things considered, the Citizens of America have in general obtained the African slaves, which they possess, on principles, which can be justified; though much cruelty has indeed been exercised towards them by many, who have been concerned in the slave-trade, and by others who have held them here, as slaves in their service; for which the authors of this cruelty are accountable. That slavery, when tempered with humanity and justice, is a state of tolerable happiness; equal, if not superior, to that which many poor enjoy in countries reputed free. That a master has a scriptural right to govern his slaves so as to keep them in subjection; to demand and receive from them a reasonable service; and to correct them for the neglect of duty, for their vices and transgressions; but that to impose on them unreasonable, rigorous services, or to inflict on them cruel punishment, he has neither a scriptural nor a moral right. At the same time it must be remembered, that, while he is receiving from them their uniform and best services, he is required by the Divine Law, to afford them protection, and such necessaries and conveniencies of life as are proper to their condition as servants; so far as he is enabled by their services to afford them these comforts, on just and rational principles. That it is the positive duty of servants to reverence their master, to be obedient, industrious, faithful to him, and careful of his interests; and without being so, they can neither be the faithful servants of God, nor be held as regular members of the Christian Church. That as claims to freedom as a right, when that right is forfeited, or has been lost, in such a manner as has been represented, would be unjust; and as all attempts to obtain it by violence and fraud would be wicked; so all representations made to them by others, on such censurable principles, or in a manner tending to make them discontented; and finally, to produce such unhappy effects and consequences, as [have] been before noticed, cannot be friendly to them (as they certainly are not to the community at large), nor consistent with righteousness: Nor can the conduct be justified, however in some it may be palliated by pleading benevolence in intention, as the motive. That masters having the disposal of the persons, time and labour of their servants, and being the heads of families, are bound, on principles of moral and religious duty, to give these servants religious instruction; or at least, to afford them opportunities, under proper regulations to obtain it: And to grant religious privileges to those, who desire them, and furnish proper evidence of their sincerity and uprightness: Due care being at the same time taken, that they receive their instructions from right sources, and from their connexions, where they will not be in danger of having their minds corrupted by sentiments unfriendly to the domestic and civil peace of the community. That, where life, comfort, safety and religious interest of so large a number of human beings, as this class of persons is among us, are concerned; and, where they must necessarily, as slaves, be so much at the disposal of their masters; it appears to be a just and necessary concern of the Government, not only to provide laws to prevent or punish insurrections, and other violent and villanous conduct among them (which are indeed necessary) but, on the other hand, laws, also, to prevent their being oppressed and injured by unreasonable, cruel masters, and others; and to afford them, in respect of morality and religion, such privileges as may comport with the peace and safety of the State, and with those relative duties existing between masters and servants, which the word of God enjoins. It is, also, believed to be a just conclusion, that the interest and security of the State would be promoted, by allowing, under proper regulations, considerable religious privileges, to such of this class, as know how to estimate them aright, and have given suitable evidence of their own good principles, uprightness and fidelity; by attaching them, from principles of gratitude and love, to the interests of their masters and the State; and thus rendering their fidelity firm and constant. While on the other hand, to lay them under an interdict, as some have supposed necessary, in a case where reason, conscience, the genius of Christianity and salvation are concerned, on account of the bad conduct of others, would be felt as oppressive, tend to sour and alienate their minds from their masters and the public, and to make them vulnerable to temptation. All which is, with deference, submitted to the consideration of your Excellency.

With high respect, I remain, personally, and on behalf of the Convention,

Sir, your very obedient and humble servant,
RICHARD FURMAN.
President of the Baptist State Convention.

His Excellency GOVERNOR WILSON.

Notes

1. See *Leviticus* XXV: 44, 45, 46, &c.
2. ὑπό ζυγον Δουλοι/hupo zugon Douloi: bond-servants, or slaves. Doulos, is the proper term for slaves; it is here in the plural and rendered more expressive by being connected with yoke—UNDER THE YOKE.

⚚ 7 ⚚

Situation of the Black Population in the United States

ALEXIS DE TOCQUEVILLE

Alexis de Tocqueville's classic analysis of nineteeenth-century American political culture, *Democracy in America* (1835), contains this judicious and prescient analysis of the problem of slavery in the United States. While de Tocqueville did not foresee, at this time, the eventual break-up of the union, he did predict that the South's position on the issue of slavery would become increasingly untenable. The strength of his argument lies in his appreciation of the impact of slavery on the culture of the South: he describes it as a source of regional impoverishment, both morally and materially. He also suggests that even abolition would not bring an end to racism, and that racial tensions would continue to plague the republic.

Situation of the Black Population in the United States,[1] and Dangers with which its Prescence threatens the Whites.

Why it is more difficult to abolish slavery, and to efface all vestiges of it among the moderns than it was among the ancients—In the United States the prejudices of the whites against the blacks seem to increase in proportion as slavery is abolished—Situation of the Negroes in the Northern and Southern states—Why the Americans abolish slavery—Servitude, which debases the slave, impoverishes the master—Contrast between the left and the right bank of the Ohio—To what attributable—The black race, as well as slavery, recedes towards the South—Explanation of this fact—Difficulties attendant upon the abolition of slavery in the South— Dangers to come—General anxiety—Foundation of a black colony in Africa— Why the Americans of the South increase the hardships of slavery while they are distressed at its continuance.

Source: Alexis de Tocqueville, *Democracy in America*, 1835,
rptd New York: Alfred A. Knopf, 1980 edition, Vol. 1. trans. Henry Reeve.

The Indians will perish in the same isolated condition in which they have lived, but the destiny of the Negroes is in some measure interwoven with that of the Europeans. These two races are fastened to each other without intermingling; and they are alike unable to separate entirely or to combine. The most formidable of all the ills that threaten the future of the Union arises from the presence of a black population upon its territory; and in contemplating the cause of the present embarrassments, or the future dangers of the United States, the observer is invariably led to this as a primary fact.

Generally speaking, men must make great and unceasing efforts before permanent evils are created; but there is one calamity which penetrated furtively into the world, and which was at first scarcely distinguishable amid the ordinary abuses of power: it originated with an individual whose name history has not preserved; it was wafted like some accursed germ upon a portion of the soil; but it afterwards nurtured itself, grew without effort, and spread naturally with the society to which it belonged. This calamity is slavery. Christianity suppressed slavery, but the Christians of the sixteenth century re-established it, as an exception, indeed, to their social system, and restricted to one of the races of mankind; but the wound thus inflicted upon humanity, though less extensive, was far more difficult to cure.

It is important to make an accurate distinction between slavery itself and its consequences. The immediate evils produced by slavery were very nearly the same in antiquity as they are among the moderns, but the consequences of these evils were different. The slave among the ancients belonged to the same race as his master, and was often the superior of the two in education[2] and intelligence. Freedom was the only distinction between them; and when freedom was conferred, they were easily confounded together. The ancients, then, had a very simple means of ridding themselves of slavery and its consequences: that of enfranchisement; and they succeeded as soon as they adopted this measure generally. Not but that in ancient states the vestiges of servitude subsisted for some time after servitude itself was abolished. There is a natural prejudice that prompts men to despise whoever has been their inferior long after he has become their equal and the real inequality that is produced by fortune or by law is always succeeded by an imaginary inequality that is implanted in the manners of the people. But among the ancients this secondary consequence of slavery had a natural limit; for the freedman bore so entire a resemblance to those born free that it soon became impossible to distinguish him from them.

The greatest difficulty in antiquity was that of altering the law; among the moderns it is that of altering the customs, and as far as we are concerned, the real obstacles begin where those of the ancients left off. This arises from the circumstance that among the moderns the abstract and transient fact of slavery is fatally united with the physical and permanent fact of color. The tradition of slavery dishonors the race, and the peculiarity of the race perpetuates the tradition of slavery. No African has ever voluntarily emigrated to the shores of the New World, whence it follows that all the blacks who are now found there are either slaves or freedmen. Thus the Negro transmits the eternal mark of his ignominy to all his descendants; and although the law may abolish slavery, God alone can obliterate the traces of its existence. The modern slave differs from his master not only in his condition but in his origin. You may set the Negro free, but you cannot make him otherwise than an alien to the European. Nor is this all; we scarcely acknowledge the common features of humanity in this stranger whom slavery has brought among us. His physiognomy is to our eyes hideous, his understanding weak, his tastes low; and we are almost inclined to look upon him as a being intermediate between man and the brutes.[3] The moderns, then, after they have abolished slavery, have three prejudices to contend against, which are less easy to attack and far less easy to conquer than the mere fact of servitude: the prejudice of the master, the prejudice of the race, and the prejudice of color.

It is difficult for us, who have had the good fortune to be born among men like ourselves by nature and our equals by law, to conceive the irreconcilable differences that separate the Negro from the European in America. But we may derive some faint notion of them from analogy. France was, formerly a country in which numerous inequalities existed that had been created by law. Nothing can be more fictitious than a purely legal inferiority, nothing more contrary to the instinct of mankind than these permanent divisions established between beings evidently similar. Yet these divisions existed for ages; they still exist in many places; and everywhere they have left imaginary vestiges, which time alone can efface. If it be so difficult to root out an inequality that originates solely in the law, how are those distinctions to be destroyed which seem to be based upon the immutable laws of Nature herself? When I remember the extreme difficulty with which aristocratic bodies, of whatever nature they may be, are commingled with the mass of the people, and the exceeding care which they take to preserve for ages the ideal boundaries of their caste inviolate, I despair of seeing an aristocracy disappear which is founded upon visible and indelible signs. Those who hope that the Europeans will ever be amalgamated with the Negroes appear to me to delude themselves. I am not led to any such conclusion by my reason or by the evidence of facts. Hitherto wherever the whites have been the most powerful, they have held the blacks in degradation or in slavery; wherever the Negroes have been strongest, they have destroyed the whites: this has been the only balance that has ever taken place between the two races.

I see that in a certain portion of the territory of the United States at the present day the legal barrier which separated the two races is falling away, but not that which exists in the manners of the country; slavery recedes, but the prejudice to which it has given birth is immovable. Whoever has inhabited the United States must have perceived that in those parts of the Union in which the Negroes are no longer slaves they have in no wise drawn nearer to the whites. On the contrary, the prejudice of race appears to be stronger in the states that have abolished slavery than in those where it still exists; and nowhere is it so intolerant as in those states where servitude has never been known.

It is true that in the North of the Union marriages may be legally contracted between Negroes and whites; but public opinion would stigmatize as infamous a man who should connect himself with a Negress, and it would be difficult to cite a single instance of such a union. The electoral franchise has been conferred upon the Negroes in almost all the states in which slavery has been abolished, but if they come forward to vote, their lives are in danger. If oppressed, they may bring an action at law, but they will find none but whites among their judges; and although they may legally serve as jurors, prejudice repels them from that office. The same schools do not receive the children of the black and of the European. In the theaters gold cannot procure a seat for the servile race beside their former masters; in the hospitals they lie apart; and although they are allowed to invoke the same God as the whites, it must be at a different altar and in their own churches, with their own clergy. The gates of heaven are not closed against them, but their inferiority is continued to the very confines of the other world. When the Negro dies, his bones are cast aside, and the distinction of condition prevails even in the equality of death. Thus the Negro is free, but he can share neither the rights, nor pleasures, nor the labor, nor the afflictions, nor the tomb of him whose equal he has been declared to be; and he cannot meet him upon fair terms in life or in death.

In the South, where slavery still exists, the Negroes are less carefully kept apart; they sometimes share the labors and the recreations of the whites; the whites consent to intermix with them to a certain extent, and although legislation treats them more harshly the habits of the people are more tolerant and compassionate. In the South the master is not afraid to raise his slave to his own standing, because he knows that he can in a moment reduce him to the dust at pleasure. In the North the white no longer distinctly perceives the barrier that separates him from the degraded race, and he shuns the Negro with the more pertinacity since he fears lest they should some day be confounded together.

Among the Americans of the South, Nature sometimes reasserts her rights and restores a transient equality between the blacks and the whites; but in the North pride restrains the most imperious of human passions. The American of the Northern states would perhaps allow the Negress to share his licentious pleasures if the laws of his country did not declare that she may aspire to be the legitimate partner of his bed, but he recoils with horror from her who might become his wife.

Thus it is in the United States that the prejudice which repels the Negroes seems to increase in proportion as they are emancipated, and inequality is sanctioned by the manners while it is effaced from the laws of the country. But if the relative position of the two races that inhabit the United States is such as I have described, why have the Americans abolished slavery in the North of the Union, why do they maintain it in the South, and why do they aggravate its hardships? The answer is easily given. It is not for the good of the Negroes, but for that of the whites, that measures are taken to abolish slavery in the United States.

The first Negroes were imported into Virginia about the year 1621.[4] In America, therefore, as well as in the rest of the globe, slavery originated in the South. Thence it spread from one settlement to another; but the number of slaves diminished towards the Northern states, and the Negro population was always very limited in

New England.[5]

A century had scarcely elapsed since the foundation of the colonies when the attention of the planters was struck by the extraordinary fact that the provinces which were comparatively destitute of slaves increased in population, in wealth, and in prosperity more rapidly than those which contained many of them. In the former, however, the inhabitants were obliged to cultivate the soil themselves or by hired laborers; in the latter they were furnished with hands for which they paid no wages. Yet though labor and expense were on the one side and ease with economy on the other, the former had the more advantageous system. This result seemed the more difficult to explain since the settlers, who all belonged to the same European race, had the same habits, the same civilization, the same laws, and their shades of difference were extremely slight.

Time, however, continued to advance, and the Anglo-Americans, spreading beyond the coasts of the Atlantic Ocean, penetrated farther and farther into the solitudes of the West. They met there with a new soil and an unwonted climate; they had to overcome obstacles of the most various character; their races intermingled, the inhabitants of the South going up towards the North, those of the North descending to the South. But in the midst of all these causes the same result occurred at every step; in general, the colonies in which there were no slaves became more populous and more prosperous than those in which slavery flourished. The farther they went, the more was it shown that slavery, which is so cruel to the slave, is prejudicial to the master.

But this truth was most satisfactorily demonstrated when civilization reached the banks of the Ohio. The stream that the Indians had distinguished by the name of Ohio, or the Beautiful River, waters one of the most magnificent valleys which have ever been made the abode of man. Undulating lands extend upon both shores of the Ohio, whose soil affords inexhaustible treasures to the laborer; on either bank the air is equally wholesome and the climate mild; and each of them forms the extreme frontier of a vast state: that which follows the numerous windings of the Ohio upon the left is called Kentucky; that upon the right bears the name of the river. These two states differ only in a single respect: Kentucky has admitted slavery, but the state of Ohio has prohibited the existence of slaves within its borders.[6] Thus the traveler who floats down the current of the Ohio to the spot where that river falls into the Mississippi may be said to sail between liberty and servitude; and a transient inspection of surrounding objects will convince him which of the two is more favorable to humanity.

Upon the left bank of the stream the population is sparse; from time to time one descries a troop of slaves loitering in the half-desert fields; the primeval forest reappears at every turn; society seems to be asleep, man to be idle, and nature alone offers a scene of activity and life. From the right bank, on the contrary, a confused hum is heard, which proclaims afar the presence of industry; the fields are covered with abundant harvests; the elegance of the dwellings announces the taste and activity of the laborers; and man appears to be in the enjoyment of that wealth and contentment which is the reward of labor.[7]

I. Introduction: Contextualising Slavery

The state of Kentucky was founded in 1775, the state of Ohio only twelve years later; but twelve years are more in America than half a century in Europe; and at the present day the population of Ohio exceeds that of Kentucky by two hundred and fifty thousand souls.[8] These different effects of slavery and freedom may readily be understood; and they suffice to explain many of the differences which we notice between the civilization of antiquity and that of our own time.

Upon the left bank of the Ohio labor is confounded with the idea of slavery, while upon the right bank it is identified with that of prosperity and improvement; on the one side, it is degraded, on the other it is honored. On the former territory no white laborers can be found, for they would be afraid of assimilating themselves to the Negroes; all the work is done by slaves; on the latter no one is idle, for the white population extend their activity and intelligence to every kind of employment. Thus the men whose task it is to cultivate the rich soil of Kentucky are ignorant and apathetic, while those who are active and enlightened either do nothing or pass over into Ohio, where they may work without shame.

It is true that in Kentucky the planters are not obliged to pay the slaves whom they employ, but they derive small profits from their labor, while the wages paid to free workmen would be returned with interest in the value of their services. The free work-man is paid, but he does his work quicker than the slave; and rapidity of execution is one of the great elements of economy. The white sells his services, but they are purchased only when they may be useful; the black can claim no remuneration for his toil, but the expense of his maintenance is perpetual; he must be supported in his old age as well as in manhood, in his profitless infancy as well as in the productive years of youth, in sickness as well as in health. Payment must equally be made in order to obtain the services of either class of men: the free workman receives his wages in money; the slave in education, in food, in care, and in clothing. The money which a master spends in the maintenance of his slaves goes gradually and in detail, so that it is scarcely perceived; the salary of the free workman is paid in a round sum and appears to enrich only him who receives it; but in the end the slave has cost more than the free servant, and his labor is less productive.[9]

The influence of slavery extends still further: it affects the character of the master and imparts a peculiar tendency to his ideas and tastes. Upon both banks of the Ohio the character of the inhabitants is enterprising and energetic, but this vigor is very differently exercised in the two states. The white inhabitant of Ohio, obliged to subsist by his own exertions, regards temporal prosperity as the chief aim of his existence; and as the country which he occupies presents inexhaustible resources to his industry, and ever varying lures to his activity, his acquisitive ardor surpasses the ordinary limits of human cupidity: he is tormented by the desire of wealth, and he boldly enters upon every path that fortune opens to him; he becomes a sailor, a pioneer, an artisan, or a cultivator with the same indifference, and supports with equal constancy the fatigues and the dangers incidental to these various professions; the resources of his intelligence are astonishing, and his avidity in the pursuit of gain amounts to a species of heroism.

135

But the Kentuckian scorns not only labor but all the undertakings that labor promotes; as he lives in an idle independence, his tastes are those of an idle man; money has lost a portion of its value in his eyes; he covets wealth much less than pleasure and excitement; and the energy which his neighbor devotes to gain turns with him to a passionate love of field sports and military exercises; he delights in violent bodily exertion, he is familiar with the use of arms, and is accustomed from a very early age to expose his life in single combat. Thus slavery prevents the whites not only from becoming opulent, but even from desiring to become so. As the same causes have been continually producing opposite effects for the last two centuries in the British colonies of North America, they have at last established a striking difference between the commercial capacity of the inhabitants of the South and those of the North. At the present day it is only the Northern states that are in possession of shipping, manufactures, railroads, and canals. This difference is perceptible not only in comparing the North with the South, but in comparing the several Southern states. Almost all those who carry on commercial operations or endeavor to turn slave labor to account in the most southern districts of the Union have emigrated from the North. The natives of the Northern states are constantly spreading over that portion of the American territory where they have less to fear from competition; they discover resources there which escaped the notice of the inhabitants; and as they comply with a system which they do not approve, they succeed in turning it to better advantage than those who first founded and who still maintain it.

Were I inclined to continue this parallel, I could easily prove that almost all the differences which may be noticed between the characters of the Americans in the Southern and in the Northern states have originated in slavery; but this would divert me from my subject, and my present intention is not to point out all the consequences of servitude, but those effects which it has produced upon the material prosperity of the countries that have admitted it.

The influence of slavery upon the production of wealth must have been very imperfectly known in antiquity, as slavery then obtained throughout the civilized world, and the nations that were unacquainted with it were barbarians. And, indeed, Christianity abolished slavery only by advocating the claims of the slave; at the present time it may be attacked in the name of the master, and upon this point interest is reconciled with morality.

As these truths became apparent in the United States, slavery receded before the progress of experience. Servitude had begun in the South and had thence spread towards the North, but it now retires again. Freedom, which started from the North, now descends uninterruptedly towards the South. Among the great states, Pennsylvania now constitutes the extreme limit of slavery to the North; but even within those limits the slave system is shaken. Maryland, which is immediately below Pennsylvania, is preparing for its abolition; and Virginia, which comes next to Maryland, is already discussing its utility and its dangers.[10] No great change takes place in human institutions without involving among its causes the law of inheritance. When the law of primogeniture obtained in the South, each family

136

was represented by a wealthy individual, who was neither compelled nor induced to labor; and he was surrounded, as by parasitic plants, by the other members of his family, who were then excluded by law from sharing the common inheritance, and who led the same kind of life as himself. The same thing then occurred in all the families of the South which still happens in the noble families of some countries in Europe: namely, that the younger sons remain in the same state of idleness as their elder brother, without being as rich as he is. This identical result seems to be produced in Europe and in America by wholly analogous causes. In the South of the United States the whole race of whites formed an aristocratic body, headed by a certain number of privileged individuals, whose wealth was permanent and whose leisure was hereditary. These leaders of the American nobility kept alive the traditional prejudices of the white race, in the body of which they were the representatives, and maintained idleness in honor. This aristocracy contained many who were poor, but none who would work; its members preferred want to labor; consequently Negro laborers and slaves met with no competition; and, whatever opinion might be entertained as to the utility of their industry, it was necessary to employ them, since there was no one else to work.

No sooner was the law of primogeniture abolished than fortunes began to diminish and all the families of the country were simultaneously reduced to a state in which labor became necessary to existence; several of them have since entirely disappeared, and all of them learned to look forward to the time when it would be necessary for everyone to provide for his own wants. Wealthy individuals are still to be met with, but they no longer constitute a compact and hereditary body, nor have they been able to adopt a line of conduct in which they could persevere and which they could infuse into all ranks of society. The prejudice that stigmatized labor was, in the first place, abandoned by common consent, the number of needy men was increased, and the needy were allowed to gain a subsistence by labor without blushing for their toil. Thus one of the most immediate consequences of the equal division of estates has been to create a class of free laborers. As soon as competition began between the free laborer and the slave, the inferiority of the latter became manifest and slavery was attacked in its fundamental principle, which is the interest of the master.

As slavery recedes, the black population follows its retrograde course and returns with it towards those tropical regions whence it originally came. However singular this fact may at first appear to be, it may readily be explained. Although the Americans abolish the principle of slavery, they do not set their slaves free. To illustrate this remark, I will quote the example of the state of New York. In 1788 this state prohibited the sale of slaves within its limits, which was an indirect method of prohibiting the importation of them. Thenceforward the number of Negroes could only increase according to the ratio of the natural increase of population. But eight years later, a more decisive measure was taken, and it was enacted that all children born of slave parents after the 4th of July 1799 should be free. No increase could then take place, and although slaves still existed, slavery might be said to be abolished.

As soon as a Northern state thus prohibited the importation, no slaves were brought from the South to be sold in its markets. On the other hand, as the sale of slaves was forbidden in that state, an owner could no longer get rid of his slave (who thus became a burdensome possession) otherwise than by transporting him to the South. But when a northern state declared that the son of the slave should be born free, the slave lost a large portion of his market value, since his posterity was no longer included in the bargain, and the owner had then a strong interest in transporting him to the South. Thus the same law prevents the slaves of the South from coming North and drives those of the North to the South.

But there is another cause more powerful than any that I have described. The want of free hands is felt in a state in proportion as the number of slaves decreases. But in proportion as labor is performed by free hands, slave labor becomes less productive; and the slave is then a useless or onerous possession, whom it is important to export to the South, where the same competition is not to be feared. Thus the abolition of slavery does not set the slave free, but merely transfers him to another master, and from the North to the South.

The emancipated Negroes and those born after the abolition of slavery do not, indeed, migrate from the North to the South; but their situation with regard to the Europeans is not unlike that of the Indians; they remain half civilized and deprived of their rights in the midst of a population that is far superior to them in wealth and knowledge, where they are exposed to the tyranny of the laws[11] and the intolerance of the people. On some accounts they are still more to be pitied than the Indians, since they are haunted by the reminiscence of slavery, and they cannot claim possession of any part of the soil. Many of them perish miserably,[12] and the rest congregate in the great towns, where they perform the meanest offices and lead a wretched and precarious existence.

If, moreover, the number of Negroes were to continue to grow in the same proportion during the period when they did not have their liberty, yet, with the number of the whites increasing at a double rate after the abolition of slavery, the Negroes would soon be swallowed up in the midst of an alien population.

A district which is cultivated by slaves is in general less populous than a district cultivated by free labor; moreover, America is still a new country, and a state is therefore not half peopled when it abolishes slavery. No sooner is an end put to slavery than the want of free labor is felt, and a crowd of enterprising adventurers immediately arrives from all parts of the country, who hasten to profit by the fresh resources which are then opened to industry. The soil is soon divided among them, and a family of white settlers takes possession of each portion. Besides, European immigration is exclusively directed to the free states; for what would a poor immigrant do who crosses the Atlantic in search of ease and happiness if he were to land in a country where labor is stigmatized as degrading?

Thus the white population grows by its natural increase, and at the same time by the immense influx of immigrants; while the black population receives no immigrants and is upon its decline. The proportion that existed between the two races is soon inverted. The Negroes constitute a scanty remnant, a poor tribe of vagrants, lost in the midst of an immense people who own the land; and the presence of the blacks is only marked by the injustice and the hardships of which they are the victims.

In several of the Western states the Negro race never made its appearance, and in all the Northern states it is rapidly declining. Thus the great question of its future condition is confined within a narrow circle, where it becomes less formidable, though not more easy of solution. The more we descend towards the South, the more difficult it becomes to abolish slavery with advantage; and this arises from several physical causes which it is important to point out.

The first of these causes is the climate: it is well known that, in proportion as Europeans approach the tropics, labor becomes more difficult to them. Many of the Americans even assert that within a certain latitude it is fatal to them, while the Negroes can work there without danger;[13] but I do not think that this opinion, which is so favorable to the indolence of the inhabitants of the South, is confirmed by experience. The southern parts of the Union are not hotter than the south of Italy and of Spain;[14] and it may be asked why the European cannot work as well there as in the latter two countries. If slavery has been abolished in Italy and in Spain without causing the destruction of the masters, why should not the same thing take place in the Union? I cannot believe that nature has prohibited the Europeans in Georgia and the Floridas, under pain of death, from raising the means of subsistence from the soil; but their labor would unquestionably be more irksome and less productive[15] to them than to the inhabitants of New England. As the free workman thus loses a portion of his superiority over the slave in the Southern states, there are fewer inducements to abolish slavery.

All the plants of Europe grow in the northern parts of the Union; the South has special products of its own. It has been observed that slave labor is a very expensive method of cultivating cereal grain. The farmer of grainland in a country where slavery is unknown habitually retains only a small number of laborers in his service, and at seed-time and harvest he hires additional hands, who live at his cost for only a short period. But the agriculturist in a slave state is obliged to keep a large number of slaves the whole year round in order to sow his fields and to gather in his crops, although their services are required only for a few weeks; for slaves are unable to wait till they are hired and to subsist by their own labor in the meantime, like free laborers; in order to have their services, they must be bought. Slavery, independently of its general disadvantages, is therefore still more inapplicable to countries in which grain is cultivated than to those which produce crops of a dffierent kind. The cultivation of tobacco, of cotton, and especially of sugar-cane demands, on the other hand, unremitting attention; and women and children are employed in it, whose services are of little use in the cultivation of wheat. Thus slavery is naturally more fitted to the countries from which these productions are derived.

Tobacco, cotton, and sugar-cane are exclusively grown in the South, and they form the principal sources of the wealth of those states. If slavery were abolished, the inhabitants of the South would be driven to this alternative: they must either change their system of cultivation, and then they would come into competition with the more active and more experienced inhabitants of the North; or, if they continued to cultivate the same produce without slave labor, they would have to support the competition of the other states of the South, which might still retain their slaves. Thus peculiar reasons for maintaining slavery exist in the South which do not operate in the North.

But there is yet another motive, which is more cogent than all the others: the South might, indeed, rigorously speaking, abolish slavery; but how should it rid its territory of the black population? Slaves and slavery are driven from the North by the same law; but this twofold result cannot be hoped for in the South.

In proving that slavery is more natural and more advantageous in the South than in the North, I have shown that the number of slaves must be far greater in the former. It was to the Southern settlements that the first Africans were brought, and it is there that the greatest number of them have always been imported. As we advance towards the South, the prejudice that sanctions idleness increases in power. In the states nearest to the tropics there is not a single white laborer; the Negroes are consequently much more numerous in the South than in the North. And, as I have already observed, this disproportion increases daily, since the Negroes are transferred to one part of the Union as soon as slavery is abolished in the other. Thus the black population augments in the South, not only by its natural fecundity, but by the compulsory emigration of the Negroes from the North; and the African race has causes of increase in the South very analogous to those which accelerate the growth of the European race in the North.

In the state of Maine there is one Negro in three hundred inhabitants; in Massachusetts, one in one hundred; in New York, two in one hundred; in Pennsylvania, three in the same number; in Maryland, thirty-four; in Virginia, forty-two; and lastly, in South Carolina,[16] fifty-five per cent of the inhabitants are black. Such was the proportion of the black population to the whites in the year 1830. But this proportion is perpetually changing, as it constantly decreases in the North and augments in the South.

It is evident that the most southern states of the Union cannot abolish slavery without incurring great dangers, which the North had no reason to apprehend when it emancipated its black population. I have already shown how the Northern states made the transition from slavery to freedom, by keeping the present generation in chains and setting their descendants free; by this means the Negroes are only gradually introduced into society; and while the men who might abuse their freedom are kept in servitude, those who are emancipated may learn the art of being free before they become their own masters. But it would be difficult to apply this method in the South. To declare that all the Negroes born after a certain period shall be free is to introduce the principle and the notion of liberty into the heart of slavery; the blacks whom the law thus maintains in a state of slavery from which their children are delivered are astonished at so unequal a fate, and their astonishment is only the prelude to their impatience and irritation. Thenceforward slavery loses, in their eyes, that kind of moral power which it derived from time and habit; it is reduced to a mere palpable abuse of force. The Northern states had nothing to fear from the contrast, because in them the blacks were few in number, and the white population was very considerable. But if this faint dawn of freedom were to show two millions of men their true position, the oppressors would have reason to tremble. After having enfranchised the children of their slaves, the Europeans of the Southern states would very shortly be obliged to extend the same benefit to the whole black population.

In the North, as I have already remarked, a twofold migration ensues upon the abolition of slavery, or even precedes that event when circumstances have rendered it probable the slaves quit the country to be transported southwards; and the whites of the Northern states, as well as the immigrants from Europe, hasten to fill their place. But these two causes cannot operate in the same manner in the Southern states. On the one hand, the mass of slaves is too great to allow any expectation of their being removed from the country; and on the other hand, the Europeans and Anglo-Americans of the North are afraid to come to inhabit a country in which labor has not yet been reinstated in its rightful honors. Besides, they very justly look upon the states in which the number of the Negroes equals or exceeds that of the whites as exposed to very great dangers; and they refrain from turning their activity in that direction. Thus the inhabitants of the South, while abolishing slavery, would not be able, like their Northern countrymen, to initiate the slaves gradually into a state of freedom; they have no means of perceptibly diminishing the black population, and they would remain unsupported to repress its excesses. Thus in the course of a few years a great people of free Negroes would exist in the heart of a white nation of equal size.

The same abuses of power that now maintain slavery would then become the source of the most alarming perils to the white population of the South. At the present time the descendants of the Europeans are the sole owners of the land and the absolute masters of all labor; they alone possess wealth, knowledge, and arms. The black is destitute of all these advantages, but can subsist without them because he is a slave. If he were free, and obliged to provide for his own subsistence, would it be possible for him to remain without these things and to support life? Or would not the very instruments of the present superiority of the white while slavery exists expose him to a thousand dangers if it were abolished?

As long as the Negro remains a slave, he may be kept in a condition not far removed from that of the brutes; but with his liberty he cannot but acquire a degree of instruction that will enable him to appreciate his misfortunes and to discern a remedy for them. Moreover, there exists a singular principle of relative justice which is firmly implanted in the human heart. Men are much more forcibly struck by those inequalities which exist within the same class than by those which may be noted between different classes. One can understand slavery, but how allow [sic] several millions of citizens to exist under a load of eternal infamy and hereditary wretchedness? In the North the population of freed Negroes feels these hardships and indignities, but its numbers and its powers are small, while in the South it would be numerous and strong.

As soon as it is admitted that the whites and the emancipated blacks are placed upon the same territory in the situation of two foreign communities, it will readily be understood that there are but two chances for the future: the Negroes and the whites must either wholly part or wholly mingle. I have already expressed my conviction as to the latter event.[17] I do not believe that the white and black races will ever live in any country upon an equal footing. But I believe the difficulty to be still greater in the United States than elsewhere. An isolated individual may surmount the prejudices of religion, of his country, or of his race; and if this individual is a king, he may effect surprising changes in society; but a whole people cannot rise, as it were, above itself. A despot who should subject the Americans and their former slaves to the same yoke might perhaps succeed in commingling their races; but as long as the American democracy remains at the head of affairs, no one will undertake so difficult a task; and it may be foreseen that the freer the white population [sic] of the United States becomes, the more isolated will it remain.[18]

I have previously observed that the mixed race is the true bond of union between the Europeans and the Indians; just so, the mulattoes are the true means of transition between the white and the Negro; so that wherever mulattoes abound, the intermixture of the two races is not impossible. In some parts of America the European and the Negro races are so crossed with one another that it is rare to meet with a man who is entirely black or entirely white; when they have arrived at this point, the two races may really be said to be combined, or, rather, to have been absorbed in a third race, which is connected with both without being identical with either.

Of all Europeans, the English are those who have mixed least with the Negroes. More mulattoes are to be seen in the South of the Union than in the North, but infinitely fewer than in any other European colony. Mulattoes are by no means numerous in the United States; they have no force peculiar to themselves, and when quarrels originating in differences of color take place they generally side with the whites, just as the lackeys of the great in Europe assume the contemptuous airs of nobility towards the lower orders.

The pride of origin, which is natural to the English, is singularly augmented by the personal pride that democratic liberty fosters among the Americans: the white citizen of the United States is proud of his race and proud of himself. But if the whites and the Negroes do not intermingle in the North of the Union, how should they mix in the South? Can it be supposed for an instant that an American of the Southern states, placed, as he must forever be, between the white man, with all his physical and moral superiority, and the Negro, will ever think of being confounded with the latter? The Americans of the Southern states have two powerful passions which will always keep them aloof: the first is the fear of being assimilated to the Negroes, their former slaves; and the second, the dread of sinking below the whites, their neighbors.

If I were called upon to predict the future, I should say that the abolition of slavery in the South will, in the common course of things, increase the repugnance of the white population for the blacks I base this opinion upon the analogous observation I have already made in the North. I have remarked that the white inhabitants of the North avoid the Negroes with increasing care in proportion as the legal barriers of separation are removed by the legislature; and why should not the same result take place in the South? In the North the whites are deterred from intermingling with the blacks by an imaginary danger; in the South, where the danger would be real, I cannot believe that the fear would be less.

If, on the one hand, it be admitted (and the fact is unquestionable) that the colored population perpetually accumulate in the extreme South and increase more rapidly than the whites; and if, on the other hand, it be allowed that it is impossible to foresee a time at which the whites and the blacks will be so intermingled as to derive the same benefits from society, must it not be inferred that the blacks and the whites will, sooner or later, come to open strife in the Southern states? But if it be asked what the issue of the struggle is likely to be, it will readily be understood that we are here left to vague conjectures. The human mind may succeed in tracing a wide circle, as it were, which includes the future; but within that circle chance rules, and eludes all our foresight. In every picture of the future there is a dim spot which the eye of the understanding cannot penetrate. It appears, however, extremely probable that in the West Indies islands the white race is destined to be subdued, and upon the continent the blacks.

In the West Indies the white planters are isolated amid an immense black population; on the continent the blacks are placed between the ocean and an innumerable people, who already extend above them, in a compact mass, from the icy confines of Canada to the frontiers of Virginia, and, from the banks of the Missouri to the shores of the Atlantic. If the white citizens of North America remain united, it is difficult to believe that the Negroes will escape the destruction which menaces them; they must be subdued by want or by the sword. But the black population accumulated along the coast of the Gulf of Mexico have a chance of success if the American Union should be dissolved when the struggle between the two races begins. The Federal tie once broken, the people of the South could not rely upon any lasting succor from their Northern countrymen. The latter are well aware that the danger can never reach them; and unless they are constrained to march to the assistance of the South by a positive obligation, it may be foreseen that the sympathy of race will be powerless.

Yet, at whatever period the strife may break out, the whites of the South, even if they are abandoned to their own resources, will enter the lists with an immense superiority of knowledge and the means of warfare; but the blacks will have numerical strength and the energy of despair upon their side, and these are powerful resources to men who have taken up arms. The fate of the white population of the Southern states will perhaps be similar to that of the Moors in Spain. After having occupied the land for centuries, it will perhaps retire by degrees to the country whence its ancestors came and abandon to the Negroes the possession of a territory which Providence seems to have destined for them, since they can subsist and labor in it more easily than the whites.

The danger of a conflict between the white and the black inhabitants of the

Southern states of the Union (a danger which, however remote it may be, is inevitable) perpetually haunts the imagination of the Americans, like a painful dream. The inhabitants of the North make it a common topic of conversation, although directly they have nothing to fear from it; but they vainly endeavor to devise some means of obviating the misfortunes which they foresee. In the Southern states the subject is not discussed: the planter does not allude to the future in conversing with strangers; he does not communicate his apprehensions to his friends; he seeks to conceal them from himself. But there is something more alarming in the tacit forebodings of the South than in the clamorous fears of the North.

This all-pervading disquietude has given birth to an undertaking as yet but little known, which, however, may change the fate of a portion of the human race. From apprehension of the dangers that I have just described, some American citizens have formed a society for the purpose of exporting to the coast of Guinea, at their own expense, such free Negroes as may be willing to escape from the oppression to which they are subject.[19]

In 1820 the society to which I allude formed a settlement in Africa, on the seventh degree of north latitude, which bears the name of Liberia. The most recent intelligence informs us that two thousand five hundred Negroes are collected there. They have introduced the democratic institutions of America into the country of their forefathers. Liberia has a representative system of government, Negro jurymen, Negro magistrates, and Negro priests; churches have been built, newspapers established, and, by a singular turn in the vicissitudes of the world, white men are prohibited from establishing themselves within the settlement.[20]

This is indeed a strange caprice of fortune. Two hundred years have now elapsed since the inhabitants of Europe undertook to tear the Negro from his family and his home in order to transport him to the shores of North America. Now the European settlers are engaged in sending back the descendants of those very Negroes to the continent whence they were originally taken: the barbarous Africans have learned civilization in the midst of bondage and have become acquainted with free political institutions in slavery. Up to the present time Africa has been closed against the arts and sciences of the whites, but the inventions of Europe will perhaps penetrate into those regions now that they are introduced by Africans themselves. The settlement of Liberia is founded upon a lofty and fruitful idea; but, whatever may be its results with regard to Africa, it can afford no remedy to the New World.

In twelve years the Colonization Society has transported two thousand five hundred Negroes to Africa; in the same space of time about seven hundred thousand blacks were born in the United States. If the colony of Liberia were able to receive thousands of new inhabitants every year, and if the Negroes were in a state to be sent thither with advantage; if the Union were to supply the society with annual subsidies,[21] and to transport the Negroes to Africa in government vessels, it would still be unable to counterpoise the natural increase of population among the blacks, and as it could not remove as many men in a year as are born upon its territory within that time, it could not prevent the growth of the evil which is daily increasing in the states.[22] The Negro race will never leave those shores of the American continent to which it was brought by the passions and the vices of Europeans; and it will not disappear from the New World as long as it continues to exist. The inhabitants of the United States may retard the calamities which they apprehend, but they cannot now destroy their efficient cause. I am obliged to confess that I do not regard the abolition of slavery as a means of warding off the struggle of the two races in the Southern states. The Negroes may long remain slaves without complaining; but if they are once raised to the level of freemen, they will soon revolt at being deprived of almost all their civil rights; and as they cannot become the equals of the whites, they will speedily show themselves as enemies. In the North everything facilitated the emancipation of the slaves, and slavery was abolished without rendering the free Negroes formidable, since their number was too small for them ever to claim their rights. But such is not the case in the South. The question of slavery was a commercial and manufacturing question for the slave-owners in the North; for those of the South it is a question of life and death. God forbid that I should seek to justify the principle of Negro slavery, as has been done by some American writers! I say only that all the countries which formerly adopted that execrable principle are not equally able to abandon it at the present time. When I contemplate the condition of the South, I can discover only two modes of action for the white inhabitants of those States: namely, either to emancipate the Negroes and to intermingle with them, or, remaining isolated from them, to keep them in slavery as long as possible. All intermediate measures seem to me likely to terminate, and that shortly, in the most horrible of civil wars and perhaps in the extirpation of one or the other of the two races. Such is the view that the Americans of the South take of the question, and they act consistently with it. As they are determined not to mingle with the Negroes, they refuse to emancipate them.

Not that the inhabitants of the South regard slavery as necessary to the wealth of the planter; on this point many of them agree with their Northern countrymen, in freely admitting that slavery is prejudicial to their interests; but they are convinced that the removal of this evil would imperil their own existence. The instruction which is now diffused in the South has convinced the inhabitants that slavery is injurious to the slave-owner, but it has also shown them, more clearly than before, that it is almost an impossibility to get rid of it. Hence arises a singular contrast: the more the utility of slavery is contested, the more firmly is it established in the laws; and while its principle is gradually abolished in the North, that selfsame principle gives rise to more and more rigorous consequences in the South.

The legislation of the Southern states with regard to slaves presents at the present day such unparalleled atrocities as suffice to show that the laws of humanity have been totally perverted, and to betray the desperate position of the community in which that legislation has been promulgated. The Americans of this portion of the Union have not, indeed, augmented the hardships of slavery; on the contrary, they have bettered the physical condition of the slaves. The only means by which the ancients maintained slavery were fetters and death; the Americans of the South of the Union have discovered more intellectual securities for the duration of their power. They have employed their despotism and their violence against the human mind. In antiquity precautions were taken to prevent the slave from breaking his chains; at the present day measures are adopted to deprive him even of the desire for freedom. The ancients kept the bodies of their slaves in bondage, but placed no restraint upon the mind and no check upon education; and they acted consistently with their established principle, since a natural termination of slavery then existed, and one day or other the slave might be set free and become the equal of his master. But the Americans of the South, who do not admit that the Negroes can ever be commingled with themselves, have forbidden them, under severe penalties, to be taught to read or write; and as they will not raise them to their own level, they sink them as nearly as possible to that of the brutes.

The hope of liberty had always been allowed to the slave, to cheer the hardships of his condition. But the Americans of the South are well aware that emancipation cannot but be dangerous when the freed man can never be assimilated to his former master. To give a man his freedom and to leave him in wretchedness and ignominy is nothing less than to prepare a future chief for a revolt of the slaves. Moreover, it has long been remarked that the presence of a free Negro vaguely agitates the minds of his less fortunate brethren, and conveys to them a dim notion of their rights. The Americans of the South have consequently taken away from slave-owners the right of emancipating their slaves in most cases.[23]

I happened to meet an old man, in the South of the Union, who had lived in illicit intercourse with one of his Negresses and had had several children by her, who were born the slaves of their father. He had, indeed, frequently thought of bequeathing to them at least their liberty; but years had elapsed before he could surmount the legal obstacles to their emancipation, and meanwhile his old age had come and he was about to die. He pictured to himself his sons dragged from market to market and passing from the authority of a parent to the rod of the stranger, until these horrid anticipations worked his expiring imagination into frenzy. When I saw him, he was a prey to all the anguish of despair; and I then understood how awful is the retribution of Nature upon those who have broken her laws.

These evils are unquestionably great, but they are the necessary and foreseen consequences of the very principle of modern slavery. When the Europeans chose their slaves from a race differing from their own, which many of them considered as inferior to the other races of mankind, and any notion of intimate union with which they all repelled with horror, they must have believed that slavery would last forever, since there is no intermediate state that can be durable between the excessive inequality produced by servitude and the complete equality that originates in independence. The Europeans did imperfectly feel this truth, but without acknowledging it even to themselves. Whenever they have had to do with Negroes, their conduct has been dictated either by their interest and their pride or by their compassion. They first violated every right of humanity by their treatment of the Negro, and they afterwards informed him that those rights were precious and inviolable. They opened their ranks to their slaves, and when the latter tried to come in, they drove them forth in scorn. Desiring slavery, they have allowed themselves unconsciously to be swayed in spite of themselves towards liberty, without having the courage to be either completely iniquitous or completely just.

If it is impossible to anticipate a period at which the Americans of the South will mingle their blood with that of the Negroes, can they allow their slaves to become free without compromising their own security? And if they are obliged to keep that race in bondage in order to save their own families, may they not be excused for availing themselves of the means best adapted to that end? The events that are taking place in the Southern states appear to me to be at once the most horrible and the most natural results of slavery. When I see the order of nature overthrown, and when I hear the cry of humanity in its vain struggle against the laws, my indignation does not light upon the men of our own time who are the instruments of these outrages; but I reserve my execration for those who, after a thousand years of freedom, brought back slavery into the world once more.

Whatever may be the efforts of the Americans of the South to maintain slavery, they will not always succeed. Slavery, now confined to a single tract of the civilized earth, attacked by Christianity as unjust and by political economy as prejudicial, and now contrasted with democratic liberty and the intelligence of our age, cannot survive. By the act of the master, or by the will of the slave, it will cease; and in either case great calamities may be expected to ensue. If liberty be refused to the Negroes of the South, they will in the end forcibly seize it for themselves; if it be given, they will before long abuse it.

Notes

1. Before treating of this matter, I would call the reader's attention to a book of which I spoke at the beginning of this work, and which is about to be published. The chief aim of M. Gustave de Beaumont, my traveling-companion, was to inform Frenchmen of the position of the Negroes among the white population in the United States. M. de Beaumont has plumbed the depths of a question which my subject has allowed me merely to touch upon. His book, the notes to which contain a great number of legislative and historical documents, extremely valuable and heretofore unpublished, furthermore presents pictures the vividness of which is ample proof of their verity. M. de Beaumont's book should be read by all those who would know into what excesses men may be driven when once they attempt to go against natural and human laws.

2. It is well known that several of the most distinguished authors of antiquity, and among them Aesop and Terence, were, or had been, slaves. Slaves were not always taken from barbarous nations; the chances of war reduced highly civilized men to servitude.

3. To induce the whites to abandon the opinion they have conceived of the moral and intellectual inferiority of their former slaves, the Negroes must change; but as long as this opinion persists, they cannot change.

4. See Beverley's *History of Virginia*. See also, in Jefferson's *Memoirs*, some curious details concerning the introduction of Negroes into Virginia, and the first Act that prohibited the importation of them, in 1778.

5. The number of slaves was less considerable in the North, but the advantages resulting from slavery were not more contested there than in the South. In 1740 the legislature of the state of New York declared that the direct importation of slaves ought to be encouraged as much as possible, and smuggling severely punished, in order not to discourage the fair trader. (Kent's *Commentaries*, Vol. II, p. 206.) Curious researches by Belknap upon slavery in New England are to be found in the *Historical Collections of Massachusetts*, Vol. IV, p. 193. It appears that Negroes were introduced there in 1630, but that the legislation and manners of the people were opposed to slavery from the first. See also, in the same work, the manner in which public opinion, and afterwards the laws, finally put an end to

147

slavery.

6. Not only is slavery prohibited in Ohio, but no free Negroes are allowed to enter the territory of that state or to hold property in it. See the statutes of Ohio.

7. The activity of Ohio is not confined to individuals, but the undertakings of the state are surprisingly great: a canal has been established between Lake Erie and the Ohio, by means of which the valley of the Mississippi communicates with the river of the North, and the European commodities which arrive at New York may be forwarded by water to New Orleans across five hundred leagues of continent.

8. The exact numbers given by the census of 1830 were: Kentucky, 688,844; Ohio, 937,679.

9. Independently of these causes, which, wherever free workmen abound, render their labor more productive and more economical than that of slaves, another cause may be pointed out which is peculiar to the United States: sugar-cane has hitherto been cultivated with success only upon the banks of the Mississippi, near the mouth of that river in the Gulf of Mexico. In Louisiana the cultivation of sugar-cane is exceedingly lucrative; nowhere does a laborer earn so much by his work; and as there is always a certain relation between the cost of production and the value of the produce, the price of slaves is very high in Louisiana. But Louisiana is one of the federal states, and slaves may be carried thither from all parts of the Union; the price given for slaves in New Orleans consequently raises the value of slaves in all the other markets. The consequence of this is that in the regions where the land is less productive, the cost of slave labor is still very considerable, which gives an additional advantage to the competition of free labor.

10. A peculiar reason contributes to detach the two last-mentioned states from the cause of slavery. The former wealth of this part of the Union was principally derived from the cultivation of tobacco. This cultivation is specially suited to slave labor; but within the last few years the market price of tobacco has diminished, while the value of the slaves remains the same. Thus the ratio between the cost of production and the value of the produce is changed. The inhabitants of Maryland and Virginia are therefore more disposed than they were thirty years ago to give up slave labor in the cultivation of tobacco, or to give up slavery and tobacco at the same time.

11. The states in which slavery is abolished usually do what they can to render their territory disagreeable to the Negroes as a place of residence; and as a kind of emulation exists between the different states in this respect, the unhappy blacks can only choose the least of the evils that beset them.

12. There is a great difference between the mortality of the blacks and of the whites in the states in which slavery is abolished; from 1820 to 1831 only one out of forty-two individuals of the white population died in Philadelphia; but one out of twenty-one of the black population died in the same time. The mortality is by no means so great among the Negroes who are still slaves. (See Emerson's *Medical Statistics*, p. 28.)

13. This is true of the places in which rice is cultivated; rice-fields, which are unhealthful in all countries, are particularly dangerous in those regions which are exposed to the rays of a tropical sun. Europeans would not find it easy to cultivate the soil in that part of the New World if they insisted on making it produce rice; but may they not exist without growing rice?

14. These states are nearer to the equator than Italy and Spain, but the temperature of the continent of America is much lower than that of Europe.

15. The Spanish government formerly caused a certain number of peasants from the Azores to be transported into a district of Louisiana called Attakapas. Slavery was not introduced among them; it was an experiment. These settlers still cultivate the soil without the assistance of slaves, but their industry is so sluggish as scarcely to supply their most necessary wants.

16. We find it asserted in an American work entitled *Letters on the Colonization Society*, by Mr. Carey (1833):

"That for the last forty years, the black race has increased more rapidly than the white race in the State of South Carolina; and that, if we take the average population of the five States of the, South into which slaves were first introduced, viz. Maryland, Virginia, South Carolina, North Carolina, and Georgia, we shall find that from 1790 to 1830 the whites have augmented in the proportion of 80 to 100, and the blacks in that of 100 to 112."

In the United States in 1830 the population of the two races stood as follows: States where slavery is abolished, 6,565,434 whites; 120,520 blacks. Slave States, 3,960,814 whites; 2,208,102 blacks.

17. This opinion is sanctioned by authorities infinitely weightier than anything that I can say. Thus, for instance, it is stated in the *Memoirs* of Jefferson: "Nothing is more clearly written in the book of destiny than the emancipation of the blacks; and it is equally certain, that the two races will never live

in a state of equal freedom under the same government, so insurmountable are the barriers which nature, habit, and opinion have established between them." (See *Extracts from the Memoirs of Jefferson*, by M. Conseil.)

18. If the British West India planters had governed themselves, they would assuredly not have passed the Slave Emancipation Bill which the mother country has recently imposed upon them.

19. This society assumed the name of "The Society for the Colonization of the Blacks." See its *Annual Reports* and more particularly the fifteenth. See also the pamphlet, to which allusion has already been made, entitled: *Letters on the Colonization Society, and on Its Probable Results*, by Mr. Carey (Philadelphia, April 1833).

20. This last regulation was laid down by the founders of the settlement; they believed that a state of things might arise in Africa similar to that which exists on the frontiers of the United States, and that if the Negroes, like the Indians, were brought into collision with a people more enlightened than themselves, they would he destroyed before they could be civilized.

21. Nor would these be the only difficulties attendant upon the undertaking; if the Union undertook to buy up the Negroes now in America in order to transport them to Africa, the price of slaves, increasing with their scarcity, would soon become enormous; and the states of the North would never consent to expend such great sums for a purpose that would profit them but little. If the Union took possession of the slaves in the Southern states by force, or at a rate determined by law, an insurmountable resistance would arise in that part of the country. Both courses are equally impossible.

22. In 1830 there were in the United States 2,010,327 slaves and 319,439 free blacks, in all 2,329,766 Negroes, who formed about one fifth of the total population of the United States at that time.

23. Emancipation is not prohibited, but surrounded with such formalities as to render it difficult.

II: Nat Turner's Revolt

❧ 8 ❧

On Nat Turner's Insurrection

WILLIAM LLOYD GARRISON

In this editorial from *The Liberator*, which he had founded earlier in 1831 and prior to Nat Turner's revolt, William Lloyd Garrison portrays the event as a vindication of his prophecy that the continuation of slavery would lead to such violent incidents. Although he was convinced that moral suasion rather than direct action was the best course to follow, the predictable lesson that Garrison extracts from the slaves' revolt is that only immediate emancipation could prevent similar incidents occurring in the South.

What we have long predicted,—at the peril of being stigmatized as an alarmist and declaimer,—has commenced its fulfillment. The first step of the earthquake, which is ultimately to shake down the fabric of oppression, leaving not one stone upon the other, has been made. The first drops of blood, which are but the prelude to a deluge from the gathering clouds, have fallen. The first flash of lightning, which is to ignite and consume, has been felt. The first wailings of a bereavement, which is to clothe the earth in sackcloth, have broken upon our ears.

In the first number of the *Liberator*, we alluded to the hour of vengeance in the following lines:

> Wo if it come with storm, and blood, and fire,
>   When midnight darkness veils the earth and sky!
> Wo to the innocent babe—*the guilty sire*—
>   Mother and daughter—*friends of kindred tie!*
>   Stranger and citizen alike shall die!
> Red-handed Slaughter his revenge shall feed,
>   And Havoc yell his ominous death-cry,
> And wild Despair in vain for mercy plead—
>   While hell itself shall shrink and sicken at the deed!

Read the account of the insurrection in Virginia, and say whether our prophecy be not fulfilled. What was poetry—imagination—in January, is now a bloody reality.

Source: William Lloyd Garrison, *The Liberator*, September 3, 1831.

"Wo to the innocent babe—to mother and daughter!" Is it not true? Turn again to the record of slaughter! Whole families have been cut off—not a mother, not a daughter, not a babe left. Dreadful retaliation! "The dead bodies of white and black lying just as they were slain, unburied"—the oppressor and the oppressed equal at last in death—what a spectacle!

True, the rebellion is quelled. Those of the slaves who were not killed in combat, have been secured, and the prison is crowded with victims destined for the gallows!

> Yet laugh not in your carnival of crime
> Too proudly, ye oppressors!

You have seen, it is to be feared, but the beginning of sorrows. All the blood which has been shed will be required at your hands. At your hands alone? No—but at the hands of the people of New England and of all the free states. The crime of oppression is national. The south is only the agent in this guilty traffic. But, remember! the same causes are at work which must inevitably produce the same effects; and when the contest shall have again begun, it must be again a war of extermination. In the present instance, no quarters have been asked or given.

But we have killed and routed them now—we can do it again and again—we are invincible! A dastardly triumph, well becoming a nation of oppressors. Detestable complacency, that can think, without emotion, of the extermination of the blacks! We have the power to kill *all*—let us, therefore, continue to apply the whip and forge new fetters!

In his fury against the revolters, who will remember their wrongs? What will it avail them, though the catalogue of their sufferings, dripping with warm blood fresh from their lacerated bodies, be held up to extenuate their conduct? It is enough that the victims were black—that circumstance makes them less precious than the dogs which have been slain in our streets! They were black—brutes, pretending to be men—legions of curses on their memories! They were black—God made them to serve us!

Ye patriotic hypocrites! ye panegyrists of Frenchmen, Greeks, and Poles! ye fustian declaimers for liberty! ye valient sticlers for equal rights among yourselves! ye haters of aristocracy ! ye assailants of monarchies! ye republican nullifiers! ye treasonable disunionists! be dumb! Cast no reproach upon the conduct of the slaves, but let your lips and cheeks wear the blisters of condemnation!

Ye accuse the pacific friends of emancipation of instigating the slaves to revolt. Take back the charge as a foul slander. The slaves need no incentives at our hands. They will find them in their stripes—in their emaciated bodies—in their ceaseless toil—in their ignorant minds—in every field, in every valley, on every hill-top and mountain, wherever you and your fathers have fought for liberty—in your speeches, your conversations, your celebrations, your pamphlets, your newspapers—voices in the air, sounds from across the ocean, invitations to resistance above, below, around them! What more do they need? Surrounded by such influences, and smarting under their newly made wounds, is it wonderful that they should rise to contend—as other "heroes" have contended—for their lost rights? It is *not* wonderful.

In all that we have written, is there aught to justify the excesses of the slaves? No. Nevertheless, they deserve no more censure than the Greeks in destroying the Turks, or the Poles in exterminating the Russians, or our fathers in slaughtering the British. Dreadful, indeed, is the standard erected by worldly patriotism!

For ourselves, we are horror-struck at the late tidings. We have exerted our utmost efforts to avert the calamity. We have warned our countrymen of the danger of persisting in their unrighteous conduct. We have preached to the slaves the pacific precepts of Jesus Christ. We have appealed to christians, philanthropists and patriots, for their assistance to accomplish the great work of national redemption through the agency of moral power—of public opinion—of individual duty. How have we been received? We have been threatened, proscribed, vilified and imprisoned—a laughing-stock and a reproach. Do we falter, in view of these things? Let time answer. If we have been hitherto urgent, and bold, and denunciatory in our efforts,—hereafter we shall grow vehement and active with the increase of danger. We shall cry, in trumphet tones, night and day,— Wo to this guilty land, unless she speedily repents of her evil doings! The blood of millions of her sons cries aloud for redress! IMMEDIATE EMANCIPATION can alone save her from the vengeance of Heaven, and cancel the debt of ages!

⊰·9·⊱

The Confessions of Nat Turner

THOMAS R. GRAY

Nat Turner's slave revolt in August 1831 caused shockwaves throughout the South. The deliberate and calculated murder of fifty-five whites—men, women and children—by Turner and his accomplices was seen by many as an act of racist fanaticism. Thomas Gray, who recorded Nat Turner's confession, interpolating it with his own questions and commentary, reveals, however, a man of considerable intelligence, a religious mystic, convinced of his mission and his destiny. The Turner of this confession is dispassionate in his account of his actions, retaining a strong belief in his cause. Also included is an account of his brief trial.

Confession

Agreeable to his own appointment, on the evening he was committed to prison, with permission of the jailor, I visited NAT on Tuesday the 1st of November, when, without being questioned at all, he commenced his narrative in the following words:

SIR,—You have asked me to give a history of the motives which induced me to undertake the late insurrection, as you call it—To do so I must go back to the days of my infancy, and even before I was born. I was thirty-one years of age the 2nd of October last, and born the property of Benj. Turner, of this county. In my childhood a circumstance occurred which made an indelible impression on my mind, and laid the ground work of that enthusiasm, which has terminated so fatally to many both white and black, and for which I am about to atone at the gallows. It is here necessary to relate this circumstance—trifling as it may seem, it was the commencement of that belief which has grown with time, and even now, sir, in this dungeon, helpless and forsaken as I am, I cannot divest myself of. Being at play with other children,

Source: *The Confessions of Nat Turner, the Leader of the late Insurrection in Southampton, Va. As fully and voluntarily made to Thomas R. Gray*, Baltimore: Lucas & Deaver, 1831.

when three or four years old, I was telling them something, which my mother overhearing, said it had happened before I was born—I stuck to my story, however, and related some things which went in her opinion to confirm it—others being called on were greatly astonished, knowing that these things had happened, and caused them to say in my hearing, I surely would be a prophet, as the Lord had shewn me things that had happened before my birth. And my father and mother strengthened me in this my first impression, saying in my presence, I was intended for some great purpose, which they had always thought from certain marks on my head and breast—[a parcel of excrescences which I believe are not at all uncommon, particularly among negroes, as I have seen several with the same. In this case he has either cut them off, or they have nearly disappeared]—My grandmother, who was very religious, and to whom I was much attached—my master, who belonged to the church, and other religious persons who visited the house, and whom I often saw at prayers, noticing the singularity of my manners, I suppose, and my uncommon intelligence for a child, remarked I had too much sense to be raised—and if I was, I would never be of any service to any one—as a slave—To a mind like mine, restless, inquisitive and observant of every thing that was passing, it is easy to suppose that religion was the subject to which it would be directed, and although this subject principally occupied my thoughts—there was nothing that I saw or heard of to which my attention was not directed—The manner in which I learned to read and write, not only had great influence on my own mind, as I acquired it with the most perfect ease, so much so, that I have no recollection whatever of learning the alphabet—but to the astonishment of the family, one day, when a book was shewn me to keep me from crying, I began spelling the names of different objects—this was a source of wonder to all in the neighborhood, particularly the blacks—and this learning was constantly improved at all opportunities—when I got large enough to go to work, while employed, I was reflecting on many things that would present themselves to my imagination, and whenever an opportunity occurred of looking at a book, when the school children were getting their lessons, I would find many things that the fertility of my own imagination had depicted to me before; all my time, not devoted to my master's service, was spent either in prayer, or in making experiments in casting different things in moulds made of earth, in attempting to make paper, gun-powder, and many other experiments, that although I could not perfect, yet convinced me of its practicability if I had the means[1]. I was not addicted to stealing in my youth, nor have ever been—Yet such was the confidence of the negroes in the neighborhood, even at this early period of my life, in my superior judgment, that they would often carry me with them when they were going on any roguery, to plan for them. Growing up among them, with this confidence in my superior judgment, and when this, in their opinions, was perfected by Divine inspiration, from the circumstances already alluded to in my infancy, and which belief was ever afterwards zealously inculcated by the austerity of my life and manners, which became the subject of remark by white and black.—Having soon discovered to be great, I must appear so, and therefore studiously avoided mixing in society, and wrapped myself in mystery, devoting my time to fasting and prayer—by this time, having arrived to man's estate, and hearing the scriptures commented on at meetings, I was struck with that particular passage which says: "Seek ye the kingdom of Heaven and all things shall be added unto you." I reflected much on this passage, and prayed daily for light on this subject—As I was praying one day at my plough, the Spirit spoke to me, saying "Seek ye the kingdom of Heaven and all things shall be added unto you."

Question—What do you mean by the Spirit.

Ans—The Spirit that spoke to the prophets in former days—and I was greatly astonished, and for two years prayed continually, whenever my duty would permit—and then again I had the same revelation, which fully confirmed me in the impression that I was ordained for some great purpose in the hands of the Almighty. Several years rolled round, in which many events occurred to strengthen me in this my belief. At this time I reverted in my mind to the remarks made of me in my childhood, and the things that had been shewn me—and as it had been said of me in my childhood by those by whom I had been taught to pray, both white and black, and in whom I had the greatest confidence, that I had too much sense to be raised, and if I was I would never be of any use to any one as a slave. Now finding I had arrived to man's estate, and was a slave, and these revelations being made known to me, I began to direct my attention to this great object, to fulfill the purpose for which, by this time, I felt assured I was intended. Knowing the influence I had obtained over the minds of my fellow servants, (not by the means of conjuring and such like tricks—for to them I always spoke of such things with contempt) but by the communion of the Spirit whose revelations I often communicated to them, and they believed and said my wisdom came from God. I now began to prepare them for my purpose, by telling them something was about to happen that would terminate in fulfilling the great promise that had been made to me—About this time I was placed under an overseer, from whom I ran away—and after remaining in the woods thirty days, I returned, to the astonishment of the negroes on the plantation, who thought I had made my escape to some other part of the country, as my father had done before. But the reason of my return was, that the Spirit appeared to me and said I had my wishes directed to the things of this world, and not to the kingdom of Heaven, and that I should return to the service of my earthly master—"For he who knoweth his Master's will, and doeth it not, shall be beaten with many stripes, and thus have I chastened you." And the negroes found fault, and murmured against me, saying that if they had my sense they would not serve any master in the world. And about this time I had a vision—and I saw white spirits and black spirits engaged in battle, and the sun was darkened—the thunder rolled in the Heavens, and blood flowed in streams—and I heard a voice saying, "Such is your luck, such you are called to see, and let it come rough or smooth, you must surely bear it." I now withdrew myself as much as my situation would permit, from the intercourse of my fellow servants, for the avowed purpose of serving the Spirit more fully—and it appeared to me, and reminded me of the things it had already shown me, and that it would then reveal to me the knowledge of the elements, the revolution of the planets, the operation of tides, and changes of the seasons. After this revelation in the year 1825, and the knowledge of the elements being made known to me, I sought more than ever to obtain true holiness before the great day of judgment should appear, and then I began to receive the true knowledge of faith. And from the first steps of righteousness until the last, was I made perfect; and the Holy Ghost was with me, and said "Behold me as I stand in the Heavens"—and I looked and saw the forms of men in different attitudes—and there were lights in the sky to which the children of darkness gave other names than what they really were— for they were the lights of the Saviour's hands, stretched forth from east to west, even as they were extended on the cross on Calvary for the redemption of sinners. And I wondered greatly at these miracles, and prayed to be informed of a certainty of the meaning thereof—and shortly afterwards, while labouring in the field, I discovered drops of blood on the corn, as though it were dew from heaven—and I communicated it to many, both white and black, in the neighbourhood—and I then found on the leaves in the woods hieroglyphic characters and numbers, with the forms of men in different attitudes, portrayed in blood, and representing the figures I had seen before in the heavens. And now the Holy Ghost had revealed itself to me, and made plain the miracles it had shown me—For as the blood of Christ had been shed on this earth, and had ascended to heaven for the salvation of sinners, and was now returning to earth again in the form of dew—and as the leaves on the trees bore the impression of the figures I had seen in the heavens, it was plain to me that the Savior was about to lay down the yoke he had borne for the sins of men, and the great day of judgement was at hand. About this time, I told these things to a white man, (Etheldred T. Brantley) on whom it had a wonderful effect—and he ceased from his wickedness, and was attacked immediately with a cutaneous eruption, and blood oozed from the pores of his skin, and after praying and fasting nine days, he was healed, and the Spirit appeared to me again, and said, as the Savior had been baptised, so should we be also—and when the white people would not let us be baptised by the church, we went down into the water together, in the sight of many who reviled us, and were baptised by the Spirit—After this I rejoiced greatly, and gave thanks to God. And on the 12th of May, 1828, I heard a loud noise in the heavens, and the Spirit instantly appeared to me and said the Serpent was loosened, and Christ had laid down the yoke he had borne for the sins of men, and that I should take it on and fight against the Serpent, for the time was fast approaching, when the first should be last and the last should be first.

Ques. Do you not find yourself mistaken now?

Ans. Was not Christ crucified? And by signs in the heavens that it would make known to me when I should commence the great work—and until the first sign appeared, I should conceal it from the knowledge of men—And on the appearance of the sign, (the eclipse of the sun last February) I should arise and prepare myself, and slay my enemies with their own weapons. And immediately on the sign appearing in the heavens, the seal was removed from my lips, and I communicated the great work laid out for me to do, to four in whom I had the greatest confidence, (Henry, Hank, Nelson and Sam)—It was intended by us to have begun the work of death on the 4th of July last—Many were the plans formed and rejected by us, and it affected my mind to such a degree, that I fell sick, and the time passed without our coming to any determination how to commence—Still forming new schemes and rejecting them, when the sign appeared again, which determined me not to wait longer.

Since the commencement of 1830, I had been living with Mr. Joseph Travis, who was to me a kind master, and placed the greatest confidence in me; in fact, I had no cause to complain of his treatment to me. On Saturday evening, the 20th of August, it was agreed between Henry, Hark and myself, to prepare a dinner the next day for the men we expected, and then to concert a plan, as we had not yet determined on any. Hark on the following morning brought a pig, and Henry brandy, and being joined by Sam, Nelson, Will and Jack, they prepared in the woods a dinner, where, about three o'clock, I joined them.

Q. Why were you so backward in joining them?

A. The same reason that had caused me not to mix with them for years before. I saluted them on coming up, and asked Will how came he there, he answered, his life was worth no more than others, and his liberty as dear to him. I asked him if he thought to obtain it? He said he would, or lose his life. This was enough to put him in full confidence. Jack, I knew, was only a tool in the hands of Hark, it was quickly agreed we should commence at home (Mr. J. Travis') on that night, and until we had armed and equipped ourselves, and gathered sufficient force, neither age nor sex was to be spared, (which was invariably adhered to). We remained at the feast until about two hours in the night, when we went to the house and found Austin; they all went to the cider press and drank, except myself. On returning to the house, Hark went to the door with an axe, for the purpose of breaking it open, as we knew we were strong enough to murder the family, if they were awaked by the noise; but reflecting that it might create an alarm in the neighborhood, we determined to enter the house secretly, and murder them whilst sleeping. Hark got a ladder and set it against the chimney, on which I ascended, and hoisting a window, entered and came down stairs, unbarred the door, and removed the guns from their places. It was then observed that I must spill the first blood. On which armed with a hatchet, and accompanied by Will, I entered my master's chamber; it being dark, I could not give a death blow, the hatchet glanced from his head, he sprang from the bed and called his wife, it was his last word. Will laid him dead, with a blow of his axe, and Mrs. Travis shared the same fate, as she lay in bed. The murder of this family five in number, was the work of a moment, not one of them awoke; there was a little infant sleeping in a cradle, that was forgotten, until we had left the house and gone some distance, when Henry and Will returned and killed it; we got here, four guns that would shoot, and several old muskets, with a pound or two of powder. We remained some time at the barn, where we paraded; I formed them in a line as soldiers, and after carrying them through all the manoeuvres I was master of, marched them off to Mr. Salathul Francis', about six hundred yards distant. Sam and Will went to the door and knocked. Mr. Francis asked who was there, Sam replied it was him, and he had a letter for him, on which he got up and came to the door; they immediately seized him, and dragging him out a little from the door, he was dispatched by repeated blows on the head; there was no other white person in the family. We started from there for Mrs. Reese's, maintaining the most perfect silence on our march, where finding the door unlocked, we entered, and murdered Mrs. Reese in her bed, while sleeping; her son awoke, but it was only to sleep the sleep of death, he had only time to say who is that, and he was no more. From Mrs. Reese's we went to Mrs. Turner's, a mile distant, which we reached about sunrise, on Monday morning. Henry, Austin, and Sam, went to the still, where, finding Mr. Peebles, Austin shot him, and the rest of us went to the house; as we approached, the family discovered us, and shut the door. Vain hope! Will, with one stroke of his axe, opened it, and we entered and found Mrs. Turner and Mrs. Newsome in the middle of a room almost frightened to death. Will immediately killed Mrs. Turner, with one blow of his axe. I took Mrs. Newsome by the hand, and with the sword I had when I was apprehended, I struck her several blows over the head, but not being able to kill her, as the sword was dull. Will turning around and discovering it, despatched her also. A general destruction of property and search for money and ammunition, always succeeded the murders. By this time my company amounted to fifteen, and nine men mounted, who started for Mrs. Whitehead's, (the other six were to go through a by way to Mr. Bryant's, and rejoin us at Mrs. Whitehead's), as we approached the house we discovered Mr. Richard Whitehead standing in the cotton patch, near the lane fence; we called him over into the lane, and Will, the executioner, was near at hand, with his fatal axe, to send him to an untimely grave. As we pushed on to the house, I discovered some one run round the garden, and thinking it was some of the white family, I pursued them, but finding it was a servant girl belonging to the house, I returned to commence the work of death, but they whom I left, had not been idle; all the family were already murdered, but Mrs. Whitehead and her daughter Margaret. As I came round to the door I saw Will pulling Mrs. Whitehead out of the house, and at the step he nearly severed her head from her body, with his broad axe. Miss Margaret, when I discovered her, had concealed herself in the corner, formed by the projection of the cellar cap from the house; on my approach she fled, but was soon overtaken, and after repeated blows with a sword, I killed her by a blow on the head, with a fence rail. By this time, the six who had gone by Mr. Bryant's, rejoined us, and informed me they had done the work of death assigned them. We again divided, part going to Mr. Richard Porter's, and from thence to Nathaniel Francis', the others to Mr. Howell Harris', and Mr. T. Doyle's. On my reaching Mr. Porter's, he had escaped with his family. I understood there, that the alarm had already spread, and I immediately returned to bring up those sent to Mr. Doyle's, and Mr. Howell Harris'; the party I left going on to Mr. Francis', having told them I would join them in that neighborhood. I met these sent to Mr. Doyle's and Mr. Harris' returning, having met Mr. Doyle on the road and killed him; and learning from some who joined them, that Mr. Harris was from home, I immediately pursued the course taken by the party gone on before; but knowing they would complete the work of death and pillage, at Mr. Francis' before I could get there, I went to Mr. Peter Edwards', expecting to find them there, but they had been here also. I then went to Mr. John

T. Barrow's, they had been here and murdered him. I pursued on their track to Capt. Newit Harris', where I found the greater part mounted, and ready to start; the men now amounting to about forty, shouted and hurraed as I rode up, some were in the yard, loading their guns, others drinking. They said Captain Harris and his family had escaped, the property in the house they destroyed, robbing him of money and other valuables. I ordered them to mount and march instantly, this was about nine or ten o'clock, Monday morning. I proceeded to Mr. Levi Waller's, two or three miles distant. I took my station in the rear, and as it was my object to carry terror and devastation wherever we went, I placed fifteen or twenty of the best armed and most to be relied on, in front, who generally approached the houses as fast as their horses could run; this was for two purposes, to prevent their escape and strike terror to the inhabitants—on this account I never got to the houses, after leaving Mrs. Whitehead's until the murders were committed, except in one case. I sometimes got in sight in time to see the work of death completed, viewed the mangled bodies as they lay, in silent satisfaction, and immediately started in quest of other victims—Having murdered Mrs. Waller and ten children, we started for Mr. William Williams'—having killed him and two little boys that were there; while engaged in this, Mrs. Williams fled and got some distance from the house, but she was pursued, overtaken, and compelled to get up behind one of the company, who brought her back, and after showing her the mangled body of her lifeless husband, she was told to get down and lay by his side, where she was shot dead. I then started for Mr. Jacob Williams, where the family were murdered—Here we found a young man named Drury, who had come on business with Mr. Williams—he was pursued, overtaken and shot. Mrs. Vaughan was the next place we visited—and after murdering the family here, I determined on starting for Jerusalem—Our number amounted now to fifty or sixty, all mounted and armed with guns, axes, swords and clubs—On reaching Mr. James W. Parker's gate, immediately on the road leading to Jerusalem, and about three miles distant, it was proposed to me to call there, but I objected, as I knew he was gone to Jerusalem, and my object was to reach there as soon as possible; but some of the men having relations at Mr. Parker's it was agreed that they might call and get his people. I remained at the gate on the road, with seven or eight; the others going across the field to the house, about half a mile off. After waiting some time for them, I became impatient, and started to the house for them, and on our return we were met by a party of white men, who had pursued our blood-stained track, and who had fired on those at the gate, and dispersed them, which I knew nothing of, not having been at that time rejoined by any of them— Immediately on discovering the whites, I ordered my men to halt and form, as they appeared to be alarmed—The white men eighteen in number, approached us in about one hundred yards, when one of them fired, (this was against the positive orders of Captain Alexander P. Peete, who commanded, and who had directed the men to reserve their fire until within thirty paces)—And I discovered about half of them retreating, I then ordered my men to fire and rush on them; the few remaining stood their ground until we approached within fifty yards, when they fired and retreated. We pursued and overtook some of them who we thought we left dead;

(they were not killed) after pursuing them about two hundred yards, and rising a little hill, I discovered they were met by another party, and had halted, and were reloading their guns, (this was a small party from Jerusalem who knew the negroes were in the field, and had just tied their horses to await their return to the road, knowing that Mr. Parker and family were in Jerusalem, but knew nothing of the party that had gone in with Captain Peete; on hearing the firing they immediately rushed to the spot and arrived just in time to arrest the progress of these barbarous villains, and save the lives of their friends and fellow citizens.) Thinking that those who retreated first, and the party who fired on us at fifty or sixty yards distant, had all only fallen back to meet others with ammunition. As I saw them reloading their guns, and more coming up than I saw at first, and several of my bravest men being wounded, the others became panic struck and squandered over the field; the white men pursued and fired on us several times. Hark had his horse shot under him, and I caught another for him as it was running by me; five or six of my men were wounded, but none left on the field; finding myself defeated here I instantly determined to go through a private way, and cross the Nottoway river at the Cypress Bridge, three miles below Jerusalem, and attack that place in the rear, as I expected they would look for me on the other road, and I had a great desire to get there to procure arms and ammunition. After going a short distance in this private way, accompanied by about twenty men, I overtook two or three who told me the others were dispersed in every direction. After trying in vain to collect a sufficient force to proceed to Jerusalem, I determined to return, as I was sure they would make back to their old neighborhood, where they would rejoin me, make new recruits, and come down again. On my way back, I called at Mrs. Thomas's, Mrs. Spencer's, and several other places, the white families having fled, we found no more victims to gratify our thirst for blood, we stopped at Majr. Ridley's quarter for the night, and being joined by four of his men, with the recruits made since my defeat, we mustered now about forty strong. After placing out sentinels, I laid down to sleep, but was quickly roused by a great racket; starting up, I found some mounted, and others in great confusion; one of the sentinels having given the alarm that we were about to be attacked, I ordered some to ride round and reconnoitre, and on their return the others being more alarmed, not knowing who they were, fled in different ways, so that I was reduced to about twenty again; with this I determined to attempt to recruit, and proceed on to rally in the neighborhood, I had left. Dr. Blunt's was the nearest house, which we reached just before day; on riding up the yard, Hark fired a gun. We expected Dr. Blunt and his family were at Maj. Ridley's, as I knew there was a company of men there; the gun was fired to ascertain if any of the family were at home; we were immediately fired upon and retreated leaving several of my men. I do not know what became of them, as I never saw them afterwards. Pursuing our course back, and coming in sight of Captain Harris's, where we had been the day before, we discovered a party of white men at the house, on which all deserted me but two, (Jacob and Nat), we concealed ourselves in the woods until near night, when I sent them in search of Henry, Sam, Nelson and Hark, and directed them to rally all they could, at the place we had had our dinner the Sunday before, where they would find me, and I accordingly returned there as soon as it was dark, and remained until Wednesday evening, when discovering white men riding around the place as though they were looking for some one, and none of my men joining me, I concluded Jacob and Nat had been taken, and compelled to betray me. On this I gave up all hope for the present; and on Thursday night, after having supplied myself with provisions from Mr. Travis's, I scratched a hole under a pile of fence rails in a field, where I concealed myself for six weeks, never leaving my hiding place but for a few minutes in the dead of night to get water, which was very near; thinking by this time I could venture out, I began to go about in the night and eaves drop the houses in the neighborhood; pursuing this course for about a fortnight and gathering little or no intelligence, afraid of speaking to any human being, and returning every morning to my cave before the dawn of day. I know not how long I might have led this life, if accident had not betrayed me, a dog in the neighborhood passing by my hiding place one night while I was out, was attracted by some meat I had in my cave, and crawled in and stole it, and was coming out just as I returned. A few nights after, two negroes having started to go hunting with the same dog, and passed that way, the dog came again to the place, and having just gone out to walk about, discovered me and barked, on which thinking myself discovered, I spoke to them to beg concealment. On making myself known, they fled from me. Knowing then they would betray me, I immediately left my hiding place, and was pursued almost incessantly until I was taken a fortnight afterwards by Mr. Benjamin Phipps, in a little hole I had dug out with my sword, for the purpose of concealment, under the top of a fallen tree. On Mr. Phipps discovering the place of my concealment, he cocked his gun and aimed at me. I requested him not to shoot, and I would give up, upon which be demanded my sword. I delivered it to him, and he brought me to prison. During the time I was pursued, I had many hair breadth escapes, which your time will not permit you to relate. I am here loaded with chains, and willing to suffer the fate that awaits me.

I here proceeded to make some inquiries of him, after assuring him of the certain death that awaited him, and that concealment would only bring destruction on the innocent as well as guilty, of his own color, if he knew of any extensive or concerted plan. His answer was, I do not. When I questioned him as to the insurrection in North Carolina happening about the same time, he denied any knowledge of it; and when I looked him in the face as though I would search his inmost thoughts, he replied, "I see sir, you doubt my word; but can you not think the same ideas, and strange appearances about this time in the heavens might prompt others, as well as myself, to this undertaking." I now had much conversation with and asked him many questions, having forborne to do so previously, except in the cases noted in parentheses; but during his statement, I had, unnoticed by him, taken notes as to some particular circumstances, and having the advantage of his statement before me in writing, on the evening of the third day that I had been with him, I began a cross examination, and found his statement corroborated by every circumstance coming within my own knowledge, or the confessions of others who had been either killed or executed, and whom he had not seen or had any knowledge since 22nd of August last, he expressed himself fully satisfied as to the impracticability of his attempt. It has been said he was ignorant and cowardly, and that his object was to murder and rob for the purpose of obtaining money to make his escape. It is notorious, that he was never known to have a dollar in his life; to swear an oath, or drink a drop of spirits. As to his ignorance, he certainly never had the advantages of education, but he can read and write (it was taught him by his parents), and for natural intelligence and quickness of apprehension, is surpassed by few men I have ever seen. As to his being a coward, his reason as given for not resisting Mr. Phipps, shews the decision of his character. When he saw Mr. Phipps present his gun, he said he knew it was impossible for him to escape, as the woods were full of men; he therefore thought it was better to surrender, and trust to fortune for his escape. He is a complete fanatic, or plays his part most admirably. On other subjects he possesses an uncommon share of intelligence, with a mind capable of attaining any thing; but warped and perverted by the influence of early impressions. He is below the ordinary stature, though strong and active, having the true negro face, every feature of which is strongly marked. I shall not attempt to describe the effect of his narrative, as told and commented on by himself, in the condemned hole of the prison. The calm, deliberate composure with which he spoke of his late deeds and intentions, the expression of his fiend-like face when excited by enthusiasm, still bearing the stains of the blood of helpless innocence about him; clothed with rags and covered with chains; yet daring to raise his manacled hands to heaven, with a spirit soaring above the attributes of man; I looked on him and my blood curdled in my veins.

I will not shock the feelings of humanity, nor wound afresh the bosoms of the disconsolate sufferers in this unparalleled and inhuman massacre, by detailing the deeds of their fiend-like barbarity. There were two or three who were in the power of these wretches, had they known it, and who escaped in the most providential manner. There were two whom they thought they had left dead on the field at Mr. Parker's, but who were only stunned by the blows of their guns, as they did not take time to re-load when they charged on them. The escape of a little girl who went to school at Mr. Waller's, and where the children were collecting for that purpose, excited general sympathy. As their teacher had not arrived, they were at play in the yard, and seeing the negroes approach, she ran up on a dirt chimney (such as are common to log houses), and remained there unnoticed during the massacre of the eleven that were killed at this place. She remained on her hiding place till just before the arrival of a party, who were in pursuit of the murderers, when she came down and fled to a swamp, where, a mere child as she was, with the horrors of the late scene before her, she lay concealed until the next day, when seeing a party go up to the house, she came up, and on being asked how she escaped, replied with the utmost simplicity, "The Lord helped her." She was taken up behind a gentleman of the party, and returned to the arms of her weeping mother. Miss Whitehead concealed herself between the bed and the mat that supported it, while they murdered her sister in the same room, without discovering her. She was afterwards carried off, and concealed for protection by a slave of the family, who gave evidence against several of them on their trial. Mrs. Nathaniel Francis, while concealed in a closet heard their blows, and the shrieks of the victims of these ruthless savages; they then entered the closet where she was concealed, and went out without discovering her. While in this hiding place, she heard two of her women in a quarrel about the division of her clothes. Mr. John T. Baron, discovering them approaching his house, told his wife to make her escape, and scorning to fly, fell fighting on his own threshold. After firing his rifle, he discharged his gun at them, and then broke it over the villain who first approached him, but he was overpowered and slain. His bravery, however, saved from the hands of these monsters, his lovely and amiable wife, who will long lament a husband so deserving of her love. As directed by him, she attempted to escape through the garden, when she was caught and held by one of her servant girls, but another coming to her rescue, she fled to the woods, and concealed herself. Few indeed, were those who escaped their work of death. But fortunately for society, the hand of retributive justice has overtaken them; and not one that was known to be concerned has escaped.

The Commonwealth, vs. Nat Turner

Charged with making insurrection, and plotting to take away the lives of divers free white persons, &c. on the 22d of August, 1831.

The court composed of ——, having met for the trial of Nat Turner, the prisoner was brought in and arraigned, and upon his arraignment pleaded *Not guilty*; saying to his counsel, that he did not feel so.

On the part of the Commonwealth, Levi Waller was introduced, who being sworn, deposed as follows: (*agreeably to Nat's own Confession.*) Col. Trezvant was then introduced, who being sworn, numerated Nat's Confession to him, as follows: (*His Confession as given to Mr. Gray.*) The prisoner introduced no evidence, and the case was submitted without argument to the court, who having found him guilty, Jeremiah Cobb, Esq. Chairman, pronounced the sentence of the court, in the following words: "Nat Turner! Stand up. Have you any thing to say why sentence of death should not be pronounced against you?"

Ans. I have not. I have made a full confession to Mr. Gray, and I have nothing more to say.

"Attend then to the sentence of the Court. You have been arraigned and tried before this court, and convicted of one of the highest crimes in our criminal code. You have been convicted of plotting in cold blood, the indiscriminate destruction of men, of helpless women, and of infant children. The evidence before us leaves not a shadow of doubt, but that your hands were often imbrued in the blood of the innocent; and your own confession tells us that they were stained with the blood of a master; in your own language, "too indulgent." Could I stop here, your crime would be sufficiently aggravated. But the original contriver of a plan, deep and deadly, one that never can be effected, you managed so far to put it into execution, as to deprive us of many of our most valuable citizens; and this was done when they were asleep, and defenceless; under circumstances shocking to humanity. And while upon this part of the subject, I cannot but call your attention to the poor misguided wretches who have gone before you. They are not few in number—they were your bosom associates; and the blood of all cries aloud, and calls upon you, as the author of their misfortune. Yes! You forced them unprepared, from Time to Eternity. Borne down by this load of guilt, your only justlfication is, that you were led away by fanaticism. If this be true, from my soul I pity you; and while you have my sympathies, I am, nevertheless called upon to pass the sentence of the court. The time between this and your execution, will necessarily be very short; and your only hope must be in another world. The judgment of the court is, that you be taken hence to the jail from whence you came, thence to the place of execution, and on Friday next, between the hours of 10 A.M. and 2 P.M. be hung by the neck until you are dead! dead! dead! and may the Lord have mercy upon your soul."

Note

1. When questioned as to the manner of manufacturing those different articles, he was found well informed on the subject.

❧10❧

Impressions of an Insurrection

JOHN FLOYD

This account of Nat Turner's rebellion, written in a letter from John Floyd, Governor of Virginia, to his counterpart in South Carolina, blames the slave revolt on abolitionists of the North and the influence of a religious revival among African–Americans. Floyd, who at one time was in favour of abolition, was, by the end of his career, a committed defender of slavery.

[From a letter to Governor James Hamilton Jr.
of South Carolina, 19th November, 1831]

I received your letter yesterday, and with great pleasure will state my impressions freely.

I will notice this affair in my annual message, but shall only give a very careless history of it, as it appears to be public.

I am fully persuaded the spirit of insubordination which has, and still manifests itself in Virginia, had its origin among, and emanated from, the Yankee population, upon their first arrival amongst us, but most especially the Yankee pedlars and traders.

The course has been by no means a direct one. They began first by making them religious; their conversations were of that character, telling the blacks, God was no respecter of persons; the black man was as good as the white; that all men were born free and equal; that they can not serve two masters; that the white people rebelled against England to obtain freedom; so have the blacks a right to do.

In the meantime I am sure without any purpose of this kind, the preachers, especially Northern, were very assiduous in operating upon our population. Day and night they were at work and religion became and is, the fashion of the times. Finally our females and of the most respectable were persuaded that it was piety to teach negroes to read and write, to the end that they might read the Scriptures.

Source: John Floyd, from a letter to Governor James Hamilton, Jr., of South Carolina,
19th November 1831, rptd   Charles H. Ambler, *Life of John Floyd*, (Randolph-Macon College, Va:,
John P. Branch Historical Papers, 1918), vol. V, No. 1.

Many of them became tutoresses in Sunday Schools and pious distributors of tracts from the New York Society.

At this point more active operations commenced; our magistrates and laws became more inactive; large assemblies of negroes were suffered to take place for religious purposes. Then commenced the efforts of the black preachers. Often from the pulpits these pamphlets and papers were read, followed by the incendiary publications of Walker, Garrison and Knapp of Boston; these too with songs and hymns of a similar character were circulated, read and commented upon, we resting in apathetic security until the Southampton affair.

From all that has come to my knowledge during and since this affair, I am fully convinced that every black preacher, in the whole country east of the Blue Ridge, was in the secret, that the plans as published by those northern prints were adopted and acted upon by them, that their congregations, as they were called knew nothing of this intended rebellion, except a few leading, and intelligent men, who may have been head men in the church. The mass were prepared by making them aspire to an equal station by such conversations as I have related as the first step.

I am informed that they had settled the form of government to be that of the white people, whom they intended to cut off to a man, with this difference that the preachers were to be their governors, generals and judges. I feel fully justified to myself, in believing the northern incendiaries, tracts, Sunday Schools, religion and reading and writing has accomplished this end.

I shall in my annual message recommend that laws be passed to confine the slaves to the estates of their masters, prohibit negroes from preaching, absolutely to drive from this state all free negroes, and to substitute the surplus revenue in our treasury annually for slaves, to work for a time upon our railroads, etc., and then sent out of the country, preparatory, or rather as the first step to emancipation. This last point will of course be tenderly and cautiously managed, and will be urged or delayed as your state and Georgia may be disposed to cooperate.

In relation to the extent of this insurrection I think it greater than will ever appear. The facts will as now considered, appear to be these: It commenced with Nat and nine others on Sunday night, two o'clock, we date it Monday morning before day, and ceased by the dispersion of the negroes on Tuesday morning at ten o'clock. During this time the negroes had murdered sixty-one persons and traversed a distance of twenty miles, and increased to about seventy men. They spared but one family and that one was so wretched as to be in all respects upon a par with them. All died bravely indicating no reluctance to lose their lives in such a cause.

I am with consideration and respect. Your obedient servant,

JOHN FLOYD.

III: The Abolitionist Mission

❦11❧

Preamble to the 'Appeal in Four Articles to the Coloured Citizens of the World'

DAVID WALKER

David Walker, born in Wilmington, North Carolina, in 1785, escaped the prospect of slavery in his native South to settle in the free labour state of Massachusetts. He became a leading figure among Boston's black community, gaining both fame and notoriety through his anti-slavery speeches. His *Appeal*, published in various editions in 1829 and 1830, focused on the rascism and injustice that underpinned the institution of slavery. With its strong assertion of Christian morality, the *Appeal* draws upon the twin traditions of religious and political radicalism which were to characterise the abolitionist movement. Banned in the South, where slaves caught in possession of Walker's pamphlet incurred the penalty of death, this work is nevertheless one of the charter documents of a militant black consciousness. In this 'Preamble' to his *Appeal*, Walker writes that he expects to be attacked as an agitator for social reform, perhaps to be imprisoned, and maybe even to be put to death. He was prophetic: he died in suspicious circumstances—perhaps of poisoning—in June 1830.

Preamble

My dearly beloved Brethren and fellow Citizens.

Having travelled over a considerable portion of these United States, and having, in the course of my travels, taken the most accurate observations of things as they exist—the result of my observations has warranted the full and unshaken conviction, that we, (coloured people of these United States,) are the most degraded, wretched, and abject set of beings that ever lived since the world began; and I pray God that

Source: David Walker, *Appeal in Four Articles; Together with a Preamble, to the Coloured Citizens of the World*, Boston: D. Walker, 1830.

none like us ever may live again until time shall be no more. They tell us of the Israelites in Egypt, the Helots in Sparta, and of the Roman Slaves, which last were made up from almost every nation under heaven, whose sufferings under those ancient and heathen nations, were, in comparison with ours, under this enlightened and Christian nation, no more than a cypher—or, in other words, those heathen nations of antiquity, had but little more among them than the name and form of slavery; while wretchedness and endless miseries were reserved, apparently in a phial, to be poured out upon our fathers, ourselves and our children, by *Christian Americans!*

These positions I shall endeavour, by the help of the Lord, to demonstrate in the course of this *Appeal*, to the satisfaction of the most incredulous mind—and may God Almighty, who is the Father of our Lord Jesus Christ, open your hearts to understand and believe the truth.

The *causes*, my brethren, which produce our wretchedness and miseries, are so very numerous and aggravating, that I believe the pen only of a Josephus or a Plutarch, can well enumerate and explain them. Upon subjects, then, of such incomprehensible magnitude, so impenetrable, and so notorious, I shall be obliged to omit a large class of, and content myself with giving you an exposition of a few of those, which do indeed rage to such an alarming pitch, that they cannot but be a perpetual source of terror and dismay to every reflecting mind.

I am fully aware, in making this appeal to my much afflicted and suffering brethren, that I shall not only be assailed by those whose greatest earthly desires are, to keep us in abject ignorance and wretchedness, and who are of the firm conviction that Heaven has designed us and our children to be slaves and *beasts of burden* to them and their children. I say, I do not only expect to be held up to the public as an ignorant, impudent and restless disturber of the public peace, by such avaricious creatures, as well as a mover of insubordination—and perhaps put in prison or to death, for giving a superficial exposition of our miseries, and exposing tyrants. But I am persuaded, that many of my brethren, particularly those who are ignorantly in league with slave-holders or tyrants, who acquire their daily bread by the blood and sweat of their more ignorant brethren—and not a few of those too, who are too ignorant to see an inch beyond their noses, will rise up and call me cursed—Yea, the jealous ones among us will perhaps use more abject subtlety by affirming that this work is not worth perusing, that we are well situated, and there is no use in trying to better our condition, for we cannot. I will ask one question here.—Can our condition be any worse?—Can it be more mean and abject? If there are any changes, will they not be for the better, though they may appear for the worst at first? Can they get us any lower? Where can they get us? The are afraid to treat us worse, for they know well, the day they do it they are gone. But against all accusations which may or can be preferred against me, I appeal to Heaven for my motive in writing—who knows that my object is, if possible, to awaken in the breasts of my afflicted, degraded and slumbering brethren, a spirit of inquiry and investigation respecting our miseries and wretchedness in this *Republican Land of Liberty!!!!!!*

The sources from which our miseries are derived, and on which I shall comment, I shall not combine in one, but shall put them under distinct heads and expose them in their turn; in doing which, keeping truth on my side, and not departing from the strictest rules of morality, I shall endeavour to penetrate, search out, and lay them open for your inspection. If you cannot or will not profit by them, I shall have done my duty to you, my country and my God.

And as the inhuman system of *slavery*, is the *source* from which most of our miseries proceed, I shall begin with that *curse to nations*, which has spread terror and devastation through so many nations of antiquity, and which is raging to such a pitch at the present day in Spain and in Portugal. It had one tug in England, in France, and in the United States of America; yet the inhabitants thereof, do not learn wisdom, and erase it entirely from their dwellings and from all with whom they have to do. The fact is, the labour of slaves comes so cheap to the avaricious usurpers, and is (as they think) of such great utility to the country where it exists, that those who are actuated by sordid avarice only, overlook the evils, which will as sure as the Lord lives, follow after the good, in fact, they are so happy to keep in ignorance and degradation, and to receive the homage and the labour of the slaves, they forget that God rules in the armies of heaven and among the inhabitants of the earth, having his ears continually open to the cries, tears and groans of his oppressed people; and being a just and holy Being will at one day appear fully in behalf of the oppressed, and arrest the progress of the avaricious oppressors; for although the destruction of the oppressors God may not effect by the oppressed, yet the Lord our God will bring other destructions upon them—for not unfrequently will he cause them to rise up one against another, to be split and divided, and to oppress each other, and sometimes to open hostilities with sword in hand. Some may ask, what is the matter with this united and happy people?—Some say it is the cause of political usurpers, tyrants, oppressors, etc. But has not the Lord an oppressed and suffering people among them? Does the Lord condescend to hear their cries and see their tears in consequence of oppression? Will he let the oppressors rest comfortably and happy always? Will he not cause the very children of the oppressors to rise up against them, and oftimes put them to death? "God works in many ways his wonders to perform."

I will not here speak of the destructions which the Lord brought upon Egypt, in consequence of the oppression and consequent groans of the oppressed—of the hundreds and thousands of Egyptians whom God hurled into the Red Sea for afflicting his people in their land—of the Lord's suffering people in Sparta or Lacedaemon, the land of the truly famous Lycurgus—nor have I time to comment upon the cause which produced the fierceness with which Sylla usurped the title, and absolutely acted as dictator of the Roman people—the conspiracy of Cataline—the conspiracy against, and murder of Caesar in the Senate house—the spirit with which Marc Anthony made himself master of the commonwealth—his associating Octavius and Lipidus with himself in power—their dividing the provinces of Rome among themselves—their attack and defeat, on the plains of Philippi, of the last defenders of their liberty, (Brutus and Cassius)—the tyranny of Tiberius, and from him to the final overthrow of Constantinople by the Turkish sultan, Mahomed II. A.D. 1453. I say, I shall not take up time to speak of the *causes* which produced so much wretchedness and massacre among those heathen nations, for I am aware that you know too well, that God is just, as well as merciful!—I shall call your attention a few moments to that *Christian* nation, the Spaniards—while I shall leave almost unnoticed, that avaricious and cruel people, the Portuguese, among whom all true hearted Christians and lovers of Jesus Christ, must evidently see the judgments of God displayed. To show the judgments of God upon the Spaniards, I shall occupy but a little time, leaving plenty of room for the candid and unprejudiced to reflect.

All persons who are acquainted with history, and particularly the Bible, who are not blinded by the God of this world, and are actuated solely by avarice—who are able to lay aside prejudice long enough to view candidly and impartially, things as they were, are, and probably will be—who are willing to admit that God made man to serve Him *alone*, and that man should have no other Lord or Lords but Himself—that God Almighty is the *sole proprietor* or *master* of the WHOLE human family, and will not on any consideration admit of a colleague, being unwilling to divide his glory with another—and who can dispense with prejudice long enough to admit that we are *men*, notwithstanding our *improminent noses* and *woolly heads*, and believe that we feel for our fathers, mothers, wives and children, as well as the whites do for theirs.—I say, all who are permitted to see and believe these things, can easily recognize the judgments of God among the Spaniards. Though others may lay the cause of the fierceness with which they cut each other's throats, to some other circumstance, yet they who believe that God is a God of justice, will believe that SLAVERY *is the principal cause.*

While the Spaniards are running about upon the field of battle cutting each other's throats, has not the Lord an afflicted and suffering people in the midst of them, whose cries and groans in consequence of oppression are continually pouring into the ears of the God of justice? Would they not cease to cut each other's throats, if they could? But how can they? The very support which they draw from government to aid them in perpetrating such enormities, does it not arise in a great degree from the wretched victims of opression among them? And yet they are calling for *Peace!—Peace!!* Will any peace be given unto them? Their destruction may indeed be procrastinated awhile, but can it continue long, while they are oppressing the Lord's people? Has He not the hearts of all men in His hand? Will he suffer one part of his creatures to go on oppressing another like brutes always, with impunity? And yet, those avaricious wretches are calling for *Peace!!!!* I declare, it does appear to me, as though some nations think God is asleep, or that he made the Africans for nothing else but to dig their mines and work their farms, or they cannot believe history, sacred or profane. I ask every man who has a heart, and is blessed with the privilege of believing—Is not God a God of justice to *all* his creatures? Do you say he is? Then if he gives peace and tranquillity to tyrants, and permits them to keep our fathers, our mothers, ourselves and our children in eternal ignorance and wretchedness, to support them and their families, would he be to us a God of *justice?*

I ask, O ye *Christians!!!* who hold us and our children in the most abject ignorance and degradation, that ever a people were afflicted with since the world began—I say, if God gives you peace and tranquillity, and suffers you thus to go on afflicting us, and our children, who have never given you the least provocation—would he be to us *a God of justice?* If you will allow that we are MEN, who feel for each other, does not the blood of our fathers and of us their children, cry aloud to the Lord of Sabaoth against you, for the cruelties and murders with which you have, and do continue to afflict us. But it is time for me to close my remarks on the suburbs, just to enter more fully into the interior of this system of cruelty and oppression.

❧12❧

An Appeal to the Women
of the Nominally Free States

ANGELINA GRIMKÉ

Angelina Grimké (1805–1879) was born in South Carolina, but made her home in the North. A Quaker, and a staunch advocate of abolitionism and rights for women, she connected the two causes in her public statements against racism. The extracts reproduced here from an appeal to Northern women indicate the sense of moral outrage she brought to the slavery debate in arguing that the South's 'peculiar institution' had a corrosive impact on the values of the nation as a whole.

From *An Appeal to the Women of the Nominally Free States*

. . . [In] a country where women are degraded and brutalized, and where their exposed persons bleed under the lash—where they are sold in the shambles of "negro brokers"—robbed of their hard earnings—torn from their husbands, and forcibly plundered of their virtue and their offspring; surely in such a country, it is very natural that women should wish to know "the reason why"—especially when these outrages of blood and nameless horror are practiced in violation of the principles of our national Bill of Rights and the Preamble of our Constitution. We do not, then, and cannot concede the position, that because this is a political subject women ought to fold their hands in idleness, and close their eyes and ears to the "horrible things" that are practiced in our land. The denial of our duty to act, is a bold denial of our right to act; and if we have no right to act, then may we well be termed "the white slaves of the North"—for, like our brethren in bonds, we must seal our lips in silence and despair . . .

Slavery exerts a most deadly influence over the morals of our country, not only over that portion of it where it actually exists as "a domestic institution," but like the miasma of some pestilential pool, it spreads its desolating influence far beyond

Source: Angelina Grimké, from *An Appeal to the Women of the Nominally Free States*,
Boston: Isaac Knapp, [1832], 1838, 2nd edition.

its own boundaries. Who does not know that licentiousness is a crying sin at the North as well as at the South? and who does not admit that the manners of the South in this respect have had a wide and destructive influence on Northern character? Can crime be fashionable and common in one part of the Union and unrebuked by the other without corrupting the very heart's blood of the nation, and lowering the standard of morality everywhere? Can Northern men go down to the well-watered plains of the South to make their fortunes, without bowing themselves in the house of Rimmon and drinking the waters of that river of pollution which rolls over the plain of Sodom and Gomorrah? Do they return uncontaminated to their homes, or does not many and many a Northerner dig the grave of his virtue in the Admahs and Zeboims of our Southern States. And can our theological and academic institutions be opened to the sons of the planter without endangering the purity of the morals of our own sons, by associations with men who regard the robbery of the poor as no crime, and oppression as no wrong? Impossible! . . .

But this is not all; our people have erected a false standard by which to judge men's character. Because in the slaveholding States colored men are plundered and kept in abject ignorance, are treated with disdain and scorn, so here, too, in profound deference to the South, we refuse to eat, or ride, or walk, or associate, or open our institutions of learning, or even our zoological institutions to people of color, unless they visit them in the capacity of servants, of menials in humble attendance upon the AngloAmerican. Who ever heard of a more wicked absurdity in a Republican country?

Have Northern women, then, nothing to do with slavery, when its demoralizing influence is polluting their domestic circles and blasting the fair character of their sons and brothers? Nothing to do with slavery when their domestics are often dragged by the merciless kidnapper from the hearth of their nurseries and the arms of their little ones? Nothing to do with slavery when Northern women are chained and driven like criminals, and incarcerated in the great prison-house of the South? Nothing to do with slavery? . . .

We have hitherto addressed you more as moral and responsible beings, than in the distinctive character of women; we have appealed to you on the broad ground of human rights and human responsibilities, rather than on that of your peculiar duties as women. We have pursued this course of argument designedly, because, in order to prove that you have any duties to perform, it is necessary first to establish the principle of moral being—for all our rights and all our duties grow out of this principle. All moral beings have essentially the same rights and the same duties, whether they be male or female . . .

Women the Victims of Slavery

Out of the millions of slaves who have been stolen from Africa, a very great number must have been women who were torn from the arms of their fathers and husbands, brothers and children, and subjected to all the horrors of the middle passage and the still greater sufferings of slavery in a foreign land. Multitudes of these were cast upon our inhospitable shores; some of them now toil out a life of bondage, "one hour of which is fraught with more misery than ages of that" which our fathers rose in rebellion to oppose. But the great mass of female slaves in the southern States are the descendants of these hapless strangers; 1,000,000 of them now wear the iron yoke of slavery in this land of boasted liberty and law. They are our country women—they are our sisters; and to us, as women, they have a right to look for sympathy with their sorrows, and effort and prayer for their rescue. Upon those of us especially who have named the name of Christ, they have peculiar claims, and claims which we must answer, or we shall incur a heavy load of guilt . . .

Women are Slaveholders

Multitudes of the Southern women hold men, women and children as property. They are pampered in luxury, and nursed in the school of tyranny; they sway the iron rod of power, and they rob the laborer of his hire. Immortal beings tremble at their nod, and bow in abject submission at their word, and under the cowskin too often wielded by their own delicate hands. Women at the South hold their own sisters and brothers in bondage. Start not at this dreadful assertion—we speak that which some of us do know—we testify that which some of us have seen. Such facts ought to be known, that the women of the North may understand their duties, and be incited to perform them.

Southern families often present the most disgusting scenes of dissension, in which the mistress acts a part derogatory to her own character as a woman . . .

There are female tyrants too, who are prompt to lay their complaints of misconduct before their husbands, brothers and sons, and to urge them to commit acts of violence against their helpless slaves. Others still more cruel, place the lash in the hands of some trusty domestic, and stand by whilst he lays the heavy strokes upon the unresisting victim, deaf to the cries for mercy which rend the air, or rather the more enraged at such appeals, which are only answered by the Southern lady with the prompt command of "give her more for that." This work of chastisement is often performed by a brother, or other relative of the poor sufferer, which circumstance stings like an adder the very heart of the slave while her body writhes under the lash. Other mistresses who cannot bear that their delicate ears should be pained by the screams of the poor sufferers, write an order to the master of the Charleston workhouse, or the New Orleans calaboose, where they are most cruelly stretched in order to render the stroke of the whip or the blow of the paddle more certain to produce cuts and wounds which cause the blood to flow at every stroke. And let it be remembered that these poor creatures are often women who are most indecently divested of their clothing and exposed to the gaze of the executioner of a woman's command.

What then, our beloved sisters, must be the effects of such a system upon the domestic character of the white females? Can a corrupt tree bring forth good fruit? Can such despotism mould the character of the Southern woman to gentleness and love? or may we not fairly conclude that all that suavity, for which slaveholding ladies are so conspicuous, is in many instances the paint and the varnish of hypocrisy, the fashionable polish of a heartless superficiality?

But it is not the character alone of the mistress that is deeply injured by the possession and exercise of such despotic power, nor is it the degradation and suffering to which the slave is continually subject; but another important consideration is, that in consequence of the dreadful state of morals at the South, the wife and the daughter sometimes find their homes a scene of the most mortifying, heart-rending preference of the degraded domestic, or the colored daughter of the head of the family. There are, alas, too many families, of which the contentions of Abraham's household is a fair example. But we forbear to lift the veil of private life any higher; let these few hints suffice to give you some idea of what is daily passing behind that curtain which has been so carefully drawn before the scenes of domestic life in Christian America.

The Colored Women of the North are Oppressed

Another reason we would urge for the interference of Northern women with the system of slavery is, that in consequence of the odium which the degradation of slavery has attached to color even in the free States, our colored sisters are dreadfully oppressed here. Our seminaries of learning are closed to them, they are almost entirely banished from our lecture rooms, and even in the house of God they are separated from their white brethren and sisters as though we were afraid to come in contact with a colored skin . . .

Here, then, are some of the bitter fruits of that inveterate prejudice which the vast proportion of northern women are cherishing towards their colored sisters; and let us remember that every one of us who denies the sinfulness of this prejudice, . . . is awfully guilty in the sight of Him who is no respecter of persons . . .

But our colored sisters are oppressed in other ways. As they walk the streets of our cities, they are continually liable to be insulted with the vulgar epithet of "nigger"; no matter how respectable or wealthy, they cannot visit the Zoological Institute of New-York except in the capacity of nurses or servants—no matter how worthy, they cannot gain admittance into or receive assistance from any of the charities of this city. In Philadelphia, they are cast out of our Widow's Asylum, and their children are refused admittance to the House of Refuge, the Orphan's House and the Infant School connected with the Alms-House, though into these are gathered the very offscouring of our population. These are only specimens of that soul-crushing influence from which the colored women of the North are daily suffering. Then, again, some of them have been robbed of their husbands and children by the heartless kidnapper, and others have themselves been dragged into slavery. If they attempt to travel, they are exposed to great indignities and great inconveniences. Instances have been known of their actually dying in consequence of the exposure to which they were subjected on board of our steamboats. No money could purchase the use of a berth for a delicate female because she had a colored skin. Prejudice, then, degrades and fetters the minds, persecutes and murders the bodies of our free colored sisters. Shall we be silent at such a time as this? . . .

Much may be done, too, by sympathizing with our oppressed colored sisters, who are suffering in our very midst. Extend to them the right hand of fellowship on the broad principles of humanity and Christianity, treat them as equals, visit them as equals, invite them to co-operate with you in Anti-Slavery and Temperance and Moral Reform Societies—in Maternal Associations and Prayer Meetings and Reading Companies. . .

Multitudes of instances will continually occur in which you will have the opportunity of identifying yourselves with this injured class of our fellow-beings: embrace these opportunities at all times and in all places, in the true nobility of our great Exemplar, who was ever found among the poor and the despised, elevating and blessing them with his counsels and presence. In this way, and this alone, will you be enabled to subdue that deep-rooted prejudice which is doing the work of oppression in the free States to a most dreadful extent.

When this demon has been cast out of your own hearts, when you can recognize the colored woman as a WOMAN—then will you be prepared to send out an appeal to our Southern sisters entreating them to "go and do likewise."

❧ 13 ❧

Declaration of Sentiments

AMERICAN ANTI-SLAVERY SOCIETY

In 1833 the American Anti-Slavery Society, led by William Lloyd Garrison, was founded in Philadelphia. The initial meeting set out the 'declaration of sentiments' upon which the society was based, arguing that slavery was illegal, if not unconstitutional, under the laws of natural justice. The abolitionists seized upon the rhetoric of the Declaration of Independence, and combined this with a strong sense of religious mission. In this, a manifesto which defined their movement, the crusading spirit is articulated in clear and compelling language.

The Convention, assembled in the City of Philadelphia to organize a national Anti-Slavery Society, promptly seize the opportunity to promulgate the following DECLARATION OF SENTIMENTS, as cherished by them in relation to the enslavement of one-sixth portion of the American people.

More than fifty-seven years have elapsed since a band of patriots convened in this place, to devise measures for the deliverance of this country from a foreign yoke. The cornerstone upon which they founded the TEMPLE OF FREEDOM was broadly this—'that all men are created equal; that they are endowed by their Creator with certain inalienable rights; that among these are life, LIBERTY, and the pursuit of happiness.' At the sound of their trumpet-call, three millions of people rose up as from the sleep of death, and rushed to the strife of blood; deeming it more glorious to die instantly as freemen, than desirable to live one hour as slaves. They were few in number—poor in resources; but the honest conviction that TRUTH, JUSTICE and RIGHT were on their side, made them invincible.

We have met together for the achievement of an enterprise, without which that of our fathers is incomplete, and which, for its magnitude, solemnity, and probable results upon the destiny of the world, as far transcends theirs, as moral truth does physical force.

In purity of motive, in earnestness of zeal, in decision of purpose, in intrepidity of action, in steadfastness of faith, in sincerity of spirit, we would not be inferior to them.

Source: *Abolitionist*, I, December 1833, pp. 178–80.

183

Their principles led them to wage war against their oppressors, and to spill human blood like water, in order to be free. *Ours* forbid the doing of evil that good may come, and lead us to reject, and to entreat the oppressed to reject, the use of all carnal weapons for deliverance from bondage—relying solely upon those which are spiritual, and mighty through God to the pulling down of strong holds.

Their measures were physical resistance—the marshalling in arms—the hostile array—the mortal encounter. *Ours* shall be such only as the opposition of moral purity to moral corruption—the destruction of error by the potency of truth—the overthrow of prejudice by the power of love—and the abolition of slavery by the spirit of repentance.

Their grievances, great as they were, were trifling in comparison with the wrongs and sufferings of those for whom we plead. Our fathers were never slaves—never bought and sold like cattle—never shut out from the light of knowledge and religion—never subjected to the lash of brutal taskmasters.

But those, for whose emancipation we are striving—constituting at the present time at least one-sixth part of our countrymen,—are recognized by the laws, and treated by their fellow beings, as brute beasts;—are plundered daily of the fruits of their toil without redress;—really enjoy no constitutional nor legal protection from licentious and murderous outrages upon their persons;—are ruthlessly torn asunder—the tender babe from the arms of its frantic mother—the heart-broken wife from her weeping husband—at the caprice or pleasure of irresponsible tyrants;—and, for the crime of having a dark complexion, suffer the pangs of hunger, the infliction of stripes, the ignominy of brutal servitude. They are kept in heathenish darkness by laws expressly enacted to make their instruction a criminal offence.

These are the prominent circumstances in the condition of more than TWO MILLIONS of our people, the proof of which may be found in thousands of indisputable facts, and in the laws of the slave-holding States.

Hence we maintain—

That, in view of the civil and religious privileges of this nation, the guilt of its oppression is unequalled by any other on the face of the earth; and, therefore,

That it is bound to repent instantly, to undo the heavy burden, to break every yoke, and to let the oppressed go free.

We further maintain—

That no man has a right to enslave or imbrute his brother—to hold or acknowledge him, for one moment, as a piece of merchndise—to keep back his hire by fraud—or to brutalize his mind by denying him the means of intellectual, social and moral improvement.

The right to enjoy liberty is inalienable. To invade it, is to usurp the prerogative of Jehovah. Every man has a right to his own body—to the products of his own labor—to the protection of law—and to the common advantages of society. It is piracy to buy or steal a native African, and subject him to servitude. Surely, the sin is as great to enslave an AMERICAN as an AFRICAN.

Therefore we believe and affirm—

That there is no difference, *in principle*, between the African slave trade and American slavery;

That every American citizen, who retains a human being in involuntary bondage, as his property, is, [according to Scripture] a MANSTEALER.

That the slaves ought instantly to be set free, and brought under the protection of law;

That if they had lived from the time of Pharaoh down to the present period, and had been entailed through successive generations, their right to be free could never have been alienated, but their claims would have constantly risen in solemnity;

That all those laws which are now in force, admitting the right of slavery, are therefore, before God, utterly null and void; being an audacious usurpation of the Divine prerogative, a daring infringement on the law of nature, a base overthrow of the very foundations of the social compact, a complete extinction of all the relations, endearments and obligations of mankind, and a presumptuous transgression of all the holy commandments—and that therefore they ought to be instantly abrogated.

We further believe and affirm—

That all persons of color who possess the qualifications which are demanded of others, ought to be admitted forthwith to the enjoyment of the same privileges, and the exercise of the same prerogatives, as others; and that the paths of preferment, of wealth and of intelligence, should be opened as widely to them as to persons of a white complexion.

We maintain that no compensation should be given to the planters emancipating their slaves—

Because it would be a surrender of the great fundamental principle, that man cannot hold property in man;

Because SLAVERY IS A CRIME, AND THEREFORE IT IS NOT AN ARTICLE TO BE SOLD;

Because the holders of slaves are not the just proprietors of what they claim;—freeing the slave is not depriving them of property, but restoring it to the right owner;—it is not wronging the master, but righting the slave—restoring him to himself;

Because immediate and general emancipation would only destroy nominal, not real property: it would not amputate a limb or break a bone of the slaves, but by infusing motives into their breasts, would make them doubly valuable to the masters as free laborers; and

Because, if compensation is to be given at all, it should be given to the outraged and guiltless slaves, and not to those who have plundered and abused them.

We regard, as delusive, cruel and dangerous, any scheme of expatriation which pretends to aid, either directly or indirectly, in the emancipation of the slaves, or to be a substitute for the immediate and total abolition of slavery.

We fully and unanimously recognize the sovereignty of each State, to legislate exclusively on the subject of the slavery which is tolerated within its limits. We concede that Congress, *under the present national compact*, has no right to interfere with any of the slave States, in relation to this momentous subject.

But we maintain that Congress has a right, and is solemnly bound, to suppress the domestic slave trade between the several States, and to abolish slavery in those portions of our territory which the Constitution has placed under its jurisdiction.

We also maintain that there are, at the present time, the highest obligations resting upon the people of the free States to remove slavery by moral and political action, as prescribed in the Constitution of the United States. They are now living under a pledge of their tremendous physical force, to fasten the galling fetters of tyranny upon the limbs of millions in the Southern States;—they are liable to be called at any moment to suppress a general insurrection of the slaves;—they authorize the slave owner to vote for three-fifths of his slaves as property, and thus enable him to perpetuate his oppression;—they support a standing army at the south for its protection;—and they seize the slave, who has escaped into their territories, and send him back to be tortured by an enraged master or a brutal driver.

This relation to slavery is criminal, and full of danger: IT MUST BE BROKEN UP.

These are our views and principles—these, our designs and measures. With entire confidence in the overruling justice of God, we plant ourselves upon the Declaration of our Independence and the truths of Divine Revelation, as upon the EVERLASTING ROCK.

We shall organize Anti-Slavery Societies, if possible, in every city, town and village in our land.

We shall send forth Agents to lift up the voice of remonstrance, of warning, of entreaty and rebuke.

We shall circulate, unsparingly and extensively, anti-slavery tracts and periodicals.

We shall enlist the PULPIT and the PRESS in the cause of the suffering and the dumb.

We shall aim at a purification of the churches from all participation in the guilt of slavery.

We shall encourage the labor of freemen over that of slaves, by giving a preference to their productions;—and

We shall spare no exertions nor means to bring the whole nation to speedy repentance.

Our trust for victory is solely in GOD. We may be personally defeated, but our principles never. TRUTH, JUSTICE, REASON, HUMANITY, must and will gloriously triumph. Already a host is coming up to the help of the Lord against the mighty, and the prospect before us is full of encouragement.

Submitting this DECLARATION to the candid examination of the people of this ountry, and of the friends of liberty all over the world, we hereby affix our signatures to it;—pledging ourselves that, under the guidance and by the help of Almighty God, we will do all that in us lies, consistently with this Declaration of our principles, to overthrow the most execrable system of slavery that has ever been witnessed upon earth—to deliver our land from its deadliest curse—to wipe out the foulest stain which rests upon our national escutheon—and to secure to the colored population of the United States, all the rights and privileges which may belong to them as men and as Americans—come what may to our persons, our interests, or our reputations—whether we live to witness the triumph of JUSTICE, LIBERTY and HUMANITY, or perish untimely as martyrs in this great, benevolent and holy cause.

⚜14⚜

The *Amistad* Case

JUSTICE JOSEPH STORY

The *Amistad* was a Spanish ship taken over by its 'cargo' of Africans who had been kidnapped in Sierra Leone and were to be sold as slaves in Puerto Principe. Eventually captured by the United States navy, the ship was taken to Connecticut. Abolitionists saw in the resulting salvage case an important opportunity to take a symbolic stand on the issue of the slave trade. John Quincy Adams, the former president, argued their case in front of the Supreme Court, which held on appeal that the Africans were free men, and that treaties with Spain in this instance were non-binding. The following is Justice Joseph Story's Opinion given to the court in 1841.

U.S. Supreme Court

40 U.S. 518

The AMISTAD.

UNITED STATES, Appellants,

v.

The LIBELLANTS AND CLAIMANTS

of the SCHOONER AMISTAD, her tackle, apparel and furniture, together with her cargo, and the AFRICANS mentioned and described in the several libels and claims, Appellees.

January Term, 1841

STORY, Justice, delivered the opinion of the court.

This is the case of an appeal from the decree of the circuit court of the district of Connecticut, sitting in admiralty. The leading facts, as they appear upon the

Source: *Records of the Supreme Court of the United States*, Washington D.C.:
National Archives and Records Administration, RG 267.

transcript of the proceedings, are as follows: On the 27th of June 1839, the schooner *L'Amistad*, being the property of Spanish subjects, cleared out from the port of Havana, in the island of Cuba, for Puerto Principe, in the same island. On board of the schooner were the master, Ramon Ferrer, and Jose Ruiz and Pedro Montez, all Spanish subjects. The former had with him a negro boy, named Antonio, claimed to be his slave. Jose Ruiz had with him forty-nine negroes, claimed by him as his slaves, and stated to be his property, in a certain pass or document, signed by the governor-general of Cuba. Pedro Montez had with him four other negroes, also claimed by him as his slaves, and stated to be his property, in a similar pass or document, also signed by the governor-general [40 U.S. 518, 588] of Cuba. On the voyage, and before the arrival of the vessel at her port of destination, the negroes rose, killed the master, and took possession of her. On the 26th of August, the vessel was discovered by Lieutenant Gedney, of the United States brig *Washington*, at anchor on the high seas, at the distance of half a mile from the shore of Long Island. A part of the negroes were then on shore, at Culloden Point, Long Island; who were seized by Lieutenant Gedney, and brought on board. The vessel, with the negroes and other persons on board, was brought by Lieutenant Gedney into the district of Connecticut, and there libelled for salvage in the district court of the United States. A libel for salvage was also filed by Henry Green and Pelatiah Fordham, of Sag Harbor, Long Island. On the 18th of September, Ruiz and Montez filed claims and libels, in which they asserted their ownership of the negroes as their slaves, and of certain parts of the cargo, and prayed that the same might be 'delivered to them, or to the representatives of her Catholic Majesty, as might be most proper.' On the 19th of September, the attorney of the United States for the district of Connecticut, filed an information or libel, setting forth, that the Spanish minister had officially presented to the proper department of the government of the United States, a claim for the restoration of the vessel, cargo and slaves, as the property of Spanish subjects, which had arrived within the jurisdictional limits of the United States, and were taken possession of by the said public armed brig of the United States, under such circumstances as made it the duty of the United States to cause the same to be restored to the true proprietors, pursuant to the treaty between the United States and Spain; and praying the court, on its being made legally to appear that the claim of the Spanish minister was well founded, to make such order for the disposal of the vessel, cargo and slaves, as would best enable the United States to comply with their treaty stipulations. But if it should appear, that the negroes were persons transported from Africa, in violation of the laws of the United States, and brought within the United States, contrary to the same laws; he then prayed the court to make such order for their removal to the coast of Africa, pursuant to the laws of the United States, as it should deem fit.

On the 19th of November, the attorney of the United States [40 U.S. 518, 589] filed a second information or libel, similar to the first, with the exception of the second prayer above set forth in his former one. On the same day, Antonio G. Vega, the vice-consul of Spain for the state of Connecticut, filed his libel, alleging that Antonio was a slave, the property of the representatives of Ramon Ferrer, and praying the court to cause him to be delivered to the said vice-consul, that he might be returned by him to his lawful owner in the island of Cuba.

On the 7th of January 1840, the negroes, Cinque and others, with the exception of Antonio, by their counsel, filed an answer, denying that they were slaves, or the property of Ruiz and Montez, or that the court could, under the constitution or laws of the United States, or under any treaty, exercise any jurisdiction over their persons, by reason of the premises; and praying that they might be dismissed. They specially set forth and insisted in this answer, that they were native-born Africans; born free, and still, of right, ought to be free and not slaves; that they were, on or about the 15th of April 1839, unlawfully kidnapped, and forcibly and wrongfully carried on board a certain vessel, on the coast of Africa, which was unlawfully engaged in the slave-trade, and were unlawfully transported in the same vessel to the island of Cuba, for the purpose of being there unlawfully sold as slaves; that Ruiz and Montez, well knowing the premises, made a pretended purchase of them; that afterwards, on or about the 28th of June 1839, Ruiz and Montez, confederating with Ferrer (master of the *Amistad*), caused them, without law or right, to be placed on board of the *Amistad*, to be transported to some place unknown to them, and there to be enslaved for life; that, on the voyage, they rose on the master, and took possession of the vessel, intending to return therewith to their native country, or to seek an asylum in some free state; and the vessel arrived, about the 26th of August 1839, off Montauk Point, near Long Island; a part of them were sent on shore, and were seized by Lieutenant Gedney, and carried on board; and all of them were afterwards brought by him into the district of Connecticut.

On the 7th of January 1840, Jose Antonio Tellincas, and Messrs. Aspe and Laca, all Spanish subjects, residing in Cuba, filed their [40 U.S. 518, 590] claims, as owners to certain portions of the goods found on board of the schooner L'*Amistad*. On the same day, all the libellants and claimants, by their counsel, except Jose Ruiz and Pedro Montez (whose libels and claims, as stated of record, respectively, were pursued by the Spanish minister, the same being merged in his claims), appeared, and the negroes also appeared by their counsel; and the case was heard on the libels, claims, answers and testimony of witnesses.

On the 23d day of January 1840, the district court made a decree. By that decree, the court rejected the claim of Green and Fordham for salvage, but allowed salvage to Lieutenant Gedney and others, on the vessel and cargo, of one-third of the value thereof, but not on the negroes, Cinque and others; it allowed the claim of Tellincas, and Aspe and Laca, with the exception of the above-mentioned salvage; it dismissed the libels and claims of Ruiz and Montez, with costs, as being included under the claim of the Spanish minister; it allowed the claim of the Spanish vice-consul, for Antonio, on behalf of Ferrer's representatives; it rejected the claims of Ruiz and Montez for the delivery of the negroes, but admitted them for the cargo, with the exception of the above-mentioned salvage; it rejected the claim made by the attorney of the United States on behalf of the Spanish minister, for the restoration of the negroes, under the treaty; but it decreed, that they should be delivered to the president of the United States, to be transported to Africa, pursuant to the act of 3d March 1819.

From this decree, the district-attorney, on behalf of the United States, appealed to the circuit court, except so far as related to the restoration of the slave Antonio. The claimants, Tellincas, and Aspe and Laca, also appealed from that part of the decree which awarded salvage on the property respectively claimed by them. No appeal was interposed by Ruiz or Montez, nor on behalf of the representatives of the owners of the *Amistad*. The circuit court by a mere pro forma decree, affirmed the decree of the district court, reserving the question of salvage upon the claims of Tellincas, and Aspe and Laca. And from that decree, the present appeal has been brought to this court.

The cause has been very elaborately argued, as well upon the [40 U.S. 518, 591] merits, as upon a motion of behalf of the appellees to dismiss the appeal. On the part of the United States, it has been contended: 1. That due and sufficient proof concerning the property has been made, to authorize the restitution of the vessel, cargo and negroes to the Spanish subjects on whose behalf they are claimed, pursuant to the treaty with Spain, of the 27th of October 1795. 2. That the United States had a right to intervene in the manner in which they have done, to obtain a decree for the restitution of the property, upon the application of the Spanish minister. These propositions have been strenuously denied on the other side. Other collateral and incidental points have been stated, upon which it is not necessary at this moment to dwell.

Before entering upon the discussion of the main points involved in this interesting and important controversy, it may be necessary to say a few words as to the actual posture of the case as it now stands before us. In the first place, then, the only parties now before the court on one side, are the United States, intervening for the sole purpose of procuring restitution of the property, as Spanish property, pursuant to the treaty, upon the grounds stated by the other parties claiming the property in their respective libels. The United States do not assert any property in themselves, nor any violation of their own rights, or sovereignty or laws, by the acts complained of. They do not insist that these negroes have been imported into the United States, in contravention of our own slave-trade acts. They do not seek to have these negroes delivered up, for the purpose of being transferred to Cuba, as pirates or robbers, or as fugitive criminals found within our territories, who have been guilty of offences against the laws of Spain. They do not assert that the seizure and bringing the vessel, and cargo and negroes, into port, by Lieutenant Gedney, for the purpose of adjudication, is a tortuous act. They simply confine themselves to the right of the Spanish claimants to the restitution of their property, upon the facts asserted in their respective allegations.

In the next place, the parties before the court, on the other side, as appellees, are Lieutenant Gedney, on his libel for salvage, and the negroes (Cinque and others), asserting themselves, in their answer, not to be slaves, but free native Africans, kidnapped [40 U.S. 518, 592] in their own country, and illegally transported by force from that country; and now entitled to maintain their freedom.

No question has been here made, as to the proprietary interests in the vessel and cargo. It is admitted, that they belong to Spanish subjects, and that they ought to be restored. The only point on this head is, whether the restitution ought to be upon the payment of salvage, or not? The main controversy is, whether these negroes are the property of Ruiz and Montez, and ought to be delivered up; and to this, accordingly, we shall first direct our attention.

It has been argued on behalf of the United States, that the court are bound to deliver them up, according to the treaty of 1795, with Spain, which has in this particular been continued in full force, by the treaty of 1819, ratified in 1821. The sixth article of that treaty seems to have had, principally in view, cases where the property of the subjects of either state had been taken possession of within the territorial jurisdiction of the other, during war. The eighth article provides for cases where the shipping of the inhabitants of either state are forced, through stress of weather, pursuit of pirates or enemies, or any other urgent necessity, to seek shelter in the ports of the other. There may well be some doubt entertained, whether the present case, in its actual circumstances, falls within the purview of this article. But it does not seem necessary, for reasons hereafter stated, absolutely to decide it. The ninth article provides,

> that all ships and merchandize, of what nature soever, which shall be rescued out of the hands of any pirates or robbers, on the high seas, shall be brought into some port of either state, and shall be delivered to the custody of the officers of that port, in order to be taken care of and restored, entire, to the true proprietor, as soon as due and sufficient proof shall be made concerning the property thereof.

This is the article on which the main reliance is placed on behalf of the United States, for the restitution of these negroes. To bring the case within the article, it is essential to establish: 1st, That these negroes, under all the circumstances, fall within the description of merchandize, in the sense of the treaty. 2d, That there has been a rescue of them on the high seas, out of the hands of the pirates and robbers; which, in the present case, can only be, by showing that they [40 U.S. 518, 593] themselves are pirates and robbers: and 3d, That Ruiz and Montez, the asserted proprietors, are the true proprietors, and have established their title by competent proof.

If these negroes were, at the time, lawfully held as slaves, under the laws of Spain, and recognized by those laws as property, capable of being lawfully bought and sold; we see no reason why they may not justly be deemed, within the intent of the treaty, to be included under the denomination of merchandize, and as such ought to be restored to the claimants; for upon that point the laws of Spain would seem to furnish the proper rule of interpretation. But admitting this, it is clear, in our opinion, that neither of the other essential facts and requisites has been established in proof; and *the onus probandi* of both lies upon the claimants to give rise to the *casus foederis*. It is plain, beyond controversy, if we examine the evidence, that these negroes never were the lawful slaves of Ruiz or Montez, or of any other Spanish subjects. They are natives of Africa, and were kidnapped there, and were unlawfully transported to Cuba, in violation of the laws and treaties of Spain, and the most solemn edicts and declarations of that government. By those laws and treaties, and edicts, the African slave-trade is utterly abolished; the dealing in that trade is deemed a heinous crime; and the negroes thereby introduced into the dominions of Spain, are declared to be free. Ruiz and Montez are proved to have made the pretended purchase of these negroes, with a full knowledge of all the circumstances. And so cogent and irresistible is the evidence in this respect, that the district-attorney has admitted in open court, upon the record, that these negroes were native Africans, and recently imported into Cuba, as alleged in their answers to the libels in the case. The supposed proprietary interest of Ruiz and Montez is completely displaced, if we are at liberty to look at the evidence, or the admissions of the district-attorney.

If then, these negroes are not slaves, but are kidnapped Africans, who, by the laws of Spain itself, are entitled to their freedom, and were kidnapped and illegally carried to Cuba, and illegally detained and restained on board the *Amistad*; there is no pretence to say, that they are pirates or robbers. We may lament the dreadful acts by which they asserted their liberty, and took possession of the *Amistad*, and endeavored to regain their native [40 U.S. 518, 594] country; but they cannot be deemed pirates or robbers, in the sense of the law of nations, or the treaty with Spain, or the laws of Spain itself; at least, so far as those laws have been brought to our knowledge. Nor do the libels of Ruiz or Montez assert them to be such.

This posture of the facts would seem, of itself, to put an end to the whole inquiry upon the merits. But it is argued, on behalf of the United States, that the ship and cargo, and negroes, were duly documented as belonging to Spanish subjects, and this court have no right to look behind these documents; that full faith and credit is to be given to them; and that they are to be held conclusive evidence in this cause, even although it should be established by the most satisfactory proofs, that they have been obtained by the grossest frauds and impositions upon the constituted authorities of Spain. To this argument, we can, in no wise, assent. There is nothing in the treaty which justifies or sustains the argument. We do not here meddle with the point, whether there has been any connivance in this illegal traffic, on the part of any of the colonial authorities or subordinate officers of Cuba; because, in our view, such an examination is unnecessary, and ought not to be pursued, unless it were indispensable to public justice, although it has been strongly pressed at the bar. What we proceed upon is this, that although public documents of the government, accompanying property found on board of the private ships of a foreign nation, certainly are to be deemed *prima facie* evidence of the facts which they purport to state, yet they are always open to be impugned for fraud; and whether that fraud be in the original obtaining of these documents, or in the subsequent fraudulent and illegal use of them, when once it is satisfactorily established, it overthrows all their sanctity, and destroys them as proof. Fraud will vitiate any, even the most solemn, transactions; and an asserted title to property, founded upon it, is utterly void. The very language of the ninth article of the treaty of 1795, requires the proprietor to make due and sufficient proof of his property. And how can that proof be deemed either due or sufficient, which is but a connected and stained tissue of fraud? This is not a mere rule of municipal jurisprudence. Nothing is more clear in the law of nations, as an established rule to regulate their rights and duties, [40 U.S. 518, 595] and intercourse, than the doctrine, that the ship's papers are but *prima facie* evidence, and that, if they are shown to be fraudulent, they are not to be held proof of any valid title. This rule is familiarly applied, and, indeed, is of every-day's occurrence in cases of prize, in the contests between belligerents and neutrals, as is apparent from numerous cases to be found in the reports of this court; and it is just as applicable to the transactions of civil intercourse between nations, in times of peace. If a private ship, clothed with Spanish papers, should enter the ports of the United States, claiming the privileges and immunities, and rights, belonging to *bona fide* subjects of Spain, under our treaties or laws, and she should, in reality, belong to the subjects of another nation, which was not entitled to any such privileges, immunities or rights, and the proprietors were seeking, by fraud, to cover their own illegal acts, under the flag of Spain; there can be no doubt, that it would be the duty of our courts to strip off the disguise, and to look at the case, according to its naked realities. In the solemn treaties between nations, it can never be presumed, that either state intends to provide the means of perpetrating or protecting frauds; but all the provisions are to be construed intended to be applied to bona fide transactions. The 17th article of the treaty with Spain, which provides for certain passports and certificates, as evidence of property on board of the ships of both states, is, in its terms, applicable only to cases where either of the parties is engaged in a war. This article required a certain form of passport to be agreed upon by the parties, and annexed to the treaty; it never was annexed; and therefore, in the case of The *Amiable Isabella*, 6 Wheat. 1, it was held inoperative.

It is also a most important consideration, in the present case, which ought not to be lost sight of, that, supposing these African negroes not to be slaves, but kidnapped, and free negroes, the treaty with Spain cannot be obligatory upon them; and the United States are bound to respect their rights as much as those of Spanish subjects. The conflict of rights between the parties, under such circumstances, becomes positive and inevitable, and must be decided upon the eternal principles of justice and international law. If the contest were about any goods on board of this ship, to which American citizens asserted a title, which was [40 U.S. 518, 596] denied by the Spanish claimants, there could be no doubt of the right to such American citizens to litigate their claims before any competent American tribunal, notwithstanding the treaty with Spain. A *fortiori*, the doctrine must apply, where human life and human liberty are in issue, and constitute the very essence of the controversy. The treaty with Spain never could have intended to take away the equal rights of all foreigners, who should contest ther claims before any of our courts, to equal justice; or to deprive such foreigners of the protection given them by other treaties, or by the general law of nations. Upon the merits of the case, then, there does not seem to us to be any ground for doubt, that these negroes ought to be deemed free; and that the Spanish treaty interposes no obstacle to the just assertion of their rights.

There is another consideration, growing out of this part of the case, which necessarily rises in judgment. It is observable, that the United States, in their original claim, filed it in the alternative, to have the negroes, if slaves and Spanish property, restored to the proprietors; or, if not slaves, but negroes who had been transported from Africa, in violation of the laws of the United States, and brought into the United States, contrary to the same laws, then the court to pass an order to enable the United States to remove such persons to the coast of Africa, to be delivered there to such agent as may be authorized to receive and provide for them. At a subsequent period, this last alternative claim was not insisted on, and another claim was interposed, omitting it; from which the conclusion naturally arises, that it was abandoned. The decree of the district court, however, contained an order for the delivery of the negroes to the United States, to be transported to the coast of Africa, under the act of the 3d of March 1819, ch. 224. The United States do not now insist upon any affirmance of this part of the decree; and in our judgment, upon the admitted facts, there is no ground to assert, that the case comes within the purview of the act of 1819, or of any other of our prohibitory slave-trade acts. These negroes were never taken from Africa, or brought to the United States, in contravention of those acts. When the *Amistad* arrived, she was in possession of the negroes, asserting their freedom; and in no sense could they possibly intend to import themselves here, as [40 U.S. 518, 597] slaves, or for sale as slaves. In this view of the matter, that part of the decree of the district court is unmaintainable, and must be reversed.

The view which has been thus taken of this case, upon the merits, under the first point, renders it wholly unnecessary for us to give any opinion upon the other point, as to the right of the United States to intervene in this case in the manner already stated. We dismiss this, therefore, as well as several minor points made at the argument.

As to the claim of Lieutenant Gedney for the salvage service, it is understood, that the United States do not now desire to interpose any obstacle to the allowance of it, if it is deemed reasonable by the court. It was a highly meritorious and useful service to the proprietors of the ship and cargo; and such as, by the general principles of maritime law, is always deemed a just foundation for salvage. The rate allowed by the court, does not seem to us to have been beyond the exercise of a sound discretion, under the very particular and embarrassing circumstances of the case.

Upon the whole, our opinion is, that the decree of the circuit court, affirming that of the district court, ought to be affirmed, except so far as it directs the negroes to be delivered to the president, to be transported to Africa, in pursuance of the act of the 3d of March 1819; and as to this, it ought to be reversed: and that the said negroes be declared to be free, and be dismissed from the custody of the court, and go without day.

❦ 15 ❦

Narrative of the Life of Frederick Douglass, An American Slave

In 1838, Frederick Douglass, who had been born into slavery in Maryland, escaped and went to New York City. In 1841, he spoke at a convention of the Massachusetts Anti-slavery Society, and his activism in the abolitionist cause led to the writing of a narrative of his life, first published in 1845, and subsequently revised as *My Bondage and My Freedom* (1855). These extracts from his original work comprise the preface, written by William Lloyd Garrison and including a testimonial letter from Wendell Phillips. Also included are Douglass's account of his escape from slavery (Chapter XI) and the appendix to his narrative, in which he inveighs against the corruption of what he terms the 'slaveholding religion' of the South.

From *Narrative of the Life of Frederick Douglass, An American Slave Written by Himself*

Entered, According to Act of Congress
In the Year 1845
By Frederick Douglass,
In the Clerk's Office of the District Court
Of Massachusetts.

Preface

In the month of August, 1841, I attended an anti-slavery convention in Nantucket, at which it was my happiness to become acquainted with FREDERICK DOUGLASS, the writer of the following Narrative. He was a stranger to nearly every member of that body; but, having recently made his escape from the southern prison-house of

Source: Frederick Douglass, *Narrative of the Life of Frederick Douglass, an American Slave, Written by Himself*, Boston: The Anti-Slavery Office, 1845.

bondage, and feeling his curiosity excited to ascertain the principles and measures of the abolitionists,—of whom he had heard a somewhat vague description while he was a slave,—he was induced to give his attendance, on the occasion alluded to, though at that time a resident in New Bedford.

Fortunate, most fortunate occurrence!—fortunate for the millions of his manacled brethren, yet panting for deliverance from their awful thraldom!—fortunate for the cause of negro emancipation, and of universal liberty!—fortunate for the land of his birth, which he has already done so much to save and bless!—fortunate for a large circle of friends and acquaintances, whose sympathy and affection he has strongly secured by the many sufferings he has endured, by his virtuous traits of character, by his ever-abiding remembrance of those who are in bonds, as being bound with them!—fortunate for the multitudes, in various parts of our republic, whose minds he has enlightened on the subject of slavery, and who have been melted to tears by his pathos, or roused to virtuous indignation by his stirring eloquence against the enslavers of men!—fortunate for himself, as it at once brought him into the field of public usefulness, "gave the world assurance of a MAN," quickened the slumbering energies of his soul, and consecrated him to the great work of breaking the rod of the oppressor, and letting the oppressed go free!

I shall never forget his first speech at the convention—the extraordinary emotion it excited in my own mind—the powerful impression it created upon a crowded auditory, completely taken by surprise—the applause which followed from the beginning to the end of his felicitous remarks. I think I never hated slavery so intensely as at that moment; certainly, my perception of the enormous outrage which is inflicted by it, on the godlike nature of its victims, was rendered far more clear than ever. There stood one, in physical proportion and stature commanding and exact—in intellect richly endowed—in natural eloquence a prodigy—in soul manifestly "created but a little lower than the angels"—yet a slave, ay, a fugitive slave,—trembling for his safety, hardly daring to believe that on the American soil, a single white person could be found who would befriend him at all hazards, for the love of God and humanity! Capable of high attainments as an intellectual and moral being—needing nothing but a comparatively small amount of cultivation to make him an ornament to society and a blessing to his race—by the law of the land, by the voice of the people, by the terms of the slave code, he was only a piece of property, a beast of burden, a chattel personal, nevertheless!

A beloved friend from New Bedford prevailed on Mr. DOUGLASS to address the convention: He came forward to the platform with a hesitancy and embarrassment, necessarily the attendants of a sensitive mind in such a novel position. After apologizing for his ignorance, and reminding the audience that slavery was a poor school for the human intellect and heart, he proceeded to narrate some of the facts in his own history as a slave, and in the course of his speech gave utterance to many noble thoughts and thrilling reflections. As soon as he had taken his seat, filled with hope and admiration, I rose, and declared that PATRICK HENRY, of revolutionary fame, never made a speech more eloquent in the cause of liberty, than the one we had just listened to from the lips of that hunted fugitive. So I believed at that time—

such is my belief now. I reminded the audience of the peril which surrounded this self-emancipated young man at the North,—even in Massachusetts, on the soil of the Pilgrim Fathers, among the descendants of revolutionary sires; and I appealed to them, whether they would ever allow him to be carried back into slavery,—law or no law, constitution or no constitution. The response was unanimous and in thunder-tones—"NO!" "Will you succor and protect him as a brother-man—a resident of the old Bay State?" "YES!" shouted the whole mass, with an energy so startling, that the ruthless tyrants south of Mason and Dixon's line might almost have heard the mighty burst of feeling, and recognized it as the pledge of an invincible determination, on the part of those who gave it, never to betray him that wanders, but to hide the outcast, and firmly to abide the consequences.

It was at once deeply impressed upon my mind, that, if Mr. DOUGLASS could be persuaded to consecrate his time and talents to the promotion of the anti-slavery enterprise, a powerful impetus would be given to it, and a stunning blow at the same time inflicted on northern prejudice against a colored complexion. I therefore endeavored to instil hope and courage into his mind, in order that he might dare to engage in a vocation so anomalous and responsible for a person in his situation; and I was seconded in this effort by warm-hearted friends, especially by the late General Agent of the Massachusetts Anti-Slavery Society, Mr. JOHN A. COLLINS, whose judgment in this instance entirely coincided with my own. At first, he could give no encouragement; with unfeigned diffidence, he expressed his conviction that he was not adequate to the performance of so great a task; the path marked out was wholly an untrodden one; he was sincerely apprehensive that he should do more harm than good. After much deliberation, however, he consented to make a trial; and ever since that period, he has acted as a lecturing agent, under the auspices either of the American or the Massachusetts Anti-Slavery Society. In labors he has been most abundant; and his success in combating prejudice, in gaining proselytes, in agitating the public mind, has far surpassed the most sanguine expectations that were raised at the commencement of his brilliant career. He has borne himself with gentleness and meekness, yet with true manliness of character. As a public speaker, he excels in pathos, wit, comparison, imitation, strength of reasoning, and fluency of language. There is in him that union of head and heart, which is indispensable to an enlightenment of the heads and a winning of the hearts of others. May his strength continue to be equal to his day! May he continue to "grow in grace, and in the knowledge of God," that he may be increasingly serviceable in the cause of bleeding humanity, whether at home or abroad!

It is certainly a very remarkable fact, that one of the most efficient advocates of the slave population, now before the public, is a fugitive slave, in the person of FREDERICK DOUGLASS; and that the free colored population of the United States are as ably represented by one of their own number, in the person of CHARLES LENOX REMOND, whose eloquent appeals have extorted the highest applause of multitudes on both sides of the Atlantic. Let the calumniators of the colored race despise themselves for their baseness and illiberality of spirit, and henceforth cease to talk of the natural inferiority of those who require nothing but time and opportunity to attain to the highest point of human excellence.

It may, perhaps, be fairly questioned, whether any other portion of the population of the earth could have endured the privations, sufferings and horrors of slavery, without having become more degraded in the scale of humanity than the slaves of African descent. Nothing has been left undone to cripple their intellects, darken their minds, debase their moral nature, obliterate all traces of their relationship to mankind; and yet how wonderfully they have sustained the mighty load of a most frightful bondage, under which they have been groaning for centuries! To illustrate the effect of slavery on the white man,—to show that he has no powers of endurance, in such a condition, superior to those of his black brother,— DANIEL O'CONNELL, the distinguished advocate of universal emancipation, and the mightiest champion of prostrate but not conquered Ireland, relates the following anecdote in a speech delivered by him in the Conciliation Hall, Dublin, before the Loyal National Repeal Association, March 31, 1845.

> "No matter," said Mr. O'CONNELL, "under what specious term it may disguise itself, slavery is still hideous. *It has a natural, an inevitable tendency to brutalize every noble faculty of man.* An American sailor, who was cast away on the shore of Africa, where he was kept in slavery for three years, was, at the expiration of that period, found to be imbruted and stultified—he had lost all reasoning power; and having forgotten his native language, could only utter some savage gibberish between Arabic and English, which nobody could understand, and which even he himself found difficulty in pronouncing. So much for the humanizing influence of THE DOMESTIC INSTITUTION!"

Admitting this to have been an extraordinary case of mental deterioration, it proves at least that the white slave can sink as low in the scale of humanity as the black one.

Mr. DOUGLASS has very properly chosen to write his own Narrative, in his own style, and according to the best of his ability, rather than to employ someone else. It is, therefore, entirely his own production; and, considering how long and dark was the career he had to run as a slave,—how few have been his opportunities to improve his mind since he broke his iron fetters,—it is, in my judgment, highly creditable to his head and heart. He who can peruse it without a tearful eye, a heaving breast, an afflicted spirit,—without being filled with an unutterable abhorrence of slavery and all its abettors, and animated with a determination to seek the immediate overthrow of that execrable system,—without trembling for the fate of this country in the hands of a righteous God, who is ever on the side of the oppressed, and whose arm is not shortened that it cannot save,—must have a flinty heart, and be qualified to act the part of a trafficker "in slaves and the souls of men." I am confident that it is essentially true in all its statements; that nothing has been set down in malice, nothing exaggerated, nothing drawn from the imagination; that it comes short of the reality, rather than overstates a single fact in regard to SLAVERY AS IT IS. The experience of FREDERICK DOUGLASS, as a slave, was not a peculiar one; his lot was not especially a hard one; his case may be regarded as a very fair specimen of the treatment of slaves in Maryland, in which State it is conceded that they are better fed and less cruelly treated than in Georgia, Alabama, or Louisiana. Many have suffered incomparably more, while very few on the plantations have suffered less, than himself. Yet how deplorable was his situation! what terrible chastisements were inflicted upon his person! what still more shocking outrages were perpetrated upon his mind! with all his noble powers and sublime aspirations, how like a brute was he treated, even by those professing to have the same mind in them that was in Christ Jesus! to what dreadful liabilities was he continually subjected! how destitute of friendly counsel and aid, even in his greatest extremities! how heavy was the midnight of woe which shrouded in blackness the last ray of hope, and filled the future with terror and gloom! what longings after freedom took possession of his breast, and how his misery aug-mented, in proportion as he grew reflective and intelligent,—thus demonstrating that a happy slave is an extinct man! how he thought, reasoned, felt, under the lash of the driver, with the chains upon his limbs! what perils he encountered in his endeavors to escape from his horrible doom! and how signal have been his deliverance and preservation in the midst of a nation of pitiless enemies!

This Narrative contains many affecting incidents, many passages of great eloquence and power; but I think the most thrilling one of them all is the description DOUGLASS gives of his feelings, as he stood soliloquizing respecting his fate, and the chances of his one day being a freeman, on the banks of the Chesapeake Bay— viewing the receding vessels as they flew with their white wings before the breeze, and apostrophizing them as animated by the living spirit of freedom. Who can read that passage, and be insensible to its pathos and sublimity? Compressed into it is a whole Alexandrian library of thought, feeling, and sentiment—all that can, all that need be urged, in the form of expostulation, entreaty, rebuke, against that crime of crimes,—making man the property of his fellow-man! O, how accursed is that system, which entombs the godlike mind of man, defaces the divine image, reduces those who by creation were crowned with glory and honor to a level with four-footed beasts, and exalts the dealer in human flesh above all that is called God! Why should its existence be prolonged one hour? Is it not evil, only evil, and that continually? What does its presence imply but the absence of all fear of God, all regard for man, on the part of the people of the United States? Heaven speed its eternal overthrow!

So profoundly ignorant of the nature of slavery are many persons, that they are stubbornly incredulous whenever they read or listen to any recital of the cruelties which are daily inflicted on its victims. They do not deny that the slaves are held as property; but that terrible fact seems to convey to their minds no idea of injustice, exposure to outrage, or savage barbarity. Tell them of cruel scourgings, of mutilations and brandings, of scenes of pollution and blood, of the banishment of all light and knowledge, and they affect to be greatly indignant at such enormous exaggerations, such wholesale misstatements, such abominable libels on the character of the southern planters! As if all these direful outrages were not the natural results of slavery! As if it were less cruel to reduce a human being to the condition of a thing, than to give him a severe flagellation, or to deprive him of necessary food and clothing! As if whips, chains, thumb-screws, paddles, bloodhounds, overseers, drivers, patrols, were not all indispensable to keep the slaves down, and to give protection to their ruthless oppressors! As if, when the marriage institution is abolished, concubinage, adultery, and incest, must not necessarily abound; when all the rights of humanity are annihilated, any barrier remains to protect the victim from the fury of the spoiler; when absolute power is assumed over life and liberty, it will not be wielded with destructive sway! Skeptics of this character abound in society. In some few instances, their incredulity arises from a want of reflection; but, generally, it indicates a hatred of the light, a desire to shield slavery from the assaults of its foes, a contempt of the colored race, whether bond or free. Such will try to discredit the shocking tales of slaveholding cruelty which are recorded in this truthful Narrative; but they will labor in vain. Mr. DOUGLASS has frankly disclosed the place of his birth, the names of those who claimed ownership in his body and soul, and the names also of those who committed the crimes which he has alleged against them. His statements, therefore, may easily be disproved, if they are untrue.

In the course of his Narrative, he relates two instances of murderous cruelty,—in one of which a planter deliberately shot a slave belonging to a neighboring plantation, who had unintentionally gotten within his lordly domain in quest of fish; and in the other, an overseer blew out the brains of a slave who had fled to a stream of water to escape a bloody scourging. Mr. DOUGLASS states that in neither of these instances was any thing done by way of legal arrest or judicial investigation. The *Baltimore American*, of March 17, 1845, relates a similar case of atrocity, perpetrated with similar impunity—as follows:—

> "*Shooting a Slave.*—We learn, upon the authority of a letter from Charles county, Maryland, received by a gentleman of this city, that a young man, named Matthews, a nephew of General Matthews, and whose father, it is believed, holds an office at Washington, killed one of the slaves upon his father's farm by shooting him. The letter states that young Matthews had been left in charge of the farm; that he gave an order to the servant, which was disobeyed, when he proceeded to the house, *obtained a gun, and, returning, shot the servant.* He immediately, the letter continues, fled to his father's residence, where he still remains unmolested."

—Let it never be forgotten, that no slaveholder or overseer can be convicted of any outrage perpetrated on the person of a slave, however diabolical it may be, on the testimony of colored witnesses, whether bond or free. By the slave code, they are adjudged to be as incompetent to testify against a white man, as though they were indeed a part of the brute creation. Hence, there is no legal protection in fact, whatever there may be in form, for the slave population; and any amount of cruelty may be inflicted on them with impunity. Is it possible for the human mind to conceive of a more horrible state of society?

The effect of a religious profession on the conduct of southern masters is vividly described in the following Narrative, and shown to be any thing but salutary. In the nature of the case, it must be in the highest degree pernicious. The testimony of Mr. DOUGLASS, on this point, is sustained by a cloud of witnesses, whose veracity is unimpeachable. "A slave-holder's profession of Christianity is a palpable imposture.

He is a felon of the highest grade. He is a man-stealer. It is of no importance what you put in the other scale."

Reader! are you with the man-stealers in sympathy and purpose, or on the side of their down-trodden victims? If with the former, then are you the foe of God and man. If with the latter, what are you prepared to do and dare in their behalf? Be faithful, be vigilant, be untiring in your efforts to break every yoke, and let the oppressed go free. Come what may—cost what it may—inscribe on the banner which you unfurl to the breeze, as your religious and political motto—"No Compromise With Slavery! No Union With Slaveholders!"

WM. LLOYD GARRISON
Boston, May 1, 1845.

Letter from Wendell Phillips, Esq.

Boston, April 22, 1845.

My Dear Friend:

You remember the old fable of "The Man and the Lion," where the lion complained that he should not be so misrepresented "when the lions wrote history."

I am glad the time has come when the "lions write history." We have been left long enough to gather the character of slavery from the involuntary evidence of the masters. One might, indeed, rest sufficiently satisfied with what, it is evident, must be, in general, the results of such a relation, without seeking farther to find whether they have followed in every instance. Indeed, those who stare at the half-peck of corn a week, and love to count the lashes on the slave's back, are seldom the "stuff" out of which reformers and abolitionists are to be made. I remember that, in 1838, many were waiting for the results of the West India experiment, before they could come into our ranks. Those "results" have come long ago; but, alas! few of that number have come with them, as converts. A man must be disposed to judge of emancipation by other tests than whether it has increased the produce of sugar,— and to hate slavery for other reasons than because it starves men and whips women,—before he is ready to lay the first stone of his anti-slavery life.

I was glad to learn, in your story, how early the most neglected of God's children waken to a sense of their rights, and of the injustice done them. Experience is a keen teacher; and long before you had mastered your A B C, or knew where the "white sails" of the Chesapeake were bound, you began, I see, to gauge the wretchedness of the slave, not by his hunger and want, not by his lashes and toil, but by the cruel and blighting death which gathers over his soul.

In connection with this, there is one circumstance which makes your recollections peculiarly valuable, and renders your early insight the more remarkable. You come from that part of the country where we are told slavery appears with its fairest features. Let us hear, then, what it is at its best estate—gaze on its bright side, if it has one; and then imagination may task her powers to add dark lines to the picture, as she travels southward to that (for the colored man) Valley of the Shadow of Death, where the Mississippi sweeps along.

Again, we have known you long, and can put the most entire confidence in your truth, candor, and sincerity. Every one who has heard you speak has felt, and, I am confident, every one who reads your book will feel, persuaded that you give them a fair specimen of the whole truth. No one-sided portrait,—no wholesale complaints,—but strict justice done, whenever individual kindliness has neutralized, for a moment, the deadly system with which it was strangely allied. You have been with us, too, some years, and can fairly compare the twilight of rights, which your race enjoy at the North, with that "noon of night" under which they labor south of Mason and Dixon's line. Tell us whether, after all, the half-free colored man of Massachusetts is worse off than the pampered slave of the rice swamps!

In reading your life, no one can say that we have unfairly picked out some rare specimens of cruelty. We know that the bitter drops, which even you have drained from the cup, are no incidental aggravations, no individual ills, but such as must mingle always and necessarily in the lot of every slave. They are the essential ingredients, not the occasional results, of the system.

After all, I shall read your book with trembling for you. Some years ago, when you were beginning to tell me your real name and birthplace, you may remember I stopped you, and preferred to remain ignorant of all. With the exception of a vague description, so I continued, till the other day, when you read me your memoirs. I hardly knew, at the time, whether to thank you or not for the sight of them, when I reflected that it was still dangerous, in Massachusetts, for honest men to tell their names!

They say the fathers, in 1776, signed the Declaration of Independence with the halter about their necks. You, too, publish your declaration of freedom with danger compassing you around. In all the broad lands which the Constitution of the United States overshadows, there is no single spot,—however narrow or desolate,—where a fugitive slave can plant himself and say, "I am safe." The whole armory of Northern Law has no shield for you. I am free to say that, in your place, I should throw the MS. into the fire.

You, perhaps, may tell your story in safety, endeared as you are to so many warm hearts by rare gifts, and a still rarer devotion of them to the service of others. But it will be owing only to your labors, and the fearless efforts of those who, trampling the laws and Constitution of the country under their feet, are determined that they will "hide the outcast," and that their hearths shall be, spite of the law, an asylum for the oppressed, if, some time or other, the humblest may stand in our streets, and bear witness in safety against the cruelties of which he has been the victim.

Yet it is sad to think, that these very throbbing hearts which welcome your story, and form your best safeguard in telling it, are all beating contrary to the "statute in such case made and provided." Go on, my dear friend, till you, and those who, like you, have been saved, so as by fire, from the dark prison-house, shall stereotype these free, illegal pulses into statutes; and New England, cutting loose from a blood-stained Union, shall glory in being the house of refuge for the oppressed,—

till we no longer merely "*hide* the outcast," or make a merit of standing idly by while he is hunted in our midst; but, consecrating anew the soil of the Pilgrims as an asylum for the oppressed, proclaim our *welcome* to the slave so loudly, that the tones shall reach every hut in the Carolinas, and make the broken-hearted bondman leap up at the thought of old Massachusetts.

God speed the day!

Till then, and ever,
Yours truly,
WENDELL PHILLIPS

Chapter XI

I now come to that part of my life during which I planned, and finally succeeded in making, my escape from slavery. But before narrating any of the peculiar circumstances, I deem it proper to make known my intention not to state all the facts connected with the transaction. My reasons for pursuing this course may be understood from the following: First, were I to give a minute statement of all the facts, it is not only possible, but quite probable, that others would thereby be involved in the most embarrassing difficulties. Secondly, such a statement would most undoubtedly induce greater vigilance on the part of slaveholders than has existed heretofore among them; which would, of course, be the means of guarding a door whereby some dear brother bondman might escape his galling chains. I deeply regret the necessity that impels me to suppress any thing of importance connected with my experience in slavery. It would afford me great pleasure indeed, as well as materially add to the interest of my narrative, were I at liberty to gratify a curiosity, which I know exists in the minds of many, by an accurate statement of all the facts pertaining to my most fortunate escape. But I must deprive myself of this pleasure, and the curious of the gratification which such a statement would afford. I would allow myself to suffer under the greatest imputations which evil-minded men might suggest, rather than exculpate myself, and thereby run the hazard of closing the slightest avenue by which a brother slave might clear himself of the chains and fetters of slavery.

I have never approved of the very public manner in which some of our western friends have conducted what they call the *underground railroad*, but which I think, by their open declarations, has been made most emphatically the *upperground railroad*. I honor those good men and women for their noble daring, and applaud them for willingly subjecting themselves to bloody persecution, by openly avowing their participation in the escape of slaves. I, however, can see very little good resulting from such a course, either to themselves or the slaves escaping; while, upon the other hand, I see and feel assured that those open declarations are a positive evil to the slaves remaining, who are seeking to escape. They do nothing towards enlightening the slave, whilst they do much towards enlightening the master. They stimulate him to greater watchfulness, and enhance his power to

205

capture his slave. We owe something to the slaves south of the line as well as to those north of it; and in aiding the latter on their way to freedom, we should be careful to do nothing which would be likely to hinder the former from escaping from slavery. I would keep the merciless slaveholder profoundly ignorant of the means of flight adopted by the slave. I would leave him to imagine himself surrounded by myriads of invisible tormentors, ever ready to snatch from his infernal grasp his trembling prey. Let him be left to feel his way in the dark; let darkness commensurate with his crime hover over him; and let him feel that at every step he takes, in pursuit of the flying bondman, he is running the frightful risk of having his hot brains dashed out by an invisible agency. Let us render the tyrant no aid; let us not hold the light by which he can trace the footprints of our flying brother. But enough of this. I will now proceed to the statement of those facts, connected with my escape, for which I am alone responsible, and for which no one can be made to suffer but myself.

In the early part of the year 1838, I became quite restless. I could see no reason why I should, at the end of each week, pour the reward of my toil into the purse of my master. When I carried to him my weekly wages, he would, after counting the money, look me in the face with a robber-like fierceness, and ask, "Is this all?" He was satisfied with nothing less than the last cent. He would, however, when I made him six dollars, sometimes give me six cents, to encourage me. It had the opposite effect. I regarded it as a sort of admission of my right to the whole. The fact that he gave me any part of my wages was proof, to my mind, that he believed me entitled to the whole of them. I always felt worse for having received any thing; for I feared that the giving me a few cents would ease his conscience, and make him feel himself to be a pretty honorable sort of robber. My discontent grew upon me. I was ever on the look-out for means of escape; and, finding no direct means, I determined to try to hire my time, with a view of getting money with which to make my escape. In the spring of 1838, when Master Thomas came to Baltimore to purchase his spring goods, I got an opportunity, and applied to him to allow me to hire my time. He unhesitatingly refused my request, and told me this was another stratagem by which to escape. He told me I could go nowhere but that he could get me; and that, in the event of my running away, he should spare no pains in his efforts to catch me. He exhorted me to content myself, and be obedient. He told me, if I would be happy, I must lay out no plans for the future. He said, if I behaved myself properly, he would take care of me. Indeed, he advised me to complete thoughtlessness of the future, and taught me to depend solely upon him for happiness. He seemed to see fully the pressing necessity of setting aside my intellectual nature, in order to contentment in slavery. But in spite of him, and even in spite of myself, I continued to think, and to think about the injustice of my enslavement, and the means of escape.

About two months after this, I applied to Master Hugh for the privilege of hiring my time. He was not acquainted with the fact that I had applied to Master Thomas, and had been refused. He too, at first, seemed disposed to refuse; but, after some reflection, he granted me the privilege, and proposed the following terms: I was to be allowed all my time, make all contracts with those for whom I worked, and find my own employment; and, in return for this liberty, I was to pay him three dollars at the end of each week; find myself in calking tools, and in board and clothing. My board was two dollars and a half per week. This, with the wear and tear of clothing and calking tools, made my regular expenses about six dollars per week. This amount I was compelled to make up, or relinquish the privilege of hiring my time. Rain or shine, work or no work, at the end of each week the money must be forthcoming, or I must give up my privilege. This arrangement, it will be perceived, was decidedly in my master's favor. It relieved him of all need of looking after me. His money was sure. He received all the benefits of slaveholding without its evils; while I endured all the evils of a slave, and suffered all the care and anxiety of a freeman. I found it a hard bargain. But, hard as it was, I thought it better than the old mode of getting along. It was a step towards freedom to be allowed to bear the responsibilities of a freeman, and I was determined to hold on upon it. I bent myself to the work of making money. I was ready to work at night as well as day, and by the most untiring perseverance and industry, I made enough to meet my expenses, and lay up a little money every week. I went on thus from May till August. Master Hugh then refused to allow me to hire my time longer. The ground for his refusal was a failure on my part, one Saturday night, to pay him for my week's time. This failure was occasioned by my attending a camp meeting about ten miles from Baltimore. During the week, I had entered into an engagement with a number of young friends to start from Baltimore to the camp ground early Saturday evening; and being detained by my employer, I was unable to get down to Master Hugh's without disappointing the company. I knew that Master Hugh was in no special need of the money that night. I therefore decided to go to camp meeting, and upon my return pay him the three dollars. I staid at the camp meeting one day longer than I intended when I left. But as soon as I returned, I called upon him to pay him what he considered his due. I found him very angry; he could scarce restrain his wrath. He said he had a great mind to give me a severe whipping. He wished to know how I dared go out of the city without asking his permission. I told him I hired my time and while I paid him the price which he asked for it, I did not know that I was bound to ask him when and where I should go. This reply troubled him; and, after reflecting a few moments, he turned to me, and said I should hire my time no longer; that the next thing he should know of, I would be running away. Upon the same plea, he told me to bring my tools and clothing home forthwith. I did so; but instead of seeking work, as I had been accustomed to do previously to hiring my time, I spent the whole week without the performance of a single stroke of work. I did this in retaliation. Saturday night, he called upon me as usual for my week's wages. I told him I had no wages; I had done no work that week. Here we were upon the point of coming to blows. He raved, and swore his determination to get hold of me. I did not allow myself a single word; but was resolved, if he laid the weight of his hand upon me, it should be blow for blow. He did not strike me, but told me that he would find me in constant employment in future. I thought the matter over during the next day, Sunday, and finally resolved upon the third day of September, as the day upon which I would make a second attempt to secure my freedom. I now had three weeks during which to prepare for my journey. Early on Monday morning, before Master Hugh had time to make any engagement for me, I went out and got employment of Mr. Butler, at his ship-yard near the drawbridge, upon what is called the City Block, thus making it unnecessary for him to seek employment for me. At the end of the week, I brought him between eight and nine dollars. He seemed very well pleased, and asked why I did not do the same the week before. He little knew what my plans were. My object in working steadily was to remove any suspicion he might entertain of my intent to run away; and in this I succeeded admirably. I suppose he thought I was never better satisfied with my condition than at the very time during which I was planning my escape. The second week passed, and again I carried him my full wages; and so well pleased was he, that he gave me twenty-five cents, (quite a large sum for a slaveholder to give a slave,) and bade me to make a good use of it. I told him I would.

Things went on without very smoothly indeed, but within there was trouble. It is impossible for me to describe my feelings as the time of my contemplated start drew near. I had a number of warm-hearted friends in Baltimore,—friends that I loved almost as I did my life,—and the thought of being separated from them forever was painful beyond expression. It is my opinion that thousands would escape from slavery, who now remain, but for the strong cords of affection that bind them to their friends. The thought of leaving my friends was decidedly the most painful thought with which I had to contend. The love of them was my tender point, and shook my decision more than all things else. Besides the pain of separation, the dread and apprehension of a failure exceeded what I had experienced at my first attempt. The appalling defeat I then sustained returned to torment me. I felt assured that, if I failed in this attempt, my case would be a hopeless one—it would seal my fate as a slave forever. I could not hope to get off with any thing less than the severest punishment, and being placed beyond the means of escape. It required no very vivid imagination to depict the most frightful scenes through which I should have to pass, in case I failed. The wretchedness of slavery, and the blessedness of freedom, were perpetually before me. It was life and death with me. But I remained firm, and, according to my resolution, on the third day of September, 1838, I left my chains, and succeeded in reaching New York without the slightest interruption of any kind. How I did so,—what means I adopted,—what direction I travelled, and by what mode of conveyance,—I must leave unexplained, for the reasons before mentioned.

I have been frequently asked how I felt when I found myself in a free State. I have never been able to answer the question with any satisfaction to myself. It was a moment of the highest excitement I ever experienced. I suppose I felt as one may imagine the unarmed mariner to feel when he is rescued by a friendly man-of-war from the pursuit of a pirate. In writing to a dear friend, immediately after my arrival at New York, I said I felt like one who had escaped a den of hungry lions. This state of mind, however, very soon subsided; and I was again seized with a feeling of great insecurity and loneliness. I was yet liable to be taken back, and subjected to all the tortures of slavery. This in itself was enough to damp the ardor of my enthusiasm. But the loneliness overcame me. There I was in the midst of thousands, and yet a perfect stranger; without home and without friends, in the midst of thousands of my own brethren—children of a common Father, and yet I dared not to unfold to any one of them my sad condition. I was afraid to speak to any one for fear of speaking to the wrong one, and thereby falling into the hands of money-loving kidnappers, whose business it was to lie in wait for the panting fugitive, as the ferocious beasts of the forest lie in wait for their prey. The motto which I adopted when I started from slavery was this—"Trust no man!" I saw in every white man an enemy, and in almost every colored man cause for distrust. It was a most painful situation; and, to understand it, one must needs experience it, or imagine himself in similar circumstances. Let him be a fugitive slave in a strange land—a land given up to be the hunting-ground for slaveholders—whose inhabitants are legalized kidnappers—where he is every moment subjected to the terrible liability of being seized upon by his fellow men, as the hideous crocodile seizes upon his prey!—I say, let him place himself in my situation—without home or friends—without money or credit—wanting shelter, and no one to give it—wanting bread, and no money to buy it,—and at the same time let him feel that he is pursued by merciless men-hunters, and in total darkness as to what to do, where to go, or where to stay,—perfectly helpless both as to the means of defence and means of escape,—in the midst of plenty, yet suffering the terrible gnawings of hunger,—in the midst of houses, yet having no home,—among fellow-men, yet feeling as if in the midst of wild beasts, whose greediness to swallow up the trembling and half-famished fugitive is only equalled by that with which the monsters of the deep swallow up the helpless fish upon which they subsist,—I say, let him be placed in this most trying situation,—the situation in which I was placed,—then, and not till then, will he fully appreciate the hardships of, and know how to sympathize with, the toil-worn and whip-scarred fugitive slave.

Thank Heaven, I remained but a short time in this distressed situation. I was relieved from it by the humane hand of Mr. DAVID RUGGLES, whose vigilance, kindness, and perseverance, I shall never forget. I am glad of an opportunity to express, as far as words can, the love and gratitude I bear him. Mr. Ruggles is now afflicted with blindness, and is himself in need of the same kind offices which he was once so forward in the performance of toward others.

I had been in New York but a few days, when Mr. Ruggles sought me out, and very kindly took me to his boarding-house at the corner of Church and Lespenard Streets. Mr. Ruggles was then very deeply engaged in the memorable *Darg* case, as well as attending to a number of other fugitive slaves, devising ways and means for their successful escape; and, though watched and hemmed in on almost every side, he seemed to be more than a match for his enemies.

Very soon after I went to Mr. Ruggles, he wished to know of me where I wanted to go; as he deemed it unsafe for me to remain in New York. I told him I was a calker, and should like to go where I could get work. I thought of going to Canada; but he decided against it, and in favor of my going to New Bedford, thinking I should be able to get work there at my trade. At this time, Anna,[1] my intended wife, came on; for I wrote to her immediately after my arrival at New York, (notwithstanding my homeless, houseless, and helpless condition), informing her of my successful flight, and wishing her to come on forthwith. In a few days after her arrival, Mr. Ruggles called in the Rev. J. W. C. Pennington, who, in the presence of Mr. Ruggles, Mrs. Michaels, and two or three others, performed the marriage ceremony, and gave us a certificate, of which the following is an exact copy:—

THIS may certify, that I joined together in holy matrimony Frederick Johnson[2] and Anna Murray, as man and wife, in the presence of Mr. David Ruggles and Mrs. Michaels.

JAMES W. C. PENNINGTON
New York, Sept. 15, 1838

Upon receiving this certificate, and a five-dollar bill from Mr. Ruggles, I shouldered one part of our baggage, and Anna took up the other, and we set out forthwith to take passage on board of the steam-boat *John W. Richmond* for Newport, on our way to New Bedford. Mr. Ruggles gave me a letter to a Mr. Shaw in Newport, and told me, in case my money did not serve me to New Bedford, to stop in Newport and obtain further assistance; but upon our arrival at Newport, we were so anxious to get to a place of safety, that, notwithstanding we lacked the necessary money to pay our fare, we decided to take seats in the stage, and promise to pay when we got to New Bedford. We were encouraged to do this by two excellent gentlemen, residents of New Bedford, whose names I afterward ascertained to be Joseph Ricketson and William C. Taber. They seemed at once to understand our circumstances, and gave us such assurance of their friendliness as put us fully at ease in their presence. It was good indeed to meet with such friends, at such a time. Upon reaching New Bedford, we were directed to the house of Mr. Nathan Johnson, by whom we were kindly received, and hospitably provided for. Both Mr. and Mrs. Johnson took a deep and lively interest in our welfare. They proved themselves quite worthy of the name of abolitionists. When the stage-driver found us unable to pay our fare, he held on upon our baggage as security for the debt. I had but to mention the fact to Mr. Johnson, and he forthwith advanced the money.

We now began to feel a degree of safety, and to prepare ourselves for the duties and responsibilities of a life of freedom. On the morning after our arrival at New Bedford, while at the breakfast-table, the question arose as to what name I should be called by. The name given me by my mother was, "Frederick Augustus Washington Bailey." I, however, had dispensed with the two middle names long before I left Maryland so that I was generally known by the name of "Frederick Bailey." I started from Baltimore bearing the name of "Stanley." When I got to New York, I again changed my name to "Frederick Johnson," and thought that would be the last change. But when I got to New Bedford, I found it necessary again to change my name. The reason of this necessity was, that there were so many Johnsons in New Bedford, it was already quite difficult to distinguish between them. I gave Mr. Johnson the privilege of choosing me a name, but told him he must not take from me the name of "Frederick." I must hold on to that, to preserve a sense of my identity. Mr. Johnson had just been reading the "Lady of the Lake," and at once suggested that my name be "Douglass." From that time until now I have been called

"Frederick Douglass;" and as I am more widely known by that name than by either of the others, I shall continue to use it as my own.

I was quite disappointed at the general appearance of things in New Bedford. The impression which I had received respecting the character and condition of the people of the north, I found to be singularly erroneous. I had very strangely supposed, while in slavery, that few of the comforts, and scarcely any of the luxuries, of life were enjoyed at the north, compared with what were enjoyed by the slaveholders of the south. I probably came to this conclusion from the fact that northern people owned no slaves. I supposed that they were about upon a level with the non-slaveholding population of the south. I knew *they* were exceedingly poor, and I had been accustomed to regard their poverty as the necessary consequence of their being non-slaveholders. I had somehow imbibed the opinion that, in the absence of slaves, there could be no wealth, and very little refinement. And upon coming to the north, I expected to meet with a rough, hard-handed, and uncultivated population, living in the most Spartan-like simplicity, knowing nothing of the ease, luxury, pomp, and grandeur of southern slaveholders. Such being my conjectures, any one acquainted with the appearance of New Bedford may very readily infer how palpably I must have seen my mistake.

In the afternoon of the day when I reached New Bedford, I visited the wharves, to take a view of the shipping. Here I found myself surrounded with the strongest proofs of wealth. Lying at the wharves, and riding in the stream, I saw many ships of the finest model, in the best order, and of the largest size. Upon the right and left, I was walled in by granite warehouses of the widest dimensions, stowed to their utmost capacity with the necessaries and comforts of life. Added to this, almost every body seemed to be at work, but noiselessly so, compared with what I had been accustomed to in Baltimore. There were no loud songs heard from those engaged in loading and unloading ships. I heard no deep oaths or horrid curses on the laborer. I saw no whipping of men; but all seemed to go smoothly on. Every man appeared to understand his work, and went at it with a sober, yet cheerful earnestness, which betokened the deep interest which he felt in what he was doing, as well as a sense of his own dignity as a man. To me this looked exceedingly strange. From the wharves I strolled around and over the town, gazing with wonder and admiration at the splendid churches, beautiful dwellings, and finely-cultivated gardens; evincing an amount of wealth, comfort, taste, and refinement, such as I had never seen in any part of slaveholding Maryland.

Every thing looked clean, new, and beautiful. I saw few or no dilapidated houses, with poverty-stricken inmates; no half-naked children and bare-footed women, such as I had been accustomed to see in Hillsborough, Easton, St. Michael's, and Baltimore. The people looked more able, stronger, healthier, and happier, than those of Maryland. I was for once made glad by a view of extreme wealth, without being saddened by seeing extreme poverty. But the most astonishing as well as the most interesting thing to me was the condition of the colored people, a great many of whom, like myself, had escaped thither as a refuge from the hunters of men. I found many, who had not been seven years out of their chains, living in finer houses,

211

and evidently enjoying more of the comforts of life, than the average of slaveholders in Maryland. I will venture to assert, that my friend Mr. Nathan Johnson (of whom I can say with a grateful heart, "I was hungry, and he gave me meat; I was thirsty, and he gave me drink; I was a stranger, and he took me in") lived in a neater house; dined at a better table; took, paid for, and read, more newspapers; better understood the moral, religious, and political character of the nation,—than nine tenths of the slaveholders in Talbot county Maryland. Yet Mr. Johnson was a working man. His hands were hardened by toil, and not his alone, but those also of Mrs. Johnson. I found the colored people much more spirited than I had supposed they would be. I found among them a determination to protect each other from the blood-thirsty kidnapper, at all hazards. Soon after my arrival, I was told of a circumstance which illustrated their spirit. A colored man and a fugitive slave were on unfriendly terms. The former was heard to threaten the latter with informing his master of his whereabouts. Straightway a meeting was called among the colored people, under the stereotyped notice, "Business of importance!" The betrayer was invited to attend. The people came at the appointed hour, and organized the meeting by appointing a very religious old gentleman as president, who, I believe, made a prayer, after which he addressed the meeting as follows: *Friends, we have got him here, and I would recommend that you young men just take him outside the door, and kill him!* With this, a number of them bolted at him; but they were intercepted by some more timid than themselves, and the betrayer escaped their vengeance, and has not been seen in New Bedford since. I believe there have been no more such threats, and should there be hereafter, I doubt not that death would be the consequence.

I found employment, the third day after my arrival, in stowing a sloop with a load of oil. It was new, dirty, and hard work for me; but I went at it with a glad heart and a willing hand. I was now my own master. It was a happy moment, the rapture of which can be understood only by those who have been slaves. It was the first work, the reward of which was to be entirely my own. There was no Master Hugh standing ready, the moment I earned the money, to rob me of it. I worked that day with a pleasure I had never before experienced. I was at work for myself and newly-married wife. It was to me the starting-point of a new existence. When I got through with that job, I went in pursuit of a job of calking; but such was the strength of prejudice against color, among the white calkers, that they refused to work with me, and of course I could get no employment.[3] Finding my trade of no immediate benefit, I threw off my calking habiliments, and prepared myself to do any kind of work I could get to do. Mr. Johnson kindly let me have his wood-horse and saw, and I very soon found myself a plenty of work. There was no work too hard—none too dirty. I was ready to saw wood, shovel coal, carry wood, sweep the chimney, or roll oil casks,—all of which I did for nearly three years in New Bedford, before I became known to the anti-slavery world.

In about four months after I went to New Bedford, there came a young man to me, and inquired if I did not wish to take the *Liberator*. I told him I did; but, just having made my escape from slavery, I remarked that I was unable to pay for it then. I, however, finally became a subscriber to it. The paper came, and I read it from week to week with such feelings as it would be quite idle for me to attempt to describe. The paper became my meat and my drink. My soul was set all on fire. Its sympathy for my brethren in bonds—its scathing denunciations of slaveholders—its faithful exposures of slavery—and its powerful attacks upon the upholders of the institution—sent a thrill of joy through my soul, such as I had never felt before!

I had not long been a reader of the *"Liberator,"* before I got a pretty correct idea of the principles, measures and spirit of the anti-slavery reform. I took right hold of the cause. I could do but little; but what I could, I did with a joyful heart, and never felt happier than when in an anti-slavery meeting. I seldom had much to say at the meetings, because what I wanted to say was said so much better by others. But, while attending an anti-slavery convention at Nantucket, on the 11th of August, 1841, I felt strongly moved to speak, and was at the same time much urged to do so by Mr. William C. Coffin, a gentleman who had heard me speak in the colored people's meeting at New Bedford. It was a severe cross, and I took it up reluctantly. The truth was, I felt myself a slave, and the idea of speaking to white people weighed me down. I spoke but a few moments, when I felt a degree of freedom, and said what I desired with considerable ease. From that time until now, I have been engaged in pleading the cause of my brethren—with what success, and with what devotion, I leave those acquainted with my labors to decide.

Appendix

I find, since reading over the foregoing Narrative, that I have, in several instances, spoken in such a tone and manner, respecting religion, as may possibly lead those unacquainted with my religious views to suppose me an opponent of all religion. To remove the liability of such misapprehension, I deem it proper to append the following brief explanation. What I have said respecting and against religion, I mean strictly to apply to the *slaveholding religion* of this land, and with no possible reference to Christianity proper; for, between the Christianity of this land, and the Christianity of Christ, I recognize the widest possible difference—so wide, that to receive the one as good, pure, and holy, is of necessity to reject the other as bad, corrupt, and wicked. To be the friend of the one, is of necessity to be the enemy of the other. I love the pure, peaceable, and impartial Christianity of Christ: I therefore hate the corrupt, slaveholding, women-whipping, cradle-plundering, partial and hypocritical Christianity of this land. Indeed, I can see no reason, but the most deceitful one, for calling the religion of this land Christianity. I look upon it as the climax of all misnomers, the boldest of all frauds, and the grossest of all libels. Never was there a clearer case of "stealing the livery of the court of heaven to serve the devil in." I am filled with unutterable loathing when I contemplate the religious pomp and show, together with the horrible inconsistencies, which every where surround me. We have men-stealers for ministers, women-whippers for missionaries, and cradle-plunderers for church members. The man who wields the blood-clotted cowskin during the week fills the pulpit on Sunday, and claims to be a minister of the meek and lowly Jesus. The man who robs me of my earnings at the end of each week meets me as a class-leader on Sunday morning, to show me the way of life, and the path of salvation. He who sells my sister, for purposes of prostitution, stands forth as the pious advocate of purity. He who proclaims it a religious duty to read the Bible denies me the right of learning to read the name of the God who made me. He who is the religious advocate of marriage robs whole millions of its sacred influence, and leaves them to the ravages of wholesale pollution. The warm defender of the sacredness of the family relation is the same that scatters whole families,—sundering husbands and wives, parents and children, sisters and brothers,—leaving the hut vacant, and the hearth desolate. We see the thief preaching against theft, and the adulterer against adultery. We have men sold to build churches, women sold to support the gospel, and babes sold to purchase Bibles for the *poor heathen! All for the glory of God and the good of souls!* The slave auctioneer's bell and the church-going bell chime in with each other, and the bitter cries of the heart-broken slave are drowned in the religious shouts of his pious master. Revivals of religion and revivals in the slave-trade go hand in hand together. The slave prison and the church stand near each other. The clanking of fetters and the rattling of chains in the prison, and the pious psalm and solemn prayer in the church, may be heard at the same time. The dealers in the bodies and souls of men erect their stand in the presence of the pulpit, and they mutually help each other. The dealer gives his blood-stained gold to support the pulpit, and the pulpit, in return, covers his infernal business with the garb of Christianity. Here we have religion and robbery the allies of each other—devils dressed in angels' robes, and hell presenting the semblance of paradise.

> "Just God! and these are they,
> Who minister at thine altar, God of right!
> Men who their hands, with prayer and blessing, lay
> On Israel's ark of light.
>
> What! preach, and kidnap men?
> Give thanks, and rob thy own afflicted poor?
> Talk of thy glorious liberty, and then
> Bolt hard the captive's door?
>
> What! servants of thy own
> Merciful Son, who came to seek and save
> The homeless and the outcast, fettering down
> The tasked and plundered slave!
>
> Pilate and Herod friends!
> Chief priests and rulers, as of old, combine!
> Just God and holy! is that church which lends
> Strength to the spoiler thine?"

The Christianity of America is a Christianity, of whose votaries it may be as truly said, as it was of the ancient scribes and Pharisees,

> "They bind heavy burdens, and grievous to be borne, and lay them on men's shoulders, but they themselves will not move them with one of their fingers. All their works they

do for to be seen of men.—They love the upper-most rooms at feasts, and the chief seats in the synagogues, ... and to be called of men, Rabbi, Rabbi.—But woe unto you, scribes and Pharisees, hypocrites! for ye shut up the kingdom of heaven against men; for ye neither go in yourselves, neither suffer ye them that are entering to go in. Ye devour widows' houses, and for a pretence make long prayers; therefore ye shall receive the greater damnation. Ye compass sea and land to make one proselyte, and when he is made, ye make him twofold more the child of hell than yourselves.—Woe unto you, scribes and Pharisees, hypocrites! for ye pay tithe of mint, and anise, and cumin, and have omitted the weightier matters of the law, judgment, mercy, and faith; these ought ye to have done, and not to leave the other undone. Ye blind guides! which strain at a gnat, and swallow a camel. Woe unto you, scribes and Pharisees, hypocrites! for ye make clean the outside of the cup and of the platter; but within, they are full of extortion and excess.—Woe unto you, scribes and Pharisees, hypocrites! for ye are like unto whited sepulchres, which indeed appear beautiful outward, but are within full of dead men's bones, and of all uncleanness. Even so ye also outwardly appear righteous unto men, but within ye are full of hypocrisy and iniquity."

Dark and terrible as is this picture, I hold it to be strictly true of the overwhelming mass of professed Christians in America. They strain at a gnat, and swallow a camel. Could any thing be more true of our churches? They would be shocked at the proposition of fellowshipping a *sheep*-stealer; and at the same time they hug to their communion a *man*-stealer, and brand me with being an infidel, if I find fault with them for it. They attend with Pharisaical strictness to the outward forms of religion, and at the same time neglect the weightier matters of the law, judgment, mercy, and faith. They are always ready to sacrifice, but seldom to show mercy. They are they who are represented as professing to love God whom they have not seen, whilst they hate their brother whom they have seen. They love the heathen on the other side of the globe. They can pray for him, pay money to have the Bible put into his hand, and missionaries to instruct him; while they despise and totally neglect the heathen at their own doors.

Such is, very briefly, my view of the religion of this land; and to avoid any misunderstanding, growing out of the use of general terms, I mean by the religion of this land, that which is revealed in the words, deeds, and actions, of those bodies, north and south, calling themselves Christian churches, and yet in union with slaveholders. It is against religion, as presented by these bodies, that I have felt it my duty to testify.

I conclude these remarks by copying the following portrait of the religion of the south, (which is, by communion and fellowship, the religion of the north), which I soberly affirm is "true to the life," and without caricature or the slightest exaggeration. It is said to have been drawn, several years before the present anti-slavery agitation began, by a northern Methodist preacher, who, while residing at the south, had an opportunity to see slaveholding morals, manners, and piety, with his own eyes. "Shall I not visit for these things? saith the Lord. Shall not my soul be avenged on such a nation as this?"

A Parody

Come, saints and sinners, hear me tell
How pious priests whip Jack and Nell,
And women buy and children sell,
And preach all sinners down to hell,
  And sing of heavenly union.

They'll bleat and baa, dona like goats,
Gorge down black sheep, and strain at motes,
Array their backs in fine black coats,
Then seize their negroes by their throats,
  And choke, for heavenly union.

 They'll church you if you sip a dram,
And damn you if you steal a lamb;
Yet rob old Tony, Doll, and Sam,
Of human rights, and bread and ham;
  Kidnapper's heavenly union.

They'll loudly talk of Christ's reward,
And bind his image with a cord,
And scold, and swing the lash abhorred,
And sell their brother in the Lord
  To handcuffed heavenly union.

They'll read and sing a sacred song,
And make a prayer both loud and long,
And teach the right and do the wrong,
Hailing the brother, sister throng,
  With words of heavenly union.

We wonder how such saints can sing,
Or praise the Lord upon the wing,
Who roar, and scold, and whip, and sting,
And to their slaves and mammon cling,
  In guilty conscience union.

They'll raise tobacco, corn, and rye,
And drive, and thieve, and cheat, and lie,
And lay up treasures in the sky,
By making switch and cowskin fly,
  In hope of heavenly union.

They'll crack old Tony on the skull,
And preach and roar like Bashan bull,
Or braying ass, of mischief full,

II. THE ABOLITIONIST MISSION

Then seize old Jacob by the wool,
* And pull for heavenly union.*

A roaring, ranting, sleek man-thief,
Who lived on mutton, veal, and beef,
Yet never would afford relief
To needy, sable sons of grief,
* Was big with heavenly union.*

'Love not the world,' the preacher said,
And winked his eye, and shook his head;
He seized on Tom, and Dick, and Ned,
Cut short their meat, and clothes, and bread,
* Yet still loved heavenly union.*

Another preacher whining spoke
Of One whose heart for sinners broke:
He tied old Nanny to an oak,
And drew the blood at every stroke,
* And prayed for heavenly union.*

Two others oped their iron jaws,
And waved their children-stealing paws;
There sat their children in gewgaws;
By stinting negroes' backs and maws,
* They kept up heavenly union.*

All good from Jack another takes,
And entertains their flirts and rakes,
Who dress as sleek as glossy snakes,
And cram their mouths with sweetened cakes;
* And this goes down for union.*

Sincerely and earnestly hoping that this little book may do something toward throwing light on the American slave system, and hastening the glad day of deliverance to the millions of my brethren in bonds—faithfully relying upon the power of truth, love, and justice, for success in my humble efforts—and solemnly pledging my self anew to the sacred cause,—I subscribe myself,

FREDERICK DOUGLASS
LYNN, *Mass., April 28, 1845.*

THE END

Notes

1. She was free.
2. I had changed my name from Frederick *Bailey* to that of *Johnson*.
3. I am told that colored persons can now get employment at calking in New Bedford—a result of anti-slavery effort.

❧ 16 ❧

The Address and Reply on the Presentation of a Testimonial to S. P. Chase

THE COLORED PEOPLE OF CINCINNATI

Samuel Portland Chase (1808–1873), nicknamed by some Kentucky opponents 'the Attorney-General of the Fugitive Slaves', worked through the courts in Ohio in an effort to define the case law affecting the status of slaves as they were in transit in free labour states. Although the verdict went against the abolitionists in Samuel Watson's case, an important legal principle was established sufficient to provide an excuse for the testimonial. Chase's advocacy in this and other cases led to the presentation of an inscribed silver pitcher in recognition of his efforts. Chase represented Ohio in the US Senate, became Governor of Ohio, and was a candidate for the presidential nomination that eventually went to Abraham Lincoln. Secretary of the Treasury in Lincoln's administration, Chase later became Chief Justice of the Supreme Court. The pamphlet is held in the Daniel A. P. Murray Collection, Library of Congress.

Address and Reply on the Presentation of a Testimonial to S.P. Chase, by the Colored People of Cincinnati, with some Account of the Case of Samuel Watson.

Introduction

It has been thought by many who are interested in the elevation and progress of the whole American People, that the recent public presentation to Mr. S. P. Chase, of a valuable and beautiful testimonial of grateful regard by the Colored People of Cincinnati, was an incident too novel in its occurrence, and far too interesting in its moral aspect, to receive only the passing record of the daily press.

Source: 'The Address and Reply on the Presentation of a Testimonial to S.P. Chase, by the Colored People of Cincinnati', Cincinnati: Henry W. Derby Co., 1845.

Attentive observers have long appreciated the fact, that our colored population are not less sensitive to kindness than patient of aggression and contumely; but the delicate and appropriate manner in which this sensibility was manifested on the occasion referred to, has attracted no inconsiderable attention in this community, and certainly indicates a refinement of sentiment, which every lover of the well-being and progress of society must regard with peculiar and cordial interest.

The immediate occasion of the offering, was the elaborate and masterly argument of Mr. Chase in the late case of Samuel Watson, although that effort was well understood to be but the sequel to other and previous services in the cause of the Oppressed, which have often marked the professional and private life of that gentleman, and have awakened a strong sense of gratitude among a class, who are the more sensible to considerate kindness and disinterested service, from experiencing so frequently the reverse.

The case of Watson deserves a passing notice. A succinct statement is as follows:

On the morning of the 21st of January, 1845, before day, one Henry Hoppess, having in charge the colored man Samuel Watson, arrived at Cincinnati on the steamer Ohio Belle. Shortly after the boat was made fast to the shore, Watson was missing. In the evening he was found by Hoppess upon the landing: not attempting, and probably not thinking of an escape. He was seized, lodged in the Watch House, and on the following morning taken before a Magistrate, in order to obtain a certificate for his removal as a fugitive from service under the Act of Congress of 1793.

At this point in the proceedings a writ of Habeas Corpus was allowed by the Honorable N. C. Read, one of the Judges of the Supreme Court of Ohio, in obedience to which Watson was taken before him and Hoppess was required to justify his detention.

With this purpose, Hoppess alleged that Watson was a slave in Virginia; that his master had taken him to Arkansas, and, having himself returned to Virginia, had died, having previously conveyed Watson to one Floyd: that as the agent of Floyd he had proceeded to Arkansas, obtained possession of Watson, and was returning with him to Virginia, when, the boat having arrived at Cincinnati very early in the morning, Watson escaped.

The proof showed that at the time of the alleged escape the boat was made fast to the Ohio shore, and was inside of low water mark: that, at the time Watson was siezed on the landing, he was making no attempt to escape: and that those who first noticed the boat on the morning of her arrival neither observed any indications, nor heard any suggestion of an escape having taken place.

The argument for Watson was opened by Messrs. Birney and Johnson, and closed by Mr. Chase. They insisted,

1. That there had been no escape.

2. That the escape, if there was one, was from one place in Ohio to another place in the same State, and so not within the constitutional provision as to escaping servants,

nor the provisions of the Act of 1793.

3. That the boat at the time of the escape was within the State of Ohio, being fastened to the Ohio shore and within low water mark; to which line by consent of all, the territory of the State extends; and beyond this line, they insisted, to the middle of the river.

4. That the holding of persons as slaves in Arkansas was repugnant to the treaty with France, which provided for the admission of all the inhabitants of the territory to the immunities of citizens of the United States; and also to the fifth amendment of the Constitution, which declares that no person shall be deprived of liberty without due process of law, and applies, at least, to all national Territories, and States created out of such: and that Watson having been taken by his alleged master from Virginia to Arkansas was free there, and could not be reclaimed.

5. That the Act of 1793, relating to fugitives from service, was unconstitutional: that no power was conferred by the Constitution upon Congress to legislate upon the subject; and if there was, yet the provisions of this Act, authorizing seizure without warrant, trial without jury and without opportunity to the defendant to cross-examine witnesses against him, and judgment by a State Magistrate, irresponsible in the exercise of this authority to the State or the United States, and compensated only according to his own bargain with the Plaintiff, were clearly unconstitutional.

6. That the ordinance of 1787 confined the right of reclaiming escaping servants, as to the Territory of the United States northwest of the River Ohio and as to the States erected out of it, to cases of escape from the original States: and that Watson, not having escaped from an original State, could not, therefore, be reclaimed as a fugitive from service.

These considerations failed to influence the Court to their whole extent. Judge Read decided that slavery might exist in Arkansas; that the treaty with France was for the cession of territory and allegiance, and did not change the relations of persons and the rights of property. He also held that a slave, escaping to Ohio from a new State, is subject to recaption precisely as though the escape had been from one of the original States. The decision also sustained the constitutionality of the Act of Congress, authorizing the present summary process against escaping servants; and upon the leading point in the case, respecting the jurisdiction on the Ohio river, the Court, although laying down the principle that slavery was strictly local, still held that a master navigating the Ohio river, whilst upon the water, is within the jurisdiction of Virginia or Kentucky for the purpose of retaining the right to his slave; and that, although the boat which contained them should be fastened to the shore of a free State, yet a slave going at large would be liable to recaption, as a fugitive from one State into another—this being an incident to the common right of navigation, secured at an early day to the people of the States bordering upon the Ohio river. The learned judge did not intimate, whether the same rule, thus applied to the Ohio, would extend to navigable streams which were wholly included within the body of a free State.

Although the result of this opinion was to subject Watson to the power of Hoppess, yet some principles were recognized of the most vital importance to the free States, and the full force of which, if applied to the case of Watson, might have reversed the issue, and vindicated his claim to himself.

His honor the Judge emphatically recognized the strictly local character of Slavery.—
"Slavery" said he,

> is wrong inflicted by force and supported alone by the municipal power of the State or
> Territory in which it exists. It is opposed to the principles of natural justice and right,
> and is the mere creature of positive law.
>
> If a master bring his slave into the State of Ohio, he loses all power over him. The
> relation of master and slave is strictly territorial. If the master take his slave beyond
> the influence of the laws which create the relation, it fails—there is nothing to support
> it, and they stand as man and man. The slave is free by the laws of the State to which
> he has been brought by the master, [who is unable] to force him back to the State
> which recognizes and enforces the relation of master and slave. At one time I was of
> the opinion he had the right to passage through a free State with his slave. This
> probably would harmonize with the spirit of the compromise upon this subject. But
> upon more careful examination, I am satisfied the master must lose his slave, if he
> brings him into a free State, unless the slave voluntarily returns to a state of slavery;
> because the master loses all power over the slave by the law of the State to which he
> has brought him; and there is no other law authorizing him to remove him. The
> Constitution of the United States only recognizes the right of recapture of a fugitive,
> held to service in one state, escaping into another. The person owing service must
> escape from the State where such service is owed, into another State. The Act of
> Congress, carrying into effect the constitutional provision, authorizes a recaption only
> where there has been an escape from the State where the service was owed into another
> State. If there has been no such escape, the master has no right of recaption, and the
> slave may go where he pleases—the master has lost all control over him.

Judge Read thus explicitly recognized a doctrine which was first fully presented to
the Courts of Ohio by Mr. Chase, in 1837, in his arguments in the case of Matilda,
before the Superior Court of Cincinnati, and in the case of The Senate against James
G. Birney, before the Supreme Court of Ohio: but which, at that time, met with
comparatively little favor. It is somewhat remarkable that Judge Read was the
opposing counsel to Mr. Chase in both these cases. This fact gives point to his
remark, which will be remembered by those present at the trial, that the transition
from his former to his present opinion, might be characterized as 'progress.' The
popular sympathy with the claimant of his liberty, and the evident impression
produced upon public sentiment, by the considerations urged in his behalf, were
indications, no less significant of 'progress.'

After the result of the case was known, it was determined at a meeting of the colored
people, that an appropriate mark of grateful respect should be tendered to each of
the counsel for Watson, who had declined the usual compensation for professional
services. As a part of these arrangements, a committee was appointed to super-
intend the preparation of a Silver Pitcher, to be presented to Mr. Chase, not merely
as a token of their gratitude for his efforts in this case, but also as a testimonial of
their grateful appreciation of other and former services. The fabrication of the gift
was entrusted to Messrs. E. D. Kinsey, whose taste and skill are fully attested by
the beauty of design, and elegance of finish, which marked the work they produced.
It was copied from a fine antique model, with little ornament beyond the slight
chasing of the borders and handle. It bore the following inscription:

TESTIMONIAL OF GRATITUDE
TO
SALMON P. CHASE,
FROM
THE COLORED PEOPLE OF CINCINNATI,
FOR HIS
Various public services in behalf of the oppressed
and particularly for his
ELOQUENT ADVOCACY OF THE RIGHTS OF MAN
in the case of Samuel Watson,
who was claimed as a fugitive slave,
Feb. 12, 1845.

The evening of Tuesday, the 6th of May, was fixed for the presentation. At the appointed time, a very large assemblage occupied the Union Baptist Church, where the ceremony was to take place. The Rev. Mr. Satchell, a colored minister, first invoked the Divine blessing upon the transactions of the evening. An address to Mr. Chase, in behalf of the colored people, by Mr. A. J. Gordon, himself one of them, accompanied the presentation.

After Mr. Chase had replied, the hymn, "America," was sung with great taste and feeling. The exercises closed with a benediction, by the Rev. Mr. Satchell.[1]

Mr. Gordon's Address.

Mr. Chase:—

Upon me, sir, has devolved the agreeable duty of presenting to you on behalf of the Colored People of Cincinnati, this Pitcher, as a token of their high regard and deep sense of gratitude towards you, for your remembrance of our brethren in bonds as bound with them; and also for your zealous and disinterested advocacy of the rights and privileges of all classes of your fellow-citizens, irrespective of clime, color or condition. In the manner of your acceptance of it, in this public manifestation of your identification with the cause of the slave, we have but another evidence, added to the many which have preceded it, of the high moral daring of your nature, and the disinterested patriotism that has led you to take sides in opposition to American slavery and American prejudice. During a period of many years, sir, we have viewed with silent admiration, and with feelings of the liveliest gratitude, the prompt and efficient aid you have rendered the cause of humanity in your professional capacity. Whenever the friendless objects of slaveholding cupidity have found themselves by the Providence of God, upon our free soil, and have sought through the instrumentality of the Ordinance of 1787, enacted by the wisdom and patriotism of the Fathers of the American Revolution, to assert their claims to those rights which our boasted Declaration of Independence declares to be inalienable; their right to themselves, to their liberty, and to the uncontroled pursuit of those objects which would alone conduce to their individual happiness, they have ever found in you, sir, a firm, zealous and devoted friend. Scorning the proffered price of blood from the hand of the oppressor, and disdaining the prostitution of your great legal talents in subserving the cause of oppression, and in riveting fetters on the limbs of a helpless fellow being, you have invariably been found ranked on the side of the oppressed, in opposition to the unrighteous claims of the oppressor. Proudly and pre-eminently conspicuous among the many cases in which you have thus distinguished yourself as a friend to the rights of man, stands the recent case of Samuel Watson: pre-eminent not only on account of the great and unsurpassed legal effort that you made to dash from his lips the bitter cup of Slavery, and the deep and heart felt sympathy you manifested for his hapless fate; but also in the marked and decisive evidence afforded in the adjudication of his case of the advance of anti-slavery sentiment in the minds of a large class of your fellow citizens, and the triumph of a principle which, for years, you have contended for, amid obloquy and reproach. Before the promulgation of anti-slavery sentiment in this State, it was of common occurrence to witness at our public landing, in their transmigration to a Southern market, coffles of human beings, manacled and chained like beasts of burden, and upon our principal streets and thoroughfares was frequently to be seen some lordling of the patriarchal institution, with his human chattels in the form of obsequious slaves, desecrating the free soil of our State, and trampling under foot her fundamental law. And strange as it may appear, during all that lengthened period, none thought to question their right, and none sought to vindicate the insulted majesty of the Law; and when, at length, you together with a noble band of coadjutors, planting yourselves on the Ordinance of 1787, enacted, as we believe, by the Patriots of the Revolution, as a barrier against the growth of the Slave Power, and as a living testimony against the foul system, but which had been suffered to lie in the grave of pro-slavery forgetfulness by their degenerate sons, sought to recall it into life, and give it that vitality necessary to vindicate the memory of the departed patriots who promulgated it, from the charge of hypocrisy, you were met by the great body of your fellow citizens with the most fierce and bitter hostility: you were denounced as officious intermeddlers with the rights of your fellow citizens of other States, plotters of treason, exciters of domestic feuds, enemies to the interest and prosperity of your native State: in short, no term of reproach was deemed too harsh, by your opponents, to express their feelings of hostility towards you, for merely enforcing a fundamental law of the State, and thereby saving from hapless bondage, from unrequited toil, from a condition of brutal degradation—which any of your opponents would willingly spill the last drop of their heart's blood, rather than submit—to fellow beings, made in the likeness of God, and destined to the same high hopes and glorious immortality as the proudest of your opponents and their oppressors. But, conscious of the purity of your motives, and the rectitude of the principles by which you were governed, and believing with the poet, that

> Thrice is he armed, who hath his quarrel just,

armed with the omnipotent panoply of Truth, and relying upon the arm of Him who maketh even the wrath of man to praise him, you pursued the even tenor of your way, unawed by the fierce and bitter opposition which marked every step of your progress, until at length you had the proud satisfaction of hearing the principle which, when you first asserted it, was pronounced a mere chimera of fanaticism, proclaimed in the adjudication of the case of Watson, as the established law of the State. And, although we cannot congratulate you that by your matchless efforts in his behalf, you won freedom for Watson, yet by this decision you won a TROPHY FOR FREEDOM: you secured the free soil of our State from further pollution by the footprints of Slavery.

Equally satisfactory must it have been to you, Sir, to mark the progress of Anti-Slavery sentiment in the minds of all classes of your fellow citizens, which this trial evinced. Instead of the reviling and reproaches which had heretofore marked your efforts in behalf of crushed humanity, the gushing sympathy of approving hearts overleaping the barrier of judicial order and decorum, attested their appreciation of your efforts, and their sympathy with the oppressed, by irrepressible applause.

But not alone in your professional capacity, have you distinguished yourself as the friend of the slave, and the opponent of American slavery, but as a private citizen of this great Confederacy in the discharge of all the duties pertaining to that high character, you have exerted all the moral influence you possess, and all the powers of your vigorous mind, for their disenthralment, and the entire extinction, in a legal and constitutional manner, of the foul system, throughout the length and breadth of the land. In your deep devotion and zealous advocacy of the rights and liberties of our enslaved brethren, you have not been unmindful of the deprivation of rights endured, and the wrongs inflicted upon the free colored people of this country. Deprived of all participation in the affairs of Government, yet compelled to bear our full share of its burdens: taxed, without a voice in the selection of those by whom the tax is imposed; and subjected, in this State, together with others, to the most invidious distinctions, created by statute, touching our dearest and most sacred rights;—our condition, by the operation of an unjust and perverted public sentiment, which meets us at the cradle and follows us to the tomb, is rendered worse than that of aliens in our native land. To right these wrongs, to redress these grievances, to wipe from off the statute books of our State and Country all invidious distinctions founded on color, to correct that unmanly and wicked public sentiment which crushes us to the earth, and which has no foundation in the naturally just and generous emotions of the human heart, but is the mere creature of a vicious education, you have labored both in your professional capacity and as a private citizen, with a zeal and devotion which commands the warmest gratitude of our hearts, and should entitle you to the gratitude and admiration of every true lover of liberty, truth, and justice.

I will not trespass too much upon the natural feeling of aversion that all good and great minds possess to the emblazonment of their virtuous deeds within their hearing, by detailing all of the many acts in which you have served the cause of our down-trodden and oppressed people; but let me assure you, sir, that each and all of them are engraven on the tablets of our hearts, and as long as memory retains her seat, will be held in grateful recollection. In conclusion, sir, permit me to add that the prayers of thousands of grateful hearts daily ascend to the God of the oppressed, imploring divine protection and blessings upon you; and that you may soon be permitted to witness the triumph of the measures you have so nobly contended for—the redemption of the slave and the removal of every vestige of oppression and prejudice from our beloved Country; and that, when in the providence of God you shall be called from your earthly labors, and, together with the oppressor and the oppressed, appear before the august Bar, you may be greeted with the welcome plaudit from the lips of Him who came on earth to open the prison doors and undo the heavy burdens, of "Well done thou good and faithful servant, enter into the joys of thy Lord;" "For inasmuch as you did it unto the least of these my brethren, you did it unto me!"

Reply of Mr. Chase

I accept, Sir, with peculiar satisfaction, the beautiful gift which you tender to me in behalf of the Colored People of Cincinnati. If I fail to express adequately my thanks to you, let me trust that you will attribute the failure, in part, at least, to the novelty of the position which I now occupy. It is, indeed, a novel position. When as a boy, I first knew the people of this city, if any one had hazarded the prediction, that in the course of some twenty years, the colored inhabitants, then hardly in a better condition than slaves, would be so far advanced as to offer to public observation, the scene witnessed here and now, he would have been looked upon as beside himself. Little did I imagine that I should ever meet you as I meet you now, and be myself an actor in such circumstances as now surround us.

Let me, however, most explicitly, and from the heart, disclaim all pretension to the praise you, sir, have bestowed upon me. I do not desire to be regarded as a leader in the contest for Universal Freedom; but simply as one of the rank and file. I see here, to-night, men who acted earlier, and have done far more than I. I can only take credit, if I take credit at all, for not being unwilling to learn and to do. Nor in what I have done can I claim to have acted from any peculiar consideration of the colored people as a separate and distinct class in the community; but from the simple conviction that all the individuals of that class, are members of the community, and in virtue of their manhood, entitled to every original right enjoyed by any other member. I am only one of a great number, who adopt the opinion that, in a country of democratic institutions, there is no reliable security for the rights of any, unless the rights of all are, also, secure. In a Monarchy or an Aristocracy, the rights, or rather privileges, of a class may be created by law and secured by law. But in a Democracy, which recognizes no classes and no privileges, every man must be protected in his just rights, or no man can be, by law. The moment the law excludes a portion of the community from its equal regard, it divides the community into higher and lower classes, and introduces all the evils of the Aristocratic principle. Henceforth, in that community, rights, in the proper sense of that word, cease to exist. Instead of rights, there are privileges for the higher classes, and restrictions for the inferior. We feel, therefore, that all legal distinctions between individuals of the same community, founded in any such circumstances as color, origin, and the like, are hostile to the genius of our institutions, and incompatible with the true theory of American Liberty. God forbid, that we should fail to sympathise, truly and deeply, with the poor, the destitute, the oppressed, the enslaved colored people of our land; or to exert ourselves strenuously in their behalf; but let us not take to ourselves too much credit for sympathy or effort, since our own rights as well as theirs, are involved in the struggle in which we are engaged, and every day's experience adds fresh strength to the conviction, that slavery and oppression must cease, or American Liberty must perish.

There are, say, three millions of colored people in this country; two and a half millions are enslaved; half a million are free. In Massachusetts, and in most if not all the New England States, the colored man and the white man are absolutely equal before the law. In New York the colored man is restricted as to the right of suffrage by a property qualification: in other respects the same equality prevails. In the other Free States they are generally excluded from the right of suffrage. In Ohio they are excluded from this right by a constitutional provision. Various legal provisions deny to them the benefits of public instruction, of testimony in courts of justice, and even of residence in the State, unless upon degrading and oppressive conditions. These legal disabilities are added in this State, to that prejudice which, every where, throughout the whole land, is as a rod of iron to smite, and a chain of iron to bind, in the hand of Oppression.

I embrace with pleasure, this opportunity of declaring my disapprobation of that clause in the constitution which denies to a portion of the colored people the right of suffrage. True Democracy makes no enquiry about the color of the skin, or the place of nativity, or other similar circumstance of condition.—Whatever it sees a man, it recognizes a being endowed by his Creator with original inalienable rights. In communities of men, it recognizes no distinctions founded on mere arbitrary will. I regard, therefore, the exclusion of the colored people as a body from the elective franchise as incompatible with true democratic principles. I am aware that this exclusion is effected by a constutional provision, and propose no action against the constitution. But, whenever a convention shall be called to revise that instrument, I trust that this antisuffrage restriction will be erased. It is, in fact, already as ridiculous in practice as it is wrong in theory. A decision of the Supreme Court has established the rule that all persons nearer white than half, are white within the meaning of the constitution and laws, and entitled to all the privileges of white citizens. It becomes necessary, therefore, in every case, when a vote is tendered at the polls, to scrutinize the complexion and ascertain the exact shade. There are voters here, doubtless—there are certainly voters in the State, distinguished too by personal worth and political position, who would have reason to fear an impartial application of such test.

The exclusion of colored children from the schools, is, in my judgment, a clear infringement of the Constitution and a palpable breach of trust. Before the organization of the State Government, the Congress of the United States appropriated one thirty-sixth of all land in the State to the purposes of public instruction. The grant was of section sixteen in each township, or an equivalent quantity of land "to the inhabitants of the township for the use of schools." When the State Constitution was formed, no person dreamed of excluding the colored inhabitants of any township from the benefits of this provision. On the contrary, the constitution expressly declares that the

> schools, colleges, and universities endowed in whole or in part from revenues arising from donations, made by the United States, shall be open for the reception of scholars, students and teachers, of every grade, without any distinction or preference whatever, contrary to the intent for which said donations were made.

For near thirty years after the adoption of the constitution, no attempt was made to exclude any portion of the inhabitants of the States from the benefits of the provision thus sacredly guaranteed to all. In 1831, for the first time, the exclusion of the colored children was effected by a legislative enactment, which is yet in force. It cannot be doubted, it seems to me, that this enactment, is repugnant to the constitution. It is certainly inconsistent with the maxims of sound policy and wise legislation, which require the highest possible instruction of every member of the community.

But exclusion from the schools is hardly so great an evil as exclusion from the witness box, in all cases where either party is a white person. Judge King, in his admirable report on the black laws, submitted to the Senate of Ohio in 1838, demonstrated to the satisfaction of all impartial men, the unconstitutionality of this provision of the law. A similar proposition for the exclusion of colored witnesses was submitted in the convention for framing the constitution, and was rejected. On the contrary the constitution declared that all courts should be open, and that every person, for any injury inflicted, should have redress without denial or delay. Where is the utility of such a provision, if the law may deny to litigants all resort to witnesses necessary to establish their rights. Suppose two persons, one white, the other colored, arraigned for crime: both are innocent, but circumstances are strong against both: the only witness who can conclusively establish the fact of innocence is a black man. In this case the white man may suffer; the colored man will escape. Reverse the case: suppose them both guilty, and the only witness to their guilt a colored man: the white man will escape, and the colored man be convicted. This law, also, enables white men to employ the agency of colored men in every description of crime with comparative impunity to themselves. It exposes the colored people to every species of violence and outrage from base and unprincipled whites, who are entirely secure from punishment, so long as they perpetrate their villanies only in the presence of colored witnesses. It is, in fact, a standing license to fraud and oppression, and a solemn legislative sanction to crime. Such a law cannot fail to exert the most disastrous influences upon public morals.

Such being the character of this legislation, it is not surprising that almost all humane and benevolent persons are opposed to it. Last winter, numerous petitions, praying for its repeal, were presented to the Legislature. The petition from this city was subscribed without party distinction, by our most respected merchants, by our most distinguished professional men, by our most venerated ministers of religion; in fine, by our best citizens, of every occupation. But the law still disgraces the statute book. The claims of humanity and justice have been postponed to the supposed interests of party.

The statute to which I have just referred, is enforced by the Courts. I am about to refer to another, which depends rather for its execution on popular sentiment represented by the trustees of the several townships. I allude to the provision requiring bonds for good behavior, and support in the case of pauperism, from colored immigrants. This provision has, for the most part, been suffered to repose as a dead letter on the statute book. Has the minister of the Gospel, who has invoked the divine blessing on the transactions of this evening, given bonds for his good behavior? Have you, sir,—who with so much feeling, and so much ability, and let me add, so much more than justice to my humble efforts, have represented the colored people here to-night,—have you given such bonds? It has not been needed. The bonds given by you are no other than those given by all good citizens—conscience, reputation, personal interest, social and domestic ties. I am glad of it; I rejoice that the public sentiment is better than the law, and has repealed the law. I trust that ere long the Legislature will be irresistibly urged, by the popular voice, to give the sanction of legal form to the repeal which has been, in fact, already effected by opinion.

I arraign the whole policy of our legislation in relation to our colored population. I deny its justice; I deny its expediency. I arraign it as wrong in principle, and demoralizing in tendency, at the bar of sound reason and enlightened opinion. I demand in the name of our common manhood, and our common Christianity, and our common destiny, the reversal of this policy, and the abrogation of this legislation. The colored people are not alone interested in this matter. Every law on the statute book so wrong and mean that it cannot be executed, or felt, if executed, to be oppressive and unjust, tends to the overthrow of all law, by separating in minds of the people, the idea of law from the idea of right. The iron of oppression, if it enters into the soul of the oppressed, poisons, with its cankering rust, the hand of the oppressor.

Let me turn now, for a moment to the condition of the enslaved. They number two millions and a half. I claim for these the rights which the Constitution and the Law, rightly interpreted, secure to them. I claim that nowhere, unless within the limits of the original States, can a single person be enslaved, except in violation of the Constitution and the Law. I maintain that the Declaration of Independence and the Constitution of the United States, are the expressions of the anti slavery sentiment of an anti slavery people. In the former, these expressions assumed the form of a solemn proclamation of the National Creed, on the subject of Human Rights. In the latter, these expressions took the shape of a permanent declaration of the National Will embodied as the Fundamental Law of the land. The Declaration assumed the natural equality of all men as the foundation principle of all just government. The constitution, acting on things as it found them, established the National government, with such powers and such limitations of power, as would, it was then thought, secure the final conformity of the actual condition of the people to the theory of the Declaration. The policy of the the Government, at that day, was clearly indicated by the Ordinance of 1787. This celebrated Ordinance excludes Slavery from the Territory of the Nation. The same instrument provides for the creation of five non-slaveholding States out of this Territory. This provision, it was supposed, would secure the permanent preponderance of anti slavery influence in the Government. It would have had this effect, had not new slaveholding Territory been subsequently acquired, out of which Congress, violating the Constitution and disregarding the established National Policy, has created five additional slaveholding States.

In the case of Watson, of which, sir, you have so feelingly spoken, the constitutional limitations of slavery were fully discussed. In that case it was my part to re-state the positions and re-iterate the reasonings of the able lawyers associated with me. I may be permitted, therefore, to say that, in my judgment, the positions were sound and the arguments unanswered. The first of these positions, and that on which the whole argument hinged, was that the Constitution was not designed to uphold slavery, and conferred no power on Congress to establish, continue, or sanction slaveholding any where. We also maintained that slaveholding could not be continued any where without the sanction and aid of positive law. Did these propositions, sir, need any other demonstration than a simple inspection of the Constitution furnishes to the first, and every man's consciousness furnishes to the second? Surely, Slavery did not descend from Heaven, as some Divine profanely teach; it came from beneath, it did not come down from above. Let us hope, however, that it will go down, and that right speedily to the place of its origin, and know no resurrection. Slavery is an institution of force. If I claim to own you, sir, and require you to do some service for me, and you refuse, and the law puts forth the power of the community, in aid of mine, to compel you to submit to my disposal, and you are compelled to submit, then you are a slave. Congress is not authorized to exert any such power in behalf of the master. Congress is expressly prohibited from exerting any such power by the fifth amendment of the Constitution, which declares that

> no person shall be deprived of Life, Liberty, or Property, without due process of law.

How, then, could Slavery continue in the territory of Louisiana, after its acquisition to the United States? There was—there could be no valid law in the Territory incompatible with the Constitution which forbade that any person should be deprived of liberty without due process of law. There was—there could be no law in the Territory which did not exist either through the adoption or by the enactment of Congress, or of the Territorial Legislature, which derived all its power from Congress. Congress could not adopt laws which it could not enact, nor confer a power on the Territorial Legislature which it did not itself possess. Congress has no power to legalize the practice of slaveholding. The practice of slaveholding, therefore, in the Territory, could not be legalized. Nor could it be legalized in any State created out of the Territory, unless it can be maintained that a part of the people of any one of the States in this Union, can convert another part into property if they can get possession of the Legislature, and have physical force enough to enforce its detestable enactments.

I have no doubt of the correctness of these positions, or of the soundness of the inevitable inference from them, that slaveholding in Arkansas is unconstitutional, and consequently that Watson, having been conveyed to Arkansas by his Virginia master, was free. But I was aware that this doctrine was too little in accordance with the received pro slavery theories of constitutional construction, to find much favor upon a first hearing, and was not disappointed that the Judge did not acquiesce in it. I expect, however, to live to see it recognized in all Courts as sound law.

I was disappointed that Watson was not set free on another ground. The Judge admitted that Slavery was strictly local, that the moment any person held as a slave, not within the constitutional exception of persons held to service in one State and escaping into another, passed out of slaveholding territory, he was beyond the reach of slaveholding law, and therefore no longer a slave, but a Man, free by Divine Right.

It was proved that the boat on which Watson was travelling, in charge of Hoppess, was within low water mark, attached to the Ohio shore, and therefore not merely within the State, but a part, as it were, of her soil. It was not pretended that Watson was a fugitive upon the boat. He was free then, there; free to go whither he pleased; free to every intent. No provision for the navigation of the river by the citizens of the different States, could prevent this consequence; for it was a necessary result of the fact that Watson was in Ohio, and not a fugitive. The distinguished Judge, who heard this case, referred to his own change of opinion. Once he thought that masters might travel with a slave through the State; now, however, he had become satisfied that if a slave was once landed on the shore, with the consent of the master, he ceased to be a slave, because beyond the reach of slave law. He said this was progress; and it was so. I only wish he had made a little more progress in the same direction. We should not, then, have had occasion to deplore, as we now do, the surrender of a man, rightfully free, by the Magistracy of Ohio, to life-long slavery.

But such occurrences as these should only arouse us to demand in more peremptory tones, the restriction of Slavery within its original limits. We ask nothing unconstitutional. We make no war on the Constitution. We defend it. We demand, for all, the rights which it guarantees. We are determined to carry out its anti slavery principles to practical consequences. We act in the spirit of our Fathers, and are guided by their example. We act as we believe they would act were they living, and not dead.

I am certainly gratified that my humble services have procured for me this token of your approbation and esteem. I trust, however, that the gratification felt by me, is not altogether personal or selfish. That ready appreciation of benefits received, or rather of efforts honestly and sincerely intended to benefit, which the proceeding of this night evinces, affords an ample refutation of the base and vulgar calumny that the colored people are incapable of refined sentiment or grateful feeling. The proceeding of this night has a value beyond this. It suggests—may I not say, proves, that the best way to ensure the peaceful dwelling together of different races, is the cordial reciprocation of benefits, not the mutual infliction of injuries. Viewed in this aspect, the occasion has a value far beyond that of the gift. I thank you for both; for the one in my own behalf; for the other in behalf of the great cause of Human Freedom and Progress.

Permit me, sir, before I close, to congratulate you upon the visibly improved condition of the colored people of Cincinnati. Debarred from the public schools, you have established schools of your own; thrust by prejudice into the obscure corners of the edifices in which white men offer prayer, you have erected churches of your own, in which you find freedom to worship God; that God who is no respecter of persons. Excluded from the witness box, you have sought that security which the law denies, in a favorable public opinion propitiated by your good conduct. It is but a few weeks since I was gratified spectator in this place, of the exercises of the Colored High School, and every intelligent countenance and every generous aspiration of that youthful band of happy scholars, added fresh strength to my desire for the advancement of the race to which they belonged. And I envy not the man who could hear without emotion that the colored people of this church, when the storm of a desolating calamity fell lately upon a neighboring city and half destroyed it, stepped forward to the relief of the suffering, with a liberality exceeded by that of few, if any, white congregations.

Such incidents as these remind us of that disinterested humanity with which so many colored people of Philadelphia, when the Yellow Fever was raging in that city, stood by the couches of the sick and the dying, refusing all compensation for their inestimable services. They may remind us also of that disinterested love of country which Jackson eulogized when he summoned the colored people of the far South, to co-operate, under his standard, with their white fellow citizens in repelling the invading foe. Let me exhort you to go forward as you have begun. Be assured that upon yourselves lies the chief responsibility of the work of your social and civil redemption. And if the white oppressor be a fit object of just indignation, what execration should pursue that colored man, who, by his unworthy vices or dishonest actions, gives ground for sweeping charges against the race, and holds back his fellows from the career of advancement. Let not this deep guilt attach to any one of you. Go forward, rather, having perfect faith in your own manhood and God's providence.

> Add to your FAITH, virtue, and to virtue, knowledge, and to knowledge, patience, and to patience, temperance, and to temperance, brotherly kindness, and to brotherly kindness, charity.

For myself I am ready to renew my pledge—and I will venture to speak also in behalf of my co-workers,—that we go straight on, without faltering or wavering, until every vestige of oppression shall be erased from the statute book: until the sun in all his journey from the utmost eastern horizon, through the mid-heaven, till he sinks beyond the western mountains into his ocean bed, shall not behold, in all our broad and glorious land, the foot print of a single slave.

Note

1. The Benediction, at the close of the Presentation, was pronounced by the Rev. W. REYNOLDS; not by the Rev. Mr. Satchell, as erroneously stated.—Ed.

·⦃·17·⦄·

Uncle Tom's Cabin

HARRIET BEECHER STOWE

Uncle Tom's Cabin was the most influential literary work of social criticism to be published in America in the nineteenth century. It was translated into thirty-seven languages (including Welsh), transforming the controversy over Southern slavery from a national into an international issue. Its dramatic vignettes of slave life raised not only public consciousness but also public sympathy. The book boosted the abolitionist cause, and contributed to the climate of opinion feeding the sectional controversies which marked the subsequent decade. When President Lincoln met Harriet Beecher Stowe in Washington, he acknowledged her as 'the little woman who made this great war'. These extracts—the preface and the concluding remarks—give a flavour of the style and the passion which animated the work, and which persuaded a receptive readership to accept its critical commentary upon the institution of slavery.

Preface

The scenes of this story, as its title indicates, lie among a race hitherto ignored by the associations of polite and refined society; an exotic race, whose ancestors, born beneath a tropic sun, brought with them, and perpetuated to their descendants, a character so essentially unlike the hard and dominant Anglo-Saxon race, as for many years to have won from it only misunderstanding and contempt.

But, another and better day is dawning; every influence of literature, of poetry and of art, in our times, is becoming more and more in unison with the great master chord of Christianity, "good will to man."

The poet, the painter, and the artist, now seek out and embellish the common and gentler humanities of life, and, under the allurements of fiction, breathe a humanising and subduing influence, favourable to the development of the great principles of Christian brotherhood.

The hand of benevolence is everywhere stretched out, searching into abuses,

Source: Harriet Beecher Stowe, *Uncle Tom's Cabin*, 1852.

righting wrongs, alleviating distresses, and bringing to the knowledge and sympathies of the world the lowly, the oppressed, and the forgotten.

In this general movement, unhappy Africa at last is remembered; Africa, who began the race of civilisation and human progress in the dim, grey dawn of early time, but who, for centuries, has lain bound and bleeding at the foot of civilised and Christianised humanity, imploring compassion in vain.

But the heart of the dominant race, who have been her conquerors, her hard masters, has at length been turned towards her in mercy; and it has been seen how far nobler it is in nations to protect the feeble than to oppress them. Thanks be to God, the world has at last outlived the slave-trade!

The object of these sketches is to awaken sympathy and feeling for the African race, as they exist among us; to show their wrongs and sorrows, under a system so necessarily cruel and unjust as to defeat and do away with the good effects of all that can be attempted for them, by their best friends, under it.

In doing this, the author can sincerely disclaim any invidious feeling towards those individuals who, often without any fault of their own, are involved in the trials and embarrassments of the legal relations of slavery.

Experience has shown her that some of the noblest of minds and hearts are often thus involved; and no one knows better than they do, that what may be gathered of the evils of slavery from sketches like these, is not the half that could be told, of the unspeakable whole.

In the northern states, these representations may, perhaps, be thought caricatures; in the southern states are witnesses who know their fidelity. What personal knowledge the author has had, of the truth of incidents such as here are related, will appear in its time.

It is a comfort to hope, as so many of the world's sorrows and wrongs have, from age to age, been lived down, so a time shall come when sketches similar to these shall be valuable only as memorials of what has long ceased to be.

When an enlightened and Christianised community shall have, on the shores of Africa, laws, language, and literature, drawn from among us, may then the scenes of the house of bondage be to them like the remembrance of Egypt to the Israelite,— a motive of thankfulness to Him who hath redeemed them!

For, while politicians contend, and men are swerved this way and that by conflicting tides of interest and passion, the great cause of human liberty is in the hands of One, of whom it is said:

"He shall not fail nor be discouraged
 Till He have set judgment in the earth."

"He shall deliver the needy when he crieth,
 The poor, and him that hath no helper."

"He shall redeem their soul from deceit and violence,
 And precious shall their blood be in His sight."

Chapter XLV
Concluding Remarks

The writer has often been inquired of, by correspondents from different parts of the country, whether this narrative is a true one; and to these inquiries she will give one general answer.

The separate incidents that compose the narrative are, to a very great extent, authentic, occurring, many of them, either under her own observation, or that of her personal friends. She or her friends have observed characters the counterpart of almost all that are here introduced; and many of the sayings are word for word as heard herself, or reported to her.

The personal appearance of Eliza, the character ascribed to her, are sketches drawn from life. The incorruptible fidelity, piety and honesty of Uncle Tom, had more than one development, to her personal knowledge. Some of the most deeply tragic and romantic, some of the most terrible incidents, have also their parallel in reality. The incident of the mother's crossing the Ohio river on the ice is a well-known fact. The story of "Old Prue" (Chapter XIX) was an incident that fell under the personal observation of a brother of the writer, then collecting-clerk to a large mercantile house, in New Orleans. From the same source was derived the character of the planter Legree. Of him her brother thus wrote, speaking of visiting his plantation, on a collecting tour: "He actually made me feel of his fist, which was like a blacksmith's hammer, or a nodule of iron, telling me that it was 'calloused with knocking down niggers.' When I left the plantation, I drew a long breath, and felt as if I had escaped from an ogre's den."

That the tragical fate of Tom, also, has too many times had its parallel, there are living witnesses, all over our land, to testify. Let it be remembered that in all Southern states it is a principle of jurisprudence that no person of colored lineage can testify in a suit against a white, and it will be easy to see that such a case may occur wherever there is a man whose passions outweigh his interests, and a slave who has manhood or principle enough to resist his will. There is actually nothing to protect the slave's life, but the *character* of the master. Facts too shocking to be contemplated occasionally force their way to the public ear, and the comment that one often hears made on them is more shocking than the thing itself. It is said, "Very likely such cases may now and then occur, but they are no sample of general practice." If the laws of New England were so arranged that a master could *now and then* torture an apprentice to death, would it be received with equal composure? Would it be said, "These cases are rare, and no samples of general practice"? This injustice is an *inherent* one in the slave system, it cannot exist without it.

The public and shameless sale of beautiful mulatto and quadroon girls has acquired a notoriety, from the incidents following the capture of the *Pearl*. We extract the following from the speech of Hon. Horace Mann, one of the legal counsel for the defendants in that case. He says: "In that company of seventy-six persons, who attempted, in 1848, to escape from the District of Columbia in the schooner *Pearl*, and whose officers I assisted in defending, there were several young and healthy girls, who had those peculiar attractions of form and feature which connoisseurs prize so highly. Elizabeth Russell was one of them. She immediately fell into the slave-trader's fangs, and was doomed for the New Orleans market. The hearts of those that saw her were touched with pity for her fate. They offered eighteen hundred dollars to redeem her; and some there were who offered to give, that would not have much left after the gift; but the fiend of a slave-trader was inexorable. She was despatched to New Orleans; but, when about half way there, God had mercy on her, and smote her with death. There were two girls named Edmundson in the same company. When about to be sent to the same market, an older sister went to the shambles to plead with the wretch who owned them, for the love of God to spare his victims. He bantered her, telling what fine dresses and fine furniture they would have. "Yes," she said, "that may do very well in this life, but what will become of them in the next?" They, too, were sent to New Orleans; but were afterwards redeemed at an enormous ransom and brought back." Is it not plain, from this, that the histories of Emmeline and Cassy may have many counterparts?

Justice, too, obliges the author to state that the fairness of mind and generosity attributed to St. Clare are not without a parallel, as the following anecdote will show. A few years since, a young Southern gentleman was in Cincinnati, with a favorite servant, who had been his personal attendant from a boy. The young man took advantage of this opportunity to secure his own freedom, and fled to the protection of a Quaker, who was quite noted in affairs of this kind. The owner was exceedingly indignant. He had always treated the slave with such indulgence, and his confidence in his affection was such, that he believed he must have been practised upon to induce him to revolt from him. He visited the Quaker, in high anger; but, being possessed of uncommon candor and fairness, was soon quieted by his arguments and representations. It was a side of the subject which he never had heard—never had thought on; and he immediately told the Quaker that, if his slave would, to his own face, say that it was his desire to be free, he would liberate him. An interview was forthwith procured, and Nathan was asked by his young master whether he had ever had any reason to complain of his treatment, in any respect.

"No, Mas'r," said Nathan; "you've always been good to me."

"Well, then, why do you want to leave me?"

"Mas'r may die, and then who get me?—I'd rather be a free man."

After some deliberation, the young master replied, "Nathan, in your place, I think I should feel very much so myself. You are free."

He immediately made him out free papers; deposited a sum of money in the hands of the Quaker, to be judiciously used in assisting him to start in life, and left a very sensible and kind letter of advice to the young man. That letter was for some time in the writer's hands.

The author hopes she has done justice to that nobility, generosity, and humanity, which in many cases characterize individuals at the South. Such instances save us from utter despair of our kind. But she asks any person, who knows the world, are such characters *common*, anywhere?

For many years of her life, the author avoided all reading upon or allusion to the subject of slavery, considering it as too painful to be inquired into, and one which advancing light and civlization would certainly live down. But, since the legislative Act of 1850, when she heard, with perfect surprise and consternation, Christian and humane people actually recommending the remanding escaped fugitives into slavery, as a duty binding on good citizens—when she heard on all hands, from kind, compassionate and estimable people, in the free states of the North, deliberations and discussions as to what Christian duty could be on this head—she could only think, these men and Christians cannot know what slavery is; if they did, such a question could never be open for discussion. And from this arose a desire to exhibit it in a *living dramatic reality*. She has endeavored to show it fairly, in its best and its worst phases. In its *best* aspect, she has, perhaps, been successful; but, oh! who shall say what yet remains untold in that valley and shadow of death, that lies the other side?

To you, generous, noble-minded men and women, of the South—you, whose virtue, and magnanimity and purity of character, are the greater for the severer trial it has encountered—to you is her appeal. Have you not, in your own secret souls, in your own private conversings, felt that there are woes and evils in this accursed system, far beyond what are here shadowed, or can be shadowed? Can it be otherwise? Is *man* ever a creature to be trusted with wholly irresponsible power? And does not the slave system, by denying the slave all legal right of testimony, make every individual owner an irresponsible despot? Can anybody fail to make the inference what the practical result will be? If there is, as we admit, a public sentiment among you, men of honor, justice and humanity, is there not also another kind of public sentiment among the ruffian, the brutal and debased? And cannot the ruffian, the brutal, the debased, by slave law, own just as many slaves as the best and purest? Are the honorable, the just, the high-minded and compassionate, the majority anywhere in this world?

The slave-trade is now, by American law, considered as piracy. But a slave-trade, as systematic as ever was carried on on the coast of Africa, is an inevitable attendant and result of American slavery. And its heart-break and its horrors, *can* they be told?

The writer has given only a faint shadow, a dim picture, of the anguish and despair that are at this very moment riving thousands of hearts, shattering thousands of families, and driving a helpless and sensitive race to frenzy and despair. There are those living who know the mothers whom this accursed traffic has driven to the murder of their children, and themselves seeking in death a shelter from woes more dreaded than death. Nothing of tragedy can be written, can be spoken, can be conceived, that equals the frightful reality of scenes daily and hourly acting on our shores, beneath the shadow of American law, and the shadow of the cross of Christ.

And now, men and women of America, is this a thing to be trifled with, apologized for, and passed over in silence? Farmers of Massachusetts, of New Hampshire, of Vermont, of Connecticut, who read this book by the blaze of your winter-evening fire—strong-hearted, generous sailors and ship-owners of Maine—is this a thing for you to countenance and encourage? Brave and generous men of New York, farmers of rich and joyous Ohio, and ye of the wide prairie states, answer, is this a thing for you to protect and countenance? And you, mothers of America— you who have learned, by the cradles of your own children, to love and feel for all mankind, by the sacred love you bear your child; by your joy in his beautiful, spotless infancy; by the motherly pity and tenderness with which you guide his growing years; by the anxieties of his education; by the prayers you breathe for his soul's eternal good—I beseech you, pity the mother who has all your affections, and not one legal right to protect, guide, or educate, the child of her bosom! By the sick hour of your child; by those dying eyes, which you can never forget; by those last cries, that wrung your heart when you could neither help nor save; by the desolation of that empty cradle, that silent nursery, I beseech you, pity those mothers that are constantly made childless by the American slave-trade! And say, mothers of America, is this a thing to be defended, sympathized with, passed over in silence?

Do you say that the people of the free state have nothing to do with it, and can do nothing? Would to God this were true! But it is not true. The people of the free states have defended, encouraged, and participated; and are more guilty for it, before God, than the South, in that they have *not* the apology of education or custom.

If the mothers of the free states had all felt as they should, in times past, the sons of the free states would not have been the holders, and, proverbially, the hardest masters of slaves; the sons of the free states would not have connived at the extension of slavery, in our national body; the sons of the free states would not, as they do, trade the souls and bodies of men as an equivalent to money, in their mercantile dealings. There are multitudes of slaves temporarily owned and sold again, by merchants in Northern cities; and shall the whole guilt or obloquy of slavery fall only on the South?

Northern men, Northern mothers, Northern Christians, have something more to do than denounce their brethren at the South; they have to look to the evil among themselves.

But, what can any individual do? Of that, every individual can judge. There is one thing that every individual can do, they can see to it that *they feel right*. An atmosphere of sympathetic influence encircles every human being; and the man or woman who *feels* strongly, healthily and justly, on the great interests of humanity, is a constant benefactor to the human race. See, then, to your sympathies in this matter! Are they in harmony with the sympathies of Christ? or are they swayed and perverted by the sophistries of worldly policy?

Christian men and women of the North; still further,—you have another power: you can *pray*! Do you believe in prayer? or has it become an indistinct apostolic tradition? You pray for the heathen abroad; pray also for the heathen at home. And pray for those distressed Christians whose whole chance of religious improvement is an accident of trade and sale;—from whom any adherence to the morals of Christianity is, in many cases, an impossibility, unless they have given them from above the courage and grace of martyrdom.

But still more. On the shores of our free states are emerging the poor, shattered, broken remnants of families, men and women, escaped, by miraculous providences from the surges of slavery, feeble in knowledge, and, in many cases, infirm in moral constitution, from a system which confounds and confuses every principle of Christianity and morality. They come to seek a refuge among you; they come to seek education, knowledge, Christianity.

What do you owe to these poor unfortunates, O Christians? Does not every American Christian owe to the African race some effort at reparation for the wrongs that the American nation has brought upon them? Shall the doors of churches and school-houses be shut upon them? Shall states arise and shake them out? Shall the church of Christ hear in silence the taunt that is thrown at them, and shrink away from the helpless hand that they stretch out, and by her silence, encourage the cruelty that would chase them from our borders? If it must be so, it will be a mournful spectacle. If it must be so, the country will have reason to tremble, when it remembers that the fate of nations is in the hands of One who is very pitiful, and of tender compassion.

Do you say, "We don't want them here; let them go to Africa"?

That the providence of God has provided a refuge in Africa, is, indeed, a great and noticeable fact; but that is no reason why the church of Christ should throw off that responsibility to this outcast race which her profession demands of her.

To fill up Liberia with an ignorant, inexperienced, half-barbarized race, just escaped from the chains of slavery, would be only to prolong, for ages, the period of struggle and conflict which attends the inception of new enterprises. Let the church of the North receive these poor sufferers in the spirit of Christ; receive them to the educating advantages of Christian republican society and schools, until they have attained to somewhat of a moral and intellectual maturity, and then assist them in their passage to those shores, where they may put in practice the lessons they have learned in America.

There is a body of men in the North, comparatively small, who have been doing this; and, as the result, this country has already seen examples of men, formerly slaves, who have rapidly acquired property, reputation, and education. Talent has been developed, which, considering the circumstances, is certainly remarkable; and, for moral traits of honesty, kindness, tenderness of feeling, for heroic efforts and self-denials, endured for the ransom of brethren and friends yet in slavery, they have been remarkable to a degree that, considering the influence under which they were born, is surprising.

The writer has lived, for many years, on the frontier-line of slave states, and has had great opportunities of observation among those who formerly were slaves. They have been in her family as servants; and, in default of any other school to receive them, she has, in many cases, had them instructed in a family school, with her own children. She has also the testimony of missionaries among the fugitives in Canada in coincidence with her own experience; and her deductions, with regard to the capabilities of the race, are encouraging in the highest degree.

The first desire of the emancipated slave, generally, is for *education*. There is nothing that they are not willing to give or do to have their children instructed; and, so far as the writer has observed herself, or taken the testimony of teachers among them, they are remarkably intelligent and quick to learn. The results of schools, founded for them by benevolent individuals in Cincinnati, fully establish this.

The author gives the following statement of facts, on the authority of Professor C. E. Stowe, then of Lane Seminary, Ohio, with regard to emancipated slaves, now resident in Cincinnati; given to show the capability of the race, even without any very particular assistance or encouragement.

The initial letters alone are given. They are all residents of Cincinnati.

"B——. Furniture maker; twenty years in this city; worth ten thousand dollars, all his own earnings; a Baptist.

"C——. Full black; stolen from Africa; sold in New Orleans; been free fifteen years; paid for himself six hundred dollars; a farmer; owns several farms in Indiana; Presbyterian; probably worth fifteen or twenty thousand dollars, all earned by himself.

"K——. Full black; dealer in real estate; worth thirty thousand dollars; about forty years old; free six years; paid eighteen hundred dollars for his family; member of the Baptist church; received a legacy from his master, which he has taken good care of, and increased.

"G——. Full black; coal dealer; about thirty years old; worth eighteen thousand dollars; paid for himself twice, being once defrauded to the amount of sixteen hundred dollars; made all his money by his own efforts—much of it while a slave, hiring his time of his master, and doing business for himself; a fine, gentlemanly fellow.

"W——. Three-fourths black; barber and waiter; from Kentucky; nineteen years free; paid for self and family over three thousand dollars; deacon in the Baptist church.

"G. D——. Three-fourths black; white-washer; from Kentucky; nine years free; paid fifteen hundred dollars for self and family; recently died, aged sixty; worth six thousand dollars."

Professor Stowe says, "With all these, except G——, I have been, for some years, personally acquainted, and make my statements from my own knowledge."

The writer well remembers an aged colored woman, who was employed as a washerwoman in her father's family. The daughter of this woman married a slave. She was a remarkably active and capable young woman, and by her industry and thrift, and the most persevering self-denial, raised nine hundred dollars for her husband's freedom, which she paid, as she raised it, into the hands of his master. She yet wanted a hundred dollars of the price, when he died. She never recovered any of the money.

These are but few facts among multitudes which might be adduced to show the self-denial, energy, patience, and honesty, which the slave has exhibited in a state of freedom.

And let it be remembered that these individuals have thus bravely succeeded in conquering for themselves comparative wealth and social position, in the face of every disadvantage and discouragement. The colored man, by the law of Ohio, cannot be a voter, and, till within a few years, was even denied the right of testimony in legal suits with the white. Nor are these instances confined to the State of Ohio. In all states of the Union we see men, but yesterday burst from the shackles of slavery, who, by a self-educating force, which cannot be too much admired, have risen to highly respectable stations in society. Pennington among clergymen, Douglas and Ward among editors, are well-known instances.

If this persecuted race, with every discouragement and disadvantage, have done thus much, how much more they might do if the Christian Church would act towards them in the spirit of her Lord!

This is an age of the world when nations are trembling and convulsed. A mighty influence is abroad, surging and heaving the world, as with an earthquake. And is America safe? Every nation that carries in its bosom great and unredressed injustice has in it the elements of this last convulsion.

For what is this mighty influence thus rousing in all nations and languages those groanings that cannot be uttered for man's freedom and equality?

O Church of Christ, read the signs of the times! Is not this power the spirit of HIM whose kingdom is yet to come, and whose will to be done on earth as it is in heaven?

But who may abide the day of his appearing? "For that day shall burn as an oven: and he shall appear as a swift witness against those that oppress the hireling in his wages, the widow and the fatherless, and that *turn aside the stranger in his right*: and he shall break in pieces the oppressor."

Are not these dread words for a nation bearing in her bosom so mighty an injustice? Christians! every time that you pray that the kingdom of Christ may come, can you forget that prophecy associates, in dread fellowship, the *day of vengeance* with the year of his redeemed?

A day of grace is yet held out to us. Both North and South have been guilty before God; and the *Christian church* has a heavy account to answer. Not by combining together, to protect injustice and cruelty, and making a common capital of sin, is this Union to be saved—but by repentance, justice and mercy; for not surer is the eternal law by which the millstone sinks in the ocean, than that stronger law, by which injustice and cruelty shall bring on nations the wrath of Almighty God!

THE END

❦18❧

Three Editorials from
The New York Tribune

As the controversy surrounding the Kansas–Nebraska Act grew, the *New York Tribune* maintained a strong editorial line against slavery and the extension of slave-holding. The three editorials from January 1854 reproduced here are representative of its views.

1. Slavery in the Field

An overt attempt is set on foot in Mr. Douglas's Nebraska bill to override the Missouri Compromise. The eighth section of the act admitting Missouri as a State is as follows:

> In all that territory ceded by France to the United States, under the name of Louisiana, which lies north of 36 degrees and 30 minutes north latitude, not included within the limits of the State contemplated by this act, slavery and involuntary servitude, otherwise than in the punishment of crime whereof the parties shall have been duly convicted, shall be, and is hereby, forever prohibited: Provided, always, that any person escaping into the same, from whom labor or service is lawfully claimed in any State or Territory of the United States, such fugitive may be lawfully reclaimed and conveyed to the person claiming his or her labor or service, as aforesaid.

This plain and unequivocal declaration that neither slavery nor involuntary servitude shall ever exist in our North-west Territories is unceremoniously hustled aside by Mr. Douglas, who makes the Compromise measures of 1850 the scape-goat for his sin in doing it. He says that:

> "A proper sense of patriotic duty enjoins upon your Committee the propriety and necessity of a strict adherence to the principles, and even a literal adoption of the enactments of that adjustment in all their Territorial bills, so far as the same are not locally inapplicable"

And hence he proceeds to incorporate the following provision respecting Nebraska into his bill at the start:

Source: 'Slavery in the Field', *New York Tribune*, 6th January 1854;
'Slavery Militant', *New York Tribune*, 11th January 1854;
'The Rascals at Washington', *New York Tribune*, 26th January 1854;

When admitted as a State, the said Territory, or any portion of the same, shall be received into the Union with or without slavery, as their Constitution may proscribe at the time of their admission.

It is not to be expected of men who live for the sole purpose of enjoying official station, that they shall ever be manly, noble or independent. They slavishly cower before every storm that threatens their opinions with popular condemnation, and make haste to trim their sails to catch the passing breeze of public favor. It is everywhere assumed among such that subjection to the slaveholding interest is now our only sure path to political honors and distinction. In the struggle of 1850, the great Northern anti-Slavery sentiment was inundated and overwhelmed in consequence of the succumbing temper and faithlessness of rotten leaders. With their own hands they destroyed the dykes and let the waters flow in and wash away the rich fruits of years. The XXXIst Congress inaugurated the era of submission to Slavery. Since then, everything has gone on swimmingly in this line. Not only was the Slavery question compromised, but the character, reputation, and principles of hundreds of our public men were also compromised by the same operation. There was a general debauch and demoralization throughout all political circles, as was clearly manifested in the triumphant run of Gen. Pierce. The demoralization continues. It is not to be expected, therefore, that we shall see, for the present, in the acts of public men who place success before principle, anything but unmanly submission to the demands of the slave power. If Gen. Taylor had lived, and the Wilmot Proviso doctrine had substantially triumphed, as it would have done through the instrumentality of his policy relative to our Mexican acquisitions, then we should have seen the reverse of what we now see. Instead of finding Mr. Douglas down on his marrow-bones at the feet of slavery, we should see the same man standing up firm and strong in behalf of the glorious old Ordinance of 1787. Freedom's battle was fought and lost in 1850, and the cowards and traitors have all run to the winning side.

But although anti-Slavery is weak in political circles, it was never stronger with the masses of the people. The great heart of the country is sound. Thousands and millions of true men all over the North wait but the occasion for a practical demonstration of their power, to show how firm is their attachment to the principles of freedom, and how deeply they scorn the shallow fools who have the impertinence to talk about "crushing out" those principles. We expect to see Slavery go on pressing and pushing the advantages it derived from the adjustment of 1850, till a reaction is created that will again convulse the country to its center. Slavery is imperious, encroaching, truculent, belligerent. Its own conduct will thus ultimately generate an explosive force that must blow it to atoms. This movement of Douglas to override and virtually repeal the Missouri Compromise is one step in this direction.

We denounce every attempt to remove the salutary restriction upon the introduction of Slavery into the North-West, and above the line of 36 [degrees] 30 [minutes] below which the Missouri Compromise confines it, whether insidious and hesitant, or open and flagrant, a breach of solemn compact between the North and the South, inevitably opening a door to a fresh and fierce agitation. Let the Country take notice that this convulsion is not commenced on the side of Freedom.

2. Slavery Militant

Slavery is an Ishmael. It is malevolent and malignant. It loves aggression, for when it ceases to be aggressive it stagnates and decays. It is the leper of modern civilization, but a leper whom no cry of "unclean" will keep from intrusion into uninfected company. Hitherto Slavery in this country has held its ground by sheltering itself behind the Constitution. It has played the role of persecuted virtue—and thus it has excited the sympathy of well-meaning persons who would never lend it aid or comfort but when it assumed the character of a distressed and wronged appellant. It has in past years pretended that it was assailed by injustice and fanaticism, which were destroying its supports and overthrowing the constitutional guards and defenses placed around it. It has appealed to the North for aid on the ground of essential justice and constitutional obligation. It has declared its right to existence within the sphere of the States where it was established, and that to assail it, or in any way to interfere with it, was to be guilty of flagrant injustice. Its great charge against Abolitionists has been that they interfered with a domestic institution for which they had no responsibility and with which they had nothing to do. Its advocates have sought to keep the position of the suffering and persecuted party, and have thus enlisted a sort of sense of justice in the Free States, which, more potent than discriminating, has borne Slavery on its shoulders through any contest.

Though it has often been urged that Slavery was aggressive in its nature, the proof of the fact to the common understanding has not been entirely conclusive. To many Northern men it has always seemed to be warring on the defensive side. But present appearances indicate that this erroneous view of Slavery will soon be removed throughout the North. We see already the encroaching steps it is taking in Congress as well as on the Pacific. It dares attempt the appropriation to its uses of territory already consecrated to Freedom by a solemn compact between the North and the South. It is manifesting a determined purpose to cross the boundary behind which its pestilent influences have hitherto been confined, and thus to disregard all considerations of justice, and trample upon its own sacred obligations. It is showing itself to be a power which refuses to adhere to its engagements, and breaks its faith at the first temptation. Not content within its own proper limits, defined after a bitter contest, in which more than its due was yielded to its imperious exactions, it now proposes to invade and overrun the soil of freedom, and to unroll the pall of its darkness over virgin territory whereon a slave has never stood. Freedom is to be elbowed out of its own home to make room for the leprous intruder. The free laborer is to be expelled that the slave may be brought in.

It is plain to see how such an aggressive spirit will be met. If Slavery is determined upon the conquest of free territory it will inevitably be resisted and paid in kind. If the conviction obtains that Slavery intends to disown its obligations and prove faithless to its own contracts, then will it follow that those who have hitherto admitted its rights under the Constitution, will admit them no longer. Let but the sentiment gain foothold that Slavery intends to make war upon the territory of freedom, and seize and appropriate whatever it can wrest from the hands of free labor, and the banner of reclamation will be raised. If Slavery may encroach upon the domain of freemen, freemen may encroach upon the domain of Slavery. If Slavery thinks this is a safe game to play at, let it be pursued as it has been begun.

3. The Rascals at Washington

If the traitorous scamps at Washington who, in a spirit no worthier than that which animated Judas Iscariot, are plotting the surrender to Slavery of the free territory west of the Mississippi, believed that a majority of the North would fail to sustain the movement, they would instantly cease their clamor, and skulk back, and we should hear no more about it.

But they have adopted the belief that the passage of the compromise measures of 1850, and the triumphant election of Frank Pierce, have taken all the spirit out of the North, and that the mass of the voters are now ready to wink at any party iniquity, and sustain any party measure, whatever its enormity.

We are not sure it is worthwhile to attempt to remove this impression. These deliberate violators of solemn compacts, these vagabond repudiators of obligations the most sacred, deserve to be roasted by the hottest fires of public indignation. They ought to have the full benefit of the verdict of an aroused and indignant constituency, and be hung upon the gallows of public opprobrium. Yet in mercy to the culprits, who are thus provoking the incensed judgment of an outraged community, we will briefly state what opposition may be expected in the Free States to the infamous proposal to repeal the Missouri Compromise, and thus expose the rotten foundations of their hopes.

There has been no time during the last seven years when the Whig and Free Soil parties have not been in a clear majority in nearly all the Northern States. The only ground upon which any doubt can be thrown on this presumption, is the result of the last Presidential election. But the vote of the Free Soil party in that contest was only partial, being but the ineffectual remonstrance (and so felt to be) of the more earnest of the Free Soilers against the settlement of the Compromise measures. And the vote of the Whigs in the North was notoriously the vote only of a party divided against itself. It was a contest utterly balked by cross purposes. The Presidential election of 1848, and the Congressional elections of 1850 furnish the only grounds of any just judgment as to the real strength of the anti-Slavery sentiment in the country; and these elections justify the statement that in every Free State, that sentiment, whenever it could be fairly reached, has shown itself to be predominant.

Assuming this to be so, the only question to be answered is, whether that sentiment can be aroused and consolidated, and brought to bear in solid phalanx against the atrocious proposition in question. The fools in Washington believe it cannot. We believe it can. And we believe further that this is by no means the whole strength of the North that will be brought into the field against this infamous project. We shall have the whole conservative force of the Free States of all parties against it. We shall have all the men who do not believe in violating contracts nor in repudiating solemn engagements, on the side of earnest opposition. The moral stamina of the Free States will be set against the measure. Fair dealing and honest purposes will everywhere frown upon such faithlessness and fraud. Sober minded men, who have leaned to the side of the South in the late contests, on the ground that the Abolitionists were the aggressors, will turn and resist this movement as a gross outrage and aggression on the part of the South. Our faith in the intelligence and sense of justice among the people is such, that on the momentous question of a Repeal of the Missouri Compromise, we believe the Free States will rise as one man and crush the repudiating and traitorous dough faces who dare to counsel it. We do not believe it is to be a question of majorities among the people. We believe the proposition will be put down by acclamation.

IV. The Rights
of
the States

⊰19⊱

From Webster's Great Reply to Hayne

DANIEL WEBSTER

Daniel Webster, (1782–1852), senator from Massachusetts, delivered on 26th January 1830 what has been regarded as the most famous speech given in the pre-Civil War period. The issue was the tariff of 1828. Senator Robert Hayne from South Carolina in his speech objecting to the measure, had discussed the doctrine of nullification, suggesting that a state could in effect disregard a federal law. With erudite wit combined with forensic intelligence, Webster here undermines that argument, and presents a powerful rhetorical appeal for the preservation of the Union. Not least among his arguments is a pragmatic one: that the collision between states' rights and federal power would result inevitably in civil war.

From Webster's Great Reply to Hayne
In which he "Expounds the Constitution," delivered in Senate, January 26, 1830

Following Mr. Hayne in the debate, Mr. Webster addressed the Senate as follows:

Mr. President: When the mariner has been tossed, for many days, in thick weather, and on an unknown sea, he naturally avails himself of the first pause in the storm, the earliest glance of the sun, to take his latitude, and ascertain how far the elements have driven him from his true course. Let us imitate this prudence, and before we float farther, refer to the point from which we departed, that we may at least be able to conjecture where we now are. I ask for a reading of the resolution.

[The Secretary read the resolution as follows:

Resolved, That the committee on public lands be instructed to inquire and report the quantity of the public lands remaining unsold within each state and territory,

Source: Thomas Cooper, *American Politics From The Beginning To Date,*
Boston: Mass.: Russell & Henderson, 1885, Book III.

and whether it be expedient to limit, for a certain period, the sales of the public lands to such lands only as have heretofore been offered for sale, and are now subject to entry at the minimum price. And, also, whether the office of suveyor general, and some of the land offices, may not be abolished without detriment to the public interest; or whether it be expedient to adopt measures to hasten the sales, and extend more rapidly the surveys of the public lands."]

We have thus heard, sir, what the resolution is, which is actually before us for consideration; and it will readily occur to every one that it is almost the only subject about which something has not been said in the speech, running through two days, by which the Senate has been now entertained by the gentleman from South Carolina. Every topic in the wide range of our public affairs,—every thing, general or local, whether belonging to national politics or party politics,—seems to have attracted more or less of the honourable member's attention, save only the resolution before us. He has spoken of every thing but the public lands. They have escaped his notice. To that subject, in all his excursions, he has not paid even the cold respect of a passing glance. ...

The honorable member complained that I had slept on his speech. I must have slept on it, or not slept at all. The moment the honorable member sat down, his friend from Missouri rose, and, with much honeyed commendation of the speech, suggested that the impressions which it had produced were too charming and delightful to be disturbed by other sentiments or other sounds, and proposed that the Senate should adjourn. Would it have been quite amiable in me, sir, to interrupt this excellent good feeling? Must I not have been absolutely malicious, if I could have thrust myself forward to destroy sensations thus pleasing? Was it not better and kinder, both to sleep upon them myself, and to allow others, also, the pleasure of sleeping upon them? But if it be meant, by sleeping upon his speech, that I took time to prepare a reply to it, it is quite a mistake; owing to other engagements, I could not employ even the interval between the adjournment of the Senate and its meeting the next morning in attention to the subject of his debate. Nevertheless, sir, the mere matter of fact is undoubtedly true—I did sleep on the gentleman's speeech, and slept soundly. And I slept equally well on his speech of yesterday, to which I am now replying. It is quite possible that, in this respect, also, I possess some advantage over the honorable member, attributable, doubtless, to a cooler temperament on my part; for in truth I slept upon his speeeches remarkably well. [...]

In the course of my observations the other day, Mr. President, I paid a passing tribute to a very worthy man, Mr. Dane of Massachusetts. It so happened that he drew the ordinance of 1787 for the government of the North-western Territory. A man of so much ability, and so little pretence; and of so great a capacity to do good, and so unmixed a disposition to do it for its own sake; a gentleman who acted an important part, forty years ago, in a measure the influence of which is still deeply felt in the very matter which was the subject of debate, might, I thought, receive from me a commendatory recognition.

But the honorable gentleman was inclined to be facetious on the subject. He was rather disposed to make it a matter of ridicule that I had introduced into the debate the name of one Nathan Dane, of whom he assures us he had never before heard. Sir, if the honorable member had never before heard of Mr. Dane, I am sorry for it. It shows him less acquainted with the public men of the country than I had supposed. Let me tell him, however, that a sneer from him at the mention of the name of Mr. Dane is in bad taste. It may well be a high mark of ambition, sir, either with the honorable gentleman or myelf, to accomplish as much to make our names known to advantage, and remembered with gratitude, as Mr. Dane has accomplished. But the truth is, sir, I suspect that Mr. Dane lives a little too far north. He is of Massachussetts, and too near the north star to be reached by the honorable gentleman's telescope. If his sphere had happened to range south of Mason and Dixon's line, he might, probably, have come within the scope of his vision!

I spoke, sir, of the ordinance of 1787, which prohibited slavery in all future times north-west of the Ohio, as a measure of great wisdom and foresight, and one which had been attended with highly beneficial and permanent consequences. I suppose that on this point no two gentlemen in the Senate could entertain different opinions. But the simple expression of this sentiment has led the gentleman, not only into a labored defence of slavery in the abstract, and on principle, but also into a warm accusation against me, as having attacked the system of slavery now existing in the Southern States. For all this there was not the slightest foundation in anything said or intimated by me. I did not utter a single word which any ingenuity could torture into an attack on the slavery of the south. I said only that it was highly wise and useful in legislating for the north-western country, while it was yet a wilderness, to prohibit the introduction of slaves; and added, that I presumed, in the neighbouring state of Kentucky, there was no reflecting and intelligent gentleman, who would doubt that, if the same prohibition had been extended, at the same early period, over that commonwealth, her strength and population would, at this day, have been far greater than they are. If these opinions be thought doubtful, they are, nevertheless, I trust, neither extraordinary nor disrespectful. They attack nobody and menace nobody. And yet, sir, the gentleman's optics have discovered, even in the mere expression of this sentiment, what he calls the very spirit of the Missouri question! He represents me as making an attack on the whole south, and manifesting a spirit which would interfere with and disturb their domestic condition. Sir, this injustice no otherwise surprises me than as it is done here, and done without the slightest pretence of ground for it. I say it only surprises me as being done here; for I know full well that it is and has been the settled policy of some persons in the south, for years, to represent the people of the north as disposed to interfere with them in their own exclusive and peculiar concerns. This is a delicate and sensitive point in southern feeling; and of late years it has always been touched, and generally with effect, whenever the object has been to unite the whole south against northern men or northern measures. This feeling, always carefully kept alive, and maintained at too intense a heat to admit discrimination or reflection, is a lever of great power in our political machine. It moves vast bodies, and gives to them one and the same direction. But the feeling is without adequate cause, and the suspicion which exists wholly groundless. There is not, and never has been, a disposition in the north to interfere with these interests of the south. Such interference has never been supposed to be within the power of the government, nor has it been in any way attempted. It has always been regarded as a matter of domestic policy, left with the states themselves, and with which the federal government had nothing to do. Certainly, sir, I am, and ever had been, of that opinion. The gentleman, indeed, argues that slavery in the abstract is no evil. Most assuredly I need not say I differ with him altogether and most widely on that point. I regard domestic slavery as one of the greatest evils, both moral and political. But, though it be a malady, and whether it be curable, and if so, by what means; or, on the other hand, whether it be the *culnus immedicabile* of the social system, I leave it to those whose right and duty it is to inquire and decide. And this I believe, sir, is, and uniformly has been, the sentiment of the north. [...]

There yet remains to be performed, Mr. President, by far the most grave and important duty; which I feel to be devolved on me by this occasion. It is to state, and to defend, what I conceive to be the true principles of the constitution under which we are here assembled. I might well have desired that so weighty a task should have fallen into other and abler hands. I could have wished that it should have been executed by those whose character and experience give weight and influence to their opinions, such as cannot possibly belong to mine. But, sir, I have met the occasion, not sought it; and I shall proceed to state my own sentiments, without challenging for them any particular regard, with studied plainness, and as much precision as possible.

I understand the honorable gentleman from South Carolina to maintain, that it is a right of the state legislatures to interfere whenever, in their judgment, this government transcends its constitutional limits, and to arrest the operation of its laws.

I understand him to maintain this right as a right existing under the constitution, not as a right to overthrow it, on the ground of extreme necessity, such as would justify violent revolution.

I understand him to maintain an authority, on the part of the states, thus to interfere for the purpose of correcting the exercise of power by the general government, of checking it, and of compelling it to conform to their opinion of the extent of its power.

I understand him to maintain that the ultimate power of judging of the constitutional extent of its own authority is not lodged exclusively in the general government, or any branch of it; but that, on the contrary, the states may lawfully decide for themselves, and each state for itself, whether, in a given case, the act of the general government transcends its power.

I understand him to insist that if the exigency of the case, in the opinion of any state government, require it, such state government may, by its own sovereign authority, annul an act of the general government which it deems plainly and palpably unconstitutional. [...]

What he contends for is that it is constitutional to interrupt the administration of the Constitution itself, in the hands of those who are chosen and sworn to administer it, by the direct interference, in form of law, of the states, in virtue of their sovereign capacity. The inherent right in the people to reform their government I do not deny; and they have another right, and that is to resist unconstitutional laws without overturning the government. It is no doctrine of mine that unconstitutional laws bind the people. The great question is, *Whose prerogative is it to decide on the constitutionality or unconstitutionality of the laws?* On that the main debate hinges. The proposition that, in the case of a supposed violation of the constitution by Congress, the states have a constitutional right to interfere, and annul the law of Congress, is the proposition of the gentleman; I do not admit it. If the gentleman had intended no more than to assert the right of revolution for justifiable cause, he would have said only what all agree to.—But I cannot conceive that there can be a middle course between submission to the laws, when regulalrly pronounced constitutional, on the one hand, and open resistance, which is revolution or rebellion on the other. I say that the right of a state to annul a law of Congress cannot be maintained but on the unalienable right of man to resist oppression; that is to say, upon the ground of revolution. I admit that there is no ultimate violent remedy, above the constitution, and defiance of the constitution, which may be resorted to, when a revolution is to be justified. But I do not admit that under the constitution, and in conformity with it, there is any mode in which a state government, as a member of the Union can interfere and stop the progress of the general government, by the force of her own laws, under any circumstances whatever.

This leads us to inquire into the origin of this government and the source of its power. Whose agent is it? Is it the creature of the state legislatures, or the creature of the people? If the government of the United States be the agent of the state governments, then they may control it, provided they can agree in the manner of controlling it; if it be the agent of the people, then the people alone can control it, restrain it, modify, or reform it. It is observable enough that the doctrine for which the honorable gentleman contends leads him to the necessity of maintaining, not only that this general government is the creature of the states, or that it is the creature of each of the states severally, so that each may assert the power for itself of determining whether it acts within the limits of its authority. It is the servant of four-and-twenty masters, of different wills and different purposes, and yet bound to obey all. This absurdity (for it seems no less) arises from a misconception as to the origin of this government and its true character. It is, sir, the people's constitution, the people's government, made for the people, made by the people, and answerable to the people. The people of the United States have declared that this constitution shall be the supreme law. We must either admit the proposition or dispute their authority. The states are, unquestionably, sovereign, so far as their sovereignty is not affected by this supreme law. But the state legislatures, as political bodies, however sovereign, are yet not sovereign over the people. So far as the people have given power to the general government, so far the grant is unquestionably good, and the government holds of the people and not of the state governments. We are all agents of the same supreme power, the people. The general government and the state governments derive their authority from the same source. Neither can, in relation to the other, be called primary, though one is definite and restricted, and the other general and residuary.

The national government possesses those powers, which it can be shown the people have conferred on it, and no more. All the rest belongs to the state governments, or to the people themselves. So far as the people have restrained state sovereignty, by the expression of their will, in the constitution of the United States, so far, it must be admitted, state sovereignty is effectually controlled. I do not contend that it is, or ought to be, controlled farther. The sentiment to which I have referred propounds that state sovereignty is only to be controlled by its own "feeling of justice;" that is to say, it is not to be controlled at all, for one who is to follow his own feelings is under no legal control. Now, however men may think this ought to be, the fact is that the people of the United States have chosen to impose control on state sovereignties. There are those, doubtless, who wish they had been left without restraint; but the constitution has ordered the matter differently. To make war, for instance, is an exercise of sovereignty; but the constitution declares that no state shall make war. To coin money is another exercise of sovereign power; but no state is at liberty to coin money. Again, the constitution says that no sovereign state shall be so sovereign as to make a treaty. These prohibitions, it must be confessed, are a control on the state sovereignty of South Carolina, as well as of the other states, which does not arise "from her own feelings of honorable justice." The opinion referred to, therefore, is in defiance of the plainest provisions of the constitution. [...]

I must now beg to ask, sir, Whence is this supposed right of the states derived? Where do they find the power to interfere with the laws of the Union? Sir, the opinion which the honorable gentleman maintains is a notion founded in a total misapprehension, in my judgment, of the origin of this government, and of the foundation on which it stands. I hold it to be a popular government, erected by the people; those who administer it, responsible to the people; and itself capable of being amended and modified, just as the people may choose it should be. It is as popular, just as truly emanating from the people, as the state governments. It is created for one purpose; the state governments for another. It has its own powers; they have theirs. There is no more authority with them to arrest the operation of a law of Congress than with Congress to arrest the operation of their laws. We are here to administer a constitution emanating immediately from the people, and trusted by them to our administration. It is not the creature of the state governments. It is of no moment to the argument that certain acts of the state legislatures are necessary to fill our seats in this body. That is not one of their original state powers, a part of the sovereignty of the state. It is a duty which the people, by the constitution itself, have imposed on the state legislatures; and which they might have left to be performed elsewhere, if they had seen fit. So they have left the choice of President with electors; but all this does not affect the proposition that this whole government—President, Senate, and House of Representatives,—is a popular government. It leaves it still all its popular character. The governor of a state (in some of the states) is chosen, not directly by the people but by those who are chosen by the people, for the purpose of performing, among other duties, that of electing a governor. Is the government of the state, on that account, not a popular government? This government, sir, is the independent offspring of the popular will. It is not the creature of state legislatures; nay, more, if the whole truth must be told, the people brought it into existence, established it, and have hitherto supported it for the very purpose, among others, of imposing certain salutary restraints on state sovereignties. The states cannot now make war; they cannot contract alliances; they cannot make, each for itself, separate regulations of commerce; they cannot lay imposts; they cannot coin money. If this constitution, sir, be the creature of state legislatures, it must be admitted that it has obtained a strange control over the volition of its creators.

The people, then, sir, erected this government. They gave it a constitution, and in that constitution they have enumerated the powers which they bestow on it. They have made it a limited government. They have defined its authority. They have restrained it to the exercise of such powers as are granted; and all others, they declare, are reserved to the states or the people. But, sir, they have not stopped here. If they had, they would have accomplished but half their work. No definition can be so clear as to avoid possibility of doubt; no limitation so precise as to exclude all uncertainty. Who, then, shall construe this grant of the people? Who shall interpret their will, where it may be supposed they have left it doubtful? With whom do they repose this ultimate right of deciding on the powers of the government? Sir, they have settled all this in the fullest manner. They have left it with the government itself, in its appropriate branches. Sir, the very chief end, the main design, for which the whole constitution was framed and adopted was to establish a government that should not be obliged to act through state agency or depend on state opinion and state discretion. The people had had quite enough of that kind of government under the confederacy. Under that system, the legal action—the application of law to individuals—belonged exclusively to the states. Congress could only recommend—their acts were not of binding force till the states had adopted and sanctioned them. Are we in that condition still? Are we yet at the mercy of state discretion and state construction? Sir, if we are, then vain will be our attempt to maintain the constitution under which we sit.

But, sir, the people have wisely provided, in the constitution itself, a proper, suitable mode and tribunal for settling questions of constitutional law. There are in the constitution grants of powers to Congress, and restrictions on these powers. There are, also, prohibitions on the states. Some authority must, therefore, necessarily exist, having the ultimate jurisdiction to fix and ascertain the interpretation of these grants, restrictions, and prohibitions. The constitution has itself pointed out, ordained, and established that authority. How has it accomplished this great and essential end? By declaring, sir, that "*the constitution, and the laws of*

257

the United States made in pursuance thereof, shall be the supreme law of the land, anything in the constitution or laws of any state to the contrary notwithstanding."

This, sir, was the first great step. By this, the supremacy of the constitution and laws of the United States is declared. The people so will it. No state law is to be valid which comes in conflict with the constitution, or any law of the United States passed in pursuance of it. But who shall decide this question of interference? To whom lies the last appeal? This, sir, the constitution itself decides also, by declaring, *"that the judicial power shall extend to all cases arising under the constitution and laws of the United States."* These two provisions cover the whole ground. They are, in truth, the keystone of the arch. With these it is a government; without them it is a confederation. In pursuance of these clear and express provisions, Congress established, at its very first session, in the judicial act, a mode for carrying them into full effect, and for bringing all questions of constitutional power to the final decision of the Supreme Court. It then, sir, became a government. It then had the means of self-protection; and but for this, it would, in all probability, have been now among things which are passed. Having constituted the government and declared its powers, the people have further said that, since somebody must decide on the extent of these powers, the government shall itself decide; subject, always, like other popular governments, to its responsibility to the people. And now, sir, I repeat, how is it that a state legislature acquires any power to interfere? Who, or what, gives them the right to say to the people, "We, who are your agents and servants for one purpose, will undertake to decide that your other agents and servants, appointed by you for another purpose, have transcended the authority you gave them"? The reply would be, I think, not impertinent, "Who made you a judge over another's servants. To their own masters they stand or fall."

Sir, I deny this power of state legislatures altogether. It cannot stand the test of examination. Gentlemen may say that, in an extreme case, a state government might protect the people from intolerable oppression. Sir, in such a case, the people might protect themselves, without the aid of the state governments. Such a case warrants revolution. It must make, when it comes, a law for itself. A nullifying act of a state legislature cannot alter the case, nor make resistance any more lawful. In maintaining these sentiments, sir, I am but asserting the rights of the people. I state what they have declared and insist on their right to declare it. They have chosen to repose this power in the general government, and I think it my duty to support it, like other constitutional powers. [...]

To avoid all possibility of being misunderstood, allow me to repeat again, in the fullest manner, that I claim no powers for the government by forced or unfair construction. I admit that it is a government of strictly limited powers; of enumerated, specified, and particularized powers; and that whatsoever is not granted, is withheld. But notwithstanding all this, and however the grant of powers may be expressed, its limit and extent may yet, in some cases, admit of doubt; and the general government would be good for nothing, it would be incapable of long existing, if some mode had not been provided in which those doubts, as they should arise, might be peaceably but authoritatively solved.

And now, Mr. President, let me run the honorable gentleman's doctrine a little into its practical application. Let us look at his probable *modus operandi*. If a thing can be done, an ingenious man can tell *how* it is to be done, and I wish to be informed *how* this state interference is to be put in practice. We will take the existing case of the tariff law. South Carolina is said to have made up her opinion upon it. If we do not repeal it, (as we probably shall not,) she will then apply to the case the remedy of her doctrine. She will, we must suppose, pass a law of her legislature, declaring the several acts of Congress, usually called the tariff laws, null and void, so far as they respect South Carolina, or the citizens thereof. So far, all is a paper transaction, and easy enough. But the collector at Charleston is collecting the duties imposed by these tariff laws—he, therefore, must be stopped. The collector will seize the goods if the tariff duties are not paid. The state authorities will undertake their rescue: the marshall, with his posse, will come to the collector's aid; and here the contest begins. The militia of the state will be called out to sustain the nullifying act. They will march, sir, under a very gallant leader; for I believe the honorable member himself commands the militia of that part of the state. He will raise the NULLIFYING ACT on his standard, and spread it out as his banner. It will have a preamble, bearing that the tariff laws are palpable, deliberate, and dangerous violations of the constitution. He will proceed, with his banner flying, to the custom house in Charleston,—

> "All the while
> Sonorous metal blowing martial sounds."

Arrived at the custom house, he will tell the collector that he must collect no more duties under any of the tariff laws. This he will be somewhat puzzled to say, by the way, with a grave countenance, considering what hand South Carolina herself had in that of 1816. But, sir, the collector would, probably, not desist at his bidding. Here would ensue a pause; for they say, that a certain stillness precedes the tempest. Before this military array should fall on custom house, collector, clerks, and all, it is very probable some of those composing it would request of their gallant commander-in-chief to be informed a little upon the point of law; for they have doubtless just respect for his opinion as a lawyer, as well as for his bravery as a soldier. They know he has read Blackstone and the constitution, as well as Turenne and Vauban. They would ask him, therefore, something concerning their rights in this matter. They would inquire whether it was not somewhat dangerous to resist a law of the United States. What would be the nature of their offence, they would wish to learn, if they, by military force and array, resisted the execution in Carolina of a law of the United States, and it should turn out, after all, that the law *was constitutional*. He would answer, of course, treason. No lawyer could give any other answer. John Fries, he would tell them, had learned that some years ago. How, then, they would ask, do you propose to defend us? We are not afraid of bullets, but treason has a way of taking people off that we do not much relish. How do you propose to defend us? "Look at my floating banner," he would reply; "see there the *nullifying law!*" Is it

259

your opinion, gallant commander, they would then say, that if we should be indicted for treason, that same floating banner of yours would make a good plea in bar? "South Carolina is a sovereign state," he would reply. That is true; but would the judge admit our plea? "These tariff laws," he would repeat, "are unconstitutional, palpably, deliberately, dangerously." That all may be so; but if the tribunals should not happen to be of that opinion, shall we swing for it? We are ready to die for our country, but it is rather an awkward business, this dying without touching the ground. After all, this is a sort of *hemp*-tax, worse than any part of the tariff.

Mr. President, the honorable gentleman would be in a dilemma like that of another great general. He would have a knot before him which he could not untie. He must cut it with his sword. He must say to his followers, Defend yourselves with your bayonets; and this is war—civil war.

Direct collision, therefore, between force and force is the unavoidable result of that remedy for the revision of unconstitutional laws which the gentleman contends for. It must happen in the very first case to which it is applied. Is not this the plain result? To resist by force the execution of a law, generally, is treason. Can the courts of the United States take notice of the indulgence of a state to commit treason? The common saying that a state cannot commit treason herself is nothing to the purpose. Can she authorize others to do it? If John Fries had produced an act of Pennsylvania annulling the law of Congress, would it have helped his case? Talk about it as we will, these doctrines go the length of revolution. They are incompatible with any peaceable administration of the government. They lead directly to disunion and civil commotion; and, therefore, it is that at their commencement, when they are first found to be maintained by respectable men, and in a tangible form, that I enter my public protest against them all.

The honorable gentleman argues that if this government be the sole judge of the extent of its own powers, whether that right of judging be in Congress or the Supreme Court, it equally subverts state sovereignty. This the gentleman sees, or thinks he sees, although he cannot perceive how the right of judging in this matter, if left to the exercise of state legislatures, has any tendency to subvert the government of the Union. The gentleman's opinion may be that the right *ought not* to have been lodged with the general government; he may like better such a constitution as we should have under the right of state interference; but I ask him to meet me on the plain matter of fact—I ask him to meet me on the constitution itself—I ask him if the power is not there—clearly and visibly found there.

But, sir, what is this danger, and what the grounds of it? Let it be remembered that the constitution of the United States is not unalterable. It is to continue in its present form no longer than the people who established it shall choose to continue it. If they shall become convinced that they have made an injudicious or inexpedient partition and distribution of power between the state governments and the general government, they can alter that distribution at will.

If anything be found in the national constitution, either by original provision or subsequent interpretation, which ought not to be in it, the people know how to get rid of it. If any construction, unacceptable to them, be established, so as to become practically, a part of the constitution, they will amend it at their own sovereign pleasure. But while the people choose to maintain it as it is, while they are satisfied with it and refuse to change it, who has given, or who can give, to the state legislatures a right to alter it, either by interference, construction, or otherwise? Gentlemen do not seem to recollect that the people have any power to do anything for themselves. They imagine there is no safety for them, any longer than they are under the close guardianship of the state legislatures. Sir, the people have not trusted their safety, in regard to the general constitution, to these hands. They have required other security, and taken other bonds. They have chosen to trust themselves, first, to the plain words of the instrument, and to such construction as the government themselves, in doubtful cases, should put on their own powers, under their oaths of office, and subject to their responsibility to them; just as the people of a state trust their own state governments with a similar power. Secondly, they have reposed their trust in the efficacy of frequent elections, and in their own power to remove their own servants and agents whenever they see cause, Thirdly, they have reposed trust in the judicial power, which, in order that it might he trustworthy, they have made as respectable, as disinterested, and as independent as practicable. Fourthly, they have seen fit to rely, in case of necessity, or high expediency, on their known and admitted power to alter or amend the constitution, peaceably and quietly, whenever experience shall point out defects or imperfections. And, finally, the people of the United States have at no time, in no way, directly or indirectly, authorized any state legislature to construe or interpret *their* instrument of government, much less to interfere, by their own power, to arrest its course and operation.

If sir, the people in these respects had done otherwise than they have done, their constitution could neither have been preserved, nor would it have been worth preserving. And if its plain provision shall now be disregarded, and these new doctrines interpolated in it, it will become as feeble and helpless a being as its enemies, whether early or more recent, could possibly desire. It will exist in every state but as a poor dependent on state permission. It must borrow leave to be, and will be, no longer than state pleasure, or state discretion, sees fit to grant the indulgence and to prolong its poor existence.

But, sir, although there are fears, there are hopes also. The people have preserved this, their own chosen constitution, for forty years and have seen their happiness, prosperity, and renown grow with its growth, and strengthen with its strength. They are now, generally, strongly attached to it. Overthrown by direct assault, it cannot be; evaded, undermined, NULLIFIED, it will not be if we, and those who shall succeed us here, as agents and representatives of the people, shall conscientiously and vigilantly discharge the two great branches of our public trust— faithfully to preserve and wisely to administer it.

Mr. President, I have thus stated the reasons of my dissent to the doctrines which have been advanced and maintained. I am conscious of having detained you and the Senate much too long. I was drawn into the debate with no previous deliberation, such as is suited to the discussion of so grave and important a subject.

But it is a subject of which my heart is full, and I have not been willing to suppress the utterance of its spontaneous sentiments.

I cannot, even now, persuade myself to relinquish it without expressing once more my deep conviction that, since it respects nothing less than the union of the states, it is of most vital and essential importance to the public happiness. I profess, sir, in my career hitherto, to have kept steadily in view the prosperity and honor of the whole country, and the preservation of our Federal Union. It is to that Union we owe our safety at home, and our consideration and dignity abroad. It is to that Union that we are chiefly indebted for whatever makes us most proud of our country. That Union we reached only by the discipline of our virtues in the severe school of adversity. It had its origin in the necessities of disordered finance, prostrate commerce, and mined credit. Under its benign influences, these great interests immediately awoke, as from the dead, and sprang forth with newness of life. Every year of its duration has teemed with fresh proofs of its utility and its blessings. And although our territory has stretched out wider and wider, and our population spread farther and farther, they have not outrun its protection or its benefits. It has been to us all a copious fountain of national, social, and personal happiness. I have not allowed myself, sir, to look beyond the Union, to see what might he hidden in the dark recess behind. I have not coolly weighed the chances of preserving liberty when the bonds that unite us together shall be broken asunder. I have not accustomed myself to hang over the precipice of disunion, to see whether, with my short sight, I can fathom the depth of the abyss below; nor could I regard him as a safe counsellor in the affairs in this government whose thoughts should be mainly bent on considering, not how the Union may be best preserved but how tolerable might be the condition of the people when it should be broken up and destroyed. While the Union lasts, we have high, exciting, gratifying prospects spread out before us, for us and our children. Beyond that I seek not to penetrate the veil. God grant that in my day, at least, that curtain may not rise! God grant that on my vision never may be opened what lies behind! When my eyes shall be turned to behold for the last time the sun in heaven, may I not see him shining on the broken and dishonored fragments of a once glorious Union; on states dissevered, discordant, belligerent; on a land rent with civil feuds, or drenched, it may be, in fraternal blood! Let their last feeble and lingering glance rather behold the gorgeous ensign of the republic, now known and honored throughout the earth, still full high advanced, its arms and trophies streaming in their original lustre, not a stripe erased or polluted, nor a single star obscured, bearing for its motto, no such miserable interrogatory as *What is all this worth?* nor those other words of delusion and folly, *Liberty first and Union afterwards*; but everywhere, spread all over in characters of living light, blazing on all its ample folds, as they float over the sea and over the land, and in every wind under the whole heavens, that other sentiment, dear to every true American heart—Liberty *and* Union, now and forever, one and inseparable!

⊹⧖·20·⧗⊹

Proclamation to the People of South Carolina

ANDREW JACKSON

In November 1832 a convention in South Carolina adopted an Ordinance of Nullification, effectively declaring that the tariff passed by the federal government earlier in the year was null and void as it applied to the state. President Jackson issued this proclamation on 10th December 1832, challenging the constitutionality of this action, and presenting in clear terms the arguments over the issue of states' rights versus federal authority. A compromise tariff enacted the following year avoided a stalemate between South Carolina and the United States. Later, as the secession crisis developed, it would be South Carolina, however, which would be the first state to leave the Union.

Proclamation
By Andrew Jackson, President of the United States

Whereas a convention assembled in the State of South Carolina have passed an ordinance by which they declare

"that the several acts and parts of acts of the Congress of the United States purporting to be laws for the imposing of duties and imposts on the importation of foreign commodities, and now having actual operation and effect within the United States, and more especially"

two acts for the same purposes passed on the 29th of May, 1828, and on the 14th of July, 1832,

"are unauthorized by the Constitution of the United States, and violate the true meaning and intent thereof, and are null and void and no law,"

nor binding on the citizens of that State or its officers; and by the said ordinance it is further declared to be unlawful for any of the constituted authorities of the State

Source: Andrew Jackson, Proclamation to the People of South Carolina, 10th December 1832, in James D. Richardson, ed., *A Compilation of the Messages and Papers of the Presidents*, New York: Bureau of National Literature, Inc., 1897, Vol. III.

or of the United States to enforce the payment of the duties imposed by the said acts within the same State, and that it is the duty of the legislature to pass such laws as may be necessary to give full effect to the said ordinance; and

Whereas by the said ordinance it is further ordained that in no case of law or equity decided in the courts of said State wherein shall be drawn in question the validity of the said ordinance, or of the acts of the legislature that may be passed to give it effect, or of the said laws of the United States, no appeal shall be allowed to the Supreme Court of the United States, nor shall any copy of the record be permitted or allowed for that purpose, and that any person attempting to take such appeal shall he punished as for contempt of court; and, finally, the said ordinance declares that the people of South Carolina will maintain the said ordinance at every hazard, and that they will consider the passage of any act by Congress abolishing or closing the ports of the said State or otherwise obstructing the free ingress or egress of vessels to and from the said ports, or any other act of the Federal Government to coerce the State, shut up her ports, destroy or harass her commerce, or to enforce the said acts otherwise than through the civil tribunals of the country, as inconsistent with the longer continuance of South Carolina in the Union, and that the people of the said State will thenceforth hold themselves absolved from all further obligation to maintain or preserve their political connection with the people of the other States, and will forthwith proceed to organize a separate government and do all other acts and things which sovereign and independent states may of right do; and

Whereas the said ordinance prescribes to the people of South Carolina a course of conduct in direct violation of their duty as citizens of the United States, contrary to the laws of their country, subversive of its Constitution. and having for its object the destruction of the Union—that Union which, coeval with our political existence, led our fathers, without any other ties to unite them than those of patriotism and a common cause, through a sanguinary struggle to a glorious Independence; that sacred Union, hitherto inviolate, which, perfected by our happy Constitution, has brought us, by the favor of Heaven, to a state of prosperity at home and high consideration abroad rarely, if ever, equated in the history of nations:

To preserve this bond of our political existence from destruction, to maintain inviolate this state of national honor and prosperity, and to justify the confidence my fellow-citizens have reposed in me, I, Andrew Jackson, President of the United States, have thought proper to issue this my proclamation, stating my views of the Constitution and laws applicable to the measures adopted by the convention of South Carolina and to the reasons they have put forth to sustain them, declaring the course which duty will require me to pursue, and, appealing to the understanding and patriotism of the people, warn them of the consequences that must inevitably result from an observance of the dictates of the convention.

Strict duty would require of me nothing more than the exercise of those powers with which I am now or may hereafter be invested for preserving the peace of the Union and for the execution of the laws; but the imposing aspect which opposition has assumed in this case, by clothing itself with State authority, and the deep interest which the people of the United States must all feel in preventing a resort to stronger measures while there is a hope that anything will be yielded to reasoning and remonstrance, perhaps demand, and will certainly justify, a full exposition to South Carolina and the nation of the views I entertain of this important question, as well as a distinct enunciation of the course which my sense of duty will require me to pursue.

The ordinance is founded, not on the indefeasible right of resisting acts which are plainly unconstitutional and too oppressive to be endured, but on the strange position that any one State may not only declare an act of Congress void, but prohibit its execution; that they may do this consistently with the Constitution; that the true construction of that instrument permits a State to retain its place in the Union and yet be bound by no other of its laws than those it may choose to consider as constitutional. It is true, they add, that to justify this abrogation of a law it must be palpably contrary to the Constitution, but it is evident that to give the right of resisting laws of that description, coupled with the uncontrolled right to decide what laws deserve that character, is to give the power of resisting all laws; for as by the theory there is no appeal, the reasons alleged by the State, good or bad, must prevail. If it should be said that public opinion is a sufficient check against the abuse of this power, it may be asked why it is not deemed a sufficient guard against the passage of an unconstitutional act by Congress? There is, however, a restraint in this last case which makes the assumed power of a State more indefensible, and which does not exist in the other. There are two appeals from an unconstitutional act passed by Congress—one to the judiciary, the other to the people and the States. There is no appeal from the State decision in theory, and the practical illustration shows that the courts are closed against an application to review it, both judges and jurors being sworn to decide in its favor. But reasoning on this subject is superfluous when our social compact, in express terms, declares that the laws of the United States, its Constitution, and treaties made under it are the supreme law of the land, and, for greater caution, adds "that the judges in every State shall be bound thereby, anything in the constitution or laws of any State to the contrary notwithstanding." And it may be asserted without fear of refutation that no federative government could exist without a similar provision. Look for a moment to the consequence. If South Carolina considers the revenue laws unconstitutional and has a right to prevent their execution in the port of Charleston, there would be a clear constitutional objection to their collection in every other port; and no revenue could be collected anywhere, for all imposts must be equal. It is no answer to repeat that an unconstitutional law is no law so long as the question of its legality is to be decided by the State itself, for every law operating injuriously upon any local interest will be perhaps thought, and certainly represented, as unconstitutional, and, as has been shown, there is no appeal.

If this doctrine had been established at an earlier day, the Union would have been dissolved in its infancy. The excise law in Pennsylvania, the embargo and nonintercourse law in the Eastern States, the carriage tax in Virginia, were all deemed unconstitutional, and were more unequal in their operation than any of the laws now complained of; but, fortunately, none of those States discovered that they had the right now claimed by South Carolina. The war into which we were forced to support the dignity of the nation and the rights of our citizens might have ended in defeat and disgrace, instead of victory and honor, if the States who supposed it a ruinous and unconstitutional measure had thought they possessed the right of nullifying the act by which it was declared and denying supplies for its prosecution. Hardly and unequally as those measures bore upon several members of the Union, to the legislatures of none did this efficient and peaceable remedy, as it is called, suggest itself. The discovery of this important feature in our Constitution was reserved to the present day. To the statesmen of South Carolina belongs the invention, and upon the citizens of that State will unfortunately fall the evils of reducing it to practice.

If the doctrine of a State veto upon the laws of the Union carries with it internal evidence of its impracticable absurdity, our constitutional history will also afford abundant proof that it would have been repudiated with indignatioin had it been proposed to form a feature in our Government.

In our colonial state, although dependent on another power, we very early considered ourselves as connected by common interest with each other. Leagues were formed for common defense, and before the declaration of independence we were known in our aggregate character as *the United Colonies of America*. That decisive and important step was taken jointly. We declared ourselves a nation by a joint, not by several acts, and when the terms of our Confederation were reduced to form it was in that of a solemn league of several States, by which they agreed that they would collectively form one nation for the purpose of conducting some certain domestic concerns and all foreign relations. In the instrument forming that Union is found an article which declares that "every State shall abide by the determinations of Congress on all questions which by that Confederation should be submitted to them."

Under the Confederation then, no State could legally annul a decision of the Congress or refuse to submit to its execution; but no provision was made to enforce these decisions. Congress made requisitions, but they were not complied with. The Government could not operate on individuals. They had no judiciary, no means of collecting revenue.

But the defects of the Confederation need not be detailed. Under its operation we could scarcely be called a nation. We had neither prosperity at home nor consideration abroad. This state of things could not be endured, and our present happy Constitution was formed, but formed in vain if this fatal doctrine prevails. It was formed for important objects that are announced in the preamble, made in the name and by the authority of the people of the United States, whose delegates framed and whose conventions approved it. The most important among these objects—that which is placed first in rank, on which all the others rest—is "*to form a more perfect union.*" Now, is it possible that even if there were no express provision giving supremacy to the Constitution and laws of the United States over those of the States, can it be conceived that an instrument made for the purpose of "*forming a more perfect union*" than that of the Confederation could be so constructed by the assembled wisdom of our country as to substitute for that Confederation a form of government dependent for its existence on the local interest, the party spirit, of a State, or of a prevailing faction in a State? Every man of plain, unsophisticated understanding who hears the question will give such an answer as will preserve the Union. Metaphysical subtlety, in pursuit of an impracticable theory, could alone have devised one that is calculated to destroy it.

I consider, then, the power to annul a law of the United States, assumed by one State, *incompatible with the existence of the Union, contradicted expressly by the letter of the Constitution, unauthorized by its spirit, inconsistent with, every principle on which it was founded, and destructive of the great object for which it was formed.*

After this general view of the leading principle; we must examine the particular application of it which is made in the ordinance.

The preamble rests its justification on these grounds: It assumes as a fact that the obnoxious laws, although they purport to be laws for raising revenue, were in reality intended for the protection of manufactures, which purpose it asserts to be unconstitutional; that the operation of these laws is unequal; that the amount raised by them is greater than is required by the wants of the Government; and, finally, that the proceeds are to be applied to objects unauthorized by the Constitution. These are the only causes alleged to justify an open opposition to the laws of the country and a threat of seceding from the Union if any attempt should be made to enforce them. The first virtually acknowledges that the law in question was passed under a power expressly given by the Constitution to lay and collect imposts; but its constitutionality is drawn in question from the *motives* of those who passed it. However apparent this purpose may be in the present case, nothing can be more dangerous than to admit the position that an unconstitutional purpose entertained by the members who assent to a law enacted under a constitutional power shall make that law void. For how is that purpose to be ascertained? Who is to make the scrutiny? How often may bad purposes be falsely imputed, in how many cases are they concealed by false professions, in how many is no declaration of motive made? Admit this doctrine, and you give to the States an uncontrolled right to decide, and every law may he annulled under this pretext. If, therefore, the absurd and dangerous doctrine should be admitted that a State may annul an unconstitutional law, or one that it deems such, it will not apply to the present case.

The next objection is that the laws in question operate unequally. This objection may be made with truth to every law that has been or can be passed. The wisdom of man never yet contrived a system of taxation that would operate with perfect equality. If the unequal operation of a law makes it unconstitutional, and if all laws of that description may be abrogated by any State for that cause, then, indeed, is the Federal Constitution unworthy of the slightest effort for its preservation. We have hitherto relied on it as the perpetual bond of our Union; we have received it as the work of the assembled wisdom of the nation; we have trusted to it as to the sheet anchor of our safety in the stormy times of conflict with a foreign or domestic foe; we have looked to it with sacred awe as the palladium of our liberties, and with all the solemnities of religion have pledged to each other our lives and fortunes here and our hopes of happiness hereafter in its defense and support. Were we mistaken, my countrymen, in attaching this importance to the constitution of our country? Was our devotion paid to the wretched, inefficient, clumsy contrivance which this new doctrine would make it? Did we pledge ourselves to the support of an airy nothing—a bubble that must be blown awayby the first breath of disaffection? Was this self-destroying, visionary theory the work of the profound statesmen, the exalted patriots, to whom the task of constitutional reform was intrusted? Did the name of Washington sanction, did the States deliberately ratify, such an anomaly in the history of fundamental legislation? No; we were not mistaken. The letter of this great instrument is free from this radical fault. Its language directly contradicts the imputation; its spirit, its evident intent, contradicts it. No; we did not err. Our Constitution does not contain the absurdity of giving power to make laws and another to resist them. The sages whose memory will always be reverenced have given us a practical and, as they hoped, a permanent constitutional compact. The Father of his Country did not affix his revered name to so palpable an absurdity. Nor did the States, when they severally ratified it, do so under the impression that a veto on the laws of the United States was reserved to them or that they could exercise it by implication. Search the debates in all their conventions, examine the speeches of the most zealous opposers of Federal authority, look at the amendments that were proposed; they are all silent—not a syllable uttered, not a vote given, not a motion made to correct the explicit supremacy given to the laws of the Union over those of the States, or to show that implication, as is now contended, could defeat it. No; we have not erred. The Constitution is still the object of our reverence, the bond of our Union, our defense in danger, the source of our prosperity in peace. It shall descend, as we have received it, uncorrupted by sophistical construction, to our posterity; and the sacrifices of local interest, of State prejudices, of personal animosities, that were made to bring it into existence, will again be patriotically offered for its support.

The two remaining objections made by the ordinance to these laws are that the sums intended to be raised by them are greater than are required and that the proceeds will be unconstitutionally employed.

The Constitution has given, expressly, to Congress the right of raising revenue and of determining the sum the public exigencies will require. The States have no control over the exercise of this right other than that which results from the power of changing the representatives who abuse it, and thus procure redress. Congress may undoubtedly abuse this discretionary power; but the same may be said of others with which they are vested. Yet the discretion must exist somewhere. The Constitution has given it to the representatives of all the people, checked by the representatives of the States and by the executive power. The South Carolina construction gives it to the legislature or the convention of a single State, where neither the people of the different States, nor the States in their separate capacity, nor the Chief Magistrate elected by the people have any representation. Which is the most discreet disposition of the power? I do not ask you, fellow-citizens, which is the constitutional disposition; that instrument speaks a language not to be misunderstood. But if you were assembled in general convention, which would you think the safest depository of this discretionary power in the last resort? Would you add a clause giving it to each of the States, or would you sanction the wise provisions already made by your Constitution? If this should be the result of your deliberations when providing for the future, are you, can you, be ready to risk all that we hold dear, to establish, for a temporary and local purpose, that which you must acknowledge to be destructive, and even absurd, as a general provision? Carry out the consequences of this right vested in the different States, and you must perceive that the crisis your conduct presents at this day would recur whenever any law of the united States displeased any of the States, and that we should soon cease to be a nation.

The ordinance, with the same knowledge of the future that characterizes a former objection, tells you that the proceeds of the tax will be constitutionally applied. If this could be ascertained with certainty, the objection would with more propriety be reserved for the law so applying the proceeds, but surely can not be urged against the laws levying the duty.

These are the allegations contained in the ordinance. Examine them seriously, my fellow citizens; judge for yourselves. I appeal to you to determine whether they are so clear, so convincing, as to leave no doubt of their correctness; and even if you should come to this conclusion, how far they justify the reckless, destructive course which you are directed to pursue. Review these objections and the conclusions drawn from them once more. What are they? Every law, then, for raising revenue, according to the South Carolina ordinance, may be rightfully annulled, unless it be so framed as no law ever will or can be framed. Congress have a right to pass laws for raising revenue and each State have a right to oppose their execution—two rights directly opposed to each other; and yet is this absurdity supposed to be contained in an instrument drawn for the express purpose of avoiding collisions between the States and the General Government by an assembly of the most enlightened statesmen and purest patriots ever embodied for a similar purpose.

In vain have these sages declared that Congress shall have the power to lay and collect taxes, duties, imposts, and excises; in vain have they provided that they shall have power to pass laws which shall be necessary and proper to carry those powers into execution, that those laws and that Constitution shall be the "supreme law of the land, and that the judges in every States shall be bound thereby, anything in the constitution or laws of any State to the contrary notwithstanding;" in vain have the people of the several States solemnly sanctioned these provisions, made them their paramount law, and individually sworn to support them whenever they were called on to execute any office. Vain provisions! ineffectual restrictions! vile profanation of oaths! miserable mockery of legislation! if a bare majority of the voters in any one State may, on a real or supposed knowledge of the intent with which a law has been passed, declare themselves free from its operation; say, here it gives too little, there, too much, and operates unequally; here it suffers articles to be free that ought to be taxed; there it taxes those that ought to be free; in this case the proceeds are intended to be applied to purposes which we do not approve; in that, the amount raised is more than is wanted. Congress, it is true, are invested by the Constitution with the right of deciding these questions according to their sound discretion. Congress is composed of the representatives of all the States and of all the people of all the States. But we, part of the people of one State, to whom the Constitution has given no power on the subject, from whom it has expressly taken it away, we, who have solemnly agreed that this Constitution shall be our law ; we, most of whom have sworn to support it—we now abrogate this law and swear, and force others to swear, that it shall not be obeyed; and we do this not because Congress have no right to pass such laws—this we do not allege—but because they have passed them with improper views. They are unconstitutional from the motives of those who passed them, which we can never with certainty know; from their unequal operation, although it is impossible, from the nature of things, that they should be equal; and from the disposition which we presume may be made of their proceeds, although that disposition has not been declared. This is the plain meaning of the ordinance in relation to laws which it abrogates for alleged unconstitutionality. But it does not stop there. It repeals in express terms an important part of the Constitution itself and of laws passed to give it effect, which have never been alleged to be unconstitutional.

The Constitution declares that the judicial powers of the United States extend to cases arising under the laws of the United States, and that such laws, the Constitution, and treaties shall be paramount to the State constitutions and laws. The judiciary act prescribes the mode by which the case may be brought before a court of the United States by appeal when a State tribunal shall decide against this provision of the Constitution. The ordinance declares there shall be no appeal—makes the State law paramount to the Constitution and laws of the United States, forces judges and jurors to swear that they will disregard their provisions, and even makes it penal in a suitor to attempt relief by appeal. It further declares that it shall not be lawful for the authorities of the United States or of that State to enforce the payment of duties imposed by the revenue laws within its limits.

Here is a law of the United States, not even pretended to be unconstitutional, repealed by the authority of a small majority of the voters of a single State. Here is a provision of the Constitution which is solemnly abrogated by the same authority.

On such expositions and reasonings the ordinance grounds not only an assertion of the right to annul the laws of which it complains, but to enforce it by a threat of seceding from the Union if any attempt is made to execute them.

This right to secede is deduced from the nature of the Constitution, which, they say, is a compact between sovereign States who have preserved their whole sovereignty and therefore are subject to no superior; that because they made the compact they can break it when in their opinion it has been departed from by the other States. Fallacious as this course of reasoning is, it enlists State pride and finds advocates in the honest prejudices of those who have not studied the nature of our Government sufficiently to see the radical error on which it rests.

The people of the United States formed the Constitution, acting through the State legislatures in making the compact, to meet and discuss its provisions, and acting in separate conventions when they ratified those provisions; but the terms used in its construction show it to be a Government in which the people of all the States, collectively, are represented. We are *one people* in the choice of President and Vice-President. Here the States have no other agency than to direct the mode in which the votes shall be given. The candidates having the majority of all the votes are chosen. The electors of a majority of States may have given their votes for one candidate, and yet another may be chosen. The people, then, and not the States, are represented in the executive branch.

In the House of Representatives there is this difference, that the people of one State do not, as in the case of President and Vice-President, all vote for the same officers. The people of all the States do not vote for all the members, each State electing only its own representatives. But this creates no material distinction. When chosen, they are all representatives of the United States, not representatives of the particular State from which they come. They are paid by the United States, not by the State; nor are they accountable to it for any act done in the performance of their legislative functions; and however they may in practice, as it is their duty to do, consult and prefer the interests of their particular constituents when they come in conflict with any other partial or local interest, yet it is their first and highest duty, as representatives of the United States, to promote the general good.

The Constitution of the United States, then, forms a *government*, not a league; and whether it be formed by compact between the States or in any other manner, its character is the same. It is a Government in which all the people are represented, which operates directly on the people individually, not upon the States; they retained all the power they did not grant. But each State, having expressly parted with so many powers as to constitute, jointly with the other States, a single nation, can not, from that period, possess any right to secede, because such secession does not break a league, but destroys the unity of a nation; and any injury to that unity is not only a breach which would result from the contravention of a compact, but it is an offense against the whole Union. To say that any State may at pleasure secede from the Union is to say that the United States are not a nation, because it would be a solecism to contend that any part of a nation might dissolve its connection with the other parts, to their injury or ruin, without committing any offense. Secession, like any other revolutionary act, may be morally justified by the extremity of oppression; but to call it a constitutional right is confounding the meaning of terms, and can only be done through gross error or to deceive those who are willing to assert a right, but would pause before they made a revolution or incur the penalties consequent on a failure.

Because the Union was formed by a compact, it is said the parties to that compact may, when they feel themselves aggrieved, depart from it; but it is precisely because it is a compact that they can not. A compact is an agreement or binding obligation. It may by its terms have a sanction or penalty for its breach, or it may not. If it contains no sanction, it may be broken with no other consequence than moral guilt; if it have a sanction, then the breach incurs the designated or implied penalty. A league between independent nations generally has no sanction other than a moral one; or if it should contain a penalty, as there is no common superior it can not be enforced. A government, on the contrary, always has a sanction, express or implied; and in our case it is both necessarily implied and expressly given. An attempt, by force of arms, to destroy a government is an offense, by whatever means the constitutional compact may have been formed; and such government has the right by the law of self-defense to pass acts for punishing the offender, unless that right is modified, restrained, or resumed by the constitutional act. In our system, although it is modified in the.case of treason, yet authority is expressly given to pass all laws necessary to carry its powers into effect, and under this grant provision has been made for punishing acts which obstruct the due administration of the laws.

It would seem superfluous to add anything to show the nature of that union which connects us, but as erroneous opinions on this subject are the foundation of doctrines the most destructive to our peace, I must give some further development to my views on this subject. No one, fellow-citizens, has a higher reverence for the reserved rights of the States than the Magistrate who now addresses you. No one would make greater personal sacrifices or official exertions to defend them from violation; but equal care must be taken to prevent, on their part, an improper interference with or resumption of the rights they have vested in the nation. The line has not been so distinctly drawn as to avoid doubts in some cases of the exercise of power. Men of the best intentions and soundest views may differ in their construction of some parts of the Constitution; but there are others on which dispassionate reflection can leave no doubt. Of this nature appears to be the assumed right of secession. It rests, as we have seen, on the alleged undivided sovereignty of the States and on their having formed in this sovereign capacity a compact which is called the Constitution, from which, because they made it, they have the right to secede. Both of these positions are erroneous, and some of the arguments to prove them so have been anticipated.

The States severally have not retained their entire sovereignty. It has been shown that in becoming parts of a nation, not members of a league, they surrendered many of their essential parts of sovereignty. The right to make treaties, declare war, levy taxes, exercise exclusive judicial and legislative powers, were all of them functions of sovereign power. The States, then, for all these important purposes were no longer sovereign. The allegiance of their citizens was transferred, in the first instance, to the Government of the United States; they became American citizens and owed obedience to the Constitution of the United States and to laws made in conformity with the powers it vested in Congress. This last position has not been and can not be denied. How, then, can that State be said to be sovereign and independent whose citizens owe obedience to laws not made by it and whose magistrates are sworn to disregard those laws when they come in conflict with those passed by another? What shows conclusively that the States can not be said to have reserved an undivided sovereignty is that they expressly ceded the right to punish treason—not treason against their separate power, but treason against the United States. Treason is an offense against *sovereignty*, and sovereignty must reside with the power to punish it. But the reserved rights of the States are not less sacred because they have, for their common interest, made the General Government the depository of these powers. The unity of our political character (as has been shown for another purpose) commenced with its very existence. Under the royal Government we had no separate character; our opposition to its oppressions began as *united colonies*. We were the *United States* under the Confederation, and the name was perpetuated and the Union rendered more perfect by the Federal Constitution. In none of these stages did we consider ourselves in any other light than as forming one nation. Treaties and alliances were made in the name of all. Troops were raised for the joint defense. How, then, with all these proofs that under all changes of our position we had, for designated purposes and with defined powers, created national governments, how is it that the most perfect of those several modes of union should now be considered as a mere league that may be dissolved at pleasure? It is from an abuse of terms. Compact is used as synonymous with league, although the true term is not employed, because it would at once show the fallacy of the reasoning. It would not do to say that our Constitution was only a league, but it is labored to prove it a compact (which in one sense it is) and then to argue that as a league is a compact every compact between nations must of course be a league, and that from such an engagement every sovereign power has a right to recede. But it has been shown that in this sense the States are not sovereign, and that even if they were, and the national Constitution had been formed by compact, there would be no right in any one State to exonerate itself from its obligations.

So obvious are the reasons which forbid this secession that it is necessary only to allude to them. The Union was formed for the benefit of all. It was produced by mutual sacrifices of interests and opinions. Can those sacrifices be recalled? Can the States who magnanimously surrendered their title to the territories of the West recall the grant? Will the inhabitants of the inland States agree to pay the duties that may be imposed without their assent by those on the Atlantic or the Gulf for their own benefit? Shall there be a free port in one State and onerous duties in another? No one believes that any right exists in a single State to involve all the others in these and countless other evils contrary to engagements solemnly made. Everyone must see that the other States, in self-defense, must oppose it at all hazards.

These are the alternatives that are presented by the convention—a repeal of all the acts for raising revenue, leaving the Government without the means of support, or an acquiescence in the dissolution of our Union by the secession of one of its members. When the first was proposed, it was known that it could not be listened to for a moment. It was known, if force was applied to oppose the execution of the laws, that it must be repelled by force; that Congress could not, without involving itself in disgrace and the country in ruin, accede to the proposition; and yet if this is not done in a given day, or if any attempt is made to execute the laws, the State is by the ordinance declared to be out of the Union. The majority of a convention assembled for the purpose have dictated these terms, or rather this rejection of all terms, in the name of the people of South Carolina. It is true that the governor of the State speaks of the submission of their grievances to a convention of all the States, which, he says, they "sincerely and anxiously seek and desire." Yet this obvious and constitutional mode of obtaining the sense of the other States on the construction of the federal compact, and amending it if necessary, has never been attempted by those who have urged the State on to this destructive measure. The State might have proposed the call for a general convention to the other States, and Congress, if a sufficient number of them concurred, must have called it. But the first magistrate of South Carolina, when he expressed a hope that "on a review by Congress and the functionaries of the General Government of the merits of the controversy" such a convention will be accorded to them, must have known that neither Congress nor any functionary of the General Government has authority to call such a convention unless it be demanded by two-thirds of the States. This suggestion, then, is another instance of the reckless inattention to the provisions of the Constitution with which this crisis has been madly hurried on, or of the attempt to persuade the people that a constitutional remedy had been sought and refused. If the legislature of South Carolina "anxiously desire" a general convention to consider their complaints, why have they not made application for it in the way the Constitution points out? The assertion that they "earnestly seek" it is completely negatived by the omission.

This, then, is the position in which we stand: A small majority of the citizens of one State in the Union have elected delegates to a State convention; that convention has ordained that all the revenue laws of the United States must be repealed, or that they are no longer a member of the Union. The governor of that State has recommended to the legislature the raising of an army to carry the secession into effect, and that he may be empowered to give clearances to vessels in the name of the State. No act of violent opposition to the laws has yet been committed, but such a state of things is hourly apprehended. And it is the intent of this instrument to *proclaim*, not only that the duty imposed on me by the Constitution "to take care that the laws be faithfully executed" shall be performed to the extent of the powers already vested in me by law, or of such others as the wisdom of Congress shall devise and intrust to me for that purpose, but to warn the citizens of South Carolina who have been deluded into an opposition to the laws of the danger they will incur by obedience to the illegal and disorganizing ordinance of the convention; to exhort those who have refused to support it to persevere in their determination to uphold the Constitution and laws of their country, and to point out to all the perilous situation into which the good people of that State have been led, and that the course they are urged to pursue is one of ruin and disgrace to the very State whose rights they affect to support.

Fellow-citizens of my native State, let me not only admonish you, as the First Magistrate of our common country, not to incur the penalty of its laws, but use the influence that a father would over his children whom he saw rushing to certain ruin. In that paternal language, with that paternal feeling, let me tell you, my countrymen, that you are deluded by men who are either deceived themselves or wish to deceive you. Mark under what pretenses you have been led on to the brink of insurrection and treason on which you stand. First, a diminution of the value of your staple commodity, lowered by overproduction in other quarters, and the consequent diminution in the value of your lands were the sole effect of the tariff laws. The effect of those laws was confessedly injurious, but the evil was greatly exaggerated by the unfounded theory you were taught to believe—that its burthens were in proportion to your exports, not to your consumption of imported articles. Your pride was roused by the assertion that a submission to those laws was a state of vassalage and that resistance to them was equal in patriotic merit to the opposition our fathers offered to the oppressive laws of Great Britain. You were told that this opposition might be peaceably, might be constitutionally, made; that you might enjoy all the advantages of the Union and bear none of its burthens. Eloquent appeals to your passions, to your State pride, to your native courage, to your sense of real injury, were used to prepare you for the period when the mask which concealed the hideous features of *disunion* should be taken off. It fell, and you were made to look with complacency on objects which not long since you would have regarded with horror. Look back, to the arts which have brought you to this state; look forward to the consequences to which it must inevitably lead ! Look back to what was first told you as an inducement to enter into this dangerous course. The great political truth was repeated to you that you had the revolutionary right of resisting all laws that were palpably unconstitutional and intolerably oppressive. It was added that the right to nullify a law rested on the same principle, but that it was a peaceable remedy. This character which was given to it made you receive with too much confidence the assertions that were made of the unconstitutionality of the law, and its oppressive effects. Mark my fellow-citizens, that by the admission of your leaders the unconstitutionality must be *palpable* or it will not justify either resistance ot nullification. What is the meaning of the word *palpable* in the sense in which it is here used? That which is apparent to everyone; that which no man of ordinary intellect will fail to perceive. Is the unconstitutionality of these laws of that description? Let those among your leaders who once approved and advocated the principle of protective duties answer the question; and let them choose whether they will be considered as incapable then of perceiving that which must have been apparent to every man of common understanding, or as imposing upon your confidence and endeavoring to mislead you now. In either case they are unsafe guides in the perilous path they urge you to tread. Ponder well on this circumstance, and you will know how to appreciate the exaggerated language they address to you. They are not champions of liberty, emulating the fame of our Revolutionary fathers, nor are you an oppressed people, contending, as they repeat to you, against worse than colonial vassalage. You are free members of a flourishing and happy Union. There is no settled design to oppress you. You have indeed felt the unequal operation of laws which may have been unwisely, not unconstitutionally, passed; but that inequality must necessarily be removed. At the very moment when you were madly urged on to the unfortunate course you have begun a change in public opinion had commenced. The nearly approaching payment of the public debt and the consequent necessity of a diminution of duties had already produced considerable reduction, and that, too, on some articles of general consumption in your State. The importance of this change was underrated and you were authoritatively told that no further alleviation of your burthens was to be expected at the very time when the condition of the country imperiously demanded such a modification of the duties as should reduce them to a just and equitable scale. But, as if apprehensive of the effect of this change in allaying your discontents, you were precipitated into the fearful state in which you now find yourselves.

I have urged you to look back to the means that were used to hurry you on to the position you have now assumed and forward to the consequences it will produce. Something more is necessary. Contemplate the condition of that country of which you still form an important part. Consider its Government, uniting in one bond of common interest and general protection so many different States, giving to all their inhabitants the proud title of *American citizen*, protecting their commerce, securing their literature and their arts, facilitating their intercom-munication, defending their frontiers, and making their name respected in the remotest parts of the earth. Consider the extent of its territory, its increasing and happy population, its advance in arts which render life agreeable, and the sciences which elevate the mind! See education spreading the lights of religion, morality, and general information into every cottage in this wide extent of our Territories and States. Behold it as the asylum where the wretched and the oppressed find a refuge and support. Look on this picture of happiness and honor and say, *We too are citizens of America*. Carolina is one of these proud States; her arms have defended, her best blood has cemented, this happy Union. And then add, if you can, without horror and remorse, This happy Union we will dissolve, this picture of peace and prosperity we will deface; this free intercourse we will interrupt; these fertile fields we will deluge with blood, the protection of that glorious flag we renounce; the very name of Americans we discard. And for what, mistaken men? For what do you throw away these inestimable blessings? For what would you exchange your share in the advantages and honor of the Union? For the dream of a separate independence—a dream interrupted by bloody conflicts with your neighbors and a vile dependence on a foreign power. If your leaders could succeed in establishing a separation, what would be your situation? Are you united at home? Are you free from the apprehension of civil discord, with all its fearful consequences? Do our neighboring republics, every day suffering some new revolution or contending with some new insurrection, do they excite your envy? But the dictates of a high duty oblige me solemnly to announce that you can not succeed. The laws of the United States must be executed. I have no discretionary power on the subject; my duty is emphatically pronounced in the Constitution. Those who told you that you might peaceably prevent their execution deceived you; they could not have been deceived themselves. They know that a forcible opposition could alone prevent the execution of the laws, and they know that such opposition must be repelled. Their object is disunion. But be not deceived by names. Disunion by armed force is *treason*. Are you really ready to incur its guilt? If you are, on the heads of the instigators of the act be the dreadful consequences; on their heads be the dishonor, but on yours may fall the punishment. On your unhappy State will inevitably fall all the evils of the conflict you force upon the Government of your country. It can not accede to the mad project of disunion, of which you would be the first victims. Its First Magistrate can not, if he would, avoid the performance of his duty. The consequence must be fearful for you, distressing to your fellow-citizens here and to the friends of good government throughout the world. Its enemies have beheld our prosperity with a vexation they could not conceal; it was a standing refutation of their slavish doctrines, and they will point to our discord with the triumph of malignant joy. It is yet in your power to disappoint them. There is yet time to show that the descendants of the Pinckneys, the Sumpters, the Rutledges, and of the thousand other names which adorn the pages of your Revolutionary history will not abandon that Union to support which so many of them fought and bled and died. I adjure you, as you honor their memory, as you love the cause of freedom, to which they dedicated their lives, as you prize the peace of your country, the lives of its best citizens, and your own fair fame, to retrace your steps. Snatch from the archives of your State the disorganizing edict of its convention; bid its members to reassemble and promulgate the decided expressions of your will to remain in the path which alone can conduct you to safety, prosperity, and honor. Tell them that compared to disunion all other evils are light, because that brings with it an accumulation of all. Declare that you will never take the field unless the star-spangled banner of your country shall float over you, that you will not be stigmatized when dead, and dishonored and scorned while you live, as the authors of the first attack on the Constitution of your country. Its destroyers you can not be. You may disturb its peace, you may interrupt the course of its prosperity, you may cloud its reputation for stability; but its tranquillity will be restored, its prosperity will return, and the stain upon its national character will be transferred and remain an eternal blot on the memory of those who caused the disorder.

Fellow-citizens of the United States, the threat of unhallowed disunion, the names of those once respected by whom it is uttered, the array of military force to support it, denote the approach of a crisis in our affairs on which the continuance of our unexampled prosperity, our political existence, and perhaps that of all free governments may depend. The conjuncture demanded a free, a full, and explicit enunciation, not only of my intentions, but of my principles of action; and as the claim was asserted of a right by a State to annul the laws of the Union, and even to secede from it at pleasure, a frank exposition of my opinions in relation to the origin and form of our Government and the construction I give to the instrument by which it was created seemed to be proper. Having the fullest confidence in the justness of the legal and constitutional opinion of my duties which has been expressed, I rely with equal confidence on your undivided support in my determination to execute the laws, to preserve the Union by all constitutional means, to arrest, if possible, by moderate and firm measures the necessity of a recourse to force, and if it be the will of Heaven that the recurrence of its primeval curse on man for the shedding of a brother's blood should fall upon our land, that it be not called down by any offensive act on the part of the United States.

Fellow-citizens, the momentous case is before you. On your undivided support of your Government depends the decision of the great question it involves—whether your sacred Union will be preserved and the blessing it secures to us as one people shall be perpetuated. No one can doubt that the unanimity with which that decision will be expressed will be such as to inspire new confidence in republican institutions, and that the prudence, the wisdom, and the courage which it will bring to their defense will transmit them unimpaired and invigorated to our children.

May the Great Ruler of Nations grant that the signal blessings with which He has favored ours may not, by the madness of party or personal ambition, be disregarded and lost; and may His wise providence bring those who have produced this crisis to see the folly before they feel the misery of civil strife, and inspire a returning veneration for that Union which, if we may dare to penetrate His designs, He has chosen as the only means of attaining the high destinies to which we may reasonably aspire.

In testimony whereof I have caused the seal of the United States to be hereunto affixed, having signed the same with my hand.

[SEAL] Done at the city of Washington, this 10th day of December, A. D. 1832, and of the Independence of the United States the fifty-seventh.

ANDREW JACKSON.

By the President:

EDW. LIVINGSTON,
Secretary of State.

❧21❧

The Address of the Southern Delegates in Congress to their Constituents

JOHN C. CALHOUN

The Address, drafted by John Calhoun, and signed by forty-eight members of Congress from twelve southern states in 1849, outlines the major grievances felt by them at this time: the gradual erosion of the Constitution's provisions for the return of fugitive slaves, the activities of the abolitionists, and the prospect of federal prohibition of slavery in the newly acquired western territories. It was evident, moreover, that the Southern states were beginning to appreciate their position as an entrenched minority within Congress, and saw that a northern majority might pass measures which they were powerless to prevent. Appealing for unity, the Address concludes with the suggestion that the South should explore every avenue open to it to preserve its position. One of the signatories was Jefferson Davis of Mississippi, later to become president of the Confederacy.

The Address

We, whose names are hereunto annexed, address you in discharge of what we believe to be a solemn duty, on the most important subject ever presented for your consideration. We allude to the conflict between the two great sections of the Union, growing out of a difference of feeling and opinion in reference to the relation existing between the two races, the European and the African, which inhabit the southern section, and the acts of aggression and encroachment to which it has led.

The conflict commenced not long after the acknowledgment of our

Source: John C. Calhoun 'The Address of the Southern Delegates in Congress to their Constituents', in Richard K. Crallé, ed., *The Works of John C. Calhoun*, Columbia, S. C: Printed by A. S. Johnston, 1851–56, Vol. VI.

independence, and has gradually increased until it has arrayed the great body of the North against the South on this most vital subject. In the progress of this conflict, aggression has followed aggression, and encroachment encroachment, until they have reached a point when a regard for your peace and safety will not permit us to remain longer silent. The object of this address is to give you a clear, correct, but brief account of the whole series of aggression and encroachments on your rights, with a statement of the dangers to which they expose you. Our object in making it is not to cause excitement, but to put you in full possession of all the facts and circumstances necessary to a full and just conception of a deep-seated disease, which threatens great danger to you and the whole body politic. We act on the impression, that in a popular government like ours, a true conception of the actual character and state of a disease is indispensable to effecting a cure.

We have made it a joint address, because we believe that the magnitude of the subject required that it should assume the most impressive and solemn form.

Not to go further back, the difference of opinion and feeling in reference to the relation between the two races, disclosed itself in the Convention that framed the Constitution, and constituted one of the greatest difficulties in forming it. After many efforts, it was overcome by a compromise, which provided in the first place, that representative and direct taxes shall be apportioned among the States according to their respective numbers; and that, in ascertaining the number of each, five slaves shall be estimated as three. In the next, that slaves escaping into States where slavery does not exist, shall not be discharged from servitude, but shall be delivered up on claim of the party to whom their labor or service is due. In the third place, that Congress shall not prohibit the importation of slaves before the year 1808; but a tax not exceeding ten dollars may be imposed on each imported. And finally, that no capitation or direct tax shall be laid, but in proportion to federal numbers; and that no amendment of the Constitution, prior to 1808, shall affect this provision, nor that relating to the importation of slaves.

So satisfactory were these provisions, that the second, relating to the delivering up of fugitive slaves, was adopted unanimously, and all the rest, except the third, relative to the importation of slaves until 1808, with almost equal unanimity. They recognize the existence of slavery, and make a specific provision for its protection where it was supposed to be the most exposed. They go further, and incorporate it, as an important element, in determining the relative weight of the several States in the Government of the Union, and the respective burden they should bear in laying capitation and direct taxes. It was well understood at the time, that without them the Constitution would not have been adopted by the Southern States, and of course that they constituted elements so essential to the system that it never would have existed without them. The Northern States, knowing all this, ratified the Constitution, thereby pledging their faith, in the most solemn manner, sacredly to observe them. How that faith has been kept and that pledge redeemed we shall next proceed to show.

With few exceptions of no great importance, the South had no cause to complain prior to the year 1819—a year, it is to be feared, destined to mark a train of events, bringing with them many, and great, and fatal disasters, on the country and its institutions. With it commenced the agitating debate on the question of the admission of Missouri into the Union. We shall pass by for the present this question, and others of the same kind, directly growing out of it, and shall proceed to consider the effects of that spirit of discord, which it roused up between the two sections. It first disclosed itself in the North, by hostility to that portion of the Constitution which provides for the delivering up of fugitive slaves. In its progress it led to the adoption of hostile acts, intended to render it of non-effect, and with so much success that it may be regarded now as practically expunged from the Constitution. How this has been effected will be next explained.

After a careful examination, truth constrains us to say, that it has been by a clear and palpable evasion of the Constitution. It is impossible for any provision to be more free from ambiguity or doubt. It is in the following words:

> No person held to service, or labor, in one State, under the laws thereof, escaping into another State, shall, in consequence of any law or regulation therein, be discharged from such service or labor, but shall be delivered up on claim of the party to whom such service or labor may be due.

All is clear. There is not an uncertain or equivocal word to be found in the whole provision. What shall not be done, and what shall be done, are fully and explicitly set forth. The former provides that the fugitive slave shall not be discharged from his servitude by any law or regulation of the State wherein he is found; and the latter, that he shall be delivered up on claim of his owner.

We do not deem it necessary to undertake to refute the sophistry and subterfuges by which so plain a provision of the Constitution has been evaded, and, in effect, annulled. It constitutes an essential part of the constitutional compact, and of course the supreme law of the land. As such it is binding on all, the Federal and State Governments, the States and the individuals composing them. The sacred obligation of compact, and the solemn injunction of the supreme law, which legislators and judges, both Federal and State, are bound by oath to support, all unite to enforce its fulfilment, according to its plain meeting and true intent. What that meaning and intent are, there was no diversity of opinion in the better days of the Republic, prior to 1819. Congress, State Legislatures, State and Federal Judges and Magistrates, and people, all spontaneously placed the same interpretation on it. During that period none interposed impediments in the way of the owner seeking to recover his fugitive slave; nor did any deny his right to have every proper facility to enforce his claim to have him delivered up. It was then nearly as easy to recover one found in a Northern State, as one found in a neighboring Southern State. But this has passed away, and the provision is defunct, except perhaps in two States.[1]

When we take into consideration the importance and clearness of this provision, the evasion by which it has been set aside may fairly be regarded as one of the most fatal blows ever received by the South and the Union. This cannot be more concisely and correctly stated, than it has been by two of the learned judges of the Supreme Court of the United States. In one of his decisions[2] Judge Story said:

281

"Historically it is well known that the object of this clause was to secure to the citizens of the slaveholding States the complete right and title of ownership in their slaves, as property, in every State of the Union, into which they might escape, from the State wherein they were held in servitude." "The full recognition of this right and title was indispensable to the security of this species of property, in all the slaveholding States, and, indeed, was so vital to the preservation of their interests and institutions, that it cannot be doubted, that it constituted a fundamental article without the adoption of which the Union would not have been formed. Its true design was to guard against the doctrines and principles prevalent in the non-slaveholding States, by preventing them from intermeddling with, or restricting, or abolishing the rights of the owners of slaves."

Again:

"The clause was therefore of the last importance to the safety and security of the Southern States, and could not be surrendered by them without endangering their whole property in slaves. The clause was accordingly adopted in the Constitution by the unanimous consent of the framers of it—a proof at once of its intrinsic and practical necessity."

Again:

"The clause manifestly contemplates the existence of a positive unqualified right on the part of the owner of the slave, which no State law or regulation can in any way regulate, control, qualify, or restrain."

The opinion of the other learned judges was not less emphatic as to the importance to this provision and the unquestionable right of the South under it. Judge Baldwin, in charging the jury, said:[3]

"If there are any rights of property which can be enforced, if one citizen have any rights of property which are inviolable under the protection of the supreme law of the State, and the Union, they are those which have been set at nought by some of these defendants. As the owner of property, which he had a perfect right to possess, protect, and take away—as a citizen of a sister State, entitled to all the privileges and immunities of citizens of any other States—Mr. Johnson stands before you on ground which cannot be taken from under him—it is the same ground on which the Government itself is based. If the defendants can be justified, we have no longer law or government."

Again, after referring more particularly to the provision for delivering up fugitive slaves, he said:

"Thus you see, that the foundations of the Government are laid, and rest on the right of property in slaves. The whole structure must fall by disturbing the corner-stone."

These are grave and solemn and admonitory words, from a high source. They confirm all for which the South has ever contended, as to the clearness, importance, and fundamental character of this provision, and the disastrous consequences which would inevitably follow from its violation. But in spite of these solemn warnings, the violation, then commenced, and which they were intended to rebuke, has been full and perfectly consummated. The citizens of the South, in their attempt to recover their slaves, now meet, instead of aid and co-operation, resistance in every form; resistance from hostile acts of legislation, intended to baffle and defeat their claims by all sorts of devices, and by interposing every description of impediment—

resistance from judges and magistrates—and finally, when all these fail, from mobs, composed of whites and blacks, which, by threats or force, rescue the fugitive slave from the possession of his rightful owner. The attempt to recover a slave, in most of the Northern States, cannot now be made without the hazard of insult, heavy pecuniary loss, imprisonment, and even of life itself. Already has a worthy citizen of Maryland lost his life[4] in making an attempt to enforce his claim to a fugitive slave under this provision.

But a provision of the Constitution may be violated indirectly as well as directly; by doing an act in its nature inconsistent with that which is enjoined to be done. Of the form of violation, there is a striking instance connected with the provision under consideration. We allude to secret combinations which are believed to exist in many of the Northern States, whose object is to entice, decoy, entrap, inveigle, and seduce slaves to escape from their owners, and to pass them secretly and rapidly, by means organized for the purpose, into Canada, where they will be beyond the reach of the provision. That to entice a slave, by whatever artifice, to abscond from his owner, into a non-slaveholding State, with the intention to place him beyond the reach of the provision, or prevent his recovery, by concealment or otherwise, is as completely repugnant to it, as its open violation would be, is too clear to admit of doubt or to require illustration. And yet, as repugnant as these combinations are to the true intent of the provision, it is believed, that, with the above exception, not one of the States, within whose limits they exist, has adopted any measure to suppress them, or to punish those by whose agency the object for which they were formed is carried into execution. On the contrary, they have looked on, and witnessed with indifference, if not with secret approbation, a great number of slaves enticed from their owners, and placed beyond the possibility of recovery, to the great annoyance and heavy pecuniary loss of the bordering Southern States.

When we take into consideration the great importance of this provision, the absence of all uncertainty as to its true meaning and intent, the many guards by which it is surrounded to protect and enforce it, and then reflect how completely the object for which it was inserted in the Constitution is defeated by these two-fold infractions, we doubt, taking all together, whether a more flagrant breach of faith is to be found on record. We know the language we have used is strong, but it is not less true than strong.

There remains to be noticed another class of aggressive acts of a kindred character, but which instead of striking at an express and specific provision of the Constitution, aims directly at destroying the relation between the two races at the South, by means subversive in their tendency of one of the ends for which the Constitution was established. We refer to the systematic agitation of the question by the Abolitionists, which, commencing about 1835, is still continued in all possible forms. Their avowed intention is to bring about a state of things that will force emancipation on the South. To unite the North in fixed hostility to slavery in the South, and to excite discontent among the slaves with their condition, are among the means employed to effect it. With a view to bring about the former, every means are resorted to in order to render the South, and the relation between the two races there, odious and hateful to the North. For this purpose societies and newspapers are everywhere established, debating clubs opened, lecturers employed, pamphlets and other publications, pictures and petitions to Congress, resorted to, and directed to that single point, regardless of truth or decency; while the circulation of incendiary publications in the South, the agitation of the subject of abolition in Congress, and the employment of emissaries are relied on to excite discontent among the slaves. This agitation, and the use of these means, have been continued with more or less activity for a series of years, not without doing much towards effecting the object intended. We regard both object and means to be aggressive and dangerous to the rights of the South, and subversive, as stated, of one of the ends for which the Constitution was established. Slavery is a domestic institution. It belongs to the States, each for itself to decide, whether it shall be established or not; and if it be established, whether it should be abolished or not. Such being the clear and unquestionable right of the States, it follows necessarily that it would be a flagrant act of aggression on a State, destructive of its rights, and subversive of its independence, for the Federal Government, or one or more States, or their people, to undertake to force on it the emancipation of its slaves. But it is a sound maxim in politics, as well as law and morals, that no one has a right to do that indirectly which he cannot do directly, and it may be added with equal truth, to aid, abet, or countenance another in doing it. And yet the Abolitionists of the North, openly avowing their intention, and resorting to the most efficient means for the purpose, have been attempting to bring about a state of things to force the Southern States to emancipate their slaves, without any act on the part of any Northern State to arrest or suppress the means by which they propose to accomplish it. They have been permitted to pursue their object, and to use whatever means they please, if without aid or countenance, also without resistance or disapprobation. What gives a deeper shade to the whole affair, is the fact, that one of the means to effect their object, that of exciting discontent among our slaves, tends directly to subvert what its preamble declares to be one of the ends for which the Constitution was ordained and established: "to ensure domestic tranquillity," and that in the only way in which domestic tranquillity is likely ever to be disturbed in the South. Certain it is, that an agitation so systematic—having such an object in view, and sought to be carried into execution by such means—would, between independent nations, constitute just cause of remonstrance by the party against which the aggression was directed, and if not heeded, an appeal to arms for redress. Such being the case where an aggression of the kind takes place among independent nations, how much more aggravated must it be between confederated States, where the Union precludes an appeal to arms, while it affords a medium through which it can operate with vastly increased force and effect? That it would be perverted to such a use, never entered into the imagination of the generation which formed and adopted the Constitution, and, if it had been supposed it would, it is certain that the South never would have adopted it.

We now return to the question of the admission of Missouri to the Union, and shall proceed to give a brief sketch of the occurrences connected with it, and the consequences to which it has directly led. In the latter part of 1819, the then territory of Missouri applied to Congress, in the usual form, for leave to form a State Constitution and Government, in order to be admitted into the Union. A bill was reported for the purpose, with the usual provisions in such cases. Amendments were offered, having for their object to make it a condition for her admission, that her Constitution should have a provision to prohibit slavery. This brought on the agitating debate, which, with the effects that followed, has done so much to alienate the South and North, and endanger our political institutions. Those who objected to the amendments, rested their opposition on the high grounds of the right of self-government. They claimed that a territory, having reached the period when it is proper for it to form a Constitution and Government for itself, becomes fully vested with all the rights of self-government; and that even the condition imposed on it by the Federal Constitution, relates not to the formation of its Constitution and Government, but its admission into the Union. For that purpose, it provides as a condition, that the Government must be Republican.

They claimed that Congress has no right to add this condition, and that to assume it would be tantamount to the assumption of the right to make its entire Constitution and Government; as no limitation could be imposed, as to the extent of the right, if it be admitted that it exists at all. Those who supported the amendment denied these grounds, and claimed the right of Congress to impose, at discretion, what conditions it pleased. In this agitating debate, the two sections stood arrayed against each other; the South in favor of the bill without amendment, and the North opposed to it without it. The debate and agitation continued until the session was well advanced; but it became apparent, towards it close, that the people of Missouri were fixed and resolved in their opposition to the proposed condition, and that they would certainly reject it, and adopt a Constitution without it, should the bill pass with the condition. Such being the case, it required no great effort of mind to perceive, that Missouri, once in possession of a Constitution and Government, not simply on paper, but with legislatures elected, and officers appointed, to carry them into effect, the grave questions would be presented, whether she was of right a Territory or State; and, if the latter, whether Congress had the right, and, if the right, the power to abrogate her Constitution, disperse her legislature, and to remand her back to the territorial condition. These were great, and, under the circumstances, fearful questions—too fearful to be met by those who had raised the agitation. From that time the only question was, how to escape from the difficulty. Fortunately, a means was afforded. A Compromise (as it was called) was offered, based on the terms, that the North should cease to oppose the admission of Missouri on the grounds for which the South contended, and that the provisions of the Ordinance of 1787, for the government of the Northwestern Territory, should be applied to all the territory acquired by the United States from France under the treaty of Louisiana lying North of 36° 30', except the portion lying in the State of Missouri. The Northern members embraced it; and although not originating with them, adopted it as their own. It was forced through Congress by the almost united votes of the North, against a minority consisting almost entirely of members from the Southern States.

Such was the termination of this, the first conflict, under the Constitution, between the two sections, in reference to slavery in connection with the territories. Many hailed it as a permanent and final adjustment that would prevent the recurrence of similar conflicts; but others, less sanguine, took the opposite and more gloomy view, regarding it as the precursor as a train of events which might rend the Union asunder, and prostrate our political system. One of these was the experienced and sagacious Jefferson. Thus far, time would seem to favor his forebodings. May a returning sense of justice and a protecting Providence, avert their final fulfilment.

For many years the subject of slavery in reference to the territories ceased to agitate the country. Indications, however, connected with the question of annexing Texas, showed clearly that it was ready to break out again, with redoubled violence, on some future occasion. The difference in the case of Texas was adjusted by extending the Missouri compromise line of 36° 30', from its terminus, on the western boundary of the Louisiana purchase, to the western boundary of Texas. The agitation again ceased for a short period.

The war with Mexico soon followed, and that terminated in the acquisition of New Mexico and Upper California, embracing an area equal to about one half of the entire valley of the Mississippi. If to this we add the portion of Oregon acknowledged to be ours by the recent treaty with England, our whole territory on the Pacific and west of the Rocky Mountains will be found to be in extent but little less than that vast valley. The near prospect of so great an addition rekindled the excitement between the North and South in reference to slavery in its connection with the territories, which has become, since those on the Pacific were acquired, more universal and intense than ever.

The effects have been to widen the difference between the two sections, and give a more determined and hostile character to their conflict. The North no longer respects the Missouri compromise line, although adopted by their almost unanimous vote. Instead of compromise, they avow that their determination is to exclude slavery from all the territories of the United States, acquired, or to be acquired; and, of course, to prevent the citizens of the Southern States from emigrating with their property in slaves into any of them. Their object, they allege, is to prevent the extension of slavery, and ours to extend it, thus making the issue between them and us to be the naked question, shall slavery be extended or not? We do not deem it necessary, looking to the object of this address, to examine the question so fully discussed at the last session, whether Congress has the right to exclude the citizens of the South from immigrating with their property into territories belonging to the confederated States of the Union. What we propose in this connection is, to make a few remarks on what the North alleges, erroneously, to be the issue between us and them.

So far from maintaining the doctrine, which the issue implies, we hold that the Federal Government has no right to extend or restrict slavery, no more than to establish or abolish it; nor has it any right whatever to distinguish between the domestic institutions of one State, or section, and another, in order to favor one and discourage the other. As the federal representative of each and all the States, it is bound to deal out, within the sphere of its powers, equal and exact justice and favor to all. To act otherwise, to undertake to discriminate between the domestic institutions of one and another, would be to act in total subversion of the end for which it was established—to be the common protection and guardian of all. Entertaining these opinions, we ask not, as the North alleges we do, for the extension of slavery. That would make a discrimination in our favor, as unjust and unconstitutional as the discrimination they ask against us in their favor. It is not for them, nor for the Federal Government to determine, whether our domestic institution is good or bad; or whether it should be repressed or preserved. It belongs to us, and us only, to decide such questions. What then we do insist on, is, not to extend slavery, but that we shall not be prohibited from immigrating with our property, into the Territories of the United States, because we are slaveholders; or, in other words, that we shall not on that account be disfranchised of a privilege possessed by all others, citizens and foreigners, without discrimination as to character, profession, or color. All, whether savage, barbarian, or civilized, may freely enter and remain, we only being excluded.

We rest our claim, not only on the high grounds above stated, but also on the solid foundation of right, justice, and equality. The territories immediately in controversy—New Mexico and California—were acquired by the common sacrifice and efforts of all the States, towards which the South contributed far more than her full share of men,[5] to say nothing of money, and is, of course, on every principle of right, justice, fairness and equality, entitled to participate fully in the benefits to be derived from their acquisition. But as impregnable as is this ground, there is another not less so. Ours is a Federal Government—a Government in which not individuals, but States as distinct sovereign communities, are the constituents. To them, as members of the Federal Union, the territories belong; and they are hence declared to be territories belonging to the United States. The States, then, are the joint owners. Now it is conceded by all writers on the subject, that in all such Governments their members are all equal—equal in rights and equal in dignity. They also concede that this equality constitutes the basis of such Government, and that it cannot be destroyed without changing their nature and character. To deprive, then, the Southern States and their citizens of their full share in territories declared to belong to them, in common with the other States, would be in derogation of the equality belonging to them as members of a Federal Union, and sink them, from being equals, into a subordinate and dependent condition. Such are the solid and impregnable grounds on which we rest our demand to an equal participation in the territories.

But as solid and impregnable as they are in the eyes of justice and reason, they oppose a feeble resistance to a majority, determined to engross the whole. At the last session of Congress, a bill was passed, establishing a territorial government for Oregon, excluding slavery therefrom. The President gave his sanction to the bill, and sent a special message to Congress assigning his reasons for doing so. These reasons presupposed that the Missouri compromise was to be, and would be, extended west of the Rocky Mountains, to the Pacific Ocean. And the President intimated his intention in his message to veto any future bill that should restrict slavery south of the line of that compromise. Assuming it to have been the purpose and intention of the North to extend the Missouri compromise line as above indicated, the passage of the Oregon bill could only be regarded as evincing the acquiescence of the South in that line. But the developments of the present session of Congress have made it manifest to all, that no such purpose or intention now exists with the North to any considerable extent. Of the truth of this, we have ample evidence in what has occurred already in the House of Representatives, where the popular feelings are soonest and most intensely felt.

Although Congress has been in session but little more than one month, a greater number of measures of an aggressive character have been introduced, and they are more aggravated and dangerous, than have been for years before. And what clearly discloses whence they take their origin, is the fact, that they all relate to the territorial aspect of the subject of slavery, or some other of a nature and character intimately connected with it.

The first of this series of aggressions is a resolution introduced by a member from Massachusetts, the object of which is to repeal all acts which recognize the existence of slavery, or authorize the selling or disposing of slaves in this District. On question of leave to bring in a bill, the votes stood 69 for and 82 against leave. The next was a resolution offered by a member from Ohio, instructing the Committee on Territories to report forthwith bills for excluding slavery from California and New Mexico.[6] It passed by a vote of 107 to 80. That was followed by a bill introduced by another member from Ohio, to take the votes of the inhabitants of this District, on the question whether slavery within its limits should be abolished.

The bill provided, according to the admission of the mover, that free negroes and slaves should vote. On the question to lay the bill on the table, the votes stood, for 106, against 79. To this succeeded the resolution of a member from New York, in the following words: "Whereas the traffic now prosecuted in this metropolis of the Republic in human beings, as chattels, is contrary to natural justice and the fundamental principles of our political system, and is notoriously a reproach to our country, throughout Christendom, and a serious hindrance to the progress of republican liberty among the nations of the earth. Therefore,

"*Resolved*, That the Committee for the District of Columbia be instructed to report a bill, as soon as practicable, prohibiting the slave trade in said District."

On the question of adopting the resolution, the votes stood 98 for, and 88 against. He was followed by a member from Illinois, who offered a resolution for abolishing slavery in the Territories, and all places where Congress has exclusive powers of legislation, that is, in all forts, magazines, arsenals, dockyards, and other needful buildings, purchased by Congress with the consent of the Legislature of the State.

This resolution was passed over under the rules of the House without being put to vote.

The votes in favor of all these measures were confined to the members from the Northern States. True, there are some patriotic members from that section who voted against all of them, and whose high sense of justice is duly appreciated; who in the progress of the aggressions upon the South have, by their votes, sustained the guaranties of the Constitution, and of whom we regret to say many have been sacrificed at home by their patriotic course.

We have now brought to a close a narrative of the series of acts of aggression and encroachment, connected with the subject of this address, including those that are consummated and those still in progress. They are numerous, great, and dangerous, and threaten with destruction the greatest and most vital of all the interests and institutions of the South. Indeed, it may be doubted whether there is a single provision, stipulation, or guaranty of the Constitution, intended for the security of the South, that has not been rendered almost perfectly nugatory. It may even be made a serious question, whether the encroachments already made, without the aid of any other, would not, if permitted to operate unchecked, end in emancipation, and that at no distant day. But be that as it may, it hardly admits of a doubt that, if the aggressions already commenced in the House, and now in progress, should be consummated, such in the end would certainly be the consequence.

Little, in truth, would be left to be done after we have been excluded from all the territories, including those to be hereafter acquired; after slavery is abolished in this District and in the numerous places dispersed all over the South, where Congress has the exclusive right of legislation, and after the other measures proposed are consummated. Every outpost and barrier would be carried, and nothing would be left but to finish the work of abolition at pleasure in the States themselves. This District, and all places over which Congress has exclusive power of legislation, would be asylums for fugitive slaves, where, as soon as they placed their feet, they would become, according to the doctrines of our Northern assailants, free, unless there should be some positive enactments to prevent it.

Under such a state of things the probability is, that emancipation would soon follow, without any final act to abolish slavery. The depressing effects of such measures on the white race at the South, and the hope they would create in the black of a speedy emancipation, would produce a state of feeling inconsistent with the much longer continuance of the existing relations between the two. But be that as it may, it is certain, if emancipation did not follow, as a matter of course, the final act in the States would not be long delayed. The want of constitutional power would oppose a feeble resistance. The great body of the North is united against our peculiar institution. Many believe it to be sinful, and the residue, with inconsiderable exceptions, believe it to be wrong. Such being the case, it would indicate a very superficial knowledge of human nature, to think that, after aiming at abolition, systematically, for so many years, and pursuing it with such unscrupulous disregard of law and Constitution, that the fanatics who have led the way and forced the great body of the North to follow them, would, when the finishing stroke only remained to be given, voluntarily suspend it, or permit any constitutional scruples or considerations of justice to arrest it. To these may be added an aggression, though not yet commenced, long meditated and threatened: to prohibit what the abolitionists call the internal slave trade, meaning thereby the transfer of slaves from one State to another, from whatever motive done, or however effected. Their object would seem to be to render them worthless by crowding them together where they are, and thus hasten the work of emancipation. There is reason for believing that it will soon follow those now in progress, unless, indeed, some decisive step should be taken in the mean time to arrest the whole.

The question then is, Will the measures of aggression proposed in the House be adopted?

They may not, and probably will not be this session. But when we take into consideration, that there is a majority now in favor of one of them, and a strong minority in favor of the other, so far as the sense of the House has been taken; that there will be in all probability a considerable increase in the next Congress of the vote in favor of them, and that it will be largely increased in the next succeeding Congress under the census to be taken next year, it amounts almost to a certainty that they will be adopted, unless some decisive measure is taken in advance to prevent it.

But, even if these conclusions should prove erroneous—if fanaticism and the love of power should, contrary to their nature, for once respect constitutional barriers, or if the calculations of policy should retard the adoption of these measures, or even defeat them altogether, there would still be left one certain way to accomplish their object, if the determination avowed by the North to monopolize all the territories, to the exclusion of the South, should be carried into effect. That of itself would, at no distant day, add to the North a sufficient number of States to give her three fourths of the whole; when, under the color of an amendment to the Constitution, she would emancipate our slaves, however opposed it might be to its true intent.

Thus, under every aspect, the result is certain, if aggression be not promptly and decidedly met. How it is to be met, it is for you to decide.

Such then being the case, it would be to insult you to suppose you could hesitate. To destroy the existing relation between the free and servile races at the South would lead to consequences unparalleled in history. They cannot be separated, and cannot live together in peace, or harmony, or to their mutual advantage, except in their present relation. Under any other, wretchedness, and misery, and desolation would overspread the whole South. The example of the British West Indies, as blighting as emancipation has proved to them, furnishes a very faint picture of the calamities it would bring on the South. The circumstances under which it would take place with us, would be entirely different from those which took place with them, and calculated to lead to far more disastrous results. There the Government of the parent country emancipated slaves in her colonial possessions—a Government rich and powerful, and actuated by views of policy (mistaken as they turned out to be), rather than fanaticism. It was besides, disposed to act justly towards the owners, even in the act of emancipating their slaves, and to protect and foster them afterwards. It accordingly appropriated nearly $100,000,000 as a compensation to them for their losses under the act, which sum, although it turned out to be far short of the amount, was thought at the time to be liberal. Since the emancipation, it has kept up a sufficient military and naval force to keep the blacks in awe, and a number of magistrates, and constables, and other civil officers, to keep order in the towns and on plantations, and enforce respect to their former owners. To a considerable extent these have served as a substitute for the police formerly kept on the plantations by the owners and their overseers, and to preserve the social and political superiority of the white race. But, notwithstanding all this, the British West India possessions are ruined, impoverished, miserable, wretched, and destined probably to be abandoned to the black race.

Very different would be the circumstances under which emancipation would take place with us. If it ever should be effected, it will be through the agency of the Federal Government, controlled by the dominant power of the Northern States of the Confederacy, against the resistance and struggle of the Southern. It can then only be effected by the prostration of the white race; and that would necessarily engender the bitterest feelings of hostility between them and the North. But the reverse would be the case between the blacks of the South and the people of the North. Owing their emancipation to them, they would regard them as friends, guardians, and patrons, and centre, accordingly, all their sympathy in them. The people of the North would not fail to reciprocate and to favor them, instead of the whites. Under the influence of such feelings, and impelled by fanaticism and love of power, they would not stop at emancipation. Another step would be taken—to raise them to a political and social equality with their former owners, by giving them the right of voting and holding public offices under the Federal Government. We see the first step toward it in the bill already alluded to—to vest the free blacks and slaves with the right to vote on the question of emancipation in this District. But when once raised to an equality, they would become the fast political associates of the North, acting and voting with them on all questions, and by this political union between them, holding the white race at the South in complete subjection. The blacks, and the profligate whites that might unite with them, would become the principal recipients of federal offices and patronage, and would, in consequence, be raised above the whites of the South in the political and social scale. We would, in a word, change conditions with them—a degradation greater than has ever yet fallen to the lot of a free and enlightened people, and one from which we could not escape, should emancipation take place (which it certainly will if not prevented), but by fleeing the homes of ourselves and ancestors, and by abandoning our country to our former slaves, to become the permanent abode of disorder, anarchy, poverty, misery, and wretchedness.

With such a prospect before us, the gravest and most solemn question that ever claimed the attention of a people is presented for your consideration: What is to be done to prevent it? It is a question belonging to you to decide. All we propose is, to give you our opinion.

We, then, are of the opinion that the first and indispensable step, without which nothing can be done, and with which every thing may be, is to be united among yourselves, on this great and most vital question. The want of Union and concert in reference to it has brought the South, the Union, and our system of government to their present perilous condition. Instead of placing it above all others, it has been made subordinate, not only to mere questions of policy, but to the preservation of party ties and ensuring of party success. As high as we hold a due respect for these, we hold them subordinate to that and other questions involving our safety and happiness. Until they are so held by the South, the North will not believe that you are in earnest in opposition to their encroachments, and they will continue to follow, one after another, until the work of abolition is finished. To convince them that you are, you must prove by your acts that you hold all other questions subordinate to it. If you become united, and prove yourselves in earnest, the North will be brought to a pause, and to a calculation of consequences; and that may lead to a change of measures, and the adoption of a course of policy that may quietly and peaceably terminate this long conflict between the two sections. If it should not, nothing would remain for you but to stand up immovably in defence of rights, involving your all—your property, prosperity, equality, liberty, and safety.

As the assailed, you would stand justified by all laws, human and divine, in repelling a blow so dangerous, without looking to consequences, and to resort to all means necessary for that purpose. Your assailants, and not you, would be responsible for consequences.

Entertaining these opinions, we earnestly entreat you *to be united*, and for that purpose adopt all necessary measures. Beyond this, we think it would not be proper to go at present.

We hope, if you should unite with any thing like unanimity, it may of itself apply a remedy to this deep-seated and dangerous disease; but, if such should not be the case, the time will then have come for you to decide what course to adopt.

R. M. T. HUNTER,	*Virginia.*	R. B. RHETT,	*South Carolina.*
JAMES M. MASON,	"	R. F. SIMPSON,	"
ARCHIBALD ATKINSON,	"	D. WALLACE,	"
THOMAS H. BAYLY,	"	J. A. WOODWARD,	"
R. L. T. BEALE,	"	H. V. JOHNSON,	*Georgia.*
HENRY BEDINGER,	"	ALFRED IVERSON,	"
THOMAS S. BOCOCK,	"	HUGH A. HARALSON,	"
WILLIAM G. BROWN,	"	DAVID L. YULEE,	*Florida.*
R. K. MEADE,	"	S. U. DOWNS,	*Louisiana.*
R. A. THOMPSON,	"	J. H. HARMANSON,	"
J. R. J. DANIEL,	*North Carolina.*	EMILE LA SERE,	*Louisiana.*
A. W. VENABLE,	"	I. E. MORSE,	"
A. P. BUTLER,	*South Carolina.*	T. PILSBURY,	*Texas*
J. C. CALHOUN,	*South Carolina.*	DAVID S. KAUFMAN	"
ARMISTEAD BURT,	"	SOLON BORLAND,	*Arkansas*
I. E. HOLMES,	"	J. K. SEBASTIAN	"

R. W. JOHNSON,   *Arkansas*
HOPKINS L. TURNEY,   *Tennessee*
F. P. STANTON   "
D. R. ATCHINSON,   *Missouri*
WILLIAM R. KING,   *Alabama*
B. FITZPATRICK,   *Alabama*
JOHN GAYLE,   "
F. W. BOWDON,   "

S. W. HARRIS,   *Alabama*
S. W. INGE,   "
JEFFERSON DAVIS,   *Mississippi*
HENRY S. FOOTE,   "
P. W. TOMPKINS,   "
A. G. BROWN,   "
W. S. FEATHERSTON,   "
JACOB THOMPSON,   "

Notes

1. Indiana and Illinois.
2. The case of Prigg vs. the Commonwealth of Pennsylvania.
3. The case of Johnson vs. Tompkins and others.
4. Mr. Kennedy, of Hagerstown, Maryland.
5. Total number of volunteers from the South—

Regiments	33
Battalions	14
Companies	120

Total number of volunteers from the South   45,640

Total number of volunteers from the North—

Regiments	22
Battalions	2
Companies	12

Total number of volunteers from the North   23,084

Being nearly two on the part of the South to one on the part of the North. But taking into consideration that the population of the North is two thirds greater than the South, the latter has furnished more than three times her due proportion of volunteers.

6. Since reported to the house.

V. Stepping to Secession: 1856–1861

22

Speech on the Slavery Question

JOHN C. CALHOUN

This was Calhoun's last formal speech to the United States Senate. Too ill to deliver it himself, it was read for him by Senator Mason. It rehearses the arguments which Calhoun had spent his life defending: the difficult position of the Southern states, faced with the pressure to abolish slavery from the growing numerical—and moral—majority in the North. Although his theme was still the need to find a formula by which to preserve the Union, Calhoun argues that its fate is in the hands of the North: it is there that the spirit of compromise must be achieved to allow the South to continue to co-exist within the framework of the federal republic. Calhoun died on March 31st, 1850.

Speech on the Slavery Question, Delivered in the Senate, 4th March 1850.

I have senators, believed from the first that the agitation of the subject of slavery would, if not prevented by some timely and effective measure, end in disunion. Entertaining this opinion, I have, on all proper occasions, endeavored to call the attention of both the two great parties which divide the country to adopt some measure to prevent so great a disaster, but without success. The agitation has been permitted to proceed, with almost no attempt to resist it, until it has reached a point when it can no longer be disguised or denied that the Union is in danger. You have thus had forced upon you the greatest and the gravest question that can ever come under your consideration—How can the Union be preserved?

To give a satisfactory answer to this mighty question it is indispensable to have an accurate and thorough knowledge of the nature and the character of the cause by which the Union is endangered. Without such knowledge it is impossible to pronounce, with any certainty, by what measure it can be saved; just as it would be

Source: John C. Calhoun, 'Speech on the Slavery Question, delivered in the Senate', 4th March 1850, in Richard K. Crallé, ed., *The Works of John C. Calhoun*, New York: Russell & Russell, 1968, Vol. IV.

impossible for a physician to pronounce, in the case of some dangerous disease, with any certainty, by what remedy the patient could be saved, without similar knowledge of the nature and character of the cause which produced it. The first question, then, presented for consideration, in the investigation I propose to make, in order to obtain such knowledge, is—What is it that has endangered the Union ?

To this question there can be but one answer,—that the immediate cause is the almost universal discontent which pervades all the States composing the Southern section of the Union. This widely-extended discontent is not of recent origin. It commenced with the agitation of the slavery question, and has been increasing ever since. The next question, going one step further back, is—What has caused this widely diffused and almost universal discontent?

It is a great mistake to suppose, as is by some, that it originated with demagogues, who excited the discontent with the intention of aiding their personal advancement, or with the disappointed ambition of certain politicians, who resorted to it as the means of retrieving their fortunes. On the contrary, all the great political influences of the section were arrayed against excitement, and exerted to the utmost to keep the people quiet. The great mass of the people of the South were divided, as in the other section, into Whigs and Democrats. The leaders and the presses of both parties in the South were very solicitous to prevent excitement and to preserve quiet; because it was seen that the effects of the former would necessarily tend to weaken, if not destroy, the political ties which united them with their respective parties in the other section. Those who know the strength of party ties will readily appreciate the immense force which this cause exerted against agitation, and in favor of preserving quiet. But, great as it was, it was not sufficient to prevent the widespread discontent which now pervades the section. No; some cause, far deeper and more powerful than the one supposed, must exist, to account for discontent so wide and deep. The question then recurs—What is the cause of this discontent ? It will be found in the belief of the people of the Southern States, as prevalent as the discontent itself, that they cannot remain, as things now are, consistently with honor and safety, in the Union. The next question to be considered is—What has caused this belief?

One of the causes is, undoubtedly, to be traced to the long-continued agitation of the slave question on the part of the North, and the many aggressions which they have made on the rights of the South during the time. I will not enumerate them at present, as it will be done hereafter in its proper place.

There is another lying back of it—with which this is intimately connected—that may be regarded as the great and primary cause. This is to be found in the fact that the equilibrium between the two sections, in the Government as it stood when the constitution was ratified and the Government put in action, has been destroyed. At that time there was nearly a perfect equilibrium between the two which afforded ample means to each to protect itself against the aggression of the other; but, as it now stands, one section has the exclusive power of controlling the Government, which leaves the other without any adequate means of protecting itself against its encroachment and oppression. To place this subject distinctly before you, I have,

Senators, prepared a brief statistical statement, showing the relative weight of the two sections in the Government under the first census of 1790 and the last census of 1840. According to the former, the population of the United States, including Vermont, Kentucky, and Tennessee, which then were in their incipient condition of becoming States, but were not actually admitted, amounted to 3,929,827. Of this number the Northern States had 1,997,899, and the Southern 1,952,072, making a difference of only 45,827 in favor of the former States. The number of States, including Vermont, Kentucky, and Tennessee, were sixteen; of which eight, including Vermont, belonged to the Northern section, and eight, including Kentucky and Tennessee, to the Southern,—making an equal division of the States between the two sections under the first census. There was a small preponderance in the House of Representatives, and in the Electoral College, in favor of the Northern, owing to the fact that, according to the provisions of the constitution, in estimating federal numbers five slaves count but three; but it was too small to affect sensibly the perfect equilibrium which, with that exception, existed at the time. Such was the equality of the two sections when the States composing them agreed to enter into a Federal Union. Since then the equilibrium between them has been greatly disturbed.

According to the last census the aggregate population of the United States amounted to 17,063,357, of which the Northern section contained 9,728,920, and the Southern 7,334,437, making a difference in round numbers, of 2,400,000. The number of States had increased from sixteen to twenty-six, making an addition of ten States. In the mean time the position of Delaware had become doubtful as to which section she properly belonged. Considering her as neutral, the Northern States will have thirteen and the Southern States twelve, making, a difference in the Senate of two Senators in favor of the former. According to the apportionment under the census of 1840, there were two hundred and twenty-three members of the House of Representatives, of which the Northern States had one hundred and thirty-five, and the Southern States (considering Delaware as neutral) eighty-seven, making a difference in favor of the former in the House of Representatives of forty-eight. The difference in the Senate of two members, added to this, gives to the North, in the electoral college, a majority of fifty. Since the census of 1840, four States have been added to the Union—Iowa, Wisconsin, Florida, and Texas. They leave the difference in the Senate as it stood when the census was taken; but add two to the side of the North in the House, making the present majority in the House in its favor fifty, and in the electoral college fifty-two.

The result of the whole is to give the Northern section a predominance in every department of the Government, and thereby concentrate in it the two elements which constitute the Federal Government,—majority of States, and a majority of their population, estimated in federal numbers.

Whatever section concentrates the two in itself possesses the control of the entire Government.

But we are just at the close of the sixth decade, and the commencement of the seventh. The census is to be taken this year, which must add greatly to the decided preponderance of the North in the House of Representatives and in the electoral college. The prospect is, also, that a great increase will be added to its present preponderance in the Senate, during the period of the decade, by the addition of new States. Two territories, Oregon and Minnesota, are already in progress, and strenuous efforts are making to bring in three additional States from the territory recently conquered from Mexico; which, if successful, will add three other States in a short time to the Northern section, making five States; and increasing the present number of its States from fifteen to twenty, and of its Senators from thirty to forty. On the contrary, there is not a single territory in progress in the Southern section, and no certainty that any additional State will be added to it during the decade. The prospect then is, that the two sections in the Senate, should the efforts now made to exclude the South from the newly acquired territories succeed, will stand, before the end of the decade, twenty Northern States to fourteen Southern (considering Delaware as neutral), and forty Northern Senators to twenty-eight Southern. This great increase of Senators, added to the great increase of members of the House of Representatives and the electoral college on the part of the North, which must take place under the next decade, will effectually and irretrievably destroy the equilibrium which existed when the Government commenced.

Had this destruction been the operation of time, without the interference of Government, the South would have had no reason to complain; but such was not the fact. It was caused by the legislation of this Government, which was appointed, as the common agent of all, and charged with the protection of the interests and security of all. The legislation by which it has been effected, may be classed under three heads. The first is, that series of acts by which the South has been excluded from the common territory belonging to all the States as members of the Federal Union—which have had the effect of extending vastly the portion allotted to the Northern section, and restricting within narrow limits the portion left the South. The next consists in adopting a system of revenue and disbursements, by which an undue proportion of the burden of taxation has been imposed upon the South, and an undue proportion of its proceeds appropriated to the North; and the last is a system of political measures, by which the original character of the Government has been radically changed. I propose to bestow upon each of these, in the order they stand, a few remarks, with the view of showing that it is owing to the action of this Government, that the equilibrum between the two sections has been destroyed, and the whole powers of the system centered in a sectional majority.

The first of the series of acts by which the South was deprived of its due share of the territories, originated with the confederacy which preceded the existence of this Government. It is to be found in the provision of the ordinance of 1787. Its effect was to exclude the South entirely from that vast and fertile region which lies between the Ohio and the Mississippi rivers, now embracing five States and one territory. The next of the series is the Missouri compromise, which excluded the South from that large portion of Louisiana which lies north of 36°30', excepting what is included in the State of Missouri. The last of the series excluded the South from the whole of the Oregon Territory. All these, in the slang of the day, were what are called slave territories, and not free soil; that is, territories belonging to slaveholding powers and open to the emigration of masters with their slaves. By these several acts, the South was excluded from 1,238,025 square miles—an extent of country considerably exceeding the entire valley of the Mississippi. To the South was left the portion of the Territory of Louisiana lying south of 36° 30', and the portion north of it included in the State of Missouri, with the portion lying south of 36° 30', including the States of Louisiana and Arkansas and the territory lying west of the latter, and south of 36° 30', called the Indian country. These, with the Territory of Florida, now the State, make, in the whole, 283,503 square miles. To this must be added the territory acquired with Texas. If the whole should be added to the Southern section, it would make an increase of 325,520, which would make the whole left to the South, 609,023. But a large part of Texas is still in contest between the two sections, which leaves it uncertain what will be the real extent of the portion of territory that may be left to the South.

I have not included the territory recently acquired by the treaty with Mexico. The North is making the most strenuous efforts to appropriate the whole to herself, by excluding the South from every foot of it. If she should succeed, it will add to that from which the South has already been excluded 526,078 square miles, and would increase the whole which the North has appropriated to herself, to 1,764,023, not including the portion that she may succeed in excluding us from in Texas. To sum up the whole, the United States, since they declared their independence, have acquired 2,373,046 square miles of territory, from which the North will have excluded the South, if she should succeed in monopolizing the newly acquired territories, about three-fourths of the whole, leaving to the South but about one-fourth.

Such is the first and great cause that has destroyed the equilibrium between the two sections in the Government.

The next is the system of revenue and disbursements which has been adopted by the Government. It is well known that the Government has derived its revenue mainly from duties on imports. 1 shall not undertake to show that such duties must necessarily fall mainly on the exporting States, and that the South, as the great exporting portion of the Union, has in reality paid vastly more than her due proportion of the revenue; because I deem it unnecessary, as the subject has on so many occasions been fully discussed. Nor shall I, for the same reason, undertake to show that a far greater portion of the revenue has been disbursed at the North, than its due share; and that the joint effect of these causes has been, to transfer a vast amount from South to North, which, under an equal system of revenue and disbursements, would not have been lost to her. If to this be added, that many of the duties were imposed, not for revenue, but for protection,—that is, intended to put money, not in the treasury, but directly into the pocket of the manufacturers,— some conception may be formed of the immense amount which, in the long course of sixty years, has been transferred from South to North. There are no data by which it can be estimated with any certainty; but it is safe to say, that it amounts to hundreds of millions of dollars. Under the most moderate estimate, it would be sufficient to add greatly to the wealth of the North, and thus greatly increase her population by attracting emigration from all quarters to that section.

This, combined with the great primary cause, amply explains why the North has acquired a preponderance in every department of the Government by its disproportionate increase of population and States. The former, as has been shown, has increased, in fifty years, 2,400,000 over that of the South. This increase of population, during so long a period, is satisfactorily accounted for, by the number of emigrants, and the increase of their descendants, which have been attracted to the Northern section from Europe and the South, in consequence of the advantages derived from the causes assigned. If they had not existed—if the South had retained all the capital which has been extracted from her by the fiscal action of the Government; and, if it had not been excluded by the ordinance of 1787 and the Missouri compromise, from the region lying between the Ohio and the Missisippi rivers, and between the Missisippi and the Rocky Mountains north of 36°30'—it scarcely admits of a doubt, that it would have divided the emigration with the North, and by retaining her own people, would have at least equalled the North in population under the census of 1840, and probably under that about to be taken. She would also, if she had retained her equal rights in those territories, have maintained an equality in the number of States with the North, and have preserved the equilibrium between the two sections that existed at the commencement of the Government. The loss, then, of the equilibrium is to be attributed to the action of this Government.

But while these measures were destroying the equilibrium between the two sections, the action of the Government was leading to a radical change in its character, by concentrating all the power of the system in itself. The occasion will not permit me to trace the measures by which this great change has been consummated. If it did, it would not be difficult to show that the process commenced at an early period of the Government; and that it proceeded, almost without interruption, step by step, until it absorbed virtually its entire powers; but without going through the whole process to establish the fact, it may be done satisfactorily by a very short statement.

That the government claims, and practically maintains the right to decide in the last resort, as to the extent of its powers, will scarcely be denied by any one conversant with the political history of the country. That it also claims the right to resort to force to maintain whatever power it claims, against all opposition, is equally certain. Indeed it is apparent, from what we daily hear, that this has become the prevailing and fixed opinion of a great majority of the community. Now, I ask, what limitation can possibly be placed upon the powers of a government claiming and exercising such rights? And, if none can be, how can the separate governments of the States maintain and protect the powers reserved to them by the constitution— or the people of the several States maintain those which are reserved to them, and among others, the sovereign powers by which they ordained and established, not only their separate State Constitutions and Governments, but also the Constitution and Government of the United States? But, if they have no constitutional means of maintaining them against the right claimed by this Government, it necessarily follows, that they hold them at its pleasure and discretion, and that all the powers of the system are in reality concentrated in it. It also follows, that the character of the Government has been changed in consequence, from a federal republic, as it originally came from the hands of its framers, into a great national consolidated democracy. It has indeed, at present, all the characteristics of the latter, and not one of the former, although it still retains its outward form.

The result of the whole of these causes combined is—that the North has acquired a decided ascendency over every department of this Government, and through it a control over all the powers of the system. A single section governed by the will of the numerical majority, has now, in fact, the control of the Government and the entire powers of the system. What was once a constitutional federal republic, is now converted, in reality, into one as absolute as that of the Autocrat of Russia, and as despotic in its tendency as any absolute government that ever existed.

As, then, the North has the absolute control over the Government, it is manifest, that on all questions between it and the South, where there is a diversity of interests, the interest of the latter will be sacrificed to the former, however oppressive the effects may be; as the South possesses no means by which it can resist, through the action of the Government. But if there was no question of vital importance to the South, in reference to which there was a diversity of views between the two sections, this state of things might be endured, without the hazard of destruction to the South. But such is not the fact. There is a question of vital importance to the Southern section, in reference to which the views and feelings of the two sections are as opposite and hostile as they can possibly be.

I refer to the relation between the two races in the Southern section, which constitutes a vital portion of her social organization. Every portion of the North entertains views and feelings more or less hostile to it. Those most opposed and hostile, regard it as a sin, and consider themselves under the most sacred obligation to use every effort to destroy it. Indeed, to the extent that they conceive they have power, they regard themselves as implicated in the sin, and responsible for not suppressing it by the use of all and every means. Those less opposed and hostile, regard it as a crime—an offence against humanity, as they call it; and, although not so fanatical, feel themselves bound to use all efforts to effect the same object; while those who are least opposed and hostile, regard it as a blot and a stain on the character of what they call the Nation, and feel themselves bound to give it no countenance or support. On the contrary, the Southern section regards the relation as one which cannot be destroyed without subjecting the two races to the greatest calamity, and the section to poverty, desolation, and wretchedness; and accordingly they feel bound, by every consideration of interest and safety, to defend it.

This hostile feeling on the part of the North towards the social organization of the South long lay dormant, but it only required some cause to act on those who felt most intensely that they were responsible for its continuance, to call it into action. The increasing power of this Government, and of the control of the Northern section over all its departments, furnished the cause. It was this which made an impression on the minds of many, that there was little or no restraint to prevent the Government from doing whatever it might choose to do. This was sufficient of itself to put the most fanatical portion of the North in action, for the purpose of destroying the existing relation between the two races in the South.

The first organized movement towards it commenced in 1835. Then, for the first time, societies were organized, presses established, lecturers sent forth to excite the people of the North, and incendiary publications scattered over the whole South, through the mail. The South was thoroughly aroused. Meetings were held everywhere, and resolutions adopted, calling upon the North to apply a remedy to arrest the threatened evil, and pledging themselves to adopt measures for their own protection, if it was not arrested. At the meeting of Congress, petitions poured in from the North, calling upon Congress to abolish slavery in the District of Columbia, and to prohibit, what they called, the internal slave trade between the States—announcing at the same time, that their ultimate object was to abolish slavery not only in the District, but in the States and throughout the Union. At this period the number engaged in the agitation was small, and possessed little or no personal influence.

Neither party in Congress had, at that time, any sympathy with them or their cause. The members of each party presented their petitions with great reluctance. Nevertheless, small and contemptible as the party then was, both of the great parties of the North dreaded them. They felt, that though small, they were organized in reference to a subject which had a great and a commanding influence over the Northern mind. Each party, on that account, feared to oppose their petitions, lest the opposite party should take advantage of the one who might do so, by favoring them. The effect was, that both united in insisting that the petitions should be received, and that Congress should take jurisdiction over the subject. To justify their course, they took the extraordinary ground, that Congress was bound to receive petitions on every subject, however objectionable they might be, and whether they had, or had not, jurisdiction over the subject. These views prevailed in the House of Representatives, and partially in the Senate; and thus the party succeeded in their first movements, in gaining what they proposed—a position in Congress, from which agitation could be extended over the whole Union. This was the commencement of the agitation, which has ever since continued, and which, as is now acknowledged, has endangered the Union itself.

As for myself, I believed at that early period, if the party who got up the petitions should succeed in getting Congress to take jurisdiction, that agitation would follow, and that it would in the end, if not arrested, destroy the Union. I then so expressed myself in debate, and called upon both parties to take grounds against assuming jurisdiction; but in vain. Had my voice been heeded, and had Congress refused to take jurisdiction, by the united votes of all parties, the agitation which followed would have been prevented, and the fanatical zeal that gives impulse to the agitation, and which has brought us to our present perilous condition, would have become extinguished, from the want of fuel to feed the flame. *That* was the time for the North to have shown her devotion to the Union; but, unfortunately, both of the great parties of that section were so intent on obtaining or retaining party ascendency, that all other considerations were overlooked or forgotten.

What has since followed are but natural consequences. With the success of their first movement, this small fanatical party began to acquire strength; and with that, to become an object of courtship to both the great parties. The necessary consequence was, a further increase of power, and a gradual tainting of the opinions of both of the other parties with their doctrines, until the infection has extended over both; and the great mass of the population of the North, who, whatever may be their opinion of the original abolition party, which still preserves its distinctive organization, hardly ever fail, when it comes to acting, to co-operate in carrying out their measures. With the increase of their influence, they extended the sphere of their action. In a short time after the commencement of their first movement, they had acquired sufficient influence to induce the legislatures of most of the Northern States to pass acts, which in effect abrogated the clause of the constitution that provides for the delivery up of fugitive slaves. Not long after, petitions followed to abolish slavery in forts, magazines, and dockyards, and all other places where Congress had exclusive power of legislation. This was followed by petitions and resolutions of legislatures of the Northern States, and popular meetings, to exclude the Southern States from all territories acquired, or to be acquired, and to prevent the admission of any State hereafter into the Union, which, by its constitution, does not prohibit slavery. And Congress is invoked to do all this, expressly with the view to the final abolition of slavery in the States. That has been avowed to be the ultimate object from the beginning of the agitation until the present time; and yet the great body of both parties of the North, with the full knowledge of the fact, although disavowing the abolitionists, have co-operated with them in almost all their measures.

Such is a brief history of the agitation, as far as it has yet advanced. Now I ask, Senators, what is there to prevent its further progress, until it fulfils the ultimate end proposed, unless some decisive measure should be adopted to prevent it? Has any one of the causes, which has added to its increase from its original small and contemptible beginning until it has attained its present magnitude, diminished in force? Is the original cause of the movement—that slavery is a sin, and ought to be suppressed—weaker now than at the commencement? Or is the abolition party less numerous or influential, or have they less influence with, or control over the two great parties of the North in elections? Or has the South greater means of influencing or controlling the movements of this Government now, than it had when the agitation commenced? To all these questions but one answer can be given: No—no—no. The very reverse is true. Instead of being weaker, all the elements in favor of agitation are stronger now than they were in 1835, when it first commenced, while all the elements of influence on the part of the South are weaker. Unless something decisive is done, I again ask, what is to stop this agitation, before the great and final object at which it aims—the abolition of slavery in the States—is consummated? Is it, then, not certain, that if something is not done to arrest it, the South will be forced to choose between abolition and secession? Indeed, as events are now moving, it will not require the South to secede, in order to dissolve the Union. Agitation will of itself effect it, of which its past history furnishes abundant proof—as I shall next proceed to show.

It is a great mistake to suppose that disunion can be effected by a single blow. The cords which bound these States together in one common Union, are far too numerous and powerful for that. Disunion must be the work of time. It is only through a long process, and successively, that the cords can be snapped, until the whole fabric falls asunder. Already the agitation of the slavery question has snapped some of the most important, and has greatly weakened all the others, as I shall proceed to show.

The cords that bind the States together are not only many, but various in character. Some are spiritual or ecclesiastical; some political; others social. Some appertain to the benefit conferred by the Union, and others to the feeling of duty and obligation.

The strongest of those of a spiritual and ecclesiastical nature, consisted in the unity of the great religious denominations, all of which originally embraced the whole Union. All these denominations, with the exception, perhaps, of the Catholics, were organized very much upon the principle of our political institutions. Beginning with smaller meetings corresponding with the political divisions of the country, their organization terminated in one great central assemblage, corresponding very much with the character of Congress. At these meetings the principal clergymen and lay members of the respective denominations, from all parts of the Union, met to transact business relating to their common concerns. It was not confined to what appertained to the doctrines and discipline of the respective denominations, but extended to plans for disseminating the Bible—establishing missions, distributing tracts—and of establishing presses for the publication of tracts, newspapers, and periodicals, with a view of diffusing religious information—and for the support of their respective doctrines and creeds. All this combined contributed greatly to strengthen the bonds of the Union. The ties which held each denomination together formed a strong cord to hold the whole Union together; but, powerful as they were, they have not been able to resist the explosive effect of slavery agitation.

The first of these cords which snapped, under its explosive force, was that of the powerful Methodist Episcopal Church. The numerous and strong ties which held it together, are all broken, and its unity gone. They now form separate churches; and, instead of that feeling of attachment and devotion to the interests of the whole church which was formerly felt, they are now arrayed into two hostile bodies, engaged in litigation about what was formerly their common property.

The next cord that snapped was that of the Baptists—one of the largest and most respectable of the denominations. That of the Presbyterian is not entirely snapped, but some of its strands have given way. That of the Episcopal Church is the only one of the four great Protestant denominations which remains unbroken and entire.

The strongest cord, of a political character, consists of the many and powerful ties that have held together the two great parties which have, with some modifications, existed from the beginning of the Government. They both extended to every portion of the Union, and strongly contributed to hold all its parts together. But this powerful cord has fared no better than the spiritual. It resisted, for a long time, the explosive tendency of the agitation but has finally snapped under its force—if not entirely, in a great measure. Nor is there one of the remaining cords which has not been greatly weakened. To this extent the Union has already been destroyed by agitation, in the only way it can be, by sundering and weakening the cords which bind it together.

If the agitation goes on, the same force, acting with increased intensity, as has been shown, will finally snap every cord, when nothing will be left to hold the States together except force. But, surely, that can, with no propriety of language, be called a Union, when the only means by which the weaker is held connected with the stronger portion is *force*. It may, indeed, keep them connected; but the connection will partake much more of the character of subjugation, on the part of the weaker to the stronger, than the union of free, independent, and sovereign States, in one confederation, as they stood in the early stages of the Government, and which only is worthy of the sacred name of Union.

Having now, Senators, explained what it is that endangers the Union, and traced it to its cause, and explained its nature and character, the question again recurs— How can the Union be saved? To this I answer, there is but one way by which it can be—and that is—by adopting such measures as will satisfy the States belonging to the Southern section, that they can remain in the Union consistently with their honor and their safety. There is, again, only one way by which this can be effected, and that is—by removing the causes by which this belief has been produced. Do *this*, and discontent will cease—harmony and kind feelings between the sections be restored—and every apprehension of danger to the Union removed. The question, then, is—How can this be done? But, before I undertake to answer this question, I propose to show by what the Union cannot be saved.

It cannot, then, be saved by eulogies on the Union, however splendid or numerous. The cry of "Union, Union—the glorious Union!" can no more prevent disunion than the cry of "Health, health—glorious health!" on the part of the physician, can save a patient lying dangerously ill. So long as the Union, instead of being regarded as a protector, is regarded in the opposite character, by not much less than a majority of the States, it will be in vain to attempt to conciliate them by pronouncing eulogies on it.

Besides this cry of Union comes commonly from those whom we cannot believe to be sincere. It usually comes from our assailants. But we cannot believe them to be sincere; for, if they loved the Union, they would necessarily be devoted to the constitution. It made the Union,—and to destroy the constitution would be to destroy the Union. But the only reliable and certain evidence of devotion to the constitution is, to abstain, on the one hand, from violating it, and to repel, on the other, all attempts to violate it. It is only by faithfully performing these high duties that the constitution can be preserved, and with it the Union.

But how stands the profession of devotion to the Union by our assailants, when brought to this test? Have they abstained from violating the constitution? Let the many acts passed by the Northern States to set aside and annul the clause of the constitution providing for the delivery up of fugitive slaves answer. I cite this, not that it is the only instance (for there are many others), but because the violation in this particular is too notorious and palpable to be denied. Again: have they stood forth faithfully to repel violations of the constitution ? Let their course in reference to the agitation of the slavery question, which was commenced and has been carried on for fifteen years, avowedly for the purpose of abolishing slavery in the States—an object all acknowledged to be unconstitutional—answer. Let them show a single instance, during this long period, in which they have denounced the agitators or their attempts to effect what is admitted to be unconstitutional or a single measure which they have brought forward for that purpose. How can we, with all these facts before us, believe that they are sincere in their profession of devotion to the Union, or avoid believing their profession is but intended to increase the vigor of their assaults and to weaken the force of our resistance ? Nor can we regard the profession of devotion to the Union, on the part of those who are not our assailants as sincere, when they pronounce eulogies upon the Union evidently with the intent of charging us with disunion, without uttering one word of denunciation against our assailants. If friends of the Union, their course should be to unite with us in repelling these assaults, and denouncing the authors as enemies of the Union. Why they avoid this, and pursue the course they do it is for them to explain. Nor can the Union be saved by invoking the name of the illustrious Southerner whose mortal remains repose on the western bank of the Potomac. He was one of us—a slave-holder and a planter. We have studied his history, and find nothing in it to justify submission to wrong. On the contrary, his great fame rests on the solid foundation, that, while he was careful to avoid doing wrong to others, he was prompt and decided in repelling wrong. I trust that, in this respect, we profited by his example.

Nor can we find any thing in his history to deter us from seceding from the Union, should it fail to fulfil the objects for which it was instituted, by being permanently and hopelessly converted into the means of oppressing instead of protecting us. On the contrary, we find much in his example to encourage us, should we be forced to the extremity of deciding between submission and disunion.

There existed then, as well as now, a union—that between the parent country and her then colonies. It was a union that had much to endear it to the people of the colonies. Under its protecting and superintending care, the colonies were planted and grew up and prospered, through a long course of years, until they became populous and wealthy. Its benefits were not limited to them. Their extensive agricultural and other productions, gave birth to a flourishing commerce, which richly rewarded the parent country for the trouble and expense of establishing and protecting them. Washington was born and grew up to manhood under that union. He acquired his early distinction in its service, and there is every reason to believe that he was devotedly attached to it. But his devotion was a rational one. He was attached to it, not as an end, but as a means to an end. When it failed to fulfil its end, and, instead of affording protection, was converted into the means of oppressing the colonies, he did not hesitate to draw his sword and head the great movement by which that union was for ever severed, and the independence of these States established. This was the great and crowning glory of his life, which has spread his fame over the whole globe, and will transmit it to the latest posterity.

Nor can the plan proposed by the distinguished Senator from Kentucky, nor that of the administration save the Union. I shall pass by, without remark, the plan proposed by the Senator, and proceed directly to the consideration of that of the administration. I however assure the distinguished and able Senator, that, in taking this course, no disrespect whatever is intended to him or his plan. I have adopted it, because so many Senators of distinguished abilities, who were present when he delivered his speech, and explained his plan, and who were fully capable to do justice to the side they support, have replied to him.

The plan of the administration cannot save the Union, because it can have no effect whatever, towards satisfying the States composing the southern section of the Union, that they can, consistently with safety and honor, remain in the Union. It is, in fact, but a modification of the Wilmot Proviso. It proposes to effect the same object,—to exclude the South from all territory acquired by the Mexican treaty. It is well known that the South is united against the Wilmot Proviso, and has committed itself by solemn resolutions, to resist, should it be adopted. Its opposition is not to the name, but that which it proposes to effect. That, the Southern States hold to be unconstitutional, unjust, inconsistent with their equality as members of the common Union, and calculated to destroy irretrievably the equilibrium between the two sections. These objections equally apply to what, for brevity, I will call the Executive Proviso. There is no difference between it and the Wilmot, except in the mode of effecting the object; and in that respect, I must say, that the latter is much the least objectionable. It goes to its object openly, boldly, and distinctly. It claims for Congress unlimited power over the territories, and proposes to assert it over the territories acquired from Mexico, by a positive prohibition of slavery. Not so the Executive Proviso. It takes an indirect course, and in order to elude the Wilmot Proviso, and thereby avoid encountering the united and determined resistance of the South, it denies, by implication, the authority of Congress to legislate for the territories, and claims the right as belonging exclusively to the inhabitants of the territories. But to effect the object of excluding the South, it takes care, in the mean time, to let in emigrants freely from the Northern States and all other quarters, except from the South, which it takes special care to exclude by holding up to them the danger of having their slaves liberated under the Mexican laws. The necessary consequence is to exclude the South from the territory, just as effectually as would the Wilmot Proviso. The only difference in this respect is, that what one proposes to effect directly and openly, the other proposes to effect indirectly and covertly.

But the Executive Proviso is more objectionable than the Wilmot in another and more important particular. The latter, to effect its object, inflicts a dangerous wound upon the constitution by depriving the Southern States, as joint partners and owners of the territories, of their rights in them; but it inflicts no greater wound than is absolutely necessary to effect its object. The former, on the contrary, while it inflicts the same wound, inflicts others equally great, and, if possible, greater, as I shall next proceed to explain.

In claiming the right for the inhabitants, instead of Congress, to legislate for the territories, the Executive Proviso, assumes that the sovereignty over the territories is vested in the former: or to express it in the language used in a resolution offered by one of the Senators from Texas (General Houston, now absent), they have "the same, inherent right of self-government as the people in the States." The assumption is utterly unfounded, unconstitutional, without example, and contrary to the entire practice of the Government, from its commencement to the present time, as I shall proceed to show.

The recent movement of individuals in California to form a constitution and a State government, and to appoint Senators and Representatives, is the first fruit of this monstrous assumption. If the individuals who made this movement had gone into California as adventurers, and if, as such, they had conquered the territory and established their independence, the sovereignty of the country would have been vested in them, as a separate and independent community. In that case, they would have had the right to form a constitution, and to establish a government for themselves; and if, afterwards, they thought proper to apply to Congress for admission into the Union as a sovereign and independent State, all this would have been regular, and according to established principles. But such is not the case. It was the United States who conquered California and finally acquired it by treaty. The sovereignty, of course, is vested in them, and not in the individuals who have attempted to form a constitution and a State without their consent. All this is clear, beyond controversy unless it can be shown that they have since lost or been divested of their sovereignty. Nor is it less clear, that the power of legislating over the acquired territory is vested in Congress, and not, as is assumed, in the inhabitants of the territories. None can deny that the Government of the United States has the power to acquire territories, either by war or treaty; but if the power to acquire exists, it belongs to Congress to carry it into execution. On this point there can be no doubt, for the constitution expressly provides, that Congress shall have power "to make all laws which shall be necessary and proper to carry into execution the foregoing powers" (those vested in Congress), and all other powers vested by this constitution in the Government of the United States, or in any department or officer thereof." It matters not, then, where the power is vested; for, if vested at all in the Government of the United States or any of its departments, or officers, the power of carrying it into execution is clearly vested in Congress. But this important provision, while it gives to Congress the power of legislating over territories, imposes important limitations on its exercise, by restricting Congress to passing laws necessary and proper for carrying the power into execution. The prohibition extends, not only to all laws not suitable or appropriate to the object of power, but also to all that are unjust, unequal, or unfair,—for all such laws would be unnecessary and improper, and, therefore, unconstitutional.

Having now established, beyond controversy, that the sovereignty over the territories is vested in the United States,—that is, in the several States composing the Union—and that the power of legislating over them is expressly vested in Congress, it follows that the individuals in California who have undertaken to form a constitution and a State, and to exercise the power of legislating without the consent of Congress, have usurped the sovereignty of the State and the authority of Congress, and have acted in open defiance of both. In other words, what they have done is revolutionary and rebellious in its character, anarchical in its tendency, and calculated to lead to the most dangerous consequences. Had they acted from premeditation and design, it would have been, in fact, actual rebellion; but such is not the case. The blame lies much less upon them them than upon those who have induced them to take a course so unconstitutional and dangerous. They have been led into it by language held here, and the course pursued by the Executive branch of the Government.

I have not seen the answer of the Executive to the calls made by the two Houses of Congress for information as to the course which it took, or the part which it acted, in reference to what was done in California. I understand the answers have not yet been printed. But there is enough known to justify the assertion, that those who profess to represent and act under the authority of the Executive, have advised, aided, and encouraged the movement, which terminated in forming, what they call a constitution and a State. General Riley, who professed to act as civil Governor, called the convention—determined on the number, and distribution of the delegates—appointed the time and place of its meeting—was present during the session—and gave its proceedings his approbation and sanction. If he acted without authority, he ought to have been tried, or at least reprimanded, and his course disavowed. Neither having been done, the presumption is, that his course has been approved. This, of itself, is sufficient to identify the Executive with his acts, and to make it responsible for them. I touch not the question, whether General Riley was appointed, or received the instructions under which he professed to act from the present Executive, or its predecessor. If from the former, it would implicate the preceding, as well as the present administration. If not, the responsibility rests exclusively on the present.

It is manifest from this statement, that the Executive Department has undertaken to perform acts preparatory to the meeting of the individuals to form their so called constitution and government, which appertain exclusively to Congress. Indeed, they are identical, in many respects, with the provisions adopted by Congress, when it gives permission to a territory to form a constitution and government, in order to be admitted as a State into the Union.

Having now shown that the assumption upon which the Executive, and the individuals in California, acted throughout this whole affair, is unfounded, unconstitutional, and dangerous; it remains to make a few remarks, in order to show that what has been done, is contrary to the entire practice of the Government, from the commencement to the present time.

From its commencement until the time that Michigan was admitted, the practice was uniform. Territorial governments were first organized by Congress. The Government of the United States appointed the governors, judges, secretaries, marshals, and other officers; and the inhabitants of the territory were represented by legislative bodies, whose acts were subject to the revision of Congress. This state of things continued until the government of a territory applied to Congress to permit its inhabitants to form a constitution and government, preparatory to admission into the Union. The act preliminary to giving permission was, to ascertain whether the inhabitants were sufficiently numerous to authorize them to be formed into a State. This was done by taking a census. That being done, and the number proving sufficient, permission was granted. The act granting it, fixed all the preliminaries—the time and place of holding the convention; the qualification of the voters; establishment of its boundaries, and all other measures necessary to be settled previous to admission. The act giving permission necessarily withdraws the sovereignty of the United States, and leaves the inhabitants of the incipient State as free to form their constitution and government as were the original States of the Union after they had declared their independence. At this stage, the inhabitants of the territory became, for the first time, a people, in legal and constitutional language. Prior to this, they were, by the old acts of Congress, called inhabitants, and not people. All this is perfectly consistent with the sovereignty of the United States, with the powers of Congress, and with the right of a people to self-government.

Michigan was the first case in which there was any departure from the uniform rule of acting. Hers was a very slight departure from established usage. The ordinance of 1787 secured to her the right of becoming a State, when she should have 60,000 inhabitants. Owing to some neglect, Congress delayed taking the census. In the mean time her population increased, until it clearly exceeded more than twice the number which entitled her admission. At this stage, she formed a constitution and government, without a census being taken by the United States, and Congress waived the omission, as there was no doubt she had more than a sufficient number to entitle her to admission. She was not admitted at the first session she applied, owing to some difficulty respecting the boundary between her and Ohio. The great irregularity, as to her admission, took place at the next session—but on a point which can have no possible connection with the case of California.

The irregularities in all other cases that have since occurred, are of a similar nature. In all, there existed territorial governments established by Congress, with officers appointed by the United States. In all, the territorial government took the lead in calling conventions, and fixing the preliminaries preparatory to the formation of a constitution and admission into the Union. They all recognized the sovereignty of the United States, and the authority of Congress over the territories; and wherever there was any departure from established usage, it was done on the presumed consent of Congress, and not in defiance of its authority, or the sovreignty of the United States over the territories. In this respect California stands alone, without usage or a single example to cover her case.

It belongs now, Senators, to you to decide what part you will act in reference to this unprecedented transaction. The Executive has laid the paper purporting to be the Constitution of California before you, and asks you to admit her into the Union as a State; and the question is, will you or will you not admit her? It is a grave question, and there rests upon you a heavy responsibility. Much, very much will depend upon your decision. If you admit her, you indorse and give your sanction to all that has been done. Are you prepared to do so? Are you prepared to surrender your power of legislation for the territories—a power expressly vested in Congress by the constitution, as has been fully established ? Can you, consistently with your oath to support the constitution, surrender the power? Are you prepared to admit that the inhabitants of the territories possess the sovereignty over them, and that any number, more or less, may claim any extent of territory they please; may form a constitution and government, and erect it into a State, without asking your permission? Are you prepared to surrender the sovereignty of the United States over whatever territory may be hereafter acquired to the first adventurers who may rush into it? Are you prepared to surrender virtually to the Executive Department all the powers which you have heretofore exercised over the territories? If not, how can you, consistently with your duty and your oaths to support the constitution, give your assent to the admission of California as a State, under a pretended constitution and government? Again, can you believe that the project of a constitution which they have adopted has the least validity? Can you believe that there is such a State in reality as the State of California? No; there is no such State. It has no legal or constitutional existence. It has no validity, and can have none, without your sanction. How, then, can you admit it as a *State*, when, according to the provision of the constitution, your power is limited to admitting new *States*. To be admitted it must be a State, —and an existing State, independent of your sanction, before you can admit it. When you give your permission to the inhabitants of a territory to form a constitution and a State, the constitution and State they form, derive their authority from the people, and not from you. The State, before it is admitted is actually a State, and does not become so by the *act of admission*, as would be the case with California, should you admit her contrary to the constitutional provisions and established usage heretofore.

The Senators on the the other side of the Chamber must permit me to make a few remarks in this connection particularly applicable to them,—with the exception of a few Senators from the South sitting on the other side of the Chamber.—When the Oregon question was before this body, not two years since, you took (if I mistake not) universally the ground, that Congress had the sole and absolute power of legislating for the territories. How, then, can you now, after the short inteval which has elapsed abandon the ground which you took, and thereby virtually admit that the power of legislating, instead of being in Congress, is in the inhabitants of the territories? How can you justify and sanction by your votes the acts of the Executive, which are in direct derogation of what you then contended for? But to approach still nearer to the present time, how can you after condemning, little more than a year since, the grounds taken by the party which you defeated at the last election, wheel round and support by your votes the grounds which, as explained recently on this floor by the candidate of the party in the last electtion, are identical with those on which the Executive has acted in reference to California? What are we to understand by all this? Must we conclude that there is no sincerity, no faith in the acts and declarations of public men, and that all is mere acting or hollow profession? Or are we to conclude that the exclusion of the South from the territory acquired from Mexico is an object of so paramount a character in your estimation, that right, justice, constitution and consistency must all yield, when they stand in the way of our exclusion?

But, it may he asked what is to be done with California, should she not be admitted? I answer, remand her back to the territorial condition, as was done in the case of Tennessee, in the early stage of the Government. Congress, in her case, had established a territorial government in the usual form, with a governor, judges, and other officers, appointed by the United States. She was entitled, under the deed of cession, to be admitted into the Union as a State as soon as she had sixty thousand inhabitants. The territorial government, believing it had that number, took a census, by which it appeared it exceeded it. She then formed a constitution, and applied for admission. Congress refused to admit her, on the ground that the census should be taken by the United States, and that Congress had not determined whether the territory should be formed into one or two States, as it was authorized to do under the cession. She returned quietly to her territorial condition. An act was passed to take a census by the United States, containing a provision that the territory should form one State. All afterwards was regularly conducted, and the territory admitted as a State in due form. The irregularities in the case of California are immeasurably greater, and offer much stronger reasons for pursuing the same course. But, it may be said, California may not submit. That is not probable; but if she should not, when she refuses, it will then be time for us to decide what is to be done.

Having now shown what cannot save the Union, I return to the question with which I commenced, How can the Union be saved? There is but one way by which it can with any certainty; and that is, by a full and final settlement, on the principle of justice, of all the questions at issue between the two sections. The South asks for justice, simple justice, and less she ought not to take. She has no compromise to offer, but the constitution; and no concession or surrender to make. She has already surrendered so much that she has little left to surrender. Such a settlement would go to the root of the evil, and remove all cause of discontent, by satisfying the South, she could remain honorably and safely in the Union, and thereby restore the harmony and fraternal feelings between the sections, which existed anterior to the Missouri agitation. Nothing else can, with any certainty, finally and for ever settle the questions at issue, terminate agitation, and save the Union.

But can this be done ? Yes, easily; not by the weaker party, for it can of itself do nothing—not even protect itself—but by the stronger. The North has only to will it to accomplish it—to do justice by conceding to the South an equal right in the acquired territory, and to do her duty by causing the stipulations relative to fugitive slaves to be faithfully fulfilled—to cease the agitation of the slave question, and to provide for the insertion of a provision in the constitution, by an amendment, which will restore to the South, in substance, the power she possessed of protecting herself, before the equilibrium between the sections was destroyed by the action of this

Government. There will be no difficulty in devising such a provision—one that will protect the South, and which, at the same tiine, will improve and strengthen the Government, instead of impairing and weakening it.

But will the North agree to this? It is for her to answer the question. But, I will say, she cannot refuse, if she has half the love of the Union which she professes to have, or without justly exposing herself to the charge that her love of power and aggrandizement is far greater than her love of the Union. At all events, the responsibility of saving the Union rests on the North and not on the South. The South cannot save it by any act of hers, and the North may save it without any sacrifice whatever, unless to do justice, and to perform her duties under the constitution, should be regarded by her as a sacrifice.

It is time, Senators, that there should be an open and manly avowal on all sides, as to what is intended to be done. If the question is not now settled, it is uncertain whether it ever can hereafter be; and we, as the representatives of the States of this Union, regarded as governments, should come to a distinct understanding as to our respective views, in order to ascertain whether the great questions at issue can be settled or not. If you, who represent the stronger portion, cannot agree to settle them on the broad principle of justice and duty, say so; and let the States we both represent agree to separate and part in peace. If you are unwilling we should part in peace, tell us so, and we shall know what to do, when you reduce the question to submission or resistance. If you remain silent, you will compel us to infer by your acts what you intend. In that case, California will become the test question. If you admit her, under all the difficulties that oppose her admission, you compel us to infer that you intend to exclude us from the whole of the acquired territories, with the intention of destroying, irretrievably, the equilibrium of the two sections. We would be blind not to perceive in that case, that your real objects are power and aggrandizement, and infatuated not to act accordingly.

I have now, Senators, done my duty in expressing my opinions fully, freely, and candidly, on this solemn occasion. In doing so, I have been governed by the motives which have governed me in all stages of the agitation of the slavery question since its commencement. I have exerted myself, during the whole period, to arrest it, with the intention of saving the Union, if it could be done; and if it could not, to save the section where it has pleased Providence to cast my lot, and which I sincerely believe has justice and the constitution on its side. Having faithfully done my duty to the best of my ability, both to the Union and my section, throughout this agitation, I shall have the consolation, let what will come, that I am free from all responsibility.

❧ 23 ❧

What to the Slave is the Fourth of July?

FREDERICK DOUGLASS

In this speech, delivered at Rochester in 1852, and subsequently reprinted in the appendix to *My Bondage and My Freedom* (1855), Douglass attacks the institution of slavery by drawing attention to the hypocrisy of a nation which can celebrate its day of independence while denying freedom to a section of its community. As a compelling contribution to the abolitionist cause, this speech is remarkable for its sustained level of forthright honesty. Douglass bears eloquent testimony to the feelings of those to whom the words of the Declaration of Independence have no meaning in reality, and presents a forceful argument for the end of slavery in a nation that professes to value liberty and equality as the animating principles of its democratic republic.

What to the Slave is the Fourth of July?

Extract from an Oration, at Rochester, July 5, 1852

Fellow-Citizens—Pardon me, and allow me to ask, why am I called upon to speak here to-day? What have I, or those I represent, to do with your national independence? Are the great principles of political freedom and of natural justice, embodied in that Declaration of Independence, extended to us? and am I, therefore, called upon to bring our humble offering to the national altar, and to confess the benefits, and express devout gratitude for the blessings, resulting from your independence to us?

Would to God, both for your sakes and ours, that an affirmative answer could be truthfully returned to these questions! Then would my task be light, and my burden easy and delightful. For who is there so cold that a nation's sympathy could not warm him? Who so obdurate and dead to the claims of gratitude, that would

Source: Frederick Douglass, 'What to the Slave is the Fourth of July?', *My Bondage and My Freedom*, 1855.

not thankfully acknowledge such priceless benefits? Who so stolid and selfish, that would not give his voice to swell the hallelujahs of a nation's jubilee, when the chains of servitude had been torn from his limbs? I am not that man. In a case like that, the dumb might eloquently speak, and the "lame man leap as an hart."

But, such is not the state of the case. I say it with a sad sense of the disparity between us. I am not included within the pale of this glorious anniversary! Your high independence only reveals the immeasurable distance between us. The blessings in which you this day rejoice, are not enjoyed in common. The rich inheritance of justice, liberty, prosperity, and independence, bequeathed by your fathers, is shared by you, not by me. The sunlight that brought life and healing to you, has brought stripes and death to me. This Fourth of July is *yours*, not *mine*. *You* may rejoice, *I* must mourn. To drag a man in fetters into the grand illuminated temple of liberty, and call upon him to join you in joyous anthems, were inhuman mockery and sacrilegious irony. Do you mean, citizens, to mock me, by asking me to speak to-day? If so, there is a parallel to your conduct. And let me warn you that it is dangerous to copy the example of a nation whose crimes, towering up to heaven, were thrown down by the breath of the Almighty, burying that nation in irrecoverable ruin! I can to-day take up the plaintive lament of a peeled and woe-smitten people.

> By the rivers of Babylon, there we sat down. Yea! we wept when we remembered Zion. We hanged our harps upon the willows in the midst thereof. For there, they that carried us away captive, required of us a song; and they who wasted us required of us mirth, saying, Sing us one of the songs of Zion. How can we sing the Lord's song in a strange land? If I forget thee, O Jerusalem, let my right hand forget her cunning. If I do not remember thee, let my tongue cleave to the roof of my mouth.

Fellow-citizens, above your national, tumultous joy, I hear the mournful wail of millions, whose chains, heavy and grievous yesterday, are to-day rendered more intolerable by the jubilant shouts that reach them. If I do forget, if I do not faithfully remember those bleeding children of sorrow this day, "may my right hand forget her cunning, and may my tongue cleave to the roof of my mouth!" To forget them, to pass lightly over their wrongs, and to chime in with the popular theme, would be treason most scandalous and shocking, and would make me a reproach before God and the world. My subject, then, fellow-citizens, is AMERICAN SLAVERY. I shall see this day and its popular characteristics from the slave's point of view. Standing there, identified with the American bondman, making his wrongs mine, I do not hesitate to declare, with all my soul, that the character and conduct of this nation never looked blacker to me than on this Fourth of July. Whether we turn to the declarations of the past, or to the professions of the present, the conduct of the nation seems equally hideous and revolting. America is false to the past, false to the present, and solemnly binds herself to be false to the future. Standing with God and the crushed and bleeding slave on this occasion, I will, in the name of humanity which is outraged, in the name of liberty which is fettered, in the name of the constitution and the bible, which are disregarded and trampled upon, dare to call in question and to denounce, with all the emphasis I can command,

317

everything that serves to perpetuate slavery—the great sin and shame of America! "I will not equivocate; I will not excuse;" I will use the severest language I can command; and yet not one word shall escape me that any man, whose judgment is not blinded by prejudice, or who is not at heart a slaveholder, shall not confess to be right and just.

But I fancy I hear some one of my audience say, it is just in this circumstance that you and your brother abolitionists fail to make a favorable impression on the public mind. Would you argue more, and denounce less, would you persuade more and rebuke less, your cause would be much more likely to succeed. But, I submit, where all is plain there is nothing to be argued. What point in the anti-slavery creed would you have me argue? On what branch of the subject do the people of this country need light? Must I undertake to prove that the slave is a man? That point is conceded already. Nobody doubts it. The slaveholders themselves acknowledge it in the enactment of laws for their government. They acknowledge it when they punish disobedience on the part of the slave. There are seventy-two crimes in the state of Virginia, which, if committed by a black man (no matter how ignorant he be), subject him to the punishment of death; while only two of these same crimes will subject a white man to the like punishment. What is this but the acknowledgement that the slave is a moral, intellectual, and responsible being. The manhood of the slave is conceded. It is admitted in the fact that southern statute books are covered with enactments forbidding, under severe fines and penalties, the teaching of the slave to read or write. When you can point to any such laws, in reference to the beasts of the field, then I may consent to argue the manhood of the slave. When the dogs in your streets, when the fowls of the air, when the cattle on your hills, when the fish of the sea, and the reptiles that crawl, shall be unable to distinguish the slave from a brute, then will I argue with you that the slave is a man!

For the present, it is enough to affirm the equal manhood of the Negro race. Is it not astonishing that, while we are plowing, planting, and reaping, using all kinds of mechanical tools, erecting houses, constructing bridges, building ships, working in metals of brass, iron, copper, silver, and gold; that, while we are reading, writing, and cyphering, acting as clerks, merchants, and secretaries, having among us lawyers, doctors, ministers, poets, authors, editors, orators, and teachers; that, while we are engaged in all manner of enterprises common to other men—digging gold in California, capturing the whale in the Pacific, feeding sheep and cattle on the hillside, living, moving, acting, thinking, planning, living in families as husbands, wives, and children, and, above all, confessing and worshiping the Christian's God, and looking hopefully for life and immortality beyond the grave—we are called upon to prove that we are men!

Would you have me argue that man is entitled to liberty? that he is the rightful owner of his own body? You have already declared it. Must I argue the wrongfulness of slavery? Is that a question for republicans? Is it to be settled by the rules of logic and argumentation, as a matter beset with great difficulty, involving a doubtful application of the principle of justice, hard to be understood? How should I look to-day in the presence of Americans, dividing and subdividing a discourse, to show that men have a natural right to freedom, speaking of it relatively and positively, negatively and affirmatively? To do so, would be to make myself ridiculous, and to offer an insult to your understanding. There is not a man beneath the canopy of heaven that does not know that slavery is wrong for *him*.

What! am I to argue that it is wrong to make men brutes, to rob them of their liberty, to work them without wages, to keep them ignorant of their relations to their fellow-men, to beat them with sticks, to flay their flesh with the lash, to load their limbs with irons, to hunt them with dogs, to sell them at auction, to sunder their families, to knock out their teeth, to burn their flesh, to starve them into obedience and submission to their masters? Must I argue that a system, thus marked with blood and stained with pollution, is wrong? No; I will not. I have better employment for my time and strength than such arguments would imply.

What, then, remains to be argued? Is it that slavery is not divine; that God did not establish it; that our doctors of divinity are mistaken? There is blasphemy in the thought. That which is inhuman cannot be divine. Who can reason on such a proposition! They that can, may! I cannot. The time for such argument is past.

At a time like this, scorching irony, not convincing argument, is needed. Oh! had I the ability, and could I reach the nation's ear, I would to-day pour out a fiery stream of biting ridicule, blasting reproach, withering sarcasm, and stern rebuke. For it is not light that is needed, but fire; it is not the gentle shower, but thunder. We need the storm, the whirlwind, and the earthquake. The feeling of the nation must be quickened; the conscience of the nation must be roused; the propriety of the nation must be startled; the hypocrisy of the nation must be exposed; and its crimes against God and man must be proclaimed and denounced.

What to the American slave is your Fourth of July? I answer, a day that reveals to him, more than all other days in the year, the gross injustice and cruelty to which he is the constant victim. To him, your celebration is a sham; your boasted liberty, an unholy license; your national greatness, swelling vanity; your sounds of rejoicing are empty and heartless; your denunciations of tyrants, brass-fronted impudence; your shouts of liberty and equality, hollow mockery; your prayers and hymns, your sermons and thanksgivings, with all your religious parade and solemnity, are to him mere bombast, fraud, deception, impiety, and hypocrisy—a thin veil to cover up crimes which would disgrace a nation of savages. There is not a nation on the earth guilty of practices more shocking and bloody, than are the people of these United States, at this very hour.

Go where you may, search where you will, roam through all the monarchies and despotisms of the old world, travel through South America, search out every abuse, and when you have found the last, lay your facts by the side of the every-day practices of this nation, and you will say with me, that, for revolting barbarity and shameless hypocrisy, America reigns without a rival.

❧ 24 ❧

Slavery Extension: The Nebraska Bill in Congress

The issue of whether slavery would extend to Kansas became a bellwether of ante-bellum controversy. The Kansas–Nebraska bill, sponsored by Stephen Douglas, became the focus of this argument in Congress. This article, which appeared in the *New York Times* on 24th January 1854, was signed by a number of independent Democrats from Ohio, among them Salmon Chase and Charles Sumner. They protested the legal and moral foundations of the bill. Four months later, Sumner's inflamatory speech in the Senate on the issue would provoke Preston Brooks to a physical assault.

Slavery Extension. The Nebraska Bill In Congress. Address to the People

Washington, Thursday Jan. 19, 1854.

Fellow-Citizens: As Senators and Representatives in Congress of the United States, it is our duty to warn our constituencies whenever imminent danger menaces the Freedom of our Institution or the Permanency of our Union.

Such danger, as we firmly believe, now impends, and we earnestly solicit your prompt attention to it.

At the last session of Congress, a bill for the organization of the Territory of Nebraska passed the House of Representatives, with an overwhelming majority. That bill was based on the principle of excluding slavery from the new territory. It was not taken up for consideration in the Senate, and consequently failed to become a law.

At the present session, a new Nebraska bill has been reported by the Senate Committee on Territories, which, should it unhappily receive the sanction of Congress, will open all the unorganized territory of the Union to the ingress of slavery.

Source: 'Slavery Extension. The Nebraska Bill in Congress. Address to the People',
New York Times, 24th January 1854.

We arraign this bill as a gross violation of a sacred pledge; as a criminal betrayal of precious rights; as part and parcel of an atrocious plot to exclude from a vast unoccupied region, emigrants from the Old World and free laborers from our own States, and convert it into a dreary region of despotism, inhabited by masters and slaves.

Take your maps, fellow citizens, we entreat you, and see what country it is which this bill gratuitously and recklessly, proposes to open to slavery.

From the southwestern corner of Missouri pursue the parallel of 36 [degrees] 30 [minutes] North latitude, westwardly across the Arkansas, across the North fork of Canadian, to the northeastern angle of Texas; then follow the northeastern boundary of Texas to the western limit of New Mexico; then proceed along that western line to its northern termination; then again turn westwardly, and follow the northern line of New Mexico to the crest of the Rocky Mountains; then ascend northwardly along the crest of that mountain range to the line which separates the United States from the British Possessions in North America, on the 49th parallel of North latitude; then pursue your course eastwardly along that line to the White Earth river, which falls into the Missouri from the North; descend that river to its confluence with the Missouri; descend the Missouri, along the western boundary of Minnesota, of Iowa, of Missouri, to the point where it ceases to be a boundary line, and enters the State to which it gives its name; then continue your southward course along the western limit of that State to the point from which you set out. You have now made the circuit of the proposed Territory of Nebraska. You have traversed the vast distance of more than three thousand miles. You have traced the outline of an area of four hundred and eighty-five thousand square miles; more than twelve times as great as that of Ohio.

This immense region, occupying the very heart of the North American Continent, and larger, by thirty three thousand square miles, than all the existing Free States, excluding California–this immense region, well watered and fertile, through which the Middle and Northern routes from the Atlantic to the Pacific must pass–this immense region, embracing all the unorganized territory of the nation, except the comparatively insignificant district of Indian territory north of Red River and between Arkansas and Texas, and now for more than thirty years regarded by the common consent of the American people as consecrated to Freedom, by statute and by compact–this immense region, the bill now before the Senate, without reason and without excuse, but in flagrant disregard of sound policy and sacred faith, proposes to open to Slavery.

We beg your attention, fellow citizens, to a few historical facts.

The *original settled policy* of the United States, clearly indicated by the Jefferson Proviso of 1784, and by the Ordinance of 1787, was NONEXTENSION OF SLAVERY.

In 1803, Louisiana was acquired by purchase from France. At that time there were some twenty-five or thirty thousand slaves in this Territory, most of them within what is now the State of Louisiana; a few only, further north, on the west bank of the Mississippi. Congress, instead of providing for the abolition of Slavery in this new Territory, permitted its continuance. In 1812 the State of Louisiana was organized, and admitted into the Union with Slavery.

In 1818, six years later, the inhabitants of the Territory of Missouri applied to Congress for authority to form a State Constitution, and for admission into the Union. There were, at that time in the whole Territory acquired from France, outside of the State of Louisiana, not three thousand slaves.

There was no apology in the circumstances of the country for the continuance of Slavery. The original national policy was against it, and, not less, the plain language of the treaty under which the Territory had been acquired from France.

It was proposed, therefore, to incorporate in the bill authorizing the formation of a State Government, a provision requiring that the Constitution of the new State should contain an article providing for the abolition of existing Slavery, and prohibiting the further introduction of slaves.

This provision was vehemently and pertinaciously opposed; but finally prevailed in the House of Representatives by a decided vote. In the Senate it was rejected, and, in consequence of the disagreement between the two Houses, the bill was lost.

At the next session of Congress the controversy was renewed with increased violence. It was terminated, at length, by a compromise. Missouri was allowed to come into the Union with Slavery, but a section was inserted in the act authorizing her admission, excluding Slavery forever, from all the territory acquired from France, not included in the new State, lying north of 36 [degrees] 30 [minutes].

We quote the prohibitory section:[1]

The question of the constitutionality of this prohibition was submitted by President MONROE to his Cabinet. JOHN QUINCY ADAMS was then Secretary of State; JOHN C. CALHOUN was Secretary of War; WILLIAM H. CRAWFORD was Secretary of the Treasury; and WILLIAM WIRT was Attorney General. Each of these eminent men, three of them being from Slave States, gave a written opinion, affirming its constitutionality, and thereupon the act received the sanction of the President, himself, also, from a Slave State.

Nothing is more certain in history than the fact that Missouri could not have been admitted as a Slave State, had not certain members from the Free States been reconciled to the measure by the incorporation of this prohibition into the act of admission. Nothing is more certain than that this prohibition has been regarded and accepted by the whole country as a solemn compact against the extension of Slavery into any part of the Territory acquired from France, lying north of 36 [degrees] 30[minutes], and not included in the new state of Missouri. The same act—let it be ever remembered—which authorized the formation of a constitution for that State, without a clause forbidding Slavery, consecrated, beyond question and beyond honest recall, the whole remainder of the Territory to Freedom and Free Institutions, forever. For more than thirty years—during more than half the period of our national existence under our present Constitution—this compact has been universally regarded and acted upon as inviolable American law. In conformity with it Iowa was admitted as a Free State, and Minnesota has been organized as a Free Territory.

It is a strange and ominous fact, well calculated to awaken the worst apprehensions, and the most fearful forebodings of future calamity, that it is now deliberately purposed to repeal this prohibition, by implication or directly—the latter certainly the manlier way—and thus to subvert this compact, and allow Slavery in all the yet unorganized territory.

We cannot, in this address, review the various pretences under which it is attempted to cloak this monstrous wrong; but we must not altogether omit to notice one.

It is said that the Territory of Nebraska sustains the same relations to slavery as did the Territory acquired from Mexico prior to 1850, and that the pro-slavery clauses of the bill are necessary to carry into effect the compromises of that year.

No assertion could be more groundless.

Three acquisitions of territory have been made by treaty. The first was from France. Out of this territory have been created the three slave States of Louisiana, Arkansas, and Missouri, and the single free State of Iowa. The controversy, which arose in relation to the then unorganized portion of this territory was closed in 1820, by the Missouri act, containing the Slavery prohibition as has been already stated. This controversy related only to territory acquired from France. The act by which it was terminated, was confined by its own express terms to the same territory, and had no relation to any other.

The second acquisition was from Spain. Florida, the territory thus acquired, was yielded to slavery without a struggle, and almost without a murmur.

The third was from Mexico. The controversy which arose from this acquisition is fresh in the remembrance of the American people. Out of it sprung the acts of Congress, commonly known as the Compromise measures of 1850, by one of which California was admitted as a free State; while two others, organizing the Territories of New Mexico and Utah, exposed all the residue of the recently acquired territory to the invasion of slavery.

These acts were never supposed to abrogate or touch the existing exclusion of Slavery from what is now called Nebraska. They applied to the Territory acquired from Mexico, and to that only. They were intended as a settlement of the controversy growing out of that acquisition, and of that controversy only. They must stand or fall by their own merits.

The statesmen, whose powerful support carried the Utah and New Mexico acts, never dreamed that their provisions would ever be applied to Nebraska. Even at the last session of Congress, Mr. ATCHISON, of Missouri, in a speech in favor of taking up the former Nebraska Bill, on the morning of the 4th of March, 1853, said: "It is evident that the Missouri Compromise cannot be repealed. So far as that question is concerned, we might as well agree to the admission of this Territory now, as next year, or five or ten years hence." These words could not have fallen from this watchful guardian of Slavery, had he proposed that this Territory was embraced by the pro-Slavery provisions of the Compromise Acts. This pretension had not then been set up. It was a palpable afterthought.

The Compromise Acts themselves refute this pretension. In the third article of the second section of the Joint Resolution for annexing Texas to the United States it is expressly declared that *"in such State or States as shall be formed out of said Territory north of said Missouri Compromise line. Slavery or involuntary servitude, except for crime, shall be prohibited;"* [2] and in the Act for organizing New Mexico and settling the boundary of Texas, a proviso was incorporated, on the motion of Mr. MASON, of Virginia, which distinctly preserves this prohibition, and flouts the bare faced pretension that all the territory of the United States, whether south or north of the Missouri Compromise line, is to be open to Slavery. It is as follows:

> *"Provided, that nothing herein contained shall be construed to impair or qualify* ANYTHING contained in the third article of the second section of the Joint Resolution for annexing Texas to the United States approved March 1, 1845, either as regards the number of States that may hereafter be formed out of the State of Texas, OR OTHERWISE."[3]

Here is proof, beyond controversy, that the principle of the Missouri Act prohibiting Slavery north of 36 [degrees] 30 [minutes], far from being abrogated by the Compromise Acts, is expressly affirmed; and that the proposed repeal of this prohibition, instead of being an affirmation of Compromise acts, is a repeal of a very prominent provision of the most important act of the series. It is solemnly declared in the very Compromise Acts *"that nothing herein contained shalt be construed to impair or qualify"* the prohibition of Slavery north of 36 [degrees] 30 [minutes], and yet, yet, in the face of this declaration, that sacred prohibition is said to be overthrown. Can presumption further go? To all who, in any way, lean upon these Compromises, we commend this exposition.

The pretences, therefore, that the Territory, covered by the positive prohibitions of 1820, sustains a similar relation to Slavery, with that acquired from Mexico, covered by no prohibition except that of disputed Constitutional or Mexican Law, and that the Compromises of 1850 require the incorporation of the proslavery clauses of the Utah and New Mexico Bill in the Nebraska Act, are mere inventions, designed to cover up from public reprehension meditated bad faith. Were he living now, no one would be more forward, more eloquent, or more indignant in his denunciation of that bad faith, than HENRY CLAY, the foremost champion of both compromises.

In 1820, the Slave States said to the Free States, "Admit Missouri with slavery, and refrain from positive exclusion south of 36 [degrees] 30 [minutes], and we will join you in perpetual prohibition north of that line." The Free States consented. In 1854, the Slave States say to the Free States, "Missouri is admitted; no prohibition of Slavery south of 36 [degrees] 30 [minutes] has been attempted; we have received the full consideration of our agreement; no more is to be gained by adherence to it on our part; we, therefore, propose to cancel the compact." If this be not Punic faith, what is it? Not without the deepest dishonor and crime can the Free States acquiesce in this demand.

We confess our total inability properly to delineate the character or describe the consequences of this measure. Language fails to express the sentiments of indignation and abhorrence which it inspires; and no vision, less penetrating and comprehensive than that of the All-Seeing, can reach its evil issues.

To some of its more immediate and inevitable consequences, however, we must attempt to direct your attention.

What will be the effect of this measure, should it unhappily become a law, upon the proposed Pacific Railroad? We have already said that two of the principal routes, the Central and the Northern, traverse this Territory. If Slavery be allowed there, the settlement and cultivation of the country must be greatly retarded. Inducements to the immigration of free laborers will be almost destroyed. The enhanced cost of construction and the diminished expectation of profitable returns will present almost insuperable obstacles to building the road at all, while even if made, the difficulty and expense of keeping it up, in a country from which the energetic and intelligent masses will be virtually excluded, will greatly impair its usefulness and value.

From the rich lands of this large Territory, also, patriotic statesmen have anticipated that a free, industrious, and enlightened population will extract abundant treasures of individual and public wealth. There, it has been expected, freedom-loving emigrants from Europe, and energetic and intelligent laborers of our own land, will find homes of comfort and fields of useful enterprise. If this bill shall become a law, all such expectation will turn to grievous disappointment. The blight of Slavery will cover the land. The Homestead Law, should Congress enact one, would be worthless there. Freemen, unless pressed by a hard and cruel necessity, will not; and should not, work beside slaves. Labor cannot be respected where any class of laborers is held in abject bondage. It is the deplorable necessity of Slavery, that to make and keep a single slave, there must be slave law; and where slave law exists, labor must necessarily be degraded.

We earnestly request the enlightened conductors of newspapers printed in the German and other foreign languages to direct the attention of their readers to this important matter.

It is of immense consequence, also, to scrutinize the geographical character of this project. We beg you, fellow-citizens, to observe that it will sever the East from the West of the United States, by a wide, Slaveholding belt of the country, extending from the Gulf of Mexico to British North America. It is a bold scheme against American Liberty, worthy of an accomplished architect of ruin. Texas is already slaveholding, and occupies the Gulf Region, from the Sabine to the Rio Grande, and from the Gulf of Mexico to the Red River. North of the Red River, and extending between Texas and Arkansas, to the parallel of 36[degrees] 30[minutes], lies the Indian Territory, about equal in extent to the latter State, in which Slavery was not prohibited by the act of 1820. From 36[degrees] 30[minutes] to the boundary line between our own country and the British Possessions, stretching from west to east through more than eleven degrees of longitude, and from south to north through more than twelve degrees of latitude, extends the great Territory, the fate of which is now to be determined by the American Congress. Thus you see, fellow-citizens, that the first operation of the proposed permission of Slavery in Nebraska, will be to stay the progress of the Free States westward, and to cut off the Free States of the Pacific from the Free States of the Atlantic. It is hoped, doubtless, by compelling the whole commerce and the whole travel between the East and the West, to pass for hundreds of miles through a Slaveholding region, in the heart of the Continent, and by the influence of a Federal Government, controlled by the Slave Power, to extinguish Freedom and establish Slavery in the States and Territories of the Pacific, and thus permanently subjugate the whole country to the yoke of a Slaveholding despotism. Shall a plot against humanity and Democracy, so monstrous and so dangerous to the interests of Liberty throughout the world, be permitted to succeed?

We appeal to the People. We warn you that the dearest interests of Freedom and the Union are in imminent peril. Servile demagogues may tell you that the Union can be maintained only by submiting to the demands of Slavery. We tell you that the safety of the Union can only be insured by the full recognition of the just claims of Freedom and Man. The Union was formed to establish justice, and secure the blessings of liberty. When it fails to accomplish these ends it will be worthless and when it becomes worthless it can not long endure.

We entreat you to be mindful of that fundamental maxim of Democracy, EQUAL RIGHTS AND JUSTICE for all men. Do not submit to become agents in extending Legalized Oppression and Systematized injustice over a vast Territory yet exempt from these terrible evils.

We implore Christians and Christian Ministers to interpose. Their Divine Religion requires them to behold in every man a brother, and to labor for the Advancement and Regeneration of the Human Race.

Whatever apologies may be offered for the toleration of Slavery in the States, none can be urged for its extension into Territories where it does not exist, and where that extension involves the repeal of ancient law, and the violation of solemn compact. Let all protest earnestly and emphatically, by correspondence, through the press, by memorials, by resolutions of public meetings and legislative bodies, and in whatever other mode may seem expedient against this enormous crime.

For ourselves, we shall resist it by speech and vote, and with all the abilities which God has given us. Even if overcome in the impending struggle, we shall not submit. We shall go home to our constituents, erect anew the standard of Freedom, and call on the People to come to the rescue of the country from the domination of Slavery. We will not despair; for the cause of Human Freedom is the cause of God.

S.P. Chase	Charles Sumner
J.R. Giddings	Edward Wade
Gerritt Smith	Alexander De Witt

Notes

1. Act March 6 1820-3, U.S. Statutes at Large, 545. "SEC. 8. *Be it further enacted, That in all that territory ceded by France to the United States, under the name of Louisiana,* which lies north of thirty-six degrees and thirty minutes of north latitude, and included within the limits of the State contemplated by this act, SLAVERY AND INVOLUNTARY SERVITUDE, otherwise than as the punishment of crimes, SHALL BE AND IS HEREBY FOREVER PROHIBITED."

2. Act of March 1, 1845-5, U.S. Statutes at Large, 127.

3. *Congressional Globe,* 1849-50, p. 1562; Act Sept. 9, 1850-9, U.S. Statutes at Large, 446.

⊷25⊷

Slavery in Massachusetts

HENRY DAVID THOREAU

Thoreau gave this lecture on Independence Day, 1854 at an 'anti-slavery celebration' at Framingham. It was subsequently reprinted in *The Liberator* by William Lloyd Garrison and in the *New York Daily Tribune* by Horace Greeley. As a leading spirit among the New England transcendentalists, Thoreau's arguments against slavery were as predictable as they were respected. Here, however, he exhorts the people of his home state of Massa-chusetts to clarify their attitudes towards slavery. Although Massachusetts was not a slave-holding state, its refusal to condemn the fugitive slave law amounted to complicit support for the institution. That law should be judged not according to its constitutionality, but against the criteria of abstract justice. For Thoreau, the failure of the Massachusetts courts to act against the provisions of the fugitive slave law confirmed their moral and political cowardice on this issue.

Slavery in Massachusetts

I lately attended a meeting of the citizens of Concord, expecting, as one among many, to speak on the subject of slavery in Massachusetts; but I was surprised and disappointed to find that what had called my townsmen together was the destiny of Nebraska, and not of Massachusetts, and that what I had to say would be entirely out of order. I had thought that the house was on fire, and not the prairie; but though several of the citizens of Massachusetts are now in prison for attempting to rescue a slave from her own clutches, not one of the speakers at that meeting expressed regret for it, not one even referred to it. It was only the disposition of some wild lands a thousand miles off which appeared to concern them. The inhabitants of Concord are not prepared to stand by one of their own bridges, but talk only of taking up a position on the highlands beyond the Yellowstone River. Our Buttricks and Davises and Hosmers are retreating thither, and I fear that they will leave no Lexington Common between them and the enemy. There is not one

Source: Henry David Thoreau, 'Slavery in Massachusetts', 1854.

slave in Nebraska; there are perhaps a million slaves in Massachusetts.

They who have been bred in the school of politics fail now and always to face the facts. Their measures are half measures and makeshifts merely. They put off the day of settlement indefinitely, and meanwhile the debt accumulates. Though the Fugitive Slave Law had not been the subject of discussion on that occasion, it was at length faintly resolved by my townsmen, at an adjourned meeting, as I learn, that the compromise compact of 1820 having been repudiated by one of the parties, "Therefore, ... the Fugitive Slave Law of 1850 must be repealed." But this is not the reason why an iniquitous law should be repealed. The fact which the politician faces is merely that there is less honor among thieves than was supposed, and not the fact that they are thieves.

As I had no opportunity to express my thoughts at that meeting, will you allow me to do so here?

Again it happens that the Boston Court House is full of armed men, holding prisoner and trying a MAN, to find out if he is not really a SLAVE. Does any one think that justice or God awaits Mr. Loring's decision? For him to sit there deciding still, when this question is already decided from eternity to eternity, and the unlettered slave himself and the multitude around have long since heard and assented to the decision, is simply to make himself ridiculous. We may be tempted to ask from whom he received his commission, and who he is that received it; what novel statutes he obeys, and what precedents are to him of authority. Such an arbiter's very existence is an impertinence. We do not ask him to make up his mind, but to make up his pack.

I listen to hear the voice of a Governor, Commander-in-Chief of the forces of Massachusetts. I hear only the creaking of crickets and the hum of insects which now fill the summer air. The Governor's exploit is to review the troops on muster days. I have seen him on horseback, with his hat off, listening to a chaplain's prayer. It chances that that is all I have ever seen of a Governor. I think that I could manage to get along without one. If he is not of the least use to prevent my being kidnapped, pray of what important use is he likely to be to me? When freedom is most endangered, he dwells in the deepest obscurity. A distinguished clergyman told me that he chose the profession of a clergyman because it afforded the most leisure for literary pursuits. I would recommend to him the profession of a Governor.

Three years ago, also, when the Sims tragedy was acted, I said to myself, there is such an officer, if not such a man, as the Governor of Massachusetts—what has he been about the last fortnight? Has he had as much as he could do to keep on the fence during this moral earthquake? It seemed to me that no keener satire could have been aimed at, no more cutting insult have been offered to that man, than just what happened—the absence of all inquiry after him in that crisis. The worst and the most I chance to know of him is that he did not improve that opportunity to make himself known, and worthily known. He could at least have *resigned* himself into fame. It appeared to be forgotten that there was such a man or such an office. Yet no doubt he was endeavoring to fill the gubernatorial chair all the while. He was no Governor of mine. He did not govern me.

But at last, in the present case, the Governor was heard from. After he and the United States government had perfectly succeeded in robbing a poor innocent black man of his liberty for life, and, as far as they could, of his Creator's likeness in his breast, he made a speech to his accomplices, at a congratulatory supper!

I have read a recent law of this State, making it penal for any officer of the "Commonwealth" to "detain or aid in the ... detention," anywhere within its limits, "of any person, for the reason that he is claimed as a fugitive slave." Also, it was a matter of notoriety that a writ of replevin to take the fugitive out of the custody of the United States Marshal could not be served for want of sufficient force to aid the officer.

I had thought that the Governor was, in some sense, the executive officer of the State; that it was his business, as a Governor, to see that the laws of the State were executed; while, as a man, he took care that he did not, by so doing, break the laws of humanity; but when there is any special important use for him, he is useless, or worse than useless, and permits the laws of the State to go unexecuted. Perhaps I do not know what are the duties of a Governor; but if to be a Governor requires to subject one's self to so much ignominy without remedy, if it is to put a restraint upon my manhood, I shall take care never to be Governor of Massachusets. I have not read far in the statutes of this Commonwealth. It is not profitable reading. They do not always say what is true; and they do not always mean what they say. What I am concerned to know is, that that man's influence and authority were on the side of the slaveholder, and not of the slave—of the guilty, and not of the innocent—of injustice, and not of justice. I never saw him of whom I speak; indeed, I did not know that he was Governor until this event occurred. I heard of him and Anthony Burns at the same time, and thus, undoubtedly, most will hear of him. So far am I from being governed by him. I do not mean that it was anything to his discredit that I had not heard of him, only that I heard what I did. The worst I shall say of him is, that he proved no better than the majority of his constituents would be likely to prove. In my opinion, he was not equal to the occasion.

The whole military force of the State is at the service of a Mr. Suttle, a slaveholder from Virginia, to enable him to catch a man whom he calls his property; but not a soldier is offered to save a citizen of Massachusetts from being kidnapped! Is this what all these soldiers, all this *training*, have been for these seventy-nine years past? Have they been trained merely to rob Mexico and carry back fugitive slaves to their masters?

These very nights I heard the sound of a drum in our streets. There were men *training* still; and for what? I could with an effort pardon the cockerels of Concord for crowing still, for they, perchance, had not been beaten that morning; but I could not excuse this rub-a-dub of the "trainers." The slave was carried back by exactly such as these; i.e., by the soldier, of whom the best you can say in this connection is that he is a fool made conspicuous by a painted coat.

Three years ago, also, just a week after the authorities of Boston assembled to carry back a perfectly innocent man, and one whom they knew to be innocent, into slavery, the inhabitants of Concord caused the bells to be rung and the cannons to be fired, to celebrate their liberty—and the courage and love of liberty of their ancestors who fought at the bridge. As if *those* three millions had fought for the right to be free themselves, but to hold in slavery three million others. Nowadays, men wear a fool's-cap, and call it a liberty-cap. I do not know but there are some who, if they were tied to a whipping-post, and could but get one hand free, would use it to ring the bells and fire the cannons to celebrate *their* liberty. So some of my townsmen took the liberty to ring and fire. That was the extent of their freedom; and when the sound of the bells died away, their liberty died away also; when the powder was all expended, their liberty went off with the smoke.

The joke could be no broader if the inmates of the prisons were to subscribe for all the powder to be used in such salutes, and hire the jailers to do the firing and ringing for them, while they enjoyed it through the grating.

This is what I thought about my neighbors.

Every humane and intelligent inhabitant of Concord, when he or she heard those bells and those cannons, thought not with pride of the events of the 19th of April, 1775, but with shame of the events of the 12th of April, 1851. But now we have half buried that old shame under a new one.

Massachusetts sat waiting Mr. Loring's decision, as if it could in any way affect her own criminality. Her crime, the most conspicuous and fatal crime of all, was permitting him to be the umpire in such a case. It was really the trial of Massachusetts. Every moment that she hesitated to set this man free, every moment that she now hesitates to atone for her crime, she is convicted. The Commissioner on her case is God; not Edward G. God, but simply God.

I wish my countrymen to consider, that whatever the human law may be, neither an individual nor a nation can ever commit the least act of injustice against the obscurest individual without having to pay the penalty for it. A government which deliberately enacts injustice, and persists in it, will at length even become the laughing-stock of the world.

Much has been said about American slavery, but I think that we do not even yet realize what slavery is. If I were seriously to propose to Congress to make mankind into sausages, I have no doubt that most of the members would smile at my proposition, and if any believed me to be in earnest, they would think that I proposed something much worse than Congress had ever done. But if any of them will tell me that to make a man into a sausage would be much worse—would be any worse—than to make him into a slave—than it was to enact the Fugitive Slave Law— I will accuse him of foolishness, of intellectual incapacity, of making a distinction without a difference. The one is just as sensible a proposition as the other.

I hear a good deal said about trampling this law under foot. Why, one need not go out of his way to do that. This law rises not to the level of the head or the reason; its natural habitat is in the dirt. It was born and bred, and has its life, only in the dust and mire, on a level with the feet; and he who walks with freedom, and does not with Hindoo mercy avoid treading on every venomous reptile, will inevitably tread on it, and so trample it under foot—and Webster, its maker, with it, like the dirt—bug and its ball.

Recent events will be valuable as a criticism on the administration of justice in our midst, or, rather, as showing what are the true resources of justice in any community. It has come to this, that the friends of liberty, the friends of the slave, have shuddered when they have understood that his fate was left to the legal tribunals of the country to be decided. Free men have no faith that justice will be awarded in such a case. The judge may decide this way or that; it is a kind of accident, at best. It is evident that he is not a competent authority in so important a case. It is no time, then, to be judging according to his precedents, but to establish a precedent for the future. I would much rather trust to the sentiment of the people. In their vote you would get something of some value, at least, however small; but in the other case, only the trammeled judgment of an individual, of no significance, be it which way it might.

It is to some extent fatal to the courts, when the people are compelled to go behind them. I do not wish to believe that the courts were made for fair weather, and for very civil cases merely; but think of leaving it to any court in the land to decide whether more than three millions of people, in this case a sixth part of a nation, have a right to be freemen or not! But it has been left to the courts of *justice*, so called—to the Supreme Court of the land—and, as you all know, recognizing no authority but the Constitution, it has decided that the three millions are and shall continue to be slaves. Such judges as these are merely the inspectors of a pick-lock and murderer's tools, to tell him whether they are in working order or not, and there they think that their responsibility ends. There was a prior case on the docket, which they, as judges appointed by God, had no right to skip; which having been justly settled, they would have been saved from this humiliation. It was the case of the murderer himself.

The law will never make men free; it is men who have got to make the law free. They are the lovers of law and order who observe the law when the government breaks it.

Among human beings, the judge whose words seal the fate of a man furthest into eternity is not he who merely pronounces the verdict of the law, but he, whoever he may be, who, from a love of truth, and unprejudiced by any custom or enactment of men, utters a true opinion or *sentence* concerning him. He it is that *sentences* him. Whoever can discern truth has received his commission from a higher source than the chiefest justice in the world who can discern only law. He finds himself constituted judge of the judge. Strange that it should be necessary to state such simple truths!

I am more and more convinced that, with reference to any public question, it is more important to know what the country thinks of it than what the city thinks. The city does not *think* much. On any moral question, I would rather have the opinion of Boxboro' than of Boston and New York put together. When the former speaks, I feel as if somebody *had* spoken, as if *humanity* was yet, and a reasonable being had asserted its rights—as if some unprejudiced men among the country's hills had at length turned their attention to the subject, and by a few sensible words redeemed the reputation of the race. When, in some obscure country town, the

331

farmers come together to a special town-meeting, to express their opinion on some subject which is vexing the land, that, I think, is the true Congress, and the most respectable one that is ever assembled in the United States.

It is evident that there are, in this Commonwealth at least, two parties, becoming more and more distinct—the party of the city, and the party of the country. I know that the country is mean enough, but I am glad to believe that there is a slight difference in her favor. But as yet she has few, if any organs, through which to express herself. The editorials which she reads, like the news, come from the seaboard. Let us, the inhabitants of the country, cultivate self-respect. Let us not send to the city for aught more essential than our broadcloths and groceries; or, if we read the opinions of the city, let us entertain opinions of our own.

Among measures to be adopted, I would suggest to make as earnest and vigorous an assault on the press as has already been made, and with effect, on the church. The church has much improved within a few years; but the press is, almost without exception, corrupt. I believe that in this country the press exerts a greater and a more pernicious influence than the church did in its worst period. We are not a religious people, but we are a nation of politicians. We do not care for the Bible, but we do care for the newspaper. At any meeting of politicians—like that at Concord the other evening, for instance—how impertinent it would be to quote from the Bible! how pertinent to quote from a newspaper or from the Constitution! The newspaper is a Bible which we read every morning and every afternoon, standing and sitting, riding and walking. It is a Bible which every man carries in his pocket, which lies on every table and counter, and which the mail, and thousands of missionaries, are continually dispersing. It is, in short, the only book which America has printed and which America reads. So wide is its influence. The editor is a preacher whom you voluntarily support. Your tax is commonly one cent daily, and it costs nothing for pew hire. But how many of these preachers preach the truth? I repeat the testimony of many an intelligent foreigner, as well as my own convictions, when I say, that probably no country was ever ruled by so mean a class of tyrants as, with a few noble exceptions, are the editors of the periodical press in this country. And as they live and rule only by their servility, and appealing to the worse, and not the better, nature of man, the people who read them are in the condition of the dog that returns to his vomit.

The *Liberator* and the *Commonwealth* were the only papers in Boston, as far as I know, which made themselves heard in condemnation of the cowardice and meanness of the authorities of that city, as exhibited in '51. The other journals, almost without exception, by their manner of referring to and speaking of the Fugitive Slave Law, and the carrying back of the slave Sims, insulted the common sense of the country, at least. And, for the most part, they did this, one would say, because they thought so to secure the approbation of their patrons, not being aware that a sounder sentiment prevailed to any extent in the heart of the Common-wealth. I am told that some of them have improved of late; but they are still eminently time-serving. Such is the character they have won.

But, thank fortune, this preacher can be even more easily reached by the weapons of the reformer than could the recreant priest. The free men of New England have only to refrain from purchasing and reading these sheets, have only to withhold their cents, to kill a score of them at once. One whom I respect told me that he purchased Mitchell's *Citizen* in the cars, and then threw it out the window. But would not his contempt have been more fatally expressed if he had not bought it?

Are they Americans? are they New Englanders? are they inhabitants of Lexington and Concord and Framingham, who read and support the Boston *Post, Mail, Journal, Advertiser, Courier,* and *Times*? Are these the Flags of our Union? I am not a newspaper reader, and may omit to name the worst.

Could slavery suggest a more complete servility than some of these journals exhibit? Is there any dust which their conduct does not lick, and make fouler still with its slime? I do not know whether the Boston *Herald* is still in existence, but I remember to have seen it about the streets when Sims was carried off. Did it not act its part well—serve its master faithfully! How could it have gone lower on its belly? How can a man stoop lower than he is low? do more than put his extremities in the place of the head he has? than make his head his lower extremity? When I have taken up this paper with my cuffs turned up, I have heard the gurgling of the sewer through every column. I have felt that I was handling a paper picked out of the public gutters, a leaf from the gospel of the gambling-house, the groggery, and the brothel, harmonizing with the gospel of the Merchants' Exchange.

The majority of the men of the North, and of the South and East and West, are not men of principle. If they vote, they do not send men to Congress on errands of humanity; but while their brothers and sisters are being scourged and hung for loving liberty, while—I might here insert all that slavery implies and is—it is the mismanagement of wood and iron and stone and gold which concerns them. Do what you will, O Government, with my wife and children, my mother and brother, my father and sister, I will obey your commands to the letter. It will indeed grieve me if you hurt them, if you deliver them to overseers to be hunted by hounds or to be whipped to death; but, nevertheless, I will peaceably pursue my chosen calling on this fair earth, until perchance, one day, when I have put on mourning for them dead, I shall have persuaded you to relent. Such is the attitude, such are the words of Massachusetts.

Rather than do thus, I need not say what match I would touch, what system endeavor to blow up; but as I love my life, I would side with the light, and let the dark earth roll from under me, calling my mother and my brother to follow.

I would remind my countrymen that they are to be men first, and Americans only at a late and convenient hour. No matter how valuable law may be to protect your property, even to keep soul and body together, if it do not keep you and humanity together.

I am sorry to say that I doubt if there is a judge in Massachusetts who is prepared to resign his office, and get his living innocently, whenever it is required of him to pass sentence under a law which is merely contrary to the law of God. I am compelled to see that they put themselves, or rather are by character, in this respect, exactly on a level with the marine who discharges his musket in any direction he is ordered to. They are just as much tools, and as little men. Certainly, they are not the more to be respected, because their master enslaves their understandings and consciences, instead of their bodies.

The judges and lawyers—simply as such, I mean—and all men of expediency, try this case by a very low and incompetent standard. They consider, not whether the Fugitive Slave Law is right, but whether it is what they call *constitutional*. Is virtue constitutional, or vice? Is equity constitutional, or iniquity? In important moral and vital questions, like this, it is just as impertinent to ask whether a law is constitutional or not, as to ask whether it is profitable or not. They persist in being the servants of the worst of men, and not the servants of humanity. The question is, not whether you or your grandfather, seventy years ago, did not enter into an agreement to serve the Devil, and that service is not accordingly now due; but whether you will not now, for once and at last, serve God—in spite of your own past recreancy, or that of your ancestor—by obeying that eternal and only just CONSTITUTION, which He, and not any Jefferson or Adams, has written in your being.

The amount of it is, if the majority vote the Devil to be God, the minority will live and behave accordingly—and obey the successful candidate, trusting that, some time or other, by some Speaker's casting-vote, perhaps, they may reinstate God. This is the highest principle I can get out or invent for my neighbors. These men act as if they believed that they could safely slide down a hill a little way—or a good way—and would surely come to a place, by and by, where they could begin to slide up again. This is expediency, or choosing that course which offers the slightest obstacles to the feet, that is, a downhill one. But there is no such thing as accomplishing a righteous reform by the use of "expediency." There is no such thing as sliding up hill. In morals the only sliders are backsliders.

Thus we steadily worship Mammon, both school and state and church, and on the seventh day curse God with a tintamar from one end of the Union to the other.

Will mankind never learn that policy is not morality—that it never secures any moral right, but considers merely what is expedient? chooses the available candidate—who is invariably the Devil—and what right have his constituents to be surprised, because the Devil does not behave like an angel of light? What is wanted is men, not of policy, but of probity—who recognize a higher law than the Constitution, or the decision of the majority. The fate of the country does not depend on how you vote at the polls—the worst man is as strong as the best at that game; it does not depend on what kind of paper you drop into the ballot-box once a year, but on what kind of man you drop from your chamber into the street every morning.

What should concern Massachusetts is not the Nebraska Bill, nor the Fugitive Slave Bill, but her own slaveholding and servility. Let the State dissolve her union with the slaveholder. She may wriggle and hesitate, and ask leave to read the Constitution once more; but she can find no respectable law or precedent which sanctions the continuance of such a union for an instant.

Let each inhabitant of the State dissolve his union with her, as long as she delays to do her duty.

The events of the past month teach me to distrust Fame. I see that she does not finely discriminate, but coarsely hurrahs. She considers not the simple heroism of an action, but only as it is connected with its apparent consequences. She praises till she is hoarse the easy exploit of the Boston tea party, but will be comparatively silent about the braver and more disinterestedly heroic attack on the Boston Court-House, simply because it was unsuccessful!

Covered with disgrace, the State has sat down coolly to try for their lives and liberties the men who attempted to do its duty for it. And this is called *justice*! They who have shown that they can behave particularly well may perchance be put under bonds for *their good behavior*. They whom truth requires at present to plead guilty are, of all the inhabitants of the State, preeminently innocent. While the Governor, and the Mayor, and countless officers of the Commonwealth are at large, the champions of liberty are imprisoned.

Only they are guiltless who commit the crime of contempt of such a court. It behoves every man to see that his influence is on the side of justice, and let the courts make their own characters. My sympathies in this case are wholly with the accused, and wholly against their accusers and judges. Justice is sweet and musical; but injustice is harsh and discordant. The judge still sits grinding at his organ, but it yields no music, and we hear only the sound of the handle. He believes that all the music resides in the handle, and the crowd toss him their coppers the same as before.

Do you suppose that that Massachusetts which is now doing these things—which hesitates to crown these men, some of whose lawyers, and even judges, perchance, may be driven to take refuge in some poor quibble, that they may not wholly outrage their instinctive sense of justice—do you suppose that she is anything but base and servile? that she is the champion of liberty?

Show me a free state, and a court truly of justice, and I will fight for them, if need be; but show me Massachusetts, and I refuse her my allegiance, and express contempt for her courts.

The effect of a good government is to make life more valuable—of a bad one, to make it less valuable. We can afford that railroad and all merely material stock should lose some of its value, for that only compels us to live more simply and economically; but suppose that the value of life itself should be diminished! How can we make a less demand on man and nature, how live more economically in respect to virtue and all noble qualities, than we do? I have lived for the last month—and I think that every man in Massachusetts capable of the sentiment of patriotism must have had a similar experience—with the sense of having suffered a vast and indefinite loss. I did not know at first what ailed me. At last it occurred to me that what I had lost was a country. I had never respected the government near to which I lived, but I had foolishly thought that I might manage to live here, minding my private affairs, and forget it. For my part, my old and worthiest pursuits have lost I cannot say how much of their attraction, and I feel that my investment in life here is worth many per cent less since Massachusetts last deliberately sent back an innocent man, Anthony Burns, to slavery. I dwelt before, perhaps, in the illusion that my life passed somewhere only *between* heaven and hell, but now I cannot persuade myself that I do not dwell *wholly within* hell. The site of that political organization called Massachusetts is to me morally covered with volcanic scoriae and cinders, such as Milton describes in the infernal regions. If there is any hell more unprincipled than our rulers, and we, the ruled, I feel curious to see it. Life itself being worth less, all things with it, which minister to it, are worth less. Suppose you have a small library, with pictures to adorn the walls—a garden laid out around—and contemplate scientific and literary pursuits and discover all at once that your villa, with all its contents is located in hell, and that the justice of the peace has a cloven foot and a forked tail—do not these things suddenly lose their value in your eyes?

I feel that, to some extent, the State has fatally interfered with my lawful business. It has not only interrupted me in my passage through Court Street on errands of trade, but it has interrupted me and every man on his onward and upward path, on which he had trusted soon to leave Court Street far behind. What right had it to remind me of Court Street? I have found that hollow which even I had relied on for solid.

I am surprised to see men going about their business as if nothing had happened. I say to myself, "Unfortunates! they have not heard the news." I am surprised that the man whom I just met on horseback should be so earnest to overtake his newly bought cows running away—since all property is insecure, and if they do not run away again, they may be taken away from him when he gets them. Fool! does he not know that his seed-corn is worth less this year—that all beneficent harvests fail as you approach the empire of hell? No prudent man will build a stone house under these circumstances, or engage in any peaceful enterprise which it requires a long time to accomplish. Art is as long as ever, but life is more interrupted and less available for a man's proper pursuits. It is not an era of repose. We have used up all our inherited freedom. If we would save our lives, we must fight for them.

I walk toward one of our ponds; but what signifies the beauty of nature when men are base? We walk to lakes to see our serenity reflected in them; when we are not serene, we go not to them. Who can be serene in a country where both the rulers and the ruled are without principle? The remembrance of my country spoils my walk. My thoughts are murder to the State, and involuntarily go plotting against her.

But it chanced the other day that I scented a white water-lily, and a season I had waited for had arrived. It is the emblem of purity. It bursts up so pure and fair to the eye, and so sweet to the scent, as if to show us what purity and sweetness reside in, and can be extracted from, the slime and muck of earth. I think I have plucked the first one that has opened for a mile. What confirmation of our hopes is in the fragrance of this flower! I shall not so soon despair of the world for it, notwithstanding slavery, and the cowardice and want of principle of Northern men. It suggests what kind of laws have prevailed longest and widest, and still prevail, and that the time may come when man's deeds will smell as sweet. Such is the odor which the plant emits. If Nature can compound this fragrance still annually, I shall believe her still young and full of vigor, her integrity and genius unimpaired, and that there is virtue even in man, too, who is fitted to perceive and love it. It reminds me that Nature has been partner to no Missouri Compromise. I scent no compromise in the fragrance of the water-lily. It is not a *Nymphaea Douglasii.* In it, the sweet, and pure, and innocent are wholly sundered from the obscene and baleful. I do not scent in this the time-serving irresolution of a Massachusetts Governor, nor of a Boston Mayor. So behave that the odor of your actions may enhance the general sweetness of the atmosphere, that when we behold or scent a flower, we may not be reminded how inconsistent your deeds are with it; for all odor is but one form of advertisement of a moral quality, and if fair actions had not been performed, the lily would not smell sweet. The foul slime stands for the sloth and vice of man, the decay of humanity; the fragrant flower that springs from it, for the purity and courage which are immortal.

Slavery and servility have produced no sweet-scented flower annually, to charm the senses of men, for they have no real life: they are merely a decaying and a death, offensive to all healthy nostrils. We do not complain that they *live,* but that they do not *get buried.* Let the living bury them: even they are good for manure.

❖26❖

The Eighteenth Presidency!

WALT WHITMAN

Whitman's commentary on the presidential election campaign of 1856 reflects his disillusionment with the political process, and draws a profoundly pessimistic portrait of American society and its leaders as the nation approaches the crisis of secession. Whitman delivers a reasoned diatribe against slavery. The poet, however, stills retains his faith in the qualities of ordinary citizens as the real repository of American democratic values.

Voice of Walt Whitman to each Young Man in the Nation,
North, South, East, and West

Before the American era, the programme of the classes of a nation read thus, first the king, second the noblemen and gentry, third the great mass of mechanics, farmers, men following the water, and all laboring persons. The first and second classes are unknown to the theory of the government of These States; the likes of the class rated third on the old programme were intended to be, and are in fact, to all intents and purposes, the American nation, the people.

Mechanics, farmers, sailors, &c., constitute some six millions of the inhabitants of These States; merchants, lawyers, doctors, teachers and priests, count up as high as five hundred thousand; the owners of slaves number three hundred and fifty thousand; the population of The States bring altogether about thirty millions, seven tenths of whom are women and children. At present, the personnel of the government of these thirty millions, in executives and elsewhere, is drawn from limber-tongued lawyers, very fluent but empty feeble old men, professional politicians, dandies, dyspeptics, and so forth, and rarely drawn from the solid body of the people; the effects now seen, and more to come. Of course the fault, if it be a fault, is for reasons, and is of the people themselves, and will mend when it should mend.

Source: Walt Whitman, 'The Eighteenth Presidency!', 1856, in
The Complete Prose Works of Walt Whitman, Philadelphia: D. McKay, 1892.

Has much been done in the theory of These States? Very good; more remains. Who is satisfied with the theory? I say, delay not, come quickly to its most courageous facts and illustrations. I say no body of men are fit to make Presidents, Judges, and Generals, unless they themselves supply the best specimens of the same, and that supplying one or two such specimens illuminates the whole body for a thousand years.

I expect to see the day when the like of the present personnel of the governments, federal, state, municipal, military, and naval, will be looked upon with derision, and when qualified mechanics and young men will reach Congress and other official stations, sent in their working costumes, fresh from their benches and tools, and return to them again with dignity. The young fellows must prepare to do credit to this destiny, for the stuff is in them. Nothing gives place, recollect, and never ought to give place except to its clean superiors. There is more rude and undeveloped bravery, friendship, conscientiousness, clear-sightedness, and practical genius for any scope of action, even the broadest and highest, now among the American mechanics and young men, than in all the official persons in These States, legislative, executive, judicial, military, and naval, and more than among all the literary persons. I would be much pleased to see some heroic, shrewd, fully-informed, healthy-bodied, middle-aged, beard-faced American blacksmith or boatman come down from the West across the Alleghanies, and walk into the Presidency, dressed in a clean suit of working attire, and with the tan all over his face, breast, and arms; I would certainly vote for that sort of man, possessing the due requirements, before any other candidate.

Such is the thought that must become familiar to you, whoever you are, and to the people of These States, and must eventually take shape in action.

At present, we are environed with nonsense under the name of respectability. Everywhere lowers that stifling atmosphere that makes all the millions of farmers and mechanics of These States the helpless supple-jacks of a comparatively few politicians. Somebody must make a bold push. The people, credulous, generous, deferential, allow the American government to be managed in many respects as is only proper under the personnel of a king and hereditary lords; or, more truly, not proper under any decent men anywhere. If this were to go on, we ought to change the title of the President, and issue patents of nobility. Of course it is not to go on. We Americans are no fools. I perceive meanwhile that nothing less than marked inconsistencies and usurpations will arouse a nation, and make ready for better things afterwards.

But what ails the present way of filling the offices of The States? Is it not good enough? I should say it was not. To-day, of all the persons in public office in These States, not one in a thousand has been chosen by any spontaneous movement of the people, nor is attending to the interests of the people; all have been nominated and put through by great or small caucuses of the politicians, or appointed as rewards for electioneering; and all consign themselves to personal and party interests. Neither in the Presidency, nor in Congress, nor in foreign ambassadorships, nor in the governorships of The States, nor in legislatures, nor in the mayoralties of cities, nor the aldermanships, nor among the police, nor on the benches of judges, do I observe a single bold muscular, young, well-informed, resolute American man, bound to do a man's duty, aloof from all parties, and with a manly scorn of all parties. Instead of that, every trustee of the people is a traitor, looking only to his own gain, and to boost up his party. The berths, the Presidency included, are bought, sold, electioneered for, prostituted, and filled with prostitutes. In the North and East, swarms of dough-faces, office-vermin, kept-editors, clerks, attachés of the ten thousand officers and their parties, aware of nothing further than the drip and spoil of politics—ignorant of principles, the true glory of a man. In the South, no end of blusterers, braggarts, windy, melodramatic, continually screaming in falsetto, a nuisance to These States, their own just as much as any; altogether the most impudent persons that have yet appeared in the history of lands, once with the most incredible successes, having pistol'd, bludgeoned, yelled and threatened America, the past twenty years into one long train of cowardly concessions, and still not through, but rather at the commencement. Their cherished secret scheme is to dissolve the union of These States.

Well, what more? Is nothing but breed upon breed like these to be represented in the Presidency? Are parties to forever usurp the government? Are lawyers, dough-faces, and the three hundred and fifty thousand owners of slaves, to sponge the mastership of thirty millions? Where is the real America? Where are the labouring persons, ploughmen, men with axes, spades, scythes, flails? Where are the carpenters, masons, machinists, drivers of horses, workmen in factories? Where is the spirit of the manliness and common-sense of These States? It does not appear in the government. It does not appear at all in the Presidency.

The sixteenth and seventeenth terms of the American Presidency have shown that the villainy and shallowness of great rulers are just as eligible to These States as to any foreign despotism, kingdom, or empire—there is not a bit of difference. History is to record these two Presidencies as so far our topmost warning and shame. Never were publicly displayed more deformed, mediocre, snivelling, unreliable, falsehearted men! Never were These States so insulted, and attempted to be betrayed! All the main purposes for which government was established are openly denied. The perfect equality of slavery with freedom is flauntingly preached in the North—nay, the superiority of slavery. The slave trade is proposed to be renewed. Everywhere frowns and misunderstandings—everywhere exasperations and humiliations. The President eats dirt and excrement for his daily meals, likes it, and tries to force it on The States. The cushions of the Presidency are nothing but filth and blood. The pavements of Congress are also bloody. The land that flushed amazed at the basest outrage of our times, grows pale with a far different feeling to see the outrage unanimously commended back again to those who only half rejected it. The national tendency toward populating the territories full of free work-peoples, established by the organic compacts of These States, promulgated by the fathers, the Presidents, the old warriors, & the earlier Congresses, a tendency vital to the life and thrift of the masses of the citizens, is violently put back under the feet of slavery, and against the free people the masters of slaves are everywhere held up by the President by the red hand. In fifteen of the States the three hundred and fifty thousand masters keep down the true people, the millions of white citizens, mechanics, farmers, boatmen, manufacturers, and the like, excluding them from politics and from office, and punishing by the lash, by tar and feathers, binding fast to rafts on the river or trees in the woods, and sometimes by death, all attempts to discuss the evils of slavery in its relations to the whites. The people of the territories are denied the power to form State governments unless they consent to fasten upon them the slave-hopple, the iron wristlet, and the neck-spike. For refusing such consent, the governor & part of the legislature of the State of Kansas are chased, seized, chained, by the creatures of the President, and are to-day in chains. Over the vast continental tracts of unorganized American territory, equal in extent to all the present organized States, and in future to give the law to all, the whole executive, judicial, military, and naval power of These States is forsworn to the people, the rightful owners, and sworn to the help of the three hundred & fifty thousand masters of slaves, to put them through this continent, with their successors, at their pleasure, and to maintain by force their mastership over their slavemen and women, slave-farmers, slave-miners, slave-cartmen, slave-sailors, and the like. Slavery is adopted as an American institution, superior, national, constitutional, right in itself, and under no circumstances to take any less than freedom takes. Nor is that all; to-day, to-night, the constables and commissioners of the President can by law step into any part of These States and pick out whom they please, deciding which man or woman they will allow to be free, and which shall be a slave, no jury to intervene, but the commissioner's mandate to be enforced by the federal troops and cannon, and has been actually so enforced.

Are The States retarded then? No; while all is drowned and desperate that the government has had to do with, all the outside influence of government, (forever the largest part,) thrives and smiles. The sun shines, corn grows, men go merrily about their affairs, houses are built, ships arrive and depart. Through evil and through good, the republic stands, and is for centuries yet to stand immovable from its foundations. No, no; out at dastards and disgraces, fortunate are the wrongs that call forth stout and angry men; then is shown what stuff there is in a nation.

The young genius of America is not going to be emasculated and strangled just as it arrives toward manly age. It shall live, and yet baffle the politicians and the three hundred and fifty thousand masters of slaves.

Now the term of the seventeenth Presidency passing hooted and spurned to its close, the delegates of the politicians have nominated for the eighteenth term, Buchanan of Pennsylvania, and Fillmore of New York, separate tickets, but men both patterned to follow and match the seventeenth term, both disunionists, both old politicians, both sworn down to the theories of special parties, and of all others the theories that balk and reverse the main purposes of the founders of These States. Such are the nominees that have arisen out of the power of the politicians, but another power has also arisen. A new race copiously appears, with resolute tread, soon to confront Presidents, congresses and parties, to look them sternly in the face, to stand no nonsense, American young men, the offspring and proof of these

341

States, the West the same as the East, and the South alike with the North.

America sends these young men in good time, for they were needed. Much waits to be done. First, people need to realize who are poisoning the politics of These States.

Whence the delegates of the politicians? Whence the Buchanan and Fillmore Conventions? Not from sturdy American freemen; not from industrious homes; not from thrifty farms; not from the ranks of fresh-bodied young men; not from among teachers, poets, savans, learned persons, beloved persons, temperate persons; not from among shipbuilders, engineers, agriculturists, scythe-swingers, corn-hoers; not from the race of mechanics; not from that great strong stock of Southerners that supplied the land in old times; not from the real West, the log-hut, the clearing, the woods, the prairie, the hill-side; not from the sensible, generous, rude Californian miners; not from the best specimens of Massachusetts, Maine, New Jersey, Pennsylvania, Ohio, Illinois, Wisconsin, Indiana, nor from the untainted unpolitical citizens of the cities.

Whence then do these nominating dictators of America year after year start out? From lawyers' offices, secret lodges, back-yards, bed-houses, and bar-rooms; from out of the custom-houses, marshals' offices, post-offices, and gambling hells; from the President's house, the jail, the venereal hospital, the station-house; from un-named by-places where devilish disunion is hatched at midnight; from political hearses, and from the coffins inside, and from the shrouds inside of the coffins; from the tumors and abcesses of the land; from the skeletons and skulls in the vaults of the federal almshouses; from the running sores of the great cities; thence to the national, state, city, and district nominating conventions of These States, come the most numerous and controlling delegates.

Who are they personally? Office-holders, office-seekers, robbers, pimps, exclusives, malignants, conspirators, murderers, fancy-men, port-masters, custom-house clerks, contractors, kept-editors, Spaniels well-trained to carry and fetch, jobbers, infidels, disunionists, terrorists, mail-riflers, slave-catchers, pushers of Slavery, creatures of the President, creatures of would-be Presidents, spies, blowers, electioneers, body-snatchers, bawlers, bribers, compromisers, runaways, lobbyers, sponges, ruined sports, expelled gamblers, policy backers, monte-dealers, duelists, carriers of concealed weapons, blind men, deaf men, pimpled men, scarred inside with the vile disorder, gaudy outside with gold chains made from the people's money and harlot's money twisted together; crawling, serpentine men, the lousy combings and born freedom sellers of the earth.

Stript of padding and paint, who are Buchanan and Fillmore? What has this age to do with them? Two galvanized old men, close on the summons to depart this life, their early contemporaries long since gone, only they two left, relics and proofs of the little political bargains, chances, combinations, resentments of a past age, having nothing in common with this age, standing for the first crop of political graves and grave-stones planted in These States, but in no sort standing for the lusty young growth of the modern times of The States. It is clear from all these two men say and do, that their hearts have not been touched in the least by the flowing fire of the humanitarianism of the new world, its best glory yet, and a moral control stronger than all its governments. It is clear that neither of these nominees of the politicians has thus far reached an inkling of the real scope and character of the contest of the day, probably now only well begun, to stretch through years, with varied temporary successes & reverses. Still the two old men live in respectable little spots, with respectable little wants. Still their eyes stop at the edges of the tables of committees and cabinets, beholding not the great round world beyond. What has this age to do with them?

You Americans who travel with such men, or who are nominated on tickets any where with them, or who support them at popular meetings, or write for them in the newspapers, or who believe that any good can come out of them, you also understand not the present age, the fibre of it, the countless currents it brings of American young men, a different superior race. All this effervescence is not for nothing; the friendlier, vaster, more vital modern spirit, hardly yet arrived at definite proportions, or to the knowledge of itself, will have the mastery. The like turmoil prevails in the expressions of literature, manners, trade, and other departments.

To butchers, sailors, stevedores, and drivers of horses—to ploughmen, wood-cutters, marketmen, carpenters, masons, and laborers—to workmen in factories—and to all in These States who live by their daily toil—Mechanics! A parcel of windy northern liars are bawling in your ears the easily-spoken words Democracy and the democratic party. Others are making a great ado with the word Americanism, a solemn and great word. What the so-called democracy are now sworn to perform would eat the faces off the succeeding generations of common people worse than the most horrible disease. The others are contributing to the like performance, and are using the great word Americanism without yet feeling the first aspiration of it, as the great word Religion has been used, probably loudest and oftenest used, by men that made indiscriminate massacres at night, and filled the world so full with hatreds, horrors, partialities, exclusions, bloody revenges, penal conscience laws and test-oaths. To the virtue of Americanism is happening to-day, what happens many days to many virtues, namely, the masses who possess them but do not understand them are sought to be sold by that very means to those who neither possess them nor understand them. What are the young men suspicious of? I will tell them what it stands them in hand to be suspicious of, and that is American craft; it is subtler than Italian craft; I guess it is about the subtlest craft upon the earth.

What is there in prospect for free farmers and work-people? A few generations ago, the general run of farmers and work-people like us were slaves, serfs, deprived of their liberty by law; they are still so deprived on some parts of the continent of Europe. Today, those who are free here, and free in the British islands and elsewhere, are free through deeds that were done, and men that lived, some of them an age or so ago, and some of them many ages ago. The men and deeds of these days also decide for generations ahead, as past men and deeds decided for us.

As the broad fat States of the West, the largest and best parts of the inheritance of the American farmers and mechanics, were ordained to common people and workmen long in advance by Jefferson, Washington, and the earlier Congresses, now a far ampler West is to be ordained. Is it to be ordained to workmen, or to the masters of workmen? Shall the future mechanics of America be serfs? Shall labor be degraded, and women be whipt in the fields for not performing their tasks? If slaves are not prohibited from all national territory by law, as prohibited in the beginning, as the organic compacts authorise and require, and if, on the contrary, the entrance and establishment of slave labor through the Continent is secured, there will steadily wheel into the Union, for centuries to come, slave state after slave state, the entire surface of the land owned by great proprietors, in plantations of thousands of acres, showing no more sight for free races of farmers and work-people than there is now in any European despotism or aristocracy; and the existence of our present Free States put in jeopardy, because out of the vast territory are to come states enough to overbalance all.

Workmen! Workwomen! Those universal National American tracts belong to you; they are in trust with you; they are latent with the populous cities, numberless farms, herds, granaries, groves, golden gardens, and inalienable homesteads, of your successors. The base political blowers and kept-editors of the North are raising a fog of prevarications around you. But the manlier Southern disunionists, the chieftains among the three hundred and fifty thousand masters, clearly distinguish the issue, and the principle it rests upon. McDuffie, disunionist governor, lays it down with candid boldness that the workingmen of a state are unsafe depositaries of political powers and rights, and that a republic cannot permanently exist unless those who ply the mechanical trades and attend to the farm-work are slaves, subordinated by strict laws to their masters. Calhoun, disunionist senator, denounces and denies, in the presence of the world, the main article of the organic compact of These States, that all men are born free and equal, and bequeaths to his followers, at present leaders of the three hundred and fifty thousand masters, guides of the so-called democracy, counsellors of Presidents, and getters-up of the nominations of Buchanan & Fillmore, his deliberate charge, to be carried out against that main article, that it is the most false and dangerous of all political errors; such being the words of that charge, spoken in the summer of the 73rd year of These States, and, indeed, carried out since the spirit of congressional legislation, executive action, and the candidates offered by the political parties to the people.

Are not political parties about played out? I say they are, all round. America has outgrown parties; henceforth it is too large, and they too small. They habitually make common cause just as soon in advocacy of the worst deeds and men as the best, or probably a little sooner for the worst. I place no reliance upon any old party, nor upon any new party. Suppose one to be formed under the noblest auspices, and getting into power with the noblest intentions, how long would it remain so? How many years? Would it remain so one year? As soon as it becomes successful, and there are offices to be bestowed, the politicians leave the unsuccessful parties, and rush toward it, and it ripens and rots with the rest.

What right has any one political party, no matter which, to wield the American government? No right at all. Not the so-called democratic, not abolition, opposition to foreigners, nor any other party, should be permitted the exclusive use of the Presidency; and every American young man must have sense enough to comprehend this. I have said the old parties are defunct; but there remains of them empty flesh, putrid mouths, mumbling and squeaking the tones of these conventions, the politicians standing back in shadow, telling lies, trying to delude and frighten the people; and nominating such candidates as Fillmore and Buchanan.

What impudence! For any one platform, section, creed, no matter which, to expect to subordinate all the rest, and rule the immense diversity of These free and equal States! Platforms are of no account. The right man is everything. With the downfall of parties go the platforms they are forever putting up, lowering, turning, repainting, and changing.

The platforms for the Presidency of These States are simply the organic compacts of The States, the Declaration of Independence, the Federal Constitution, the action of the earlier Congresses, the spirit of the fathers and warriors, the official lives of Washington, Jefferson, Madison, and the now well-understood and morally established rights of man, wherever the sun shines, the rain falls, and the grass grows.

Much babble will always be heard in the land about the Federal Constitution, this, that, and the other concerning it. The Federal Constitution is a perfect and entire thing, an edifice put together, not for the accommodation of a few persons, but for the whole human race; not for a day or a year, but for many years, perhaps a thousand, perhaps many thousand. Its architecture is not a single brick, a beam, an apartment, but only the whole. It is the grandest piece of moral building ever constructed; I believe its architects were some mighty prophets and gods. Few appreciate it, Americans just as few as any. Like all perfect works or persons, time only is great enough to give its area. Five or six centuries hence, it will be better understood from results, growths.

The Federal Constitution is the second of the American organic compacts. The premises, outworks, guard, defense, entrance of the Federal Constitution, is the primary compact of These States, sometimes called the Declaration of Independence; and the groundwork, feet, understratum of that again, is its deliberate engagement, in behalf of the States, thenceforward to consider all men to be born free and equal into the world, each one possessed of inalienable rights to his life and liberty, (namely, that no laws passed by any government could be considered to alienate or take away those born rights, the penalties upon criminals being, of course, for the very purpose of preserving those rights). This is the covenant of the Republic from the beginning, now and forever. It is not a mere opinion; it is the most venerable pledge, with all forms observed, signed by the commissioners, ratified by the States, and sworn to by Washington at the head of his army, with his hand upon the Bible. It is supreme over all American law, and greater than Presidents, Congresses, elections, and what not, for they hurry out of the way, but it remains. Above all, it is carefully to be observed in all that relates to the continental territories. When they are organized into States, it is to be passed over to the good faith of those States.

One or 2 radical parts of the American theory of government: man can not hold property in man. As soon as there are clear-brained original American judges, this saying will be simplified by their judgements, and no State out of the whole confederacy but will confirm and approve those judgements.

Any one of These States is perfect mistress of itself; and each additional State the same. When states organize themselves, the Federal government withdraws, also absolved from its duties, except certain specific ones under the Constitution, and only in behalf of them can it interfere in The States.

Every rational uncriminal person, twenty-one years old, should be eligible to vote, on actual residence, no other requirement needed. The day will come when this will prevail.

The whole American Government is itself simply a compact with each individual of the thirty millions of persons now inhabitants of These States, and prospectively with each individual of the hundred millions and five hundred millions that are in time to become inhabitants, to protect each one's life, liberty, industry, acquisitions, without excepting one single individual out of the whole number, and without making ignominious distinctions. Thus is government sublime; thus is it equal; otherwise it is a government of castes, on exactly the same principles with the kingdoms of Europe.

I said the National obligation is passed over to the States. Then if they are false to it and impose upon certain persons, can the national government interfere? It can not under any circumstances whatever. We must wait, no matter how long. There is no remedy, except in The State itself. A corner-stone of the organic compacts of America is that a State is perfect mistress of itself. If that is taken away, all the rest may just as well be taken away—When that is taken away, this Union is dissolved.

Must run-away slaves be delivered back? They must. Many things may have the go-by, but good faith shall never have the go-by.

By a section of the fourth article of the Federal Constitution, These States compact each with the other, that any person held to service or labor in one State under its laws, and escaping into another State, shall not be absolved from service by any law of that other State, but shall be delivered up to the person to whom such service or labor is due. This part of the second organic compact between the original States should be carried out by themselves in their usual forms, but in spirit and in letter. Congress has no business to pass any law upon the subject, any more than upon the hundred other of the compacts between the States, left to be carried out by their good faith. Why should Congress pick out this particular one? I had quite as lief depend on the good faith of any of These States, as on the law of Congress and the President. Good faith is irresistible among men, and friendship is; which lawyers can not understand, thinking nothing but compulsion will do.

But can not that requirement of the fourth article of the Second Compact be evaded, on any plea whatever, even the plea of its unrighteousness? Nay, I perceive it is not to be evaded on any plea whatever, not even the plea of its unrighteousness. It should be observed by The States, in spirit and in letter, whether it is pleasant to them or unpleasant, beholding in it one item among many items, each of the rest as important as it, and each to be so carried out as not to contravene the rest. As to what is called the Fugitive Slave Law, insolently put over the people by their Congress and President, it contravenes the whole of the organic compacts, and is at all times to be defied in all parts of These States, South or North, by speech, by men, and, if need be, by the bullet and the sword.

Shall we determine upon such things, then, and not leave them to the great judges and the scholars? Yes, it is best that we determine upon such things.

Whenever the day comes for him to appear, the man who shall be the Redeemer President of These States, is to be the one that fullest realizes the rights of individuals, signified by the impregnable rights of The States, the substratum of the Union. The Redeemer President of These States is not to be exclusive, but inclusive. In both physical and political America there is plenty of room for the whole human race; if not, more room can be provided.

To the American young men, mechanics, farmers, etc. How much longer do you intend to submit to the espionage and terrorism of the three hundred and fifty thousand owners of slaves? Are you too their slaves, and their most obedient slaves? Shall no one among you dare open his mouth to say he is opposed to slavery, as a man should be, on account of the whites, and wants it abolished for their sake? Is not a writer, speaker, teacher to be left alive, but those who lick up the spit that drops from the mouths of the three hundred and fifty thousand masters? Is there hardly one free, courageous soul left in fifteen large and populous States? Do the ranks of the owners of slaves themselves contain no men desperate and tired of that service and sweat of the mind, worse than any service in sugar-fields or corn-fields, under the eyes of overseers? Do the three hundred and fifty thousand expect to bar off forever all preachers, poets, philosophers—all that makes the brain of These States, free literature, free thought, the good old cause of liberty? Are they blind? Do they not see those unrelaxed circles of death narrowing and narrowing every hour around them?

You young men of the Southern States! is the word abolitionist so hateful to you, then? Do you not know that Washington, Jefferson, Madison, and all the great Presidents and primal warriors and sages were declared abolitionists?

You young men! American mechanics, farmers, boatmen, manufacturers, and all work-people of the South, the same as the North! You are either to abolish slavery, or it will abolish you.

To the three hundred and fifty thousand owners of slaves: Suppose you get Kansas, do you think it would be ended? Suppose you and the politicians put Buchanan into the Eighteenth Presidency, or Fillmore into the Presidency, do you think it would be ended? I know nothing more desirable for those who contend against you than that you should get Kansas. Then would the melt begin in These States that would not cool till Kansas should be redeemed, as of course it would be.

O gentlemen, you do not know whom Liberty has nursed in These States, and depends on in time of need. You have not received any report of the Free States, but have received only the reports of the trustees who have betrayed the Free States. Do you suppose they will betray many thousand men, and stick at betraying a few more like you? Raised on plantations or in towns full of menial workmen and workwomen, you do not know as I know, these fierce and turbulent races that fill the Northeast, the East, the West, the Northwest, the Pacific shores, the great cities, Manhattan island, Brooklyn, Newark, Boston, Worcester, Hartford, New Haven, Providence, Portland, Bangor, Augusta, Albany, Buffalo, Rochester, Syracuse, Lockport, Cleveland, Detroit, Milwaukee, Racine, Sheboygan, Madison, Galena, Burlington, Iowa City, Chicago, St.Louis, Cincinnati, Columbus, Pittsburgh, Philadelphia, San Francisco, Sacramento, and many more. From my mouth hear the will of These States taking form in the great cities. Where slavery is, there it is. The American compacts, common sense, all things unite to make it the affair of the States diseased with it, to cherish the same as long as they see fit, and to apply the remedy when they see fit. But not one square mile of continental territory shall henceforward be given to slavery, to slaves, or to the masters of slaves—not one square foot. If any laws are passed giving up such territory those laws will be repealed. In organizing the territories, what laws are good enough for the American freeman must be good enough for you; if you come in under the said laws, well and good; if not, stay away. What is done, is done; henceforth there is no further compromise. All this is now being cast in the stuff that makes the tough national resolves of These States, that every hour only anneals tougher. It is not that putty you see in Congress and in the Presidency; it is iron—it is the undissuadable swift metal of death.

To editors of the independent press, and to rich persons. Circulate and reprint this Voice of mine for the workingmen's sake. I hereby permit and invite any rich person, anywhere, to stereotype it, or re-produce it in any form, to deluge the cities of The States with it, North, South, East and West. It is those millions of mechanics you want; the writers, thinkers, learned and benevolent persons, merchants, are already secured about to a man. But the great masses of the mechanics, and a large portion of the farmers, are unsettled, hardly know whom to vote for, or whom to believe. I am not afraid to say that among them I seek to initiate my name, Walt Whitman, and that I shall in future have much to say to them. I perceive that the best thoughts they have wait unspoken, impatient to be put in shape; also that the character, pride, friendship, conscience of America have yet to be proved to the remainder of the world.

The times are full of great portents in These States and in the whole world. Freedom against slavery is not issuing here alone, but is issuing everywhere. The horizon rises, it divides I perceive, for a more august drama than any of the past. Old men have played their parts, the act suitable to them is closed, and if they will not withdraw voluntarily, must be bid to do so with unmistakeable voice. Landmarks of masters, slaves, kings, aristocracies, are moth-eaten, and the peoples of the earth are planting new vast land marks for themselves. Frontiers and boundaries are less and less able to divide men. The modern inventions, the wholesale engines of war, the world-spreading instruments of peace, the steamship, the locomotive, the electric telegraph, the common newspaper, the cheap book, the ocean mail, are interlinking the inhabitants of the earth together as groups of one family—America standing, and for ages to stand, as the host and champion of the same, the most welcome spectacle ever presented among nations. Everything indicates unparalleled reforms. Races are marching and countermarching by swift millions and tens of millions. Never was justice so mighty amid injustice; never did the idea of equality erect itself so haughty and uncompromising amid inequality, as to-day. Never were such sharp questions asked as to-day. Never was there more eagerness to know. Never was the representative man more energetic, more like a god, than to-day. He urges on the myriads before him, he crowds them aside, his daring step approaches the arctic and antarctic poles, he colonizes the shores of the Pacific, the Asiatic Indias, the birthplace of languages and of races, the Archipelagoes, Australia; he explores Africa, he unearths Assyria and Egypt, he re-states history, he enlarges morality, he speculates anew upon the soul, upon original premises; nothing is left quiet, nothing but he will settle by demonstrations for himself. What whispers are these running through the eastern Continents, and crossing the Atlantic and Pacific? What historic denouements are these we are approaching? On all sides tyrants tremble, crowns are unsteady, the human race restive, on the watch for some better era, some divine war. No man knows what will happen next, but all know that some such things are to happen as mark the greatest moral convulsions of the earth. Who shall play the hand for America in these tremendous games?

❦ 27 ❧

Inaugural Address

JAMES BUCHANAN

James Buchanan was the last President to take office before the secession crisis. In his inaugural address on Wednesday, 4th March 1857, he identified himself as a strict constructionist, and took the view that the Kansas–Nebraska controversy remained a states' rights issue. He did foresee, however, that the slavery question, if not resolved, would threaten the constitutional integrity of the nation.

Fellow citizens:

I appear before you this day to take the solemn oath "that I will faithfully execute the office of President of the United States and will to the best of my ability preserve, protect, and defend the Constitution of the United States."

In entering upon this great office I must humbly invoke the God of our fathers for wisdom and firmness to execute its high and responsible duties in such a manner as to restore harmony and ancient friendship among the people of the several States and to preserve our free institutions throughout many generations. Convinced that I owe my election to the inherent love for the Constitution and the Union which still animates the hearts of the American people, let me earnestly ask their powerful support in sustaining all just measures calculated to perpetuate these, the richest political blessings which Heaven has ever bestowed upon any nation. Having determined not to become a candidate for reelection, I shall have no motive to influence my conduct in administering the Government except the desire ably and faithfully to serve my country and to live in the grateful memory of my countrymen.

We have recently passed through a Presidential contest in which the passions of our fellow-citizens were excited to the highest degree by questions of deep and vital importance; but when the people proclaimed their will the tempest at once subsided and all was calm.

The voice of the majority, speaking in the manner prescribed by the Constitution, was heard, and instant submission followed. Our own country could alone

Source: James Buchanan, 'Inaugural Address', in James D. Richardson, ed., *A Compilation of Messages and Papers of the Presidents*, New York: Bureau of National Literature Inc., 1897, Vol. VI.

have exhibited so grand and striking a spectacle of the capacity of man for self-government.

What a happy conception, then, was it for Congress to apply this simple rule, that the will of the majority shall govern, to the settlement of the question of domestic slavery in the Territories. Congress is neither "to legislate slavery into any Territory or State nor to exclude it therefrom, but to leave the people thereof perfectly free to form and regulate their domestic institutions in their own way, subject only to the Constitution of the United States."

As a natural consequence, Congress has also prescribed that when the Territory of Kansas shall be admitted as a State it "shall be received into the Union with or without slavery, as their constitution may prescribe at the time of their admission."

A difference of opinion has arisen in regard to the point of time when the people of a Territory shall decide this question for themselves.

This is, happily, a matter of but little practical importance. Besides, it is a judicial question, which legitimately belongs to the Supreme Court of the United States, before whom it is now pending, and will, it is understood, be speedily and finally settled. To their decision, in common with all good citizens, I shall cheerfully submit, whatever this may be, though it has ever been my individual opinion that under the Nebraska-Kansas act the appropriate period will be when the number of actual residents in the Territory shall justify the formation of a constitution with a view to its admission as a State into the Union. But be this as it may, it is the imperative and indispensable duty of the Government of the United States to secure to every resident inhabitant the free and independent expression of his opinion by his vote. This sacred right of each individual must be preserved. That being accomplished, nothing can be fairer than to leave the people of a Territory free from all foreign interference to decide their own destiny for themselves, subject only to the Constitution of the United States.

The whole Territorial question being thus settled upon the principle of popular sovereignty—a principle as ancient as free government itself—everything of a practical nature has been decided. No other question remains for adjustment, because all agree that under the Constitution slavery in the States is beyond the reach of any human power except that of the respective States themselves wherein it exists. May we not, then, hope that the long agitation on this subject is approaching its end, and that the geographical parties to which it has given birth, so much dreaded by the Father of his Country, will speedily become extinct? Most happy will it be for the country when the public mind shall be diverted from this question to others of more pressing and practical importance. Throughout the whole progress of this agitation, which has scarcely known any intermission for more than twenty years, whilst it has been productive of no positive good to any human being it has been the prolific source of great evils to the master, to the slave, and to the whole country. It has alienated and estranged the people of the sister States from each other, and has even seriously endangered the very existence of the Union. Nor has the danger yet entirely ceased. Under our system there is a remedy for all mere political evils in the sound sense and sober judgment of the people. Time is a great corrective. Political subjects which but a few years ago excited and exasperated the public mind have passed away and are now nearly forgotten. But this question of domestic slavery is of far graver importance than any mere political question, because should the agitation continue it may eventually endanger the personal safety of a large portion of our countrymen where the institution exists. In that event no form of government, however admirable in itself and however productive of material benefits, can compensate for the loss of peace and domestic security around the family altar. Let every Union-loving man, therefore, exert his best influence to suppress this agitation, which since the recent legislation of Congress is without any legitimate object.

It is an evil omen of the times that men have undertaken to calculate the mere material value of the Union. Reasoned estimates have been presented of the pecuniary profits and local advantages which would result to different States and sections from its dissolution and of the comparative injuries which such an event would inflict on other States and sections. Even descending to this low and narrow view of the mighty question, all such calculations are at fault. The bare reference to a single consideration will be conclusive on this point. We at present enjoy a free trade throughout our extensive and expanding country such as the world has never witnessed. This trade is conducted on railroads and canals, on noble rivers and arms of the sea, which bind together the North and the South, the East and the West, of our Confederacy. Annihilate this trade, arrest its free progress by the geographical lines of jealous and hostile States, and you destroy the prosperity and onward march of the whole and every part and involve all in one common ruin. But such considerations, important as they are in themselves, sink into insignificance when we reflect on the terrific evils which would result from disunion to every portion of the Confederacy—to the North, not more than to the South, to the East not more than to the West. These I shall not attempt to portray, because I feel an humble confidence that the kind Providence which inspired our fathers with wisdom to frame the most perfect form of government and union ever devised by man will not suffer it to perish until it shall have been peacefully instrumental by its example in the extension of civil and religious liberty throughout the world.

Next in importance to the maintenance of the Constitution and the Union is the duty of preserving the Government free from the taint or even the suspicion of corruption. Public virtue is the vital spirit of republics, and history proves that when this has decayed and the love of money has usurped its place, although the forms of free government may remain for a season, the substance has departed forever.

Our present financial condition is without a parallel in history. No nation has ever before been embarrassed from too large a surplus in its treasury. This almost necessarily gives birth to extravagant legislation. It produces wild schemes of expenditure and begets a race of speculators and jobbers, whose ingenuity is exerted in contriving and promoting expedients to obtain public money. The purity of official agents, whether rightfully or wrongfully, is suspected, and the character of the government suffers in the estimation of the people. This is in itself a very great evil.

The natural mode of relief from this embarrassment is to appropriate the surplus in the Treasury to great national objects for which a clear warrant can be found in the Constitution. Among these I might mention the extinguishment of the public debt, a reasonable increase of the Navy, which is at present inadequate to the protection of our vast tonnage afloat, now greater than that of any other nation, as well as to the defense of our extended seacoast.

It is beyond all question the true principle that no more revenue ought to be collected from the people than the amount necessary to defray the expenses of a wise, economical, and efficient administration of the Government. To reach this point it was necessary to resort to a modification of the tariff, and this has, I trust, been accomplished in such a manner as to do as little injury as may have been practicable to our domestic manufactures, especially those necessary for the defense of the country. Any discrimination against a particular branch for the purpose of benefiting favored corporations, individuals, or interests would have been unjust to the rest of the community and inconsistent with that spirit of fairness and equality which ought to govern in the adjustment of a revenue tariff.

But the squandering of the public money sinks into comparative insignificance as a temptation to corruption when compared with the squandering of the public lands.

No nation in the tide of time has ever been blessed with so rich and noble an inheritance as we enjoy in the public lands. In administering this important trust, whilst it may be wise to grant portions of them for the improvement of the remainder, yet we should never forget that it is our cardinal policy to reserve these lands, as much as may be, for actual settlers, and this at moderate prices. We shall thus not only best promote the prosperity of the new States and Territories, by furnishing them a hardy and independent race of honest and industrious citizens, but shall secure homes for our children and our children's children, as well as for those exiles from foreign shores who may seek in this country to improve their condition and to enjoy the blessings of civil and religious liberty. Such emigrants have done much to promote the growth and prosperity of the country. They have proved faithful both in peace and in war. After becoming citizens they are entitled, under the Constitution and laws, to be placed on a perfect equality with native-born citizens, and in this character they should ever be kindly recognized.

The Federal Constitution is a grant from the States to Congress of certain specific powers, and the question whether this grant should be liberally or strictly construed has more or less divided political parties from the beginning. Without entering into the argument, I desire to state at the commencement of my Administration that long experience and observation have convinced me that a strict construction of the powers of the Government is the only true, as well as the only safe, theory of the Constitution. Whenever in our past history doubtful powers have been exercised by Congress, these have never failed to produce injurious and unhappy consequences. Many such instances might be adduced if this were the proper occasion. Neither is it necessary for the public service to strain the language of the Constitution, because all the great and useful powers required for a successful administration of the Government, both in peace and in war, have been granted, either in express terms or by the plainest implication.

Whilst deeply convinced of these truths, I yet consider it clear that under the war-making power Congress may appropriate money toward the construction of a military road when this is absolutely necessary for the defense of any State or Territory of the Union against foreign invasion. Under the Constitution Congress has power "to declare war," "to raise and support armies," "to provide and maintain a navy," and to call forth the militia to "repel invasions." Thus endowed, in an ample manner, with the war-making power, the corresponding duty is required that "the United States shall protect each of them [the States] against invasion." Now, how is it possible to afford this protection to California and our Pacific possessions except by means of a military road through the Territories of the United States, over which men and munitions of war may be speedily transported from the Atlantic States to meet and to repel the invader? In the event of a war with a naval power much stronger than our own we should then have no other available access to the Pacific Coast, because such a power would instantly close the route across the isthmus of Central America. It is impossible to conceive that whilst the Constitution has expressly required Congress to defend all the States it should yet deny to them, by any fair construction, the only possible means by which one of these States can be defended. Besides, the Government, ever since its origin, has been in the constant practice of constructing military roads. It might also be wise to consider whether the love for the Union which now animates our fellow-citizens on the Pacific Coast may not be impaired by our neglect or refusal to provide for them, in their remote and isolated condition, the only means by which the power of the States on this side of the Rocky Mountains can reach them in sufficient time to "protect" them "against invasion." I forbear for the present from expressing an opinion as to the wisest and most economical mode in which the Government can lend its aid in accomplishing this great and necessary work. I believe that many of the difficulties in the way, which now appear formidable, will in a great degree vanish as soon as the nearest and best route shall have been satisfactorily ascertained.

It may be proper that on this occasion I should make some brief remarks in regard to our rights and duties as a member of the great family of nations. In our intercourse with them there are some plain principles, approved by our own experience, from which we should never depart. We ought to cultivate peace, commerce, and friendship with all nations, and this not merely as the best means of promoting our own material interests, but in a spirit of Christian benevolence toward our fellow-men, wherever their lot may be cast. Our diplomacy should be direct and frank, neither seeking to obtain more nor accepting less than is our due. We ought to cherish a sacred regard for the independence of all nations, and never attempt to interfere in the domestic concerns of any unless this shall be imperatively required by the great law of self-preservation. To avoid entangling alliances has been a maxim of our policy ever since the days of Washington, and its wisdom no one will attempt to dispute. In short, we ought to do justice in a kindly spirit to all nations and require justice from them in return.

It is our glory that whilst other nations have extended their dominions by the sword we have never acquired any territory except by fair purchase or, as in the case of Texas, by the voluntary determination of a brave, kindred, and independent people to blend their destinies with our own. Even our acquisitions from Mexico form no exception. Unwilling to take advantage of the fortune of war against a sister republic, we purchased these possessions under the treaty of peace for a sum which was considered at the time a fair equivalent. Our past history forbids that we shall in the future acquire territory unless this be sanctioned by the laws of justice and honor. Acting on this principle, no nation will have a right to interfere or to complain if in the progress of events we shall still further extend our possessions. Hitherto in all our acquisitions the people, under the protection of the American flag, have enjoyed civil and religious liberty, as well as equal and just laws, and have been contented, prosperous, and happy. Their trade with the rest of the world has rapidly increased, and thus every commercial nation has shared largely in their successful progress.

I shall now proceed to take the oath prescribed by the Constitution, whilst humbly invoking the blessing of Divine Providence on this great people.

❧ 28 ❧

Cannibals All!
Or Slaves Without Masters

GEORGE FITZHUGH

The South found an able advocate in defence of its 'peculiar institution' in George Fitzhugh. In a series of polemics, he argued that the North was hypocritical in attempting to seize the moral high-ground over the issue of slavery. Capitalism created a class of 'wage slaves' in the north, who, Fitzhugh claimed, were in many respects worse off than their slave counterparts in the south. Southerners respected their slaves as property, and their treatment of them was benign in comparison to those in thrall to the demands of capitalist enterprise. These extracts give a flavour of his style, and end with a warning to the North that the abolitionists were the vanguard of a movement towards the creation of a socialist republic in the United States.

I
The Universal Trade

We are all, North and South, engaged in the White Slave Trade, and he who succeeds best is esteemed most respectable. It is far more cruel than the Black Slave Trade, because it exacts more of its slaves, and neither protects nor governs them. We boast that it exacts more when we say, "that the *profits* made from employing free labor are greater than those from slave labor." The profits, made from free labor, are the amount of the products of such labor, which the employer, by means of the command which capital or skill gives him, takes away, exacts, or "exploitates" from the free laborer. The profits of slave labor are that portion of the products of such labor which the power of the master enables him to appropriate. These profits are less, because the master allows the slave to retain a larger share of the results of his own labor than do the employers of free labor. But we not only boast that the White Slave Trade is more exacting and fraudulent (in

Source: George Fitzhugh, *Cannibals All! Or, Slaves Without Masters*, 1857.

fact, though not in intention) than Black Slavery; but we also boast that it is more cruel, in leaving the laborer to take care of himself and family out of the pittance which skill or capital have allowed him to retain. When the day's labor is ended, he is free, but is overburdened with the cares of family and household, which make his freedom an empty and delusive mockery. But his employer is really free, and may enjoy the profits made by others' labor, without a care, or a trouble, as to their well-being. The negro slave is free, too, when the labors of the day are over, and free in mind as well as body; for the master provides food, raiment, house, fuel, and everything else necessary to the physical well-being of himself and family. The master's labors commence just when the slave's end. No wonder men should prefer white slavery to capital, to negro slavery, since it is more profitable, and is free from all the cares and labors of black slave-holding.

Now, reader, if you wish to know yourself–to "descant on your own deformity"– read on. But if you would cherish self-conceit, self-esteem, or self-appreciation, throw down our book; for we will dispel illusions which have promoted your happiness, and show you that what you have considered and practiced as virtue is little better than moral Cannibalism. But you will find yourself in numerous and respectable company; for all good and respectable people are "Cannibals all" who do not labor, or who are successfully trying to live on the unrequited labor of other people:– Whilst low, bad, and disreputable people, are those who labor to support themselves, and to support said respectable people besides. Throwing the negro slaves out of the account, and society is divided in Christendom into four classes: the rich, or independent respectable people, who live well and labor not at all, the professional and skillful respectable people, who do a little light work, for enormous wages; the poor hard-working people, who support everybody, and starve themselves; and the poor thieves, swindlers, and sturdy beggars, who live like gentlemen, without labor, on the labor of other people. The gentlemen exploitate, which being done on a large scale and requiring a great many victims, is highly respectable–whilst the rogues and beggars take so little from others that they fare little better than those who labor.

But, reader, we do not wish to fire into the flock. "Thou art the man!" You are a Cannibal! and if a successful one, pride yourself on the number of your victims quite as much as any Fiji chieftain, who breakfasts, dines, and sups on human flesh– and your conscience smites you, if you have failed to succeed, quite as much as his, when he returns from an unsuccessful foray.

Probably, you are a lawyer, or a merchant, or a doctor, who has made by your business fifty thousand dollars, and retired to live on your capital. But, mark! not to spend your capital. That would be vulgar, disreputable, criminal. That would be, to live by your own labor; for your capital is your amassed labor. That would be to do as common working men do; for they take the pittance which their employers leave them to live on. They live by labor; for they exchange the results of their own labor for the products of other people's labor. It is, no doubt, an honest, vulgar way of living, but not at all a respectable way. The respectable way of living is to make other people work for you, and to pay them nothing for so doing–and to have no concern about them after their work is done. Hence, white slave-holding is much more respectable than negro slavery—for the master works nearly as hard for the negro as he for the master. But you, my virtuous, respectable reader, exact three thousand dollars per annum from white labor (for your income is the product of white labor) and make not one cent of return in any form. You retain your capital, and never labor, and yet live in luxury on the labor of others. Capital commands labor, as the master does the slave. Neither pays for labor; but the master permits the slave to retain a larger allowance from the proceeds of his own labor, and hence "free labor is cheaper than slave labor." You, with the command over labor which your capital gives you, are a slave owner—a master, without the obligations of a master. They who work for you, who create your income, are slaves, without the rights of slaves. Slaves without a master! Whilst you were engaged in amassing your capital, in seeking to become independent, you were in the White Slave Trade. To become independent is to be able to make other people support you, without being obliged to labor for *them*. Now, what man in society is not seeking to attain this situation? He who attains it is a slave owner, in the worst sense. He who is in pursuit of it is engaged in the slave trade. You, reader, belong to the one or other class. The men without property, in a free society, are theoretically in a worse condition than slaves. Practically, their condition corresponds with this theory, as history and statistics everywhere demonstrate. The capitalists, in free society, live in ten times the luxury and show that Southern masters do, because the slaves to capital work harder and cost less than negro slaves.

The negro slaves of the South are the happiest, and, in some sense, the freest people in the world. The children and the aged and infirm work not at all, and yet have all the comforts and necessities of life provided for them. They enjoy liberty, because they are oppressed neither by care nor labor. The women do little hard work, and are protected from the despotism of their husbands by their masters. The negro men and stout boys work, on the average, in good weather, not more than nine hours a day. The balance of their time is spent in perfect abandon. Besides, they have their Sabbaths and holidays. White men, with so much license and liberty, would die of ennui; but negroes luxuriate in corporeal and mental repose. With their faces upturned to the sun, they can sleep at any hour; and quiet sleep is the greatest of human enjoyments. "Blessed be the man who invented sleep." 'Tis happiness in itself—and results from contentment with the present, and confident assurance of the future. We do not know whether free laborers ever sleep. They are fools to do so; for, whilst they sleep, the wily and watchful capitalist is devising means to ensare and exploitate them. The free laborer must work or starve. He is more of a slave than the negro, because he works longer and harder for less allowance than the slave, and has no holiday, because the cares of life with him begin when its labors end. He has no liberty, and not a single right. We know, 'tis often said, air and water are common property, which all have equal right to participate and enjoy; but this is utterly false. The appropriation of the lands carries with it the appropriation of all on or above the lands, *usque ad coelum, aut ad inferos.*[1] A man cannot breathe the air without a place to breathe it from, and all places are appropriated. All water is private property "to the middle of the stream," except the ocean, and that is not fit to drink.

Free laborers have not a thousandth part of the rights and liberties of negro slaves. Indeed, they have not a single liberty, unless it be the right or liberty to die. But the reader may think that he and other capitalists and employers are freer than negro slaves. Your capital would soon vanish, if you dared indulge in the liberty and abandon of negroes. You hold your wealth and position by the tenure of constant watchfulness, care, and circumspection. You never labor; but you are never free.

Where a few own the soil, they have unlimited power over the balance of society, until domestic slavery comes in to compel them to permit this balance of society to draw a sufficient and comfortable living from *terra mater*. Free society asserts the right of a few to the earth—slavery maintains that it belongs, in different degrees, to all. But, reader, well may you follow the slave trade. It is the only trade worth following, and slaves the only property worth owning. All other is worthless, a mere *caput mortuum*,[2] except in so far as it vests the owner with the power to command the labors of others—to enslave them. Give you a palace, ten thousand acres of land, sumptuous clothes, equipage, and every other luxury; and with your artificial wants you are poorer than Robinson Crusoe, or the lowest working man, if you have no slaves to capital, or domestic slaves. Your capital will not bring you an income of a cent, nor supply one of your wants, without labor. Labor is indispensable to give value to property, and if you owned every thing else, and did not own labor, you would be poor. But fifty thousand dollars means, and is, fifty thousand dollars worth of slaves. You can command, without touching on that capital, three thousand dollars worth of labor per annum. You could do no more were you to buy slaves with it, and then you would be cumbered with the cares of governing and providing for them. You are a slaveholder now, to the amount of fifty thousand dollars, with all the advantages, and none of the cares and responsibilities of a master.

"Property in man" is what all are struggling to obtain. Why should they not be obliged to take care of man, their property, as they do of their horses and their hounds, their cattle and their sheep. Now, under the delusive name of liberty, you work him "from morn to dewy eve"—from infancy to old age—then turn him out to starve. You treat your horses and hounds better. Capital is a cruel master. The free slave trade, the commonest, yet the cruellest of trades.

XXI
Negro Slavery

Until the lands of America are appropriated by a few, population becomes dense, competition among laborers active, employment uncertain, and wages low, the personal liberty of all the whites will continue to be a blessing. We have vast unsettled territories; population may cease to increase slowly, as in most countries, and many centuries may elapse before the question will be practically suggested, whether slavery to capital be preferable to slavery to human masters. But the negro has neither energy nor enterprise, and, even in our sparser population, finds, with his improvident habits, that his liberty is a curse to himself, and a greater curse to the society around him. These considerations, and others equally obvious, have induced the South to attempt to defend negro slavery as an exceptional institution, admitting, nay asserting, that slavery, in the general or in the abstract, is morally wrong, and against common right. With singular inconsistency, after making this admission, which admits away the authority of the Bible, of profane history, and of the almost universal practice of mankind—they turn round and attempt to bolster up the cause of negro slavery by these very exploded authorities. If we mean not to repudiate all divine, and almost all human authority in favor of slavery, we must vindicate that institution in the abstract.

To insist that a status of society, which has been almost universal, and which is expressly and continually justified by holy Writ, is its natural, normal, and necessary status, under the ordinary circumstances, is on its face a plausible and probable proposition. To insist on less, is to yield our cause, and to give up our religion; for if white slavery be morally wrong, be a violation of natural rights, the Bible cannot be true. Human and divine authority do seem in the general to concur, in establishing the expediency of having masters and slaves of different races. The nominal servitude of the Jews to each other, in its temporary character, and no doubt in its mild character, more nearly resembled our wardship and apprenticeship, than ordinary domestic slavery. In very many nations of antiquity, and in some of modern times, the law has permitted the native citizens to become slaves to each other. But few take advantage of such laws; and the infrequency of the practice, establishes the general truth that master and slave should be of different national descent. In some respects, the wider the difference the better, as the slave will feel less mortified by his position. In other respects, it may be that too wide a difference hardens the hearts and brutalizes the feelings of both master and slave. The civilized man hates the savage, and the savage returns the hatred with interest. Hence, West India slavery of newly caught negroes is not a very humane, affectionate, or civilizing institution. Virginia Negroes have become moral and intelligent. They love their master and his family, and the attachment is reciprocated. Still, we like the idle, but intelligent house-servants, better than the hard-used, but stupid outhands; and we like the mulatto better than the negro; yet the negro is generally more affectionate, contented and faithful.

The world at large looks on negro slavery as much the worst form of slavery; because it is only acquainted with West India slavery. Abolition never arose till negro slavery was instituted; and now abolition is only directed against negro slavery. There is no philanthropic crusade attempting to set free the white slaves of Eastern Europe and of Asia. The world, then, is prepared for the defence of slavery in the abstract—it is prejudiced only against negro slavery. These prejudices were in their origin well founded. The Slave Trade, the horrors of the Middle Passage, and West India slavery were enough to rouse the most torpid philanthropy.

But our Southern slavery has become a benign and protective institution, and our negroes are confessedly better off than any free laboring population in the world.

How can we contend that white slavery is wrong, whilst all the great body of free laborers are starving; and slaves, white or black, throughout the world, are enjoying comfort? We write in the cause of Truth and Humanity, and will not play the advocate for master or for slave.

The aversion to negroes, the antipathy of race, is much greater at the North than at the South; and it is very probable that this antipathy to the person of the negro, is confounded with or generates hatred of the institution with which he is usually connected. Hatred to slavery is very generally little more than hatred of negroes.

There is one strong argument in favor of negro slavery over all other slavery: that he, being unfitted for the mechanic arts, for trade, and all skillful pursuits, leaves those pursuits to be carried on by the whites; and does not bring all industry into disrepute, as in Greece and Rome, where the slaves were not only the artists and mechanics, but also the merchants. Whilst, as a general and abstract question, negro slavery has no other claims over other forms of slavery, except that from inferiority, or rather peculiarity, of race, almost all negroes require masters, whilst only the children, the women, the very weak, poor, and ignorant, &c., among the whites, need some protective and governing relation of this kind; yet as a subject of temporary, but worldwide importance, negro slavery has become the most necessary of all human institutions.

The African slave trade to America commenced three centuries and a half since. By the time of the American Revolution, the supply of slaves had exceeded the demand for slave labor, and the slaveholders, to get rid of a burden, and to prevent the increase of a nuisance, became violent opponents of the slave trade, and many of them abolitionists. New England, Bristol, and Liverpool, who reaped the profits of the trade, without suffering from the nuisance, stood out for a long time against its abolition. Finally, laws and treaties were made, and fleets fitted out to abolish it; and after a while, the slaves of most of South America, of the West Indies, and of Mexico were liberated. In the meantime, cotton, rice, sugar, coffee, tobacco, and other products of slave labor, came into universal rise as necessaries of life. The population of Western Europe, sustained and stimulated by those products, was trebled, and that of the North increased tenfold. The products of slave labor became scarce and dear, and famines frequent. Now, it is obvious, that to emancipate all the negroes would be to starve Western Europe and our North. Not to extend and increase negro slavery, *pari passu*, with the extension and multiplication of free society, will produce much suffering. If all South America, Mexico, the West Indies, and our Union south of Mason and Dixon's line, of the Ohio and Missouri, were slaveholding, slave products would he abundant and cheap in free society; and their market for their merchandise, manufactures, commerce, &c., illimitable. Free white laborers might live in comfort and luxury on light work, but for the exacting and greedy landlords, bosses and other capitalists.

We must confess, that overstock the world as you will with comforts and with

361

luxuries, we do not see how to make capital relax its monopoly—how to do aught but tantalize the hireling. Capital, irresponsible capital, begets, and ever will beget, the *immedicabile vulnus*[3] of so-called Free Society. It invades every recess of domestic life, infects its food, its clothing, its drink, its very atmosphere, and pursues the hireling, from the hovel to the poorhouse, the prison and the grave. Do what he will, go where he will, capital pursues and persecutes him. "*Haeret lateri lethalis arundo!*"[4] Capital supports and protects the domestic slave; taxes, oppresses and persecutes the free laborer.

XXV
In What Anti-Slavery Ends

Mr. Carlyle very properly contends that abolition and all the other social movements of the day, propose little or no government as the moral panacea that is to heal and save a suffering world. Proudhon expressly advocates anarchy; and Stephen Pearl Andrews, the ablest of American socialistic and abolition philosophers, elaborately attacks all existing social relations, and all legal and governmental restraints, and proposes No-Government as their substitute. He is the author of the Free Love experiment in New York, and a co-laborer and eulogist of similar experiments in villages or settlements in Ohio, Long Island and other places in the North and Northwest. He is a follower of Josiah Warren, who was associated with Owen of Lanark at New Harmony. We do not know that there is any essential difference between his system and that which has been for many years past practically carried out in Oneida County, New York, by the Perfectionists, who construe the Bible into authority for the unrestrained indulgence of every sensual appetite. The doctrines of Fourier, of Owen and Fanny Wright, and the other early Socialists, all lead to No-Government and Free Love. 'Tis probable they foresaw and intended this result, but did not suggest or propose it to a world then too wicked and unenlightened to appreciate its beatific purity and loveliness. The materials, as well as the proceedings of the infidel, woman's rights, negro's rights, free-everything and anti-every school, headed and conducted in Boston, by Garrison, Parker, Phillips, and their associate women and negroes, show that they too are busy with "assiduous wedges" in loosening the whole frame of society, and preparing for the glorious advent of Free Love and No-Government. All the Infidel and Abolition papers in the North betray a similar tendency. The Abolitionists of New York, headed by Gerrit Smith and Wm. Goodell, are engaged in precisely the same projects, but being Christians, would dignify Free Love and No-Government with the appellation of a Millennium. Probably half the Abolitionists at the North expect a great social revolution soon to occur by the advent of the Millennium. If they would patiently await that event, instead of attempting to get it up themselves, their delusions, however ridiculous, might at least be innocuous. But these progressive Christian Socialists differ not at all from the Infidel Socialists of Boston. They are equally intent and busy in pulling down the priesthood, and abolishing or dividing all property—seeing that whether the denouement be Free Love or a Millennium, the destruction of all existing human relations and human institutions is prerequisite to their full fruition.

Many thousand as have been of late years the social experiments attempting to practice community of property, of wives, children, &c., and numerous as the books inculcating and approving such practices, yet the existence and growth of Mormonism is of itself stronger evidence than all other of the tendency of modern free society towards No-Government and Free Love. In the name of polygamy, it has practically removed all restraints to the intercourse of sexes, and broken up the Family. It promises, too, a qualified community of property and a fraternal association of labor. It beats up monthly thousands of recruits from free society in Europe and America, but makes not one convert in the slaveholding South. Slavery is satisfied and conservative. Abolition, finding that all existing legal, religious, social and governmental institutions restrict liberty and occasion a quasi-slavery, is resolved not to stop short of the subversion of all those institutions, and the inauguration of Free Love and No-Government. The only cure for all this is for free society sternly to recognize slavery as right in principle and necessary in practice, with more or less of modification, to the very existence of government, of property, of religion, and of social existence.

We shall not attempt to reconcile the doctrines of the Socialists, which propose to remove all legal restraints, with their denunciations of Political Economy. Let Alone is the essence of Political Economy and the whole creed of most of the Socialists. The Political Economists, Let Alone, for a fair fight, for universal rivalry, antagonism, competition, and cannibalism. They say the eating up the weaker members of society, the killing them out by capital and competition will improve the breed of men and benefit society. They foresee the consequences of their doctrine, and are consistent. Hobbes saw men devouring one another, under their system, two hundred years ago, and we all see them similarly engaged now. The Socialists promise that when society is wholly disintegrated and dissolved, by inculcating good principles and "singing fraternity over it" all men will co-operate, love, and help one another.

They place men in positions of equality, rivalry, and antagonism, which must result in extreme selfishness of conduct, and yet propose this system as a cure for selfishness. To us their reasonings seem absurd.

Yet the doctrines so prevalent with Abolitionists and Socialists, of Free Love and Free Lands, Free Churches, Free Women and Free Negroes—of No-Marriage, No-Religion, No-Private Property, No-Law and No-Government, are legitimate deductions, if not obvious corollaries from the leading and distinctive axiom of political economy—Laissez Faire, or Let Alone.

All the leading Socialists and Abolitionists of the North, we think, agree with Fanny Wright, that the gradual changes which have taken place in social organization from domestic slavery to praedial serfdom and thence to the present system of free and competitive society, have been mere transitive states, each placing the laborer in a worse condition than that of absolute slavery, yet valuable as preparing the way for a new and more perfect social state. They value the present state of society the more highly because it is intolerable, and must the sooner usher in a Millenium or Utopia.

XXVII
Slavery—Its Effect On The Free

Beaten at every other quarter, we learn that a distinguished writer at the North, is about to be put forward by the Abolitionists, to prove that the influence of slavery is deleterious on the whites who own no slaves.

Now, at first view it elevates those whites; for it makes them not the bottom of society, as at the North—not the menials, the hired day laborer, the work scavengers and scullions—but privileged citizens, like Greek and Roman citizens, with a numerous class far beneath them. In slave society, one white man does not lord it over another; for all are equal in privilege, if not in wealth; and the poorest would not become a menial—hold your horse, and then extend his hand or his hat for a gratuity, were you to proffer him the wealth of the Indies. The menial, the exposed and laborious, and the disgraceful occupations are all filled by slaves. But filled they must be by someone, and in free society, half of its members are employed in occupations that are not considered or treated as respectable. Our slaves till the land, do the coarse and hard labor on our roads and canals, sweep our streets, cook our food, brush our boots, wait on our tables, hold our horses, do all hard work, and fill all menial offices. Your freemen at the North do the same work and fill the same offices. The only difference is, we love our slaves, and we are ready to defend, assist and protect them; you hate and fear your white servants, and never fail, as a moral duty, to screw down their wages to the lowest, and to starve their families, if possible, as evidence of your thrift, economy and management—the only English and Yankee virtues.

In free society, miscalled freemen fulfill all the offices of slaves for less wages than slaves, and are infinitely less liked and cared for by their superiors than slaves. Does this elevate them and render them happy?

The trades, the professions, the occupations that pay well, and whose work is light, is reserved for freemen in slave society. Does this depress them?

The doctor, the lawyer, the mechanic, the dentist, the merchant, the overseer, every trade and profession, in fact, live from the proceeds of slave labor at the South. They divide the profits with the owner of the slaves. He has nothing to pay them except what his slaves make. But you Yankees and Englishmen more than divide the profits—you take the lion's share. You make more money from our cotton, and tobacco, and sugar, and indigo, and wheat, and corn, and rice, than we make ourselves. You live by slave labor—would perish without it—yet you abuse it. Cut off England and New England from the South American, East and West India and our markets, from which to buy their food, and in which to sell their manufactures, and they would starve at once. You live by our slave labor. It elevates your whites as well as ours, by confining them, in a great degree, to skillful, well-paying, light, and intellectual employments—and it feeds and clothes them. Abolish slavery, and you will suffer vastly more than we, because we have all the lands of the South, and can command labor as you do, and a genial soil and climate, that require less labor. But while in the absence of slavery, we could support ourselves, we should cease to support you. We would neither send you food and clothing, nor buy your worse than useless notions.

XXXVI
Warning To The North

Banquo—   *But 'tis strange:*
And oftentimes, to win us to our harm,
The instruments of darkness tell us truths;
Win us with honest trifles, to betray us
In deepest consequences.
                                   Macbeth

The reader must have remarked our propensity of putting scraps of poetry at the head of our chapters, or of interweaving them with the text. It answers as a sort of chorus or refrain, and, when skillfully handled, has as fine an effect as the fiddle at a feast, or the brass band on the eve of an engagement. It nerves the author for greater effort, and inspires the reader with resolution to follow him in his most profound ratiocinations and airiest speculations. We learnt it from "our Masters in the art of war" when we carried their camp and their whole park of artillery (which we are now using with such murderous effect against their own ranks). We also captured their camp equipage, books of military strategy, &c. In them we found rules laid down for the famous songs which are so harmoniously blended with the speeches at all Infidel and Abolition conventions, and Women's Rights and Free Love assemblages. They are intended to inspire enthusiasm, confirm conviction, and to "screw the courage to the sticking point." Besides, sometimes they answer admirably the opposite purpose of a sedative. Often, when Sister This One has, by her imprudent speech, outraged decency, propriety, religion, and morality, and drawn down upon her head hisses, and cries of "Turn, her out! Turn her out!" Brother That One bursts forth in "strains of sweetest melody," and like another Orpheus quells and quiets another hell. Not that we intend by any means to intimate that this musical brother would play Orpheus throughout, and take as long and perilous a trip to rescue his sister as Orpheus did for Eurydice. On the contrary, we suspect in such contingency he would pray to Pluto to double bar the gates, and bribe Cerberus to keep closer watch. We derive this impression from the triangular correspondence of Greeley, Andrews, and James, entitled "Love, Marriage and Divorce"; and from the actings and doings of the courts and legislature of Massachusetts—who from the number of the divorces they grant, we should think could hardly find time to send Hiss on a visit of purification to the Convents.

Now it may be, that sometimes, when we "have gone it rather strong" (as we are very apt to do) and offended the reader, our scraps of poetry may answer the purpose of the Abolition songs, and soothe and propitiate him. Besides, they afford a sort of interlude or by-play, like that of Sancho where he slipped off from the flying horse, Clavileno, just as he and the Don had reached the constellation of the Goat, and went to playing with the little goats to relieve the giddiness of his head. I am sure, when we have, as we often do, mounted with our reader into the highest regions of metaphysics, that his head becomes a little giddy (at least ours does) and that he is thankful for a little poetry or a turn at play with our Abolition Goats. "Goats, indeed!" quoth Mr. G——, "Lions, you had better say." Well, be it lions! We are no more afraid of you than if you were lambs; and you will no sooner dare to attack us than you did the Knight of La Mancha when he vainly challenged you to mortal combat.

Let not the reader suppose that we either emulate the chivalry of the Don or the wisdom of his Squire. A Northern crime has congealed the courage of our lions and they are afraid of the "paper bullets of the brain"; yet they are vastly fond of shooting them at others, provided they are sure the shot will not be returned.

As for Sancho, we think him the wisest man we ever read after, except Solomon. Indeed, in the world of Fiction, all the wisdom issues from the mouths of fools—as witness Shakspeare's Falstaff and his fools. There is at least vrai semblance in all this; for, as in the Real world, the philosophers (e.g. our Masters in the art of war) have monopolized all the folly—where so likely to find the wisdom as among the fools?

We fear our "Little Cannibals" are growing impatient, and may be, a little jealous of our seeming preference for our goats. They are young yet and require nursing. But they are young Herculeses, born with teeth, and if any Abolition serpents attempt to strangle them in the cradle, they'll be apt to get the worst of it. The danger is, however, that the Abolitionists will steal and adopt them—for they are vastly fond of young cannibals, and employ much of their time in sewing and knitting, and getting up subscriptions, to send shirts and trousers to the little fellows away over in Africa, who as indignantly repel them as King Lear did when he stripped in the storm and resolved to be his "unsophisticated self."

Now, seeing that the Abolitionists are so devoted to the uncouth, dirty, naked little cannibals of Africa, haven't we good reason to fear that they will run away with and adopt ours, when they come forth neatly dressed in black muslin and all shining with gold from the master hands of Morris and Wynne? They will be sure at least to captivate the hearts of the strong-minded ladies, and if they will treat them well in infancy, we don't know but what, if they will wait till they grow up, we may spare them a husband or two from the number.

Mr. Morris has promised they shall be black as Erebus without, and white as "driven snow" within.

If they can get over the trying time of infancy—if the critics don't smother them in the cradle, the boys will make their own way in the world, and get a name famous as Toussaint or Dessalines.

To be candid with the reader, we have learned lately that the physique of a book is quite as important as its metaphysique—the outside as the inside. Figure, size, proportion are all to be consulted; for books are now used quite as much for center table ornaments as for reading. We have a marble one on our center table that answers the former purpose admirably, because nobody can put puzzling questions about its contents. Now, we must write the exact amount, and no more, to enable Mr. Morris and Mr. Wynne to make our book appear externally *comme il faut*. We write this chapter in part for that purpose. The reader would not object to a page, or so, more or less of it, and Mr. Morris and Mr. Wynne will know how to curtail or omit, for they are not only masters of their own trades, but can render us valuable assistance in ours.

We return to our Cannibals, with this single remark to that morose and demure reader who is snarling at our occasional levity—"You, sir, never throw off your dignity; because you would be sure to uncover your folly."

We warn the North, that everyone of the leading Abolitionists is agitating the negro slavery question merely as a means to attain ulterior ends, and those ends nearer home. They would not spend so much time and money for the mere sake of the negro or his master, about whom they care little. But they know that men once fairly committed to negro slavery agitation—once committed to the sweeping principle "that man being a moral agent, accountable to God for his actions, should not have those actions controlled and directed by the will of another," are, in effect, committed to Socialism and Communism, to the most ultra doctrines of Garrison, Goodell, Smith and Andrews—to no private property, no church, no law, no government,—to free love, free lands, free women and free churches.

There is no middle ground—not an inch of ground of any sort, between the doctrines which we hold and those which Mr. Garrison holds. If slavery, either white or black, be wrong in principle or practice, then is Mr. Garrison right—then is all human government wrong.

Socialism, not Abolition, is the real object of Black Republicanism. The North, not the South, the true battleground. Like Fanny Wright, the author of American Socialism, the agitators of the North look upon free society as a mere transition state to be a better, but untried, form of society. The reader will not fully comprehend the ideas we would convey, without reading *England the Civilizer*, by Miss Fanny Wright. It is worth reading, not only as far the best history of the British constitution, but as the most correct and perfect analysis and delineation of free society—of that form of society which all Socialists and all thinking men agree cannot stand as it is. The Abolition School of Socialists like it because it is intolerable—because they consider it a transition state to a form of society without law or government. Miss Wright has the honesty to admit, that a *transition* has never taken place. No; and never will take place: because the expulsion of human nature is a pre-requisite to its occurrence.

But we solemnly warn the North that what she calls a *transition* is what every leading Abolitionist is moving heaven and earth to attain. This is their real object—negro emancipation a mere gull-trap.

In the attempt to attain "transition" seas of gore may be shed, until military despotism comes in to restore peace and security. We (for we are a Socialist) agree with Mr. Carlyle, that the action of free society must be reversed. That, instead of relaxing more and more the bonds that bind man to man, you must screw them up more closely. That, instead of no government, you must have more government. And this is eminently true in America, where from the nature of things, as society becomes older and population more dense, more of government will be required. To prevent the attempt at transition, which would only usher in revolution, you must begin to govern more vigorously.

But we will be asked, How is this to be effected? The answer is easy. The means are at hand, and the work is begun.

The Democratic party, purged of its radicalism and largely recruited from the ranks of the old line Whigs, has become eminently and actively conservative. It is the antipodes of the Democratic party of the days of Jefferson, in the grounds which it occupies and the opinions which it holds, (what it professes to hold is another thing). Yet it has been a consistent party throughout. Consistent, in wisely and boldly adapting its action to the emergencies of the occasion. It is pathological, and practices according to prevailing symptoms. 'Tis true, it has a mighty Nosology in its Declaration of Independence, Bills of Rights, Constitutions, Platforms, and Preambles and Resolutions; but, like a good physician, it watches the state of the patient, and casts Nosology to the dogs when the symptoms require it. When we entered the party we were radicals, and half Abolitionists, and found inscribed on its banner, "*The world is too much governed!*" Now, we are sure the conviction has fastened itself on the heart of every good citizen, that "the world is too little governed."

The true and honorable distinction of the Democratic party is, that it has but one unbending principle—"The safety of the people is the supreme law." To this party we think the Nation and the North may confidently look for a happy exodus from our difficulties. It is pure, honest, active, and patriotic now, and will continue so as long as the dark cloud of Abolition and Socialism lowers and threatens at the North. Long and quiet possession of power will be sure to corrupt it. It will be then time to cast it aside. It is now able, and it alone is able, to grapple with and strangle the treasons of the North.

Times change, and men change with them.

Good and brave men are proud, not ashamed, of such changes. Let no false pride of seeming consistency deter us from an avowal, which omitted, may trammel and impede our action.

Our old Nosology is an effective arsenal and armory for the most ultra Abolitionists, and the more effective, because we have not formally repudiated it. Let "*The world is too little governed*" be adopted as our motto, inscribed upon our flag and run up to the masthead.

NOTE.—We learn that many of the old Federalists of the North, and some of the South, are joining our ranks. We welcome them. Their principles were wrong when they adopted them, but (barring their consolidation doctrines) will answer pretty well now. It was ever the misfortune of the old Federal party and the lately deceased Whig party, to be right at the wrong time. They were, as the doctors say, nosological and not pathological in practice. The Whig party of England, like the Democratic party of America, is eminently pathological, active, observant, and impressible.

Notes

1. "Even to heaven or to hell."
2. "Worthless residue."
3. "Irreparable injury"
4. "The lethal arrow clings to her side." Virgil, *Aeneid,* IV, 73.

VI. Schism

VI. Schism

⟨⟩·29·⟨⟩

Opinion in the Dred Scott Case

JUSTICE ROGER TANEY

Two days after Buchanan's inaugural speech in 1857, Chief Justice Taney delivered the Supreme Court's opinion in the Dred Scott case. This case had political and legal implications of great significance in the context of the debate over slavery that was dividing the Union. Scott's case concerned a slave who had accompanied his owner on his travels in free labour states and the free territories—where slavery was barred by the Missouri Compromise of 1820— and hinged upon whether his residence outside the South effectively meant he had been freed. In deciding against Scott, Taney argued that he had no rights that needed to be respected by whites; that in any event, he was permanently resident in the slave state of Missouri when he filed suit; and that the Missouri Compromise was unconstitutional. The case sparked intense controversy among abolitionists, and again highlighted the difficulties of deciding an individual's status in a nation half-slave and half-free.

Scott v. Sandford: Opinion

Mr. Chief Justice Taney delivered the opinion of the court:

This case has been twice argued. After the argument at the last term, differences of opinion were found to exist among the members of the court; and as the questions in controversy are of the highest importance, and the court was at that time much pressed by the ordinary business of the term, it was deemed advisable to continue the case and direct a re-argument on some of the points, in order that we might have an opportunity of giving to the whole subject a more deliberate consideration. It has accordingly been again argued by counsel, and considered by the court, and I now proceed to deliver its opinion.

There are two leading questions presented by the record:

Source: *Records of the Supreme Court of the United States*, Washington D.C.:
National Archives and Records Administration, RG 267.

1. Had the Circuit Court of the United States jurisdiction to hear and determine the case between these parties? And,

2. If it had jurisdiction, is the judgment it has given erroneous or not?

The plaintiff in error, who was also the plaintiff in the court below, was, with his wife and children, held as slaves by the defendant, in the State of Missouri, and he brought this action in the Circuit Court of the United States for that district to assert the title of himself and his family to freedom.

The declaration is in the form usually adopted in that State to try questions of this description, and contains the averment necessary to give the court jurisdiction: that he and the defendant are citizens of diferent States; that is, he is a citizen of Missouri, and the defendant a citizen of New York.

The defendant pleaded in abatement to the jurisdiction of the court, that the plaintiff was not a citizen of the State of Missouri, as alleged in his declaration, being a negro of African descent, whose ancestors were of pure African blood, and who were brought into this country and sold as slaves.

To this plea the plaintiff demurred, and the defendant joined in demurrer. The court overruled the plea, and gave judgment that the defendant should answer over. And he thereupon put in sundry pleas in bar, upon which issues were joined, and at the trial the verdict and judgment were in his favor. Whereupon the plaintiff brought this writ of error.

Before we speak of the pleas in bar, it will be proper to dispose of the questions which have arisen on the plea in abatement.

That plea denies the right of the plaintiff to sue in a court of the United States, for the reasons therein stated.

If the question raised by it is legally before us, and the court should be of opinion that the facts stated in it disqualify the plaintiff from becoming a citizen, in the sense in which that word is used in the Constitution of the United States, then the judgment of the Circuit Court is erroneous, and must be reversed.

It is suggested, however, that this plea is not before us; and that as the judgment in the court below on this plea was in favor of the plaintiff, he does not seek to reverse it, or bring it before the court for revision by his writ of error; and also that the defendant waived this defense by pleading over, and thereby admitted the jurisdiction of the court. But in making this objection, we think the peculiar and limited jurisdiction of courts of the United States has not been adverted to. This peculiar and limited jurisdiction has made it necessary, in these courts to adopt different rules and principles of pleading, so far as jurisdiction is concerned, from those which regulate courts of common law in England and in the different States of the Union which have adopted the common law rules.

In these last mentioned courts, where their character and rank are analogous to that of a circuit court of the United States; in other words, where they are what the law terms courts of general jurisdiction, they are presumed to have jurisdiction unless the contrary appears. No averment in the pleadings of the plaintiff is necessary, in order to give jurisdiction. If the defendant objects to it, he must plead it specially, and unless the fact on which he relies is found to be true by a jury, or admitted to be true by the plaintiff, the jurisdiction cannot be disputed in an appellate court.

Now, it is not necessary to inquire whether in courts of that description a party who pleads over in bar, when a plea to the jurisdiction has been ruled against him, does or does not waive his plea; nor whether upon a judgment in his favor on the pleas in bar, and a writ of error brought by the plaintiff, the question upon the plea in abatement would be open for revision in the appellate court. Cases that may have been decided in such courts, or rules that may have been laid down by common law pleaders, can have no influence in the decision in this court. Because, under the Constitution and laws of the United States, the rules which govern the pleadings in its courts, in questions of jurisdiction, stand on different principles and are regulated by different laws.

This difference arises, as we have said, from the peculiar character of the government of the United States. For although it is sovereign and supreme in its appropriate sphere of action, yet it does not possess all the powers which usually belong to the sovereignty of a nation. Certain specified powers, enumerated in the Constitution, have been conferred upon it; and neither the Legislative, Executive nor Judicial Departments of the Government can lawfully exercise any authority beyond the limits marked out in the Constitution. And in regulating the Judicial Department, the cases in which the courts of the United States shall have jurisdiction are particularly and specifcally enumerated and defined; and they are not authorized to take cognizance of any case which does not come within the description therein specified. Hence, when a plaintiff sues in a court of the United States, it is necessary that he should show, in his pleading, that the suit he brings is within the jurisdiction of the court, and that he is entitled to sue there. And if he omits to do this, and should, by an oversight of the Circuit Court, obtain a judgment in his favor, the judgment would be reversed in the appellate court for want of jurisdiction in the court below. The jurisdiction would not be presumed, as in the case of a common law, English, or state court, unless the contrary appeared. But the record, when it comes before the appellate court, must show affirmatively, that the inferior court had authority, under the Constitution, to hear and determine the case. And if the plaintiff claims a right to sue in a circuit court of the United States, under that provision of the Constitution which gives jurisdiction in controversies between citizens of different states, he must distinctly aver in his pleading that they are citizens of different states, and he cannot maintain his suit without showing that fact in the pleading.

This point was decided in the case of Bingham v. Cabot, in 3 Dall. 382, and ever since adhered to by the court. And in Jackson v. Ashton, 8 Pet. 148, it was held that the objection to which it was open could not be waived by the opposite party, because consent of parties could not give jurisdiction.

It is needless to accumulate cases on this subject. Those already referred to, and the cases of Capron v. Van Noorden, in 2 Cranch, 126, and Montalet v. Murray, 4 Cranch, 40, are sufficient to show the rule of which we have spoken. The case of Capron v. Van Noorden strikingly illustrates the diference between a common law court and a court of the United States.

If however, the fact of citizenship is averred in the declaration, and the defendant does not deny it, and put it in issue by plea in abatement, he cannot offer evidence at the trial to disprove it, and consequently cannot avail himself of the objection in the appellate court, unless the defect should be apparent in some other part of the record. For if there is no plea in abatement, and the want of jurisdiction does not appear in any other part of the transcript brought up by the writ of error, the undisputed averment of citizenship in the declaration must be taken in this court to be true. In this case the citizenship is averred, but it is denied by the defendant in the manner required by the rules of pleading, and the fact upon which the denial is based is admitted by the demurrer. And if the plea and demurrer, and judgmemt of the court below upon it, are before us upon this record, the question to be decided is, whether the facts stated in the plea are sufficient to show that the plaintiff is not entitled to sue as a citizen in a court of the Untied States.

We think they are before us. The plea in abatement and the judgment of the court upon it, are a part of the judicial proceedings in the Circuit Court, and are there recorded as such; and a writ of error always brings up to the superior court the whole record of the pleadings in the court below. And in the case of The Bank of the U. S. v. Smith, 11 Wheat. 172, this court said, that the case being brought up by writ of error, the whole record was under the consideration of this court. And this being the case in the present instance, the plea in abatement is necessarily under consideration; and it becomes, therefore, our duty to decide whether the facts stated in the plea are or are not sufficient to show that the plaintiff is not entitled to sue as a citizen in a court of the United States.

This is certainly a very serious question, and one that now for the first time has been brought for decision before this court. But it is brought here by those who have a right to bring it, and it is our duty to meet it and decide it.

The question is simply this: can a negro, whose ancestors were imported into this country and sold as slaves, become a member of the political community formed and brought into existence by the Constitution of the United States, and as such become entitled to all the rights, and privileges, and immunities, guarantied by that Instrument to the citizen. One of these rights is the privilege of suing in a court of the United States in the cases specified in the Constitution.

It will be observed, that the plea applies to that class of persons only whose ancestors were negroes of the African race, and imported into this country, and sold and held as slaves. The only matter in issue before the court, therefore, is, whether the descendants of such slaves, when they shall be emancipated, or who are born of parents who had become free before their birth, are citizens of a state, in the sense in which the word "citizen" is used in the Constitution of the United States. And this being the only matter in dispute on the pleadings, the court must be understood as speaking in this opinion of that class only; that is, of those persons who are the descendants of Africans who were imported into this country and sold as slaves.

The situation of this population was altogether unlike that of the Indian race.

The latter, it is true, formed no part of the colonial communities, and never amalgamated with them in social connections or in government. But although they were uncivilized, they were yet a free and independent people, associated together in nations or tribes, and governed by their own laws. Many of these political communities were situated in territories to which the white race claimed the ultimate right of dominion. But that claim was acknowledged to be subject to the right of the Indians to occupy it as long as they thought proper, and neither the English nor Colonial governments claimed or exercised any dominion over the tribe or nation by whom it was occupied, nor claimed the right to the possession of the territory, until the tribe or nation consented to cede it. These Indian governments were regarded and treated as foreign governments, as much so as if an ocean had separated the red man from the white; and their freedom has constantly been acknowledged, from the time of the first emigration to the English Colonies to the present day, by the different governments which suceeded each other. Treaties have been negotiated with them, and their alliance sought for in war; and the people who compose these Indian political communities have always been treated as foreigners not living under our government. It is true that the course of events has brought the Indian tribes within the limits of the United States under supjection to the white race; and it has been found necessary, for their sake as well as our own, to regard them as in a state of pupilage, and to legislate to a certain extent over them and the territory they occupy. But they may, without doubt, like the subjects of any other foreign govemment, be naturalized by the authority of Congress, and become citizens of a State and of the United States; and if an individual should leave his nation or tribe, and take up his abode among the white population, he would be entitled to all the rights and privileges which would belong to an emigrant from any other foreign people.

We proceed to examine the case as presented by the pleadings.

The words "people of the United States" and "citizens" are synonymous terms, and mean the same thing. They both describe the political body, who, according to our republican institutions, form the sovereignty, and who hold the power and conduct the government through their representatives. They are what we familiarly call the "sovereign people," and every citizen is one of this people and a constituent member of this sovereignty. The question before us is, whether the class of persons described in the plea in abatement compose a portion of this people, and are constituent members of this sovereignty. We think they are not, and that they are not included, and were not intended to be included, under the word "citizens" in the Constitution, and can, therefore, claim none of the rights and privileges which that instrument provides for and secures to citizens of the United States. On the contrary, they were at that time considered as a subordinate and inferior class of beings, who had been subjugated by the dominant race, and whether emancipated or not, yet remained subject to their authority, and had no rights or privileges but such as those who held the power and the government might choose to grant them.

It is not the province of this court to decide upon the justice or injustice, the policy or impolicy of these laws. The decision of that question belonged to the political or policy-making power; to those who formed the sovereignty and framed the Constitution. The duty of the court is to interpret the instrument they have framed, with the best lights we can obtain on the subject, and to administer it as we find it, according to its true intent and meaning when it was adopted.

In discussing this question we must not confound the rights of citizenship which a state may confer within its own limits, and the rights of citizenship as a member of the Union. It does not by any means follow, because he has all the rights and privileges of a State, that he must be a citizen of the United States. He may have all the rights and privileges of the citizen of a State, and yet not be entitled to the rights and privileges of a citizen in any other State. For, previous to the adoption of the Constitution of the United States, every State had the undoubted right to confer on whomever it pleased the character of a citizen, and to endow him with all its rights. But this character, of course, was confined to the borders of the State and gave him no rights or privileges in other States beyond those secured to him by the laws of nations and the comity of States. Nor have the several States surrendered the power of conferring these rights and privileges by adopting the Constitution of the United States. Each State may still confer them upon an alien, or any one it thinks proper, or upon any class or description of persons; yet he would not be a citizen in the sense in which that word is used in the Constitution of the United States, nor entitled to sue as such in one of its courts, nor to the privileges and immunities of a citizen in the other States. The rights which he would acquire would be restricted to the State which gave them. The Constitution has conferred on Congress the right to establish an uniform rule of naturalization, and this right is evidently exclusive, and has always been held by this court to be so. Consequently no State, since the adoption of the Constitution, can, by naturalizing an alien, invest him with the rights and privileges secured to a citizen of a State under the federal government, although, so far as the State alone was concerned, he would undoubtedly be entitled to the rights of a citizen, and clothed with all the rights and immunities which the Constitution and laws of the State attached to that character.

It is very clear, therefore, that no State can, by any Act or law of its own, passed since the adoption of the Constitution, introduce a new member into the political community created by the Constitution of the United States. It cannot make him a member of this community by making him a member of its own. And for the same reason it cannot introduce any person, or description of persons, who were not intended to be embraced in this new political family, which the Constitution brought into existence, but were intended to be excluded from it.

The question then arises, whether the provisions of the Constitution, in relation to the personal rights and privileges to which the citizen of a state should be entitled, embraced the negro African race, at that time in this country, or who might afterwards be imported, who had then or should afterwards be made free in any Slate; and to put it in the power of a single State to make him a citizen of the United States, and endue him with the full rights of citizenship in every other State without their consent. Does the Constitution of the United States act upon him whenever he shall be made free under the laws of a State, and raised there to the rank of a citizen, and immediately clothe him with all the privileges of a citizen in every other State, and in its own courts?

The court thinks the affirmative of these propositions cannot be maintained. And if it cannot, the plaintiff in error could not be a citizen of the State of Missouri, within the meaning of the Constitution of the United States, and consequently was not entitled to sue in its courts.

It is true, every person, and every class and description of persons, who were at the time of the adoption of the Constitution recognized as citizens in the several States, became also citizens of this new political body; but none other; it was formed by them, and for them and their posterity, but for no one else. And the personal rights and privileges guaranteed to citizens of this new sovereignty were intended to embrace those only who were then members of the several state communities or who should afterwards, by birthright or otherwise, become members according to the provisions of the Constitution and the principles on which it was founded. It was the union of those who were at that time members of distinct and separate political communities into one political family, whose power for certain specified purposes was to extend over the whole territory of the United States. And it gave to each citizen rights and privileges outside of his State, which he did not before possess, and placed him in every other State upon a perfect equality with its own citizens as to rights of person and rights of property; it made him a citizen of the United States.

It becomes necessary, therefore, to determine who were citizens of the several States when the Constitution was adopted. And in order to do this, we must recur to the governments and institutions of the thirteen Colonies, when they separated from Great Britain and formed new sovereignties, and took their places in the family of independent nations. We must inquire who, at that time, were recognized as the people or citizens of a State, whose rights and liberties had been outraged by the English Government; and who declared their independence, and assumed the powers of government to defend their rights by force of arms.

In the opinion of the court, the legislation and histories of the times, and the language used in the Declaration of Independence, show, that neither the class of persons who had been imported as slaves, nor their descendents, whether they had become free or not, were then acknowledged as a part of the people, nor intended to be included in the general words used in that memorable instrument.

It is difficult at this day to realize the state of public opinion in relation to that unfortunate race, which prevailed in the civilized and enlightened portions of the world at the time of the Declaration of Independence, and when the Constitution of the United States was written and adopted. But the public history of every European nation displays it, in manner too plain to be mistaken.

They had for more than a century before been regarded as beings of an inferior order and altogether unfit to associate with the white race, either in social or political relations; and so far inferior, that they had no rights which the white man was bound to respect; and that the negro might justly and lawfully be reduced to slavery for his benefit. He was bought and sold, and treated as an ordinary article of merchandise and traffic, whenever a profit could be made by it. This opinion was at that time fixed and universal in the civilized portion of the white race. It was regarded as an axiom in morals as well as in politics, which no one thought of disputing, or supposed to be open to dispute; and men in every grade and position in society daily and habitually acted upon it in their private pursuits, as well as in matters of public concern, without doubting for a moment the correctness of this opinion.

And in no nation was this opinion more firmly fixed or more uniformly acted upon than by the English government and English people. They not only seized them on the coast of Africa, and sold them or held them in slavery for their own use, but they took them as ordinary articles of merchandise to every country where they could make a profit on them, and were far more extensively engaged in this commerce than any other nation in the world.

The opinion thus entertained and acted upon in England was naturally impressed upon the colonies they founded on this side of the Atlantic. And, accordingly, a negro of the African race was regarded by them as an article of property, and held, and bought and sold as such, in every one of the thirteen Colonies which united in the Declaration of Independence, and afterwards formed the Constitution of the United States. The slaves were more or less numerous in the different Colonies, as slave labor was found more or less profitable. But no one seems to have doubted the correctness of the prevailing opinion of the time.

The legislation of the different Colonies furnishes positive and indisputable proof of this fact.

It would be tedious, in this opinion, to enumerate the various laws they passed upon this subject. It will be sufficient, as a sample of the legislation which then generally prevailed throughout the British Colonies, to give the laws of two of them; one being still a large slaveholding State, and the other the first State in which slavery ceased to exist.

The Province of Maryland, in 1717 (ch. 13, sec. 5), passed a law declaring "that if any free negro or mulatto intermarry with any white woman, or if any white man shall intermarry with any negro or mulatto woman, such negro or mulatto shall become a slave during life, excepting mulattoes born of white women who, for such intermarriage, shall only become servants for seven years, to be disposed of as the Justices of the County Court, where such marriage so happens, shall think fit; to be applied by them towards the support of a public school within the said county. And any white man or white woman who shall intermarry as aforesaid, with any negro or mulatto, such white man or white woman shall become servants during the term of seven years, and shall be disposed of by the justices aforesaid, and be applied to the uses aforesaid."

The other colonial law to which we refer was passed by Massachusetts in 1705 (chap. 6). It is entitled "An Act for the better preventing of a spurious and mixed issue," etc.; and it provides, that "if any negro or milatto shall presume to smite or strike any person of the English or other Christian nation, such negro or mulatto shall he severely whipped, at the discretion of the justices before whom the offender shall be convicted."

And "that none of Her Majesty's English or Scottish subjects, nor of any other Christian nation, within this province, shall contract matrimony with any negro or mulatto; nor shall any person, duly authorized to solemnize marriage, presume to join any such in marriage, on pain of forfeiting the sum of fifty pounds; one moiety thereof to Her Majesty, for and towards the support of the government within this province, and the other moiety to him or them that shall inform and sue for the same in any of Her Majesty's courts of record within the Province, by will, plaint, or information."

We give both of these laws in the words used by the respective legislative bodies, because the language in which they are framed, as well as the provisions contained in them, show, too plainly to be misunderstood, the degraded condition of this unhappy race. They were still in force when the Revolution began, and are a faithful index to the state of feeling towards the class of persons of whom they speak, and of the position they occupied throughout the thirteen colonies, in the eyes and thoughts of the men who framed the Declaration of Independence and established the State constitutions and governments. They show that a perpetual and impassable barrier was intended to be erected between the white race and the one which they had reduced to slavery, and governed as subjects with absolute and despotic power, and which they then looked upon as so far below them in the scale of created beings, that intermarriages between white persons and negroes or mulattoes were regarded as unnatural and immoral, and punished as crimes, not only on the parties, but in the person who joined them in marriage. And no distinction in this respect was made between the free negro or mulatto and the slave, but this stigma, of the deepest degradation, was fixed upon the whole race.

We refer to these historical facts for the purpose of showing the fixed opinions concerning this race, upon which the statesmen of that day spoke and acted. It is necessary to do this, in order to determine whether the general terms used in the Constitution of the United States, as to the rights of man and the rights of the people, was intended to include them, or to give to them or their posterity the benefit of any of its provisions.

The language of the Declaration of Independence is equally conclusive.

It begins by declaring that, "when in the course of human events it becomes necessary for one people to dissolve the political bands which have connected them with another, and to assume among the powers of the earth the separate and equal station to which the laws of nature and nature's God entitle them, a decent respect for the opinions of mankind requires that they should declare the causes which impel them to the separation."

It then proceeds to say: "We hold these truths to be self-evident: that all men are created equal, that they are endowed by their Creator with certain inalienable rights; that among them is life, liberty, and pursuit of happiness; that to secure these rights, governments are instituted, deriving their just powers from the consent of the governed."

The general words above quoted would seem to embrace the whole human family, and if they were used in a similar instrument at this day, would be so understood. But it is too clear for dispute, that the enslaved African race were not intended to be included, and formed no part of the people who framed and adopted this Declaration; for if the language, as understood in that day, would embrace them, the conduct of the distinguished men who framed the Declaration of Independence would have been utterly and flagrantly inconsistent with the principles they asserted; and instead of the sympathy of mankind, to which they so confidently appealed, they would have deserved and received universal rebuke and repropation.

Yet the men who framed this Declaration were great men—high in literary acquirements—high in their sense of honor, and incapable of asserting principles inconsistent with those on which they were acting. They perfectly understood the meaning of the language they used, and how it would be understood by others; and they knew that it would not, in any part of the civilized world, be supposed to embrace the negro race, which, by common consent, had been excluded from civilized governments and the family of nations, and doomed to slavery. They spoke and acted according to the then established doctrines and principles, and in the ordinary language of the day, and no one misunderstood them. The unhappy black race were separated from the white by indelible marks, and laws long before established, and were never thought of or spoken of except as property, and when the claims of the owner or the profit of the trader were supposed to need protection.

This state of public opinion had undergone no change when the Constitution was adopted, as is equally evident from its provisions and language.

The brief preamble sets forth by whom it was formed, for what purposes, and for whose benefit and protection. It declares that it is formed by the people of the United States, that is to say, by those who were members of the different political communities in the several States; and its great object is declared to be to secure the blessings of liberty to themselves and their posterity. It speaks in general terms of the people of the United States and of citizens of the several States, when it is providing for the exercise of the powers granted or the privileges secured to the citizen. It does not define what description of persons are intended to be included under these terms, or who shall be regarded as a citizen and one of the people. It uses them as terms so well understood that no further description or definition was necessary.

But there are two clauses in the Constitution which point directly and specifically to the negro race as a separate class of persons, and show clearly that they were not regarded as a portion of the people or citizens of the government then formed.

One of these clauses reserves to each of the thirteen states the right to import slaves until the year 1808, if it thinks proper. And the importation which it thus sanctions was unquestionably of persons of the race of which we are speaking, as the traffic in slaves in the United States had always been confined to them. And by the other provision the states pledge themselves to each other to maintain the right of property of the master, by delivering up to him any slave who may have escaped from his service, and be found within their respective territories. By the first above-mentioned clause, therefore, the right to purchase and hold this property is directly sanctioned and authorized for twenty years by the people who framed the Constitution. And by the second, they pledge themselves to maintain and uphold the right of the master in the manner specified, as long as the government they then formed should endure. And these two provisions show, conclusively, that neither the description of persons therein referred to, nor their descendents, were embraced in any of the other provisions of the Constitution; for certainly these two clauses were not intended to confer on them or their posterity the blessings of liberty, or any of the personal rights so carefully provided for the citizen.

No one of that race had ever migrated to the United States voluntarily; all of them had been brought here as articles of merchandise. The number that had been emancipated at that time were but few in comparison with those held in slavery; and they were identified in the public mind with the race to which they belonged, and regarded as a part of the slave population rather than the free. It is obvious that they were not even in the minds of the framers of the Constitution when they were conferring special rights and privileges upon the citizens of a State in every other part of the Union.

Indeed, when we look to the condition of this race in the several States at the time, it is impossible to believe that these rights and privileges were intended to be extended to them.

It is very true, that in that portion of the Union where the labor of the negro race was found to be unsuited to the climate, and unprofitable to the master, but few slaves were held at the time of the Declaration of Independence; and when the Constitution was adopted, it had entirely worn out in one of them, and measures had been taken for its gradual abolition in several others. But this change had not been producod by any change of opinion in relation to this race; but because it was discovered, from experience, that slave labor was unsuited to the climate and productions of those States: for some of the States, where it had ceased or nearly ceased to exist, were actively engaged in the slave trade, procuring cargoes on the coast of Africa, and transporting them for sale to those parts of the Union where their labor was found to be profitable, and suited to the climate and productions. And this traffic was openly carried on, and fortunes accumulated by it, without reproach from the people of the States where they resided. And it can hardly be supposed that, in the states where it was then countenanced in its worst form—that is, in the seizure and transportation—the people could have regarded those who were emancipated as entitled to actual rights with themselves.

And we may here again refer in support of this proposition, to the plain and unequivocal language of the laws of the several States, some passed after the Declaration of Independence and before the Constitution was adopted, and some since the government went into operation.

We need not refer. on this point, particularly, to the laws of the present slaveholding States. Their statue books are full of provisions in relation to this class, in the same spirit with the Mary and law which we have before quoted. They have continued to treat them as an inferior class, and to subject them to strict police regulation, drawing a broad line of distinction between the citizen and the slave races, and legislating in relation to them upon the same principle which prevailed at the time of the Declaration of Independence. As relates to these states, it is too plain for argument, that they have never been regarded as a part of the people or citizens of the State, nor supposed to possess any political rights which the dominant race might not withhold or grant at their pleasure. And as long ago as 1822, the Court of Appeals of Kentucky decided that free negroes and mulattoes were not citizens within the meaning of the Constitution of the United States; and the correctness of this decision is recognized, and the same doctrine affirmed, in 1 Meigs' Tenn. 321.

And if we turn to the legislation of the States where slavery had worn out, or measures taken for its speedy abolition, we shall find the same opinions and principles equally fixed and equally acted upon.

Thus, Massachusetts, in 1786, passed a law similar to the colonial one of which we have spoken. The Law of 1786, like the Law of 1705, forbids the marriage of any white person with any negro, Indian or mulatto, and inflicts a penalty of £50 upon anyone who shall join them in marriage, and declares all such marriages absolutely null and void, and degrades thus the unhappy issue of the marriage by fixing upon it the stain of bastardy. And this mark of degradation was renewed, and again impressed upon the race, in the careful and deliberate preparation of their Revised Code published in 1836. This Code forbids any person from joining in marriage any white person with any Indian, negro or mulatto, and subjects the party who shall offend in this respect to imprisonment, not exceeding six months, in the common jail, or to hard labor, and to a fine of not less than fifty nor more than two hundred dollars; and, like the Law of 1780, it declares the marriage to be absolutely null and void. It will be seen that the punishment is increased by the Code upon the person who shall marry them, by adding imprisonment to a pecuniary penalty.

So, too, in Connecticut. We refer more particularly to the legislation of this State, because it was not only among the first to put an end to slavery within its own territory, but was the first to fix a mark of reprobation upon the African slave trade. The law last mentioned was passed in October, 1788, about nine months after the State had ratified and adopted the present Constitution of the United States; and by that law it prohibited its own citizens, under severe penalties, from engaging in the trade, and declared all policies of insurance on the vessel or cargo made in the State to be null and void. But, up to the time of the adoption of the Constitution, there is nothing in the legislation of the State indicating any change of opinion as to the relative rights and position of the white and black races in this country, or indicating that it meant to place the latter, when free, upon a level with its citizens. And certainly nothing which would have led the slaveholding States to suppose that Connecticut designed to claim for them, under the new Constitution, the equal rights and privileges and rank of citizens in every other state.

The first step taken by Connecticut upon this subject was as early as 1774, when it passed an Act forbidding the further importation of slaves into the State. But the section containing the prohibition is introduced by the following preamble:

"And whereas the increase of slaves in this State is injurious to the poor, and inconvenient."

This recital would appear to have been carefully introduced, in order to prevent any misunderstanding of the motive which induced the Legislature to pass the law, and places it distinctly upon the interest and convenience of the white population—excluding the inference that it might have been intended in any degree for the benefit of the other.

And in the Act of 1784, by which the issue of slaves born after the time therein mentioned, were to be free at a certain age, the section is again introduced by a preamble assigning a similar motive for the Act. It is in these words:

"Whereas sound policy requires that the abolition of slavery should be effected as soon as may be consistent with the rights of individuals, and the public safety and welfare"—showing that the right of property in the master was to be protected, and that the measure was one of policy, and to prevent the injury and inconvenience, to the whites, of a slave population in the State.

And still further pursuing its legislation, we find that in the same Statute passed in 1774, which prohibited the further importation of slaves into the State, there is also a provision by which any negro, Indian or mulatto servant, who was found wandering out of the town or place to which he belonged, without a written pass such as is therein described, was made liable to be seized by anyone, and taken before the next authority to be examined and delivered up to his master—who was required to pay the charge which had accrued thereby. And a subsequent section of the same law provides, that if any free negro shall travel without such pass, and shall be stopped, seized or taken up, be shall pay all charges arising thereby. And this law was in full operation when the Constitution of the United States was adopted, and was not repealed until 1797. So that up to that time free negroes and mulattoes were associated with servants and slaves in the police regulations established by the laws of the State.

And again, in 1833, Connecticut passed another law, which made it penal to set up or establish any school in that State for the instruction of persons of the African race not inhabitants of the State, or to instruct or teach in any such school or institution, or board or harbor for that purpose any such person, without the previous consent in writing of the civil authority of the town in which such school or institution might be.

And it appears by the case of Crandall v. The State, reported in 10 Conn. 340, that upon an information filed against Prudence Crandall for a violation of this law, one of the points raised in the defense was, that the law was a violation of the Constitution of the United States; and that the persons instructed, although of the African race, were citizens of other States, and therefore entitled to the rights and privileges of citizens in the State of Connecticut. But Chief Justice Daggett, before whom the case was tried, held, that persons of that description were not citizens of a State, within the meaning of the word "citizen" in the Constitution of the United

States, and were not, therefore, entitled to the privileges and immunities of citizens in other States.

The case was carried up to the Supreme Court of Errors of the State, and the question fully argued there. But the case went off upon another point, and no opinion was expressed on this question.

We have made this particular examination into the legislative and judicial action of Connecticut, because, from the early hostility it displayed to the slave trade on the coast of Africa, we may expect to find the laws of that State as lenient and favorable to the subject race as those of any other State in the Union; and if we find that at the time the Constitution was adopted, they were not even there raised to the rank of citizens, but were still held and treated as property, and the laws relating to them passed with reference altogether to the interest and convenience of the white race, we shall hardly find them elevated to a higher rank anywhere else.

A brief notice of the laws of two other States, and we shall pass on to other considerations.

By the laws of New Hampshire, collected and finally passed in 1816, no one was permitted to be enrolled in the militia of the State but free white citizens, and the same provision is found in a subsequent collection of the laws made in 1856. Nothing could more strongly mark the entire repudiation of the African race. The alien is excluded, because, being born in a foreign country he cannot be a member of the community until he is naturalized. But why are the African race, born in the State, not permitted to share in one of the highest duties of the citizen? The answer is obvious; he is not by the institutions and laws of the State numbered among its people. He forms no part of the sovereignty of the State, and is not, therefore, called on to uphold and defend it.

Again in 1822, Rhode Island in its Revised Code, passed a law forbidding persons who were authorized to join persons in marriage from joining in marriage any white person with any negro, Indian or mulatto, under the penalty of $200, and declaring all such marriages absolutely null and void, and the same law was again re-enacted in its Revised Code of 1844. So that, down to the last mentioned period, the strongest mark of inferiority and degradation was fastened upon the African race in that State.

It would be impossible to enumerate and compress, in the space usually allotted to an opinion of a court, the various laws, marking the condition of this race, which were passed from time to time after the Revolution, and before and since the adoption of the Constitution of the United States. In addition to those already referred to, it is sufficient to say that Chancellor Kent, whose accuracy and research no one will question, states in the sixth edition of his Commentaries, published in 1848, 2d vol. 258, note b, that in no part of the country, except Maine, did the African race, in point of fact, participate equally with the whites in the exercise of civil and political rights.

The legislation of the States therefore shows, in a manner not to be mistaken, the inferior and subject condition of that race at the time the Constitution was adopted, and long afterwards, throughout the thirteen States by which that instrument was framed; and it is hardly consistent with the respect due to these States, to suppose that they regarded at that time, as fellow citizens and members of the sovereignty, a class of beings whom they had thus stigmatized; whom, as we are bound, out of respect to the State sovereignties, to assume they had deemed it just and necessary thus to stigmatize, and upon whom they had impressed such deep and enduring marks of inferiority and degradation; or that when they met in convention to form the Constitution, they looked upon them as a portion of their constituents, or designed to include them in the provisions so carefully inserted for the security and protection of the liberties and rights of their citizens. It cannot be supposed that they intended to secure to them rights and privileges, and rank, in the new political body throughout the Union, which every one of them denied within the limits of its own dominion. More especially, it cannot be believed that the large slaveholding States regarded them as included in the word "citizens," or would have consented to a Constitution which might compel them to receive them in that character from another State. For if they were so received, and entitled to the privileges and immunities of citizens, it would exempt them from the operation of the special laws and from the police regulations which they considered to be necessary for their own safety. It would give to persons of the negro race, who were recognized as citizens in any one State of the Union, the right to enter every other State whenever they pleased, singly or in companies, without pass or passport, and without obstructions to sojourn there as long as they pleased, to go where they pleased at every hour of the day or night without molestation, unless they committed some violation of law for which a white man would be punished; and it would give them the full liberty of speach in public and in private upon all subjects upon which its own citizens might speak; to hold public meetings upon political affairs, and to keep and carry arms wherever they went. And all of this would be done in the face of the subject race of the same color, both free and slaves, inevitably producing discontent and insubordination among them, and endangering the peace and safety of the State.

It is impossible, it would seem, to believe that the great men of the slaveholding States, who took so large a share in framing the Constitution of the United States, and exercised so much influence in procuring its adoption, could have been so forgetful or regardless of their own safety and the safety of those who trusted and confided in them.

Besides, this want of foresight and care would have been utterly inconsistent with the caution displayed in providing for the admission of new members into this political family. For, when they gave to the citizens of each State the privileges and immunities of citizens in the several States, they at the same time took from the several States the power of naturalization, and confined that power exclusively to the Federal government. No state was willing to permit another State to determine who should or should not be admitted as one of its citizens, and entitled to demand equal rights and privileges with their own people, within their own territories. The right of naturalization was therefore, with one accord, surrendered by the States, and confined to the Federal Government. And this power granted to

Congress to establish an uniform rule of naturalization is, by the well-understood meaning of the word, confined to persons born in a foreign country, under a foreign government. It is not a power to raise to the rank of a citizen anyone born in the United States, who, from birth or parentage, by the laws of the country, belongs to an inferior and subordinate class. And when we find the States guarding themselves from the indiscreet or improper admission by other states of emigrants from other countries by giving the power exclusively to Congress, we cannot fail to see that they could never have left with the States a much more important power—that is, the power of transforming into citizens a numerous class of persons who in that character would be much more dangerous to the peace and safety of a large portion of the Union than the few foreigners one of the States might improperly naturalize. The Constitution, upon its adoption, obviously took from the States all power by any subsequent legislation to introduce as a citizen into the political family of the United States anyone, no matter where he was born, or what might be his character or condition; and it gave to Congress the power to confer this character upon those only who were born outside of the dominions of the United States. And no law of a State, therefore, passed since the Constitution was adopted, can give any right of citizenship outside of its own territory.

A clause similar to the one in the Constitution, in relation to the rights and immunities of citizens of one State in the other States, was contained in the Articles of Confederation. But there is a difference of language, which is worthy of note. The provision in the Articles of Confederation was, "that the free inhabitants of each of the States, paupers, vagabonds, and fugitives from justice excepted, should be entitled to all the privileges and immunities of free citizens, in the several States."

It will be observed, that under this Confederation each State had the right to decide for itself, and in its own tribunals, whom it would acknowledge as a free inhabitant of another State. The term "free inhabitant," in the generality of its terms, would certainly include one of the African race who had been manumitted. But no example, we think, can be found of his admission to all the privileges of citizenship in any State of the Union after these Articles were formed, and while they continued in force. And notwithstanding the generality of the words "free inhabitants," it is very clear that, according to their accepted meaning in that day, they did not include the African race, whether free or not; for the 5th section of the 9th article provides that Congress should have the power "to agree upon the number of land forces to be raised, and to make requisitions from each State for its quota in proportion to the number of white inhabitants in such State, which requisition shall be binding."

Words could hardly have been used which more strongly mark the line of distinction between the citizen and the subject—the free and the subjugated races. The latter were not even counted when the inhabitants of a State were to be embodied in proportion to its numbers for the general defense. And it cannot for a moment be supposed, that a class of persons thus separated and rejected from those who formed the sovereignty of the States were yet intended to be included under the words "free inhabitants," in the preceding article, to whom privileges and immunities were so carefully secured in every State.

But although this clause of the Articles of Confederation is the same in principle with that inserted in the Constitution, yet the comprehensive word "inhabitant," which might be construed to include an emancipated slave, is omitted, and the privilege is confined to "citizens" of the State. And this alteration in words would hardly have been made unless a different meaning was intended to be conveyed, or a possible doubt removed. The just and fair inference is, that as this privilege was about to be placed under the protection of the general government, and the words expounded by its tribunals, and all power in relation to it taken from the State and its courts, it was deemed prudent to describe with precision and caution the persons to whom this high privilege was given—and the word "citizen" was on that account substituted for the words "free inhabitant." The word "citizen" excluded, and no doubt intended to exclude, foreigners who had not become citizens of some one of the States when the Constitution was adopted; and also every descrption of persons who were not fully recognized as citizens in the several States. This, upon any fair construction of the instruments to which we have referred, was evidently the object and purpose of this change of words.

To all this mass of proof we have still to add, that Congress has repeatedly legislated upon the same construction of the Constitution that we have given. Three laws, two of which were passed almost immediately after the government went into operation, will be abundantly sufficient to show this. The first two are particularly worthy of notice, because many of the men who assisted in framing the Constitution, and took an active part in procuring its adoption, were then in the halls of legislation, and certainly understood what they meant when they used the words "people of the United States" and "citizen" in that well considered instrument.

The first of these Acts is the Naturalization Law, which was passed at the second session of the first Congress, March 26, 1790, and confines the right of becoming citizens "to aliens being free white persons."

Now, the Constitution does not limit the power of Congress in this respect to white persons. And they may, if they think proper, authorize the naturalization of anyone, of any color, who was born under allegiance to another government. But the language of the law above quoted shows that citizenship at that time was perfectly understood to be confined to the white race; and that they alone constituted the sovereignty in the government.

Congress might, as we before said, have authorized the naturalization of Indians, because they were aliens and foreigners. But, in their then untutored and savage state, no one would have thought of admitting them as citizens in a civilized community. And, moreover the atrocities they had but recently committed, when they were the allies of Great Britain in the Revolutionary War, were yet fresh in the recollection of the people of the United States, and they were even then guarding themselves against the threatened renewal of Indian hostilities. No one supposed then that any Indian would ask for, or was capable of enjoying, the privileges of an American citizen, and the word "white" was not used with any particular reference to them.

Neither was it used with any reference to the African race imported into or born in this country, because Congress had no power to naturalize them, and therefore there was no necessity for using particular words to exclude them.

It would seem to have been used merely because it followed out the line of division which the Constitution has drawn between the citizen race, who formed and held the government, and the African race, which they held in subjection and slavery, and governed at their own pleasure.

Another of the early laws of which we have spoken, is the first Militia Law, which was passed in 1792, at the first session of the second Congress. The language of this law is equally plain and significant with the one just mentioned. It directs that every "free able-bodied white male citizen" shall be enrolled in the militia. The word "white" is evidently used to exclude the African race, and the word "citizen" to exclude unnaturalized foreigners, the latter forming no part of the sovereignty, owing it no allegiance, and therefore under no obligation to defend it. The African race however, born in the country, did owe allegiance to the government, whether they were slave or free; but it is repudiated, and rejected from the duties and obligations of citizenship in marked language.

The third Act to which we have alluded is even still more decisive; it was passed as late as 1813 (2 Stat. 809), and it provides: "that from and after the termination of the war in which the United States are now engaged with Great Britain, it shall not be lawful to employ on board of any public or private vessels of the United States, any person or persons except citizens of the United States, or persons of color, natives of the United States.

Here the line of distinction is drawn in express words. Persons of color, in the judgment of Congress, were not included in the word "citizen," and they are described as another and different class of persons, and authorized to be employed, if born in the United States.

And even as late as 1820 (chap. 104, sec. 8), in the charter to the City of Washington, the Corporation is authorized "to restrain and prohibit the nightly and other disorderly meetings of slaves, free negroes, and mulattoes," thus associating them together in its legislation; and after prescribing the punishment that may be initiated on the slaves, proceeds in the following words: "And to punish such free negroes and mulattoes by penalties not exceeding twenty dollars for any one offense, and in case of the inability of any such free negro or mulatto to pay any such penalty and cost thereon, to cause him or her to be confined to labor for any time not exceeding six calendar months." And in a subsequent part of the same section, the Act authorizes the Corporation "to prescribe the terms and conditions upon which free negroes and mulattoes may reside in the city."

This law, like the laws of the States, shows that this class of persons were governed by special legislation directed expressly to them, and always connected with provisions for the government of slaves, and not with those for the government of free white citizens. And after such an uniform course of legislation as we have stated, by the Colonies, by the States, and by Congress, running through a period of more than a century, it would seem that to call persons thus marked and stigmatized, "citizens" of the United States, "fellow citizens," a constituent part of the sovereignty, would be an abuse of terms, and not calculated to exalt the character of an American citizen in the eyes of other nations.

The conduct of the Executive Department of the government has been in perfect harmony upon this subject with this course of legislation. The question was brought officially before the late William Witt when he was the Attorney-General of the United States, in 1821, and he decided that the words "citizen of the United States" were used in the Acts of Congress in the same sense as in the Constitution; and that free persons of color were not citizens, within the meaning of the Constitution and laws; and this opinion has been confirmed by that of the late Attorney-General, Caleb Cushing, in a recent case, and acted upon by the Secretary of State, who refused to grant passports to them as "citizens of the United States."

But it is said that a person may be a citizen, and entitled to that character, although he does not possess all the rights which may belong to other citizens; as, for example, the right to vote, or to hold particular office; and that yet, when he goes into another State, he is entitled to be recognized there as a citizen, although the State may measure his rights by the rights which it allows to persons of a like character or class, resident in the State, and refuse to him the full rights of citizenship.

This argument overlooks the language of the provision in the Constitution of which we are speaking.

Undoubtedly, a person may be a citizen, that is, a member of the community who form the sovereignty, although he exercizes no share of the political power, and is incapacitated from holding particular offices. Women and minors, who form a part of the political family, cannot vote; and when a property qualification is required to vote or hold a particular office, those who have not the necessary qualification cannot vote or hold the office, yet they are citizens.

So, too, a person may be entitled to vote by the law of the State, who is not a citizen even of the State itself. And in some of the States of the Union foreigners not naturalized are allowed to vote. And the State may give the right to free negroes and mulattoes, but that does not make them citizens of the State, and still less of the United States. And the provision in the Constitution giving privileges and immunities in other States, does not apply to them.

Neither does it apply to a person who, being the citizen of a State, migrates to another State. For then he becomes subject to the laws of the State in which he lives, and he is no longer a citizen of the State from which he removed. And the State in which he resides may then, unquestionably, determine his status or condition, and place him among the class of persons who are not recognized as citizens, but belong to an inferior and subject race; and may deny him the privileges and immunities enjoyed by its citizens.

But so far as mere rights of person are concerned, the provision in question is confined to citizens of a State who are temporarily in another State without taking up their residence there. It gives them no political rights in the state as to voting or holding office, or in any other respect. For a citizen of one State has no right to participate in the government of another. But if he ranks as a citizen of the State to which he belongs, within the meaning of the Constitution of the United States, then, whenever he goes into another State, the Constitution clothes him, as to the rights of person, with all the privileges and immunities which belong to citizens of the State. And if persons of the African race are citizens of a state, and of the United States, they would be entitled to all of these privileges and immunities in every State, and the State could not restrict them; for they would hold these privileges and immunities, under the paramount authority of the Federal Government, and its courts would be bound to maintain and enforce them, the Constitution and laws of the State to the contrary notwithstanding. And if the State could limit or restrict them, or place the party in an inferior grade, this clause of the Constitution would be unmeaning, and could have no operation; and would give no rights to the citizen when in another State. He would have none but what the State itself chose to allow him. This is evidently not the construction or meaning of the clause in question. It guarantees rights to the citizen, and the State cannot withhold them. And these rights are of a character and would lead to consequences which make it absolutely certain that the African race were not intended under the name of citizens of a State, and were not in the contemplation of the framers of the Constitution when these privileges and immunities were provided for the citizens of other States.

The case of Legrand v Darnall, 2 Pet. 664, has been referred to for the purpose of showing that this court has decided that the descendant of a slave may sue as a citizen in a court of the United States; but the case itself shows that the question did not arise and could not have arisen in the case.

It appears from the report that Darnall was born in Maryland and was the son of a white man by one of his slaves, and his father executed certain instruments to manumit him, and devised to him some landed property in the State. This property Darnall afterwards sold to Legrand, the appellant, who gave his notes for the puchase money. But becoming afterwards apprehensive that the appellee had not been emancipated according to the laws of Maryland, he refused to pay the note until he could be better satisfied as to Darnall's right to convey. Darnall in the meantime, had taken up his residence in Pennsylvania, and brought suit on the notes and recovered judgment in the Circuit Court for the District of Maryland.

The whole proceeding, as appears by the report, was an amicable one; Legrand being perfectly willing to pay the money if he could obtain a title, and Darnall not wishing him to pay unless he could make him a good one. In point of fact, the whole proceeding was under the direction of the counsel who argued the case for the appellee, who was the mutual friend of the parties, and confided in by both of them, and whose only object was to have the rights of both parties established by judicial decision in the most speedy and least expensive manner.

Legrand, therefore, raised no objection to the jurisdiction of the court in the suit at law, because he was himself anxious to obtain the judgment of the court upon his title. Consequently there was nothing in the record before the court to show that Darnall was of African descent, and the usual judgment and award of execution was entered. And Legrand thereupon filed his bill on the equity side of the Circuit Court, stating that Darnall was born a slave, and had not been legally emancipated, and could not, therefore, take the land devised to him, nor make Legrand a good title; and praying an injuction to restrain Darnall from proceeding to execution on the judgment, which was granted. Darnall answered, averring in his answer that he was a free man, and capable of conveying a good title. Testimony was taken on this point, and at the hearing the Circuit Court was of opinion that Darnall was a free man and his title good, and disolved the injunction and dismissed the bill; and that decree was affirmed here, upon the appeal of Legrand.

Now, it is difficult to imagine how any question about citizenship of Darnell, or his right to sue in that character, can be supposed to have arisen or been decided in that case. The fact that he was of African descent was first brought before the court upon the bill in equity. The suit at law had then passed into judgment and award of execution, and the Circuit Court, as a court of law, had no longer any authority over it. It was a valid and legal judgment, which the court that rendered it had not the power to reverse or set aside. And unless it had jurisdiction as a court of equity to restrain him from using its process as a court of law, Darnall, if he thought proper, would have been at liberty to proceed on his judgment, and compel the payment of the money, although the allegations in the bill were true, and he was incapable of making a title. No other court could have enjoined him, for certainly no State equity court could interfere in that way with the judgment of a circuit court of the United States.

But the Circuit Court as a court of equity certainly had equity jurisdiction over its own judgment as a court of law, without regard to the character of the parties; and had not only the right, but it was its duty—no matter who were the parties in the judgment—to prevent them from proceeding to enforce it by execution, if the court was satisfied that the money was not justly and equitably due. The ability of Darnall to convey did not depend upon his citizenship, but upon his title to freedom. And if he was free, he could hold and convey property, by the laws of Maryland, although he was not a citizen. But if he was by law still a slave, he could not. It was, therefore, the duty of the court, sitting as a court of equity in the latter case, to prevent him from using its process, as a court of common law, to compel the payment of the purchase money, when it was evident that the purchaser must lose the land. But if he was free, and could make a title, it was equally the duty of the court not to suffer Legrand to keep the land, and refuse the payment of the money, upon the ground that Darnall was incapable of suing or being sued as a citizen in a court of the United States. The character or citizenship of the parties had no connection with the question of jurisdiction, and the matter in dispute had no relation to the citizenship of Darnall. Nor is such a question alluded to in the opinion of the court.

Besides, we are by no means prepared to say that there are not many cases, civil as well as criminal, in which a circuit court of the United States may exercise jurisdiction, although one of the African race is a party; that broad question is not before the court. The question with which we are now dealing is, Whether a person of the African race can be a citizen of the United States, and become thereby entitled to a special privilege, by virtue to his title to that character, and which, under the Constitution, no one but a citizen can claim. It is manifest that the case of Legrand v. Darnall has no bearing on that question, and can have no application to the case now before the court.

This case, however, strikingly illustrates the consequences that would follow the construction of the Constitution which would give the power contended for, to a State. It would, in effect, give it also to an individual. For if the father of young Darnall had manumitted him in his lifetime, and sent him to reside in a State which recognized him as a citizen, he might have visited and sojourned in Maryland when he pleased, and as long as he pleased, as a citizen of the United States; and the state officers and tribunals would be compelled, by the paramount authority of the Constitution, to receive him and treat him as one of its citizens, exempt from the laws and police of the state in relation to a person of that description, and allow him to enjoy all the rights and privileges of citizenship, without respect to the laws of Maryland, although such laws were deemed by it absolutely essential to its own safety.

The only two provisions which point to them and include them, treat them as property, and make it the duty of the government to protect it; no other power, in relation to this race, is to be found in the Constitution; and as it is a government of special, delegated powers, no authority beyond these two provisions can be constitutionally exercised. The Government of the United States had no right to interfere in any other purpose but that of protecting the rights of the owner, leaving it altogether with the several States to deal with this race, whether emancipated or not, as each State may think justice, humanity, and the interests and safety of society, require. The States evidently intended to reserve this power exclusively to themselves.

No one, we presume, supposes that any change in public opinion or feeling in relation to this unfortunate race, in the civilized nations of Europe or in this country, should induce the court to give to the words of the Constitution a more liberal construction in their favor than they were intended to bear when the instrument was framed and adopted. Such an argument would be altogether inadmissible in any tribunal called on to interpret it. If any of its provisions are deemed unjust, there is a mode prescribed in the instrument itself by which it may be amended; but while it remains unaltered, it must be construed now as it was understood at the time of its adoption. It is not only the same in words, but the same in meaning, and delegates the same powers to the government, and reserves and secures the same rights and privileges to the citizen; and as long as it continues to exist in its present form, it speaks not only in the same words, but with the same meaning and intent with which it spoke when it came from the hands of its framers, and was voted on and adopted by the people of the the United States. Any other rule of construction would abrogate the judicial character of this court, and make it the mere reflex of the popular opinion or passion of the day. This court was not created by the Constitution for such purposes. Higher and graver trusts have been confided to it, and it must not falter in the path of duty.

What the construction was at that time, we think can hardly admit of doubt. We have the language of the Declaration of Independence and of the Articles of Confederation, in addition to the plain words of the Constitution itself; we have the legislation of the different States, before, about the time, and after the Constitution was adopted; we have the legislation of Congress, from the time of its adoption to a recent period; and we have the constant and uniform action of the Executive Department, all concurring together, and leading to the same result. And if anything in relation to the construction of the Constitution can be regarded as settled, it is that which we now give to the word "citizen" and the word "people."

And upon a full and careful consideration of the subject, the court is of opinion that, upon the facts stated in plea in abatement, Dred Scott is not a citizen of Missouri within the meaning of the Constitution of the United States, and not entitled as such to sue in its courts; and consequently, that the Circuit Court had no jurisdiction of the case, and that the judgment on the plea in abatement is erroneous.

We are aware that doubts are entertained by some of the members of the court, whether the plea in abatement is legally before the court upon this writ of error, but if that plea is regarded as waived, or out of the case upon any other ground, yet the question as to the jurisdiction of the Circuit Court is presented on the face of the bill of exception itself, taken by the plaintiff at the trial; for he admits that he and his wife were born slaves, but endeavors to make out his title to freedom and citizenship by showing that they were taken by their owner to certain places, hereinafter mentioned, where slavery could not by law exist, and that they thereby became free, and upon their return to Missouri became citizens of that State.

Now if the removal of which he speaks did not give them their freedom, then by his own admission he is still a slave; and whatever opinions may be entertained in favor of the citizenship of a free person of the African race, no one supposes that a slave is a citizen of the State or of the United States. If, therefore, the acts done by his owner did not make them free persons, he is still a slave, and certainly incapable of suing in the character of a citizen.

The principle of law is too well settled to be disputed that a court can give no judgment for either party, where it has no jurisdiction; and if upon the showing of Scott himself, it appeared he was still a slave, the case ought to have been dismissed, and the judgment against him and in favor of the defendant for costs is, like that on the plea in abatement, erroneous and the suit ought to have been dismissed by the Circuit Court for want of jurisdiction in that court.

But, before we proceed to examine this part of the case, it may be proper to notice an objection taken to the judicial authority of this court to decide it; and it has been said, that as this court has decided against the jurisdiction of the Circuit Court on the plea in abatement, it has no right to examine any question presented by the exception; and that anything it may say upon that part of the case will be extrajudicial and mere obiter dicta.

This is a manifest mistake; there can be no doubt as to the jurisdiction of this court to revise the judgment of a circuit court, and to reverse it for any error apparent on the record, whether it be the error of giving judgment in a case over which it had no jurisdiction, or any other material error; and this too, whether there is a plea in abatement or not.

The objection appears to have arisen from confounding writs of error to a state court with writs of error to a circuit court of the United States. Undoubtedly, upon a writ of error to a state court, unless the record shows a case that gives jurisdiction, the case must be dismissed for want of jurisdiction in this court. And if it is dismissed on that ground, we have no right to examine and decide upon any question presented by the bill of exceptions or any other part of the record. But writs of error to a state court, and to a circuit court of the United States, are regulated by different laws, and stand upon entirely different principles. And in a writ of error to a circuit court of the United States, the whole record is before this court for examination and decision; and if the sum in controversy is large enough to give jurisdiction, it is not only the right but it is the judicial duty of the court, to examine the whole case as presented by the record, and if it appears upon its face that any material error or errors have been committed by the court below, it is the duty of this court to reverse the judgment, and remand the case. And certainly an error in passing a judgment upon the merits in favor of either party, in a case which it was not authorized to try and over which it had no jurisdiction, is as grave an error as a court can commit.

The plea in abatement is not a plea to the jurisdiction of this court, but to the jurisdiction of the Circuit Court. And it appears by the record before us, that the Circuit Court committed an error, in deciding that it had jurisdiction, upon the facts in the case, admitted by the pleadings. It is the duty of the appellate tribunal to correct this error; but that could not be done by dismissing the case for want of jurisdiction here—for that would leave the erroneous judgment in full force, and the injured party without remedy. And the appellate court, therefore, exercises the power for which alone appellate courts are constituted by reversing the judgment of the court below for this error. It exercises its proper and appropriate jurisdiction over the judgment and proceedings of the Circuit Court as they appear upon the record brought up by the writ of error.

The correction of one error in the court below does not deprive the appellate court of the power of examining further into the record, and correcting any other material errors which may have been committed by the inferior court. There is certainly no rule of law—nor any practice—nor any decision of a court—which even questions this power in the appellate tribunal. On the contrary, it is the daily practice of this court, and of all appellate courts where they reverse the judgment of an inferior court for error, to correct by its opinions whatever errors may appear on the record material to the case; and they have always held it to be their duty to do so where the silence of the court might lead to misconstruction or future controversy, and the point has been relied on by either side, and argued before the court.

In the case before us we have already decided that the Circuit Court erred in deciding that it had jurisdiction upon the facts admitted by the pleadings. And it appears that, in the further progress of the case, it acted upon the erroneous principle it had decided on the pleadings, and gave judgment for the defendant, where, upon the facts admitted in the exception, it had no jurisdiction.

We are at a loss to understand upon what principle of law applicable to appellate jurisdiction it can be supposed that this court has not judicial authority to correct the last mentioned error because they had before corrected the former; or by what process of reasoning it can be made out, that the error of an inferior court in actually pronouncing judgment for one of the parties in a case in which it had no jurisdiction cannot be looked into or corrected by this court, because we have decided a similar question presented in the pleadings. The last point is distinctly presented by the facts contained in the plaintiff's own bill of exceptions, which he himself brings here by this writ of error. It was the point which chiefly occupied the attention of the counsel on both sides in the argument—and the judgment which this court must render upon both errors is precisely the same. It must, in each of them, exercise jurisdiction over the judgment and reverse it for the errors committed by the court below; and issue a mandate to the Circuit Court to conform its judgment to the opinion pronounced by this court, by dismissing the case for want of jurisdiction in the Circuit Court. This is the constant and invariable practice of this court where it reverses a judgment for want of jurisdiction in the Circuit Court.

It can scarcely be necessary to pursue such a question further. The want of jurisdiction in the court below may appear on the record without any plea in abatement. This is familiarly the case where a court of chancery has exercised jurisdiction in a case where the plaintiff had a plain and adequate remedy at law, and it so appears by the transcript when brought here by appeal. So also where it appears that a court of admiralty has exercised jurisdiction in a case belonging exclusively to a court of common law. In these cases there is no plea in abatement. And for the same reason and upon the same principles where the defect of jurisdiction is patent on the record, this court is bound to reverse the judgment although the defendant has not pleaded in abatement to the jurisdiction of the inferior court.

The cases of Jackson v. Aspton, 8 Pet. 148, and of Capron v. Van Noorden, 2 Cranch, 126, to which we have referred in a previous part of this opinion, are directly in point. In the last mentioned case, Capron brought an action against Van Noorden in a circuit court of the United States without showing, by the usual averments of citizenship, that the court had jurisdiction. There was no plea in abatement put in and the parties went to trial upon the merits. The court gave judgment in favor of the defendant with costs. The plaintiff thereupon brought his writ of error, and this court reversed the judgment given in favor of the defendant, and remanded the case with directions to dismiss it, because it did not appear by the transcript that the Circuit Court had jurisdiction.

The case before us still more strongly imposes upon this court the duty of examining whether the court below has not committed an error, in taking jurisdiction and giving a judgment for costs in favor of the defendant; for in Capron

v. Van Noorden the judgment was reversed, because it did not appear that the parties were citizens of different States. They might or might not be. But in this case it does appear that the plaintiff was born a slave; and if the facts upon which he relies have not made him free, then it appears affirmatively on the record that he is not a citizen and consequently his suit against Sandford was not a suit between citizens of different States, and the court had no authority to pass any judgment between the parties. The suit ought in this view of it, to have been dismissed by the Circuit Court, and its judgment in favor of Sandford is erroneous and must be reversed.

It is true that the result either way, by dismissal or by a judgment for the defendant, makes very little, if any difference in a pecuniary or personal point of view to either party. But the fact that the result would be very nearly the same to the parties in either form or judgment, would not justify this court in sanctioning an error in the judgment which is patent on the record, and which, if sanctioned, might be drawn into precedent, and lead to serious mischief and injustice in some other suit.

We proceed, therefore, to inquire whether the facts relied on by the plaintiff entitled him to his freedom.

The case, as he himself states it, on the record, brought here by his writ of error, is this:

The plaintiff was a negro slave, belonging to Dr. Emerson, who was a surgeon in the Army of the United States. In the year 1834 he took the plaintiff from the State of Missouri to the military post at Rock Island, in the State of Illinois, and held him there as a slave until the month of April or May, 1836. At the time last mentioned, said Dr. Emerson removed the plaintiff from said military post at Rock Island to the military post at Fort Snelling, situate on the west bank of the Mississippi River, in the Territory known an Upper Louisiana, acquired by the United States of France, and situate north of the latitude of thirty-six degrees thirty minutes north and north of the State of Missouri. Said Dr. Emerson held the plaintiff in slavery at said Fort Snelling, from said last mentioned date until the year 1838.

In the year 1835, Harriet, who is named in the second count of the plaintiff's declaration, was a negro slave of Major Taliaferro, who belonged to the Army of the United States. In that year, 1835, said Major Taliaferro took said Harriet to said Fort Snelling, a military post, situated as herebefore stated, and kept her there as a slave until the year 1836, and then held and delivered her as a slave, at said Fort Snelling, unto the said Dr. Emerson hereinbefore named. Said Dr. Emerson held said Harriet in slavery at said Fort Snelling, until the year 1838.

In the year 1836, the plaintiff and Harriet intermarried, at Fort Snelling, with the consent of Dr. Emerson, who then claimed to be their master and owner. Eliza and Lizzie, named in the third count of the plaintiff's declaration, are the fruit of that marriage. Eliza is about fourteen years old, and was born on board the steamboat Gipsey, north of the north line of the State of Missouri, and upon the River Mississippi. Lizzie is about seven years old and was born in the State of

Missouri at the military post called Jefferson Barracks.

In the year 1838 said Dr. Emerson removed the plaintiff and said Harriet, and their said daughter Eliza, from said Fort Snelling, to the State of Missouri, where they have ever since resided.

Before the commencement of this suit, said Dr. Emerson sold and conveyed the plaintiff and Harriet, Eliza, and Lizzie, to the defendant, as slaves, and the defendant has ever since claimed to hold them, and each of them, as slaves.

In considering this part of the controversy, two questions arise: 1st. Was he, together with his family, free in Missouri by reason of the stay in the territory of the United States hereinbefore mentioned? And 2d. If they were not, is Scott himself free by reason of his removal to Rock Island, in the State of Illinois, as stated in the above admissions?

We proceed to examine the first question.

The Act of Congress, upon which the plaintiff relies, declares that slavery and involuntary servitude, except as a punishment for crime, shall be forever prohibited in all that part of that territory ceded by France under the name of Louisiana, which lies north of thirty six degrees thirty minutes north latitude, and not included within the limits of Missouri. And the difficulty which meets us at the threshold of this part of the inquiry is whether Congress was authorized to pass this law under any of the powers granted to it by the Constitution; for if the authority is not given by that instrument, it is the duty of this court to declare it void and inoperative, and incapable of conferring freedom upon one who is held as a slave under the laws of any one of the States.

The counsel for the plaintiff has laid much stress upon that article in the Constitution which confers on Congress the power "to dispose of and make all necessary rules and regulations respecting the territory or other property belonging to the United States," but in the judgment of the court, that provision has no bearing on the present controversy, and the power there given, whatever it may be, is confined, and was intended to be confined, to the territory which at that time belonged to, or was claimed by, the United States, and was within their boundaries as settled by the Treaty with Great Britain, and can have no influence upon a territory afterwards acquired from a foreign government. It was a special provision for a known and particular Territory, and to meet a present emergency, and nothing more.

A brief summary of the history of the times, as well as the careful and measured terms in which the article is framed, will show the correctness of this proposition.

It will be remembered that, from the commencement of the Revolutionary War, serious difficulties existed between the States, in relation to the disposition of large and unsettled territores which were included in the chartered limits of some of the States. And some of the other States, and more especially Maryland, which had no unsettled lands, insisted that as the unoccupied lands, if wrested from Great Britain, would owe their preservation to the common purse and the common sword, the money arising from them ought to be applied in just proportion among the several States, to pay the expenses of the war, and ought not to be appropriated to the use of State in whose chartered limits they might happen to lie, to the exclusion of the other States by whose combined efforts and common expense the territory was defended and preserved against the claim of the British Government.

These difficulties caused much uneasiness during the War, while the issue was in some degree doubtful, and the future boundaries of the United States yet to he defined by treaty, if we achieved our independence.

The majority of the Congress of the Confederation obviously concurred in opinion with the State of Maryland, and desired to obtain from the States which claimed it a cession of this territory, in order that Congress might raise money on this security to carry on the War. This appears by the resolution passed on the 6th of September, 1780, strongly urging the States to cede these lands to the United States, both for the sake of peace and union among themselves, and to maintain the public credit; and this was followed by the resolution of October 10th, 1780, by which Congress pledged itself, that if the lands were ceded, as recommended by the resolution above mentioned, they should be disposed of for the common benefit of the United States, and be settled and formed into distinct republican States, which should become members of the Federal Union, and have the same rights of sovereignty, and freedom, and independence as other States.

But these difficulties became much more serious after peace took place, and the boundaries of the United States were established. Every State, at that time, felt severely the pressure of its war debt; but in Virginia, and some other States there were large territories of unsettled lands, the sale of which would enable them to discharge their obligations without much inconvenience; while other States which had no such resource, saw before them many years of heavy and burdensome taxation, and the latter insisted, for the reasons before stated, that these unsettled lands should be treated as the common property of the States, and the proceeds applied to their common benefit.

The letters from the statesmen of that day will show how much this controversy occupied their thoughts, and the dangers that were apprehended from it. It was the disturbing element of the time, and fears were entertained that it might dissolve the Confederation by which the States were then united.

These fears and dangers were, however, at once removed, when the State of Virginia, in 1784, voluntarily ceded to the United States the immense tract of country lying northwest of the River Ohio, and which was within the acknowledged limits of the State. The only object of the State, in making this cession, was to put an end to the threatening and exciting controversy, and to enable the Congress of that time to dispose of the lands, and appropriate the proceeds as a common fund for the common benefit of the States. It was not ceded because it was inconvenient to the State to hold and govern it, nor from any expectation that it could be better or more conveniently governed by the United States.

The example of Virginia was soon afterwards followed by other States, and, at the time of the adoption of the Constitution, all of the States similarly situated had ceded their unappropriated lands, except North Carolina and Georgia. The main object for which these cessions were desired and made, was on account of their money value, and to put an end to a dangerous controversy, as to who was justly entitled to the proceeds when the lands should be sold. It is necessary to bring this part of the history of these cessions thus distinctly into view, because it will enable us the better to comprehend the phraseology of the Article of the Constitution so often referred to in the argument.

Undoubtedly the powers of Sovereignty and the eminent domain were ceded with the land. This was essential in order to make it effectual, and to accomplish its objects. But it must be remembered that, at that time, there was no Government of the United States in existence with enumerated and limited powers; what was then called the United States, were thirteen separate, sovereign, independent States, which had entered into a league or confederation for their mutual protection and advantage, and the Congress of the United States was composed of the representatives of these separate sovereignties, meeting together, as equals, to discuss and decide on certain measures which the States, by the Articles of Confederation, had agreed to submit to their decision. But this Confederation had none of the attributes of sovereignty in legislative, executive, or judicial power. It was little more than a congress of ambassadors, authorized to represent separate nations, in matters in which they had a common concern.

It was this Congress that accepted the cession from Virginia. They had no power to accept it under the Articles of Confederation. But they had an undoubted right, as independent sovereignties, to accept any cession of territory for their common benefit, which all of them assented to; and it is equally clear, that as their common property, and having no superior to control them, they had the right to exercise absolute dominion over it, subject only to the restrictions which Virginia had imposed in her Act of Cession. There was, as we have said, no Government of the United States then in existence with special enumerated powers. The territory belonged to sovereignties, who, subject to the limitations above mentioned, had a right to establish any form of government they pleased, by compact or treaty among themselves, and to regulate the rights of person and property in the territory as they might deem proper. It was by a Congress, representing the authority of these several and separate sovereignties, and acting under their authority and command, (but not from any authority derived from the Articles of Confederation), that the instrument, usually called the Ordinance of 1787, was adopted; regulating in much detail the principles and the laws by which this Territory should be governed; and among other provisions, slavery is prohibited in it. We do not question the power of the States, by agreement among themselves, to pass this Ordinance, nor its obligatory force in the Territory, while the confederation or league of the States in their separate sovereign character continued to exist.

This was the state of things when the Constitution of the United States was formed. The territory ceded by Virginia belonged to the several confederated States as common property, and they had united in establishing in it a system of government and jurisprudence, in order to prepare it for admission as States, according to the terms of the cession. They were about to dissolve this federative Union, and to surrender a portion of their independent sovereignty to a new government, which, for certain purposes, would make the people of the several States one people, and which was to be supreme and controlling, within its sphere of action throughout the United States; but this government was to be carefully limited in its powers, and to exercise no authority beyond those expressly granted by the Constitution, or necessarily to be implied from the language of the instrument, and the objects it was intended to accomplish; and as this league of States would, upon the adoption of the new government, cease to have any power over the territory, and the Ordinance they had all agreed upon be incapable of execution, and a mere nullity, it was obvious that some provision was necessary to give the new government sufficient power to enable it to carry into effect the objects for which it was ceded, and the compacts and agreements which the States had made each other in the exercise of their powers of sovereignty. It was necessary that the lands should be sold to pay the war debt; that a government and system of jurisprudence should be maintained in it, to protect the citizens of the United States, who should migrate to the Territory, in their rights of person and of property. It was also necessary that the new government, about to be adopted, should be authorized to maintain the claim of the United States to the unappropriated lands in North Carolina and Georgia, which had not then been ceded, but the cession of which was confidently anticipated upon some terms that would be arranged between the general government and these two States. And, moreover, there were many articles of value besides this property in land, such as arms, military stores, munitions, and ships of war, which were the common property of the States, when acting in their independent characters as confederates, which neither the new government nor anyone else would have a right to take possession of, or control, without authority from them; and it was to place these things under the guardianship and protection of the new government, and to clothe it with the necessary powers, that the clause was inserted in the Constitution which gives Congress the power "to dispose of and make all needful rules and regulations respecting the territory or other property belonging to the United States." It was intended for a specific purpose, to provide for the things we have mentioned. It was to transfer to the new government the property then held in common by the States, and to give to that government power to apply it to the objects for which it had been destined by mutual agreement among the States before their league was desolved. It applied only to the property which the States held in common at that time, and has no reference whatever to any territory or other property which the new sovereignty might afterwards itself acquire.

The language used in the clause, the arrangement and combination of the powers, and the somewhat unusual phraseology it uses, when it speaks of the political power to be exercised in this government of the territory, all indicate the design and meaning of the clause to be such as we have mentioned. It does not speak of any Territory, nor of Territories, but uses language which, according to its legitimate meaning, points to a particular thing. The power is given in relation only to the territory of the United States—that is, to a Territory then in existence, and then known or claimed as the territory of the United States. It begins its enumeration of powers by that of disposing, in other words, making sale of the lands, or raising money from them, which, as we have already said, was the main object of the cession, and which is accordingly the first things provided for in the Article. It then gives the power which was necessarily associated with the disposition and sale of the lands—that is, the power of making needful rules and regulations respecting the Territory. And whatever construction may now be given to these words, everyone, we think, must admit that they are not the words usually employed by statesmen in giving supreme power of legislation. They are certainly very unlike the words used in the power granted to legislate over territory which the new government might afterwards itself obtain by cession from a state, either for its seat of government, or for forts, magazines, arsenals, dockyards, and other needful buildings.

And the same power of making needful rules respecting the Territory is, in precisely the same language, applied to the other property belonging to the United States—associating the power over the Territory in this respect with the power over movable or personal property, that is, the ships, arms, and munitions of war, which then belonged in common to the State sovereignties. And it will hardly be said, that this power, in relation to the last mentioned objects, was deemed necessary to be thus specially given to the new government, in order to authorize it to make needful rules and regulations respecting the ships it might itself build, or arms and munitions of war it might itself manufacture or provide for the public service.

No one, it is believed, would think a moment of deriving the power of Congress to make needful rules and regulations in relation to property of this kind from this clause of the Constitution. Nor can it, upon any fair construction, be applied to any property but that which the new government was about to receive from the confederated States. And if this be true as to this property, it must be equally true and limited as to the territory, which is so carefully and precisely coupled with it—and like it referred to as property in the power granted. The concluding words of the clause appear to render this construction irresistible; for, after the provisions we have mentioned, it proceeds to say, "that nothing in the Constitution shall be so construed as to prejudice any claims of the United States, or of any particular State."

Now, as we have before said, all of the States except North Carolina and Georgia, had made the cession before the Constitution was adopted, according to the resolution of Congress of October 10, 1780. The claims of other States that the unappropriated lands in these two States should be applied to the common benefit, in like manner, was still insisted on, but refused by the States. And this member of clause in question evidently applies to them, and can apply to nothing else. It was to exclude the conclusion that either party, by adopting the Constitution, would surrender what they deemed their rights. And when the latter provision relates so obviously to the unapropriated lands not yet ceded by the States, and the first clause makes provision for those then actually ceded, it is imposible, by any just rule of construction, to make the first provision general, and extend to all territories, which the Federal Government might in any way afterwards acquire, when the latter is plainly and unequivocally confined to a particular territory; which was a part of the same controversy, and involved in the same dispute, and depended upon the same principles. The union of the two provisions in the same clause shows that they were kindred subjects, and that the whole clause is local, and relates only to lands, within the limits of the United States, which had been or then were claimed by a State; and that no other Territory was in the mind of the framers of the Constitution, or intended to be embraced in it. Upon any other construction it would be impossible to account for the insertion of the last provision in the place where it is found, or to comprehend why, or for what object, it was associated with the previous provision.

This view of the subject is confirmed by the manner in which the present Government of the United States dealt with the subject as soon as it came into existence. It must be borne in mind that the same States that adopted the Confederation also formed and adopted the new government, to which so large a portion of their former sovereign powers were surrendered. It must also be borne in mind that all of these same States which had then ratified the new Constitution were represented in the Congress which passed the first law for the government of this territory; and many of the members of that legislative body had been deputies from the States under the Confederation—had united in adopting the Ordinance of 1787, and assisted in forming the new government under which they were then acting, and whose powers they were then exercising. And it is obvious from the law they passed to carry into effect the principles and provisions of the Ordinance, that they regarded it as the Act of the States done in the exercise of their legitimate powers at the time. The new government took the territory as it found it, in the condition in which it was transferred, and did not attempt to undo anything that had been done. And among the earliest laws passed under the new government, is one reviving the Ordinance of 1787, which had become inoperative and a nullity upon the adoption of the Constitution. This law introduces no new form or principle for its government, but recites, in the preamble, that it is passed in order that this Ordinance may continue to have full effect, and proceeds to make only those rules and regulations which were needful to adapt it to the new government, into whose hands the power had fallen.

It appears, therefore, that this Congress regarded the purposes to which the land in this territory was to be applied, and the form of government and principles of jurisprudence which were to prevail there, while it remained in the territorial state, as already determined by the States when they had full power and right to make the decision; and that the new government, having received it in this condition, ought to carry substanially into effect the plans and principles which had been previously adopted by the States, and which no doubt the States anticipated when they surrendered their power to the new government. And if we regard this clause of the Constitution as pointing to this Territory, with a territorial government already established in it, which had been ceded to the States for the purposes hereinbefore mentioned—every word in it is perfectly appropriate and easily understood, and the provisions it contains are in perfect harnony with the objects for which it was ceded, and with the condition of its government as a

Territory at the time. We can, then, easily account for the manner in which the first Congress legislated on the subject—and can also understand why this power over the Territory was associated in the same clause with the other property of the United States, and subjected to the like power of making needful rules and regulations. But if the clause is construed in the expanded sense contended for, so as to embrace any territory acquired from a foreign nation by the present government, and to give it in such territory a despotic and unlimited power over persons and property, such as the confederated States might exercise in their common property, it would be difficult to account for grants of power—and also for its association with the other provisions in the same clause.

The Constitution has always been remarkable for the felicity of its arrangement of different subjects, and the perspicuity and appropriateness of the language it uses. But if this clause is construed to extend to territory acquired by the present government from a foreign nation, outside of the limits of any charter from the British Government to a Colony, it would be dificult to say, why it was deemed necessary to give the government the power to sell any vacant lands belonging to the sovereignty which might be found within it; and if this was necessary, why the grant of this power should precede the power to legislate over it and establish a government there, and still more difficult to say, why it was deemed necessary so specially and particularly to grant the power to make needful rules and regulations in relation to any person or movable property it might acquire there. For the words, "other property," necessarily, by every known rule of interpretation, must mean property of a different description from territory or land. And the difficulty would perhaps be insurmountable in endeavoring to account for the last member of the sentence, which provides that "nothing in this Constitution shall be so contstrued as to prejudice any claims of the United States or any particular State," or to say how any particular State could have claims in or to a Territory ceded by a foreign government, or to account for associating this provision with the preceding provisions of the clause, with which it would appear to have no connection.

The words "needful rules and regulations" would seem, also, to have been cautiously used for some definite object. They are not the words usually employed by statesmen, when they mean to give the powers of sovereignty, or to establish a government, or to authorize its establishment. Thus, in the law to renew and keep alive the Ordinance of 1787, and to re-establish the government, the title of the law is: "An Act to provide for the government of the territory northwest of the River Ohio." And in the Constitution, when granting the power to legislate over the territory that may be selected for the seat of government, independently of a State, it does not say Congress shall have power "to make all needful rules and regulations respecting the territory;" but it declares that "Congress shall have power to exercise exclusive legislation in all cases whatsoever over such District (not exceeding ten miles square) as may, by cession of particular States and the acceptance of Congress, become the seat of the Governmnent of the United States."

The words "rules and regulations" are usually employed in the Constitution in speaking of some particular specified power which it means to confer on the government, and not, as we have seen, when granting general powers of legislation. As, for example, in the particular power of Congress "to make rules for the government and regulation of the land and naval forces, or the particular and specific power to regulate commerce;" "to establish an uniform rule of naturalization;" "to coin money and regulate the value thereof." And to construe the words of which we are speaking as a general and unlimited grant of sovereignty over territories which the government might afterwards acquire, is to use them in a sense and for a purpose for which they were not used in any other part of the instrument. But if confined to a particular territory, in which a government and laws have already been established, but which would require some alterations to adopt it to the new government, the words are peculiarly applicable appropriate [sic] for that purpose.

The necessity of this special provision in relation to property and the rights or property held in common by the confederated States, is illustrated by the 1st clause of the 6th article. This clause provides that "all debts, contracts and engagements entered into before the adoption of this Constitution, shall be as valid against the United States under this government as under the Confederation." This provision, like the one under consideration, was indispensable if the new Constitution was adopted. The new government was not a mere change in a dynasty, or in a form of government, leaving the nation or sovereignty same, and clothed with all the same rights, and bound by all the obligations of the preceding one. But, when the present United States came into existence under the new government, it was a new political body, a new nation, then for the first time taking its place in the family of nations. It took nothing by succession from the Confederation. It had no right, as its successor, to any property or rights of property which it had acquired, and was not liable for any of its obligations. It was evidently viewed in this light by the framers of the Constitution. And as the several States would cease to exist in their former confederated character upon the adoption of the Constitution, and could not, in that character, again assemble together, special provisions were indispensable to transfer to the new government the property and rights which at that time they held in common; and at the same time to authorize it to lay taxes and appropriate money to pay the common debt which they had contracted; and this power could only be given to it by special provisions in the Constitution.

The clause in relation to the territory and other property of the United States provided for the first, and the clause last quoted provided for the other. They have no connection with the general powers and rights of sovereignty delegated to the new government, and can neither enlarge nor diminish them. They were inserted to meet a present emergency, and not to regulate its powers as a government.

Indeed, a similar provision was deemed necessary, in relation to treaties made by the Confederation; and when in the clause next succeeding the one of which we have last spoken, it is declared that treaties shall be the supreme law of the land, care is taken to include, by express words, the Treaties made by the confederation and States. The language is: "and all treaties made, or which shall be made, under the authority of the United States, shall be the supreme law of the land."

Whether, therefore, we take the particular clause in question, by itself, or in connection with the other provisions of the Constititution, we think it clear, that it applies only to the particular territory of which we have spoken, and cannot, by any just rule of interpretation, be extended to a territory which the new government might afterwards obtain from a foreign nation. Consequently, the power which Congress may have lawfully exercised in this territory, while it remained under a territorial government, and which may have been sanctioned by judicial decision, can furnish no justification and no argument to support a similar exercise of power over territory afterwards acquired by the Federal government. We put aside, therefore, any argument, drawn from precedents, showing the extent of the power which the general government exercised over slavery in this territory, as altogether inapplicable in the case before us.

But the case of the American and Ocean Insurance Companies v. Canter, 1 Pet. 511, has been quoted as establishing a different construction of this clause of the Constitution. There is, however, not the slightest conflict between the opinion now given and the one referred to; and it is only by taking a single sentence out of the latter and separating it from the context, that even an appearance of conflict can be shown. We need not comment on such a mode of expounding an opinion of the court. Indeed it most commonly misrepresents instead of expounding it. And this is fully exemplified in the case referred to, where, if one sentence is taken by itself, the opinion would appear to be in direct conflict with that now given; but the words which immediately follow that sentence show that the court did not mean to decide the point, but merely affirmed the power of Congress to establish a government in the Territory, leaving it an open question, whether that power was derived from this clause in the Constitution, or was to be necessarily inferred from a power to acquire territory by cession from a foreign government. The opinion on this part of the case is short, and we give the whole of it to show how well the selection of a single sentence is calculated to mislead.

The passage referred to is in page 542, in which the court, in speaking of the power of Congress to establish a territorial govenment in Florida until it should become a State, uses the following language:

> In the meantime Florida continues to be a Territory of the United States, governed by that clause of the Constitution which empowers Congress to make all needful rules and regulations respecting the territory or other property of the United States. Perhaps the power of governing a territory belonging to the United States, which has not, by becoming a State, acquired the means of self-government, may result necessarily from the facts that it is not within the jurisdiction of any State, and is within the power and jurisdiction of the United States. The right to govern may be the inevitable consequence of the right to acquire territory. Whichever may be the source from which the power is derived, the possession of it is unquestionable.

It is thus clear, from the whole opinion on this point, that the court did not mean to decide whether the power was derived from the clause in the Constitution or was the necessary consequence of the right to acquire. They do decide that the power in Congress is unquestionable, and in this we entirely concur, and nothing will be found in this opinion to the contrary. The power stands firmly on the latter alternative put by the court, that is, as "the inevitable consequence of the right to acquire territory."

And what still more clearly demonstrates that the court did not mean to decide the question, but leave it open for future consideration, is the fact that the case was decided in the Circuit Court by Mr. Justice Johnson, and his decision was affirmed by the Supreme Court. His opinion at the Circuit is given in full in a note to the case, and in that opinion he states, in explicit terms, that the clause of the Constitution applies only to the territory then within the limits of the United States, and not to Florida, which had been acquired by cession from Spain. This part of his opinion will be found in the note in page 517 of of the report. But he does not dissent from the opinion of the Supreme Court; thereby showing that, in his judgment, as well as that of the court, the case before them did not call for a decision on that particular point, and the court abstained from deciding it. And in a part of its opinion subsequent to the passage we have quoted, where the court speak of the legislative power of Congress in Florida, they still speak with the same reserve. And in page 546, speaking of the power of Congress to authorize the Territorial legislature to establish courts there, the court say: "They are legislative courts, created in virtue of the general right of sovereignty which exists in the government, or in virtue of that clause which enables Congress to make all needful rules and regulations respecting the territory belonging to the United States."

It has been said that the construction given to this clause is new, and now for the first time brought forward. The case of which we are speaking, and which has been so much discussed, shows that the fact is otherwise. It shows that precisely the same question came before Mr. Justice Johnson, at his circuit, thirty years ago—was fully considered by him, and the same construction given to the clause in the Constitution which is now given by this court. And that upon an appeal from his decision the same question was brought before this court, but, was not decided because a decision upon it was not required by the case before the court.

There is another sentence in the opinion which has been commented on, which even in a still more striking manner shows how one may mislead or be misled by taking out a single sentence from the opinion of a court, and leaving out of view what precedes and follows. It is in page 546, near the close of the opinion, in which the court say: "In legislating for them" (the Territories of the United States), "Congress exercises the combined powers of the general and of a state government." And it is said, that as a State may unquestionably prohibit slavery within its territory, this sentence decides in effect that Congress may do the same in a Territory of the United States, exercising there the powers of a State as well as the power of the general government.

The examination of this passage in the case referred to, would be more appropriate when we come to consider in another part of this opinion what power Congress can constitutionally exercise in a Territory, over the rights of person or rights of property of a citizen. But as it is in the same case with the passage we have before commented on, we dispose of it now, as it will save the court from the necessity of referring again to the case. And it will be seen upon reading the page in which this sentence is found, that it has no reference whatever to the power of Congress over rights of person or rights of property—but relates altogether to the power of establishing judicial tribunals to administer the laws constitutionally passed, and defining the jurisdiction they may exercise.

The law of Congress establishing a territorial government in Florida, provided that the legislature of the Territory should have legislative powers over "all rightful objects of legislation; but no law should be valid which was inconsistent with the laws and Constitution of the United States."

Under the power thus conferred, the Legislature of Florida passed an Act, erecting a tribunal at Key West to decide cases of salvage. And in the case of which we are speaking, the question arose whether the Territorial Legislature could be authorized by Congress to establish such a tribunal, with such powers; and one of the parties, among other objections, insisted that Congress could not under the Constitution authorize the Legislature of the Territory to establish such a tribunal with such powers, but that it must be established by Congress itself; and that a sale of cargo made under its order, to pay salvors, was void, as made without legal authority, and passed no property to the purchaser.

It is in disposing of this objection that the sentence relied on occurs, and the court begin that part of the opinion by stating with great precision the point which they are about to decide.

They say:

> It has been contended that by the Constitution of the United States, the judicial power of the United Strates extends to all cases of admiralty and maritime jurisdiction; and that the whole of the judicial power must be vested 'in one Supreme Court, and in such inferior courts as Congress shall from time to time ordain and establish.' Hence it has been argued that Congress cannot vest admiralty jurisdiction in courts created by the Territorial Legistature.

And after thus clearly stating the point before them, and which they were about to decide, they proceed to show that these territorial tribunals were not constitutional courts, but merely legislative, and that Congress might, therefore, delegate the power to the territorial government to establish the court in question; and they conclude that part of the opinion in the following words:

> Although admiralty jurisdiction can be exercised in the states in those courts only which are established in pursuance of the 3d article of the Constitution, the same limitation does not extend to the Territories. In legislating for them, Congress exercises the combined powers of the general and state governments.

Thus it will be seen by these quotations from the opinion, that the court, after stating the question it was about to decide, in a manner too plain to be misunderstood, proceeded to decide it, and announced, as the opinion of the tribunal, that in organizing the Judicial Department of the government in a Territory of the United States, Congress does not act under, and is not restricted by, the 3d article in the Constitution, and is not bound, in a Territory, to ordain and establish courts in which the judges hold their offices during good behavior; but may exercise the discretionary power which a state exercises in establishing its judicial department, and regulating the jurisdiction of its courts, and may authorize the territorial government to establish, or may itself establish, courts in which the judges hold their offices for a term of years only, and may vest in them judicial power upon subjects confided to the judiciary of the United States. And in doing this, Congress undoubtedly exercises the combined power of the general and a state government. It exercises the discretionary power of a state government in authorizing the establishment of a court in which the judges hold their appointments for a term of years only, and not during good behavior; and it exercises the power of the general government in investing that court with admiralty jurisdiction, over which the general government had executive jurisdiction in the Territory.

No one, we presume, will question the correctness of that opinion; nor is there anything in conflict with it in the opinion now given. The point decided in the case cited has no relation to the question now before the court. That depended on the construction of the 3d article of the Constitution, in relation to the judiciary of the United States, and the power which Congress might exercise in a territory in organizing the Judicial Department of the government. The case before us depends upon other and different provisions of the Constitution, altogether separate and apart from the one above mentioned. The question as to what courts Congress may ordain or establish in a territory to administer laws which the Constitution authorizes it to pass, and what laws it is or is not authorized by the Constitution to pass, are widely different—are regulated by different and separate articles of the Constitution, and stand upon different principles. And we are satisfied that no one who reads attentively the page in Peters' Reports to which we have referred, can suppose that the attention of the court was drawn for a moment to the quesion now before this court, or that it meant in that case to say that Congress had a right to prohibit a citizen of the United States from taking any property which he lawfully held, into a Territory of the United States.

This brings us to examine by what provision of the Constitution the present Federal Government under its delegated and restricted powers, is authorized to acquire territory outside of the original limits of the United States, and what powers it may exercise therein over the person or property of a citizen of the United States, while it remans a territory, and until it shall be admitted as one of the States of the Union.

There is certainly no power given by the Constitution to the Federal Government to establish or maintain Colonies bordering on the United States or at a distance, to be ruled and governed at its own pleasure; nor to enlarge its territorial limits in any way, except by the admission of new States. That power is plainly given; and if a new State is admitted it needs no further legislation by Congress, because the Constitution itself defines the relative rights and powers and duties of the State, and the citizens of the State, and the Federal Government. But no power is given to acquire Territory to be held and governed permanently in that character.

And indeed the power exercised by Congress to acquire territory and establish a government there, according to its own unlimited discretion, was viewed with great jealousy by the leading statesmen of the day. And in the Federalist, No. 38, written

410

by Mr. Madison, he speaks of the acquisition of the Northwestern Territory by the confederated States, by the cession from Virginia and the establishment of a government there, as an exercise of power not warranted by the Articles of Confederation, and dangerous to the liberties of the people. And he urges the adoption of the Constitution as a security and safeguard against such an exercise of power.

We do not mean, however, to question the power of Congress in this respect. The power to expand the territory of the United States by the admission of new States is plainly given; and in the construction of this power by all the departments of the government, it has been held to authorize the acquisition of territory, not fit for admission at the time, but to be admitted as soon as its population and situation would entitle it to admission. It is acquired to become a State, and not to be held as a colony and governed by Congress with absolute authority; and as the propriety of admiting a new State is committed to the sound discretion of Congress, the power to acquire territory for that purpose, to be held by the United States until it is in a suitable condition to become a state upon an equal footing with the other States, must rest upon the same discretion. It is a question for the Political Department of the government, and not the judicial; and whatever the Political department of the government shall recognize as within the limits of the United States the Judicial Department is also bound to recognize, and to administer in it the laws of the United States, so far as they apply, and to maintain in the territory the authority and rights of the government; and also the personal rights and rights of property of individual citizens, as secured by the Constitution. All we mean to say on this point is, that, as there is no express regulation in the Constitution defining the power which the general government may exercise over the person or property of a citizen in a territory thus acquired, the court must necessarily look to the provisions and principles of the Constitution, and its distribution of powers, for the rules and principles by which its decision must be governed.

Taking this rule to guide us, it may be safely assumed that citizens of the United States who migrate to a territory belonging to the people of the United States, cannot be ruled as mere colonists, dependent upon the will of the general government, and to be governed by any laws it may think proper to impose. The principle upon which our governments rest, and upon which alone they continue to exist, is the union of States, sovereign and independent within their own limits in their internal and domestic concerns, and bound together as one people by a general government, possessing certain enumerated and restricted powers, delegated to it by the people of the several States and exercising supreme authority within the scope of the powers granted to it, throughout the dominion of the United States. A power, therefore, in the general government to obtain and hold Colonies and dependent Territories, over which they might legislate without restriction, would be inconsistent with its own existence in its present form. Whatever it acquires, it acquires for the benefit of the people of the several States who created it. It is their trustee acting for them, and charged with the duty of promoting the interests of the whole people of the Union in the exercise of the powers specifically granted.

At the time when the Territory in question was obtained by cession from France, it contained no population fit to be associated together and admitted as a State; and it therefore was absolutely necessary to hold possession of it as a Territory belonging to the United States until it was settled and inhabited by a civilized community capable of self-government, and in a condition to be admitted on equal terms with the other States as a member of the Union. But, as we have before said, it was acquired by the general government as the representative and trustee of the people of the United States, and it must, therefore, be held in that character for their common and equal benefit; for it was the people of the several States, acting through the agent and representative, the Federal Government, who in fact acquired the territory in question, and the government holds it for their common use until it shall be associated with the other States as a member of the Union.

But until that time arrives, it is undoubtedly necessary that some government should be established, in order to organize society, and to protect the inhabitants in their persons and property; and as the people of the United States could act in this matter only through the government which represented them and through which they spoke and acted when the territory was obtained, it was not only within the scope of its powers, but it was its duty to pass such laws and establish such a government as would enable those by whose authority they acted to reap the advantages anticipated from its acquisition, and to gather there a population which would enable it to assume the position to which it was destined among the States of the Union. The power to acquire, necessarily carries with it the power to preserve and apply to the purposes for which it was acquired. The form of government to be established necessarily rested in the discetion of Congress. It was their duty to establish the one that would be best suited for the protection and security of the citizens of the United States and other inhabitants who might be authorized to take up their abode there, and that must always depend upon the existing condition of the Territory, as to the number and character of its inhabitants, and the situation in the Territory. In some cases a government, consisting of persons appointed by the Federal Government, would best subserve the interests of the Territory, when the inhabitants were few and scattered, and new to one another. In other instances, it would be more advisable to commit the powers of self-government to the people who resided in the territory, as being the most competent to determine what was best for their own interests. But some form of civil authority would be absolutely necessary to organize and preserve civilized society, and prepare it to become a state; and what is the best form must always depend on the condition of the territory at the time, and the choice of the mode must depend upon the exercise of a discretionary power by Congress acting within the scope of its constitutional authority, and not infringing upon the rights of person or rights of property of the citizen who might go there to reside or for any other lawful purpose. It was acquired by the exercise of this discretion and it must be held and governed in like manner, until it is fitted to be a state.

But the power of Congress over the person or property of a citizen can never be a mere discretionary power under our Constitution and form of government. The powers of the government and the rights and privileges of the citizen are regulated and plainly defined by the Constitution itself. And when the territory becomes a part of the United States, the Federal government enters into possession in the character impressed upon it by those who created it. It enters upon it with its powers over the citizen strictly limited by the Constitution, from which it derives its own existence, and by virtue of which alone it continues to exist and act as a government and sovereignty. It has no power of any kind beyond it; and it cannot, when it enters a territory of the United States, put off its character, and assume discretionary or despotic powers which the Constitution has denied to it. It cannot create for itself a new character separated from the citizens of the United States, and the duties it owes them under the provisions of the Constitution. The territory being a part of the United States, the government and the citizen both enter it under the authority of the Constitution, with their respective rights defined and marked out; and the Federal Government can exercise no power over his person or property, beyond what that instrument confers, nor lawfully deny any right which it has reserved.

A reference to a few of the provisions of the Constitution will illustrate this proposition. For no one, we presume, will contend that Congress can make any law in a territory respecting the establishment of religion or the free exercise thereof, or abridging the freedom of speech or of the press, or the right of the people of the territory peaceably to assemble and to petition the government for the redress of grievances.

Nor can Congress deny to the people the right to keep and bear arms, nor the right to trial by jury, nor compel anyone to be a witness against himself in a criminal proceeding.

These powers, and others in relation to rights of person, which it is not necessary here to enumerate, are, in express and positive terms, denied to the general government; and the rights of private property have been guarded with equal care. Thus the rights of property are united with the rights of person, and placed on the same ground by the fifth amendment to the Constitution, which provides that no person shall be deprived of life, liberty and property, without due process of law. And an Act of Congress which deprives a citizen of the United States of his liberty or property, merely because he came himself or brought his property into a particular Territory of the United States, and who had committed no offense against the laws, could hardly be dignified with the name of due process of law.

So, too, it will hardly be contended that Congress could by law quarter a soldier in a house in a territory without the consent of the owner, in time of peace; nor in time of war, but in a manner prescribed by law. Nor could they by law forfeit the property of a citizen in a territory who was convicted of treason, for a longer period than the life of the person convicted; nor take private property for public use without just compensation.

The powers over person and property of which we speak are not only not granted to Congress, but are in express terms denied, and they are forbidden to exercise them. And this prohibition is not confined to the States, but the words are general, and extend to the whole territory over which the Constitution gives it power to legislate, including those portions of it remaining under territorial government, as well as that covered by States. It is a total absence of power everywhere within the dominion of the United States, and places the citizens of a territory, so far as these rights are concerned, on the same footing with citizens of the States, and guards them as firmly and plainly against any inroads which the general government might attempt, under the plea of implied or incidental powers. And if Congress itself cannot do this—if it is beyond the powers conferred on the Federal Government—it will be admitted, we presume, that it could not authorize a territorial government to exercise them. It could confer no power on any local government, established by its authority, to violate the provisions of the Constitution.

It seems, however, to be supposed, that there is a difference between property in a slave and other property, and that different rules may be applied to it in expounding the Constitution of the United States. And the laws and usage of nations, and the writings of eminent jurists upon the relation of master and slave and their mutual rights and duties, and the power which governments may exercise over it, have been dwelt upon in the argument.

But in considering the question before us, it must be borne in mind that there is no law of nations standing between the people of the United States and their government and interfering with their relation to each other. The powers of the government, and the rights of the citizen under it, are positive and practical regulations plainly written down. The people of the United States have delegated to it certain enumerated powers, and forbidden it to exercise others. It has no power over the person or property of a citizen but what the citizens of the United States have granted. And no law or usages of other nations, or reasoning of statesmen or jurists upon the relations of master and slave, can enlarge the powers of the government, or take from the citizens the rights they have reserved. And if the Constitution recognizes the right of property of the master in a slave, and makes no distinction between that description of property and other property owned by a citizen, no tribunal, acting under the authority of the United States, whether it be legislative, executive, or judicial, has a right to draw such a distinction, or deny to it the benefit of the provisions and guarantees which have been provided for the protection of private property against the encroachments of the governments.

Now, as we have already said in an earlier part of this opinion, upon a different point, the right of property in a slave is distinctly and expressly affirmed in the Constitution. The right to traffic in it, like an ordinary article of merchandise and property, was guaranteed to the citizens of the United States, in every State that might desire it, for twenty years. And the government in express terms is pledged to protect it in all future time, if the slave eacapes from his owner. This is done in plain words—too plain to be misunderstood. And no word can be found in the Constitution which gives Congress a greater power over slave property, or which entitles property of that kind to less protection than property of any other description. The only power conferred is the power coupled with the duty of

414

guarding and protecting the owner in his rights.

Upon these considerations, it is the opinion of the court that the Act of Congress which prohibited a citizen from holding and owning property of this kind in the territory of the United States north of the line therein mentioned, is not warranted by the Constitution, and is therefore void; and that neither Dred Scott himself, nor any of his family, were made free by being carried into this territory; even if they had been carried there by the owner, with the intention of becoming a permanent resident.

We have so far examined the case, as it stands under the Constitution of the United States, and the powers thereby delegated to the Federal Government.

But there is another point in the case which depends on state power and state law. And it is contended, on the part of the plaintiff, that he is made free by being taken to Rock Island, in the State of Illinois, independently of his residence in the territory of the United States; and being so made free he was not again reduced to a state of slavery by being brought back to Missouri.

Our notice of this part of the case will be very brief; for the principle on which it depends was decided in this court, upon much consideration, in the case of Strader et al. v. Graham, reported in 10th Howard, 82. In that case, the slaves had been taken from Kentucky to Ohio, with the consent of the owner, and afterwards brought back to Kentucky. And this court held that their status or condition, as free or slave, depended upon the laws of Kentucky, when they were brought back into that State, and not of Ohio; and that this court had no jurisdiction to revise the judgment of a state court upon its own laws. This was the point directly before the court, and the decision that this court had not jurisdiction, turned upon it, as will be seen by the report of the case.

So in this case: as Scott was a slave when taken into the State of Illinois by his owner, and was there held as such, and brought back in that character, his status, as free or slave, depended on the laws of Missouri, and not of Illinois.

It has, however, been urged in the argument, that by the laws of Missouri he was free on his return, and that this case, therefore, cannot be governed by the case of Strader et al. v. Graham, where it appeared, by the laws of Kentucky, that the plaintiffs continued to be slaves on their return from Ohio. But whatever doubts or opinions may, at one time, have been entertained upon this subject, we are satisfied, upon a careful examination of all the cases decided in the State courts of Missouri referred to, that it is now firmly settled by the decisions of the highest court in the State, that Scott and his family upon their return were not free, but were, by the laws of Missouri, the property of the defendant; and that the Circuit Court of the United States had no jurisdiction, when, by the laws of the State, the plaintiff was a slave and not a citizen.

Moreover, the plaintiff, it appears, brought a similar action against the defendant in the State court of Missouri, claiming the freedom of himself and his family upon the same grounds and the same evidence upon which he now relies in the case before the court. The case was carried before the Supreme Court of the State; was fully argued there; and that court decided that neither the plaintiff nor his family were entitled to freedom, and were still the slaves of the defendant; and reversed the judgment of the inferior State court, which had given a different decision. If the plaintiff supposed that this judgment of the Supreme Court of the State was erroneous, and that this court had jurisdiction to revise and reverse it, the only mode by which he could legally bring it before this court was by writ of error directed to the Supreme Court of the State, requiring it to transmit the record to this court. If this had been done, it is too plain for argument that the writ must have been dismissed for want of jurisdiction in this court. The case of Strader et al. v. Graham is directly in point; and, indeed, independent of any decision, the language of the 25th section of the Act of 1789 is too clear and precise to admit of controversy.

But the plaintiff did not pursue the mode prescribed by law for bringing the judgment of a state court before this court for revision, but suffered the case to be remanded to the inferior State court, where it is still continued, and is, by agreement of parties, to await the judgment of this court on the point. All of this appears on the record before us and by the printed report of the case.

And while the case is yet open and pending, in the inferor State court, the plaintiff goes into the Circuit Court of the United States, upon the same case and the same evidence, and against the same party, and proceeds to judgment, and then brings here the same case from the Circuit Court, which the law would not have permitted him to bring directly from the State court. And if this court takes jurisdiction in this form, the result, so far as the rights of the respective parties are concerned, is in every respect substantially the same as if it had, in open violation of law, entertained jurisdiction over the judgment of the State court upon a writ of error, and revised and reversed its judgment upon the ground that its opinion upon the question of law was erroneous. It would ill become this court to sanction such an attempt to evade the law, or to exercise an appellate power in this circuitous way, which it is forbidden to exercise in the direct and regular and invariable forms of judicial proceedings.

Upon the whole, therefore, it is the judgment of this court, that it appears by the record before us that the plaintiff in error is not a citizen of Missouri, in the sense in which that word is used in the Constitution; and that the Circuit Court of the United States, for that reason, had no jurisdiction in the case, and could give no judgment in it.

Its judgment for the defendant must, consequently, be reversed, and a mandate issued directing the suit to be dismissed for want of jurisdiction.

Ꭸ·30·Ꭸ

On the Dred Scott Decision

ABRAHAM LINCOLN

In 1856 Abraham Lincoln had become the leader of the Republican party in Illinois and was positioning himself to contest the election for the Senate in the following year. Here, in a speech given in the immediate aftermath of the Dred Scott decision in 1857, he argues that the status of the Afro–American population has declined since the founding of the republic. He also dissects the Supreme Court's decision, and particularly its justification in terms of its interpretation of the Declaration of Independence with a scholarly and witty argument that points out the manifest absurdities of the judgment.

Fellow citizens:—I am here to-night, partly by the invitation of some of you, and partly by my own inclination. Two weeks ago Judge Douglas spoke here on the several subjects of Kansas, the Dred Scott decision, and Utah. I listened to the speech at the time, and have read the report of it since. It was intended to controvert opinions which I think just, and to assail (politically, not personally,) those men who, in common with me, entertain those opinions. For this reason I wished then, and still wish, to make some answer to it, which I now take the opportunity of doing. [. . .]

I have said, in substance, that the Dred Scott decision was, in part, based on assumed historical facts which were not really true; and I ought not to leave the subject without giving some reasons for saying this; I therefore give an instance or two, which I think fully sustain me. Chief Justice Taney, in delivering the opinion of the majority of the Court, insists at great length that negroes were no part of the people who made, or for whom was made, the Declaration of Independence, or the Constitution of the United States.

On the contrary, Judge Curtis, in his dissenting opinion, shows that in five of the then thirteen states, to wit: New Hampshire, Massachusetts, New York. New Jersey and North Carolina, free negroes were voters, and, in proportion to their

Source: Abraham Lincoln, Speech, 1957, rptd in Roy P. Brassler, ed., *The Collected Works of Abraham Lincoln*, New Brunswick, N.J.: Rutgers University Press, 1953.

numbers, had the same part in making the Constitution that the white people had. He shows this with so much particularity as to leave no doubt of its truth; and, as a sort of conclusion on that point, holds the following language:

> "The Constitution was ordained and established by the people of the United States, through the action, in each State, of those persons who were qualified by its laws to act thereon in behalf of themselves and all other citizens of the State. In some of the States, as we have seen, colored persons were among those qualified by law to act on the subject. These colored persons were not only included in the body of 'the people of the United States,' by whom the Constitution was ordained and established; but in at least five of the States they had the power to act, and, doubtless, did act, by their suffrages, upon the question of its adoption."

Again, Chief Justice Taney says:

> "It is difficult, at this day to realize the state of public opinion in relation to that unfortunate race, which prevailed in the civilized and enlightened portions of the world at the time of the Declaration of Independence, and when the Constitution of the United States was framed and adopted."

And again, after quoting from the Declaration, he says:

> "The general words above quoted would seem to include the whole human family, and if they were used in a similar instrument at this day, would be so understood."

In these the Chief Justice does not directly assert, but plainly assumes, as a fact, that the public estimate of the black man is more favorable *now* than it was in the days of the Revolution. This assumption is a mistake. In some trifling particulars, the condition of that race has been ameliorated; but, as a whole, in this country, the change between then and now is decidedly the other way; and their ultimate destiny has never appeared so hopeless as in the last three or four years. In two of the five States—New Jersey and North Carolina—that then gave the free negro the right of voting, the right has since been taken away; and in a third—New York—it has been greatly abridged; while it has not been extended, so far as I know, to a single additional State, though the number of the States has more than doubled. In those days, as I understand, masters could, at their own pleasure, emancipate their slaves; but since then, such legal restraints have been made upon emancipation, as to amount almost to prohibition. In those days, Legislatures held the unquestioned power to abolish slavery in their respective States; but now it is becoming quite fashionable for State Constitutions to withhold that power from the Legislatures. In those days, by common consent, the spread of the black man's bondage to new countries was prohibited; but now, Congress decides that it *will* not continue the prohibition, and the Supreme Court decides that it *could* not if it would. In those days, our Declaration of Independence was held sacred by all, and thought to include all; but now, to aid in making the bondage of the negro universal and eternal, it is assailed, and sneered at, and construed, and hawked at, and torn, till, if its framers could rise from their graves, they could not at all recognize it. All the powers of earth seem rapidly combining against him. Mammon is after him; ambition follows, and philosophy follows, and the Theology of the day is fast joining the cry. They have him in his prison house; they have searched his person, and left no prying instrument with him. One after another they have closed the heavy iron doors upon him, and now they have him, as it were, bolted in with a lock of a hundred keys, which can never be unlocked without the concurrence of every key; the keys in the hands of a hundred different men, and they scattered to a hundred different and distant places; and they stand musing as to what invention, in all the dominions of mind and matter, can be produced to make the impossibility of his escape more complete than it is.

It is grossly incorrect to say or assume, that the public estimate of the negro is more favorable now than it was at the origin of the government. [. . .]

There is a natural disgust in the minds of nearly all white people, to the idea of an indiscriminate amalgamation of the white and black races; and Judge Douglas evidently is basing his chief hope, upon the chances of being able to appropriate the benefit of this disgust to himself. If he can, by much drumming and repeating, fasten the odium of that idea upon his adversaries, he thinks he can struggle through the storm. He therefore clings to this hope, as a drowning man to the last plank. He makes an occasion for lugging it in from the opposition to the Dred Scott decision. He finds the Republicans insisting that the Declaration of Independence includes ALL men, black as well as white; and forthwith he boldly denies that it includes negroes at all, and proceeds to argue gravely that all who contend it does, do so only because they want to vote, and eat, and sleep, and marry with negroes! He will have it that they cannot be consistent else. Now I protest against that counterfeit logic which concludes that, because I do not want a black woman for a *slave* I must necessarily want her for a *wife*. I need not have her for either, I can just leave her alone. In some respects she certainly is not my equal; but in her natural right to eat the bread she earns with her own hands without asking leave of any one else, she is my equal, and the equal of all others.

Chief Justice Taney, in his opinion in the Dred Scott case, admits that the language of the Declaration is broad enough to include the whole human family, but he and Judge Douglas argue that the authors of that instrument did not intend to include negroes, by the fact that they did not at once, actually place them on an equality with the whites. Now this grave argument comes to just nothing at all, by the other fact, that they did not at once, *or ever afterwards*, actually place all white people on an equality with one or another. And this is the staple argument of both the Chief Justice and the Senator, for doing this obvious violence to the plain un-mistakable language of the Declaration. I think the authors of that notable instrument intended to include *all* men, but they did not intend to declare all men equal *in all respects*. They did not mean to say all were equal in color, size, intellect, moral developments, or social capacity. They defined with tolerable distinctness, in what respects they did consider all men created equal—equal in "certain inalienable rights, among which are life, liberty, and the pursuit of happiness." This they said, and this meant. They did not mean to assert the obvious untruth, that all were then actually enjoying that equality, nor yet, that they were about to confer it immediately upon them. In fact they had no power to confer such a boon. They meant simply to declare the *right*, so that the *enforcement* of it might follow as fast as circumstances should permit. They meant to set up a standard maxim for free society, which should be familiar to all, and revered by all; constantly looked to, constantly labored for, and even though never perfectly attained, constantly approximated, and thereby constantly spreading and deepening its influence, and augmenting the happiness and value of life to all people of all colors everywhere. The assertion that "all men are created equal" was of no practical use in effecting our separation from Great Britain; and it was placed in the Declaration, not for that, but for future use. Its authors meant it to be, thank God, it is now proving itself, a stumbling block to those who in after times might seek to turn a free people back into the hateful paths of despotism. They knew the proneness of prosperity to breed tyrants, and they meant when such should re-appear in this fair land and commence their vocation they should find left for them at least one hard nut to crack.

I have now briefly expressed my view of the *meaning* and *objects* of that part of the Declaration of Independence which declares that "all men are created equal."

Now let us hear Judge Douglas's view of the same subject, as I find it in the printed report of his late speech. Here it is:

> "No man can vindicate the character, motives and conduct of the signers of the Declaration of Independence, except upon the hypothesis that they referred to the white race alone, and not to the African, when they declared all men to have been created equal—that they were speaking of British subjects on this continent being equal to British subjects born and residing in Great Britain—that they were entitled to the same inalienable rights, and among them were enumerated life, liberty and the pursuit of happiness. The Declaration was adopted for the purpose of justifying the colonists in the eyes of the civilized world in withdrawing their allegiance from the British crown, and dissolving their connection with the mother country."

My good friends, read that carefully over some leisure hour, and ponder well upon it—see what a mere wreck—mangled ruin—it makes of our once glorious Declaration.

"They were speaking of British subjects on this continent being equal to British subjects born and residing in Great Britain!" Why, according to this, not only negroes but white people outside of Great Britain and America are not spoken of in that instrument. The English, Irish and Scotch, along with white Americans, were included to be sure, but the French, Germans and other white people of the world are all gone to pot along with the Judge's inferior races.

I had thought the Declaration promised something better than the condition of British subjects; but no, it only meant that we should be *equal* to them in their own oppressed and *unequal* condition. According to that, it gave no promise that having kicked off the King and Lords of Great Britain, we should not at once be saddled with a King and Lords of our own.

I had thought the Declaration contemplated the progressive improvement in the condition of all men everywhere; but no, it merely

> was adopted for the purpose of justifying the colonists in the eyes of the civilized world in withdrawing their allegiance from the British crown, and dissolving their connection with the mother country.

Why, that object having been effected some eighty years ago, the Declaration is of no practical use now—mere rubbish—old wadding left to rot on the battle-field after the victory is won.

I understand you are preparing to celebrate the "Fourth," tomorrow week. What for? The doings of that day had no reference to the present; and quite half of you are not even descendants of those who were referred to at that day. But I suppose you will celebrate; and will even go so far as to read the Declaration. Suppose after you read it once in the old fashioned way, you read it once more with Judge Douglas' version. It will then run thus:

> We hold these truths to be self-evident that all British subjects who were on this continent eighty-one years ago, were created equal to all British subjects born and then residing in Great Britain.

And now I appeal to all—to Democrats as well as others,—are you really willing that the Declaration shall be thus frittered away?— thus left no more at most, than an interesting memorial of the dead past? thus shorn of its vitality, and practical value; and left without the *germ* or even the *suggestion* of the individual rights of man in it?

But Judge Douglas is especially horrified at the thought of the mixing blood by the white and black races: agreed for once—a thousand times agreed. There are white men enough to marry all the white women, and black men enough to marry all the black women; and so let them be married. On this point we fully agree with the Judge; and when he shall show that his policy is better adapted to prevent amalgamation than ours we shall drop ours, and adopt his. Let us see. In 1850 there were in the United States 405,751 mulattoes. Very few of these are the offspring of whites and *free* blacks; nearly all have sprung from black *slaves* and white masters. A separation of the races is the only perfect preventive of amalgamation but as an immediate separation is impossible the next best thing is to *keep* them apart *where* they are not already together. If white and black people never get together in Kansas, they will never mix blood in Kansas. That is at least one self-evident truth. A few free colored persons may get into the free States, in any event; but their number is too insignificant to amount to much in the way of mixing blood. In 1850 there were in the free states 56,649 mulattoes; but for the most part they were not born there—they came from the slave States, ready made up. In the same year the slave States had 348,874 mulattoes all of home production. The proportion of free mulattoes to free blacks—the only colored classes in the free states—is much greater in the slave than in the free states. It is worthy of note too, that among the free states those which make the colored man the nearest to equal the white, have, proportionably the fewest mulattoes the least of amalgamation. In New Hampshire, the State which goes farthest towards equality between the races, there are just 184 mulattoes while there are in Virginia—how many do you think? 79,775, being 23,126 more than in all the free States together.

These statistics show that slavery is the greatest source of amalgamation; and next to it, not the elevation, but the degeneration of the free blacks. Yet Judge

Douglas dreads the slightest restraints on the spread of slavery, and the slightest human recognition of the negro, as tending horribly to amalgamation.

I have said that the separation of the races is the only perfect preventive of amalgamation. I have no right to say all the members of the Republican party are in favor of this, nor to say that as a party they are in favor of it. There is nothing in their platform directly on the subject. But I can say a very large proportion of its members are for it, and that the chief plank in their platform—opposition to the spread of slavery—is most favorable to that separation.

Such separation, if ever effected at all, must be effected by colonization; and no political party, as such, is now doing anything directly for colonization. Party operations at present only favor or retard colonization incidentally. The enterprise is a difficult one; but "when there is a will there is a way;" and what colonization needs most is a hearty will. Will springs from the two elements of moral sense and self-interest. Let us be brought to believe it is morally right, and, at the same time, favorable to, or, at least, not against, our interest, to transfer the African to his native clime, and we shall find a way to do it, however great the task may be. The children of Israel, to such numbers as to include four hundred thousand fighting men, went out of Egyptian bondage in a body.

How differently the respective courses of the Democratic and Republican parties incidentally bear on the question of forming a will—a public sentiment—for colonization, is easy to see. The Republicans inculcate, with whatever of ability they can, that the negro is a man; that his bondage is cruelly wrong, and that the field of his oppression ought not to be enlarged. The Democrats deny his manhood; deny, or dwarf to insignificance, the wrong of his bondage; so far as possible, crush all sympathy for him, and cultivate and excite hatred and disgust against him; compliment themselves as Union-savers for doing so; and call the indefinite outspreading of his bondage "a sacred right of self-government."

The plainest print cannot be read through a gold eagle; and it will be ever hard to find many men who will send a slave to Liberia, and pay his passage while they can send him to a new country, Kansas for instance, and sell him for fifteen hundred dollars, and the rise.

ৡ 31 ৡ

Speech at Springfield
16th June 1858

ABRAHAM LINCOLN

This speech opened Lincoln's campaign for the US Senate against the incumbent, Stephen Douglas, in 1858. It serves as a prelude to the debates between the two candidates, which commenced the following month, and marked the election campaign. In it, Lincoln outlined the main themes which he would develop in the course of the contest. He also showed his skill as a phrase-maker: the speech included the famous observation that "A house divided against itself cannot stand". For Lincoln, then, the future was clear. There would be no compromise between north and south that would allow the two sections to co-exist within the existing political and moral conventions of the Union.

Mr. President and Gentlemen of the Convention:

If we could first know *where* we are, and *whither* we are tending, we could better judge *what* to do, and *how* to do it.

We are now far into the *fifth* year since a policy was initiated with the *avowed* object, and *confident* promise, of putting an end to slavery agitation.

Under the operation of that policy, that agitation has not only *not ceased*, but has *constantly augmented*.

In *my* opinion, it *will* not cease, until a *crisis* shall have been reached and passed.

"A house divided against itself cannot stand." I believe this government cannot endure permanently half *slave* and half *free*.

I do not expect the Union to be *dissolved*—I do not expect the house to *fall*—but I *do* expect it will cease to be divided.

It will become *all* one thing, or *all* the other.

Either the *opponents* of slavery will arrest the further spread of it, and place it where the public mind shall rest in the belief that it is in the course of ultimate

Source: Abraham Lincoln, Speech, 1858, rptd in *Illinois State Journal*, June 18, 1858.

extinction; or its *advocates* will push it forward, till it shall become alike lawful in *all* the States, *old* as well as new—*North* as well as *South*.

Have we no *tendency* to the latter condition?

Let any one who doubts, carefully contemplate that now almost complete legal combination—piece of *machinery*, so to speak—compounded of the Nebraska doctrine, and the Dred Scott decision. Let him consider not only *what work* the machinery is adapted to do, and *how well* adapted; but also, let him study the *history* of its construction, and trace, if he can, or rather *fail*, if he can, to trace the evidences of design, and concert of action, among its chief architects, from the beginning.

But, so far, *Congress* only had acted; and an *indorsement* by the people, *real* or apparent, was indispensable, to *save* the point already gained, and give chance for more.

The new year of 1854 found slavery excluded from more than half the states by state constitutions, and from most of the national territory by congressional prohibition.

Four days later, commenced the struggle which ended in repealing that congressional prohibition.

This opened all the national territory to slavery, and was the first point gained.

This necessity had not been overlooked; but had been provided for, as well as might be, in the notable argument of "*squatter sovereignty*," otherwise called "*sacred right of self-government*," which latter phrase, though expressive of the only rightful basis of any government, was so perverted in this attempted use of it as to amount to just this: That if any *one* man choose to enslave *another*, no third man shall be allowed to object.

That argument was incorporated into the Nebraska Bill itself, in the language which follows: "*It being the true intent and meaning of this act not to legislate slavery into any Territory or State, nor to exclude it therefrom; but to leave the people thereof perfectly free to form and regulate their domestic institutions in their own way, subject only to the Constitution of the United States.*"

Then opened the roar of loose declamation in favor of "Squatter Sovereignty," and "Sacred right of self-government."

"But," said opposition members, "let us be more *specific* -- let us *amend* the bill so as to expressly declare that the people of the Territory *may* exclude slavery." "Not we," said the friends of the measure; and down they voted the amendment.

While the Nebraska Bill was passing through Congress, a law case involving the question of a negro's freedom, by reason of his owner having voluntarily taken him first into a free State and then into a Territory covered by the Congressional prohibition, and held him as a slave for a long time in each, was passing through the U. S. Circuit Court for the District of Missouri; and both Nebraska Bill and law suit were brought to a decision in the same month of May, 1854. The negro's name was "Dred Scott," which name now designates the decision finally made in the case. *Before* the *then* next presidential election, the law case came to, and was argued in, the Supreme Court of the United States; but the *decision* of it was deferred until *after* the election. Still, before the election, Senator Trumbull, on the floor of the Senate, requested the leading advocate of the Nebraska Bill to state *his opinion* whether the people of a territory can constitutionally exclude slavery from their limits; and the latter answers: "That is a question for the Supreme Court."

The election came. Mr. Buchanan was elected, and the *indorsement*, such as it was, secured. That was the *second* point gained. The indorsement, however, fell short of a clear popular majority by nearly four hundred thousand votes, and so, perhaps, was not overwhelmingly reliable and satisfactory.

The *outgoing* President, in his last annual message, as impressively as possible *echoed back* upon the people the *weight* and *authority* of the indorsement.

The Supreme Court met again; *did not* announce their decision, but ordered a re-argument.

The presidential inauguration came, and still no decision of the court; but the *incoming* President in his inaugural address, fervently exhorted the people to abide by the forthcoming decision, *whatever it might be.*

Then, in a few days, came the decision.

The reputed author of the Nebraska Bill finds an early occasion to make a speech at this capital indorsing the Dred Scott decision, and vehemently denouncing all opposition to it.

The new President, too, seizes the early occasion of the Silliman letter to *indorse* and strongly *construe* that decision, and to express his *astonishment* that any different view had ever been entertained.

At length a squabble springs up between the President and the author of the Nebraska Bill, on the *mere* question of *fact*, whether the Lecompton Constitution was or was not, in any just sense, made by the people of Kansas; and in that quarrel the latter declares that all he wants is a fair vote for the people, and that he *cares* not whether slavery be voted *down* or voted *up*. I do not understand his declaration that he cares not whether slavery be voted down or voted up, to be intended by him other than as an *apt definition* of the *policy* he would impress upon the public mind—the *principle* for which he declares he has suffered so much, and is ready to suffer to the end.

And well may he cling to that principle. If he has any parental feeling, well may he cling to it. That principle is the only *shred* left of his original Nebraska doctrine. Under the Dred Scott decision "squatter sovereignty" squatted out of existence, tumbled down like temporary scaffolding—like the mould at the foundry served through one blast and fell back into loose sand—helped to carry an election, and then was kicked to the winds. His late *joint* struggle with the Republicans, against the Lecompton Constitution, involves nothing of the original Nebraska doctrine. That struggle was made on a point—the right of a people to make their own constitution—upon which he and the Republicans have never differed.

The several points of the Dred Scott decision, in connection, with Senator Douglas's "care not" policy, constitute the piece of machinery, in its *present* state of advancement. This was the third point gained.

The *working* points of that machinery are:

First, that no negro slave, imported as such from Africa, and no descendant of such slave, can ever be a citizen of any State, in the sense of that term as used in the Constitution of the United States.

This point is made in order to deprive the negro, in every possible event, of the benefit of that provision of the United States Constitution, which declares that --

"The citizens of each state, shall be entitled to all privileges and immunities of citizens in the several states."

Secondly, that "subject to the Constitution of the United States," neither *Congress* nor a *territorial legislature* can exclude slavery from any United States territory.

This point is made in order that individual men may *fill up* the territories with slaves, without danger of losing them as property, and thus to enhance the chances of *permanency* to the institution through all the future.

Thirdly, that whether the holding a negro in actual slavery in a free state, makes him free, as against the holder, the United States courts will not decide, but will leave to be decided by the courts of any slave state the negro may be forced into by the master.

This point is made, not to be pressed *immediately*; but, if acquiesced in for a while, and apparently *indorsed* by the people at an election, then to sustain the logical conclusion that what Dred Scott's master might lawfully do with Dred Scott, in the free state of Illinois, every other master may lawfully do with any other *one*, or one *thousand* slaves, in Illinois, or in any other free state.

Auxiliary to all this, and working hand in hand with it, the Nebraska doctrine, or what is left of it, is to *educate* and *mould* public opinion, at least *Northern* public opinion, not to *care* whether slavery is voted *down* or voted *up*.

This shows exactly where we now *are*; and *partially*, also, whither we are tending.

It will throw additional light on the latter, to go back, and run the mind over the string of historical facts already stated. Several things will *now* appear less *dark* and *mysterious* than they did when they were transpiring. The people were to be left "perfectly free," "subject only to the Constitution." What the *Constitution* had to do with it, outsiders could not *then* see. Plainly enough *now*, it was an exactly fitted *niche*, for the Dred Scott decision to afterwards come in, and declare the *perfect freedom* of the people to be just no freedom at all.

Why was the amendment, expressly declaring the right of the people, voted down? Plainly enough *now*: the adoption of it would have spoiled the niche for the Dred Scott decision.

Why was the court decision held up? Why even a Senator's individual opinion withheld, till *after* the presidential election? Plainly enough *now*: the speaking out *then* would have damaged the *"perfectly free"* argument upon which the election was to be carried.

Why the *outgoing* President's felicitation on the indorsement? Why the delay of a reargument? Why the incoming President's *advance* exhortation in favor of the decision?

These things *look* like the cautious *patting* and *petting* of a spirited horse preparatory to mounting him, when it is dreaded that he may give the rider a fall.

And why the hasty after-indorsements of the decision by the President and others?

We can not absolutely *know* that all these exact adaptations are the result of preconcert. But when we see a lot of framed timbers, different portions of which we know have been gotten out at different times and places and by different workmen—Stephen, Franklin, Roger and James, for instance—and when we see these timbers joined together, and see they exactly make the frame of a house or a mill, all the tenons and mortices exactly fitting, and all the lengths and proportions of the different pieces exactly adapted to their respective places, and not a piece too many or too few—not omitting even scaffolding—or, if a single piece be lacking, we see the place in the frame exactly fitted and prepared yet to bring such a piece in—in *such* a case, we find it impossible not to *believe* that Stephen and Franklin and Roger and James all understood one another from the beginning, and all worked upon a common *plan* or *draft* drawn up before the first blow was struck.

It should not be overlooked that, by the Nebraska Bill, the people of a *state* as well as *territory*, were to be left *"perfectly free"* " *subject only to the Constitution.*"

Why mention a *state?* They were legislating for *territories*, and not *for* or *about* states. Certainly the people of a state *are* and *ought to be* subject to the Constitution of the United States; but why is mention of this *lugged* into this merely *territorial* law? Why are the people of a *territory* and the people of a *state* therein *lumped* together, and their relation to the Constitution therein treated as being *precisely* the same?

While the opinion of the *Court*, by Chief Justice Taney, in the Dred Scott case, and the separate opinions of all the concurring Judges, expressly declare that the Constitution of the United States neither permits Congress nor a Territorial Legislature to exclude slavery from any United States Territory, they all *omit* to declare whether or not the same Constitution permits a *state*, or the people of a *state*, to exclude it.

Possibly, this is a mere *omission*; but who can be quite sure, if McLean or Curtis had sought to get into the opinion a declaration of unlimited power in the people of a *state* to exclude slavery from their limits, just as Chase and Mace sought to get such declaration, in behalf of the people of a Territory, into the Nebraska Bill—I ask, who can be quite *sure* that it would not have been voted down in the one case as it had been in the other?

The nearest approach to the point of declaring the power of a State over slavery, is made by Judge Nelson. He approaches it more than once, using the precise idea, and *almost* the language, too, of the Nebraska Act. On one occasion, his exact language is, "except in cases where the power is restrained by the Constitution of the United States, the law of the State is supreme over the subject of slavery within its jurisdiction."

In what *cases* the power of the *states* is so restrained by the U. S. Constitution, is left an *open* question, precisely as the same question, as to the restraint on the power of the *territories*, was left open in the Nebraska Act. Put *that* and *that* together, and we have another nice little niche, which we may, ere long, see filled with another

Supreme Court decision, declaring that the Constitution of the United States does not permit a *state* to exclude slavery from its limits.

And this may especially be expected if the doctrine of "care not whether slavery be voted *down* or voted *up*," shall gain upon the public mind sufficiently to give promise that such a decision can be maintained when made.

Such a decision is all that slavery now lacks of being alike lawful in all the states.

Welcome or unwelcome, such decision *is* probably coming, and will soon be upon us, unless the power of the present political dynasty shall be met and overthrown.

We shall *lie down* pleasantly dreaming that the people of *Missouri* are on the verge of making their state *free*, and we shall *awake* to the *reality* instead, that the *Supreme* Court has made *Illinois* a *slave* state.

To meet and overthrow the power of that dynasty, is the work now before all those who would prevent that consummation.

That is *what* we have to do.

But *how* can we best do it?

There are those who denounce us *openly* to their *own* friends, and yet whisper *us* *softly*, that *Senator Douglas* is the *aptest* instrument there is with which to effect that object. *They* do not *tell* us, nor has *he* told us, that he *wishes* any such object to be effected. They wish us to *infer* all, from the fact that he now has a little quarrel with the present head of the dynasty; and that he has regularly voted with us on a single point, upon which he and we have never differed.

They remind us that *he* is a very *great* man, and that the largest of *us* are very small ones. Let this be granted. But "a *living dog* is better than a *dead lion*." Judge Douglas, if not a *dead* lion, for *this work*, is at least a *caged* and *toothless* one. How can he oppose the advances of slavery? He don't *care* anything about it. His avowed *mission is impressing* the "*public heart*" to *care* nothing about it.

A leading Douglas democratic newspaper thinks Douglas's superior talent will be needed to resist the revival of the African slave trade.

Does Douglas believe an effort to revive that trade is approaching? He has not said so. Does he *really* think so? But if it is, how can he resist it? For years he has labored to prove it a *sacred right* of white men to take negro slaves into the new territories. Can he possibly show that it is *less* a sacred right to *buy* them where they can be bought cheapest? And unquestionably they can be bought *cheaper in Africa* than in *Virginia*.

He has done all in his power to reduce the whole question of slavery to one of a mere *right of property*; and as such, how can *he* oppose the foreign slave trade—how can he refuse that trade in that "property" shall be "perfectly free"—unless he does it as a *protection* to the home production? And as the home *producers* will probably not *ask* the protection, he will be wholly without a ground of opposition.

Senator Douglas holds, we know, that a man may rightfully be *wiser to-day* than he was *yesterday*—that he may rightfully *change* when he finds himself wrong.

But can we, for that reason, run ahead, and *infer* that he *will* make any particular change, of which he, himself, has given no intimation? Can we *safely* base *our* action upon any such *vague* inference?

Now, as ever, I wish not to *misrepresent* Judge Douglas's *position*, question his *motives*, or do aught that can be personally offensive to him.

Whenever, *if ever*, he and we can come together on *principle* so that *our great cause* may have assistance from *his great ability*, I hope to have interposed no adventitious obstacle.

But clearly, he is not *now* with us—he does not *pretend* to be—he does not *promise* to *ever* be.

Our cause, then, must be intrusted to, and conducted by, its own undoubted friends—those whose hands are free, whose hearts are in the work—who *do care* for the result.

Two years ago the Republicans of the nation mustered over thirteen hundred thousand strong. We did this under the single impulse of resistance to a common danger, with every external circumstance against us.

Of *strange, discordant*, and even *hostile* elements, we gathered from the four winds, and *formed* and fought the battle through, under the constant hot fire of a disciplined, proud and pampered enemy.

Did we brave all *then*, to *falter* now?—now—when that same enemy is *wavering*, dissevered and belligerent?

The result is not doubtful. We shall not fail—if we stand firm, we shall not fail.

Wise counsels may *accelerate*, or *mistakes delay* it, but, sooner or later, the victory is *sure* to come.

❧ 32 ❧

Speech at Springfield 17th July 1858

STEPHEN DOUGLAS

Stephen Douglas came to Springfield, Illinois, early in his re-election campaign for the United States Senate. This speech foreshadowed the themes he would address during his series of debates with his opponent, Abraham Lincoln. Douglas was a staunch advocate of states' rights, and saw any attempt by the federal government to legislate on the question of slavery as unconstitutional. He supported the Dred Scott decision, convinced that the Declaration of Independence had been written by Jefferson as an expression of the exclusive rights and privileges of the white male community. His audience appreciated such sentiments, and Douglas would go on to be re-elected to the Senate from Illinois.

M r. Chairman and Fellow-citizens of Springfield and old Sangamon:

My heart is filled with emotions at the allusions which have been so happily and so kindly made in the welcome just extended to me—a welcome so numerous and so enthusiastic, bringing me to my home among my old friends, that language cannot express my gratitude. I do feel at home whenever I return to old Sangamon and receive those kind and friendly greetings which have never failed to meet me when I have come among you; but never before have I had such occasion to be grateful and to be proud of the manner of the reception as on the present. While I am willing, sir, to attribute a part of this demonstration to those kind and friendly personal relations to which you have referred, I cannot conceal from myself that the controlling and pervading element in this great mass of human beings is devotion to that principle of self-government to which so many years of my life have been devoted; and rejoice more in considering it an approval of my support of a cardinal principle than I would if I could appropriate it to myself as a personal compliment.

Source: *Illinois State Register*, 19 July 1858

You but speak rightly when you assert that during the last session of Congress there was an attempt to violate one of the fundamental principles upon which our free institutions rest. The attempt to force the Lecompton constitution upon the people of Kansas against their will, would have been, if successful, subversive of the great fundamental principles upon which all our institutions rest. If there is any one principle more sacred and more vital to the existence of a free government than all others, it is the right of the people to form and ratify the constitution under which they are to live. It is the corner stone of the temple of liberty, it is the foundation upon which the whole structure rests, and whenever it can be successfully evaded self-government has received a vital stab. I deemed it my duty, as a citizen and as a representative of the state of Illinois, to resist, with all my energies and with whatever of abil ity I could command, the consummation of that effort to force a constitution upon an unwilling people. [*Applause.*]

I am aware that other questions have been connected, or attempted to be connected, with that great struggle, but they were mere collateral questions, not affecting the main point. My opposition to the Lecompton constitution rested solely upon the fact that it was not the act and deed of that people, and that it did not embody their will. I did not object to it upon the ground of the slavery clause contained in it. I should have resisted it with the same energy and determination even if it had been a free state instead of a slaveholding state; and as an evidence of this fact I wish you to bear in mind that my speech against that Lecompton act was made on the 9th day of December, nearly two weeks before the vote was taken on the acceptance or rejection of the slavery clause. I did not then know, I could not have known, whether the slavery clause would be accepted or rejected, the general impression was that it would be rejected, and in my speech I assumed that impression to be true; that probably it would be voted down; and then I said to the U.S. Senate, as I now proclaim to you, my constituents, that you have no more right to force a free state upon an unwilling people than you have to force a slave state upon them against their will. [*"That's so,"and cheers.*] You have no right to force either a good or a bad thing upon a people who do not choose to receive it. And then, again, the highest privilege of our people is to determine for themselves what kind of institutions are good and what kind of institutions are bad, and it may be true that the same people, situated in a different latitude and different climate, and with different productions and different interests, might decide the same question one way in the North and another way in the South, in order to adapt their institutions to the wants and wishes of the people to be affected by them.

You are all familiar with the Lecompton struggle, and I will occupy no more time upon the subject, except to remark that when we drove the enemies of the principle of popular sovereignty from the effort to force the Lecompton constitution upon the people of Kansas, and when we compelled them to abandon the attempt and to refer that constitution to that people for acceptance or rejection, we obtained a concession of the principle for which I had contended throughout the struggle. When I saw that the principle was conceded, and that the constitution was not to be forced on Kansas against the wishes of the people, I felt anxious to give the proposition my support; but, when I examined it, I found that the mode of reference to the people and the form of submission, upon which the vote was taken, was so objectionable as to make it unfair and unjust.

Sir, it is an axiom with me that in every free government an unfair election is no election at all. Every election should be free, should be fair, with the same privileges and the same inducements for a negative as for an affirmative vote. The objection to what is called the "English" proposition, by which the Lecompton constitution was referred back to the people of Kansas was this, that if the people chose to accept the Lecompton constitution they could come in with only 35,000 inhabitants, while if they determined to reject it in order to form another more in accordance with their wishes and sentiments. they were compelled to stay out until they should have 93,420 inhabitants. In other words, it was making a distinction and discrimination between free states and slave states under the federal constitution. I deny the justice, I deny the right, of any distinction or discrimination between the states North or South, free or slave. Equality among the states is a fundamental principle of this government. [*"Stand up to that," and cheers.*] Hence while I will never consent to the passage of a law that a slave state may come in with 35,000 while a free state shall not come in unless it have 93,000, on the other hand I shall not consent to admit a free state with a population of 35,000, and require 93,000 in a slaveholding state. [*"Good," and cheers.*]

My principle is to recognize each state of the Union as independent, sovereign and equal in its sovereignty. I will apply that principle not only to the original thirteen states, but to the states which have since been brought into the Union, and also to every state that shall hereafter be received, "as long as water shall run and grass grow." [*Cheers.*] For these reasons I felt compelled by a sense of duty, by a conviction of principle, to record my vote against what is called the English Bill; but yet the bill became a law, and under that law an election has been ordered to be held on the first Monday in August for the purpose of determining the question of the acceptance or rejection of the proposition submitted by Congress. I have no hesitation in saying to you, as the chairman of your committee has justly said in his address, that whatever the decision of the people of Kansas may be at that election, it must be final and conclusive of the whole subject; [*"that's it"*] for if at that election a majority of the people of Kansas shall vote for the acceptance of the congressional proposition, Kansas at that moment becomes a state of the Union, the law admitting her becomes irrepealable, and thus the controversy terminates forever; if, on the other hand, the people of Kansas shall vote down that proposition, as it is now generally admitted they will, by a large majority, then from that instant the Lecompton constitution is *dead*, dead beyond the power of resurrection, and thus the controversy terminates. [*Cheers.*] And when the monster shall die I shall be willing, and trust that all of you will be willing, to acquiesce in the death of the Lecompton constitution. [*Cheers.*] The controversy may now be considered as terminated, for in three weeks from now it will be finally settled, and all the ill feeling, all the embittered feeling which grew out of it shall cease, unless an attempt should be made in the future to repeat the same outrage upon popular rights. I need not tell you that my past course is a sufficient guarantee that if the occasion shall ever arise again whilst I occupy a seat in the United States Senate, you will find me carrying out the same principle, [*"good"*] that I have this winter, with all the energy and all the power I may be able to command. [*"We will stand by you,"* *"That's it "Good," &c.*] I have the gratification of saying to you that I do not believe that that controversy will ever arise again; first, because the fate of Lecompton is a *warning* to the people of every territory and of every state to be cautious how the example is repeated, [*"that's so," and laughter.*] and secondly, because the President of the United States, in his annual message has said that he trusts the example in the Minnesota case, wherein Congress passed a law, called an enabling act, requiring the constitution to be submitted to the people for acceptance or rejection, will be followed in all future cases. [*"That was right."*] I agree with you that it was right. I said so on the day after the message was delivered, in my speech in the Senate on the Lecompton constitution, and I have frequently in the debate tendered to the President and his friends, tendered to the Lecomptonites, my voluntary pledge that if he will stand by that recommendation, and they will stand by it, that they will find me working hand in hand with them in the effort to carry it out. [*Cheers.*] All we have to do, therefore, is to adhere firmly in the future, as we have done in the past, to the principle contained in the recommendation of the President in his annual message, that the example in the Minnesota case shall be carried out in all future cases of the admission of territories into the Union as states. [*"That's the doctrine."*] Let that be done and the principle of popular sovereignty will be maintained in all of its vigor and all of its integrity. I rejoice to know that Illinois stands prominently and proudly forward among the states which first took their position firmly and immovably upon this principle of popular sovereignty, applied to the territories as well as to the states. You all recollect when in 1850 the peace of the country was disturbed in consequence of the agitation of the slavery question, and the effort to force the Wilmot proviso upon all the territories, that it required all the talent and all the energy, all the wisdom, all the patriotism, of a Clay and a Webster, united with other great party leaders, to devise a system of measures by which peace and harmony could be restored to our distracted country. Those compromise measures eventually passed and were recorded on the statute book, not only as the settlement of the then existing difficulties but as furnishing a rule of action which should prevent in all future time the recurrence of like evils, if they were firmly and fairly carried out. Those compromise measures rested, as I said in my speech at Chicago, on my return home that year, upon the principle that every people ought to have the right to form and regulate their own domestic institutions in their own way, subject only to the Constitution. They were founded upon the principle that, while every state possessed that right under the Constitution, that the same right ought to be extended to and exercised by the people of the territories. [*"Good."*] When the Illinois legislature assembled, a few months after the adoption of these measures, the first thing the members did was to review their action upon this slavery agitation and to correct the errors into which their predecessors had fallen. You remember that their first act was to repeal the Wilmot proviso instructions to our U.S. Senators, which had been previously passed, and in lieu of them to record another resolution upon the journal, with which you must all be familiar—a resolution brought forward by Mr. Ninian Edwards, and adopted by the House of Representatives by a vote of 61 in the affirmative and 4 in the negative. That resolution I can quote to you in almost its precise language. It declared that the great principle of self-government was the birth right of freemen; was the gift of heaven, was achieved by the blood of our Revolutionary fathers and must be continued and carried out in the organization of all the territories and the admission of all new states. That became the Illinois platform by the united voices of the Democratic party and of the Whig party in 1851; all the Whigs and all the Democrats in the legislature uniting in an affirmative vote upon it and there being only 4 votes in the negative, of Abolitionists, of course, [*"of course"* *"They could not be anything else,"and laughter*]. That resolution stands upon the journal of your legislature to this day and hour unrepealed, and a standing, living, perpetual instruction to the Senators from Illinois in all time to come to carry out that principle of self-government and allow no limitation upon it in the organization of any territories or the admission of any new states. In 1854 when it became my duty as the chairman of the Committee on Territories to bring forward a bill for the organization of Kansas and Nebraska, I incorporated that principle in it and Congress passed it, thus carrying the principle into practical effect. I will not recur to the scenes which took place all over this country in 1854 when that Nebraska Bill passed. I could then travel from Boston to Chicago by the light of my own effigies, in consequence of having stood up for it. [*"It did not hurt you,"* *"Hurra for Douglas,"* *&c.*] I leave it to you to say how I met that storm, and whether I quailed under it; [*"never,"* *"no"*] whether I did not "face the music," justify the principle and no pledge my life to carry it out. [*"You did,"* *and three cheers.*] A friend here reminds me, too, that when making speeches then, justifying the Nebraska Bill and the great principle of self-government, that I predicted that in less than five years you would have to get out a search warrant to find an anti-Nebraska man. [*"That's so,"* *"good,"* *&c.*] Well, I believe I did make that prediction. I did not claim the power of a prophet, but it occurred to me that among a free people, and an honest people and an intelligent people, that five years was long enough for them to come to an understanding that the great principle of self-government was right, not only in the states, but in the territories. I rejoiced this year to see my prediction, in that respect, carried out and fulfilled, by the unanimous vote, in one form or another, of both Houses of Congress. If you will remember that pending this Lecompton controversy that gallant old Roman, Kentucky's favorite son, the worthy successor of the immortal Clay—I allude, as you know, to the gallant John J. Crittenden—[*cheers*] brought forward a bill, now known as the Crittenden–Montgomery Bill, in which it was proposed that the Lecompton constitution should be referred back to the people of Kansas, to be decided for or against it, at a fair election, and if a majority of the people were in favor of it, that Kansas should come into the Union as a slaveholding state, but that if a majority were against it that they should make a new constitution and come in with slavery or without it, as they thought proper. [*"That* *was right.*"] Yes, my dear sir, it was not only right, but it was carrying out the principle of the Nebraska Bill in its letter and in its spirit. Of course I voted for it, [*cheers,*] and so did every Republican Senator and Representative in Congress. [*Laughter.*] I have found some Democrats so perfectly straight that they blame me for voting for the principle of the Nebraska Bill because the Republicans voted the same way. [*Great laughter. "What did they say?"*]

What did they say? Why, many of them said that Douglas voted with the Republicans. Yes! not only that, but with the *Black* Republicans. [*Renewed laughter.*] Well, there are different modes of stating that proposition. The New York *Tribune* says that Douglas did not vote with the Republicans, but that on that question the Republicans went over to Douglas and voted with him. [*"Good," and cheers.*]

My friends, I have never yet abandoned a principle because of the support I found men yielding to it, and I shall never abandon my Democratic principles, merely because Republicans come to them. [*Great applause.*] For what do we travel over the country and make speeches in every political canvass, if it is not to enlighten the minds of these Republicans; [*"Good," great laughter and cheers,*] to remove the scales from their eyes, and to impart to them the light of Democratic vision, so that they may be able to carry out the constitution of our country as our fathers made it. [*"Good, good."*] And if by preaching our principles to the people we succeed in convincing the Republicans of the errors of their ways, and bring them over to us, are we bound to turn traitors to our principles, merely because they give them their support? [*"Never," and cheers.*] All I have to say is that I hope the Republican party will stand firm, in the future, by the vote they gave on the Crittenden–Montgomery Bill [*Cheers.*] I hope we will find, in the resolutions of their county and congressional conventions, no declarations of "no more slave states to be admitted into this Union," but in lieu of that declaration that we will find the principle that the people of every state and every territory shall come into the Union with slavery or without it, just as they please, without any interference on the part of Congress. [*"That's the doctrine."*]

My friends, whilst I was at Washington, engaged in this great battle for sound constitutional principles, I find from the newspapers that the Republican party of this state assembled in this capital, in state convention, and not only nominated, as it was wise and proper for them to do, a man for my successor in the Senate, but laid down a platform, and their nominee made a speech, carefully written and prepared, and well delivered, which that convention accepted as containing the Republican creed. I have no comment to make on that part of Mr. Lincoln's speech, in which he represents me as forming a conspiracy with the Supreme Court and with the late President of the United States and the present chief magistrate, having for my object the passage of the Nebraska Bill, the Dred Scott decision and the extension of slavery—a scheme of political tricksters, composed of Chief Justice Taney and his eight associates, two Presidents of the United States, and one Senator of Illinois. [*"Hit him again," cheers and great laughter.*] If Mr. Lincoln deems me a conspirator of that kind, all I have to say is that I do not think so badly of the President of the United States and the Supreme Court of the United States, the highest judicial tribunal on earth, as to believe that they were capable in their action and decision of entering into political intrigues for partisan purposes. [*Three cheers were here given for the Supreme Court of the United States.*] I therefore shall only notice those parts of Mr. Lincoln's speech, in which he lays down his platform of principles and tells you what he intends to do if he is elected to the Senate of the United States.

[*An old gentleman here rose on the platform and said. "Be particular now judge, be particular."*]

MR. DOUGLAS—My venerable friend here says that he will be gratified if I will be particular, and in order that I may be so I will read the language of Mr. Lincoln as reported by himself and published to the country. [*"Good, good."*] Mr. Lincoln lays down his main proposition in these words:

> "A house divided against itself cannot stand." I believe this Union cannot endure permanently half free and half slave. I do not expect the Union will be dissolved, I do not expect the house to fall, but I do expect it will cease to be divided. It will become all one thing or all the other. [*Laughter.*]

Mr. Lincoln does not think this Union can continue to exist composed of half slave and half free states; they must all be free or all slave. [*"That's Abolition doctrine."*] I do not doubt that this is Mr. Lincoln's conscientious conviction. [*"Nor I."*] I do not doubt that he thinks it is the highest duty of every patriotic citizen to preserve this glorious Union, and to adopt these measures as necessary to its preservation. He tells you that the only mode to preserve the Union is to make all the states free or all slave. [*"God forbid."*] It must be the one or it must be the other. Now that being essential, in his estimation, to the preservation of this glorious union, how is he going to accomplish it? He says that he wants to go to the Senate in order to carry out this favorite patriotic policy of his, of making all the states free, so that the house shall no longer be divided against itself. [*Great laughter.*] When he gets to the Senate by what means is he going to accomplish it? By an act of Congress. Will he contend that Congress has any power under the Constitution to abolish slavery in any state of this Union, or to interfere with, it directly or indirectly? Of course he will not contend that. [*"Hurra for Douglas."*] Then what is to be his mode of carrying out his principle, by which slavery shall be abolished in all the states? Mr. Lincoln certainly does not speak at random. He is a lawyer, an eminent lawyer, and his profession is to know the remedy for every wrong. What is his remedy for this imaginary wrong which he supposes to exist? The Constitution of the United States provides that it may be amended by Congress passing an amendment by a two-thirds majority of each House, which shall be ratified by three-fourths of the states, and the inference is that Mr. Lincoln intends to carry this slavery agitation into Congress with the view of amending the Constitution so that slavery can be abolished in all the states of the Union. In other words he is not going to allow one portion of the Union to be slave and another portion to be free; he is not going to permit the house to be divided against itself. [*"He can't help it."*] He is going to remedy it by lawful and constitutional means. What are to be these means? How can he abolish slavery in those states where it exists? There is but one mode by which a political organization, composed of men in the free states, can abolish slavery in the slaveholding states, and that would be to abolish the state legislatures, blot out of existence the state sovereignties, invest Congress with full and plenary power over all the local and domestic police regulations of the different states of this Union. Then there would be uniformity in the local concerns and domestic institutions of the different states; then the house would no longer be divided against itself; then the states would all be free, or they would all be slave, then you would have uniformity prevailing throughout this whole land in the local and domestic institutions, but it would be a uniformity not of liberty but a uniformity of despotism that would triumph. [*Three cheers.*] I submit to you, my fellow citizens, whether this is not the logical consequence of Mr. Lincoln's proposition. ["*Right.*"] I have called on Mr. Lincoln to explain what he did mean, if he did not mean this, and he has made a speech at Chicago, in which he attempts to explain. And how does he explain? I will give him the benefit of his own language, precisely as it was reported in the Republican papers of that city, after undergoing his revision. [*Laughter.*]

> I have said a hundred times, and have now no inclination to take it back, that I believe there is no right and ought to be no inclination in the people of the free states to enter into the slave sates and interfere with the question of slavery at all.

He believes there is no right on the part of the free people of the free states to enter the slave states and interfere with the question of slavery, hence he does not propose to go into Kentucky and stir up a civil war and a servile war between the blacks and the whites. All he proposes is to invite the people of Illinois and every other free state to band together as one sectional party, governed and divided by a geographical line, to make war upon the institution of slavery in the slaveholding states. He is going to carry it out by means of a political party, that has its adherents only in the free states; a political party, that does not pretend that it can give [get?] a solitary vote in the slave states of the Union, and by this sectional vote he is going to elect a President of the United States, form a cabinet and administer the government on sectional grounds, being the power of the North over that of the South. In other words, he invites a war of the North against the South, a warfare of the free states against the slaveholding states. He asks all men in the free states to conspire to exterminate slavery in the Southern states so as to make them all free, and then he notifies the South that unless they are going to submit to our efforts to exterminate their institutions, they must band together and plant slavery in Illinois and every Northern state. He says that the states must all be free or must all be slave. On this point I take issue with him directly. I assert that Illinois has a right to decide the slavery question for herself. We have decided it, and I think we have done it wisely, but whether wisely or unwisely it is our business, and the people of no other state have any right to interfere with us directly or indirectly. Claiming as we do this right for ourselves we must concede it to every other state to be exercised by them respectively. ["*That's the doctrine.*"]

Now, Mr. Lincoln says, that he will not enter into Kentucky to abolish slavery there, but that all he will do is to fight slavery in Kentucky from Illinois. [*Laughter.*]

437

He will not go over there to set fire to the match. I do not think he would. Mr. Lincoln is a very prudent man. [*Laughter.*] He would not deem it wise to go over into Kentucky to stir up this strife but he would do it from this side of the river. [*Great laughter and cheers.*] Permit me to inquire whether the wrong, the outrage of interference by one state with the local concerns of another is worse when you actually invade them than it would be if you carried on the warfare from another state. For the purpose of illustration, suppose the British government should plant a battery on the Niagara River opposite Buffalo and throw their shells over into Buffalo, where they should explode and blow up the houses and destroy the town. We call the British government to an account and they say, in the language of Mr. Lincoln, we did not enter into the limits of the United States to interfere with you, [*great laughter*] we planted the battery on our own soil and had a right to shoot from our own soil, and if our shells and balls fell in Buffalo and killed your inhabitants, why, it is your lookout, not ours. Thus, Mr. Lincoln is going to plant his Abolition batteries all along the banks of the Ohio River and throw his shells into Virginia and Kentucky and into Missouri, and blow up the institution of slavery, and when we arraign him for his unjust interference with the institutions of the other states, he says, "Why, I never did enter into Kentucky to interfere with her; I do not propose to do it, I only propose to take care of my own head by keeping on this side of the river, out of harm's way." [*Shouts of laughter and cheers.*] But yet, he says he is going to persevere in this system of sectional warfare, and I have no doubt he is sincere in what he says. [*Laughter.*] He says that the existence of the Union depends upon his success in firing into these slave states until he exterminates them. [*Renewed laughter.*] He says that unless he shall play his batteries successfully, so as to abolish slavery in every one of the states, that the Union shall be dissolved; [*Laughter*] and he says that a dissolution of the Union would be a terrible calamity. Of course it would. We are all friends of the Union. We all believe—I do—that our lives, our liberties, our hopes in the future depend upon the preservation and perpetuity of this glorious Union. I believe that the hopes of the friends of liberty throughout the world depend upon the perpetuity of the American Union. [*"Hear him,"* and intense enthusiasm.] But while I believe that my mode of preserving the Union is a very different one from that of Mr. Lincoln, I believe that the Union can only be preserved by maintaining inviolate the Constitution of the U.S. as our fathers have made it. [*"That's it,"* and cheers.] That Constitution guarantees to the people of every state the right to have slavery or not have it; to have negroes or not have them; to have Maine liquor laws or not have them; to have just such institutions as they choose, each state being left free to decide for itself. [*"That's right,"* and cheers.] The framers of that Constitution never conceived the idea that uniformity in the domestic institutions of the different states was either desirable or possible. They well understood that the laws and institutions which would be well adapted to the granite hills of New Hampshire would be unfit for the rice plantations of South Carolina; they well understood that each one of the thirteen states had distinct and separate interests, and required distinct and separate local laws and local institutions. [*"That's sound doctrine; hurrah for Douglas."*]

And in view of that fact they provided that each state should retain its sovereign power within its own limits, with the right to make just such laws and just such institutions as it saw proper, under the belief that no two of them would be alike. If they had supposed that uniformity was desirable and possible, why did they provide for a separate legislature for each state? Why did they not blot out state sovereignty and state legislatures, and give all the power to Congress, in order that the laws might be uniform? For the very reason that uniformity, in their opinion, was neither desirable or possible. We have increased from thirteen states to thirty-two states, and just in proportion as the number of states increases and our territory expands, there will be a still greater variety and dissimilarity of climate, of production, and of interest, requiring a corresponding dissimilarity and variety in the local laws and institutions adapted thereto. The laws that are necessary in the mining regions of California, would be totally useless and vicious on the prairies of Illinois; the laws that would suit the lumber regions of Maine or of Minnesota, would be totally useless and valueless in the tobacco regions of Virginia and Kentucky; the laws which would suit the manufacturing districts of New England, would be totally unsuited to the planting regions of the Carolinas, of Georgia and of Louisiana. Each state is supposed to have interests separate and distinct from each and every other, and hence must have laws different from each and every other state, in order that its laws shall be adapted to the condition and necessities of the people. ["*Hurrah for Douglas.*"] Hence I insist that our institutions rest on the theory that there shall be dissimilarity and variety in the local laws and institutions of the different states instead of all being uniform; and you find, my friends, that Mr. Lincoln and myself differ radically and totally on the fundamental principles of this government. He goes for consolidation, for uniformity in our local institutions, for blotting out state rights and state sovereignty, and consolidating all the power in the federal government, for converting these thirty-two sovereign states into one empire, and making uniformity throughout the length and breadth of the land. On the other hand, I go for maintaining the authority of the federal government within the limits marked out by the Constitution, and then for maintaining and preserving the sovereignty of each and all of the states of the Union, in order that each state may regulate and adopt its own local institutions in its own way, without interference from any power whatsoever. [*Cheers.*] Thus you find there is a distinct issue of principles—principles irreconcilable—between Mr. Lincoln and myself. He goes for consolidation and uniformity in our government. I go for maintaining the confederation of the sovereign states under the Constitution, as our fathers made it, leaving each state at liberty to manage its own affairs and own internal institutions.

Mr. Lincoln makes another point upon me, and rests his whole case upon these two points. His last point is, that he will wage a warfare upon the Supreme Court of the United States because of the Dred Scott decision. He takes occasion, in his speech made before the Republican convention, in my absence, to arraign me, not only for having expressed my acquiescence in that decision, but to charge me with being a conspirator with that court in devising that decision three years before Dred

Scott ever thought of commencing a suit for his freedom. [*Laughter.*] The object of his speech was to convey the idea to the people that the court could not be trusted, that the late President could not be trusted, that the present one could not be trusted, and that Mr. Douglas could not be trusted; that they were all conspirators in bringng about that corrupt decision, to which Mr. Lincoln is determined he will never yield a willing obedience.

He makes two points upon the Dred Scott decision. The first is that he objects to it because the court decided that negroes descended of slave parents are not citizens of the United States; and secondly, because they have decided that the act of Congress, passed 8th of March, 1820, prohibiting slavery in all of the territories north of 36°30', was unconstitutional and void, and hence did not have effect in emancipating a slave brought into that territory. And he will not submit to that decision. He says that he will not fight the judges or the United States marshals in order to liberate Dred Scott, but that he will not respect that decision, as a rule of law binding on this country, in the future. Why not? Because, he says, it is unjust. How is he going to remedy it? Why, he says he is going to reverse it. How? He is going to take an appeal. To whom is he going to appeal? [*Laughter.*] The Constitution of the United States provides that the Supreme Court is the ultimate tribunal, the highest judicial tribunal on earth, and Mr. Lincoln is going to appeal from that. To whom? I know he appealed to the Republican State Convention of Illinois, [*laughter,*] and I believe that convention reversed the decision, but I am not aware that they have yet carried it into effect. [*Renewed laughter.*] How are they going to make that reversal effectual? Why, Mr. Lincoln tells us in his late Chicago speech. He explains it as clear as light. He says to the people of Illinois that if you elect him to the Senate he will introduce a bill to re-enact the law which the court pronounced unconstitutional. [*Shouts of laughter, and voices, "spot the law."*] Yes, he is going to spot the law. The court pronounces that law, prohibiting slavery, unconstitutional and void, and Mr. Lincoln is going to pass an act reversing that decision and making it valid. I never heard before of an appeal being taken from the Supreme Court to the Congress of the United States to reverse its decision. I have heard of appeals being taken from Congress to the Supreme Court to declare a statute void. That has been done from the earliest days of Chief Justice Marshall, down to the present time.

The supreme court of Illinois do not hesitate to pronounce an act of the legislature void, as being repugnant to the constitution, and the Supreme Court of the United States is vested by the Constitution with that very power. The Constitution says that the judicial power of the United States shall be vested in the Supreme Court, and such inferior courts as Congress shall, from time to time ordain and establish. Hence it is the province and duty of the Supreme Court to pronounce judgment on the validity and constitutionality of an act of Congress. In this case they have done so, and Mr. Lincoln will not submit to it, and he is going to reverse it by another act of Congress of the same tenor. [*Laughter.*] My opinion is that Mr. Lincoln ought to be on the supreme bench himself, when the Republicans get into power, if that kind of law knowledge qualifies a man for the bench. But Mr.

Lincoln intimates that there is another mode by which he can reverse the Dred Scott decision. How is that? Why, he is going to appeal to the people to elect a President who will appoint judges who will reverse the Dred Scott decision. Well let us see how that is going to be done. First, he has to carry on his sectional organization, a party confined to the free states, making war upon the slaveholding states until he gets a Republican President elected. [*"He never will, sir,"* and great cheering.] I do not believe he ever will. [*"Bravo,"* and applause.] But suppose he should; when that Republican President shall have taken his seat—Mr. Seward, for instance—will he then proceed to appoint judges? No! he will have to wait until the present judges die before he can do that, and perhaps his four years would be out before a majority of these judges found it agreeable to die; [*laughter and cheers,*] and it is very possible, too, that Mr. Lincoln's senatorial term would expire before these judges would be accommodating enough to die. [*"That's right."*] If it should so happen I do not see a very great prospect for Mr. Lincoln to reverse the Dred Scott decision. But suppose they should die, then how are the new judges to be appointed? Why, the Republican President is to call up the candidates and catechise them, and ask them, "How will you decide this case if I appoint you judge?" [*Shouts of laughter.*] Suppose, for instance, Mr. Lincoln to be a candidate for a vacancy on the supreme bench to fill Chief Justice Taney's place, [*renewed laughter*] and when he applied to Seward, the latter would say, "Mr. Lincoln, I cannot appoint you until I know how you will decide the Dred Scott case." Mr. Lincoln tells him, and then [Seward] asks him how he will decide Tom Jones' case, and Bill Wilson's case, and thus catechises the judge as to how he will decide any case which may arise before him. Suppose you get a Supreme Court composed of such judges, who have been appointed by a partisan President upon their giving pledges how they would decide a case before it arise, what confidence would you have in such a court? [*"None, none."*] Would not your court be prostituted beneath the contempt of all mankind! What man would feel that his liberties were safe; his right of person or property was secure if the supreme bench, that august tribunal, the highest on earth, was brought down to that low, dirty pool wherein the judges are to give pledges in advance how they will decide all the questions which may be brought before them. [*"Hurra for Douglas."*] It is a proposition to make that court the corrupt, unscrupulous tool of a political party. But Mr. Lincoln cannot conscientiously submit, he thinks, to the decision of a court composed of a majority of Democrats. If he cannot, how can he expect us to have confidence in a court composed of a majority of Republicans, selected for the purpose of deciding against the Democracy, and in favor of the Republicans? [*Cheers.*] The very proposition carries with it the demoralization and degradation destructive of the judicial department of the federal government.

I say to you, fellow citizens, that I have no warfare to make upon the Supreme Court because of the Dred Scott decision. I have no complaints to make against that court, because of that decision. My private opinions on some points of the case may have been one way and on other points of the case another; in some things concurring with the court and in others dissenting, but what have my private opinions in a question of law to do with the decision after it has been pronounced by the highest judicial tribunal known to the Constitution? [*Cheers.*] You, sir, [*addressing the chairman*], as an eminent lawyer, have a right to entertain your opinions on any question that comes before the court and to appear before the tribunal and maintain them boldly and with tenacity until the final decision shall have been pronounced, and then, sir, whether you are sustained or overruled your duty as a lawyer and a citizen is to bow in deference to that decision. I intend to yield obedience to the highest tribunals in the land in all cases whether their opinions are in conformity with my views as a lawyer or not. When we refuse to abide by judicial decisions what protection is there left for life and property? To whom shall you appeal? To mob law, to partisan caucuses, to town meetings, to revolution? Where is the remedy when you refuse obedience to the constituted authorities? I will not stop to inquire whether I agree or disagree with all the opinions expressed by Judge Taney or any other judge. It is enough for me to know that the decision has been made. It has been made by a tribunal appointed by the Constitution to make it; it was a point within their jurisdiction, and I am bound by it. [*Cheers.*]

But, my friends, Mr. Lincoln says that this Dred Scott decision destroys the doctrine of popular sovereignty, for the reason that the court has decided that Congress had no power to prohibit slavery in the territories, and hence he infers that it would decide that the territorial legislatures could not prohibit slavery there. I will not stop to inquire whether the court will carry the decision that far or not. It would be interesting as a matter of theory, but of no importance in practice; for this reason, that if the people of a territory want slavery they will have it, ["*that's so,*"] and if they do not want it they will drive it out, and you cannot force it on them. ["*That's good," "That's the doctrine," and cheers.*] Slavery cannot exist a day in the midst of an unfriendly people with unfriendly laws. There is truth and wisdom in a remark made to me by an eminent Southern Senator, when speaking of this technical right to take slaves into the territories. Said he:

> I do not care a fig which way the decision shall be, for it is of no particular consequence; slavery cannot exist a day or an hour in any territory or state unless it has affirmiative laws sustaining and supporting it, furnishing police regulations and remedies, and an omission to furnish them would be as fatal as a constitutional prohibition. Without affirmative legislation in its favor slavery could not exist any longer than a new born infant could survive under the beat of the sun on a barren rock without protection. It would wilt and die for the want of support.

So it would be in the territories. See the illustration in Kansas. The Republicans have told you, during the whole history of that territory, down to last winter, that the pro-slavery party in the legislature had passed a pro-slavery code, establishing and sustaining slavery in Kansas, but that this pro-slavery legislature did not truly represent the people, but was imposed upon them by an invasion from Missouri, and hence the legislature were one way and the people another. Granting all this, and what has been the result? With laws supporting slavery, but the people against, there are not as many slaves in Kansas today as there were on the day the Nebraska Bill passed and the Missouri Compromise was repealed. [*Cheers.*] Why? Simply because slave owners knew that if they took their slaves into Kansas, where a majority of the people were opposed to slavery, that it would soon be abolished, and that they would lose their right of property in consequence of taking them there. For that reason they would not take or keep them there. If there had been a majority of the people in favor of slavery and the climate had been favorable, they would have taken them there, but the climate not being suitable, the interest of the people being opposed to it, and a majority of them against it, the slave owner did not find it profitable to take his slaves there, and consequently there are not as many slaves there today as on the day the Missouri Compromise was repealed. This shows clearly that if the people do not want slavery they will keep it out and that if they do want it they will protect it.

You have a good illustration of this in the territorial history of this state. You all remember that by the Ordinance of 1787 slavery was prohibited in Illinois, yet you all know, particularly you old settlers, who were here in territorial times, that the territorial legislature, in defiance of that ordinance, passed a law allowing you to go into Kentucky, buy slaves and bring them into the territory, having them sign indentures to serve you and your posterity 99 years, and their posterity thereafter to do the same. This hereditary slavery was introduced in defiance of the act of Congress. That was the exercise of popular sovereignty, the right of a territory to decide the question for itself in defiance of the act of Congress. On the other hand, if the people of a territory are hostile to slavery they will drive it out. Consequently this theoretical question raised upon the Dred Scott decision, is worthy of no consideration whatsoever, for it is only brought into these political discussions and used as a hobby upon which to ride into office, or out of which to manufacture political capital.

But Mr. Lincoln's main objection to the Dred Scott decision I have reserved for my conclusion. His principal objection to that decision is that it was intended to deprive the negro of the rights of citizenship in the different states of the Union. Well, suppose it was, and there is no doubt that that was its legal effect, what is his objection to it? Why, he thinks that a negro ought to be permitted to have the rights of citizenship. He is in favor of negro citizenship, and opposed to the Dred Scott decision, because it declares that a negro is not a citizen, and hence is not entitled to vote. Here I have a direct issue with Mr. Lincoln. I am not in favor of negro citizenship. [*"Nor I,"* responded the crowd,, *"Hurrah for Douglas,"* *"good, good,"&c.*] I do not believe that a negro is a citizen or ought to be a citizen. [*"Hurrah for Douglas."*] I believe that this government of ours was founded, and wisely founded, upon the white basis. [*"That's right,"* *"Hurrah,"* and *"Bravo,"* &c.] It was made by white men for the benefit of white men and their posterity, to be executed and managed by white men, [*"Glory to you,"* *"Hurrah for Douglas,"* and great applause]. I freely concede that humanity requires us to extend all the protection, all the privileges, all the immunities, to the Indian and the negro which they are capable of enjoying consistent with the safety of society. [*"That's right."*] You may then ask me what are those rights, what is the nature and extent of the rights which a negro ought to have. My answer is that this is a question for each state and each territory to decide for itself. ["*Good.*"] In Illinois we have decided that a negro is not a slave, but we have at the same tirne determined that he is not a citizen and shall not enjoy any political rights. ["*That's right.*"] I concur in the wisdom of that policy and am content with it. ["*Hurrah for Douglas.*"] I assert that the sovereignty of Illinois had a right to determine that question as we have decided it, and I deny that any other state has a right to interfere with us or call us to account for that decision. In the state of Maine they have decided by their constitution that the negro shall exercise the elective franchise and hold office on an equality with the white man. Whilst I do not concur in the good sense or correct taste of that decision on the part of Maine, I have no disposition to quarrel with her. It is her business and not ours. If the people of Maine desire to be put on an equality with the negro [*laughter*], I do not know that anybody in this state will attempt to prevent it. ["*Not at all.*"] If the white people of Maine think a negro their equal and that he has a right to come and kill their vote by a negro vote, they have a right to think so, I suppose, and I have no disposition to interfere with them. Then again, passing over to New York we find in that state they have provided that a negro may vote provided he holds $250 worth of property, but that he shall not unless he does; that is to say, they will allow a negro to vote if he is rich, but a poor fellow they will not allow to vote. In New York they think a rich negro is equal to a white man. Well, that is a matter of taste with them. [*Laughter.*] If they think so in that state and do not carry the doctrine outside of it and propose to interfere with us, I have no quarrel to make with them. It is their business. There is a great deal of philosophy and good sense in a saying of Fridley of Kane. Fridley had a law suit before a justice of the peace, and the justice decided it against him. This he did not like, and standing up and looking at the justice for a moment, "Well, Square," said he, "if a man chooses to make darnation fool of himself I suppose there is no law against it." [*Laughter.*] That is all I have to say about these negro regulations and this negro voting in other states where they have systems different from ours. If it is their wish to have it so, be it so. There is no cause to complain. Kentucky has decided that it is not consistent with her safety and her prosperity to allow a negro to have either political rights or his freedom, and hence she makes him a slave. That is her business, not mine. It is her right under the constitution of the country. The sovereignty of Kentucky, and that alone, can decide that question, and when she decides it there is no power on earth to which you can appeal to reverse it. ["*Hurrah for old Kaintuck.*"] Therefore, leave Kentucky as the Constitution has left her, a sovereign, independent state, with the exclusive right to have slavery or not, as she chooses, and so long as I hold power I will maintain and defend her right against any assaults from whatever quarter they may come. [*Cheers.*]

I will never stop to inquire whether I approve or disapprove of the domestic institutions of a state. I maintain her sovereign rights. I defend her sovereignty from all assault, in the hope that she will join in defending us when we are assailed by any outside power. ["*Good, good,*" *and cheers.*] How are we to protect our sovereign rights to keep slavery out, unless we protect the sovereign rights of every other state to decide the question for itself. Let Kentucky, or South Carolina, or any other state, attempt to intefere in Illinois and tell us that we shall establish slavery, in order to make it uniform, according to Mr. Lincoln's proposition, throughout the Union. [*Laughter.*] Let them come here and tell us that we must and shall have slavery, and I will call on you to follow me and shed the last drop of our heart's blood in repelling the invasion and chastising their insolence. [*Cheers.*] And if we would fight for our reserved rights and sovereign power in our own limits, we must respect the sovereignty of each other state. [*"That's the doctrine."*]

Hence, you find that Mr. Lincoln and myself come to a direct issue on this whole doctrine of slavery. He is going to wage a war against it everywhere, not only in Illinois but in his native state of Kentucky. And why? Because he says that the Declaration of Independence contains this language:

We hold these truths to be self-evident, that all men are created equal; that they are endowed by their Creator with certain inalienable rights; that among these are life, liberty and the pursuit of happiness,

and he asks whether that instrument does not declare that all men are created equal. [*"Not niggers."*] Mr. Lincoln then goes on to say that that clause of the Declaration of Independence includes negroes. [*"I say not."*] Well, if you say not I do not think you will vote for Mr. Lincoln. [*Laughter, and the same voice, "I'll be d—d if I do."*] Mr. Lincoln goes on to argue that the language "all men" included the negroes, Indians, and all inferior races.

In his Chicago speech he says in so many words that it includes the negroes, that they were endowed by the Almighty with the right of equality with the white man, and therefore that that right is divine—a right under the higher law; that the law of God makes them equal to the white man, and therefore that the law of the white man cannot deprive them of that right. This is Mr. Lincoln's argument. He is conscientious in his belief. I do not question his sincerity, I do not doubt that he, in his conscience, believes that the Almighty made the negro equal to the white man. He thinks that the negro is his brother. [*Laughter.*] I do not think that the negro is any kin of mine at all. [*Laughter and cheers.*] And here is the difference between us. I believe that the Declaration of Independence, in the words "all men are created equal," was intended to allude only to the people of the United States, to men of European birth or descent, being white men, that they were created equal, and hence that Great Britain had no right to deprive them of their political and religious priviliges; but the signers of that paper did not intend to include the Indian or the negro in that declaration, [*"never,"* &c.] for if they had would they not have been bound to abolish slavery in every state and colony from that day? [*"Certainly,"* and cheers.] Remember, too, that at the time the Declaration was put forth every one of the thirteen colonies were slave-holding colonies; every man who signed the Declaration represented slaveholding constituents. [*"Hurrah for Douglas."*] Did those signers mean by that act to charge themselves and all their constituents with having violated the law of God, in holding the negro in an inferior condition to the white man? [*"No, certainly not."*] And yet, if they included negroes in that term they were bound, as conscientious men, that day and that hour, not only to have abolished slavery throughout the land, but to have conferred political rights and privileges on the negro, and elevated him to an equality with the white man. [*"They did not do it."*] I know they did not do it, and the very fact that they did not shows that they did not understand the language they used to include any but the white race. Did they mean to say that the Indian, on this continent, was created equal to the white man, and that he was endowed by the Almighty with inalienable rights—rights so sacred that they could not be taken away by any constitution or law that man could pass? Why, their whole action towards the Indian showed that they never dreamed that they were bound to put him on an equality. I am not only opposed to negro equality, but I am opposed to Indian equality. I am opposed to putting the coolies, now importing into this country, on an equality with us, or putting the Chinese or any other inferior race on an equality with us. I hold that the white race, the European race, I care not whether Irish, German, French, Scotch, English, or to what nation they belong, so they are the white race to be our equals, [*"Good, that's the doctrine,"* and cheers,] and I am for placing them, as our fathers did, on an equality with us. [*Cheers.*] Emigrants from Europe and their descendants constitute the people of the U.S. [*Renewed applause.*] The Declaration of Independence only included the white people of the U.S. [*"Not the negro."*] The Constitution of the U.S. was framed by the white people, it ought to be administered by them, leaving each state to make such regulations concerning the negro as it chooses, allowing him political rights or not as it chooses, and allowing him civil rights or not as it may determine for itself. Let us only carry out those principles, and we will have peace and harmony in the different states. But Mr. Lincoln's conscientious scruples on this point govern his action and I honor him for following them, although I abhor the doctrine which he preaches. [*Laughter.*] His conscientious scruples lead him to believe that the negro is entitled by divine right to the civil and political privileges of citizenship on an equality with the white man. [*"Hurra for Douglas."*]

For that reason he says he wishes the Dred Scott decision reversed. He wishes to confer those priviliges of citizenship on the negro. Let us see how he will do it. He will first be called upon to strike out of the constitution of Illinois that clause which prohibits free negroes and slaves from Kentucky or any other state coming into Illinois. When he blots out that clause, when he lets down the door or opens the gate for all the negro population to flow in and cover our prairies in mid-day they will look dark and black as night [*laughter*], when we shall have done this, his mission will yet be unfulfilled. Then it will be that he will apply his principles of negro equality, that is if he can get the Dred Scott decision reversed in the meantime. He will then change the constitution again, and allow negroes to vote and hold office, and will make them eligible to the legislature so that thereafter they can have the right men for U.S. Senators. [*Laughter.*] He will allow them to vote to elect the legislature, the judges and the governor, and will make them eligible to the office of judge or governor, or to the legislature. He will put them on an equality with the white man. What then? Of course, after making them eligible to the judiciary, when he gets Cuffee elevated to the bench, he certainly will not refuse his judge the privilege of marrying any woman he may select! I submit to you whether these are not the legitimate consequences of his doctrine. [*"Certainly."*] If it be true, as he says, that by the Declaration of Independence and by divine law, the negro is created the equal of the white man; if it be true that the Dred Scott decision is unjust and wrong, because it deprives the negro of citizenship and equality with the white man, then does it not follow that if he had the power he would make negroes citizens, and give them all the rights and privileges of citizenship on an equality with white men? I think that is the inevitable conclusion. I do not doubt Mr. Lincoln's conscientious conviction on the subject, and I do not doubt that he will carry out that doctrine if he ever has the power; but I resist it because I am utterly opposed to any political amalgamation or any other amalgamation on this continent. We are witnessing the result of giving civil and political rights to inferior races in Mexico, in Central America, in South America, and in the West India Islands. Those young men who went from here to Mexico to fight the battles of their country in the Mexican war, can tell you the fruits of negro equality with the white man. They will tell you that the result of that equality is social amalgamation, demoralization and degradation, below the capacity for self-government.

My friends, if we wish to preserve this government we must maintain it on the basis on which it was established, to wit: the white basis. We must preserve the purity of the race not only in our politics but in our domestic relations. We must then preserve the sovereignty of the states, and we must maintain the federal Union by preserving the federal constitution inviolate. Let us do that and our Union will not only be perpetual but may extend until it shall spread over the entire continent.

Fellow-citizens—I have already detained you too long. ["Go on, go on, do not stop yet."] I have exhausted myself and wearied you, and owe you an apology for the desultory manner in which I have discussed these topics. I will have an opportunity of addressing you again before the November election comes off. ["You will be welcome," &c.] I come to you to appeal to your judgment as American citizens, to take your verdict of approval or disapproval upon the discharge of my public duty and my principles as compared with those of Mr. Lincoln. ["We'll return you," and cheers.] If you conscientiously believe that his principles are more in harmony ["we do not"] with the feelings of the American people and the interests and honor of the Republic, elect him. ["We'll not do it, never, never."] If, on the contrary, you believe that my principles are more consistent with those great principles upon which our fathers framed this government, then I shall ask you to so express your opinion at the polls. ["Hurrah for Douglas, we will do it," &c.] I am aware that it is a bitter and severe contest, but I do not doubt what the decision of the people of Illinois will be. ["We do not doubt it. It will be for you."] I do not anticipate any personal collision between Mr. Lincoln and myself. You all know that I am an amiable, good-natured man, ["Hurrah for Douglas"] and I take great pleasure in bearing testimony to the fact that Mr. Lincoln is a kind-hearted, amiable, good-natured gentleman, with whom no man has a right to pick a quarrel, even if he wanted one. He is a worthy gentleman. I have known him for twenty-five years, and there is no better citizen, no kinder hearted man. He is a fine lawyer, possesses high ability and there is no objection to him, except the monstrous revolutionary doctrines with which he is identified and which he conscientiously entertains, and is determined to carry out if he gets the power. [*"He never shall, &c.*]

He has one element of strength upon which he relies to accomplish his object, and that is his alliance with certain men in this state claiming to be Democrats, whose avowed object is to use their power to prostrate the Democratic nominees. [*"Hurrah for Douglas; they can't do it,"&c.*] He hopes he can secure the few men claiming to be friends of the Lecompton constitution, and for that reason you will find he does not say a word against the Lecompton constitution or its supporters. He is as silent as the grave upon that subject. Behold Mr. Lincoln courting Lecompton votes, in order that he may go to the Senate as the representative of Republican principles! [*Laughter.*] You know that that alliance exists. I think you will find that it will ooze out before the contest is over. [*"That's my opinion," and cheers.*] It must be a contest of principle.— Either the radical Abolition principles of Mr. Lincoln must be maintained, or the strong, constitutional, national Democratic principles with which I am identified must be carried out. I shall be satisfied whatever way you decide. I have been sustained by the people of Illinois with a steadiness, a firmness and an enthusiasm which makes my heart overflow with gratitude. If I was now to be consigned to private life, I would have nothing to complain of. I would even then owe you a debt of gratitude which the balance of my life could not repay. But, my friends, you have discharged every obligation you owe to me. I have been a thousand times paid by the welcome you have extended to me since I have entered the state on my return home this time. Your reception not only discharges all obligations, but it furnishes inducement to renewed efforts to serve you in the future. If you think Mr. Lincoln will do more to advance the interests and elevate the character of Illinois than myself, it is your duty to elect him; if you think he would do more to preserve the peace of the country and perpetuate the Union than myself, then elect him. [*"No," "no," "never."*] I leave the question in your hands and again tender you my profound thanks for the cordial and heartfelt welcome tendered to me this evening.

⚜-33-⚜

Speech at Springfield
17th July 1858

ABRAHAM LINCOLN

As part of the 1858 election campaign which Abraham Lincoln contested with Stephen Douglas for a seat in the United States Senate, a series of seven debates was staged betwen the two candidates. These debates, which entered into the grand tradition of American political oratory, focused on the issue which divided the two men: that of slavery. Lincoln's reply to Douglas at Springfield, Illinois on 17th July 1858 is a good summary of the position he took throughout the debates. Although he lost this election against the incumbent, Douglas, Lincoln would use this experience as a springboard into his successful presidential campaign two years later.

Fellow Citizens:

Another election, which is deemed an important one, is approaching, and, as I suppose, the Republican party will, without much difficulty elect their state ticket. But in regard to the legislature, we, the Republicans, labor under some disadvantages. In the first place, we have a legislature to elect upon an apportionment of the representation made several years ago, when the proportion of the population was far greater in the south (as compared with the north) than it now is; and inasmuch as our opponents hold almost entire sway in the south, and we a correspondingly large majority in the north, the fact that we are now to be represented as we were years ago, when the population was different, is to us a very great disadvantage. We had, in the year 1855, according to law, a census or enumeration of the inhabitants, taken for the purpose of a new apportionment of representation. We know what a fair apportionment of representation upon that census would give us. We know that it could not if fairly made, fail to give the Republican party from six to ten more members of the legislature than they can

Source: Abraham Lincoln, Speech at Springfield, 17th July 1858 and printed in *Illinois State Journal*, 20-21st July 1858

probably get as the law now stands. It so happened at the last session of the legislature, that our opponents, holding the control of both branches of the legislature, steadily refused to give us such an apportionment as we were rightfully entitled to have upon the census already taken. [*A rocket goes up near the window.*] I expect that we shall have as much of that as we can conveniently get along with. I was saying that the legislature steadily refused to give us such an apportionment as we were rightfully entitled to have upon the census taken of the population of the state. The legislature would pass no bill upon that subject, except such as was at least as unfair to us as the old one, and in which in some instances, two men in the Democratic regions were allowed to go as far towards sending a member of the legislature as three were in the Republican regions. Comparison was made at the time as to representative and senatorial districts, which completely demonstrated that such was the fact. Such a bill was passed, and tendered to the Republican Governor for his signature; but principally for the reasons I have stated, he withheld his approval, and the bill fell without becoming a law.

Another disadvantage under which we labor is, that there are one or two Democratic Senators who will be members of the next legislature, and will vote for the election of Senator, who are holding over in districts in which we could, on all reasonable calculation, elect men of our own, if we only had the chance of an election. When we consider that there are but twenty-five Senators in the Senate, taking two from the side where they rightfully belong and adding them to the other, is to us a disadvantage not to be lightly regarded. Still, so it is; we have this to contend with. Perhaps there is no ground of complaint on our part. In attending to the many things involved in the last general election for President, Governor, Auditor, Treasurer, Superintendent of Public Instruction, Members of Congress, of the legislature, county officers, and so on, we allowed these things to happen by want of sufficient attention, and we have no cause to complain of our adversaries, so far as this matter is concerned. But we have some cause to complain of the refusal to give us a fair apportionment.

There is still another disadvantage under which we labor, and to which I will ask your attention. It arises out of the relative positions of the two persons who stand before the state as candidates for the Senate. Senator Douglas is of world wide renown. All the anxious politicians of his party, or who have been of his party for years past, have been looking upon him as certainly, at no distant day, to be the President of the United States. They have seen in his round, jolly, fruitful face, postoffices, landoffices, marshalships, and cabinet appointments, chargeships and foreign missions, bursting and sprouting out in wonderful exuberance ready to be laid hold of by their greedy hands. [*Great laughter.*] And as they have been gazing upon this attractive picture so long, they cannot, in the little distraction that has taken place in the party, bring themselves to give up the charming hope; but with greedier anxiety they rush about him, sustain him, and give him marches, triumphal entries, and receptions beyond what even in the days of his highest prosperity they could have brought about in his favor. On the contrary nobody has ever expected me to be President. In my poor, lean, lank, face, nobody has ever seen that any cabbages were sprouting out. [*Tremendous cheering and laughter.*] These are disadvantages all, taken together, that the Republicans labor under. We have to fight this battle upon principle, and upon principle alone. I am, in a certain sense, made the standard-bearer in behalf of the Republicans. I was made so merely because there had to be some one so placed—I being in no wise, preferable to any other one of the twenty-five—perhaps a hundred we have in the Republican ranks. Then I say I wish it to be distinctly understood and borne in mind, that we have to fight this battle without many—perhaps without any—of the external aids which are brought to bear against us. So I hope those with whom I am surrounded have principle enough to nerve themselves for the task and leave nothing undone, that can be fairly done, to bring about the right result.

After Senator Douglas left Washington, as his movements were made known by the public prints, he tarried a considerable time in the city of New York; and it was heralded that, like another Napoleon, he was lying by, and framing the plan of his campaign. It was telegraphed to Washington City, and published in the *Union*, that he was framing his plan for the purpose of going to Illinois to pounce upon and annihilate the treasonable and disunion speech which Lincoln had made here on the 16th of June. Now, I do suppose that the Judge really spent some time in New York maturing the plan of the campaign, as his friends heralded for him. I have been able, by noting his movements since his arrival in Illinois, to discover evidences confirmatory of that allegation. I think I have been able to see what are the material points of that plan. I will, for a little while, ask your attention to some of them. What I shall point out, though not showing the whole plan, are, nevertheless, the main points, as I suppose.

They are not very numerous. The first is popular sovereignty. The second and third are attacks upon my speech made on the 16th of June. Out of these three points—drawing within the range of popular sovereignty the question of the Lecompton constitution—he makes his principal assault. Upon these his successive speeches are substantially one and the same. On this matter of popular sovereignty I wish to be a little careful. Auxiliary to these main points, to be sure, are their thunderings of cannon, their marching and music, their fizzlegigs and fireworks; but I will not waste time with them. They are but the little trappings of the campaign.

Coming to the substance—the first point—"Popular Sovereignty." It is to be labelled upon the cars in which he travels; put upon the hacks he rides in; to be flaunted upon the arches he passes under, and the banners which wave over him. It is to be dished up in as many varieties as a French cook can produce soups from potatoes. Now, as this is so great a staple of the plan of the campaign, it is worth while to examine it carefully; and if we examine only a very little, and do not allow ourselves to be misled, we shall be able to see that the whole thing is the most arrant quixotism that was ever enacted before a community. What is the matter of popular sovereignty? The first thing, in order to understand it, is to get a good definition of what it is, and after that to see how it is applied.

I suppose almost every one knows, that in this controversy, whatever has been said, has had reference to the question of negro slavery. We have not been in a controversy about the right of the people to govern themselves in the *ordinary* matters of domestic concern in the states and territories. Mr. Buchanan in one of his late messages, (I think when he sent up the Lecompton constitution,) urged that the main points to which the public attention had been directed, was not in regard to the great variety of small domestic matters, but was directed to the question of negro slavery; and he asserts, that if the people had had a fair chance to vote on that question, there was no reasonable ground of objection in regard to minor questions. Now, while I think that the people had *not* had given, or offered them, a fair chance upon that slavery question; still, if there had been a fair submission to a vote upon that main question, the President's proposition would have been true to the uttermost. Hence, when hereafter, I speak of popular sovereignty, I wish to be understood as applying what I say to the question of slavery only, not to other minor domestic matters of a territory or a state.

Does Judge Douglas, when he says that several of the past years of his life have been devoted to the question of "popular sovereignty," and that all the remainder of his life shall be devoted to it, does he mean to say that he has been devoting his life to securing to the people of the territories the right to exclude slavery from the territories? If he means so to say, he means to deceive; because he and every one knows that the decision of the Supreme Court, which he approves and makes especial ground of attack upon me for disapproving, forbids the people of a territory to exclude slavery. This covers the whole ground, from the settlement of a territory till it reaches the degree of maturity entitling it to form a state constitution. So far as all that ground is concerned, the Judge is not sustaining popular sovereignty, but absolutely opposing it. He sustains the decision which declares that the popular will of the territories has no constitutional power to exclude slavery during their territorial existence. [*Cheers.*] This being so, the period of time from the first settlement of a territory till it reaches the point of forming a state constitution, is not the thing that the Judge has fought for or is fighting for, but on the contrary, he has fought for, and is fighting for, the thing that annihilates and crushes out that same popular sovereignty,

Well, so much being disposed of, what is left? Why, he is contending for the right of the people, when they come to make a state constitution, to make it for themselves, and precisely as best suits themselves. I say again, that is quixotic. I defy contradiction when I declare that the Judge can find no one to oppose him on that proposition. I repeat, there is nobody opposing that proposition on *principle*. Let me not be misunderstood. I know that, with reference to the Lecompton constitution, I may be misunderstood; but when you understand me correctly, my proposition will be true and accurate. Nobody is opposing, or has opposed, the right of the people, when they form a constitution, to form it for themselves. Mr. Buchanan and his friends have not done it; they, too, as well as the Republicans and the anti-Lecompton Democrats, have not done it; but, on the contrary, they together have insisted on the right of the people to form a constitution for themselves. The difference between the Buchanan men on the one hand, and the

Douglas men and the Republicans on the other, has not been on a question of principle, but on a question of *fact*.

The dispute was upon the question of fact, whether the Lecompton constitution had been fairly formed by the people or not. Mr. Buchanan and his friends have not contended for the contrary principle any more than the Douglas men or the Republicans. They have insisted that whatever of small irregularities existed in getting up the Lecompton constitution, were such as happen in the settlement of all new territories. The question was, was it a fair emanation of the people? It was a question of fact, and not of principle. As to the principle, all were agreed. Judge Douglas voted with the Republicans upon that matter of fact.

He and they, by their voices and votes, denied that it was a fair emanation of the people. The administration affirmed that it was. With respect to the evidence bearing upon that question of fact, I readily agree that Judge Douglas and the Republicans had the right on their side, and that the administration was wrong. But I state again that as a matter of principle there is no dispute upon the light of a people in a territory, merging into a state to form a constitution for themselves without outside interference from any quarter. This being so, what is Judge Douglas going to spend his life for? Is he going to spend his life in maintaining a principle that nobody on earth opposes? [*Cheers.*] Does he expect to stand up in majestic dignity, and go through his *apotheosis* and become a god, in the maintaining of a principle which neither a man nor a mouse in all God's creation is opposing? [*Tremendous cheering.*] Now something in regard to the Lecompton constitution more specially; for I pass from this other question of popular sovereignty as the most errant humbug that has ever been attempted on an intelligent community.

As to the Lecompton constitution, I have already said that on the question of fact as to whether it was a fair emanation of the people or not, Judge Douglas with the Republicans and some Americans had greatly the argument against the administration; and while I repeat this, I wish to know what there is in the opposition of Judge Douglas to the Lecompton constitution that entitles him to be considered the only opponent to it—as being *par excellence* the very *quintessence* of that opposition. I agree to the rightfulness of his opposition. He in the Senate and his class of men there formed the number *three* and no more. In the House of Representatives his class of men—the anti-Lecompton Democrats—formed a number of about twenty. It took one hundred and twenty to defeat the measure against one hundred and twelve. Of the votes of that one hundred and twenty, Judge Douglas' friends furnished twenty, to add to which, there were six Americans and ninety-four Republicans. I do not say that I am precisely accurate in their numbers, but I am sufficiently so for any use I am making of it.

Why is it that twenty shall be entitled to all the credit of doing that work, and the hundred none of it? Why, if, as Judge Douglas says, the honor is to be divided and due credit is to be given to other parties, why is just so much given as is consonant with the wishes, the interests and advancement of the twenty? My understanding is, when a common job is done, or a common enterprise prosecuted, if I put in five dollars to your one, I have a right to take out five dollars to your one. But he does not so understand it. He declares the dividend of credit for defeating Lecompton upon a basis which seems unprecedented and incomprehensible.

Let us see. Lecompton in the raw was defeated. It afterwards took a sort of cooked up shape, and was passed in the English Bill. It is said by the Judge that the defeat was a good and proper thing. If it was a good thing, why is he entitled to more credit than others, for the performance of that good act, unless there was something in the antecedents of the Republicans that might induce every one to expect them to join in that good work, and at the same time, something leading them to doubt that he would? Does he place his superior claim to credit, on the ground that he performed a good act which was never expected of him? He says I have a proneness for quoting scripture. If I should do so now, it occurs that perhaps he places himself somewhat upon the ground of the parable of the lost sheep which went astray upon the mountains, and when the owner of the hundred sheep found the one that was lost, and threw it upon his shoulders, and came home rejoicing, it was said that there was more rejoicing over the one sheep that was lost and had been found, than over the ninety and nine in the fold. [*Great cheering, renewed cheering.*] The application is made by the Saviour in this parable, thus, "Verily, I say unto you, there is more rejoicing in heaven over one sinner that repenteth, than over ninety and nine just persons that need no repentance." [*Cheering.*]

And now, if the Judge claims the benefit of this parable, *let him repent.* [*Vociferous applause.*] Let him not come up here and say: I am the only just person; and you are the ninety-nine sinners! *Repentance*, before *forgiveness* is a provision of the Christian system, and on that condition alone will the Republicans grant his forgiveness. [*Laughter and cheers.*]

How will he prove that we have ever occupied a different position in regard to the Lecompton constitution or any principle in it? He says he did not make his opposition on the ground as to whether it was a free or slave constitution, and he would have you understand that the Republicans made the opposition because it ultimately became a slave constitution. To make proof in favor of himself on this point, he reminds us that he opposed Lecompton before the vote was taken declaring whether the state was to be free or slave. But he forgets to say that our Republican Senator Trumbull, made a speech against Lecompton, even before he did.

Why did he oppose it? Partly, as he declares, because the members of the convention who framed it were not fairly elected by the people; that the people were not allowed to vote unless they had been registered; and that the people of whole counties, in some instances, were not registered. For these reasons he declares the constitution was not an emanation, in any true sense, from the people. He also has an additional objection as to the mode of submitting the constitution back to the people. But bearing on the question of whether the delegates were fairly elected, a speech of his, made something more than twelve months ago, from this stand, becomes important. It was made a little while before the election of the delegates who made Lecompton. In that speech he declared there was every reason to hope and believe the election would be fair; and if any one failed to vote, it would be his own culpable fault.

I, a few days after, made a sort of answer to that speech. In that answer, I made, substantially, the very argument with which he combatted his Lecompton adversaries in the Senate last winter. I pointed to the facts that the people could not vote without being registered, and that the time for registering had gone by. I commented on it as wonderful that Judge Douglas could be ignorant of these facts, which every one else in the nation so well knew.

I now pass from popular sovereignty and Lecompton. I may have occasion to refer to one or both.

When he was preparing his plan of campaign, Napoleon like, in New York, as appears by two speeches I have heard him deliver since his arrival in Illinois, he gave special attention to a speech of mine, delivered here on the 16th of June last. He says that he carefully read that speech. He told us that at Chicago a week ago last night, and he repeated it at Bloomington last night. Doubtless, he repeated it again to-day, though I did not hear him. In the two first places—Chicago and Bloomington—I heard him; to-day I did not. [A voice—"Yes; he said the same thing."] He said he had carefully examined that speech; when, he did not say; but there is no reasonable doubt it was when he was in New York preparing his plan of campaign. I am glad he did read it carefully. He says it was evidently prepared with great care. I freely admit it was prepared with care. I claim not to be more free from errors than others—perhaps scarcely so much; but I was very careful not to put anything in that speech as a matter of fact, or make any inferences which did not appear to me to be true, and fully warrantable. If I had made any mistake I was willing to be corrected; if I had drawn any inference in regard to Judge Douglas, or any one else, which was not warranted, I was fully prepared to modify it as soon as discovered. I planted myself upon the truth, and the truth only, so far as I knew it, or could be brought to know it.

Having made that speech with the most kindly feeling towards Judge Douglas, as manifested therein, I was gratified when I found that he had carefully examined it, and had detected no error of fact, nor any inference against him, nor any misrepresentations, of which he thought fit to complain. In neither of the two speeches I have mentioned, did he make any such complaint. I will thank any one who will inform me that he, in his speech to day, pointed out anything I had stated, respecting him, as being erroneous. I presume there is no such thing. I have reason to be gratified that the care and caution used in that speech, left it so that he, most of all others interested in discovering error, has not been able to point out one thing against him which he could say was wrong. He seizes upon the doctrines he supposes to be included in that speech, and declares that upon them will turn the issues of this campaign. He then quotes, or attempts to quote, from my speech. I will not say that he willfully misquotes, but he does fail to quote accurately. His attempt at quoting is from a passage which I believe I can quote accurately from memory. I shall make the quotation now, with some comments upon it, as I have already said, in order that the Judge shall be left entirely without excuse for misrepresenting me. I do so now, as I hope, for the last time. I do this in great caution, in order that if he repeats his misrepresentation, it shall be plain to all that he does so willfully. If, after all, he still persists, I shall be compelled to reconstruct the course I have marked out for myself, and draw upon such humble resources as I have, for a new course, better suited to the real exigencies of the case. I set out in this campaign, with the intention of conducting it strictly as a gentleman, in substance at least, if not in the outside polish. The latter I shall never be, but that which constitutes the inside of a gentleman I hope I understand, and am not less inclined to practice than others. [*Cheers.*] It was my purpose and expectation that this canvass would be conducted upon principle, and with fairness on both sides; and it shall not be my fault, if this purpose and expectation shall be given up.

He charges, in substance, that I invite a war of sections; that I propose all the local institutions of the different states shall become consolidated and uniform. What is there in the language of that speech which expresses such purpose, or bears such construction? I have again and again said that I would not enter into any of the states to disturb the institution of slavery. Judge Douglas said, at Bloomington, that I used language most able and ingenious for concealing what I really meant; and that while I had protested against entering into the slave states, I nevertheless did mean to go on the banks of [the] Ohio and throw missiles into Kentucky to disturb them in their domestic institutions.

I said, in that speech, and I meant no more, that the institution of slavery ought to be placed in the very attitude where the framers of this government placed it, and left it. I do not understand that the framers of our Constitution left the people of the free states in the attitude of firing bombs or shells into the slave states. I was not using that passage for the purpose for which he infers I did use it. I said: "We are now far advanced into the fifth year since a policy was created for the avowed object and with the confident promise of putting an end to slavery agitation. Under the operation of that policy that agitation has not only not ceased, but has constantly augmented. In my opinion it will not cease till a crisis shall have been reached and passed. 'A house divided against itself can not stand.' I believe that this government cannot endure permanently half slave and half free. It will become all one thing or all the other. Either the opponents of slavery will arrest the further spread of it, and place it where the public mind shall rest in the belief that it is in the course of ultimate extinction, or its advocates will push it forward till it shall become alike lawful in all the states, old as well as new, North as well as South."

Now you all see, from that quotation, I did not express my *wish* on anything. In that passage I indicated no wish or purpose of my own; I simply expressed my *expectation*. Cannot the Judge perceive the distinction between a *purpose* and an *expectation*? I have often expressed an expectation to die, but I have never expressed a *wish* to die. I said at Chicago, and now repeat, that I am quite aware this government has endured, half slave and half free, for eighty-two years. I understand that little bit of history. I expressed the opinion I did, because I perceived—or thought I perceived—a new set of causes introduced. I did say, at Chicago, in my speech there, that I do wish to see the spread of slavery arrested and to see it placed where the public mind shall rest in the belief that it is in course of ultimate extinction. I said that because I supposed, when the public mind shall rest in that belief, we shall have peace on the slavery question. I have believed—and now believe—the public mind did rest in that belief up to the introduction of the Nebraska Bill.

Although I have ever been opposed to slavery, so far I rested in the hope and belief that it was in course of ultimate extinction. For that reason, it had been a minor question with me. I might have been mistaken; but I had believed, and now believe, that the whole public mind, that is the mind of the great majority, had rested in that belief up to the repeal of the Missouri Compromise. But upon that event, I became convinced that either I had been resting in a delusion, or the institution was being placed on a new basis—a basis for making it perpetual, national and universal. Subsequent events have greatly confirmed me in that belief. I believe that bill to be the beginning of a conspiracy for that purpose. So believing, I have since then considered that question a paramount one. So believing, I have thought the public mind will never rest till the power of Congress to restrict the spread of it, shall again be acknowledged and exercised on the one hand, or on the other, all resistance be entirely crushed out. I have expressed that opinion, and I entertain it to-night. It is denied that there is any tendency to the nationalization of slavery in these states.

Mr. Brooks, of South Carolina, in one of his speeches, when they were presenting him with canes, silver plate, gold pitchers and the like, for assaulting Senator Sumner, distinctly affirmed his opinion that when this Constitution was formed, it was the belief of no man that slavery would last to the present day.

He said, what I think, that the framers of our Constitution placed the institution of slavery where the public mind rested in the hope that it was in course of ultimate extinction. But he went on to say that the men of the present age, by their experience, have become wiser than the framers of the Constitution; and the invention of the cotton gin has made the perpetuity of slavery a necessity in this country.

As another piece of evidence tending to the same point:—Quite recently in Virginia, a man—the owner of slaves—made a will providing that after his death certain of his slaves should have their freedom if they should so choose, and go to Liberia, rather than remain in slavery. They chose to be liberated. But the persons to whom they would descend as property, claimed them as slaves. A suit was instituted, which finally came to the Supreme Court of Virginia, and was therein decided against the slaves, upon the ground that a negro cannot make a choice— that they had no legal power to choose—could not perform the condition upon which their freedom depended.

I do not mention this with any purpose of criticizing, but to connect it with the arguments as affording additional evidence of the change of sentiment upon this question of slavery in the direction of making it perpetual and national. I argue now as I did before, that there is such a tendency, and I am backed not merely by the facts, but by the open confession in the slave states.

And now as to the Judge's inference, that because I wish to see slavery placed in the course of ultimate extinction—placed where our fathers originally placed it—I wish to annihilate the state legislatures—to force cotton to grow upon the tops of the Green Mountains—to freeze ice in Florida—to cut lumber on the broad Illinois prairies—that I am in favor of all these ridiculous and impossible things.

It seems to me it is a complete answer to all this, to ask, if, when Congress did have the fashion of restricting slavery from free territory; when courts did have the fashion of deciding that taking a slave into a free country made him free—I say it is a sufficient answer, to ask, if any of this ridiculous nonsense about consolidation, and uniformity, did actually follow. Who heard of any such thing, because of the Ordinance of '87? because of the Missouri Restriction? because of the numerous court decisions of that character?

Now, as to the Dred Scott decision; for upon that he makes his last point at me. He boldly takes ground in favor of that decision.

This is one-half the onslaught, and one-third of the entire plan of the campaign. I am opposed to that decision in a certain sense, but not in the sense which he puts on it. I say that in so far as it decided in favor of Dred Scott's master and against Dred Scott and his family, I do not propose to disturb or resist the decision.

I never have proposed to do any such thing. I think, that in respect for judicial authority, my humble history would not suffer in a comparison with that of Judge Douglas. He would have the citizen conform his vote to that decision; the member of Congress, his; the President, his use of the veto power. He would make it a rule of political action for the people and all the departments of the government. I would not. By resisting it as a political rule, I disturb no right of property, create no disorder, excite no mobs.

When he spoke at Chicago, on Friday evening of last week, he made this same point upon me. On Saturday evening I replied and reminded him of a Supreme Court decision which he opposed for at least several years. Last night, at Bloomington, he took some notice of that reply; but entirely forgot to remember that part of it.

He renews his onslaught upon me, forgetting to remember that I have turned the tables against himself on that very point. I renew the effort to draw his attention to it. I wish to stand erect before the country as well as Judge Douglas, on this question of judicial authority; and therefore I add something to the authority in favor of my own position. I wish to show that I am sustained by authority, in addition to that heretofore presented. I do not expect to convince the Judge. It is part of the plan of his campaign, and he will cling to it with a desperate gripe. Even, turn it upon him—turn the sharp point against him, and gaff him through— he will still cling to it till he can invent some new dodge to take the place of it.

In public speaking it is tedious reading from documents; but I must beg to indulge the practice to a limited extent. I shall read from a letter written by Mr. Jefferson in 1820, and now to be found in the seventh volume of his correspondence, at page 177. It seems he had been presented by a gentleman by the name of Jarvis with a book, or essay, or periodical, called the "Republican," and he was writing in acknowledgement of the present, and noting some of its contents. After expressing the hope that the work will produce a favorable effect upon the minds of the young, he proceeds to say:

That it will have this tendency may be expected, and for that reason I feel an urgency to note what I deem an error in it, the more requiring notice as your opinion is strengthened by that of many others. You seem in pages 84 and 148, to consider the judges as the ultimate arbiters of all constitutional questions—a very dangerous doctrine indeed and one which would place us under the despotism of an oligarchy. Our judges are as honest as other men, and not more so. They have, with others, the same passions for party, for power, and the privilege of their corps. Their maxim is, "*boni judicis est ampliare jurisdictionem*"; and their power is the more dangerous as they are in office for life, and not responsible, as the other functionaries are, to the elective control. The constitution has erected no such single tribunal, knowing that to whatever hands confided, with the corruptions of time and party, its members would become despots. It has more wisely made all the departments co-equal and co-sovereign within themselves.

Thus we see the power claimed for the Supreme Court by Judge Douglas, Mr. Jefferson holds, would reduce us to the despotism of an oligarchy.

Now, I have said no more than this—in fact, never quite so much as this—at least I am sustained by Mr. Jefferson.

Let us go a little further. You remember we once had a national bank. Some one owed the bank a debt; he was sued and sought to avoid payment, on the ground that the bank was unconstitutional. The case went to the Supreme Court, and therein it was decided that the bank was constitutional. The whole Democratic party revolted against that decision. General Jackson himself asserted that he, as President, would not be bound to hold a national bank to be constitutional, even though the Court had decided it to be so. He fell in precisely with the view of Mr. Jefferson, and acted upon it under his official oath, in vetoing a charter for a national bank. The declaration that Congress does not possess this constitutional power to charter a bank, has gone into the Democratic platform, at their national conventions, and was brought forward and reaffirmed in their last convention at Cincinnati. They have contended for that declaration, in the very teeth of the Supreme Court, for more than a quarter of a century. In fact, they have reduced the decision to an absolute nullity. That decision, I repeat, is repudiated in the Cincinnati platform; and still, as if to show that effrontery can go no farther, Judge Douglas vaunts in the very speeches in which he denounces me for opposing the Dred Scott decision, that he stands on the Cincinnati platform.

Now, I wish to know what the Judge can charge upon me, with respect to decisions of the Supreme Court which does not lie in all its length, breadth, and proportions at his own door. The plain truth is simply this: Judge Douglas is for Supreme Court decisions when he likes and against them when he does not like them. He is for the Dred Scott decision because it tends to nationalize slavery — because it is part of the original combination for that object. It so happens, singularly enough, that I never stood opposed to a decision of the Supreme Court till this. On the contrary, I have no recollection that he was ever particularly in favor of one till this. He never was in favor of any, nor opposed to any, till the present one, which helps to nationalize slavery.

Free men of Sangamon—free men of Illinois—free men everywhere judge ye between him and me, upon this issue.

He says this Dred Scott case is a very small matter at most—that it has no practical effect; that at best, or rather, I suppose, at worst, it is but an abstraction. I submit that the proposition that the thing which determines whether a man is free or a slave, is rather *concrete* than *abstract*. I think you would conclude that it was, if your liberty depended upon it, and so would Judge Douglas if his liberty depended upon it. But suppose it was on the question of spreading slavery over the new territories that he considers it as being merely an abstract matter, and one of no practical importance. How has the planting of slavery in new countries always been effected? It has now been decided that slavery cannot be kept out of our new territories by any legal means. In what does our new territories now differ in this respect, from the old colonies when slavery was first planted within them? It was planted as Mr. Clay once declared, and as history proves true, by individual men in spite of the wishes of the people; the mother government refusing to prohibit it, and withholding from the people of the colonies the authority to prohibit it for themselves. Mr. Clay says this was one of the great and just causes of complaint against Great Britain by the colonies, and the best apology we can now make for having the institution amongst us. In that precise condition our Nebraska politicians have at last succeeded in placing our own new territories; the government will not prohibit slavery within them, nor allow the people to prohibit it.

I defy any man to find any difference between the policy which originally planted slavery in these colonies and that policy which now prevails in our own new territories. If it does not go into them, it is only because no individual wishes it to go. The Judge indulged himself, doubtless, to-day, with the question as to what I am going to do with or about the Dred Scott decision. Well, Judge, will you please tell me what you did about the bank decision? Will you not graciously allow us to do with the Dred Scott decision precisely as you did with the bank decision? You succeeded in breaking down the moral effect of that decision; did you find it necessary to amend the Constitution? or to set up a court of negroes in order to do it?

There is one other point. Judge Douglas has a very affectionate leaning towards the Americans and Old Whigs. Last evening, in a sort of weeping tone, he described to us a death bed scene. He had been called to the side of Mr. Clay, in his last moments, in order that the genius of "popular sovereignty" might duly descend from the dying man and settle upon him, the living and most worthy successor. He could do no less than promise that he would devote the remainder of his life to "popular sovereignty"; and then the great statesman departs in peace. By this part of the "plan of the campaign," the Judge has evidently promised himself that tears shall be drawn down the cheeks of all Old Whigs, as large as half grown apples.

Mr. Webster, too, was mentioned; but it did not quite come to a death-bed scene, as to him. It would be amusing, if it were not disgusting, to see how quick these compromise-breakers administer on the political effects of their dead adversaries, trumping up claims never before heard of, and dividing the assets among themselves. If I should be found dead tomorrow morning, nothing but my insignificance could prevent a speech being made on my authority, before the end of next week. It so happens that in that "popular sovereignty" with which Mr. Clay was identified, the Missouri Compromise was expressly reserved; and it was a little singular if Mr. Clay cast his mantle upon Judge Douglas on purpose to have that compromise repealed.

Again, the Judge did not keep faith with Mr. Clay when he first brought in his Nebraska bill. He left the Missouri Compromise unrepealed, and in his report accompanying the bill, he told the world he did it on purpose. The *manes* of Mr. Clay must have been in great agony, till thirty days later, when "popular sovereignty" stood forth in all its glory.

One more thing. Last night Judge Douglas tormented himself with horrors about my disposition to make negroes perfectly equal with white men in social and political relations. He did not stop to show that I have said any such thing, or that it legitimately follows from any thing I have said, but he rushes on with his assertions. I adhere to the Declaration of Independence. If Judge Douglas and his friends are not willing to stand by it, let them come up and amend it. Let them make it read that all men are created equal except negroes. Let us have it decided, whether the Declaration of Independence, in this blessed year of 1858, shall be thus amended. In his construction of the Declaration last year he said it only meant that Americans in America were equal to Englishmen in England. Then, when I pointed out to him that by that rule he excludes the Germans, the Irish, the Portuguese, and all the other people who have come amongst us since the Revolution, he reconstructs his construction. In his last speech he tells us it meant Europeans.

I press him a little further, and ask if it meant to include the Russians in Asia? or does he mean to exclude that vast population from the principles of our Declaration of Independence? I expect ere long he will introduce another amendment to his definition. He is not at all particular. He is satisfied with any thing which does not endanger the nationalizing of negro slavery. It may draw white men down, but it must not lift negroes up. Who shall say, "I am the superior, and you are the inferior?"

My declarations upon this subject of negro slavery may be misrepresented, but can not be misunderstood. I have said that I do not understand the Declaration to mean that all men were created equal in all respects. They are not our equal in color; but I suppose that it does mean to declare that all men are equal in some respects; they are equal in their right to "life, liberty, and the pursuit of happiness." Certainly the negro is not our equal in color— perhaps not in many other respects; still, in the right to put into his mouth the bread that his own hands have earned, he is the equal of every other man, white or black. In pointing out that more has been given you, you can not be justified in taking away the little which has been given him. All I ask for the negro is that if you do not like him, let him alone. If God gave him but little, that little let him enjoy.

When our government was established, we had the institution of slavery among us. We were in a certain sense compelled to tolerate its existence. It was a sort of necessity. We had gone through our struggle and secured our own independence.

The framers of the Constitution found the institution of slavery amongst their other institutions at the time. They found that by an effort to eradicate it, they might lose much of what they had already gained. They were obliged to bow to the necessity. They gave power to Congress to abolish the slave trade at the end of twenty years. They also prohibited it in the territories where it did not exist. They did what they could and yielded to the necessity for the rest. I also yield to all which follows from that necessity. What I would most desire would be the separation of the white and black races.

One more point on this Springfield speech which Judge Douglas says he has read so carefully. I expressed my belief in the existence of a conspiracy to perpetuate and nationalize slavery. I did not profess to know it, nor do I now. I showed the part Judge Douglas had played in the string of facts, constituting to my mind, the proof of that conspiracy. I showed the parts played by others.

I charged that the people had been deceived into carrying the last presidential election, by the impression that the people of the territories might exclude slavery if they chose, when it was known in advance by the conspirators, that the Court was to decide that neither Congress nor the people could so exclude slavery. These charges are more distinctly made than any thing else in the speech.

Judge Douglas has carefully read and re-read that speech. He has not, so far as I know, contradicted those charges. In the two speeches which I heard he certainly did not. On his own tacit admission I renew that charge. I charge him with having been a party to that conspiracy and to that deception for the sole purpose of nationalizing slavery.

❧ 34 ❧

Speech in Rochester
25 October 1858

WILLIAM H. SEWARD

William Seward, who held office as Governor of New York, and who represented the state in the Senate, was to lose the Republican presidential nomination to Lincoln in 1860. His views on the slavery issue echoed Lincoln's, but his rhetoric was, if anything, more forceful.. In this speech he warns famously of "the irrepressible conflict" between North and South that would lead to a situation in which the United States would inevitably become either entirely slave-holding or a free-labour nation. A senior figure in the Republican party, Seward would subsequently serve as President Lincoln's Secretary of State.

"The Irrepressible Conflict"

The unmistakable outbreaks of zeal which occur all around me, show that you are earnest men—and such a man am I. Let us therefore, at least for a time, pass by all secondary and collateral questions, whether of a personal or of a general nature, and consider the main subject of the present canvass. The democratic party—or, to speak more accurately, the party which wears that attractive name—is in possession of the federal government. The republicans propose to dislodge that party, and dismiss it from its high trust.

The main subject, then, is, whether the democratic party deserves to retain the confidence of the American people. In attempting to prove it unworthy, I think that I am not actuated by prejudices against that party, or by prepossessions in favor of its adversary; for I have learned, by some experience, that virtue and patriotism, vice and selfishness, are found in all parties, and that they differ less in their motives than in the policies they pursue.

Our country is a theatre, which exhibits, in full operation, two radically different

Source: William H. Seward, speech in Rochester, New York, 25th October 1858 repr. in George Baker, ed., *The Works of William H. Seward*, Boston: Houghton, Mifflin and Company, 1884, vol. 4, new edition.

political systems; the one resting on the basis of servile or slave labor, the other on the basis of voluntary labor of freemen.

The laborers who are enslaved are all negroes, or persons more or less purely of African derivation. But this is only accidental. The principle of the system is, that labor in every society, by whomsoever performed, is necessarily unintellectual, groveling and base; and that the laborer, equally for his own good and for the welfare of the state, ought to be enslaved The white laboring man, whether native or foreigner, is not enslaved, only because he cannot, as yet, be reduced to bondage.

You need not be told now that the slave system is the older of the two, and that once it was universal.

The emancipation of our own ancestors, Caucasians and Europeans as they were, hardly dates beyond a period of five hundred years. The great melioration of human society which modern times exhibit, is mainly due to the incomplete substitution of the system of voluntary labor for the old one of servile labor, which has already taken place. This African slave system is one which, in its origin and in its growth, has been altogether foreign from the habits of the races which colonized these states, and established civilization here. It was introduced on this new continent as an engine of conquest, and for the establishment of monarchical power, by the Portuguese and the Spaniards, and was rapidly extended by them all over South America, Central America, Louisiana and Mexico. Its legitimate fruits are seen in the poverty, imbecility, and anarchy, which now pervade all Portuguese and Spanish America. The free-labor system is of German extraction, and it was established in our country by emigrants from Sweden, Holland, Germany, Great Britain and Ireland.

We justly ascribe to its influences the strength, wealth, greatness, intelligence, and freedom, which the whole American people now enjoy. One of the chief elements of the value of human life is freedom in the pursuit of happiness. The slave system is not only intolerable, unjust, and inhuman, towards the laborer, whom, only because he is a laborer, it loads down with chains and converts into merchandise, but is scarcely less severe upon the freeman, to whom, only because he is a laborer from necessity, it denies facilities for employment, and whom it expels from the community because it cannot enslave and convert him into merchandise also. It is necessarily improvident and ruinous, because, as a general truth, communities prosper and flourish or droop and decline in just the degree that they practice or neglect to practice the primary duties of justice and humanity. The free-labor system conforms to the divine law of equality, which is written in the hearts and consciences of man, and therefore is always and everywhere beneficent.

The slave system is one of constant danger, distrust, suspicion, and watchfulness. It debases those whose toil alone can produce wealth and resources for defense, to the lowest degree of which human nature is capable, to guard against mutiny and insurrection, and thus wastes energies which otherwise might be employed in national development and aggrandizement.

The free-labor system educates all alike, and by opening all the fields of industrial employment, and all the departments of authority, to the unchecked and equal rivalry of all classes of men, at once secures universal contentment, and brings into the highest possible activity all the physical, moral and social energies of the whole state. In states where the slave system prevails, the masters, directly or indirectly, secure all political power, and constitute a ruling aristocracy. In states where the free-labor system prevails, universal suffrage necessarily obtains, and the state inevitably becomes, sooner or later, a republic or democracy.

Russia yet maintains slavery, and is a despotism. Most of the other European states have abolished slavery, and adopted the system of free labor. It was the antagonistic political tendencies of the two systems which the first Napoleon was contemplating when he predicted that Europe would ultimately be either all Cossack or all republican. Never did human sagacity utter a more pregnant truth. The two systems are at once perceived to be incongruous. But they are more than incongruous—they are incompatible. They never have permanently existed together in one country, and they never can. It would be easy to demonstrate this impossibility, from the irreconcilable contrast between their great principles and characteristics. But the experience of mankind has conclusively established it. Slavery, as I have already intimated, existed in every state in Europe. Free labor has supplanted it everywhere except in Russia and Turkey. State necessities developed in modern times, are now obliging even those two nations to encourage and employ free labor; and already, despotic as they are, we find them engaged in abolishing slavery. In the United States, slavery came into collision with free labor at the close of the last century, and fell before it in New England, New York, New Jersey and Pennsylvania, but triumphed over it effectually, and excluded it for a period yet undetermined, from Virginia, the Carolinas and Georgia. Indeed, so incompatible are the two systems, that every new state which is organized within our ever extending domain makes its first political act a choice of the one and the exclusion of the other, even at the cost of civil war, if necessary. The slave states, without law, at the last national election, successfully forbade, within their own limits, even the casting of votes for a candidate for president of the United States supposed to be favorable to the establishment of the free-labor system in new states.

Hitherto, the two systems have existed in different states, but side by side within the American Union. This has happened because the Union is a confederation of states. But in another aspect the United States constitute only one nation. Increase of population, which is filling the states out to their very borders, together with a new and extended net-work of railroads and other avenues, and an internal commerce which daily becomes more intimate, is rapidly bringing the states into a higher and more perfect social unity or consolidation. Thus, these antagonistic systems are continually coming into closer contact, and collision results.

Shall I tell you what this collision means? They who think that it is accidental, unnecessary, the work of interested or fanatical agitators, and therefore ephemeral, mistake the case altogether. It is an irrepressible conflict between opposing and enduring forces, and it means that the United States must and will, sooner or later, become either entirely a slaveholding nation, or entirely a free-labor nation. Either the cotton and rice-fields of South Carolina and the sugar plantations of Louisiana will ultimately be tilled by free labor, and Charleston and New Orleans become marts for legitimate merchandise alone, or else the rye-fields and wheat-fields of Massachusetts and New York must again be surrendered by their farmers to slave culture and to the production of slaves, and Boston and New York become once more markets for trade in the bodies and souls of men. It is the failure to apprehend this great truth that induces so many unsuccessful attempts at final compromise between the slave and free states, and it is the existence of this great fact that renders all such pretended compromises, when made, vain and ephemeral. Startling as this saying may appear to you, fellow citizens, it is by no means an original or even a moderate one. Our forefathers knew it to be true, and unanimously acted upon it when they framed the constitution of the United States. They regarded the existence of the servile system in so many of the states with sorrow and shame, which they openly confessed, and they looked upon the collision between them, which was then just revealing itself, and which we are now accustomed to deplore, with favor and hope. They knew that either the one or the other system must exclusively prevail.

Unlike too many of those who in modern time invoke their authority, they had a choice between the two. They preferred the system of free labor, and they determined to organize the government, and so to direct its activity, that that system should surely and certainly prevail. For this purpose, and no other, they based the whole structure of government broadly on the principle that all men are created equal, and therefore free—little dreaming that, within the short period of one hundred years, their descendants would bear to be told by any orator, however popular, that the utterance of that principle was merely a rhetorical rhapsody; or by any judge, however venerated, that it was attended by mental reservations, which rendered it hypocritical and false. By the ordinance of 1787, they dedicated all of the national domain not yet polluted by slavery to free labor immediately, thenceforth and forever; while by the new constitution and laws they invited foreign free labor from all lands under the sun, and interdicted the importation of African slave labor, at all times, in all places, and under all circumstances whatsoever. It is true that they necessarily and wisely modified this policy of freedom, by leaving it to the several states, affected as they were by differing circumstances, to abolish slavery in their own way and at their own pleasure, instead of confiding that duty to congress; and that they secured to the slave states, while yet retaining the system of slavery, a three-fifths representation of slaves in the federal government, until they should find themselves able to relinquish it with safety. But the very nature of these modifications fortifies my position that the fathers knew that the two systems could not endure within the Union, and expected that within a short period slavery would disappear forever. Moreover, in order that these modifications might not altogether defeat their grand design of a republic maintaining universal equality, they provided that two-thirds of the states might amend the constitution.

It remains to say on this point only one word, to guard against misapprehension. If these states are to again become universally slaveholding, I do not pretend to say with what violations of the constitution that end shall be accomplished. On the other hand, while I do confidently believe and hope that my country will yet become a land of universal freedom, I do not expect that it will be made so otherwise than through the action of the several states cooperating with the federal government, and all acting in strict conformity with their respective constitutions.

The strife and contentions concerning slavery, which gently-disposed persons so habitually deprecate, are nothing more than the ripening of the conflict which the fathers themselves not only thus regarded with favor, but which they may be said to have instituted.

It is not to be denied, however, that thus far the course of that contest has not been according to their humane anticipations and wishes. In the field of federal politics, slavery, deriving unlooked-for advantages from commercial changes, and energies unforeseen from the facilities of combination between members of the slaveholding class and between that class and other property classes, early rallied, and has at length made a stand, not merely to retain its original defensive position, but to extend its sway throughout the whole Union. It is certain that the slaveholding class of American citizens indulge this high ambition, and that they derive encouragement for it from the rapid and effective political successes which they have already obtained. The plan of operation is this: By continued appliances of patronage and threats of disunion, they will keep a majority favorable to these designs in the senate, where each state has an equal representation. Through that majority they will defeat, as they best can, the admission of free states and secure the admission of slave states. Under the protection of the judiciary, they will, on the principle of the Dred Scott case, carry slavery into all the territories of the United States now existing and hereafter to be organized. By the action of the president and the senate, using the treaty-making power, they will annex foreign slaveholding states. In a favorable conjecture they will induce congress to repeal the act of 1808, which prohibits the foreign slave trade, and so they will import from Africa, at the cost of only twenty dollars a head, slaves enough to fill up the interior of the continent. Thus relatively increasing the number of slave states, they will allow no amendment to the constitution prejudicial to their interest; and so, having permanently established their power, they expect the federal judiciary to nullify all state laws which shall interfere with internal or foreign commerce in slaves. When the free states shall be sufficiently demoralized to tolerate these designs, they reasonably conclude that slavery will be accepted by those states themselves. I shall not stop to show how speedy or how complete would be the ruin which the accomplishment of these slaveholding schemes would bring upon the country. For one, I should not remain in the country to test the sad experiment. Having spent my manhood, though not my whole life, in a free state, no aristocracy of any kind, much less an aristocracy of slaveholders, shall ever make the laws of the land in which I shall be content to live. Having seen the society around me universally engaged in agriculture, manufactures and trade, which were innocent and beneficent, I shall never be a denizen of a state where men and women are reared as cattle, and bought and sold as merchandise. When that evil day shall come, and all further effort at resistance shall be impossible, then, if there shall be no better hope for redemption than I can now foresee, I shall say with Franklin, while looking abroad over the whole earth for a new and more congenial home, "Where liberty dwells, there is my country."

You will tell me that these fears are extravagant and chimerical. I answer, they are so; but they are so only because the designs of the slaveholders must and can be defeated. But it is only the possibility of defeat that renders them so. They cannot be defeated by inactivity. There is no escape from them, compatible with non-resistance. How, then, and in what way, shall the necessary resistance be made. There is only one way. The democratic party must be permanently dislodged from the government. The reason is, that the democratic party is inextricably committed to the designs of the slaveholders, which I have described. Let me be well understood. I do not charge that the democratic candidates for public office now before the people are pledged to—much less that the democratic masses who support them really adopt—those atrocious and dangerous designs. Candidates may, and generally do, mean to act justly, wisely and patriotically, when they shall be elected; but they become the ministers and servants, not the dictators, of the power which elects them. The policy which a party shall pursue at a future period is only gradually developed, depending on the occurrence of events never fully foreknown. The motives of men, whether acting as electors or in any other capacity, are generally pure. Nevertheless, it is not more true that "hell is paved with good intentions," than it is that earth is covered with wrecks resulting from innocent and amiable motives.

The very constitution of the democratic party commits it to execute all the designs of the slaveholders, whatever they may be. It is not a party of the whole Union, of all the free states and of all the slave states; nor yet is it a party of the free states in the north and in the northwest; but it is a sectional and local party, having practically its seat within the slave states, and counting its constituency chiefly and almost exclusively there. Of all its representatives in congress and in the electoral colleges, two-thirds uniformly come from these states. Its great element of strength lies in the vote of the slaveholders, augmented by the representation of three-fifths of the slaves. Deprive the democratic party of this strength, and it would be a helpless and hopeless minority, incapable of continued organization. The democratic party, being thus local and sectional, acquires new strength from the admission of every new slave state, and loses relatively by the admission of every new free state into the Union.

A party is in one sense a joint stock association, in which those who contribute most direct the action and management of the concern. The slaveholders contributing in an overwhelming proportion to the capital strength of the democratic party, they necessarily dictate and prescribe its policy. The inevitable caucus system enables them to do so with a show of fairness and justice. If it were possible to conceive for a moment that the democratic party should disobey the behests of the slaveholders, we should then see a withdrawal of the slaveholders, which would leave the party to perish. The portion of the party which is found in the free states is a mere appendage, convenient to modify its sectional character, without impairing its sectional constitution, and is less effective in regulating its movement than the nebulous tail of the comet is in determining the appointed though apparently eccentric course of the fiery sphere from which it emanates.

To expect the democratic party to resist slavery and favor freedom, is as unreasonable as to look for protestant missionaries to the catholic propaganda of Rome. The history of the democratic party commits it to the policy of slavery. It has been the democratic party, and no other agency, which has carried that policy up to its present alarming culmination. Without stopping to ascertain, critically, the origin of the present democratic party, we may concede its claim to date from the era of good feeling which occurred under the administration of President Monroe. At that time, in this state, and about that time in many others of the free states, the democratic party deliberately disfranchised the free colored or African citizen, and it has pertinaciously continued this disfranchisement ever since. This was an effective aid to slavery; for, while the slaveholder votes for his slaves against freedom, the freed slave in the free states is prohibited from voting against slavery.

In 1824, the democracy resisted the election of John Quincy Adams—himself before that time an acceptable democrat and in 1828 it expelled him from the presidency and put a slaveholder in his place, although the office had been filled by slaveholders thirty-two out of forty years.

In 1836, Martin Van Buren—the first non-slaveholding citizen of a free state to whose election the democratic party ever consented—signalized his inauguration into the presidency by a gratuitous announcement, that under no circumstances would he ever approve a bill for the abolition of slavery in the District of Columbia. From 1838 to 1844, the subject of abolishing slavery in the District of Columbia and in the national dock-yards and arsenals, was brought before congress by repeated popular appeals. The democratic party thereupon promptly denied the right of petition, and effectually suppressed the freedom of speech in congress, so far as the institution of slavery was concerned.

From 1840 to 1843, good and wise men counseled that Texas should remain outside the Union until she should consent to relinquish her self instituted slavery; but the democratic party precipitated her admission into the Union, not only without that condition, but even with a covenant that the state might be divided and reorganized so as to constitute four slave states instead of one.

In 1846, when the United States became involved in a war with Mexico, and it was apparent that the struggle would end in the dismemberment of that republic, which was a non-slaveholding power, the democratic party rejected a declaration that slavery should not be established within the territory to be acquired. When, in 1850, governments were to be instituted in the territories of California and New Mexico, the fruits of that war, the democratic party refused to admit New Mexico as a free state, and only consented to admit California as a free state on the condition, as it has since explained the transaction, of leaving all of New Mexico and Utah open to slavery, to which was also added the concession of perpetual slavery in the District of Columbia, and the passage of an unconstitutional, cruel and humiliating law, for the recapture of fugitive slaves, with a further stipulation that the subject of slavery should never again be agitated in either chamber of congress. When, in 1854, the slaveholders were contentedly reposing on these great advantages, then so recently won, the democratic party unnecessarily, officiously and with super-serviceable liberality, awakened them from their slumber, to offer and force on their acceptance the abrogation of the law which declared that neither slavery nor involuntary servitude should ever exist within that part of the ancient territory of Louisiana which lay outside of the state of Missouri, and north of the parallel of 36° 30' of north latitude—a law which, with the exception of one other, was the only statute of freedom then remaining in the federal code.

In 1856, when the people of Kansas had organized a new state within the region thus abandoned to slavery, and applied to be admitted as a free state into the Union, the democratic party contemptuously rejected their petition, and drove them with menaces and intimidations from the halls of congress, and armed the president with military power to enforce their submission to a slave code, established over them by fraud and usurpation. At every subsequent stage of the long contest which has since raged in Kansas, the democratic party has lent its sympathies, its aid, and all the powers of the government which it controlled, to enforce slavery upon that unwilling and injured people. And now, even at this day, while it mocks us with the assurance that Kansas is free, the democratic party keeps the state excluded from her just and proper place in the Union, under the hope that she may be dragooned into the acceptance of slavery.

The democratic party, finally, has procured from a supreme judiciary, fixed in its interest, a decree that slavery exists by force of the constitution in every territory of the United States, paramount to all legislative authority, either within the territory, or residing in congress.

Such is the democratic party. It has no policy, state or federal, for finance, or trade, or manufacture, or commerce, or education, or internal improvements, or for the protection or even the security of civil or religious liberty. It is positive and uncompromising in the interest of slavery—negative, compromising, and vacillating, in regard to everything else. It boasts its love of equality, and wastes its strength, and even its life, in fortifying the only aristocracy known in the land. It professes fraternity, and, so often as slavery requires, allies itself with proscription. It magnifies itself for conquests in foreign lands, but it sends the national eagle forth always with chains, and not the olive branch, in his fangs.

This dark record shows you, fellow citizens, what I was unwilling to announce at an earlier stage of this argument, that of the whole nefarious schedule of slaveholding designs which I have submitted to you, the democratic party has left only one yet to be consummated—the abrogation of the law which forbids the African slave trade.

Now, I know very well that the democratic party has, at every stage of these proceedings, disavowed the motive and the policy of fortifying and extending slavery, and has excused them on entirely different and more plausible grounds. But the inconsistency and frivolity of these pleas prove still more conclusively the guilt I charge upon that party. It must, indeed, try to excuse such guilt before mankind, and even to the consciences of its own adherents. There is an instinctive abhorrence of slavery, and an inborn and inhering love of freedom in the human heart, which render palliation of such gross misconduct indispensable. It disfranchised the free African on the ground of a fear that, if left to enjoy the right of suffrage, he might seduce the free white citizens into amalgamation with his wronged and despised race. The democratic party condemned and deposed John Quincy Adams, because he expended twelve millions a year, while it justifies his favored successor in spending seventy, eighty and even one hundred millions, a year. It denies emancipation in the District of Columbia, even with compensation to masters and the consent of the people, on the ground of an implied constitutional inhibition, although the constitution expressly confers upon congress sovereign legislative power in that district, and although the democratic party is tenacious of the principle of strict construction. It violated the express provisions of the constitution in suppressing petition and debate on the subject of slavery, through fear of disturbance of the public harmony, although it claims that the electors have a right to instruct their representatives, and even demand their resignation in cases of contumacy. It extended slavery over Texas, and connived at the attempt to spread it across the Mexican territories, even to the shores of the Pacific ocean, under a plea of enlarging the area of freedom. It abrogated the Mexican slave law and the Missouri compromise prohibition of slavery in Kansas, not to open the new territories to slavery, but to try therein the new and fascinating theories of non-intervention and popular sovereignty; and, finally, it overthrew both these new and elegant systems by the English Lecompton bill and the Dred Scott decision, on the ground that the free states ought not to enter the Union without a population equal to the representative basis of one member of congress, although slave states might come in without inspection as to their numbers.

Will any member of the democratic party now here claim that the authorities chosen by the suffrages of the party transcended their partisan platforms, and so misrepresented the party in the various transactions, I have recited? Then I ask him to name one democratic statesman or legislator, from Van Buren to Walker, who, either timidly or cautiously like them, or boldly and defiantly like Douglas, ever refused to execute a behest of the slaveholders and was not therefore, and for no other cause, immediately denounced, and deposed from his trust, and repudiated by the democratic party for that contumacy.

I think, fellow citizens, that I have shown you that it is high time for the friends of freedom to rush to the rescue of the constitution, and that their very first duty is to dismiss the democratic party from the administration of the government.

Why shall it not be done? All agree that it ought to be done. What, then, shall prevent its being done? Nothing but timidity or division of the opponents of the democratic party.

Some of these opponents start one objection, and some another. Let us notice these objections briefly. One class say that they cannot trust the republican party; that it has not avowed its hostility to slavery boldly enough, or its affection for freedom earnestly enough.

I ask, in reply, is there any other party which can be more safely trusted? Every one knows that it is the republican party, or none, that shall displace the democratic party. But I answer, further, that the character and fidelity of any party are determined, necessarily, not by its pledges, programmes, and platforms, but by the public exigencies, and the temper of the people when they call it into activity. Subserviency to slavery is a law written not only on the forehead of the democratic party, but also in its very soul—so resistance to slavery, and devotion to freedom, the popular elements now actively working for the republican party among the people, must and will be the resources for its ever-renewing strength and constant invigoration.

Others cannot support the republican party, because it has not sufficiently exposed its platform, and determined what it will do, and what it will not do, when triumphant. It may prove too progressive for some, and too conservative for others. As if any party ever foresaw so clearly the course of future events as to plan a universal scheme of future action, adapted to all possible emergencies. Who would ever have joined even the whig party of the revolution, if it had been obliged to answer, in 1770, whether it would declare for independence in 1776, and for this noble federal constitution of ours in 1787, and not a year earlier or later? The people will be as wise next year, and even ten years hence, as we are now. They will oblige the republican party to act as the public welfare and the interests of justice and humanity shall require, through all the stages of its career, whether of trial or triumph.

Others will not venture an effort, because they fear that the Union would not endure the change. Will such objectors tell me how long a constitution can bear a strain directly along the fibres of which it is composed? This is a constitution of freedom. It is being converted into a constitution of slavery. It is a republican constitution. It is being made an aristocratic one. Others wish to wait until some collateral questions concerning temperance, or the exercise of the elective franchise are properly settled. Let me ask all such persons, whether time enough has not been wasted on these points already, without gaining any other than this single advantage, namely, the discovery that only one thing can be effectually done at one time, and that the one thing which must and will be done at any one time is just that thing which is most urgent, and will no longer admit of postponement or delay. Finally, we are told by faint-hearted men that they despond; the democratic party, they say is unconquerable, and the dominion of slavery is consequently inevitable. I reply that the complete and universal dominion of slavery would be intolerable enough, when it should have come, after the last possible effort to escape should have been made. There would then be left to us the consoling reflection of fidelity to duty.

But I reply further, that I know—few, I think, know better than I—the resources and energies of the democratic party, which is identical with the slave power. I do ample prestige to its traditional popularity. I know, further—few, I think, know better than I—the difficulties and disadvantages of organizing a new political force, like the republican party, and the obstacles it must encounter in laboring without prestige and without patronage. But, understanding all this, I know that the democratic party must go down, and that the republican party must rise into its place. The democratic party derived its strength, originally, from its adoption of the principles of equal and exact justice to all men. So long as it practiced this principle faithfully, it was invulnerable. It became vulnerable when it renounced the principle, and since that time it has maintained itself, not by virtue of its own strength, or even of its traditional merits, but because there as yet had appeared in the political field no other party that had the conscience and the courage to take up, and avow, and practice the life-inspiring principle which the democratic party had surrendered. At last, the republican party has appeared. It avows, now, as the republican party of 1800 did, in one word, its faith and its works, "Equal and exact justice to all men." Even when it first entered the field, only half organized, it struck a blow which only just failed to secure complete and triumphant victory. In this, its second campaign, it has already won advantages which render that triumph now both easy and certain.

The secret of its assured success lies in that very characteristic which, in the mouth of scoffers, constitutes its great and lasting imbecility and reproach. It lies in the fact that it is a party of one idea; but that idea is a noble one—an idea that fills and expands all generous souls; the idea of equality—the equality of all men before human tribunals and human laws, as they all are equal before the Divine tribunal and Divine laws.

I know, and you know, that a revolution has begun. I know, and all the world knows, that revolutions never go backward. Twenty senators and a hundred representatives proclaim boldly in congress to-day sentiments and opinions and principles of freedom which hardly so many men, even in this free state, dared to utter in their own homes twenty years ago. While the government of the United States, under the conduct of the democratic party, has been all that time surrendering one plain and castle after another to slavery, the people of the United States have been no less steadily and perseveringly gathering together the forces with which to recover back again all the fields and all the castles which have been lost, and to confound and overthrow, by one decisive blow, the betrayers of the constitution and freedom forever.

VII. John Brown's Raid at Harper's Ferry: 1859

2. John Brown, 1856.

❧·35·❧

The Capture of John Brown

ISRAEL GREEN

This eye-witness account of the capture of John Brown at Harper's Ferry was published more than twenty-five years after the raid. Israel Green recalls his role in the event, and provides vignettes not only of Brown himself, but also of Robert E. Lee who commanded the detachment of federal troops despatched to recapture the U.S. armory that had been seized by Brown and his followers. This laconic description of the incident in the language used to report a military encounter avoids any reflection upon the symbolic significance of Brown's raid and its impact upon the tension that was building between Southerners and Northern abolitionists.

At noon of Monday, October 18, 1859, Chief Clerk Walsh, of the Navy Department, drove rapidly into the Washington Navy-yard, and, meeting me, asked me how many marines we had stationed at the barracks available for immediate duty. I happened to be the senior officer present and in command that day. I instantly replied to Mr. Walsh that we had ninety men available, and then asked him what was the trouble. He told me that Ossawatomie Brown, of Kansas, with a number of men, had taken the arsenal at Harper's Ferry, and was then besieged there by the Virginia State troops. Mr. Walsh returned speedily to the Navy Department building, and, in the course of an hour, orders came to me from Secretary Tousey to proceed at once to Harper's Ferry and report to the senior officer; and, if there should be no such officer at the Ferry, to take charge and protect the government property. With a detachment of ninety marines, I started for Harper's Ferry that afternoon on the 3:30 train, taking with me two howitzers. It was a beautiful, clear autumn day, and the men, exhilarated by the excitement of the occasion, which came after a long, dull season of confinement in the barracks, enjoyed the trip exceedingly.

At Frederick Junction I received a dispatch from Colonel Robert E. Lee, who turned out to be the army officer to whom I was to report. He directed me to proceed

Source: Israel Green, 'The Capture of John Brown', *The North American Review*, December 1885.

to Sandy Hook, a small place about a mile this side of the Ferry, and there await his arrival. At ten o'clock in the evening he came up on a special train from Washington. His first order was to form the marines out of the car, and march from the bridge to Harper's Ferry. This we did, entering the enclosure of the arsenal grounds through a back gate. At eleven o'clock Colonel Lee ordered the volunteers to march out of the grounds, and gave the control inside to the marines, with instructions to see that none of the insurgents escaped during the night. There had been hard fighting all the preceding day, and Brown and his men kept quiet during the night. At half-past six in the morning Colonel Lee gave me orders to select a detail of twelve men for a storming party, and place them near the engine-house in which Brown and his men had intrenched themselves. I selected twelve of my best men, and a second twelve to be employed as a reserve. The engine-house was a strong stone [actually brick] building, which is still in a good state of preservation at the Ferry, in spite of the three days' fighting in the building by Brown and his men, and the ravages of the recent war between the States. The building was . . . perhaps thirty feet by thirty-five. In the front were two large double doors, between which was a stone abutment. Within were two old-fashioned, heavy fire-engines, with a hose-cart and reel standing between them, and just back of the abutment between the doors. They were double-battened doors, very strongly made, with heavy wrought-iron nails.

Lieutenant J.E.B. Stewart [Stuart], afterwards famous as a cavalry commander on the side of the South, accompanied Colonel Lee as a volunteer aid. He was ordered to go with a part of the troops to the front of the engine-house and demand the surrender of the insurgent party. Colonel Lee directed him to offer protection to Brown and his men, but to receive no counter-proposition from Brown in regard to the surrender. On the way to the engine-house, Stewart and myself agreed upon a signal for attack in the event that Brown should refuse to surrender. It was simply that Lieutenant Stewart would wave his hat, which was then, I believe, one very similar to the famous chapeau which he wore throughout the war. I had my storming party ranged alongside of the engine-house, and a number of men were provided with sledge-hammers with which to batter in the doors. I stood in front of the abutment between the doors. Stewart hailed Brown and called for his surrender, but Brown at once began to make a proposition that he and his men should be allowed to come out of the engine-house and be given the length of the bridge start, so that they might escape. Suddenly Lieutenant Stewart waved his hat, and I gave the order to my men to batter in the door. Those inside fired rapidly at the point where the blows were given upon the door. Very little impression was made with the hammers, as the doors were tied on the inside with ropes and braced by the hand-brakes of the fire- engines, and in a few minutes I gave the order to desist. Just then my eye caught sight of a ladder, lying a few feet from the engine-house, in the yard, and I ordered my men to catch it up and use it as a battering-ram. The reserve of twelve men I employed as a supporting column for the assaulting party. The men took hold bravely and made a tremendous assault upon the door. The second blow broke it in. This entrance was a ragged hole low down in the right-hand door, the door being splintered and cracked some distance upward. I instantly stepped from my position in front of the stone abutment, and entered the opening made by the ladder. At the time I did not stop to think of it, but upon reflection I should say that Brown had just emptied his carbine at the point broken by the ladder, and so I passed in safely. Getting to my feet, I ran to the right of the engine which stood behind the door, passed quickly to the rear of the house, and came up between the two engines. The first person I saw was Colonel Lewis Washington, who was standing near the hose-cart, at the front of the engine-house. On one knee, a few feet to the left, knelt a man with a carbine in his hand, just pulling the lever to reload.

"Hello, Green," said Colonel Washington, and he reached out his hand to me. I grasped it with my left hand, having my saber uplifted in my right, and he said, pointing to the kneeling figure, "This is Ossawatomie."

As he said this, Brown turned his head to see who it was to whom Colonel Washington was speaking. Quicker than thought I brought my saber down with all my strength upon his head. He was moving as the blow fell, and I suppose I did not strike him where I intended, for he received a deep saber cut in the back of the neck. He fell senseless on his side, then rolled over on his back. He had in his hand a short Sharpe's cavalry carbine. I think he had just fired as I reached Colonel Washington, for the marine who followed me into the aperture made by the ladder received a bullet in the abdomen, from which he died in a few minutes. The shot might have been fired by some one else in the insurgent party, but I think it was from Brown. Instinctively as Brown fell I gave him a saber thrust in the left breast. The sword I carried was a light uniform weapon, and, either not having a point or striking something hard in Brown's accouterments, did not penetrate. The blade bent double.

By that time three or four of my men were inside. They came rushing in like tigers, as a storming assault is not a play-day sport. They bayoneted one man skulking under the engine, and pinned another fellow up against the rear wall, both being instantly killed. I ordered the men to spill no more blood. The other insurgents were at once taken under arrest, and the contest ended. The whole fight had not lasted over three minutes. My only thought was to capture, or, if necessary, kill, the insurgents, and take possession of the engine-house.

I saw very little of the situation within until the fight was over. Then I observed that the engine-house was thick with smoke, and it was with difficulty that a person could be seen across the room. In the rear, behind the left-hand engine, were huddled the prisoners whom Brown had captured and held as hostages for the safety of himself and his men. Colonel Washington was one of these. All during the fight, as I understood afterward, he kept to the front of the engine-house. When I met him he was as cool as he would have been on his own veranda entertaining guests. He was naturally a very brave man. I remember that he would not come out of the engine-house, begrimed and soiled as he was from his long imprisonment, until he had put a pair of kid gloves upon his hands. The other prisoners were the sorriest lot of people I ever saw. They had been without food for over sixty hours, in constant dread of being shot, and were huddled up in the corner where lay the body of Brown's son and one or two others of the insurgents who had been killed. Some of them have endeavored to give an account of the storming of the engine-house and the capture of Brown, but none of the reports have been free from a great many misstatements, and I suppose that Colonel Washington and myself were the only persons really able to say what was done. Other stories have been printed by people on the outside, describing the fight within. What they say must be taken with a great deal of allowance, for they could not have been witnesses of what occurred within the engine-house. One recent account describes me as jumping over the right-hand engine more like a wild beast than a soldier. Of course nothing of the kind happened. The report made by Colonel Lee at the time, which is now on file in the War department, gives a more succinct and detailed account than any I have seen.

I can see Colonel Lee now, as he stood on a slight elevation about forty feet from the engine-house, during the assault. He was in civilian dress, and looked then very little as he did during the war. He wore no beard, except a dark mustache, and his hair was slightly gray. He had no arms upon his person, and treated the affair as one of no very great consequence, which would be speedily settled by the marines. A part of the scene, giving color and life to the picture, was the bright blue uniform of the marines. They wore blue trousers then, as they do now, and a dark-blue frock-coat. Their belts were white, and they wore French fatigue caps. I do not remember the names of the twelve men in the storming party, nor can I tell what became of them in later life. We had no use for the howitzers, and, in fact, they were not taken from the car.

Immediately after the fight, Brown was carried out of the engine-house, and recovered consciousness while lying on the ground in front. A detail of men carried him up to the paymaster's office, where he was attended to and his wants supplied. On the following day, Wednesday, with an escort, I removed him to Charleston [Charles Town], and turned him over to the civil authorities. No handcuffs were placed upon him, and he supported himself with a self-reliance and independence which were characteristic of the man. He had recovered a great deal from the effects of the blow from my saber, the injury of which was principally the shock, as he only received a flesh wound. I had little conversation with him, and spent very little time with him.

I have often been asked to describe Brown's appearance at the instant he lifted his head to see who was talking with Colonel Washington. It would be impossible for me to do so. The whole scene passed so rapidly that it hardly made a distinct impression upon my mind. I can only recall the fleeting picture of an old man kneeling with a carbine in his hand, with a long gray beard falling away from his face, looking quickly and keenly toward the danger that he was aware had come upon him. He was not a large man, being perhaps five feet ten inches when he straightened up in full. His dress, even, I do not remember distinctly. I should say that he had his trousers tucked in his boots, and that he wore clothes of gray— probably no more than trousers and shirt. I think he had no hat upon his head.

None of the prisoners were hurt. They were badly frightened and somewhat starved. I received no wounds except a slight scratch on one hand as I was getting through the hole in the door. Colonel Lee and the people on the outside thought I was wounded. Brown had, at the time, only five or six fighting men, and I think he himself was the only one who showed fight after I entered the engine-house. There were no provisions in the building, and it would have been only a question of time when Brown would have had to surrender. Colonel Washington was the only person inside the house that I knew.

I have been asked what became of Brown's carbine. That I do not know. My sword was left in Washington, among people with whom I lived, and I lost trace of it. A few years ago, after having come out of the war and gone west to Dakota, where I now live, I received a letter from a gentleman in Washington, saying that he knew where the sword was, and that it was still bent double, as it was left by the thrust upon Brown's breast. He said that it was now a relic of great historic value, and asked me to assent to the selling of it upon the condition that I should receive a portion of the price of the weapon. To me the matter had very little interest, and I replied indifferently. Since then I have heard nothing of the matter. I presume the saber could be found somewhere in Washington.

ᕙ·36·ᕗ

Correspondence of Lydia Mary Child on the subject of John Brown and Slavery

LYDIA MARY CHILD, HENRY A WISE, JOHN BROWN, and M. J. C. MASON

Lydia Child, a staunch abolitionist, had a lengthy correspondence with the Governor of Virginia over the John Brown case in 1859. Some of this was published in the *New York Tribune*, together with her correspondence with John Brown himself. Mrs. M J. C. Mason also became involved in the argument: her attempt to tie the case against Brown to Biblical references resulted in Lydia Child responding with a plethora of Biblical citations in condemnation of slavery.

---

1. Letter to Gov. Wise from Lydia Mary Child

Wayland, Mass.,
Oct. 26th, 1859.

Governor Wise: I have heard that you were a man of chivalrous sentiments, and I know you were opposed to the iniquitous attempt to force upon Kansas a Constitution abhorrent to the moral sense of her people. Relying upon these indications of honor and justice in your character, I venture to ask a favor of you. Enclosed is a letter to Capt. John Brown. Will you have the kindness, after reading it yourself, to transmit it to the prisoner?

I and all my large circle of abolition acquaintances were taken by surprise when news came of Capt. Brown's recent attempt; nor do I know of a single person who would have approved of it, had they been apprised of his intention. But I and thousands of others feel a natural impulse of sympathy for the brave and suffering man. Perhaps God, who sees the inmost of our souls, perceives some such sentiment

Source: Anti-Slavery Tracts, New York: American Anti-Slavery Society, 1860, No. 1. New Series, Daniel A. P. Murray collection in the Library of Congress.

in your heart also. He needs a mother or sister to dress his wounds, and speak soothingly to him. Will you allow me to perform that mission of humanity? If you will, may God bless you for the generous deed!

I have been for years an uncompromising Abolitionist, and I should scorn to deny it or apologize for it as much as John Brown himself would do. Believing in peace principles, I deeply regret the step that the old veteran has taken, while I honor his humanity towards those who became his prisoners. But because it is my habit to be as open as the daylight, I will also say, that if I believed our religion justified men in fighting for freedom, I should consider the enslaved every where as best entitled to that right. Such an avowal is a simple, frank expression of my sense of natural justice.

But I should despise myself utterly if any circumstances could tempt me to seek to advance these opinions in any way, directly or indirectly, after your permission to visit Virginia has been obtained on the plea of sisterly sympathy with a brave and suffering man. I give you my word of honor, which was never broken, that I would use such permission solely and singly for the purpose of nursing your prisoner, and for no other purpose whatsoever.

Yours, respectfully,
L. Maria Child.

2. Gov. Wise's Reply

Richmond, Va.,
Oct. 29th, 1859.

Madam: Yours of the 26th was received by me yesterday, and at my earliest leisure I respectfully reply to it, that I will forward the letter for John Brown, a prisoner under our laws, arraigned at the bar of the Circuit Court for the country of Jefferson, at Charlestown, Va., for the crimes of murder, robbery and treason, which you ask me to transmit to him. I will comply with your request in the only way which seems to me proper, by enclosing it to the Commonwealth's attorney, with the request that he will ask the permission of the Court to hand it to the prisoner. Brown, the prisoner, is now in the hands of the judiciary, not of the executive, of this Commonwealth.

You ask me, further, to allow you to perform the mission "of mother or sister, to dress his wounds, and speak soothingly to him." By this, of course, you mean to be allowed to visit him in his cell, and to minister to him in the offices of humanity. Why should you not be so allowed, Madam? Virginia and Massachusetts are involved in no civil war, and the Constitution which unites them in one confederacy guarantees to you the privileges and immunities of a citizen of the United States in the State of Virginia. That Constitution I am sworn to support, and am, therefore, bound to protect your privileges and immunities as a citizen of Massachusetts coming into Virginia for any lawful and peaceful purpose.

Coming, as you propose, to minister to the captive in prison, you will be met, doubtless, by all our people, not only in a chivalrous, but in a Christian spirit. You have the right to visit Charlestown. Va., Madam; and your mission being merciful and humane, will not only be allowed, but respected if not welcomed. A few unenlightened and inconsiderate persons, fanatical in their modes of thought and action, to maintain justice and right, might molest you, or be disposed to do so; and this might suggest the imprudence of risking any experiment upon the peace of a society very much excited by the crimes with whose chief author you seem to sympathize so much. But still, I repeat, your motives and avowed purpose are lawful and peaceful, and I will, as far as I am concerned, do my duty in protecting your rights in our limits. Virginia and her authorities would be weak indeed—weak in point of folly, and weak in point of power—if her State faith and constitutional obligations cannot be redeemed in her own limits to the letter of morality as well as of law; and if her chivalry cannot courteously receive a lady's visit to a prison, every arm which guards Brown from rescue on the one hand, and from Lynch law on the other, will be ready to guard your person in Virginia.

I could not permit an insult even to woman in her walk of charity among us, though it be to one who whetted knives of butchery for our mothers, sisters, daughters and babes. We have no sympathy with your sentiments of sympathy with Brown, and are surprised that you were "taken by surprise when news came of Capt. Brown's recent attempt." His attempt was a natural consequence of your sympathy, and the errors of that sympathy ought to make you doubt its virtue from the effect on his conduct. But it is not of this I should speak. When you arrive at Charlestown, if you go there, it will be for the Court and its officers, the Commonwealth's attorney, sheriff and jailer, to say whether you may see and wait on the prisoner. But whether you are thus permitted or not, (and you will be, if my advice can prevail) you may rest assured that he will be humanely, lawfully and mercifully dealt by in prison and on trial.

Respectfully,
HENRY A. WISE.

3. Mrs. Child to Gov. Wise

In your civil but very diplomatic reply to my letter, you inform me that I have a constitutional right to visit Virginia, for peaceful purposes, in common with every citizen of the United States. I was perfectly well aware that such was the theory of constitutional obligation in the Slave States; but I was also aware of what you omit to mention, viz.; that the Constitution has, in reality, been completely and systematically nullified, whenever it suited the convenience or the policy of the Slave Power. Your constitutional obligation, for which you profess so much respect, has never proved any protection to citizens of the Free States, who happened to have a black, brown, or yellow complexion; nor to any white citizen whom you even suspected of entertaining opinions opposite to your own, on a question of vast importance to the temporal welfare and moral example of our common country. This total disregard of constitutional obligation has been manifested not merely by the Lynch Law of mobs in the Slave States, but by the deliberate action of magistrates and legislators. What regard was paid to constitutional obligation in South Carolina, when Massachusetts sent the Hon. Mr. Hoar there as an envoy, on a purely legal errand? Mr. Hedrick, Professor of Political Economy in the University of North Carolina, had a constitutional right to reside in that State. What regard was paid to that right, when he was driven from his home, merely for declaring that he considered Slavery an impolitic system, injurious to the prosperity of States? What respect for constitutional rights was manifested by Alabama, when a bookseller in Mobile was compelled to flee for his life, because he had, at the special request of some of the citizens, imported a few copies of a novel that every body was curious to read? Your own citizen, Mr. Underwood, had a constitutional right to live in Virginia, and vote for whomsoever he pleased. What regard was paid to his rights, when he was driven from your State for declaring himself in favor of the election of Fremont? With these, and a multitude of other examples before your eyes, it would seem as if the less that was said about respect for constitutional obligations at the South, the better. Slavery is, in fact, an infringement of all law, and adheres to no law, save for its own purposes of oppression.

You accuse Captain John Brown of "whetting knives of butchery for the mothers, sisters, daughters and babes" of Virginia; and you inform me of the well-known fact that he is "arraigned for the crimes of murder, robbery and treason." I will not here stop to explain why I believe that old hero to be no criminal, but a martyr to righteous principles which he sought to advance by methods sanctioned by his own religious views, though not by mine. Allowing that Capt. Brown did attempt a scheme in which murder, robbery and treason were, to his own consciousness, involved, I do not see how Gov. Wise can consistently arraign him for crimes he has himself commended. You have threatened to trample on the Constitution, and break the Union, if a majority of the legal voters in these Confederated States dared to elect a President unfavorable to the extension of Slavery. Is not such a declaration proof of premeditated treason? In the Spring of 1842, you made a speech in Congress, from which I copy the following:—

> Once set before the people of the Great Valley the conquest of the rich Mexican Provinces, and you might as well attempt to stop the wind. This Government might send its troops, but they would run over them like a herd of buffalo. Let the work once begin, and I do not know that this House would hold me very long. Give me five millions of dollars, and I would undertake to do it myself. Although I do not know how to set a single squadron in the field, I could find men to do it. Slavery should pour itself abroad, without restraint, and find no limit but the Southern Ocean. The Camanches should no longer hold the richest mines of Mexico. Every golden image which had received the profanation of a false worship, should soon be melted down into good American eagles. I would cause as much gold to cross the Rio del Norte as the mules of Mexico could carry; aye, and I would make better use of it, too, than any lazy, bigoted priesthood under heaven.

When you thus boasted that you and your "booted loafers" would overrun the troops of the United States "like a herd of buffalo," if the Government sent them to arrest your invasion of a neighboring nation, at peace with the United States, did you not pledge yourself to commit treason? Was it not by robbery, even of churches, that you proposed to load the mules of Mexico with gold for the United States? Was it not by the murder of unoffending Mexicans that you expected to advance those schemes of avarice and ambition? What humanity had you for Mexican "mothers and babes," whom you proposed to make childless and fatherless? And for what purpose was this wholesale massacre to take place? Not to right the wrongs of any oppressed class; not to sustain any great principles of justice, or of freedom; but merely to enable "Slavery to pour itself forth without restraint."

Even if Captain Brown were as bad as you paint him, I should suppose he must naturally remind you of the words of Macbeth:

> We but teach
> Bloody instructions, which, being taught, return
> To plague the inventor: This even-handed justice
> Commends the ingredients of our poisoned chalice
> To our own lips.

If Captain Brown intended, as you say, to commit treason, robbery and murder, I think I have shown that he could find ample authority for such proceedings in the public declarations of Gov. Wise. And if, as he himself declares, he merely intended to free the oppressed, where could he read a more forcible lesson than is furnished by the State Seal of Virginia? I looked at it thoughtfully before I opened your letter; and though it had always appeared to me very suggestive, it never seemed to me so much so as it now did in connection with Captain John Brown. A liberty-loving hero stands with his foot upon a prostrate despot; under his strong arm, manacles and chains lie broken; and the motto is, *"Sic Semper Tyrannis"*; "Thus be it ever done to Tyrants." And this is the blazon of a State whose most profitable business is the Internal Slave-Trade!—in whose highways coffles of human chattels, chained and manacled, are frequently seen! And the Seal and the Coffles are both looked upon by other chattels, constantly exposed to the same fate! What if some Vezey, or Nat Turner, should be growing up among those apparently quiet spectators? It is in no spirit of taunt or of exultation that I ask this question. I never think of it but with anxiety, sadness, and sympathy. I know that a slave-holding community necessarily lives in the midst of gunpowder; and, in this age, sparks of free thought are flying in every direction. You cannot quench the fires of free thought and human sympathy by any process of cunning or force; but there is a method by which you can effectually wet the gunpowder. England has already tried it, with safety and success. Would that you could be persuaded to set aside the prejudices of education, and candidly examine the actual working of that experiment! Virginia is so richly endowed by nature that Free Institutions alone are wanting to render her the most prosperous and powerful of the States.

In your letter, you suggest that such a scheme as Captain Brown's is the natural result of the opinions with which I sympathize. Even if I thought this to be a correct statement, though I should deeply regret it, I could not draw the conclusion that humanity ought to be stifled, and truth struck dumb, for fear that long-successful despotism might be endangered by their utterance. But the fact is, you mistake the source of that strange outbreak. No abolition arguments or denunciations, however earnestly, loudly, or harshly proclaimed, would have produced that result. It was the legitimate consequence of the continual and constantly increasing aggressions of the Slave Power. The Slave States, in their desperate efforts to sustain a bad and dangerous institution, have encroached more and more upon the liberties of the Free States. Our inherent love of law and order, and our superstitious attachment to the Union, you have mistaken for cowardice; and rarely have you let slip any opportunity to add insult to aggression.

The manifested opposition to Slavery began with the lectures and pamphlets of a few disinterested men and women, who based their movements upon purely moral and religious grounds; but their expostulations were met with a storm of rage, with tar and feathers, brickbats, demolished houses, and other applications of Lynch Law. When the dust of the conflict began to subside a little, their numbers were found to be greatly increased by the efforts to exterminate them. They had become an influence in the State too important to be overlooked by shrewd calculators. Political economists began to look at the subject from a lower point of view. They used their abilities to demonstrate that slavery was a wasteful system, and that the Free States were taxed, to an enormous extent, to sustain an institution which, at heart, two-thirds of them abhorred. The forty millions, or more, of dollars, expended in hunting Fugitive Slaves in Florida, under the name of the Seminole War, were adduced, as one item in proof, to which many more were added. At last, politicians were compelled to take some action on the subject. It soon became known to all the people that the Slave States had always managed to hold in their hands the political power of the Union, and that while they constituted only one-third of the white population of these States, they held more than two-thirds of all the lucrative, and once honorable offices; an indignity to which none but a subjugated people had ever submitted. The knowledge also became generally diffused, that while the Southern States owned their Democracy at home, and voted for them, they also systematically bribed the nominally Democratic party, at the North, with the offices adroitly kept at their disposal.

Through these, and other instrumentalities, the sentiments of the original Garrisonian Abolitionist became very widely extended, in forms more or less diluted. But by far the most efficient co-labors we have ever had have been the Slave States themselves. By denying us the sacred Right of Petition, they roused the free spirit of the North, as it never could have been roused by the loud trumpet of Garrison, or the soul-animating bugle of Phillips. They bought the great slave, Daniel, and according to their established usage, paid him no wages for his labor. By his cooperation, they forced the Fugitive Slave Law upon us, in violation of all our humane instincts and all our principles of justice. And what did they procure for the Abolitionist by that despotic process? A deeper and wider detestation of Slavery throughout the Free States, and the publication of Uncle Tom's Cabin, an eloquent outburst of moral indignation, whose echoes wakened the world to look upon their shame.

By fillibustering and fraud, they dismembered Mexico, and having thus obtained the soil of Texas, they tried to introduce it as a Slave State into the Union. Failing to effect their purpose by constitutional means, they accomplished it by a most open and palpable violation of the Constitution, and by obtaining the votes of Senators on the false pretences. [1]

Soon afterward, a Southern Slave Administration ceded to the powerful monarchy of Great Britain several hundred thousands of square miles, that must have been made into Free States, to which that same Administration had declared that the United States had "an unquestionable right;" and then they turned upon the weak Republic of Mexico, and, in order to make more Slave States, wrested from her twice as many hundred thousands of square miles, to which we had not a shadow of right.

Notwithstanding all these extra efforts, they saw symptoms that the political power so long held with a firm grasp was in danger of slipping from their hands, by reason of the extension of Abolition sentiments, and the greater prosperity of Free States. Emboldened by continual success in aggression, they made use of the pretence of "Squatter Sovereignty" to break the league into which they had formerly cajoled the servile representatives of our blinded people, by which all the territory of the United States south of 36° 30' was guaranteed to Slavery, and all north of it to Freedom. Thus Kansas became the battle-ground of the antagonistic elements in our Government. Ruffians hired by the Slave Power were sent thither temporarily, to do the voting, and drive from the polls the legal voters, who were often murdered in the process. Names, copied from the directories of cities in other States, were returned by thousands as legal voters in Kansas, in order to establish a Constitution abhorred by the people. This was their exemplification of Squatter Sovereignty. A Massachusetts Senator, distinguished for candor, courtesy, and stainless integrity, was half murdered by slaveholders, merely for having the manliness to state these facts to the assembled Congress of the nation. Peaceful emigrants from the North, who went to Kansas for no other purpose than to till the soil, erect mills, and establish manufactories, schools, and churches, were robbed, outraged, and murdered. For many months, a war more ferocious than the warfare of wild Indians was carried on against a people almost unresisting, because they relied upon the Central Government for aid. And all this while, the power of the United States, wielded by the Slave Oligarchy, was on the side of the aggressors. They literally tied the stones, and let loose the mad dogs. This was the state of things when the hero of Osawatomie and his brave sons went to the rescue. It was he who first turned the tide of Border-Ruffian triumph, by showing them that blows were to be taken as well as given.

You may believe it or not, Gov. Wise, but it is certainly the truth that, because slaveholders so recklessly sowed the wind in Kansas, they reaped a whirlwind at Harper's Ferry.

The people of the North had a very strong attachment to the Union; but, by your desperate measures, you have weakened it beyond all power of restoration. They are not your enemies, as you suppose, but they cannot consent to be your tools for any ignoble task you may choose to propose. You must not judge of us by the crawling sinuosities of an Everett; or by our magnificent hound, whom you trained to hunt your poor cripples, and then sent him sneaking into a corner to die—not with shame for the base purposes to which his strength had been applied, but with vexation because you withheld from him the promised bone. Not by such as these must you judge the free, enlightened yeomanry of New England. A majority of them would rejoice to have the Slave States fulfil their oft-repeated threat of withdrawal from the Union. It has ceased to be a bugbear, for we begin to despair of being able, by any other process, to give the world the example of a real republic. The moral sense of these States is outraged by being accomplices in sustaining an institution vicious in all its aspects; and it is now generally understood that we purchase our disgrace at great pecuniary expense. If you would only make the offer of a separation in serious earnest, you would here the hearty response of millions, "Go, gentlemen, and

> Stand not upon the order of your going,
> But go at once!"

Yours, with all due respect,
L. Maria Child.

4. Explanatory Letter to The Editor of The *New York Tribune* from Mrs Child

Boston, Nov. 10, 1859.

Sir: I was much surprised to see my correspondence with Governor Wise published in your columns. As I have never given any person a copy, I presume you must have obtained it from Virginia. My proposal to go and nurse that brave and generous old man, who so willingly gives his life a sacrifice for God's oppressed poor, originated in a very simple and unmeritorious impulse of kindness. I heard his friends inquiring, "Has he no wife, or sister, that can go to nurse him? We are trying to ascertain, for he needs some one." My niece said she would go at once, if her health were strong enough to be trusted. I replied that my age and state of health rendered me a more suitable person to go, and that I would go most gladly. I accordingly wrote to Captain Brown, and enclosed the letter to Governor Wise. My intention was to slip away quietly, without having the affair made public. I packed my trunk and collected a quantity of old linen for lint, and awaited tidings from Virginia. When Governor Wise answered, he suggested the "imprudence of trying any experiment upon the peace of a society already greatly excited." My husband and I took counsel together, and we both concluded that, as the noble old veteran was said to be fast recovering from his wounds, and as my presence might create a popular excitement unfavorable to such chance as the prisoner had for a fair trial, I had better wait until I received a reply from Captain Brown himself. Fearing to do him more harm than good by following my impulse, I waited for his own sanction. Meanwhile, his wife, said to be a brave-hearted Roman matron, worthy of such a mate, has gone to him, and I have received the following reply.

Respectfully yours,
L. Maria Child.

5. Mrs. Child to John Brown

Wayland, Mass.,
Oct. 26, 1859.

Dear Capt. Brown: Though personally unknown to you, you will recognize in my name an earnest friend of Kansas, when circumstances made that Territory the battle-ground between the antagonistic principles of slavery and freedom, which politicians so vainly strive to reconcile in the government of the United States.

Believing in peace principles, I cannot sympathize with the method you chose to advance the cause of freedom. But I honor your generous intentions—I admire your courage, moral and physical. I reverence you for the humanity which tempered your zeal. I sympathize with you in your cruel bereavement, your sufferings, and your wrongs. In brief, I love you and bless you.

Thousands of hearts are throbbing with sympathy as warm as mine. I think of you night and day, bleeding in prison, surrounded by hostile faces, sustained only by trust in God and your own heart. I long to nurse you—to speak to you sisterly words of sympathy and consolation. I have asked permission of Governor Wise to do so. If the request is not granted, I cherish the hope that these few words may at least reach your hands, and afford you some little solace. May you be strengthened by the conviction that no honest man ever sheds blood for freedom in vain, however much he may be mistaken in his efforts. May God sustain you, and carry you through whatsoever may be in store for you!

Yours, with heartfelt respect, sympathy and affection,
L. Maria Child.

6. John Brown's Reply

Mrs. L. Maria Child:

My Dear Friend—Such you prove to be, though a stranger—your most kind letter has reached me, with the kind offer to come here and take care of me. Allow me to express my gratitude for your great sympathy, and at the same time to propose to you a different course, together with my reasons for wishing it. I should certainly be greatly pleased to become personally acquainted with one so gifted and so kind, but I cannot avoid seeing some objections to it, under present circumstances. First, I am in charge of a most humane gentleman, who, with his family, has rendered me every possible attention I have desired, or that could be of the least advantage; and I am so recovered of my wounds as no longer to require nursing. Then, again, it would subject you to great personal inconvenience and heavy expense, without doing me any good. Allow me to name to you another channel through which you may reach me with your sympathies much more effectually. I have at home a wife and three young daughters, the youngest but little over five years old, the oldest nearly sixteen. I have also two daughters-in-law, whose husbands have both fallen near me here. There is also another widow, Mrs. Thompson, whose husband fell here. Whether she is a mother or not, I cannot say. All these, my wife included, live at North Elba, Essex county, New York. I have a middle-aged son, who has been, in some degree, a cripple from his childhood, who would have as much as he could well do to earn a living. He was a most dreadful sufferer in Kansas, and lost all he had laid up. He has not enough to clothe himself for the winter comfortably. I have no living son, or son-in-law, who did not suffer terribly in Kansas.

Now, dear friend, would you not as soon contribute fifty cents now, and a like sum yearly, for the relief of those very poor and deeply afflicted persons, to enable them to supply themselves and their children with bread and very plain clothing, and to enable the children to receive a common English education? Will you also devote your own energies to induce others to join you in giving a like amount, or any other amount, to constitute a little fund for the purpose named?

I cannot see how your coming here can do me the least good; and I am quite certain you can do immense good where you are. I am quite cheerful under all my afflicting circumstances and propects; having, as I humbly trust, "the peace of God which passeth all understanding" to rule in my heart. You may make such use of this as you see it fit. God Almighty bless and reward you a thousand fold!

Yours in sincerity and truth,

John Brown.

7. Letter from Mrs. Mason to Mrs. Child

Alto, King George's Co., Va.,
Nov. 11th, 1859.

[. . .] Do you read your Bible, Mrs. Child? If you do, read there, "Woe unto you, hypocrites," and take to yourself with two-fold damnation that terrible sentence; for, rest assured, in the day of judgment it shall be more tolerable for those thus scathed by the awful denunciation of the Son of God, than for you. You would soothe with sisterly and motherly care the hoary-headed murderer of Harper's Ferry! A man whose aim and intention was to incite the horrors of a servile war—to condemn women of your own race, ere death closed their eyes on their sufferings from violence and outrage, to see their husbands and fathers murdered, their children butchered, the ground strewed with the brains of their babes. The antecedents of Brown's band proved them to have been the offscourings of the earth; and what would have been our fate had they found as many sympathizers in Virginia as they seem to have in Massachusetts?

Now, compare yourself with those your "sympathy" would devote to such ruthless ruin, and say, on that "word of honor, which never has been broken," would you stand by the bedside of an old negro, dying of a hopeless disease, to alleviate his sufferings as far as human aid could? Have you ever watched the last, lingering illness of a consumptive, to soothe, as far as in you lay, the inevitable fate? Do you soften the pangs of maternity in those around you by all the care and comfort you can give? Do you grieve with those near you, even though the sorrows resulted from their own misconduct? Did you ever sit up until the "wee hours" to complete a dress for a motherless child, that she might appear on Christmas day in a new one, along with her more fortunate companions? We do these and more for our servants, and why? Because we endeavor to do our duty in that state of life it has pleased God to place us. In his revealed word we read our duties to them—theirs to us are there also—"Not only to the good and gentle, but to the forward."—(Peter 2: 18.) Go thou and do likewise, and keep away from Charlestown. If the stories read in the public prints be true, of the sufferings of the poor of the North, you need not go far for objects of charity. "Thou hypocrite! take first the beam out of thine own eye, then shalt thou see clearly to pull the mote out of thy neighbor's." But if, indeed, you do lack objects of sympathy near you, go to Jefferson county, to the family of George Turner, a noble, true-hearted man, whose devotion to his friend (Col. Washington) causing him to risk his life, was shot down like a dog. Or to that of old Beckham, whose grief at the murder of his negro subordinate made him needlessly expose himself to the aim of the assassin Brown. And when you can equal in deeds of love and charity to those around you, what is shown by nine-tenths of the Virginia plantations, then by your "sympathy" whet the knives for our throats, and kindle the torch that fires our homes. You reverence Brown for his clemency to his prisoners! Prisoners! and how taken? Unsuspecting workmen, going to their daily duties; unarmed gentlemen, taken from their beds at the dead hour of the night, by six men doubly and trebly armed. Suppose he had hurt a hair of their heads, do you suppose one of the band of desperadoes would have left the engine-house alive? And did he not know that his treatment of them was [their] only hope of life then, or of clemency afterward? Of course he did. The United States troops could not have prevented him from being torn limb from limb.

I will add, in conclusion, no Southerner ought, after your letter to Governor Wise and to Brown, to read a line of your composition, or to touch a magazine which bears your name in its lists of contributors; and in this we hope for the "sympathy," at least of those at the North who deserve the name of woman.

M. J. C. MASON.

8. Mrs. Child's Reply.

Wayland, Mass.,
Dec. 17th, 1859.

Prolonged absence from home has prevented my answering your letter so soon as I intended. I have no disposition to retort upon you the "two-fold damnation" to which you consign me. On the Contrary, I sincerely wish you well, both in this world and the next. If the anathema proved a safety valve to your own boiling spirit, it did some good to you, while it fell harmless upon me. Fortunately for all of us, the Heavenly Father rules His universe by laws, which the passions or the prejudices of mortals have no power to change.

As for John Brown, his reputation may be safety trusted to the impartial pen of History; and his motives will be righteously judged by Him who knoweth the secrets of all hearts. Men, however great they may be, are of small consequence in comparison with principles; and the principle for which John Brown died is the question issue between us.

You refer me to the Bible, from which you quote the favorite text of slaveholders:—

> Servants, be subject to your masters with all fear; not only to the good and gentle, but also to the forward.—1 Peter, 2:18.

Abolitionists also have favorite texts, to some of which I would call your attention:—

> Remember those that are in bonds as bound with them.—Heb. 13:3.

> Hide the outcasts. Betray not him that wandereth. Let mine outcasts dwell with thee. Be thou a convert to them from the face of the spoiler.—Isa. 16: 3, 4.

> Thou shalt not deliver unto his master the servant which is escaped from his master unto thee. He shall dwell with thee where it liketh him best. Thou shalt not oppress him.—Deut. 23: 15, 16.

> Open thy mouth for the dumb, in the cause of all such are appointed to destruction. Open thy mouth judge righteously, and plead the cause of the poor and needy.—Prov. 29: 8,9.

> Cry aloud, spare not, lift up thy voice like a trumpet, and show my people their transgression, and the house of Jacob their sins.—Isa. 58: 1.

I would especially commend to slaveholders the following portions of that volume, wherein you say God has revealed the duty of masters:—

> Masters, give unto your servants that which is just and equal, knowing that ye also have a Master in heaven.—Col. 4:1.

> Neither be ye called masters; for one is your master, even Christ; and all ye are brethren.—Matt 23: 8, 10.

> Whatsoever ye would that men should do unto you, do ye even so unto them.—Matt. 7: 12.

> Is not this the fast that I have chosen, to loose the bands of wickedness, to undo the heavy burdens and to let the oppressed go free, and that ye break every yoke?—Isa. 58: 6.

> They have given a boy for a harlot, and sold a girl for wine, that they might drink.—Joel 3: 3.

> He that oppresseth the poor, reproacheth his Maker.—Prov. 14: 31.

> Rob not the poor, because he is poor; neither oppress the afflicted. For the Lord will plead their cause, and spoil the soul of those who spoiled them.—Prov. 22: 22, 23.

> Woe unto him that useth his neighbor's service without wages, and giveth him not for his work.—Jer. 22: 13.

Let him that stole, steal no more, but rather let him labor, working with his hands.—Eph. 4: 28.

Woe unto them that decree unrighteous decrees, and that write grievousness which they have prescribed; to turn aside the needy from judgment, and to take away the right from the poor, that widows may be their prey, and that they may rob the fatherless.—Isa. 10: 1, 2.

If I did despise the cause of my man-servant or my maid-servant, when they contend with me, what then shall I do when God riseth up? and when he visiteth, what shall I answer Him?—Job 31: 13, 14.

Thou hast sent widows away empty, and the arms of the fatherless have been broken. Therefore snares are round about thee, and sudden fear troubleth thee; and darkness, that thou canst not see.—Job 22: 9, 10, 11.

Behold, the hire of your laborers, who have reaped down your fields, which is of you kept back by fraud, crieth; and the cries of them which have reaped are entered into the ears of the Lord of saboath. Ye have lived in pleasure on the earth, and been wanton; ye have nourished your hearts as in a day of slaughter; ye have condemned and killed the just.—James 5: 4.

If the appropriateness of these texts is not apparent, I will try to make it so, by evidence drawn entirely from Southern sources. The Abolitionists are not such an ignorant set of fanatics as you suppose. They know whereof they affirm. They are familiar with the laws of the Slave States, which are alone sufficient to inspire abhorrence in any humane heart or reflecting mind not perverted by the prejudices of education and custom. I might fill many letters with significant extracts from your statute-books; but I have space only to glance at a few, which indicate the leading features of the system you cherish so tenaciously.

The universal rule of the slave State is, that "the child follows the condition of its mother." This is an index to many things. Marriages between white and colored people are forbidden by law; yet a very large number of the slaves are brown or yellow. When Lafayette visited this country in his old age, he said he was very much struck by the great change in the colored population of Virginia; that in the time of the Revolution, nearly all the household slaves were black, but when he returned to America, he found very few of them black. The advertisements in Southern newspapers often describe runaway slaves that "pass themselves for white men." Sometimes they are descibed as having "straight, light hair blue eyes, and clear complexion." This could not be, unless their fathers, grandfathers, and great-grandfathers had been white men. But as their mothers were slaves, the law pronounces them slaves, subject to be sold on the auction-block whenever the necessities or convenience of their masters or mistresses required it. The sale of one's own children, brother, or sisters, has an ugly aspect to those who are unaccustomed to it; and, obviously, it cannot have a good moral influence, that law and custom should render licentiousness a profitable vice.

Throughout the Slave States, the testimony of no colored person, bond or free, can be received against a white man. You have some laws, which, on the face of them, would seem to restrain inhuman men from murdering or mutilating slaves;

494

but they are rendered nearly null by the law I have cited. Any drunken master, overseer, or patrol, may go into the negro cabins, and commit what outrages he pleases, with perfect impunity, if no white person is present who chooses to witness against him. North Carolina and Georgia leave a large loophole for escape, even if white persons are present, when murder is committed. A law to punish persons for "maliciously killing a slave" has this remarkable qualification: "Always provided that this act shall not extend to any dying of moderate correction." We at the North find it difficult to understand how moderate punishment can cause death. I have read several of your law books attentively, and I find no cases of punishment for the murder of a slave, except by fines paid to the owner to indemnify him for the loss of his property: the the same as if his horse or cow had been killed. In South Carolina Reports is a case where the State had indited Guy Raines for the murder of slave Isaac. It was proved that William Gray, the owner of Isaac, had given him a thousand lashes. The poor creature made his escape, but was caught, and delivered to the custody of Raines, to be carried to the county jail. Because he refused to go, Raines gave him five hundred lashes, and he died soon after. The counsel for Raines proposed that he should be allowed to acquit himself by his own oath . The Court decided against it, because white witnesses had testified; but the Court afterward decided he ought to have been exculpated by his own oath, and he was acquitted . Small indeed is the chance for justice to a slave, when his own color are not allowed to testify, if they see him maimed or his children murdered; when he has slaveholders for Judges and Jurors; when the murderer can exculpate himself by his own oath; and when the law provides that it is no murder to kill a slave by "moderate correction"!

Your laws uniformly declare that "slave shall be deemed a chattel personal in the hands of his master, to all intents, constructions, and purposes whatsoever." This, of course, involves the right to sell his children, as if they were pigs; also, to take his wife from him "for any intent or purpose whatsoever." Your laws also make it death for him to resist a white man, however brutally he may be treated, or however much his family may be outraged before his eyes. If he attempts to run away, your laws allow any man to shoot him.

By your laws, all a slave's earnings belong to his master. He can neither receive donations or transmit property. If his master allows him some hours to work for himself, and by great energy and perseverance he earns enough to buy his own bones and sinews, his master may make him pay two or three times over, and he has no redress. Three such cases have come within my knowledge. Even a written promise from his master has no legal value, because a slave can make no contracts.

Your laws also systematically aim at keeping the minds of the colored people in the most abject state of ignorance. If white people attempt to teach them to read or write, they are punished by imprisonment or fines; if they attempt to teach each other, they are punished with from twenty to thirty-nine lashes each. It cannot be said that the anti-slavery agitation produced such laws, for they date much further back; many of them when we were Provinces. They are the necessities of the system, which, being itself an outrage upon human nature, can be sustained only by perpetual outrages.

The next reliable source of information is the advertisements in the Southern papers. In the North Carolina (Raleigh) *Standard*, Mr. Mieajah Ricks advertises, "Runaway, a negro woman and her two children. A few days before went off, I burned her with a hot iron on the left side of her face. I tried to make the letter M." in the Natchez *Courier*, Mr. J. P. Ashford advertises a runaway negro girl, with "a good many teeth missing, and the letter A branded on her cheek and forehead." In the Lexington (Ky.) *Observer*, Mr. William Overstreet advertises a runaway negro with "his left eye out, scars from a drik on his left arm, and much scarred with the whip." I might quote from hundreds of such advertisements, offering rewards for runaways, "dead or alive," and describing them with "ears cut off," "jaws broken," "scarred by rifle-balls," &c.

Another source of information is afforded by your "Fugitives from Injustice," with many of whom I have conversed freely. I have seen scars of the whip and marks of the branding-iron, and I have listened to their heart-breaking sobs, while they told of "piccaninnies" torn from their arms and sold.

Another source of information is furnished by emancipated slaveholders. Sarah M. Grimké, daughter of the late Judge Grimké, of the Supreme Court of South Carolina, testifies as follows:

> As I left my native State on account account of Slavery, and deserted the home of my fathers to escape the sound of the lash and the shrieks of tortured victims, I would gladly bury in oblivion the recollection of those seens [sic] with which I have been familiar. But this cannot be. They come over my memory like gory spectres, and implore me, with resistless power, in the name of a God of mercy, in the name of a crucified Saviour, in the name of humanity, for the sake of the slaveholder, as well as the slave, to bear witness to the horrors of the Southern prison-house.

She proceeds to describe dreadful tragedies, the actors in which she says were "men and women of the families in South Carolina;" and that their cruelties did not, in the slightest degree, affect their standing in society. Her sister, Angelina Grimké; declared:

> While I live, and Slavery lives, I must testify against it. Not merely for the sake of my poor brothers and sisters in bonds; for even were Slavery no curse to its victims, the exercise of arbitrary power works such fearful ruin upon the hearts of slaveholders, that I should feel impelled to labor and pray for its overthrow with my latest breath.

Among the horrible barbarities she enumerates is the case of a girl thirteen years old, who was flogged to death by her master. She says:

> I asked a prominent lawyer, who belonged to one of the first families in the State, whether the murderer of this helpless child could not be indicted, and he coolly replied that the slave was Mr.——'s property, and if he chose to suffer the loss , no one else had any thing to do with it.

She proceeds to say:

> I felt there could be for me no rest in the midst of such outrages and pollutions. Yet I saw nothing of Slavery in its most vulgar and repulsive forms. I saw it in the city, among the fashionable and the honorable, where it was garnished by refinement and

decked out for show. It is my deep, solemn, deliberate conviction, but this is a cause worth dying for. I say so from what I have seen, and heard, and known, in a land of Slavery, whereon rest the darkness of Egypt and the sin of Sadom.

I once asked Miss Angelina if she thought Abolitionists exaggerated the horrors of Slavery. She replied, with earnest emphasis: "They cannot be exaggerated. It is impossible for imagination to go beyond the fact." To a lady who observed that the time had not yet come for agitating the subject, she answered: "I apprehend if thou wert a slave, toiling in the fields of Carolina, thou wouldst think the time had fully come."

Mr. Thome, of Kentucky, in the course of his eloquent lectures on this subject, said:

I breathed my first breath in an atmosphere of Slavery. But though I am heir to a slave inheritance, I am bold to denounce the whole system as an outrage, a complication of crimes, and wrongs, and cruelties, that make angels weep.

Mr. Allen, of Alabama, in a discussion with the students at Lane Seminary, in 1834, told of a slave who was tied up and beaten all day, with a paddle full of holes.

At night, his flesh was literally pounded to a jelly. The punishment was inflicted within hearing of the Academy and the Public Green. But no one took any notice of it. No one thought any wrong was done. At our house, it is so common to hear screams from a neighboring plantation, that we think nothing of it. Lest any one should think that the slaves are generally well treated, and that the cases I have mentioned are exceptions, let me be distinctly understood that cruelty is the rule and kindness is the exception.

In the same discussion, a student from Virginia, after relating cases of great cruelty, said:

Such things are common all over Virginia; at least, so far as I am acquainted. But the planters generally avoid punishing their slaves before strangers.

Miss Mattie Griffith, of Kentucky, whose entire property consisted in slaves, emancipated them all. The noble-hearted girl wrote to me:

I shall go forth into the world penniless; but I shall work with a heart, and, best of all, I shall live with an easy consience.

Previous to this generous resolution, she had never read any Abolition document, and entertained the common Southern prejudice against them. But her own observation so deeply impressed her with the enormities of Slavery, that she was impelled to publish a book, called *The Autobiography of a Female Slave*. I read it with thrilling interest; but some of the scenes made my nerves quiver so painfully, that I told her I hoped they were too highly colored. She shook her head sadly, and replied: "I am sorry to say that every incident in the book has come within my own knowledge."

St. George Tucker, Judge and Professor of Law in Virginia, speaking of the legalized murder of runaways, said:

Such are the cruelties to which a state of Slavery gives birth—such the horrors to which the human mind is capable of being reconciled by its adoption.

Alluding to our struggle in '76, he said:

> While we proclaimed our resolution to live free or die, we imposed on our fellow-men, of different complexion, a Slavery ten thousand times worse than the utmost extremity of the oppressions of which we complained.

Governor Giles, in a Message to the Legislature of Virginia, referring to the custom of selling free colored people into Slavery, as a punishment for offences not capital, said:

> Slavery must be admitted to be a punishment of the highest order; and, according to the just rule for the apportionment of punishment to crimes, it ought to be applied only to crimes of the highest order. The most distressing reflection in the application of this punishment to female offenders, is that it extends to their offspring; and the innocent are thus punished with the guilty.

Yet one hundred and twenty thousand innocent babies in this country are annually subjected to a punishment which your Governor declared "ought to be applied only to crimes of the highest order."

Jefferson said: "One day of American Slavery is worse than a thousand years of that which we rose in arms to oppose." Alluding to insurrections, he said: "The Almighty has no attribute that can take side with us in such a contest."

John Randolph declared: "Every planter is a sentinel at his own door. Every Southern mother, when she hears an alarm of fire in the night, instinctively presses her infant closer to her bosom."

Looking at the system of slavery in the light of all this evidence, do you candidly think we deserve "two-fold damnation" for detesting it? Can you not believe that we may hate the system, and yet be truly your friends? I make allowance for the excited state of your mind, and for the prejudices induced by education. I do not care to change your opinion of me; but I so wish you could be persuaded to examine this subject dispassionately, for the sake of the prosperity of Virginia, and the welfare of unborn generations, both white and colored. For thirty years, Abolitionists have been trying to reason with slaveholders, through the press, and in the halls of Congress. Their efforts, though directed to the masters only, have been met with violence and abuse almost equal to that poured on head of John Brown. Yet surely we, as a portion of the Union, involved in the expense, the degeneracy, the danger, and the disgrace, of the iniquitious and fatal system, have a right to speak about it, and a right to be heard also. At the North, we willingly publish pro-slavery arguments, and ask only a fair field and no favor for the other side. But you will not even allow your own citizens a chance to examine this important subject. Your letter to me is published in Northern papers, as well as Southern; my reply will not be allowed to appear in any Southern paper. The despotic measures you take to silence investigation, and shut out the light from your own white population, prove how little reliance you have on the strength of your cause. In this enlightened age, all despotisms ought to come to an end by the agency of moral and rational means. But if they resist such agencies, it is in the order of Providence that they must come to an end by violence. History is full of such lessons.

Would that the evil of prejudice could be removed from your eyes. If you would candidly examine the statements of Governor Hincks of the British West Indies, and of the Rev. Mr. Bleby, long time a Missionary in those Islands, both before and after emancipation, you could not fail to be convinced that Cash is a more powerful incentive to labor than the Lash, and far safer also. One fact in relation to those Islands is very significant. While the working people were slaves, it was always necessary to order out the military during the Christmas holidays; but since emancipation, not a soldier is to be seen. A hundred John Browns might land there, without exciting the slightest alarm.

To the personal questions you ask me, I will reply in the name of all the women of New England. It would be extremely difficult to find any woman in our villages who does not sew for the poor, and watch with the sick, whenever occasion requires. We pay our domestics generous wages, with which they can purchase as many Christmas gowns as they please; a process far better for their characters, as well as our own, than to receive their clothing as a charity, after being deprived of just payment for their labor. I have never known an instance where the "pangs of maternity" did not meet with requisite assistance; and here at the North, after we have helped the mothers, we do not sell the babies

I readily believe what you state concerning the kindness of many Virginia matrons. It is creditable to their hearts: but after all, the best that can be done in that way is a poor equivalent for the perpetual wrong done to the slaves, and the terrible liabilities to which they are always subject. Kind masters and mistresses among you are merely lucky accidents.

If any one chooses to be a brutal despot, your laws and customs give him complete power to do so. And the lot of those slaves who have the kindest masters is exceedingly precarious. In case of death, or pecuniary difficulties, or marriages in the family, they may at any time be suddenly transferred from protection and indulgence to personal degradation, or extreme severity; and if they should try to escape from such sufferings, any body is authorized to shoot them down like dogs.

With regard to your declaration that "no Southerner ought henceforth to read a line of my composition," I reply that I have great satisfaction in the consciousness of having nothing to lose in that quarter. Twenty-seven years ago, I published a book called "An Appeal in behalf of that class of Americans called Africans." It influenced the minds of several young men, afterward conspicuous in public life, through whose agency the cause was better served than it could have been by me. From that time to this, I have labored too earnestly for the slave to be agreeable to slaveholders. Literary popularity was never a paramount object with me, even in my youth; and, now that I am old, I am utterly indifferent to it. But, if I cared for the exclusion you threaten I should at least have the consolation of being exiled with honorable company. Dr. Channing's writings, mild and candid as they are, breathe what you would call arrant treason. William C. Bryant, in his capacity of editor, is openly on our side. The inspired muse of Whittier has incessantly sounded the trumpet for moral warfare with your iniquitous institution; and his stirring tones have been answered, more or less loudly, by Pierpont, Lowell, and Longfellow. Emerson, the Plato of America, leaves the scholastic seclusion he loves so well, and disliking noise with all his poetic soul, bravely takes his stand among the trumpeters. George W. Curtis, the brilliant wealth of his talent on the altar of Freedom, and makes common cause with rough-shod reformers.

The genius of Mrs. Stowe carried the outworks of your institution at one dash, and left the citadel open to besiegers, who are pouring in amain. In the church, on the ultra-liberal side, it is assailed by the powerful battering-ram of Theodore Parker's eloquence. On the extreme orthodox side is set a huge fire, kindled by the burning words of Dr. Cheever. Between them is Henry Ward Beecher, sending a shower of keen arrows into your entrenchments; and with him ride a troop of sharp-shooters from all sects. If you turn to the literature of England or France, you will find your institution treated with as little favor. The fact is, the whole civilized world proclaims Slavery an outlaw, and the best intellect of the age is active in hunting it down.

L. Maria Child

Note

1. The following Senators, Mr. Niles, of Connecticut, Mr. Dix, of New York, and Mr. Tappan, of Ohio, published statements that their votes had been obtained by false representations; and they declared that the case was the same with Mr. Heywood, of North Carolina.

A Plea for Captain John Brown

HENRY DAVID THOREAU

This lecture was first given to an audience in Concord, Massachusetts on October 30th 1859. In it, Thoreau presents a powerful polemic in support of John Brown and his actions at Harper's Ferry. Claiming Brown as a fellow transcendentalist whose conscience was informed by a higher code of ethics than that implied by the laws of the United States, Thoreau praises him as a sincere and robust exponent of Christian moral values. He also foresees that Brown's actions mark him not simply as a hero, but also as a martyr for the abolitionist cause.

I trust that you will pardon me for being here. I do not wish to force my thoughts upon you, but I feel forced myself. Little as I know of Captain Brown, I would fain do my part to correct the tone and the statements of the newspapers, and of my countrymen generally, respecting his character and actions. It costs us nothing to be just. We can at least express our sympathy with, and admiration of, him and his companions, and that is what I now propose to do.

First, as to his history.

I will endeavor to omit, as much as possible, what you have already read. I need not describe his person to you, for probably most of you have seen and will not soon forget him. I am told that his grandfather, John Brown, was an officer in the Revolution; that he himself was born in Connecticut about the beginning of this century, but early went with his father to Ohio. I heard him say that his father was a contractor who furnished beef to the army there, in the war of 1812; that he accompanied him to the camp, and assisted him in that employment, seeing a good deal of military life, more, perhaps, than if he had been a soldier, for he was often present at the councils of the officers. Especially, he learned by experience how armies are supplied and maintained in the field—a work which, he observed, requires at least as much experience and skill as to lead them in battle. He said that few

Source: Henry David Thoreau, 'A Plea for Captain John Brown', 30 October 1859.

persons had any conception of the cost, even the pecuniary cost, of firing a single bullet in war. He saw enough, at any rate, to disgust him with a military life, indeed to excite in him a great abhorrence of it; so much so, that though he was tempted by the offer of some petty office in the army, when he was about eighteen, he not only declined that, but he also refused to train when warned, and was fined for it. He then resolved that he would never have anything to do with any war, unless it were a war for liberty.

When the troubles in Kansas began, he sent several of his sons thither to strengthen the party of the Free State men, fitting them out with such weapons as he had; telling them that if the troubles should increase, and there should be need of him, he would follow to assist them with his hand and counsel. This, as you all know, he soon after did; and it was through his agency, far more than any others, that Kansas was made free.

For a part of his life he was a surveyor, and at one time he was engaged in wool-growing, and he went to Europe as an agent about that business. There, as every where, he had his eyes about him, and made many original observations. He said, for instance, that he saw why the soil of England was so rich, and that of Germany (I think it was) so poor, and he thought of writing to some of the crowned heads about it. It was because in England the peasantry live on the soil which they cultivate, but in Germany they are gathered into villages, at night. It is a pity that he did not make a book of his observations.

I should say that he was an old-fashioned man in his respect for the Constitution, and his faith in the permanence of this Union. Slavery he deemed to be wholly opposed to these, and he was its determined foe.

He was by descent and birth a New England farmer, a man of great common sense, deliberate and practical as that class is, and tenfold more so. He was like the best of those who stood at Concord Bridge once, on Lexington Common, and on Bunker Hill, only he was firmer and higher principled than any that I have chanced to hear of as there. It was no abolition lecturer that converted him. Ethan Allen and Stark, with whom he may in some respects be compared, were rangers in a lower and less important field. They could bravely face their country's foes, but he had the courage to face his country herself, when she was in the wrong. A Western writer says, to account for his escape from so many perils, that he was concealed under a "rural exterior;" as if, in that prairie land, a hero should, by good rights, wear a citizen's dress only.

He did not go to the college called Harvard, good old Alma Mater as she is. He was not fed on the pap that is there furnished. As he phrased it, "I know no more of grammar than one of your calves." But he went to the great university of the West, where he sedulously pursued the study of Liberty, for which he had early betrayed a fondness, and having taken many degrees, he finally commenced the public practice of Humanity in Kansas, as you all know. Such were *his humanities*, and not any study of grammar. He would have left a Greek accent slanting the wrong way, and righted up a falling man.

He was one of that class of whom we hear a great deal, but, for the most part, see nothing at all—the Puritans. It would be in vain to kill him. He died lately in the time of Cromwell, but he reappeared here. Why should he not? Some of the Puritan stock are said to have come over and settled in New England. They were a class that did something else than celebrate their forefathers' day, and eat parched corn in remembrance of that time. They were neither Democrats nor Republicans, but men of simple habits, straightforward, prayerful; not thinking much of rulers who did not fear God, not making many compromises, nor seeking after available candidates.

"In his camp," as one has recently written, and as I have myself heard him state, "he permitted no profanity; no man of loose morals was suffered to remain there, unless, indeed, as a prisoner of war. 'I would rather,' said he, 'have the small-pox, yellow fever, and cholera, all together in my camp, than a man without principle. . . . It is a mistake, sir, that our people make, when they think that bullies are the best fighters, or that they are the fit men to oppose these Southerners. Give me men of good principles,—God-fearing men,—men who respect themselves, and with a dozen of them I will oppose any hundred such men as these Buford ruffians.'" He said that if one offered himself to be a soldier under him, who was forward to tell what he could or would do, if he could only get sight of the enemy, he had but little confidence in him.

He was never able to find more than a score or so of recruits whom he would accept, and only about a dozen, among them his sons, in whom he had perfect faith. When he was here, some years ago, he showed to a few a little manuscript book,—his "orderly book" I think he called it,—containing the names of his company in Kansas, and the rules by which they bound themselves; and he stated that several of them had already sealed the contract with their blood. When some one remarked that, with the addition of a chaplain, it would have been a perfect Cromwellian troop, he observed that he would have been glad to add a chaplain to the list, if he could have found one who could fill that office worthily. It is easy enough to find one for the United States army. I believe that he had prayers in his camp morning and evening, nevertheless.

He was a man of Spartan habits, and at sixty was scrupulous about his diet at your table, excusing himself by saying that he must eat sparingly and fare hard, as became a soldier or one who was fitting himself for difficult enterprises, a life of exposure.

A man of rare common sense and directness of speech, as of action; a transcendentalist above all, a man of ideas and principles,—that was what distinguished him. Not yielding to a whim or transient impulse, but carrying out the purpose of a life. I noticed that he did not overstate any thing, but spoke within bounds. I remember, particularly, how, in his speech here, he referred to what his family had suffered in Kansas, without ever giving the least vent to his pent-up fire. It was a volcano with an ordinary chimney-flue. Also referring to the deeds of certain Border Ruffians, he said, rapidly paring away his speech, like an experienced soldier, keeping a reserve of force and meaning, "They had a perfect right to be hung." He was not in the least a rhetorician, was not talking to Buncombe or his constituents any where, had no need to invent any thing, but to tell the simple truth, and communicate his own resolution; therefore he appeared incomparably strong, and eloquence in Congress and elsewhere seemed to me at a discount. It was like the speeches of Cromwell compared with those of an ordinary king.

As for his tact and prudence, I will merely say, that at a time when scarcely a man from the Free States was able to reach Kansas by any direct route, at least without having his arms taken from him, he, carrying what imperfect guns and other weapons he could collect, openly and slowly drove an ox-cart through Missouri, apparently in the capacity of a surveyor, with his surveying compass exposed in it, and so passed unsuspected, and had ample opportunity to learn the designs of the enemy. For some time after his arrival he still followed the same profession. When, for instance, he saw a knot of the ruffians on the prairie, discussing, of course, the single topic which then occupied their minds, he would, perhaps, take his compass and one of his sons, and proceed to run an imaginary line right through the very spot on which that conclave had assembled, and when he came up to them, he would naturally pause and have some talk with them, learning their news, and, at last, all their plans perfectly; and having thus completed his real survey, he would resume his imaginary one, and run on his line till he was out of sight.

When I expressed surprise that he could live in Kansas at all, with a price set upon his head, and so large a number, including the authorities, exasperated against him, he accounted for it by saying, "It is perfectly well understood that I will not be taken." Much of the time for some years he has had to skulk in swamps, suffering from poverty and from sickness, which was the consequence of exposure, befriended only by Indians and a few whites. But though it might be known that he was lurking in a particular swamp, his foes commonly did not care to go in after him. He could even come out into a town where there were more Border Ruffians than Free State men, and transact some business, without delaying long, and yet not be molested; for said he, "No little handful of men were willing to undertake it, and a large body could not be got together in season."

As for his recent failure, we do not know the facts about it. It was evidently far from being a wild and desperate attempt. His enemy, Mr. Vallandigham, is compelled to say, that "it was among the best planned and executed conspiracies that ever failed."

Not to mention his other successes, was it a failure, or did it show a want of good management, to deliver from bondage a dozen human beings, and walk off with them by broad daylight, for weeks if not months, at a leisurely pace, through one State after another, for half the length of the North, conspicuous to all parties, with a price set upon his head, going into a court room on his way and telling what he had done, thus convincing Missouri that it was not profitable to try to hold slaves in his neighborhood?—and this, not because the government menials were lenient, but because they were afraid of him.

Yet he did not attribute his success, foolishly, to "his star," or to any magic. He said, truly, that the reason why such greatly superior numbers quailed before him, was, as one of his prisoners confessed, because they *lacked a cause*—a kind of armor which he and his party never lacked. When the time came, few men were found willing to lay down their lives in defence of what they knew to be wrong; they did not like that this should be their last act in this world.

But to make haste to *his* last act, and its effects.

The newspapers seem to ignore, or perhaps are really ignorant of the fact, that there are at least as many as two or three individuals to a town throughout the North, who think much as the present speaker does about him and his enterprise. I do not hesitate to say that they are an important and growing party. We aspire to be something more than stupid and timid chattels, pretending to read history and our bibles, but desecrating every house and every day we breathe in. Perhaps anxious politicians may prove that only seventeen white men and five negroes were concerned in the late enterprise, but their very anxiety to prove this might suggest to themselves that all is not told. Why do they still dodge the truth? They are so anxious because of a dim consciousness of the fact, which they do not distinctly face, that at least a million of the free inhabitants of the United States would have rejoiced if it had succeeded. They at most only criticise the tactics. Though we wear no crape, the thought of that man's position and probable fate is spoiling many a man's day here at the North for other thinking. If any one who has seen him here can pursue successfully any other train of thought, I do not know what he is made of. If there is any such who gets his usual allowance of sleep, I will warrant him to fatten easily under any circumstances which do not touch his body or purse. I put a piece of paper and a pencil under my pillow, and when I could not sleep, I wrote in the dark.

On the whole, my respect for my fellow-men, except as one may outweigh a million, is not being increased these days. I have noticed the cold-blooded way in which newspaper writers and men generally speak of this event, as if an ordinary malefactor, though one of unusual "pluck,"—as the Governor of Virginia is reported to have said, using the language of the cock-pit, "the gamest man he ever saw,"—had been caught, and were about to be hung. He was not dreaming of his foes when the governor thought he looked so brave. It turns what sweetness I have to gall, to hear, or hear of, the remarks of some of my neighbors. When we heard at first that he was dead, one of my townsmen observed that "he died as the fool dieth;" which, pardon me, for an instant suggested a likeness in him dying to my neighbor living. Others, craven-hearted, said disparagingly, that "he threw his life away," because he resisted the government. Which way have they thrown *their* lives, pray?—Such as would praise a man for attacking singly an ordinary band of thieves or murderers. I hear another ask, Yankee-like, "What will he gain by it?" as if he expected to fill his pockets by this enterprise. Such a one has no idea of gain but in this worldly sense. If it does not lead to a "surprise" party, if he does not get a new pair of boots, or a vote of thanks, it must be a failure. "But he won't gain any thing by it." Well, no, I don't suppose he could get four-and-sixpence a day for being hung, take the year round; but then he stands a chance to save a considerable part of his soul—and *such* a soul!—when *you* do not. No doubt you can get more in your market for a quart of milk than for a quart of blood, but that is not the market that heroes carry their blood to.

Such do not know that like the seed is the fruit, and that, in the moral world, when good seed is planted, good fruit is inevitable, and does not depend on our watering and cultivating; that when you plant, or bury, a hero in his field, a crop of heroes is sure to spring up. This is a seed of such force and vitality, that it does not ask our leave to germinate.

The momentary charge at Balaclava, in obedience to a blundering command, proving what a perfect machine the soldier is, has, properly enough, been celebrated by a poet laureate; but the steady, and for the most part successful charge of this man, for some years, against the legions of Slavery, in obedience to an infinitely higher command, is as much more memorable than that, as an intelligent and conscientious man is superior to a machine. Do you think that that will go unsung?

"Served him right"—"A dangerous man"—"He is undoubtedly insane." So they proceed to live their sane, and wise, and altogether admirable lives, reading their Plutarch a little, but chiefly pausing at that feat of Putnam, who was let down into a wolf's den; and in this wise they nourish themselves for brave and patriotic deeds some time or other. The Tract Society could afford to print that story of Putnam. You might open the district schools with the reading of it, for there is nothing about Slavery or the Church in it; unless it occurs to the reader that some pastors are wolves in sheep's clothing. "The American Board of Commissioners for Foreign Missions" even, might dare to protest against that wolf. I have heard of boards, and of American boards, but it chances that I never heard of this particular lumber till lately. And yet I hear of Northern men, women, and children, by families, buying a "life membership" in such societies as these;—a life-membership in the grave! You can get buried cheaper than that. Our foes are in our midst and all about us. There is hardly a house but is divided against itself, for our foe is the all but universal woodenness of both head and heart, the want of vitality in man, which is the effect of our vice; and hence are begotten fear, superstition, bigotry, persecution, and slavery of all kinds. We are mere figure-heads upon a hulk, with livers in the place of hearts. The curse is the worship of idols, which at length changes the worshipper into a stone image himself; and the New Englander is just as much an idolater as the Hindoo. This man was an exception, for he did not set up even a political graven image between him and his God.

A church that can never have done with excommunicating Christ while it exists! Away with your broad and flat churches, and your narrow and tall churches! Take a step forward, and invent a new style of out-houses. Invent a salt that will save you, and defend our nostrils.

The modern Christian is a man who has consented to say all the prayers in the liturgy, provided you will let him go straight to bed and sleep quietly afterward. All his prayers begin with "Now I lay me down to sleep," and he is forever looking forward to the time when he shall go to his "long rest." He has consented to perform certain old established charities, too, after a fashion, but he does not wish to hear of any new-fangled ones; he doesn't wish to have any supplementary articles added to the contract, to fit it to the present time. He shows the whites of his eyes on the

Sabbath, and the blacks all the rest of the week. The evil is not merely a stagnation of blood, but a stagnation of spirit. Many, no doubt, are well disposed, but sluggish by constitution and by habit, and they cannot conceive of a man who is actuated by higher motives than they are. Accordingly they pronounce this man insane, for they know that *they* could never act as he does, as long as they are themselves.

We dream of foreign countries, of other times and races of men, placing them at a distance in history or space; but let some significant event like the present occur in our midst, and we discover, often, this distance and this strangeness between us and our nearest neighbors. *They* are our Austrias, and Chinas, and South Sea Islands. Our crowded society becomes well spaced all at once, clean and handsome to the eye, a city of magnificent distances. We discover why it was that we never got beyond compliments and surfaces with them before; we become aware of as many versts between us and them as there are between a wandering Tartar and a Chinese town. The thoughtful man becomes a hermit in the thoroughfares of the market-place. Impassable seas suddenly find their level between us, or dumb steppes stretch themselves out there. It is the difference of constitution, of intelligence, and faith, and not streams and mountains, that make the true and impassable boundaries between individuals and between states. None but the like-minded can come plenipotentiary to our court.

I read all the newspapers I could get within a week after this event, and I do not remember in them a single expression of sympathy for these men. I have since seen one noble statement, in a Boston paper, not editorial. Some voluminous sheets decided not to print the full report of Brown's words to the exclusion of other matter. It was as if a publisher should reject the manuscript of the New Testament, and print Wilson's last speech. The same journal which contained this pregnant news, was chiefly filled, in parallel columns, with the reports of the political conventions that were being held. But the descent to them was too steep. They should have been spared this contrast, been printed in an extra at least. To turn from the voices and deeds of earnest men to the cackling of political conventions! Office seekers and speechmakers, who do not so much as lay an honest egg, but wear their breasts bare upon an egg of chalks! Their great game is the game of straws, or rather that universal aboriginal game of the platter, at which the Indians cried *hub, bub!* Exclude the reports of religious and political conventions, and publish the words of a living man.

But I object not so much to what they have omitted as to what they have inserted. Even the *Liberator* called it "a misguided, wild, and apparently insane ... effort." As for the herd of newspapers and magazines, I do not chance to know an editor in the country who will deliberately print anything which he knows will ultimately and permanently reduce the number of his subscribers. They do not believe that it would be expedient. How then can they print truth? If we do not say pleasant things, they argue, nobody will attend to us. And so they do like some travelling auctioneers, who sing an obscene song in order to draw a crowd around them. Republican editors, obliged to get their sentences ready for the morning edition, and accustomed to look at every thing by the twilight of politics, express no admiration, nor true sorrow even, but call these men "deluded fanatics"—"mistaken men"—"insane," or "crazed." It suggests what a sane set of editors we are blessed with, not "mistaken men"; who know very well on which side their bread is buttered, at least.

A man does a brave and humane deed, and at once, on all sides, we hear people and parties declaring, "I didn't do it, nor countenance *him* to do it, in any conceivable way. It can't be fairly inferred from my past career." I, for one, am not interested to hear you define your position. I don't know that I ever was, or ever shall be. I think it is mere egotism, or impertinent at this time. Ye needn't take so much pains to wash your skirts of him. No intelligent man will ever be convinced that he was any creature of yours. He went and came, as he himself informs us, "under the auspices of John Brown and nobody else." The Republican party does not perceive how many his *failure* will make to vote more correctly than they would have them. They have counted the votes of Pennsylvania &. Co., but they have not correctly counted Captain Brown's vote. He has taken the wind out of their sails, the little wind they had, and they may as well lie to and repair.

What though he did not belong to your clique! Though you may not approve of his method or his principles, recognize his magnanimity. Would you not like to claim kindredship with him in that, though in no other thing he is like, or likely, to you? Do you think that you would lose your reputation so? What you lost at the spile, you would gain at the bung.

If they do not mean all this, then they do not speak the truth, and say what they mean. They are simply at their old tricks still. "It was always conceded to him," *says one who calls him crazy,* "that he was a conscientious man, very modest in his demeanor, apparently inoffensive, until the subject of Slavery was introduced, when he would exhibit a feeling of indignation unparalleled."

The slave-ship is on her way, crowded with its dying victims; new cargoes are being added in mid ocean; a small crew of slaveholders, countenanced by a large body of passengers, is smothering four millions under the hatches, and yet the politician asserts that the only proper way by which deliverance is to be obtained, is by "the quiet diffusion of the sentiments of humanity," without any "outbreak." As if the sentiments of humanity were ever found unaccompanied by its deeds, and you could disperse them, all finished to order, the pure article, as easily as water with a watering-pot, and so lay the dust. What is that that I hear cast overboard? The bodies of the dead that have found deliverance. That is the way we are "diffusing" humanity, and its sentiments with it.

Prominent and influential editors, accustomed to deal with politicians, men of an infinitely lower grade, say, in their ignorance, that he acted "on the principle of revenge." They do not know the man. They must enlarge themselves to conceive of him. I have no doubt that the time will come when they will begin to see him as he was. They have got to conceive of a man of faith and of religious principle, and not a politician or an Indian; of a man who did not wait till he was personally interfered with, or thwarted in some harmless business, before he gave his life to the cause of the oppressed.

If Walker may be considered the representative of the South, I wish I could say that Brown was the representative of the North. He was a superior man. He did not value his bodily life in comparison with ideal things. He did not recognize unjust human laws, but resisted them as he was bid. For once we are lifted out of the trivialness and dust of politics into the region of truth and manhood. No man in America has ever stood up so persistently and effectively for the dignity of human nature, knowing himself for a man, and the equal of any and all governments. In that sense he was the most American of us all. He needed no babbling lawyer, making false issues, to defend him. He was more than a match for all the judges that American voters, or office-holders of whatever grade, can create. He could not have been tried by a jury of his peers, because his peers did not exist. When a man stands up serenely against the condemnation and vengeance of mankind, rising above them literally *by a whole body*,—even though he were of late the vilest murderer, who has settled that matter with himself,—the spectacle is a sublime one,—didn't ye know it, ye Liberators, ye Tribunes, ye Republicans?—and we become criminal in comparison. Do yourselves the honor to recognize him. He needs none of your respect.

As for the Democratic journals, they are not human enough to affect me at all. I do not feel indignation at any thing they may say.

I am aware that I anticipate a little, that he was still, at the last accounts, alive in the hands of his foes; but that being the case, I have all along found myself thinking and speaking of him as physically dead.

I do not believe in erecting statues to those who still live in our hearts, whose bones have not yet crumbled in the earth around us, but I would rather see the statue of Captain Brown in the Massachusetts State-House yard, than that of any other man whom I know. I rejoice that I live in this age—that I am his contemporary.

What a contrast, when we turn to that political party which is so anxiously shuffling him and his plot out of its way, and looking around for some available slaveholder, perhaps, to be its candidate, at least for one who will execute the Fugitive Slave Law, and all those other unjust laws which he took up arms to annul!

Insane! A father and six sons, and one son-in-law, and several more men besides,—as many at least as twelve disciples,—all struck with insanity at once; while the sane tyrant holds with a firmer grip than ever his four millions of slaves, and a thousand sane editors, his abettors, are saving their country and their bacon! Just as insane were his efforts in Kansas. Ask the tyrant who is his most dangerous foe, the sane man or the insane. Do the thousands who know him best, who have rejoiced at his deeds in Kansas, and have afforded him material aid there, think him insane? Such a use of this word is a mere trope with most who persist in using it, and I have no doubt that many of the rest have already in silence retracted their words.

Read his admirable answers to Mason and others. How they are dwarfed and defeated by the contrast! On the one side, half brutish, half timid questioning; on the other, truth, clear as lightning, crashing into their obscene temples. They are made to stand with Pilate, and Gessler, and the Inquisition. How ineffectual their speech and action! and what a void their silence! They are but helpless tools in this great work. It was no human power that gathered them about this preacher.

What have Massachusetts and the North sent a few *sane* representatives to Congress for, of late years?—to declare with effect what kind of sentiments? All their speeches put together and boiled down,—and probably they themselves will confess it,—do not match for manly directness and force, and for simple truth, the few casual remarks of crazy John Brown, on the floor of the Harper's Ferry engine house;—that man whom you are about to hang, to send to the other world, though not to represent *you* there. No, he was not our representative in any sense. He was too fair a specimen of a man to represent the like of us. Who, then, *were* his constituents? If you read his words understandingly you will find out. In his case there is no idle eloquence, no made, nor maiden speech, no compliments to the oppressor. Truth is his inspirer, and earnestness the polisher of his sentences. He could afford to lose his Sharps' rifles, while he retained his faculty of speech, a Sharps' rifle of infinitely surer and longer range.

And the *New York Herald* reports the conversation *"verbatim"!* It does not know of what undying words it is made the vehicle. I have no respect for the penetration of any man who can read the report of that conversation, and still call the principal in it insane. It has the ring of a saner sanity than an ordinary discipline and habits of life, than an ordinary organization, secure. Take any sentence of it—"Any questions that I can honorably answer, I will; not otherwise. So far as I am myself concerned, I have told every thing truthfully. I value my word, sir." The few who talk about his vindictive spirit, while they really admire his heroism, have no test by which to detect a noble man, no amalgam to combine with his pure gold. They mix their own dross with it.

It is a relief to turn from these slanders to the testimony of his more truthful, but frightened, jailers and hangmen. Governor Wise speaks far more justly and appreciatingly of him than any Northern editor, or politician, or public personage, that I chance to have heard from. I know that you can afford to hear him again on this subject. He says: "They are themselves mistaken who take him to be a madman. . . . He is cool, collected, and indomitable, and it is but just to him to say, that he was humane to his prisoners. . . . And he inspired me with great trust in his integrity as a man of truth. He is a fanatic, vain and garrulous," (I leave that part to Mr. Wise) "but firm, truthful, and intelligent. His men, too, who survive, are like him. . . . Colonel Washington says that he was the coolest and firmest man he ever saw in defying danger and death. With one son dead by his side, and another shot through, he felt the pulse of his dying son with one hand, and held his rifle with the other, and commanded his men with the utmost composure, encouraging them to be firm, and to sell their lives as dear as they could. Of the three white prisoners, Brown, Stevens, and Coppoc, it was hard to say which was most firm. . . . ."

Almost the first Northern men whom the slave-holder has learned to respect!

The testimony of Mr. Vallandigham, though less valuable, is of the same purport, that "it is vain to underrate either the man or his conspiracy. . . . He is the farthest possible remove from the ordinary ruffian, fanatic, or madman."

"All is quiet at Harper's Ferry," say the journals. What is the character of that calm which follows when the law and the slaveholder prevail? I regard this event as a touchstone designed to bring out, with glaring distinctness, the character of this government. We needed to be thus assisted to see it by the light of history. It needed to see itself. When a government puts forth its strength on the side of injustice, as ours to maintain Slavery and kill the liberators of the slave, it reveals itself a merely brute force, or worse, a demoniacal force. It is the head of the Plug Uglies. It is more manifest than ever that tyranny rules. I see this government to be effectually allied with France and Austria in oppressing mankind. There sits a tyrant holding fettered four millions of slaves; here comes their heroic liberator. This most hypocritical and diabolical government looks up from its seat on the gasping four millions, and inquires with an assumption of innocence, "What do you assault me for? Am I not an honest man? Cease agitation on this subject, or I will make a slave of you, too, or else hang you."

We talk about a *representative* government; but what a monster of a government is that where the noblest faculties of the mind, and the whole heart, are not *represented*. A semi-human tiger or ox, stalking over the earth, with its heart taken out and the top of its brain shot away. Heroes have fought well on their stumps when their legs were shot off, but I never heard of any good done by such a government as that.

The only government that I recognize,—and it matters not how few are at the head of it, or how small its army,—is that power that establishes justice in the land, never that which establishes injustice. What shall we think of a government to which all the truly brave and just men in the land are enemies, standing between it and those whom it oppresses? A government that pretends to be Christian and crucifies a million Christs every day!

Treason! Where does such treason take its rise? I cannot help thinking of you as you deserve, ye governments. Can you dry up the fountains of thought? High treason, when it is resistance to tyranny here below, has its origin in, and is first committed by the power that makes and forever recreates man. When you have caught and hung all these human rebels, you have accomplished nothing but your own guilt, for you have not struck at the fountain head. You presume to contend with a foe against whom West Point cadets and rifled cannon *point* not. Can all the art of the cannon-founder tempt matter to turn against its maker? Is the form in which the founder thinks he casts it more essential than the constitution of it and of himself?

The United States have a coffle of four millions of slaves. They are determined to keep them in this condition; and Massachusetts is one of the confederated overseers to prevent their escape. Such are not all the inhabitants of Massachusetts, but such are they who rule and are obeyed here. It was Massachusetts, as well as Virginia, that put down this insurrection at Harper's Ferry. She sent the marines there, and she will have to pay the penalty of her sin.

Suppose that there is a society in this State that out of its own purse and magnanimity saves all the fugitive slaves that run to us, and protects our colored fellow-citizens, and leaves the other work to the Government, so-called. Is not that government fast losing its occupation, and becoming contemptible to mankind? If private men are obliged to perform the offices of government, to protect the weak and dispense justice, then the government becomes only a hired man, or clerk, to perform menial or indifferent services. Of course, that is but the shadow of a government whose existence necessitates a Vigilant Committee. What should we think of the oriental Cadi even, behind whom worked in secret a Vigilant Committee? But such is the character of our Northern States generally; each has its Vigilant Committee. And, to a certain extent, these crazy governments recognize and accept this relation. They say, virtually, "We'll be glad to work for you on these terms, only don't make a noise about it." And thus the government, its salary being insured, withdraws into the back shop, taking the constitution with it, and bestows most of its labor on repairing that. When I hear it at work sometimes, as I go by, it reminds me, at best, of those fanners who in winter contrive to turn a penny by following the coopering business. And what kind of spirit is their barrel made to hold? They speculate in stocks, and bore holes in mountains, but they are not competent to lay out even a decent highway. The only *free* road, the Underground Railroad, is owned and managed by theVigilant Committee. *They* have tunnelled under the whole breadth of the land. Such a government is losing its power and respectability as surely as water runs out of a leaky vessel, and is held by one that can contain it.

I hear many condemn these men because they were so few. When were the good and the brave ever in a majority? Would you have had him wait till that time came?— till you and I came over to him? The very fact that he had no rabble or troop of hirelings about him would alone distinguish him from ordinary heroes. His company was small indeed, because few could be found worthy to pass muster. Each one who there laid down his life for the poor and oppressed, was a picked man, called out of many thousands, if not millions; apparently a man of principle, of rare courage and devoted humanity, ready to sacrifice his life at any moment for the benefit of his fellow man. It may be doubted if there were as many more their equals in these respects in all the country—I speak of his followers only—for their leader, no doubt, scoured the land far and wide, seeking to swell his troop. These alone were ready to step between the oppressor and the oppressed. Surely, they were the very best men you could select to be hung. That was the greatest compliment which this country could pay them. They were ripe for her gallows. She has tried a long time, she has hung a good many, but never found the right one before.

When I think of him, and his six sons, and his son in law,—not to enumerate the others,—enlisted for this fight; proceeding coolly, reverently, humanely to work, for months if not years, sleeping and waking upon it, summering and wintering the thought, without expecting any reward but a good conscience, while almost all America stood ranked on the other side, I say again that it affects me as a sublime spectacle. If he had had any journal advocating *"his cause,"* any organ as the phrase is, monotonously and wearisomely playing the same old tune, and then passing round the hat, it would have been fatal to his efficiency. If he had acted in any way so as to be let alone by the government, he might have been suspected. It was the fact that the tyrant must give place to him, or he to the tyrant, that distinguished him from all the reformers of the day I know.

It was his peculiar doctrine that a man has a perfect right to interfere by force with the slaveholder, in order to rescue the slave. I agree with him. They who are continually shocked by slavery have some right to be shocked by the violent death of the slaveholder, but no others. Such will be more shocked by his life than by his death. I shall not be forward to think him mistaken in his method who quickest succeeds to liberate the slave. I speak for the slave when I say, that I prefer the philanthropy of Captain Brown to that philanthropy which neither shoots me nor liberates me. At any rate, I do not think it is quite sane for one to spend his whole life in talking or writing about this matter, unless he is continuously inspired, and I have not done so. A man may have other affairs to attend to. I do not wish to kill nor to be killed, but I can foresee circumstances in which both these things would be by me unavoidable. We preserve the so-called "peace" of our community by deeds of petty violence every day. Look at the policeman's billy and hand cuffs! Look at the jail! Look at the gallows! Look at the chaplain of the regiment! We are hoping only to live safely on the outskirts of this provisional army. So we defend ourselves and our hen roosts, and maintain slavery. I know that the mass of my countrymen think that the only righteous use that can be made of Sharps' rifles and revolvers is to fight duels with them, when we are insulted by other nations, or to hunt Indians, or shoot fugitive slaves with them, or the like. I think that for once the Sharps' rifles and the revolvers were employed in a righteous cause. The tools were in the hands of one who could use them.

The same indignation that is said to have cleared the temple once will clear it again. The question is not about the weapon, but the spirit in which you use it. No man has appeared in America as yet who loved his fellow man so well, and treated him so tenderly. He lived for him. He took up his life and he laid it down for him. What sort of violence is that which is encouraged, not by soldiers but by peaceable citizens, not so much by lay-men as by ministers of the gospel, not so much by the fighting sects as by the Quakers, and not so much by Quaker men as by Quaker women?

This event advertises me that there is such a fact as death—the possibility of a man's dying. It seems as if no man had ever died in America before, for in order to die you must first have lived. I don't believe in the hearses and pains and funerals that they have had. There was no death in the case, because there had been no life; they merely rotted or sloughed off, pretty much as they had rotted or sloughed along. No temple's vail was rent, only a hole dug somewhere. Let the dead bury their dead. The best of them fairly ran down like a clock. Franklin—Washington—they were let off without dying; they were merely missing one day. I hear a good many pretend that they are going to die;—or that they have died for aught that I know. Nonsense! I'll defy them to do it. They haven't got life enough in them. They'll deliquesce like fungi, and keep a hundred eulogists mopping the spot where they left off. Only half a dozen or so have died since the world began. Do you think that you are going to die, sir? No! there's no hope of you. You haven't got your lesson yet. You've got to stay after school. We make a needless ado about capital punishment—taking lives, when there is no life to take. *Memento mori!* We don't understand that sublime sentence which some worthy got sculptured on his gravestone once. We've interpreted it in a grovelling and snivelling sense; we've wholly forgotten how to die.

But be sure you do die, neverthless. Do your work, and finish it. If you know how to begin, you will know when to end.

These men, in teaching us how to die, have at the same time taught us how to live. If this man's acts and words do not create a revival, it will be the severest possible satire on the acts and words that do. It is the best news that America has ever heard. It has already quickened the feeble pulse of the North, and infused more and more generous blood into her veins and heart, than any number of years of what is called commercial and political prosperity could. How many a man who was lately contemplating suicide has now something to live for!

One writer says that Brown's peculiar monomania made him to be "dreaded by the Missourians as a supernatural being." Sure enough, a hero in the midst of us cowards is always so dreaded. He is just that thing. He shows himself superior to nature. He has a spark of divinity in him.

> *Unless above himself he can*
> *Erect himself, how poor a thing is man!*

Newspaper editors argue also that it is a proof of his *insanity* that he thought he was appointed to do this work which he did—that he did not suspect himself for a moment! They talk as if it were impossible that a man could be "divinely appointed" in these days to do any work whatever; as if vows and religion were out of date as connected with any man's daily work,—as if the agent to abolish Slavery could only be somebody appointed by the President, or by some political party. They talk as if a man's death were a failure, and his continued life, be it of whatever character, were a success.

When I reflect to what a cause this man devoted himself, and how religiously, and then reflect to what cause his judges and all who condemn him so angrily and fluently devote themselves, I see that they are as far apart as the heavens and earth are asunder.

The amount of it is, our *"leading men"* are a harmless kind of folk, and they know *well enough* that *they* were not divinely appointed, but elected by the votes of their party.

Who is it whose safety requires that Captain Brown be hung? Is it indispensable to any Northern man? Is there no resource but to cast these men also to the Minotaur? If you do not wish it say so distinctly. While these things are being done, beauty stands veiled and music is a screeching lie. Think of him—of his rare qualities! such a man as it takes ages to make, and ages to understand; no mock hero, nor the representative of any party. A man such as the sun may not rise upon again in this benighted land. To whose making went the costliest material, the finest adamant; sent to be the redeemer of those in captivity. And the only use to which you can put him is to hang him at the end of a rope! You who pretend to care for Christ crucified, consider what you are about to do to him who offered himself to be the savior of four millions of men.

Any man knows when he is justified, and all the wits in the world cannot enlighten him on that point. The murderer always knows that he is justly punished; but when a government takes the life of a man without the consent of his conscience, it is an audacious government, and is taking a step towards its own dissolution. Is it not possible that an individual may be right and a government wrong? Are laws to be enforced simply because they were made? or declared by any number of men to be good, if they are *not* good? Is there any necessity for a man's being a tool to perform a deed of which his better nature disapproves? Is it the intention of law-makers that *good* men shall be hung ever? Are judges to interpret the law according to the letter, and not the spirit? What right have *you* to enter into a compact with yourself that you *will* do thus or so, against the light within you? Is it for *you* to *make up* your mind—to form any resolution whatever—and not accept the convictions that are forced upon you, and which ever pass your understanding? I do not believe in lawyers, in that mode of attacking or defending a man, because you descend to meet the judge on his own ground, and, in cases of the highest importance, it is of no consequence whether a man breaks a human law or not. Let lawyers decide trivial cases. Business men may arrange that among themselves. If they were the interpreters of the everlasting laws which rightfully bind man, that would be another thing. A counterfeiting law-factory, standing half in a slave land and half in a free! What kind of laws for free men can you expect from that?

I am here to plead his cause with you. I plead not for his life, but for his character—his immortal life; and so it becomes your cause wholly, and is not his in the least. Some eighteen hundred years ago Christ was crucified; this morning, perchance, Captain Brown was hung. These are the two ends of a chain which is not without its links. He is not Old Brown any longer; he is an Angel of Light.

I see now that it was necessary that the bravest and humanest man in all the country should be hung. Perhaps he saw it himself. I *almost fear* that I may yet hear of his deliverance, doubting if a prolonged life, if *any* life, can do as much good as his death.

"Misguided"! "Garrulous"! "Insane"! Vindictive"! So ye write in your easy chairs, and thus he wounded responds from the floor of the Armory, clear as a cloudless sky, true as the voice of nature is: "No man sent me here; it was my own prompting and that of my Maker. I acknowledge no master in human form."

And in what a sweet and noble strain he proceeds, addressing his captors, who stand over him: "I think, my friends, you are guilty of a great wrong against God and humanity, and it would be perfectly right for any one to interfere with you so far as to free those you wilfully and wickedly hold in bondage."

And referring to his movement: "It is, in my opinion, the greatest service a man can render to God."

"I pity the poor in bondage that have none to help them; that is why I am here; not to gratify any personal animosity, revenge, or vindictive spirit. It is my sympathy with the oppressed and the wronged, that are as good as you, and as precious in the sight of God."

You don't know your testament when you see it.

"I want you to understand that I respect the rights of the poorest and weakest of colored people, oppressed by the slave power, just as much as I do those of the most wealthy and powerful."

"I wish to say, furthermore, that you had better, all you people at the South, prepare yourselves for a settlement of that question, that must come up for settlement sooner than you are prepared for it. The sooner you are prepared the better. You may dispose of me very easily. I am nearly disposed of now; but this question is still to be settled—this negro question, I mean; the end of that is not yet."

I foresee the time when the painter will paint that scene, no longer going to Rome for a subject; the poet will sing it; the historian record it; and, with the Landing of the Pilgrims and the Declaration of Independence, it will be the ornament of some future national gallery, when at least the present form of Slavery shall be no more here. We shall then be at liberty to weep for Captain Brown. Then, and not till then, we will take our revenge.

⚜ 38 ⚜

Last Speech

JOHN BROWN

Following the raid at Harper's Ferry, John Brown was put on trial for treason and then executed. In his last words to the court on 2nd November 1859, he accepts full responsibility for his actions, but argues that he was acting according to divine will. As slavery represents an offense to God's law, he is prepared to be judged by a higher authority than that which he is confronted with on earth. Again, the combination of religiosity and abolitionist sentiment is evident in his statement, which to his supporters would confirm his status as a martyr for their cause.

I have, may it please the Court, a few words to say.

In the first place, I deny everything but what I have all along admitted,—the design on my part to free the slaves. I intended certainly to have made a clean thing of that matter, as I did last winter, when I went into Missouri and there took slaves without the snapping of a gun on either side, moved them through the country, and finally left them in Canada. I designed to have done the same thing again, on a larger scale. That was all I intended. I never did intend murder, or treason, or the destruction of property, or to excite or incite slaves to rebellion, or to make insurrection.

I have another objection; and that is, it is unjust that I should suffer such a penalty. Had I interfered in the manner which I admit, and which I admit has been fairly proved (for I admire the truthfulness and candor of the greater portion of the witnesses who have testified in this case),—had I so interfered in behalf of the rich, the powerful, the intelligent, the so-called great, or in behalf of any of their friends,—either father, mother, brother, sister, wife, or children, or any of that class,—and suffered and sacrificed what I have in this interference, it would have been all right; and every man in this court would have deemed it an act worthy of reward rather than punishment.

Source: John Brown, Last speech to the court, 2 November, 1859, repr. in Henry Steele Commager, ed., *Documents of American History*, New York: Appleton-Century-Crofts, 1968.

This court acknowledges, as I suppose, the validity of the law of God. I see a book kissed here which I suppose to be the Bible, or at least the New Testament. That teaches me that all things whatsoever I would that men should do to me, I should do even so to them. It teaches me, further, to "remember them that are in bonds, as bound with them." I endeavored to act up to that instruction. I say, I am yet too young to understand that God is any respecter of persons. I believe that to have interfered as I have done—as I have always freely admitted I have done—in behalf of His despised poor, was not wrong but right. Now, if it is deemed necessary that I should forfeit my life for the furtherance of the ends of justice, and mingle my blood further with the blood of my children and with the blood of millions in this slave country whose rights are disregarded by wicked, cruel, and unjust enactments,—I submit; so let it be done!

Let me say one word further.

I feel entirely satisfied with the treatment I have received in my trial. Considering all the circumstances, it has been more generous than I expected. But I feel no consciousness of my guilt. I have stated from the first what was my intention, and what was not. I never had any design against the life of any person, nor any disposition to commit treason, or excite slaves to rebel, or make any general insurrection. I never encouraged any man to do so, but always discouraged any idea of that kind.

Let me say, also, a word in regard to the statements made by some of those connected with me. I hear it has been stated by some of them that I induced them to join me. But the contrary is true. I do not say this to injure them, but as regretting their weakness. There is not one of them but joined me of his own accord, and the greater part of them at their own expense. A number of them I never saw, and never had a word of conversation with, till the day they came to me; and that was for the purpose I have stated.

Now I have done.

ᛤ 39 ᛤ

A Letter to *The London News*

VICTOR HUGO

John Brown's raid was an event reported not simply nationally but internationally as well. This letter to *The London News* from the eminent French novelist, Victor Hugo, contains a powerful plea for clemency on Brown's behalf. Hugo assumes that there had been a stay of execution so that John Brown was still alive as he was making the case for mercy. In fact, his letter, dated December 2nd, was written on the day that Brown's sentence was carried out in America. Hugo's attempt to mobilise public opinion in support of John Brown nevertheless demonstrates the extent to which the slavery issue within the southern states was becoming an issue debated and discussed beyond America's borders. The letter is contained in a pamphlet in the Daniel A. P.Murray Collection in the Library of Congress.

To The Editor Of The London News:

Sir: When our thoughts dwell upon the United States of America, a majestic form rises before the eye of imagination. It is a Washington!

Look, then, to what is taking place in that country of Washington at this present moment.

In the Southern States of the Union there are slaves; and this circumstance is regarded with indignation, as the most monstrous of inconsistencies, by the pure and logical conscience of the Northern States. A white man, a free man, John Brown, sought to deliver these negro slaves from bondage. Assuredly, if insurrection is ever a sacred duty, it must be when it is directed against Slavery. John Brown endeavored to commence the work of emancipation by the liberation of slaves in Virginia. Pious, austere, animated with the old Puritan spirit, inspired by the spirit of the Gospel, he sounded to these men, these oppressed brothers, the rallying cry of Freedom. The slaves, enervated by servitude, made no response to the appeal. Slavery afflicts the soul with weakness. Brown, though deserted, still fought at the

Source: Victor Hugo, Letter, *The London News*, 1859, repr. in *Letters on American Slavery*, Boston: The American Anti-Slavery Society, 1860.

head of a handful of heroic men; he was riddled with balls; his two young sons, sacred martyrs, fell dead at his side, and he himself was taken. This is what they call the affair at Harper's Ferry.

John Brown has been tried, with four of his comrades, Stephens, Cowpoke, Green and Copeland. What has been the character of his trial? Let us sum it up in a few words:—

John Brown, upon a wretched pallet, with six half gaping wounds, a gun-shot wound in his arm, another in his loins, and two in his head, scarcely conscious of surrounding sounds, bathing his mattress in blood, and with the ghastly presence of his two dead sons ever beside him; his four fellow-sufferers wounded, dragging themselves along by his side; Stephens bleeding from four sabre wounds; justice in a hurry, and over-leaping all obstacles; an attorney, Hunter, who wishes to proceed hastily, and a judge, Parker, who suffers him to have his way; the hearing cut short, almost every application for delay refused, forged and mutilated documents produced, the witnesses for the defence kidnapped, every obstacle thrown in the way of the prisoner's counsel, two cannon loaded with canister stationed in the Court, orders given to the jailers to shoot the prisoners if they sought to escape, forty minutes of deliberation, and three men sentenced to die! I declare on my honor that all this took place, not in Turkey, but in America!

Such things cannot be done with impunity in the face of the civilized world. The universal conscience of humanity is an ever-watchful eye. Let the judges of Charlestown, and Hunter and Parker, and the slaveholding jurors, and the whole population of Virginia, ponder it well: they are watched! They are not alone in the world. At this moment, America attracts the eyes of the whole of Europe.

John Brown, condemned to die, was to have been hanged on the 2d of December—this very day.

But news has just reached us. A respite has been granted to him. It is not until the 16th that he is to die. The interval is a brief one. Before it has ended, will a cry of mercy have had time to make itself effectually heard?

No matter! It is our duty to speak out.

Perhaps a second respite may be granted. America is a noble nation. The impulse of humanity springs quickly into life among a free people. We may yet hope that Brown will be saved.

If it were otherwise, if Brown should die on the scaffold on the 16th of December, what a terrible calamity! The executioner of Brown, let us avow it openly (for the day of the kings is past, and the day of the peoples dawns, and to the people we are bound frankly to speak the truth) —the executioner of Brown would be neither the attorney Hunter, nor the judge Parker, nor the Governor Wise, nor the State of Virginia; it would be, though we can scarce think or speak of it without a shudder, the whole American Republic.

The more one loves, the more one admires, the more one venerates that Republic, the more heart-sick one feels at the contemplation of such a catastrophe. A single State ought not to have the power to dishonor all the rest, and in this case there is an obvious justification for a federal intervention. Otherwise, by hesitating to interfere when it might prevent a crime, the Union becomes a participator in its guilt. No matter how intense may be the indignation of the generous Northern States, the Southern States force them to share the opprobrium of this murder. All of us, no matter who we may be, who are bound together as compatriots by the common tie of a democratic creed, feel ourselves in some measure compromised. If the scaffold should be erected on the 16th of December, the incorruptible voice of history would thenceforward testify that the august Confederation of the New World, had added to all its rites of holy brotherhood a brotherhood of blood, and the fasces of that splendid Republic would be bound together with the running noose that hung from the gibbet of Brown!

This is a bond that kills.

When we reflect on what Brown, the liberator, the champion of Christ, has striven to effect, and when we remember that he is about to die, slaughtered by the American Republic, the crime assumes an importance co-extensive with that of the nation which commits it—and when we say to ourselves that this nation is one of the glories of the human race; that like France, like England, like Germany, she is one of the great agents of civilization; that she sometimes even leaves Europe in the rear by the sublime audacity of some of her progressive movements; that she is the Queen of an entire world, and that her brow is irradiated with a glorious halo of freedom, we declare our conviction that John Brown will not die; for we recoil horror-struck from the idea of so great a crime committed by so great a people.

Viewed in a political light, the murder of Brown would be an irreparable fault. It would penetrate the Union with a gaping fissure which would lead in the end to its entire disruption. It is possible that the execution of Brown might establish slavery on a firm basis in Virginia, but it is certain that it would shake to its centre the entire fabric of American democracy. You preserve your infamy, but you sacrifice your glory. Viewed in a moral light, it seems to me that a portion of the enlightenment of humanity would be eclipsed, that even the ideas of justice and injustice would be obscured on the day which should witness the assassination of Emancipation by Liberty.

As for myself, though I am but a mere atom, yet being, as I am, in common with all other men, inspired with the conscience of humanity, I fall on my knees, weeping before the great starry banner of the New World; and with clasped hands, and with profound and filial respect, I implore the illustrious American Republic, sister of the French Republic, to see to the safety of the universal moral law, to save John Brown, to demolish the threatening scaffold of the 16th of December, and not to suffer that beneath its eyes, and I add, with a shudder, almost by its fault a crime should be perpetrated surpassing the first fratricide in iniquity.

For—yes, let America know it, and ponder on it well— there is something more terrible than Cain slaying Abel: It is Washington slaying Spartacus!

VICTOR HUGO.
Hauteville House, Dec. 2d, 1859.

❧ 40 ❧

John Brown

RALPH WALDO EMERSON

This speech by Ralph Waldo Emerson, the inspirational spirit among New England transcendentalists, was made on 6th January 1860, some two months after John Brown's trial and execution for the events at Harper's Ferry. It demonstrates nonetheless the continuing impact of the event on the abolitionist movement. Beginning his eulogy with a description of Brown's childhood—including the incident that gave him his life-long aversion to slavery—Emerson draws a portrait of a Christian hero whose example is one that should command widespread respect. The speech ends with a powerful defense of abolitionism, connecting it with the Christian value of love, and the democratic principle of justice.

Mr. Chairman:
I have been struck with one fact, that the best orators who have added their praise to his fame,—and I need not go out of this house to find the purest eloquence in the country,—have one rival who copies off a little better, and that is JOHN BROWN. Every thing that is said of him leaves people a little dissatisfied; but as soon as they read his own speeches and letters they are heartily contented,—such is the singleness of purpose which justifies him to the head and the heart of all. Taught by this experience, I mean, in the few remarks I have to make, to cling to his history, or let him speak for himself.

John Brown, the founder of liberty in Kansas, was born in Torrington, Litchfield County, Conn., in 1800. When he was five years old his father emigrated to Ohio, and the boy was there set to keep sheep and to look after cattle and dress skins; he went bareheaded and barefooted, and clothed in buckskin. He said that he loved rough play, could never have rough play enough; could not see a seedy hat without wishing to pull it off. But for this it needed that the playmates should be equal; not one in fine clothes and the other in buckskin; not one his own master, hale and hearty, and the other watched and whipped. But it chanced that in Pennsylvania,

Source: Ralph Waldo Emerson, *Complete Works Vol. XI :Miscellanies*,
London: George Routledge and Sons, Ltd, 1903 edition.

where he was sent by his father to collect cattle, he fell in with a boy whom he heartily liked and whom he looked upon as his superior. This boy was a slave; he saw him beaten with an iron shovel, and otherwise maltreated; he saw that this boy had nothing better to look forward to in life, whilst he himself was petted and made much of; for he was much considered in the family where he then stayed, from the circumstance that this boy of twelve years had conducted alone a drove of cattle a hundred miles. But the colored boy had no friend, and no future. This worked such indignation in him that he swore an oath of resistance to Slavery as long as he lived. And thus his enterprise to go into Virginia and run off five hundred or a thousand slaves was not a piece of spite or revenge, a plot of two years or of twenty years, but the keeping of an oath made to Heaven and earth forty-seven years before. Forty-seven years at least, though I incline to accept his own account of the matter at Charlestown, which makes the date a little older, when he said, "This was all settled millions of years before the world was made."

He grew up a religious and manly person, in severe poverty; a fair specimen of the best stock of New England; having that force of thought and that sense of right which are the warp and woof of greatness. Our farmers were Orthodox Calvinists, mighty in the Scriptures; had learned that life was a preparation, a "probation," to use their word, for a higher world, and was to be spent in loving and serving mankind.

Thus was formed a romantic character absolutely without any vulgar trait; living to ideal ends, without any mixture of self-indulgence or compromise, such as lowers the value of benevolent and thoughtful men we know; abstemious, refusing luxuries, not sourly and reproachfully but simply as unfit for his habit; quiet and gentle as a child in the house. And, as happens usually to men of romantic character, his fortunes were romantic. Walter Scott would have delighted to draw his picture and trace his adventurous career. A shepherd and herdsman, he learned the manners of animals, and knew the secret signals by which animals communicate. He made his hard bed on the mountains with them; he learned to drive his flock through thickets all but impassable; he had all the skill of a shepherd by choice of breed and by wise husbandry to obtain the best wool, and that for a course of years. And the anecdotes preserved show a far-seeing skill and conduct which, in spite of adverse accidents, should secure, one year with another, an honest reward, first to the farmer, and afterwards to the dealer. If he kept sheep, it was with a royal mind; and if he traded in wool, he was a merchant prince, not in the amount of wealth, but in the protection of the interests confided to him.

I am not a little surprised at the easy effrontery with which political gentlemen, in and out of Congress, take it upon them to say that there were not a thousand men in the North who sympathize with John Brown. It would be far safer and nearer the truth to say that all people, in proportion to their sensibility and self-respect, sympathize with him. For it is impossible to see courage, and disinterestedness, and the love that casts out fear, without sympathy. All women are drawn to him by their predominance of sentiment. All gentlemen, of course, are on his side. I do not mean by "gentlemen," people of scented hair and perfumed handkerchiefs, but men of gentle blood and generosity, "fulfilled with all nobleness," who, like the Cid, give the outcast leper a share of their bed; like the dying Sidney, pass the cap of cold water to the wounded soldier who needs it more. For what is the oath of gentle blood and knighthood? What but to protect the weak and lowly against the strong oppressor?

Nothing is more absurd than to complain of this sympathy, or to complain of a party of men united in opposition to Slavery. As well complain of gravity, or the ebb of the tide. Who makes the Abolitionist? The Slaveholder. The sentiment of mercy is the natural recoil which the laws of the universe provide to protect mankind from destruction by savage passions. And our blind statesmen go up and down, with committees of vigilance and safety, hunting for the origin of this new heresy. They will need a very vigilant committee indeed to find its birthplace, and a very strong force to root it out. For the arch-Abolitionist, older than Brown, and older than the Shenandoah Mountains, is Love, whose other name is Justice, which was before Alfred, before Lycurgus, before Slavery, and will be after it.

VIII. The House Divides

3. Robert E. Lee, 1864.
Photograph by J. Vannerson.

⚘41⚘

Address at Cooper Institute

ABRAHAM LINCOLN

Following his unsuccessful campaign against Stephen Douglas in Illinois, Lincoln began to reach out to a national constituency as part of his progress towards the presidential nomination for the Republicans in 1860. This speech, his first of any significance to an audience outside the mid-west, attracted widespread publicity. In it, he analyses the attitudes of the Founders towards slavery, before moving on to assess the current state of the nation. The speech, carefully crafted, and an outstanding example of Lincoln's sense of history as well as his political sensibility, was widely reprinted as campaign literature.

Mr. President and Fellow-Citizens of New York: The facts with which I shall deal this evening are mainly old and familiar; nor is there anything new in the general use I shall make of them. If there shall be any novelty, it will be in the mode of presenting the facts, and the inferences and observations following that presentation. In his speech last autumn, at Columbus, Ohio, as reported in *The New-York Times*, Senator Douglas said:

> Our fathers, when they framed the Government under which we live, understood this question just as well, and even better, than we do now.

I fully indorse this, and I adopt it as a text for this discourse. I so adopt it because it furnishes a precise and an agreed starting point for a discussion between Republicans and that wing of the Democracy headed by Senator Douglas. It simply leaves the inquiry: What was the understanding those fathers had of the question mentioned?

What is the frame of government under which we live? The answer must be: "The Constitution of the United States." That Constitution consists of the original, framed in 1787, (and under which the present government first went into operation), and twelve subsequently framed amendments, the first ten of which were framed in 1789.

Source: Abraham Lincoln, Address at Cooper Institute, New York, 27th February 1860.

Who were our fathers that framed the Constitution? I suppose the "thirty-nine" who signed the original instrument may be fairly called our fathers who framed that part of the present Government. It is almost exactly true to say they framed it, and it is altogether true to say they fairly represented the opinion and sentiment of the whole nation at that time. Their names, being familiar to nearly all, and accessible to quite all, need not now be repeated.

I take these "thirty-nine," for the present, as being "our fathers who framed the Government under which we live." What is the question which, according to the text, those fathers understood "just as well, and even better than we do now"?

It is this: Does the proper division of local from federal authority, or anything in the Constitution, forbid our Federal Government to control as to slavery in our Federal Territories?

Upon this, Senator Douglas holds the affirmative, and Republicans the negative. This affirmation and denial form an issue; and this issue—this question—is precisely what the text declares our fathers understood "better than we." Let us now inquire whether the "thirty-nine," or any of them, ever acted upon this question; and if they did, how they acted upon it—how they expressed that better understanding? In 1784, three years before the Constitution—the United States then owning the Northwestern Territory, and no other, the Congress of the Confederation had before them the question of prohibiting slavery in that Territory; and four of the "thirty-nine" who afterward framed the Constitution, were in that Congress, and voted on that question. Of these, Roger Sherman, Thomas Mifflin, and Hugh Williamson voted for the prohibition, thus showing that, in their understanding, no line dividing local from federal authority, nor anything else, properly forbade the Federal Government to control as to slavery in federal territory. The other of the four—James McHenry—voted against the prohibition, showing that, for some cause, he thought it improper to vote for it.

In 1787, still before the Constitution, but while the Convention was in session framing it, and while the Northwestern Territory still was the only territory owned by the United States, the same question of prohibiting slavery in the territory again came before the Congress of the Confederation; and two more of the "thirty-nine" who afterward signed the Constitution, were in that Congress, and voted on the question. They were William Blount and William Few; and they both voted for the prohibition—thus showing that, in their understanding, no line dividing local from federal authority, nor anything else, properly forbids the Federal Government to control as to slavery in Federal territory. This time the prohibition became a law, being part of what is now well known as the Ordinance of '87.

The question of Federal control of slavery in the territories, seems not to have been directly before the Convention which framed the original Constitution; and hence it is not recorded that the "thirty-nine," or any of them, while engaged on that instrument, expressed any opinion on that precise question.

In 1789, by the first Congress which sat under the Constitution, an act was passed to enforce the Ordinance of '87, including the prohibition of slavery in the Northwestern Territory. The bill for this act was reported by one of the "thirty-nine"—Thomas Fitzsimmons, then a member of the House of Representatives from Pennsylvania. It went through all its stages without a word of opposition, and finally passed both branches without yeas and nays, which is equivalent to a unanimous passage. In this Congress there were sixteen of the thirty-nine fathers who framed the original Constitution. They were John Langdon, Nicholas Gilman, Wm. S. Johnson, Roger Sherman, Robert Morris, Thos. Fitzsimmons, William Few, Abraham Baldwin, Rufus King, William Paterson, George Clymer, Richard Bassett, George Read, Pierce Butler, Daniel Carroll, James Madison.

This shows that, in their understanding, no line dividing local from federal authority, nor anything in the Constitution, properly forbade Congress to prohibit slavery in the federal territory; else both their fidelity to correct principle, and their oath to support the Constitution, would have constrained them to oppose the prohibition.

Again, George Washington, another of the "thirty-nine," was then President of the United States, and as such approved and signed the bill; thus completing its validity as a law, and thus showing that, in his understanding, no line dividing local from federal authority, nor anything in the Constitution, forbade the Federal Government, to control as to slavery in federal territory.

No great while after the adoption of the original Constitution, North Carolina ceded to the Federal Government the country now constituting the State of Tennessee; and a few years later Georgia ceded that which now constitutes the States of Mississippi and Alabama. In both deeds of cession it was made a condition by the ceding States that the Federal Government should not prohibit slavery in the ceded territory. Besides this, slavery was then actually in the ceded country. Under these circumstances, Congress, on taking charge of these countries, did not absolutely prohibit slavery within them. But they did interfere with it—take control of it—even there, to a certain extent. In 1798, Congress organized the Territory of Mississippi. In the act of organization, they prohibited the bringing of slaves into the Territory, from any place without the United States, by fine, and giving freedom to slaves so brought. This act passed both branches of Congress without yeas and nays. In that Congress were three of the "thirty-nine" who framed the original Constitution. They were John Langdon, George Read and Abraham Baldwin. They all, probably, voted for it. Certainly they would have placed their opposition to it upon record, if, in their understanding, any line dividing local from federal authority, or anything in the Constitution, properly forbade the Federal Government to control as to slavery in federal territory.

In 1803, the Federal Government purchased the Louisiana country. Our former territorial acquisitions came from certain of our own States; but this Louisiana country was acquired from a foreign nation. In 1804, Congress gave a territorial organization to that part of it which now constitutes the State of Louisiana. New Orleans, lying within that part, was an old and comparatively large city. There were other considerable towns and settlements, and slavery was extensively and thoroughly intermingled with the people. Congress did not, in the Territorial Act, prohibit slavery; but they did interfere with it—take control of it—in a more marked and extensive way than they did in the case of Mississippi. The substance of the provision therein made, in relation to slaves, was:

1st. That no slave should be imported into the territory from foreign parts.

2d. That no slave should be carried into it who had been imported into the United States since the first day of May, 1798.

3d. That no slave should be carried into it, except by the owner, and for his own use as a settler; the penalty in all the cases being a fine upon the violator of the law, and freedom to the slave.

This act also was passed without yeas and nays. In the Congress which passed it, there were two of the "thirty-nine." They were Abraham Baldwin and Jonathan Dayton. As stated in the case of Mississippi, it is probable they both voted for it. They would not have allowed it to pass without recording their opposition to it, if, in their understanding, it violated either the line properly dividing local from federal authority, or any provision of the Constitution.

In 1819-20, came and passed the Missouri question. Many votes were taken, by yeas and nays, in both branches of Congress, upon the various phases of the general question. Two of the "thirty-nine"—Rufus King and Charles Pinckney—were members of that Congress. Mr. King steadily voted for slavery prohibition and against all compromises, while Mr. Pinckney as steadily voted against slavery prohibition and against all compromises. By this, Mr. King showed that, in his understanding, no line dividing local from federal authority, nor anything in the Constitution, was violated by Congress prohibiting slavery in federal territory; while Mr. Pinckney, by his votes, showed that, in his understanding, there was some sufficient reason for opposing such prohibition in that case.

The cases I have mentioned are the only acts of the "thirty-nine," or of any of them, upon the direct issue, which I have been able to discover.

To enumerate the persons who thus acted, as being four in 1784, two in 1787, seventeen in 1789, three in 1798, two in 1804, and two in 1819-20—there would be thirty of them. But this would be counting John Langdon, Roger Sherman, William Few, Rufus King, and George Read each twice, and Abraham Baldwin, three times. The true number of those of the "thirty-nine" whom I have shown to have acted upon the question, which, by the text, they understood better than we, is twenty-three, leaving sixteen not shown to have acted upon it in any way.

Here, then, we have twenty-three out of our thirty-nine fathers "who framed the government under which we live," who have, upon their official responsibility and their corporal oaths, acted upon the very question which the text affirms they "understood just as well, and even better than we do now;" and twenty-one of them—a clear majority of the whole "thirty-nine"—so acting upon it as to make them guilty of gross political impropriety and willful perjury, if, in their understanding, any proper division between local and Federal authority, or anything in the Constitution they had made themselves, and sworn to support, forbade the Federal Government to control as to slavery in the federal territories. Thus the twenty-one acted; and, as actions speak louder than words, so actions, under such responsibility, speak still louder.

Two of the twenty-three voted against Congressional prohibition of slavery in the federal territories, in the instances in which they acted upon the question. But for what reasons they so voted is not known. They may have done so because they thought a proper division of local from federal authority, or some provision or principle of the Constitution, stood in the way; or they may, without any such question, have voted against the prohibition, on what appeared to them to be sufficient grounds of expediency. No one who has sworn to support the Constitution can conscientiously vote for what he understands to be an unconstitutional measure, however expedient he may think it; but one may and ought to vote against a measure which he deems constitutional, if, at the same time, he deems it inexpedient. It, therefore, would be unsafe to set down even the two who voted against the prohibition, as having done so because, in their understanding, any proper division of local from Federal authority, or anything in the Constitution, forbade the Federal Government to control as to slavery in Federal territory.

The remaining sixteen of the "thirty-nine," so far as I have discovered, have left no record of their understanding upon the direct question of federal control of slavery in the federal territories. But there is much reason to believe that their understanding upon that question would not have appeared different from that of their twenty-three compeers, had it been manifested at all.

For the purpose of adhering rigidly to the text, I have purposely omitted whatever understanding may have been manifested by any person, however distinguished, other than the thirty-nine fathers who framed the original Constitution; and, for the same reason, I have also omitted whatever understanding may have been manifested by any of the "thirty-nine" even on any other phase of the general question of slavery. If we should look into their acts and declarations on those other phases, as the foreign slave trade, and the morality and policy of slavery generally, it would appear to us that on the direct question of federal control of slavery in federal territories, the sixteen, if they had acted at all, would probably have acted just as the twenty-three did. Among that sixteen were several of the most noted anti-slavery men of those times—as Dr. Franklin, Alexander Hamilton and Gouverneur Morris—while there was not one now known to have been otherwise, unless it may be John Rutledge, of South Carolina.

The sum of the whole is, that of our thirty-nine fathers who framed the original Constitution, twenty-one—a clear majority of the whole—certainly understood that no proper division of local from federal authority, nor any part of the Constitution, forbade the Federal Government to control slavery in the federal territories; while all the rest probably had the same understanding. Such, unquestionably, was the understanding of our fathers who framed the original Constitution; and the text affirms that they understood the question "better than we."

But, so far, I have been considering the understanding of the question manifested by the framers of the original Constitution. In and by the original instrument, a mode was provided for amending it; and, as I have already stated, the present frame of "the Government under which we live" consists of that original, and twelve amendatory articles framed and adopted since. Those who now insist that Federal control of slavery in Federal Territories violates the Constitution, point us to the provisions which they suppose it thus violates; and, as I understand, they all fix upon provisions in these amendatory articles, and not in the original instrument. The Supreme Court, in the Dred Scott case, plant themselves upon the fifth amendment, which provides that no person shall be deprived of "life, liberty or property without due process of law;" while Senator Douglas and his peculiar adherents plant themselves upon the tenth amendment, providing that "the powers not delegated to the United States by the Constitution" "are reserved to the States respectively, or to the people."

Now, it so happens that these amendments were framed by the first Congress which sat under the Constitution—the identical Congress which passed the act already mentioned, enforcing the prohibition of slavery in the Northwestern Territory. Not only was it the same Congress, but they were the identical, same individual men who, at the same session, and at the same time within the session, had under consideration, and in progress toward maturity, these Constitutional amendments, and this act prohibiting slavery in all the territory the nation then owned. The Constitutional amendments were introduced before, and passed after the act enforcing the Ordinance of '87; so that, during the whole pendency of the act to enforce the Ordinance, the Constitutional amendments were also pending.

The seventy-six members of that Congress, including sixteen of the framers of the original Constitution, as before stated, were pre-eminently our fathers who framed that part of "the Government under which we live," which is now claimed as forbidding the Federal Government to control slavery in the Federal Territories.

Is it not a little presumptuous in any one at this day to affirm that the two things which that Congress deliberately framed, and carried to maturity at the same time, are absolutely inconsistent with each other? And does not such affirmation become impudently absurd when coupled with the other affirmation from the same mouth, that those who did the two things, alleged to be inconsistent, understood whether they really were inconsistent better than we—better than he who affirms that they are inconsistent?

It is surely safe to assume that the thirty-nine framers of the original Constitution, and the seventy-six members of the Congress which framed the amendments thereto, taken together, do certainly include those who may be fairly called "our fathers who framed the Government under which we live." And so assuming, I defy any man to show that any one of them ever, in his whole life, declared that, in his understanding, any proper division of local from federal authority, or any part of the Constitution, forbade the Federal Government to control as to slavery in the federal territories. I go a step further. I defy any one to show that any living man in the whole world ever did, prior to the beginning of the present century, (and I might almost say prior to the beginning of the last half of the present century), declare that, in his understanding, any proper division of local from federal authority, or any part of the Constitution, forbade the Federal Government to control as to slavery in the Federal Territories. To those who now so declare, I give, not only "our fathers who framed the Government under which we live," but with them all other living men within the century in which it was framed, among whom to search, and they shall not be able to find the evidence of a single man agreeing with them.

Now, and here, let me guard a little against being misunderstood. I do not mean to say we are bound to follow implicitly in whatever our fathers did. To do so, would be to discard all the lights of current experience—to reject all progress—all improvement. What I do say is, that if we would supplant the opinions and policy of our fathers in any case, we should do so upon evidence so conclusive, and argument so clear, that even their great authority, fairly considered and weighed, cannot stand; and most surely not in a case whereof we ourselves declare they understood the question better than we.

If any man at this day sincerely believes that a proper division of local from federal authority, or any part of the Constitution, forbids the Federal Government to control as to slavery in the federal territories, he is right to say so, and to enforce his position by all truthful evidence and fair argument which he can. But he has no right to mislead others, who have less access to history, and less leisure to study it, into the false belief that "our fathers who framed the Government under which we live" were of the same opinion—thus substituting falsehood and deception for truthful evidence and fair argument. If any man at this day sincerely believes "our fathers who framed the Government under which we live," used and applied principles, in other cases, which ought to have led them to understand that a proper division of local from federal authority or some part of the Constitution, forbids the Federal Government to control as to slavery in the federal territories, he is right to say so. But he should, at the same time, brave the responsibility of declaring that, in his opinion, he understands their principles better than they did themselves; and especially should he not shirk that responsibility by asserting that they "understood the question just as well, and even better, than we do now."

But enough! Let all who believe that "our fathers, who framed the Government under which we live, understood this question just as well, and even better, than we do now," speak as they spoke, and act as they acted upon it. This is all Republicans ask—all Republicans desire—in relation to slavery. As those fathers marked it, so let it be again marked, as an evil not to be extended, but to be tolerated and protected only because of and so far as its actual presence among us makes that toleration and protection a necessity. Let all the guarantees those fathers gave it, be, not grudgingly, but fully and fairly, maintained. For this Republicans contend, and with this, so far as I know or believe, they will be content.

And now, if they would listen—as I suppose they will not—I would address a few words to the Southern people.

I would say to them:—You consider yourselves a reasonable and a just people; and I consider that in the general qualities of reason and justice you are not inferior to any other people. Still, when you speak of us Republicans, you do so only to denounce us as reptiles, or, at the best, as no better than outlaws. You will grant a hearing to pirates or murderers, but nothing like it to "Black Republicans." In all your contentions with one another, each of you deems an unconditional condemnation of "Black Republicanism" as the first thing to be attended to. Indeed, such condemnation of us seems to be an indispensable prerequisite—license, so to speak—among you to be admitted or permitted to speak at all. Now, can you, or not, be prevailed upon to pause and to consider whether this is quite just to us, or even to yourselves? Bring forward your charges and specifications, and then be patient long enough to hear us deny or justify.

You say we are sectional. We deny it. That makes an issue; and the burden of proof is upon you. You produce your proof; and what is it? Why, that our party has no existence in your section—gets no votes in your section. The fact is substantially true; but does it prove the issue? If it does, then in case we should, without change of principle, begin to get votes in your section, we should thereby cease to be sectional. You cannot escape this conclusion; and yet, are you willing to abide by it? If you are, you will probably soon find that we have ceased to be sectional, for we shall get votes in your section this very year. You will then begin to discover, as the truth plainly is, that your proof does not touch the issue. The fact that we get no votes in your section, is a fact of your making, and not of ours. And if there be fault in that fact, that fault is primarily yours, and remains until you show that we repel you by some wrong principle or practice. If we do repel you by any wrong principle or practice, the fault is ours; but this brings you to where you ought to have started— to a discussion of the right or wrong of our principle. If our principle, put in practice, would wrong your section for the benefit of ours, or for any other object, then our principle, and we with it, are sectional, and are justly opposed and denounced as such. Meet us, then, on the question of whether our principle, put in practice, would wrong your section; and so meet it as if it were possible that something may be said on our side. Do you accept the challenge? No! Then you really believe that the principle which "our fathers who framed the Government under which we live" thought so clearly right as to adopt it, and indorse it again and again, upon their official oaths, is in fact so clearly wrong as to demand your condemnation without a moment's consideration.

Some of you delight to flaunt in our faces the warning against sectional parties given by Washington in his Farewell Address. Less than eight years before Washington gave that warning, he had, as President of the United States, approved and signed an act of Congress, enforcing the prohibition of slavery in the Northwestern Territory, which act embodied the policy of the Government upon that subject up to and at the very moment he penned that warning; and about one year after he penned it, he wrote Lafayette that he considered that prohibition a wise measure, expressing in the same connection his hope that we should at some time have a confederacy of free States.

Bearing this in mind, and seeing that sectionalism has since arisen upon this same subject, is that warning a weapon in your hands against us, or in our hands against you? Could Washington himself speak, would he cast the blame of that sectionalism upon us, who sustain his policy, or upon you who repudiate it? We respect that warning of Washington, and we commend it to you, together with his example pointing to the right application of it.

But you say you are conservative—eminently conservative—while we are revolutionary, destructive, or something of the sort. What is conservatism? Is it not adherence to the old and tried, against the new and untried? We stick to, contend for, the identical old policy on the point in controversy which was adopted by "our fathers who framed the Government under which we live;" while you with one accord reject, and scout, and spit upon that old policy, and insist upon substituting something new. True, you disagree among yourselves as to what that substitute shall be. You are divided on new propositions and plans, but you are unanimous in rejecting and denouncing the old policy of the fathers. Some of you are for reviving the foreign slave trade; some for a Congressional Slave-Code for the Territories; some for Congress forbidding the Territories to prohibit Slavery within their limits; some for maintaining Slavery in the Territories through the judiciary; some for the "gur-reat pur-rinciple" that "if one man would enslave another, no third man should object," fantastically called "Popular Sovereignty"; but never a man among you is in favor of federal prohibition of slavery in Federal Territories, according to the practice of "our fathers who framed the Government under which we live." Not one of all your various plans can show a precedent or an advocate in the century within which our Government originated. Consider, then, whether your claim of conservatism for yourselves, and your charge of destructiveness against us, are based on the most clear and stable foundations.

Again, you say we have made the slavery question more prominent than it formerly was. We deny it. We admit that it is more prominent, but we deny that we made it so. It was not we, but you, who discarded the old policy of the fathers. We resisted, and still resist, your innovation; and thence comes the greater prominence of the question. Would you have that question reduced to its former proportions? Go back to that old policy. What has been will be again, under the same conditions. If you would have the peace of the old times, readopt the precepts and policy of the old times.

You charge that we stir up insurrections among your slaves. We deny it; and what is your proof? Harper's Ferry! John Brown!! John Brown was no Republican; and you have failed to implicate a single Republican in his Harper's Ferry enterprise. If any member of our party is guilty in that matter, you know it or you do not know it. If you do know it, you are inexcusable for not designating the man and proving the fact. If you do not know it, you are inexcusable for asserting it, and especially for persisting in the assertion after you have tried and failed to make the proof. You need to be told that persisting in a charge which one does not know to be true, is simply malicious slander.

Some of you admit that no Republican designedly aided or encouraged the Harper's Ferry affair, but still insist that our doctrines and declarations necessarily lead to such results. We do not believe it. We know we hold to no doctrine, and make no declaration, which were not held to and made by "our fathers who framed the Government under which we live." You never dealt fairly by us in relation to this affair. When it occurred, some important State elections were near at hand,

and you were in evident glee with the belief that, by charging the blame upon us, you could get an advantage of us in those elections. The elections came, and your expectations were not quite fulfilled. Every Republican man knew that, as to himself at least, your charge was a slander, and he was not much inclined by it to cast his vote in your favor. Republican doctrines and declarations are accompanied with a continual protest against any interference whatever with your slaves, or with you about your slaves. Surely, this does not encourage them to revolt. True, we do, in common with "our fathers, who framed the Government under which we live," declare our belief that slavery is wrong; but the slaves do not hear us declare even this. For anything we say or do, the slaves would scarcely know there is a Republican party. I believe they would not, in fact, generally know it but for your misrepresentations of us, in their hearing. In your political contests among yourselves, each faction charges the other with sympathy with Black Republicanism; and then, to give point to the charge, defines Black Republicanism to simply be insurrection, blood and thunder among the slaves.

Slave insurrections are no more common now than they were before the Republican party was organized. What induced the Southampton insurrection, twenty-eight years ago, in which at least three times as many lives were lost as at Harper's Ferry? You can scarcely stretch your very elastic fancy to the conclusion that Southampton was "got up by Black Republicanism." In the present state of things in the United States, I do not think a general, or even a very extensive slave insurrection is possible. The indispensable concert of action cannot be attained. The slaves have no means of rapid communication; nor can incendiary freemen, black or white, supply it. The explosive materials are everywhere in parcels; but there neither are, nor can be supplied, the indispensable connecting trains.

Much is said by Southern people about the affection of slaves for their masters and mistresses; and a part of it, at least, is true. A plot for an uprising could scarcely be devised and communicated to twenty individuals before some one of them, to save the life of a favorite master or mistress, would divulge it. This is the rule; and the slave revolution in Hayti was not an exception to it, but a case occurring under peculiar circumstances. The gunpowder plot of British history, though not connected with slaves, was more in point. In that case, only about twenty were admitted to the secret; and yet one of them, in his anxiety to save a friend, betrayed the plot to that friend, and, by consequence, averted the calamity. Occasional poisonings from the kitchen, and open or stealthy assassinations in the field, and local revolts extending to a score or so, will continue to occur as the natural results of slavery; but no general insurrection of slaves, as I think, can happen in this country for a long time. Whoever much fears, or much hopes for such an event, will be alike disappointed.

In the language of Mr. Jefferson, uttered many years ago, "It is still in our power to direct the process of emancipation, and deportation, peaceably, and in such slow degrees, as that the evil will wear off insensibly; and their places be, *pari passu*, filled up by free white laborers. If, on the contrary, it is left to force itself on, human nature must shudder at the prospect held up."

Mr. Jefferson did not mean to say, nor do I, that the power of emancipation is in the Federal Government. He spoke of Virginia; and, as to the power of emancipation, I speak of the slaveholding States only. The Federal Government, however, as we insist, has the power of restraining the extension of the institution—the power to insure that a slave insurrection shall never occur on any American soil which is now free from slavery.

John Brown's effort was peculiar. It was not a slave insurrection. It was an attempt by white men to get up a revolt among slaves, in which the slaves refused to participate. In fact, it was so absurd that the slaves, with all their ignorance, saw plainly enough it could not succeed. That affair, in its philosophy, corresponds with the many attempts, related in history, at the assassination of kings and emperors. An enthusiast broods over the oppression of a people till he fancies himself commissioned by Heaven to liberate them. He ventures the attempt, which ends in little else than his own execution. Orsini's attempt on Louis Napoleon, and John Brown's attempt at Harper's Ferry were, in their philosophy, precisely the same. The eagerness to cast blame on old England in the one case, and on New England in the other, does not disprove the sameness of the two things.

And how much would it avail you, if you could, by the use of John Brown, Helper's Book, and the like, break up the Republican organization? Human action can be modified to some extent, but human nature cannot be changed. There is a judgment and a feeling against slavery in this nation, which cast at least a million and a half of votes. You cannot destroy that judgment and feeling—that sentiment—by breaking up the political organization which rallies around it. You can scarcely scatter and disperse an army which has been formed into order in the face of your heaviest fire; but if you could, how much would you gain by forcing the sentiment which created it out of the peaceful channel of the ballot-box, into some other channel? What would that other channel probably be? Would the number of John Browns be lessened or enlarged by the operation?

But you will break up the Union rather than submit to a denial of your Constitutional rights.

That has a somewhat reckless sound; but it would be palliated, if not fully justified, were we proposing, by the mere force of numbers, to deprive you of some right, plainly written down in the Constitution. But we are proposing no such thing.

When you make these declarations, you have a specific and well-understood allusion to an assumed Constitutional right of yours, to take slaves into the federal territories, and to hold them there as property. But no such right is specifically written in the Constitution. That instrument is literally silent about any such right. We, on the contrary, deny that such a right has any existence in the Constitution, even by implication.

Your purpose, then, plainly stated, is that you will destroy the Government, unless you be allowed to construe and enforce the Constitution as you please, on all points in dispute between you and us. You will rule or ruin in all events.

This, plainly stated, is your language. Perhaps you will say the Supreme Court has decided the disputed Constitutional question in your favor.[1] Not quite so. But waiving the lawyer's distinction between dictum and decision, the Court have decided the question for you in a sort of way. The Court have substantially said, it is your Constitutional right to take slaves into the federal territories, and to hold them there as property. When I say the decision was made in a sort of way, I mean it was made in a divided Court, by a bare majority of the Judges, and they not quite agreeing with one another in the reasons for making it; that it is so made as that its avowed supporters disagree with one another about its meaning, and that it was mainly based upon a mistaken statement of fact—the statement in the opinion that "the right of property in a slave is distinctly and expressly affirmed in the Constitution."

An inspection of the Constitution will show that the right of property in a slave is not "distinctly and expressly affirmed" in it. Bear in mind, the Judges do not pledge their judicial opinion that such right is impliedly affirmed in the Constitution; but they pledge their veracity that it is "distinctly and expressly" affirmed there—"distinctly," that is, not mingled with anything else—"expressly," that is, in words meaning just that, without the aid of any inference, and susceptible of no other meaning.

If they had only pledged their judicial opinion that such right is affirmed in the instrument by implication, it would be open to others to show that neither the word "slave" nor "slavery" is to be found in the Constitution, nor the word "property" even, in any connection with language alluding to the things slave, or slavery; and that wherever in that instrument the slave is alluded to, he is called a "person";— and wherever his master's legal right in relation to him is alluded to, it is spoken of as "service or labor which may be due,"—as a debt payable in service or labor. Also, it would be open to show, by contemporaneous history, that this mode of alluding to slaves and slavery, instead of speaking of them, was employed on purpose to exclude from the Constitution the idea that there could be property in man.

To show all this, is easy and certain.

When this obvious mistake of the Judges shall be brought to their notice, is it not reasonable to expect that they will withdraw the mistaken statement, and reconsider the conclusion based upon it?

And then it is to be remembered that "our fathers, who framed the Government under which we live"—the men who made the Constitution—decided this same Constitutional question in our favor, long ago—decided it without division among themselves, when making the decision; without division among themselves about the meaning of it after it was made, and, so far as any evidence is left, without basing it upon any mistaken statement of facts.

Under all these circumstances, do you really feel yourselves justified to break up this Government unless such a court decision as yours is, shall be at once submitted to as a conclusive and final rule of political action? But you will not abide the election of a Republican president! In that supposed event, you say, you will destroy the Union; and then, you say, the great crime of having destroyed it will be upon us! That is cool. A highwayman holds a pistol to my ear, and mutters through his teeth, "Stand and deliver, or I shall kill you, and then you will be a murderer!"

To be sure, what the robber demanded of me—my money—was my own; and I had a clear right to keep it; but it was no more my own than my vote is my own; and the threat of death to me, to extort my money, and the threat of destruction to the Union, to extort my vote, can scarcely be distinguished in principle.

A few words now to Republicans. It is exceedingly desirable that all parts of this great Confederacy shall be at peace, and in harmony, one with another. Let us Republicans do our part to have it so. Even though much provoked, let us do nothing through passion and ill temper. Even though the southern people will not so much as listen to us, let us calmly consider their demands, and yield to them if, in our deliberate view of our duty, we possibly can. Judging by all they say and do, and by the subject and nature of their controversy with us, let us determine, if we can, what will satisfy them.

Will they be satisfied if the Territories be unconditionally surrendered to them? We know they will not. In all their present complaints against us, the Territories are scarcely mentioned. Invasions and insurrections are the rage now. Will it satisfy them, if, in the future, we have nothing to do with invasions and insurrections? We know it will not. We so know, because we know we never had anything to do with invasions and insurrections; and yet this total abstaining does not exempt us from the charge and the denunciation.

The question recurs, what will satisfy them? Simply this: We must not only let them alone, but we must somehow convince them that we do let them alone. This, we know by experience, is no easy task. We have been so trying to convince them from the very beginning of our organization, but with no success. In all our platforms and speeches we have constantly protested our purpose to let them alone; but this has had no tendency to convince them. Alike unavailing to convince them, is the fact that they have never detected a man of us in any attempt to disturb them.

These natural, and apparently adequate means all failing, what will convince them? This, and this only: cease to call slavery wrong, and join them in calling it right. And this must be done thoroughly—done in acts as well as in words. Silence will not be tolerated—we must place ourselves avowedly with them. Senator Douglas' new sedition law must be enacted and enforced, suppressing all declarations that slavery is wrong, whether made in politics, in presses, in pulpits, or in private. We must arrest and return their fugitive slaves with greedy pleasure. We must pull down our Free State constitutions. The whole atmosphere must be disinfected from all taint of opposition to slavery, before they will cease to believe that all their troubles proceed from us.

I am quite aware they do not state their case precisely in this way. Most of them would probably say to us, "Let us alone, do nothing to us, and say what you please about slavery." But we do let them alone—have never disturbed them—so that, after all, it is what we say, which dissatisfies them. They will continue to accuse us of doing, until we cease saying.

I am also aware they have not, as yet, in terms, demanded the overthrow of our Free-State Constitutions. Yet those Constitutions declare the wrong of slavery, with more solemn emphasis, than do all other sayings against it; and when all these other sayings shall have been silenced, the overthrow of these Constitutions will be demanded, and nothing be left to resist the demand. It is nothing to the contrary, that they do not demand the whole of this just now. Demanding what they do, and for the reason they do, they can voluntarily stop nowhere short of this consummation. Holding, as they do, that slavery is morally right, and socially elevating, they cannot cease to demand a full national recognition of it, as a legal right, and a social blessing.

Nor can we justifiably withhold this, on any ground save our conviction that slavery is wrong. If slavery is right, all words, acts, laws, and constitutions against it, are themselves wrong, and should be silenced, and swept away. If it is right, we cannot justly object to its nationality—its universality; if it is wrong, they cannot justly insist upon its extension—its enlargement. All they ask, we could readily grant, if we thought slavery right; all we ask, they could as readily grant, if they thought it wrong. Their thinking it right, and our thinking it wrong, is the precise fact upon which depends the whole controversy. Thinking it right, as they do, they are not to blame for desiring its full recognition, as being right; but, thinking it wrong, as we do, can we yield to them? Can we cast our votes with their view, and against our own? In view of our moral, social, and political responsibilities, can we do this?

Wrong as we think slavery is, we can yet afford to let it alone where it is, because that much is due to the necessity arising from its actual presence in the nation; but can we, while our votes will prevent it, allow it to spread into the National Territories, and to overrun us here in these Free States? If our sense of duty forbids this, then let us stand by our duty, fearlessly and effectively. Let us be diverted by none of those sophistical contrivances wherewith we are so industriously plied and belabored—contrivances such as groping for some middle ground between the right and the wrong, vain as the search for a man who should be neither a living man nor a dead man—such as a policy of "don't care" on a question about which all true men do care—such as Union appeals beseeching true Union men to yield to Disunionists, reversing the divine rule, and calling, not the sinners, but the righteous to repentance—such as invocations to Washington, imploring men to unsay what Washington said, and undo what Washington did.

Neither let us be slandered from our duty by false accusations against us, nor frightened from it by menaces of destruction to the Government nor of dungeons to ourselves. Let us have faith that right makes might, and in that faith let us to the end dare to do our duty as we understand it.

Note

1. In the Dred Scott Decision.—ed,

❦42❧

1860 Presidential Election: Party Platforms

The 1860 Presidential election effectively became two separate contests when the Democrats divided, running separate candidates in the dividing nation. Abraham Lincoln faced Stephen Douglas in the north, and John Breckinridge, Buchanan's vice-president, ran against John Bell in the south. Party platforms were framed in the context of the debate on slavery and the threat of secession.

1. Republican Party Platform (Candidate: Abraham Lincoln) Adopted at Chicago, 1860

Resolved, That we, the delegated representatives of the Republican electors of the United States, in Convention assembled, in discharge of the duty we owe to our constituents and our country, unite in the following declarations:

1. That the history of the nation, during the last four years, has fully established the propriety and necessity of the organization and perpetuation of the Republican party, and that the causes which called it into existence are permanent in their nature, and now, more than ever before, demand its peaceful and constitutional triumph.

2. That the maintenance of the principles promulgated in the Declaration of Independence and embodied in the Federal Constitution,

That all men are created equal; that they are endowed by their Creator with certain inalienable rights; that among these are life, liberty, and the pursuit of happiness; that to secure these rights, governments are instituted among men, deriving their just powers from the consent of the governed,

is essential to the preservation of our Republican institutions; and that the Federal Constitution, the Rights of the States, and the Union of the States, must and shall be preserved.

3. That to the Union of the States this nation owes its unprecedented increase in population, its surprising development of material resources, its rapid

Source: *The Tribune Almanac*, 1861, New York: *New York Tribune*, 1868, (facsimile), pp. 30–32, 34.

augmentation of wealth, its happiness at home and its honor abroad; and we hold in abhorrence all schemes for Disunion, come from whatever source they may: And we congratulate the country that no Republican member of Congress has uttered or countenanced the threats of Disunion so often made by Democratic members without rebuke and with applause from their political associates; and we denounce those threats of Disunion, in case of a popular overthrow of their ascendency, as denying the vital principles of a free government, and as an avowal of contemplated treason, which it is the imperative duty of an indignant People sternly to rebuke and forever silence.

4. That the maintenance inviolate of the rights of the States, and especially the right of each State to order and control its own domestic institutions according to its own judgment exclusively, is essential to that balance of powers on which the perfection and endurance of our political fabric depends; and we denounce the lawless invasion by armed force of the soil of any State or Territory, no matter under what pretext, as among the gravest of crimes.

5. That the present Democratic Administration has far exceeded our worst apprehensions, in its measureless subserviency to the exactions of a sectional interest, as especially evinced in its desperate exertions to force the infamous Lecompton Constitution upon the protesting people of Kansas; in construing the personal relation between master and servant to involve an unqualified property in persons; in its attempted enforcement, everywhere, on land and sea, through the intervention of Congress and of the Federal Courts of the extreme pretensions of a purely local interest; and in its general and unvarying abuse of the power intrusted to it by a confiding people.

6. That the people justly view with alarm the reckless extravagance which pervades every department of the Federal Government; that a return to rigid economy and accountability is indispensible to arrest the systematic plunder of the public treasury by favored partisans, while the recent startling developments of frauds and corruptions at the Federal metropolis, show that an entire change of administration is imperatively demanded.

7. That the new dogma, that the Constitution, of its own force, carries Slavery into any or all of the Territories of the United States, is a dangerous political heresy, at variance with the explicit provisions of that instrument itself, with contemporaneous exposition, and with legislative and judicial precedent; is revolutionary in its tendency, and subversive of the peace and harmony of the country.

8. That the normal condition of all the territory of the United States is that of freedom; That as our Republican fathers, when they had abolished Slavery in all our national territory, ordained that "no person should be deprived of life, liberty, or property, without due process of law," it becomes our duty, by legislation, whenever such legislation is necessary, to maintain this provision of the Constitution against all attempts to violate it; and we deny the authority of Congress, of a territorial legislature, or of any individuals, to give legal existence to Slavery in any Territory of the United States.

9. That we brand the recent re-opening of the African slave-trade, under the cover of our national flag, aided by perversions of judicial power, as a crime against humanity and a burning shame to our country and age; and we call upon Congress to take prompt and efficient measures for the total and final suppression of that execrable traffic.

10. That in the recent vetoes, by their Federal Governors, of the acts of the Legislatures of Kansas and Nebraska, prohibiting Slavery in those Territories, we find a practical illustration of the boasted Democratic principle of Non-Intervention and Popular Sovereignty, embodied in the Kansas-Nebraska bill, and a demonstration of the deception and fraud involved therein.

11. That Kansas should, of right, be immediately admitted as a State under the Constitution recently formed and adopted by her people, and accepted by the House of Representatives.

12. That, while providing revenue for the support of the General Government by duties upon imports, sound policy requires such an adjustment of these imposts as to encourage the development of the industrial interest of the whole country; and we commend that policy of national exchanges which secures to the working men liberal wages, to agriculture remunerative prices, to mechanics and manufactures an adequate reward for their skill, labor, and enterprise, and to the nation commercial prosperity and independence.

13. That we protest against any sale or alienation to others of the Public Lands held by actual settlers, and against any view of the Homestead policy which regards the settlers as paupers or suppliants for public bounty; and we demand the passage by Congress of the complete and satisfactory Homestead measure which has already passed the House.

14. That the Republican party is opposed to any change in our Naturalization Laws or any State legislation by which the rights of citizenship hitherto accorded to immigrants from foreign lands shall be abridged or impaired; and in favor of giving a full and efficient protection to the rights of all classes of citizens, whether native or naturalized, both at home and abroad.

15. That appropriations by Congress for River and Harbor improvements of a National character, required for the accommodation and security of an existing commerce, are authorized by the Constitution, and justified by the obligations of Government to protect the lives and property of its citizens.

16. That a Railroad to the Pacific Ocean is imperatively demanded by the interest of the whole country; that the Federal Government ought to render immediate and efficient aid in its construction; and that, as preliminary thereto, a daily Overland Mail should be promply established.

17. Finally, having thus set forth our distinctive principles and views, we invite the coöperation of all citizens, however differing on other questions, who substantially agree with us in their affirmance and support.

2. (Northern) National Democratic Party Platform (Candidate: Stephen Douglas) Adopted at Charleston and Baltimore, 1860.

1. Resolved, That we, the Democracy of the Union, in Convention assembled, hereby declare our affirmation of the resolutions unanimously adopted and declared as a platform of principles by the Democratic Convention at Cincinnati, in the year 1856, believing that Democratic principles are unchangeable in their nature, when applied to the same subject matters; and we recommend, as the only further resolutions, the following:

Inasmuch as differences of opinion exist in the Democratic party as to the nature and extent of the Powers of a Territorial Legislature, and as to the powers and duties of Congress, under the Constitution of the United States, over the institution of Slavery within the Territories:

2. Resolved, That the Democratic party will abide by the decisions of the Supreme Court of the United States on the questions of Constitutional law.

3. Resolved, That it is the duty of the United States to afford ample and complete protection to all its citizens, whether at home or abroad, and whether native or foreign.

4. Resolved, That one of the necessities of the age, in a military, commercial, and postal point of view, is speedy communication between the Atlantic and Pacific States; and the Democratic party pledge such Constitutional Government aid as will insure the construction of a Railroad to the Pacific coast, at the earliest practicable period.

5. Resolved, That the Democratic party are in favor of the acquisition of the island of Cuba, on such terms as shall be honorable to ourselves and just to Spain.

6. Resolved, That the enactments of State Legislatures to defeat the faithful execution of the Fugitive Slave Law, are hostile in character, subversive of the Constitution, and revolutionary in their effect.

7. Resolved, That it is in accordance with the true interpretation of the Cincinnati Platform, that, during the existence of the Territorial Governments, the measure of restriction, whatever it may be, imposed by the Federal Constitution on the power of the Territorial Legislature over the subject of the domestic relations, as the same has been, or shall hereafter be, finally determined by the Supreme Court of the United States, shall be respected by all good citizens, and enforced with promptness and fidelity by every branch of the General Government.

3. (Southern) National Democratic Party
(Candidate: John Breckinridge)
Adopted at Charleston and Baltimore, 1860.

Resolved, That the Platform adopted by the Democratic party at Cincinnati be affirmed, with the following explanatory Resolutions:

1. That the Government of a Territory organized by an act of Congress, is provisional and temporary; and during its existence, all citizens of the United States have an equal right to settle with their property in the Territory, without their rights, either of person or property, being destroyed or impaired by Congressional or Territorial legislation.

2. That it is the duty of the Federal Government, in all its departments, to protect, when necessary, the rights of persons and property in the Territories, and wherever else its Constitutional authority extends.

3. That when the settlers in a Territory having an adequate population, form a State Constitution, in pursuance of law, the right of sovereignty commences, and, being consummated by admission into the Union, they stand on an equal footing with the people of other States; and the State thus organized ought to be admitted into the Federal Union, whether its Constitution prohibits or recognizes the institution of Slavery.

4. That the Democratic party are in favor of the acquisition of the island of Cuba, on such terms as shall be honorable to ourselves and just to Spain, at the earliest practicable moment.

5. That the enactments of State Legislatures to defeat the faithful execution of the Fugitive Slave Law are hostile in character, subversive of the Constitution, and revolutionary in their effect.

6. That the democracy of the United States recognize it as the imperative duty of this Government to protect the naturalized citizen in all his rights, whether at home or in foreign lands, to the same exent as its native-born citizens.

Whereas, one of the greatest necessities of the age in a Political, Commercial, Postal, and Military point of view, is a speedy communication between the Pacific and Atlantic coasts; therefore, be it

Resolved, That the Democratic party do hereby pledge themselves to use every means in their power to secure the passage of some bill to the extent of the Constitutional authority of Congress for the Construction of a Pacific Railroad from the Mississippi River to the Pacific Ocean, at the earliest practicable moment.

4. Constitutional Union Platform (Candidate: John Bell)
Adopted at Baltimore, 1860

Whereas, Experience has demonstrated that Platforms adopted by the partisan conventions of the country have had the effect to mislead and deceive the people, and at the same time to widen the political divisions of the country, by the creation and encouragement of geographical and sectional parties; therefore,

Resolved, That it is both the part of patriotism and of duty to recognise no political principle other than THE CONSTITUTION OF THE COUNTRY, THE UNION OF THE STATES, AND THE ENFORCEMENT OF THE LAWS, and that as representatives of the Constitutional Union men of the country in National Convention assembled, we hereby pledge ourselves to maintain, protect, and defend, separately and unitedly, these great principles of public liberty and national safety, against all enemies at home and abroad, believing that thereby peace may once more be restored to the country, the rights of the People and of the States reëstablished, and the Government again placed in that condition, of justice, fraternity and equality, which under the example and Constitution of our fathers, has solemnly bound every citizen of the United States to maintain a more perfect union, establish justice, insure domestic tranquility, provide for the common defence, promote the general welfare, and secure the blessings of liberty to ourselves and our posterity.

❧43❧

The Crittenden Compromise
December 1860

Two days before South Carolina seceded, Senator John Crittenden (Kentucky)
suggested the adoption of a number of constitutional amendments which would
have clearly defined the extent of slave-holding and non-slave-holding areas in
the territories. When the Senate rejected this, Crittenden proposed a national
referendum on his compromise plan, but this too was blocked by Republicans
in the Senate.

A joint resolution (S. No. 50) proposing certain amendments to the Constitution of the United States.

Whereas serious and alarming dissensions have arisen between the northern
and southern states, concerning the rights and security of the rights of the
slaveholding States, and especially their rights in the common territory of the
United States; and whereas it is eminently desirable and proper that these
dissensions, which now threaten the very existence of this Union, should be
permanently quieted and settled by constitutional provisions, which shall do equal
justice to all sections, and thereby restore to all the people that peace and good-will
which ought to prevail between all the citizens of the United States: Therefore,

Resolved by the Senate and House of Representatives of the United States of
America in Congress assembled, (two thirds of both Houses concurring); That the
following articles be, and are hereby, proposed and submitted as amendments to
the Constitution of the United States, which shall be valid to all intents and
purposes, as part of said Constitution, when ratified by conventions of three-fourths
of the several States:

Article 1: In all the territory of the United States now held, or hereafter acquired,
situated north of 36 degrees 30 minutes, slavery or involuntary servitude, except as
a punishment for crime, is prohibited while such territory shall remain under
territorial government. In all the territory south of said line of latitude, slavery of
the African race is hereby recognized as existing, and shall not be interfered with

Source: *Congressional Globe*, 18th December, 1860.

by Congress, but shall be protected as property by all the departments of the territorial government during its continuance. And when any territory, north or south of said line, within such boundaries as Congress may prescribe, shall contain the population requisite for a member of Congress according to the then Federal ratio of representation of the people of the United States, it shall, if its form of government be republican, be admitted into the Union, on an equal footing with the original States, with or without slavery, as the constitution of such new States may provide.

Article 2: Congress shall have no power to abolish slavery in places under its exclusive jurisdiction, and situate within the limits of States that permit the holding of slaves.

Article 3: Congress shall have no power to abolish slavery within the District of Columbia, so long as it exists in the adjoining States of Virginia and Maryland, or either, nor without the consent of the inhabitants, nor without just compensation first made to such owners of slaves as do not consent to such abolishment. Nor shall Congress at any time prohibit officers of the Federal Government, or members of Congress, whose duties require them to be in said District, from bringing with them their slaves, and holding them as such during the time their duties may require them to remain there, and afterwards taking them from the District.

Article 4: Congress shall have no power to prohibit or hinder the transportation of slaves from one State to another, or to a Territory, in which slaves are by law permitted to be held, whether that transportation be by land, navigable river, or by the sea.

Article 5: That in addition to the provisions of the third paragraph of the second section of the fourth article of the Constitution of the United States, Congress shall have power to provide by law, and it shall be its duty so to provide, that the United States shall pay to the owner who shall apply for it, the full value of his fugitive slave in all cases where the marshall or other officer whose duty it was to arrest said fugitive was prevented from so doing by violence or intimidation, or when, after arrest, said fugitive was rescued by force, and the owner thereby prevented and obstructed in the pursuit of his remedy for the recovery of his fugitive slave under the said clause of the Constitution and the laws made in pursuance thereof. And in all such cases, when the United States shall pay for such fugitive, they shall have the right, in their own name, to sue the county in which said violence, intimidation, or rescue was committed, and to recover from it, with interest and damages, the amount paid by them for said fugitive slave. And the said county, after it has paid said amount to the United States, may, for its indemnity, sue and recover from the wrong-doers or rescuers by whom the owner was prevented from the recovery of his fugitive slave, in like manner as the owner himself might have sued and recovered.

Article 6: No future amendment of the Constitution shall affect the five preceding articles; nor the third paragraph of the second section of the first article of the Constitution; nor the third paragraph of the second section of the fourth article of said Constitution; and no amendment will be made to the Constitution which shall authorize or give to Congress any power to abolish or interfere with slavery in any of the States by whose laws it is, or may be, allowed or permitted.

And whereas, also, besides those causes of dissension embraced in the foregoing amendments proposed to the Constitution of the United States, there are others which come within the jurisdiction of Congress, and may be remedied by its legislative power; and whereas it is the desire of Congress, so far as its power will extend, to remove all just cause for the popular discontent and agitation which now disturb the peace of the country, and threaten the stability of its institutions; Therefore,

1. Resolved by the Senate and House of Representatives of the United States of America, in Congress assembled, That the laws now in force for the recovery of fugitive slaves are in strict pursuance of the plain and mandatory provisions of the Constitution, and have been sanctioned as valid and constitutional by the judgement of the Supreme Court of the United States; that the slaveholding States are entitled to the faithful observance and execution of those laws, and that they ought not to be repealed, or so modified or changed as to impair their efficiency; and that laws ought to be made for the punishment of those who attempt by rescue of the slave, or other illegal means, to hinder or defeat the due execution of said laws.

2. That all State laws which conflict with the fugitive slave acts of Congress, or any other constitutional acts of Congress, or which, in their operation, impede, hinder, or delay the free course and due execution of any of said acts, are null and void by the plain provisions of the Constitution of the United States; yet those State laws, void as they are, have given color to practices, and led to consequences, which have obstructed the due administration and execution of acts of Congress, and especially the acts for the delivery of fugitive slaves, and have thereby contributed much to the discord and commotion now prevailing. Congress, therefore, in the present perilous juncture, does not deem it improper, respectfully and earnestly to recommend the repeal of those laws to the several States which have enacted them, or such legislative corrections or explanations of them as may prevent their being used or perverted to such mischievous purposes.

3. That the act of the 18th of September, 1850, commonly called the fugitive slave law, ought to be so amended as to make the fee of the commissioner, mentioned in the eighth section of the act, equal in amount in the cases decided by him, whether his decision be in favor of or against the claimant. And to avoid misconstruction, the last clause of the fifth section of said act, which authorizes the person holding a warrant for the arrest or detention of a fugitive slave, to summon to his aid the posse comitatus, and which declares it to be the duty of all good citizens to assist him in its execution, ought to be so amended as to expressly limit the authority and duty to cases in which there shall be resistance or danger of resistance or rescue.

4. That the laws for the suppression of the African slave trade, and especially

those prohibiting the importation of slaves in the United States, ought to be made effectual, and ought to be thoroughly executed; and all further enactments necessary to those ends ought to be promptly made.

⚜·44·⚜

Declaration of the Immediate Causes which Induce and Justify the Secession of South Carolina from the Federal Union

South Carolina's secession from the Union signalled the end of argument and the beginning of the final stages of the process that would culminate in the Civil War. The Declaration effectively sought to recreate the state of South Carolina as a separate independent nation. This step was rationalised by reference to the founding documents of American nationhood—connecting South Carolina's move to secession with the Declaration of Independence itself.

The people of the State of South Carolina, in Convention assembled, on the 26th day of April, A.D., 1852, declared that the frequent violations of the Constitution of the United States, by the Federal Government, and its encroachments upon the reserved rights of the States, fully justified this State in then withdrawing from the Federal Union; but in deference to the opinions and wishes of the other slaveholding States, she forbore at that time to exercise this right. Since that time, these encroachments have continued to increase, and further forbearance ceases to be a virtue.

And now the State of South Carolina having resumed her separate and equal place among nations, deems it due to herself, to the remaining United States of America, and to the nations of the world, that she should declare the immediate causes which have led to this act.

In the year 1765, that portion of the British Empire embracing Great Britain, undertook to make laws for the government of that portion composed of the thirteen American Colonies. A struggle for the right of self-government ensued, which resulted, on the 4th of July, 1776, in a Declaration, by the Colonies,

Source: *State of South Carolina, Journal of the Convention of the People of South Carolina, Held in 1860, 1861, and 1862. Together with the Ordinances, Reports, Resolutions, etc.,* Columbia, S.C.: R. W. Gibbes, Printer to the Convention, 1862.

"that they are, and of right ought to be, FREE AND INDEPENDENT STATES; and that, as free and independent States, they have full power to levy war, conclude peace, contract alliances, establish commerce, and to do all other acts and things which independent States may of right do."

They further solemnly declared that whenever any

"form of government becomes destructive of the ends for which it was established, it is the right of the people to alter or abolish it, and to institute a new government."

Deeming the Government of Great Britain to have become destructive of these ends, they declared that the Colonies

"are absolved from all allegiance to the British Crown, and that all political connection between them and the State of Great Britain is, and ought to be, totally dissolved."

In pursuance of this Declaration of Independence, each of the thirteen States proceeded to exercise its separate sovereignty; adopted for itself a Constitution, and appointed officers for the administration of government in all its departments—Legislative, Executive and Judicial. For purposes of defense, they united their arms and their counsels; and, in 1778, they entered into a League known as the Articles of Confederation, whereby they agreed to entrust the administration of their external relations to a common agent, known as the Congress of the United States, expressly declaring, in the first Article

"that each State retains its sovereignty, freedom and independence, and every power, jurisdiction and right which is not, by this Confederation, expressly delegated to the United States in Congress assembled."

Under this Confederation the war of the Revolution was carried on, and on the 3rd September, 1783, the contest ended, and a definite Treaty was signed by Great Britain, in which she acknowledged the independence of the Colonies in the following terms:

"ARTICLE 1.—His Britannic Majesty acknowledges the said United States, viz: New Hampshire, Massachusetts Bay, Rhode Island and Providence Plantations, Connecticut, New York, New Jersey, Pennsylvania, Delaware, Maryland, Virginia, North Carolina, South Carolina and Georgia, to be FREE, SOVEREIGN AND INDEPENDENT STATES; that he treats with them as such; and for himself, his heirs and successors, relinquishes all claims to the government, proprietary and territorial rights of the same and every part thereof."

Thus were established the two great principles asserted by the Colonies, namely: the right of a State to govern itself; and the right of a people to abolish a Government when it becomes destructive of the ends for which it was instituted. And concurrent with the establishment of these principles, was the fact, that each Colony became and was recognized by the mother Country as a FREE, SOVEREIGN AND INDEPENDENT STATE.

In 1787, Deputies were appointed by the States to revise the Articles of Confederation, and on 17th September, 1787, these Deputies recommended, for the adoption of the States, the Articles of Union, known as the Constitution of the United States.

The parties to whom this Constitution was submitted, were the several sovereign States; they were to agree or disagree, and when nine of them agreed the compact was to take effect among those concurring; and the General Government, as the common agent, was then invested with their authority.

If only nine of the thirteen States had concurred, the other four would have remained as they then were—separate, sovereign States, independent of any of the provisions of the Constitution. In fact, two of the States did not accede to the Constitution until long after it had gone into operation among the other eleven; and during that interval, they each exercised the functions of an independent nation.

By this Constitution, certain duties were imposed upon the several States, and the exercise of certain of their powers was restrained, which necessarily implied their continued existence as sovereign States. But to remove all doubt, an amendment was added, which declared that the powers not delegated to the United States by the Constitution, nor prohibited by it to the States, are reserved to the States, respectively, or to the people. On the 23d May, 1788, South Carolina, by a Convention of her People, passed an Ordinance assenting to this Constitution, and afterwards altered her own Constitution, to conform herself to the obligations she had undertaken.

Thus was established, by compact between the States, a Government with defined objects and powers, limited to the express words of the grant. This limitation left the whole remaining mass of power subject to the clause reserving it to the States or to the people, and rendered unnecessary any specification of reserved rights.

We hold that the Government thus established is subject to the two great principles asserted in the Declaration of Independence; and we hold further, that the mode of its formation subjects it to a third fundamental principle, namely: the law of compact. We maintain that in every compact between two or more parties, the obligation is mutual; that the failure of one of the contracting parties to perform a material part of the agreement, entirely releases the obligation of the other; and that where no arbiter is provided, each party is remitted to his own judgment to determine the fact of failure, with all its consequences.

In the present case, that fact is established with certainty. We assert that fourteen of the States have deliberately refused, for years past, to fulfill their constitutional obligations, and we refer to their own Statutes for the proof.

The Constitution of the United States, in its fourth Article, provides as follows:

> "No person held to service or labor in one State, under the laws thereof, escaping into another, shall, in consequence of any law or regulation therein, be discharged from such service or labor, but shall be delivered up, on claim of the party to whom such service or labor may be due."

This stipulation was so material to the compact, that without it that compact would not have been made. The greater number of the contracting parties held slaves, and they had previously evinced their estimate of the value of such a stipulation by making it a condition in the Ordinance for the government of the territory ceded by Virginia, which now composes the States north of the Ohio River.

The same article of the Constitution stipulates also for rendition by the several States of fugitives from justice from the other States.

The General Government, as the common agent, passed laws to carry into effect these stipulations of the States. For many years these laws were executed. But an increasing hostility on the part of the non-slaveholding States to the institution of slavery, has led to a disregard of their obligations, and the laws of the General Government have ceased to effect the objects of the Constitution. The States of Maine, New Hampshire, Vermont, Massachusetts, Connecticut, Rhode Island, New York, Pennsylvania, Illinois, Indiana, Michigan, Wisconsin and Iowa, have enacted laws which either nullify the Acts of Congress or render useless any attempt to execute them. In many of these States the fugitive is discharged from service or labor claimed, and in none of them has the State Government complied with the stipulation made in the Constitution. The State of New Jersey, at an early day, passed a law in conformity with her constitutional obligation; but the current of anti-slavery feeling has led her more recently to enact laws which render inoperative the remedies provided by her own law and by the laws of Congress. In the State of New York even the right of transit for a slave has been denied by her tribunals; and the States of Ohio and Iowa have refused to surrender to justice fugitives charged with murder, and with inciting servile insurrection in the State of Virginia. Thus the constituted compact has been deliberately broken and disregarded by the non-slaveholding States, and the consequence follows that South Carolina is released from her obligation.

The ends for which this Constitution was framed are declared by itself to be

"to form a more perfect union, establish justice, insure domestic tranquillity, provide for the common defence, promote the general welfare, and secure the blessings of liberty to ourselves and our posterity."

These ends it endeavored to accomplish by a Federal Government, in which each State was recognized as an equal, and had separate control over its own institutions. The right of property in slaves was recognized by giving to free persons distinct political rights, by giving them the right to represent, and burthening them with direct taxes for three-fifths of their slaves; by authorizing the importation of slaves for twenty years; and by stipulating for the rendition of fugitives from labor.

We affirm that these ends for which this Government was instituted have been defeated, and the Government itself has been made destructive of them by the action of the non-slaveholding States. Those States have assumed the right of deciding upon the propriety of our domestic institutions; and have denied the rights of property established in fifteen of the States and recognized by the Constitution; they have denounced as sinful the institution of slavery; they have permitted open establishment among them of societies, whose avowed object is to disturb the peace and to eloign the property of the citizens of other States. They have encouraged and assisted thousands of our slaves to leave their homes; and those who remain, have been incited by emissaries, books and pictures to servile insurrection.

For twenty-five years this agitation has been steadily increasing, until it has now secured to its aid the power of the common Government. Observing the forms of the Constitution, a sectional party has found within that Article establishing the Executive Department, the means of subverting the Constitution itself. A geographical line has been drawn across the Union, and all the States north of that line have united in the election of a man to the high office of President of the United States, whose opinions and purposes are hostile to slavery. He is to be entrusted with the administration of the common Government, because he has declared that that "Government cannot endure permanently half slave, half free," and that the public mind must rest in the belief that slavery is in the course of ultimate extinction.

This sectional combination for the subversion of the Constitution, has been aided in some of the States by elevating to citizenship, persons who, by the supreme law of the land, are incapable of becoming citizens; and their votes have been used to inaugurate a new policy, hostile to the South, and destructive of its peace and safety.

On the 4th of March next, this party will take possession of the Government. It has announced that the South shall be excluded from the common territory, that the judicial tribunals shall be made sectional, and that a war must be waged against slavery until it shall cease throughout the United States.

The guaranties of the Constitution will then no longer exist; the equal rights of the States will be lost. The slaveholding States will no longer have the power of self-government, or self-protection, and the Federal Government will have become their enemy.

Sectional interest and animosity will deepen the irritation, and all hope of remedy is rendered vain, by the fact that public opinion at the North has invested a great political error with the sanctions of a more erroneous religious belief.

We, therefore, the People of South Carolina, by our delegates in Convention assembled, appealing to the Supreme Judge of the world for the rectitude of our intentions, have solemnly declared that the Union heretofore existing between this State and the other States of North America, is dissolved, and that the State of South Carolina has resumed her position among the nations of the world, as a separate and independent State; with full power to levy war, conclude peace, contract alliances, establish commerce, and to do all other acts and things which independent States may of right do.

✥45✥

Brother Jonathan's Lament
for Sister Caroline

OLIVER WENDELL HOLMES

Oliver Wendell Holmes (1809–1894) here expresses in poetical form the impact of South Carolina's secession from the union. Holmes makes reference to the turbulent and fractious relationship that had existed between the state and the federal government. He looks upon secession as a family quarrel. It is a temporary crisis: the union will survive, and eventually South Carolina will return as a part of the federal whole.

She has gone,—she has left us in passion and pride—
Our stormy-browed sister, so long at our side!
She has torn her own star from our firmament's glow,
And turned on her brother the face of a foe!

O Caroline, Caroline, child of the sun,
We can never forget that our hearts have been one,—
Our foreheads both sprinkled in Liberty's name,
From the fountain of blood with the finger of flame!

You were always too ready to fire at a touch;
But we said: "She is hasty,—she does not mean much."
We have scowled when you uttered some turbulent threat;
But Friendship still whispered: "Forgive and forget!"

Has our love all died out? Have its altars grown cold?
Has the curse come at last which the fathers foretold?
Then Nature must teach us the strength of the chain
That her petulant children would sever in vain.

Source: Oliver Wendell Holmes, 'Brother Jonathan's Lament for Sister Caroline',
March 25, 1861, repr. in *The Poetical Works of Oliver Wendell Holmes*,
Boston: H.O. Houghton & Co., 1908 edition.

VIII: THE HOUSE DIVIDES

They may fight till the buzzards are gorged with their spoil,
Till the harvest grows black as it rots in the soil,
Till the wolves and the catamounts troop from their caves,
And the shark tracks the pirate, the lord of the waves:

In vain is the strife! When its fury is past,
Their fortunes must flow in one channel at last,
As the torrents that rush from the mountains of snow
Roll mingled in peace through the valleys below.

Our Union is river, lake, ocean, and sky;
Man breaks not the medal when God cuts the die!
Though darkened with sulphur, though cloven with steel,
The blue arch will brighten, the waters will heal!

O Caroline, Caroline, child of the sun,
There are battles with Fate that can never be won!
The star-flowering banner must never be furled,
For its blossoms of light are the hope of the world!

Go, then, our rash sister! afar and aloof,
Run wild in the sunshine away from our roof,
But when your heart aches and your feet have grown sore,
Remember the pathway that leads to our door!

⚬46⚬

Farewell Speech to the US Senate, 21st January 1861

JEFFERSON DAVIS

As the Southern States seceded from the Union, their representatives in the federal government had necessarily to resign their positions. Jefferson Davis, as senator for Mississippi, made his farewell speech to the Senate prior to taking office as president of the Confederacy.

I rise, Mr. President, for the purpose of announcing to the Senate that I have satisfactory evidence that the State of Mississippi, by a solemn ordinance of her people, in convention assembled, has declared her separation from the United States. Under these circumstances, of course, my functions are terminated here. It has seemed to me proper, however, that I should appear in the Senate to announce that fact to my associates, and I will say but very little more. The occasion does not invite me to go into argument; and my physical condition would not permit me to do so, if it were otherwise; and yet it seems to become me to say something on the part of the State I here represent on an occasion as solemn as this.

It is known to Senators who have served with me here that I have for many years advocated, as an essential attribute of State sovereignty, the right of a State to secede from the Union. Therefore, if I had thought that Mississippi was acting without sufficient provocation, or without an existing necessity, I should still, under my theory of the Government, because of my allegiance to the State of which I am a citizen, have been bound by her action. I, however, may be permitted to say that I do think she has justifiable cause, and I approve of her act. I conferred with her people before that act was taken, counseled them then that, if the state of things which they apprehended should exist when their Convention met, they should take the action which they have now adopted.

I hope none who hear me will confound this expression of mine with the advocacy of the right of a State to remain in the Union, and to disregard its

Source: Thomas Cooper and Hector Fenton, *American Politics (Non-Partisan): From The Beginning to Date*, Boston: Mass., Russell & Henderson, 1885 edition, Book III.

constitutional obligation by the nullification of the law. Such is not my theory. Nullification and secession, so often confounded, are, indeed, antagonistic principles. Nullification is a remedy which it is sought to apply within the Union, against the agent of the States. It is only to be justified when the agent has violated his constitutional obligations, and a State, assuming to judge for itself, denies the right of the agent thus to act, and appeals to the other states of the Union for a decision; but, when the States themselves and when the people of the States have so acted as to convince us that they will not regard our constitutional rights, then, and then for the first time, arises the doctrine of secession in its practical application.

A great man who now reposes with his fathers, and who has often been arraigned for want of fealty to the Union, advocated the doctrine of nullification because it preserved the Union. It was because of his deep-seated attachment to the Union—his determination to find some remedy for existing ills short of a severance of the ties which bound South Carolina to the other States—that Mr. Calhoun advocated the doctrine of nullification, which he proclaimed to be peaceful, to be within the limits of State power, not to disturb the Union, but only to be a means of bringing the agent before the tribunal of the States for their judgement.

Secession belongs to a different class of remedies. It is to be justified upon the basis that the states are sovereign. There was a time when none denied it. I hope the time may come again when a better comprehension of the theory of our Government, and the inalienable rights of the people of the States, will prevent any one from denying that each State is a sovereign, and thus may reclaim the grants which it has made to any agent whomsoever.

I, therefore, say I concur in the action of the people of Mississippi, believing it to be necessary and proper, and should have been bound by their action if my belief had been otherwise; and this brings me to the important point which I wish, on this last occasion, to present to the Senate. It is by this confounding of nullification and secession that the name of a great man whose ashes now mingle with his mother earth has been invoked to justify coercion against a seceded State. The phrase, "to execute the laws," was an expression which General Jackson applied to the case of a State refusing to obey the laws while yet a member of the Union. That is not the case which is now presented. The laws are to be executed over the United States, and upon the people of the United States. They have no relation to any foreign country. It is a perversion of terms—at least, it is a great mis-apprehension of the case—which cites that expression for application to a State which has withdrawn from the Union. You may make war on a foreign state. If it be the purpose of gentlemen, they may make war against a State which has withdrawn from the Union; but there are no laws of the United States to be executed within the limits of a seceded State. A State, finding herself in the condition in which Mississippi has judged she is—in which her safety requires that she should provide for the maintenance of her rights out of the Union—surrenders all the benefits (and they are known to be many), deprives herself of the advantages (and they are known to be great), severs all the ties of affection (and they are close and enduring), which have bound her to the Union; and thus divesting herself of every benefit—taking upon herself every burden—she claims to be exempt from any power to execute the laws of the United States within her limits.

I well remember an occasion when Massachusetts was arraigned before the bar of the Senate, and when the doctrine of coercion was rife, and to be applied against her, because of the rescue of a fugitive slave in Boston. My opinion then was the same that it is now. Not in a spirit of egotism, but to show that I am not influenced in my opinions because the case is my own, I refer to that time and that occasion as containing the opinion which I then entertained, and on which my present conduct is based. I then said that if Massachusetts—following her purpose through a stated line of conduct—chose to take the last step, which separates her from the Union, it is her right to go, and I will neither vote one dollar nor one man to coerce her back; but I will say to her, "God speed," in memory of the kind associations which once existed between her and the other States.

It has been a conviction of pressing necessity—it has been a belief that we are to be deprived in the Union of the rights which our fathers bequeathed to us— which has brought Mississippi to her present decision. She has heard proclaimed the theory that all men are created free and equal, and this made the basis of an attack upon her social institutions; and the sacred Declaration of Independence has been invoked to maintain the position of the equality of the races. That Declaration is to be construed by the circumstances and purposes for which it was made. The communities were declaring their independence; the people of those communities were asserting that no man was born—to use the language of Mr. Jefferson—booted and spurred, to ride over the rest of mankind; that men were created equal—meaning the men of the political community; that there was no divine right to rule; that no man inherited the right to govern; that there were no classes by which power and place descended to families; but that all stations were equally within the grasp of each member of the body politic. These were the great principles they announced; these were the purposes for which they made their declaration; these were the ends to which their enunciation was directed. They have no reference to the slave; else, how happened it that among the items of arraignment against George III was that he endeavored to do just what the North has been endeavoring of late to do, to stir up insurrection among our slaves? Had the Declaration announced that the negroes were free and equal, how was the prince to be arraigned for raising up insurrection among them? And how was this to be enumerated among the high crimes which caused the colonies to sever their connection with the mother-country? When our Constitution was formed, the same idea was rendered more palpable; for there we find provision made for that very class of persons as property; they were not put upon the equality of footing with white men—not even upon that of paupers and convicts; but, so far as representation was concerned, were discriminated against as a lower caste, only to be represented in the numerical proportion of three-fifths. So stands the compact which binds us together.

Then, Senators, we recur to the principles upon which our Government was founded; and when you deny them, and when you deny us the right to withdraw from a Government which, thus perverted, threatens to be destructive of our rights, we but tread in the path of our fathers when we proclaim our independence and take the hazard. This is done, not in hostility to others, not to injure any section of the country, not even for our own pecuniary benefit, but from the high and solemn motive of defending and protecting the rights we inherited, and which it is our duty to transmit unshorn to our children.

I find in myself perhaps a type of the general feeling of my constituents towards yours. I am sure I feel no hostility toward you, Senators from the North. I am sure there is not one of you, whatever sharp discussion there may have been between us, to whom I cannot now say, in the presence of my God, I wish you well; and such, I feel, is the feeling of the people whom I represent toward those whom you represent. I, therefore, feel that I but express their desire when I say I hope, and they hope, for peaceable relations with you, though we must part. They may be mutually beneficial to us in the future, as they have been in the past, if you so will it. The reverse may bring disaster on every portion of the country, and, if you will have it thus, we will invoke the God of our fathers, who delivered them from the power of the lion, to protect us from the ravages of the bear; and thus, putting our trust in God and in our firm hearts and strong arms, we will vindicate the right as best we may.

In the course of my service here, associated at different times with a variety of Senators, I see now around me some with whom I have served long; there have been points of collision, but, whatever of offense there has been to me, I leave here. I carry with me no hostile remembrance. Whatever offense I have given which has not been redressed, or for which satisfaction has not been demanded, I have, Senators, in this hour of our parting, to offer you my apology for any pain which, in the heat of discussion, I have inflicted. I go hence unencumbered by the remembrance of any injury received, and having discharged the duty of making the only reparation in my power for any injury offered.

Mr. President and Senators, having made the announcement which the occasion seemed to me to require, it only remains for me to bid you a final adieu.

IX. Union and Confederacy: 1861

4 . Young Southerners at Richmond, 1861.

❦·47·❦

The Washington Peace Conference Proposals: February 1861

The Washington Peace Conference met at the Willard Hotel, during the month of February 1861. The conference convened on the initiative of the Virginia legislature. Not all the states sent representatives. John Tyler of Virginia, the former President, was the presiding officer. The proposals represent another last ditch effort at compromise.

Article 13, Sec. 1. In all the present territory of the United States, north of the parallel of 36 degrees 30 minutes of north latitude, involuntary servitude, except in punishment of crime, is prohibited. In all the present Territory south of that line, the status of persons held to involuntary servitude or labor, as it now exists, shall not be changed; nor shall any law be passed by Congress or the Territorial Legislature to hinder or prevent the taking of such persons from any of the States of this Union to said Territory, nor to impair the rights arising from said relation; but the same shall be subject to judicial cognizance in the Federal courts, according to the course of the common law. When any territory north or south of said line, within such boundary as Congress may prescribe, shall contain a population equal to that required for a member of Congress, it shall, if its form of government be republican, be admitted into the Union on an equal footing with the original States, with or without slavery, as the constitution of such new State may provide.

Sec. 2. No Territory shall be acquired by the United States, except by discovery and for naval and commercial stations, depots, and transit routes, without the concurrence of a majority of all the Senators from States which allow involuntary servitude, and a majority of all the Senators from States which prohibit that relation; nor shall Territory be acquired by treaty, unless the votes of a majority of the Senators from States from each class of States heretobefore mentioned be cast as a part of the two-thirds majority necessary to the ratification of such treaty.

Sec. 3. Neither the Constitution nor any amendment thereof shall be construed to give Congress power to regulate, abolish, or control, within any State the relation

Source: E. McPherson, *Political History of the United States of America during the Great Rebellion,* Washington D.C.: Philp & Solomons, 1865.

established or recognized by the laws thereof touching persons held to labor or involuntary service therein, nor to interfere with or abolish involuntary service in the District of Columbia without the consent of Maryland and without the consent of the owners, or making the owners who do not consent just compensation; nor the power to interfere with or prohibit Representatives and others from bringing with them to the District of Columbia, retaining, and taking away, persons so held to labor or service; nor the power to interfere with or abolish involuntary service in places under the exclusive jurisdiction of the United States within those States and Territories where the same is established or recognized; nor the power to prohibit the removal or transportation of persons held to labor or involuntary service in any State or Territory of the United States to any other State or Territory thereof where it is established or recognized by law or usage, and the right during transportation, by sea or river, of touching at ports, shores, and landings, and of landing in case of distress, shall exist; but not the right of transit in or through any State or Territory, or of sale or traffic, against the laws thereof. Nor shall Congress have power to authorize any higher rate of taxation on persons held to labor or service than on land. The bringing into the District of Columbia of persons held to labor or service, for sale, or placing them in depots to be afterwards transferred to other places for sale as merchandize, is prohibited.

Sec. 4. The third paragraph of the second section of the fourth article of the Constitution shall not be construed to prevent any of the States, by appropriate legislation, and through the action of their judicial and ministerial officers from enforcing the delivery of fugitives from labor to the person to whom such service or labor is due.

Sec. 5. The foreign slave trade is hereby forever prohibited; and it shall be the duty of Congress to pass laws to prevent the importation of slaves, coolies, or persons held to service or labor, into the United States and the Territories from places beyond the limits thereof.

Sec. 6. The first, third, and fifth sections, together with this section of these amendments and the third paragraph of the second section of the first article of the Constitution, and the third paragraph of the second section of the fourth article thereof, shall not be amended or abolished without the consent of all the States.

Sec. 7. Congress shall provide by law that the United States shall pay to the owner the full value of his fugitive from labor, in all cases when the marshall or other officer, whose duty it was to arrest such fugitive, was prevented from so doing by violence or intimidation from mobs or riotous assemblages, or when, after arrest, such fugitive was rescued by like violence and intimidation, and the owner thereby deprived of the same; and the acceptance of such payment shall preclude the owner from further claim to such fugitive. Congress shall provide by law for securing to the citizens of each State the privileges and immunities of citizens in the several States.

⟨⟩48⟨⟩

First Inaugural Address

ABRAHAM LINCOLN

Lincoln's first inaugural address on 4th March 1861 was couched in the language of conciliation, even as the southern states were seceding from the Union. He reiterated his belief that he did not have the legal power to intervene in those states where slavery existed to abolish the 'peculiar institution', and concluded with a powerful appeal to nationalist sentiment in the hope of preserving the union.

Fellow-Citizens of the United States:

In compliance with a custom as old as the Government itself, I appear before you to address you briefly and to take in your presence the oath prescribed by the Constitution of the United States to be taken by the President "before he enters on the execution of this office."

I do not consider it necessary at present for me to discuss those matters of administration about which there is no special anxiety or excitement.

Apprehension seems to exist among the people of the Southern States that by the accession of a Republican Administration their property and their peace and personal security are to be endangered. There has never been any reasonable cause for such apprehension. Indeed, the most ample evidence to the contrary has all the while existed and been open to their inspection. It is found in nearly all the published speeches of him who now addresses you. I do but quote from one of those speeches when I declare that—

> I have no purpose, directly or indirectly, to interfere with the institution of slavery in the States where it exists. I believe I have no lawful right to do so, and I have no inclination to do so.

Those who nominated and elected me did so with full knowledge that I had made this and many similar declarations and had never recanted them; and more than this, they placed in the platform for my acceptance, and as a law to themselves

Source: Abraham Lincoln, 'First Inaugural Address', 4th March 1861, in James D. Richardson, ed., *A Compilation of the Messages and Papers of the Presidents*, New York: Bureau of National Literature, Inc., 1897, Volume VII.

and to me, the clear and emphatic resolution which I now read:

> *Resolved*, That the maintenance inviolate of the rights of the States, and especially the right of each State to order and control its own domestic institutions according to its own judgment exclusively, is essential to that balance of power on which the perfection and endurance of our political fabric depend; and we denounce the lawless invasion by armed force of the soil of any State or Territory, no matter under what pretext, as among the gravest of crimes.

I now reiterate these sentiments, and in doing so I only press upon the public attention the most conclusive evidence of which the case is susceptible that the property, peace, and security of no section are to be in any wise endangered by the now incoming Administration. I add, too, that all the protection which, consistently with the Constitution and the laws, can be given will be cheerfully given to all the States when lawfully demanded, for whatever cause—as cheerfully to one section as to another. There is much controversy about the delivering up of fugitives from service or labor. The clause I now read is as plainly written in the Constitution as any other of its provisions:

> No person held to service or labor in one State, under the laws thereof, escaping into another, shall in consequence of any law or regulation therein be discharged from such service or labor, but shall be delivered up on claim of the party to whom such service or labor may be due.

It is scarcely questioned that this provision was intended by those who made it for the reclaiming of what we call fugitive slaves; and the intention of the lawgiver is the law. All members of Congress swear their support to the whole Constitution—to this provision as much as to any other. To the proposition, then, that slaves whose cases come within the terms of this clause "shall be delivered up" their oaths are unanimous. Now, if they would make the effort in good temper, could they not with nearly equal unanimity frame and pass a law by means of which to keep good that unanimous oath?

There is some difference of opinion whether this clause should be enforced by national or by State authority, but surely that difference is not a very material one. If the slave is to be surrendered, it can be of but little consequence to him or to others by which authority it is done. And should anyone in any case be content that his oath shall go unkept on a merely unsubstantial controversy as to how it shall be kept?

Again: In any law upon this subject ought not all the safeguards of liberty known in civilized and humane jurisprudence to be introduced, so that a free man be not in any case surrendered as a slave? And might it not be well at the same time to provide by law for the enforcement of that clause in the Constitution which guarantees that "the citizens of each State shall be entitled to all privileges and immunities of citizens in the several States"?

I take the official oath to-day with no mental reservations and with no purpose to construe the Constitution or laws by any hypercritical rules; and while I do not choose now to specify particular acts of Congress as proper to be enforced, I do suggest that it will be much safer for all, both in official and private stations, to conform to and abide by all those acts which stand unrepealed than to violate any of them trusting to find impunity in having them held to be unconstitutional.

It is seventy-two years since the first inauguration of a President under our National Constitution. During that period fifteen different and greatly distinguished citizens have in succession administered the executive branch of the Government. They have conducted it through many perils, and generally with great success. Yet, with all this scope of precedent, I now enter upon the same task for the brief constitutional term of four years under great and peculiar difficulty. A disruption of the Federal Union, heretofore only menaced, is now formidably attempted.

I hold that in contemplation of universal law and of the Constitution the Union of these States is perpetual. Perpetuity is implied, if not expressed, in the fundamental law of all national governments. It is safe to assert that no government proper ever had a provision in its organic law for its own termination. Continue to execute all the express provisions of our National Constitution, and the Union will endure forever, it being impossible to destroy it except by some action not provided for in the instrument itself.

Again: If the United States be not a government proper, but an association of States in the nature of contract merely, can it, as a contract, be peaceably unmade by less than all the parties who made it? One party to a contract may violate it—break it, so to speak—but does it not require all to lawfully rescind it?

Descending from these general principles, we find the proposition that in legal contemplation the Union is perpetual confirmed by the history of the Union itself. The Union is much older than the Constitution. It was formed, in fact, by the Articles of Association in 1774. It was matured and continued by the Declaration of Independence in 1776. It was further matured, and the faith of all the then thirteen States expressly plighted and engaged that it should be perpetual, by the Articles of Confederation in 1778. And finally, in 1787, one of the declared objects for ordaining and establishing the Constitution was "*to form a more perfect Union.*" But if destruction of the Union by one or by a part only of the States be lawfully possible, the Union is less perfect than before the Constitution, having lost the vital element of perpetuity.

It follows from these views that no State upon its own mere motion can lawfully get out of the Union; that *resolves* and *ordinances* to that effect are legally void, and that acts of violence within any State or States against the authority of the United States are insurrectionary or revolutionary, according to circumstances.

I therefore consider that in view of the Constitution and the laws the Union is unbroken, and to the extent of my ability, I shall take care, as the Constitution itself expressly enjoins upon me, that the laws of the Union be faithfully executed in all the States. Doing this I deem to be only a simple duty on my part, and I shall perform it so far as practicable unless my rightful masters, the American people, shall withhold the requisite means or in some authoritative manner direct the contrary. I trust this will not be regarded as a menace, but only as the declared purpose of the Union that it *will* constitutionally defend and maintain itself.

In doing this there needs to be no bloodshed or violence, and there shall be none unless it be forced upon the national authority. The power confided to me will be used to hold, occupy, and possess the property and places belonging to the Government and to collect the duties and imposts; but beyond what may be necessary for these objects, there will be no invasion, no using of force against or among the people anywhere. Where hostility to the United States in any interior locality shall be so great and universal as to prevent competent resident citizens from holding the Federal offices, there will be no attempt to force obnoxious strangers among the people for that object. While the strict legal right may exist in the Government to enforce the exercise of these offices, the attempt to do so would be so irritating and so nearly impracticable withal that I deem it better to forego for the time the uses of such offices.

The mails, unless repelled, will continue to be furnished in all parts of the Union. So far as possible the people everywhere shall have that sense of perfect security which is most favorable to calm thought and reflection. The course here indicated will be followed unless current events and experience shall show a modification or change to be proper, and in every case and exigency my best discretion will be exercised, according to circumstances actually existing and with a view and a hope of a peaceful solution of the national troubles and the restoration of fraternal sympathies and affections.

That there are persons in one section or another who seek to destroy the Union at all events and are glad of any pretext to do it I will neither affirm nor deny; but if there be such, I need address no word to them. To those, however, who really love the Union may I not speak?

Before entering upon so grave a matter as the destruction of our national fabric, with all its benefits, its memories, and its hopes, would it not be wise to ascertain precisely why we do it? Will you hazard so desperate a step while there is any possibility that any portion of the ills you fly from have no real existence? Will you, while the certain ills you fly to are greater than all the real ones you fly from, will you risk the commission of so fearful a mistake?

All profess to be content in the Union if all constitutional rights can be maintained. Is it true, then, that any right plainly written in the Constitution has been denied? I think not. Happily, the human mind is so constituted that no party can reach to the audacity of doing this. Think, if you can, of a single instance in which a plainly written provision of the Constitution has ever been denied. If by the mere force of numbers a majority should deprive a minority of any clearly written constitutional right, it might in a moral point of view justify revolution; certainly would if such right were a vital one. But such is not our case. All the vital rights of minorities and of individuals are so plainly assured to them by affirmations and negations, guaranties and prohibitions, in the Constitution that controversies never arise concerning them. But no organic law can ever be framed with a provision specifically applicable to every question which may occur in practical adminis-tration. No foresight can anticipate nor any document of reasonable length contain express provisions for all possible questions. Shall fugitives from labor be surrendered by national or by State authority? The Constitution does not expressly say. *May* Congress prohibit slavery in the Territories? The Constitution does not expressly say. *Must* Congress protect slavery in the Territories? The Constitution does not expressly say.

From questions of this class spring all our constitutional controversies, and we divide upon them into majorities and minorities. If the minority will not acquiesce, the majority must, or the Government must cease. There is no other alternative, for continuing the Government is acquiescence on one side or the other. If a minority in such case will secede rather than acquiesce, they make a precedent which in turn will divide and ruin them, for a minority of their own will secede from them whenever a majority refuses to be controlled by such minority. For instance, why may not any portion of a new confederacy a year or two hence arbitrarily secede again, precisely as portions of the present Union now claim to secede from it? All who cherish disunion sentiments are now being educated to the exact temper of doing this.

Is there such perfect identity of interests among the States to compose a new union as to produce harmony only and prevent renewed secession?

Plainly the central idea of secession is the essence of anarchy. A majority held in restraint by constitutional checks and limitations, and always changing easily with deliberate changes of popular opinions and sentiments, is the only true sovereign of a free people. Whoever rejects it does of necessity fly to anarchy or to despotism. Unanimity is impossible. The rule of a minority, as a permanent arrangement, is wholly inadmissible; so that, rejecting the majority principle, anarchy or despotism in some form is all that is left.

I do not forget the position assumed by some that constitutional questions are to be decided by the Supreme Court, nor do I deny that such decisions must be binding in any case upon the parties to a suit as to the object of that suit, while they are also entitled to very high respect and consideration in all parallel cases by all other departments of the Government. And while it is obviously possible that such decision may be erroneous in any given case, still the evil effect following it, being limited to that particular case, with the chance that it may be overruled and never become a precedent for other cases, can better be borne than could the evils of a different practice. At the same time, the candid citizen must confess that if the policy of the Government upon vital questions affecting the whole people is to be irrevocably fixed by decisions of the Supreme Court, the instant they are made in ordinary litigation between parties in personal actions the people will have ceased to be their own rulers, having to that extent practically resigned their Government into the hands of that eminent tribunal. Nor is there in this view any assault upon the court or the judges. It is a duty from which they may not shrink to decide cases properly brought before them, and it is no fault of theirs if others seek to turn their decisions to political purposes.

One section of our country believes slavery is *right* and ought to be extended, while the other believes it is *wrong* and ought not to be extended. This is the only substantial dispute. The fugitive-slave clause of the Constitution and the law for the suppression of the foreign slave trade are each as well enforced, perhaps, as any law can ever be in a community where the moral sense of the people imperfectly supports the law itself. The great body of the people abide by the dry legal obligation in both cases, and a few break over in each. This, I think, can not be perfectly cured, and it would be worse in both cases *after* the separation of the sections than before. The foreign slave trade, now imperfectly suppressed, would be ultimately revived without restriction in one section, while fugitive slaves, now only partially surrendered, would not be surrendered at all by the other.

Physically speaking, we can not separate. We can not remove our respective sections from each other nor build an impassable wall between them. A husband and wife may be divorced and go out of the presence and beyond the reach of each other, but the different parts of our country can not do this. They can not but remain face to face, and intercourse, either amicable or hostile, must continue between them. Is it possible, then, to make that intercourse more advantageous or more satisfactory after separation than before? Can aliens make treaties easier than friends can make laws? Can treaties be more faithfully enforced between aliens than laws can among friends? Suppose you go to war, you can not fight always; and when, after much loss on both sides and no gain on either, you cease fighting, the identical old questions, as to terms of intercourse, are again upon you.

This country, with its institutions, belongs to the people who inhabit it. Whenever they shall grow weary of the existing Government, they can exercise their *constitutional* right of amending it or their *revolutionary* right to dismember or overthrow it. I can not be ignorant of the fact that many worthy and patriotic citizens are desirous of having the National Constitution amended. While I make no recommendation of amendments, I fully recognize the rightful authority of the people over the whole subject, to be exercised in either of the modes prescribed in the instrument itself; and I should, under existing circumstances, favor rather than oppose a fair opportunity being afforded the people to act upon it. I will venture to add that to me the convention mode seems preferable, in that it allows amendments to originate with the people themselves, instead of only permitting them to take or reject propositions originated by others, not especially chosen for the purpose, and which might not be precisely such as they would wish to either accept or refuse. I understand a proposed amendment to the Constitution—which amendment, however, I have not seen—has passed Congress, to the effect that the Federal Government shall never interfere with the domestic institutions of the States, including that of persons held to service. To avoid misconstruction of what I have said, I depart from my purpose not to speak of particular amendments so far as to say that, holding such a provision to now be implied constitutional law, I have no objection to its being made express and irrevocable.

The Chief Magistrate derives all his authority from the people, and they have referred none upon him to fix terms for the separation of the States. The people themselves can do this if also they choose, but the Executive as such has nothing to do with it. His duty is to administer the present Government as it came to his hands and to transmit it unimpaired by him to his successor.

Why should there not be a patient confidence in the ultimate justice of the people? Is there any better or equal hope in the world? In our present differences, is either party without faith of being in the right? If the Almighty Ruler of Nations, with His eternal truth and justice, be on your side of the North, or on yours of the South, that truth and that justice will surely prevail by the judgment of this great tribunal of the American people.

By the frame of the Government under which we live this same people have wisely given their public servants but little power for mischief, and have with equal wisdom provided for the return of that little to their own hands at very short intervals. While the people retain their virtue and vigilance no Administration by any extreme of wickedness or folly can very seriously injure the Government in the short space of four years.

My countrymen, one and all, think calmly and *well* upon this whole subject. Nothing valuable can be lost by taking time. If there be an object to *hurry* any of you in hot haste to a step which you would never take *deliberately*, that object will be frustrated by taking time; but no good object can be frustrated by it. Such of you as are now dissatisfied still have the old Constitution unimpaired, and, on the sensitive point, the laws of your own framing under it; while the new Administration will have no immediate power, if it would, to change either. If it were admitted that you who are dissatisfied hold the right side in the dispute, there still is no single good reason for precipitate action. Intelligence, patriotism, Christianity, and a firm reliance on Him who has never yet forsaken this favored land are still competent to adjust in the best way all our present difficulty.

In *your* hands, my dissatisfied fellow-countrymen, and not in *mine*, is the momentous issue of civil war. The Government will not assail *you*. You can have no conflict without being yourselves the aggressors. *You* have no oath registered in heaven to destroy the Government, while *I* shall have the most solemn one to "preserve, protect, and defend it."

I am loath to close. We are not enemies, but friends. We must not be enemies. Though passion may have strained it must not break our bonds of affection. The mystic chords of memory, stretching from every battlefield and patriot grave to every living heart and hearthstone all over this broad land, will yet swell the chorus of the Union, when again touched, as surely they will be, by the better angels of our nature.

❦49❧

The Constitution of the Confederate States of America

A provisional constitution for the Confederacy was unanimously adopted on the night of 8th February, 1861, at a Congress held in Montgomery, Alabama. A little over a month later on 11th March, this formal version was presented for formal ratification. The Constitution of the Confederate States was not radically different from that of the United States that it replaced. It did, however, provide for an executive elected for a six year single term of office, and, while prohibiting the African slave trade, it did insist upon the status of slaves as property.

The Constitution of the Confederate States of America
March 11, 1861

We, the people of the Confederate States, each State acting in its sovereign and independent character, in order to form a permanent federal government, establish justice, insure domestic tranquillity, and secure the blessings of liberty to ourselves and our posterity—invoking the favor and guidance of Almighty God—do ordain and establish this Constitution for the Confederate States of America.

ART. I.

SEC. 1.—All legislative powers herein delegated shall be vested in a Congress of the Confederate States, which shall consist of a Senate and House of Representatives.

SEC. 2. (1) The House of Representatives shall be chosen every second year by the people of the several States; and the electors in each State shall be citizens of the Confederate States, and have the qualifications requisite for electors of the most numerous branch of the State Legislature; but no person of foreign birth, not a citizen of the Confederate States, shall be allowed to vote for any officer, civil or

Source: Henry Steele Commager, ed., *Documents of American History*, New York: Meredith Corporation, 1968 edition.

political, State or Federal.

(2) No person shall be a Representative who shall not have attained the age of twenty-five years, and be a citizen of the Confederate States, and who shall not, when elected, be an inhabitant of that State in which he shall be chosen.

(3) Representatives and direct taxes shall be apportioned among the several States, which may be included within this Confederacy, according to their respective numbers, which shall be determined by adding to the whole number of free persons, including those bound to service for a term of years, and excluding Indians not taxed, three-fifths of all slaves. The actual enumeration shall be made within three years after the first meeting of the Congress of the Confederate States, and within every subsequent term of ten years, in such manner as they shall by law direct. The number of Representatives shall not exceed one for every fifty thousand, but each State shall have at least one Representative; and until such enumeration shall be made, the State of South Carolina shall be entitled to choose six; the State of Georgia ten; the State of Alabama nine; the State of Florida two; the State of Mississippi seven; the State of Louisiana six; and the State of Texas six.

(4) When vacancies happen in the representation from any State, the Executive authority thereof shall issue writs of election to fill such vacancies.

(5) The House of Representatives shall choose their Speaker and other officers; and shall have the sole power of impeachment; except that any judicial or other federal officer, resident and acting solely within the limits of any State, may be impeached by a vote of two-thirds of both branches of the Legislature thereof.

SEC. 3. (1) The Senate of the Confederate States shall be composed of two Senators from each State, chosen for six years by the Legislature thereof, at the regular session next immediately preceding the commencement of the term of service; and each Senator shall have one vote.

(2) Immediately after they shall be assembled, in consequence of the first election, they shall be divided as equally as may be into three classes. The seats of the Senators of the first class shall be vacated at the expiration of the second year; of the second class at the expiration of the fourth year; and of the third class at the expiration of the sixth year; so that one-third may be chosen every second year; and if vacancies happen by resignation, or otherwise, during the recess of the Legislature of any State, the Executive thereof may make temporary appointments until the next meeting of the Legislature, which shall then fill such vacancies.

(3) No person shall be a Senator who shall not have attained the age of thirty years, and be a citizen of the Confederate States; and who shall not, when elected, be an inhabitant of the State for which he shall be chosen.

(4) The Vice-President of the Confederate States shall be President of the Senate, but shall have no vote unless they be equally divided.

(5) The Senate shall choose their other officers; and also a president *pro tempore* in the absence of the Vice-President, or when he shall exercise the office of President of the Confederate States.

(6) The Senate shall have sole power to try all impeachments. When sitting for

that purpose, they shall be on oath or affirmation. When the President of the Confederate States is tried, the Chief Justice shall preside; and no person shall be convicted without the concurrence of two-thirds of the members present.

(7) Judgment in cases of impeachment shall not extend further than to removal from office, and disqualification to hold and enjoy any office of honor, trust, or profit under the Confederate States; but the party convicted shall, nevertheless, be liable and subject to indictment, trial, judgment and punishment according to law.

SEC. 4. (1) The times, places, and manner of holding elections for Senators and Representatives shall be prescribed in each State by the Legislature thereof, subject to the provisions of this Constitution; but the Congress may, at any time, by law, make or alter such regulations, except as to the times and places of choosing Senators.

(2) The Congress shall assemble at least once in every year; and such meeting shall be on the first Monday in December, unless they shall, by law, appoint a different day.

SEC. 5. (1) Each House shall be the judge of the elections, returns, and qualifications of its own members, and a majority of each shall constitute a quorum to do business; but a smaller number may adjourn from day to day, and may be authorized to compel the attendance of absent members, in such manner and under such penalties as each House may provide.

(2) Each House may determine the rules of its proceedings, punish its members for disorderly behavior, and with the concurrence of two-thirds of the whole number expel a member.

(3) Each House shall keep a journal of its proceedings, and from time to time publish the same, excepting such parts as may in their judgment require secrecy; and the ayes and nays of the members of either House, on any question, shall, at the desire of one-fifth of those present, be entered on the journal.

(4) Neither House, during the session of Congress, shall, without the consent of the other, adjourn for more than three days, nor to any other place than that in which the two Houses shall be sitting.

SEC. 6. (1) The Senators and Representatives shall receive a compensation for their services, to be ascertained by law, and paid out of the Treasury of the Confederate States. They shall, in all cases, except treason, felony, and breach of the peace, be privileged from arrest during their attendance at the session of their respective Houses, and in going to and returning from the same; and for any speech or debate in either House, they shall not be questioned in any other place.

(2) No Senator or Representative shall, during the time for which he was elected, be appointed to any civil office under the authority of the Confederate States, which shall have been created, or the emoluments whereof shall have been increased during such time; and no person holding any office under the Confederate States shall be a member of either House during his continuance in office. But Congress

may, by law, grant to the principal officer in each of the Executive Departments a seat upon the floor of either House, with the privilege of discussing any measures appertaining to his department.

SEC. 7. (1) All bills for raising revenue shall originate in the House of Representatives; but the Senate may propose or concur with amendments, as on other bills.

(2) Every bill which shall have passed both Houses shall, before it becomes a law, be presented to the President of the Confederate States; if he approve, he shall sign it; but if not, he shall return it, with his objections, to that House in which it shall have originated, who shall enter the objections at large on their journal, and proceed to reconsider it. If, after such reconsideration, two-thirds of that House shall agree to pass the bill, it shall be sent, together with the objections, to the other House, by which it shall likewise be reconsidered, and if approved by two-thirds of that House, it shall become a law. But in all such cases, the votes of both Houses shall be determined by yeas and nays, and the names of the persons voting for and against the bill shall be entered on the journal of each House respectively. If any bill shall not be returned by the President within ten days (Sundays excepted) after it shall have been presented to him, the same shall be a law, in like manner as if he had signed it, unless the Congress, by their adjournment, prevent its return; in which case it shall not be a law. The President may approve any appropriation and disapprove any other appropriation in the same bill. In such case he shall, in signing the bill, designate the appropriations disapproved; and shall return a copy of such appropriations, with his objections, to the House in which the bill shall have originated; and the same proceedings shall then be had as in case of other bills disapproved by the President.

(3) Every order, resolution or vote, to which the concurrence of both Houses may be necessary (except on a question of adjournment) shall be presented to the President of the Confederate States; and before the same shall take effect, shall be approved by him; or being disapproved by him, shall be repassed by two-thirds of both Houses, according to the rules and limitations prescribed in case of a bill.

SEC. 8.—The Congress shall have power—

(1) To lay and collect taxes, duties, imposts, and excises, for revenue, necessary to pay the debts, provide for the common defense, and carry on the Government of the Confederate States; but no bounties shall be granted from the treasury; nor shall any duties or taxes on importations from foreign nations be laid to promote or foster any branch of industry; and all duties, imposts, and excises shall be uniform throughout the Confederate States.

(2) To borrow money on the credit of the Confederate States.

(3) To regulate commerce with foreign nations, and among the several States, and with the Indian tribes; but neither this, nor any other clause contained in the Constitution, shall ever be construed to delegate the power to Congress to appropriate money for any internal improvement intended to facilitate commerce;

except for the purpose of furnishing lights, beacons, and buoys, and other aids to navigation upon the coasts, and the improvement of harbors and the removing of obstructions in river navigation; in all which cases such duties shall be laid on the navigation facilitated thereby as may be necessary to pay the costs and expenses thereof.

(4) To establish uniform laws of naturalization, and uniform laws on the subject of bankruptcies, throughout the Confederate States; but no law of Congress shall discharge any debt contracted before the passage of the same.

(5) To coin money, regulate the value thereof, and of foreign coin, and fix the standard of weights and measures.

(6) To provide for the punishment of counterfeiting the securities and current coin of the Confederate States.

(7) To establish post-offices and post-routes; but the expenses of the Post-office Department, after the first day of March in the year of our Lord eighteen hundred and sixty-three, shall be paid out of its own revenues.

(8) To promote the progress of science and useful arts, by securing for limited times to authors and inventors the exclusive right to their respective writings and discoveries.

(9) To constitute tribunals inferior to the Supreme Court.

(10) To define and punish piracies and felonies committed on the high seas, and offenses against the law of nations.

(11) To declare war, grant letters of marque and reprisal, and make rules concerning captures on land and water.

(12) To raise and support armies; but no appropriation of money to that use shall be for a longer term than two years.

(13) To provide and maintain a navy.

(14) To make rules for the government and regulation of the land and naval forces.

(15) To provide for calling forth the militia to execute the laws of the Confederate States; suppress insurrections, and repel invasions:

(16) To provide for organizing, arming, and disciplining the militia, and for governing such part of them as may be employed in the service of the Confederate States; reserving to the States, respectively, the appointment of the officers, and the authority of training the militia according to the discipline prescribed by Congress.

(17) To exercise exclusive legislation, in all cases whatsoever, over such district (not exceeding ten miles square) as may, by cession of one or more States and the acceptance of Congress, become the seat of the Government of the Confederate States; and to exercise like authority over all places purchased by the consent of the Legislature of the State in which the same shall be, for the erection of forts, magazines, arsenals, dockyards, and other needful buildings, and

(18) To make all laws which shall be necessary and proper for carrying into execution the foregoing powers, and all other powers vested by this Constitution in the Government of the Confederate States, or in any department or officer thereof.

Sec. 9. (1) The importation of negroes of the African race, from any foreign country other than the slave-holding States or Territories of the United States of America, is hereby forbidden; and Congress is required to pass such laws as shall effectually prevent the same.

(2) Congress shall also have power to prohibit the introduction of slaves from any State not a member of, or Territory not belonging to, this Confederacy.

(3) The privilege of the writ of *habeas corpus* shall not be suspended, unless when in cases of rebellion or invasion the public safety may require it.

(4) No bill of attainder, or *ex post facto* law, or law denying or impairing the right of property in negro slaves shall be passed.

(5) No capitation or other direct tax shall be laid, unless in proportion to the census or enumeration hereinbefore directed to be taken.

(6) No tax or duty shall be laid on articles exported from any State, except by a vote of two-thirds of both Houses.

(7) No preference shall be given by any regulation of commerce or revenue to the ports of one State over those of another.

(8) No money shall be drawn from the treasury, but in consequence of appropriations made by law; and a regular statement and account of the receipts and expenditures of all public money shall be published from time to time.

(9) Congress shall appropriate no money from the treasury except by a vote of two-thirds of both Houses, taken by yeas and nays, unless it be asked and estimated for by some one of the heads of departments and submitted to Congress by the President; or for the purpose of paying its own expenses and contingencies; or for the payment of claims against the Confederate States, the justice of which shall have been judicially declared by a tribunal for the investigation of claims against the Government, which it is hereby made the duty of Congress to establish.

(10) All bills appropriating money shall specify in Federal currency the exact amount of each appropriation and the purposes for which it is made; and Congress shall grant no extra compensation to any public contractor, officer, agent or servant, after such contract shall have been made or such service rendered.

(11) No title of nobility shall be granted by the Confederate States; and no person holding any office of profit or trust under them shall, without the consent of the Congress, accept of any present, emoluments, office, or title of any kind whatever, from any king, prince, or foreign state.

(12) Congress shall make no law respecting an establishment of religion, or prohibiting the free exercise thereof; or abridging the freedom of speech, or of the press; or the right of the people peaceably to assemble and petition the Government for a redress of grievances.

(13) A well-regulated militia being necessary to the security of a free State, the right of the people to keep and bear arms shall not be infringed.

(14) No soldier shall, in time of peace, be quartered in any house without the consent of the owner; nor in time of war, but in a manner prescribed by law.

(15) The right of the people to be secure in their persons, houses, papers, and against unreasonable searches and seizures, shall not be violated; and no warrant

shall issue but upon probable cause, supported by oath or affirmation, and particularly describing the place to be searched and the persons or things to be seized.

(16) No person shall be held to answer for a capital or otherwise infamous crime, unless on a presentment or indictment of a grand jury, except in cases arising in the land or naval forces, or in the militia, when in actual service in time of war or public danger; nor shall any person be subject for the same offense to be twice put in jeopardy of life or limb; nor be compelled, in any criminal case, to be a witness against himself; nor be deprived of life, liberty, or property without due process of law; nor shall private property be taken for public use, without just compensation.

(17) In all criminal prosecutions the accused shall enjoy the right to a speedy and public trial, by an impartial jury of the State and district wherein the crime shall have been committed, which district shall have been previously ascertained by law, and to be informed of the nature and cause of the accusation; to be confronted with the witnesses against him; to have compulsory process for obtaining witnesses in his favor; and to have the assistance of counsel for his defense.

(18) In suits at common law, where the value in controversy shall exceed twenty dollars, the right of trial by jury shall be preserved; and no fact so tried by a jury shall be otherwise reexamined in any court of the Confederacy, than according to the rules of common law.

(19) Excessive bail shall not be required, nor excessive fines imposed, nor cruel and unusual punishments inflicted.

(20) Every law, or resolution having the force of law, shall relate to but one subject, and that shall be expressed in the title.

SEC. 10. (1) No State shall enter into any treaty, alliance, or confederation; grant letters of marque and reprisals; coin money; make anything but gold and silver coin a tender in payment of debts; pass any bill of attainder, or *ex post facto* law, or law impairing the obligation of contracts; or grant any title of nobility.

(2) No State shall, without the consent of the Congress, lay any imposts or duties on imports or exports, except what may be absolutely necessary for executing its inspection laws; and the net produce of all duties and imposts, laid by any State on imports or exports, shall be for the use of the Treasury of the Confederate States; and all such laws shall be subject to the revision and control of Congress.

(3) No State shall, without the consent of Congress, lay any duty of tonnage, except on seagoing vessels, for the improvement of its rivers and harbors navigated by the said vessels; but such duties shall not conflict with any treaties of the Confederate States with foreign nations; and any surplus revenue, thus derived, shall, after making such improvement, be paid into the common treasury; nor shall any State keep troops or ships of war in time of peace, enter into any agreement or compact with another State, or with a foreign power, or engage in war, unless actually invaded, or in such imminent danger as will not admit of delay. But when any river divides or flows through two or more States they may enter into compacts with each other to improve the navigation thereof.

ART II.

Sec. 1. (1) The executive power shall be vested in a President of the Confederate States of America. He and the Vice-President shall hold their offices for the term of six years; but the President shall not be reeligible. The President and Vice-President shall be elected as follows:

(2) Each State shall appoint, in such manner as the Legislature thereof may direct, a number of electors equal to the whole number of Senators and Representatives to which the State may be entitled in Congress; but no Senator or Representative or person holding an office of trust or profit under the Confederate States, shall be appointed an elector.

(3) The electors shall meet in their respective States and vote by ballot for President and Vice-President, one of whom, at least, shall not be an inhabitant of the same State with themselves; they shall name in their ballots the person voted for as President, and in distinct ballots the person voted for as Vice-President, and they shall make distinct lists of all persons voted for as President, and of all persons voted for as Vice-President, and of the number of votes for each, which list they shall sign and certify, and transmit, sealed, to the seat of the Government of the Confederate States, directed to the President of the Senate; the President of the Senate shall, in the presence of the Senate and House of Representatives, open all the certificates, and the votes shall then be counted; the person having the greatest number of votes for President shall be the President, if such number be a majority of the whole number of electors appointed; and if no person have such majority, then from the persons having the highest numbers, not exceeding three, on the list of those voted for as President, the House of Representatives shall choose immediately, by ballot, the President. But in choosing the President the votes shall be taken by States, the representation from each State having one vote; a quorum for this purpose shall consist of a member or members from two-thirds of the States, and a majority of all the States shall be necessary to a choice. And if the House of Representatives shall not choose a President, whenever the right of choice shall devolve upon them, before the fourth day of March next following, then the Vice-President shall act as President, as in case of the death, or other constitutional disability of the President.

(4) The person having the greatest number of votes as Vice-President shall be the Vice-President, if such number be a majority of the whole number of electors appointed; and if no person have a majority, then from the two highest numbers on the list, the Senate shall choose the Vice-President; a quorum for the purpose shall consist of two-thirds of the whole number of Senators, and a majority of the whole number shall be necessary for a choice.

(5) But no person constitutionally ineligible to the office of President shall be eligible to that of Vice-President of the Confederate States.

(6) The Congress may determine the time of choosing the electors, and the day on which they shall give their votes; which day shall be the same throughout the Confederate States.

(7) No person except a natural born citizen of the Confederate States, or a citizen thereof at the time of the adoption of this Constitution, or a citizen thereof born in the United States prior to the 20th December, 1860, shall be eligible to the office of President; neither shall any person be eligible to that office who shall not have attained the age of thirty-five years, and been fourteen years a resident within the limits of the Confederate States, as they may exist at the time of his election.

(8) In case of the removal of the President from office, or of his death, resignation, or inability to discharge the powers and duties of the said office, the same shall devolve on the Vice-President; and the Congress may, by law, provide for the case of removal, death, resignation, or inability, both of the President and Vice-President, declaring what officer shall then act as President; and such officer shall act accordingly until the disability be removed or a President shall be elected.

(9) The President shall, at stated times, receive for his services a compensation, which shall neither be increased nor diminished during the period for which he shall have been elected; and he shall not receive within that period any other emolument from the Confederate States, or any of them.

(10) Before he enters on the execution of his office he shall take the following oath or affirmation:

> "I do solemnly swear (or affirm) that I will faithfully execute the office of President of the Confederate States, and will, to the best of my ability, preserve, protect, and defend the Constitution thereof."

SEC. 2. (1) The President shall be Commander-in-Chief of the army and navy of the Confederate States, and of the militia of the several States, when called into the actual service of the Confederate States; he may require the opinion, in writing, of the principal officer in each of the Executive Departments, upon any subject relating to the duties of their respective offices; and he shall have power to grant reprieves and pardons for offenses against the Confederate States, except in cases of impeachment.

(2) He shall have power, by and with the advice and consent of the Senate, to make treaties; provided two-thirds of the Senators present concur; and he shall nominate, and, by and with the advice and consent of the Senate, shall appoint ambassadors, other public ministers and consuls, Judges of the Supreme Court, and all other officers of the Confederate States whose appointments are not herein otherwise provided for, and which shall be established by law; but the Congress may, by law, vest the appointment of such inferior officers, as they think proper, in the President alone, in the courts of law, or in the heads of departments.

(3) The principal officer in each of the Executive Departments, and all persons connected with the diplomatic service, may be removed from office at the pleasure of the President. All other civil officers of the Executive Department may be removed at any time by the President, or other appointing power, when their services are unnecessary, or for dishonesty, incapacity, inefficiency, misconduct, or neglect of duty; and when so removed, the removal shall be reported to the Senate, together with the reasons therefor.

(4) The President shall have power to fill all vacancies that may happen during the recess of the Senate, by granting commissions which shall expire at the end of their next session; but no person rejected by the Senate shall be reappointed to the same office during their ensuing recess.

Sec. 3. (1) The President shall, from time to time, give to the Congress information of the state of the Confederacy, and recommend to their consideration such measures as he shall judge necessary and expedient; he may, on extraordinary occasions, convene both Houses, or either of them; and in case of disagreement between them, with respect to the time of adjournment, he may adjourn them to such time as he shall think proper; he shall receive ambassadors and other public ministers; he shall take care that the laws be faithfully executed, and shall commission all the officers of the Confederate States.

Sec. 4. (1) The President, Vice-President, and all civil officers of the Confederate States, shall be removed from office on impeachment, for and conviction of, treason, bribery, or other high crimes and misdemeanors.

ART. III.

Sec 1. (1) The judicial power of the Confederate States shall be vested in one Supreme Court, and in such inferior courts as the Congress may, from time to time, ordain and establish. The judges, both of the Supreme and inferior courts, shall hold their offices during good behavior, and shall, at stated times, receive for their services a compensation which shall not be diminished during their continuance in office.

Sec. 2. (1) The judicial power shall extend to all cases arising under this Constitution, the laws of the Confederate States, or treaties made or which shall be made under their authority; to all cases affecting ambassadors, other public ministers and consuls; to all cases of admiralty and maritime jurisdiction; to controversies to which the Confederate States shall be a party; to controversies between two or more States; between a State and citizens of another State, where the State is plaintiff; between citizens claiming lands under grants of different States; and between a State or the citizens thereof, and foreign States, citizens, or subjects; but no State shall be sued by a citizen or subject of any foreign state.

(2) In all cases affecting ambassadors, other public ministers, and consuls, and those in which a State shall be a party, the Supreme Court shall have original jurisdiction. In all the other cases before mentioned, the Supreme Court shall have appellate jurisdiction, both as to law and fact, with such exceptions, and under such regulations as the Congress shall make.

(3) The trial of all crimes, except in cases of impeachment, shall be by jury, and such trial shall be held in the State where the said crimes shall have been committed; but when not committed within any State, the trial shall be at such place or places

as the Congress may by law have directed.

SEC. 3. (1) Treason against the Confederate States shall consist only in levying war against them, or in adhering to their enemies, giving them aid and comfort. No person shall be convicted of treason unless on the testimony of two witnesses to the same overt act, or on confession in open court.

(2) The Congress shall have power to declare the punishment of treason; but no attainder of treason shall work corruption of blood, or forfeiture, except during the life of the person attainted.

ART. IV.

SEC. 1. (1) Full faith and credit shall be given in each State to the public acts, records, and judicial proceedings of every other State. And the Congress may, by general laws, prescribe the manner in which such acts, records, and proceedings shall be proved, and the effect thereof.

SEC. 2. (1) The citizens of each State shall be entitled to all the privileges and immunities of citizens of the several States; and shall have the right of transit and sojourn in any State of this Confederacy, with their slaves and other property; and the right of property in said slaves shall not be thereby impaired.

(2) A person charged in any State with treason, felony, or other crime against the laws of such State, who shall flee from justice, and be found in another State, shall, on demand of the executive authority of the State from which he fled, be delivered up, to be removed to the State having jurisdiction of the crime.

(3) No slave or other person held to service or labor in any State or Territory of the Confederate States, under the laws thereof, escaping or lawfully carried into another, shall, in consequence of any law or regulation therein, be discharged from such service or labor; but shall be delivered up on claim of the party to whom such slave belongs, or to whom such service or labor may be due.

SEC. 3. (1) Other States may be admitted into this Confederacy by a vote of two-thirds of the whole House of Representatives and two-thirds of the Senate, the Senate voting by States; but no new State shall be formed or erected within the jurisdiction of any other State, nor any State be formed by the junction of two or more States, or parts of States, without the consent of the Legislatures of the States concerned, as well as of the Congress.

(2) The Congress shall have power to dispose of and make all needful rules and regulations concerning the property of the Confederate States, including the lands thereof.

(3) The Confederate States may acquire new territory; and Congress shall have power to legislate and provide governments for the inhabitants of all territory belonging to the Confederate States, lying without the limits of the several States, and may permit them, at such times, and in such manner as it may by law provide,

to form States to be admitted into the Confederacy. In all such territory, the institution of negro slavery, as it now exists in the Confederate States, shall be recognized and protected by Congress and by the territorial government; and the inhabitants of the several Confederate States and Territories shall have the right to take to such Territory any slaves lawfully held by them in any of the States or Territories of the Confederate States.

(4) The Confederate States shall guarantee to every State that now is, or hereafter may become a member of this Confederacy, a Republican form of government, and shall protect each of them against invasion; and on application of the Legislature, (or of the Executive when the Legislature is not in session,) against domestic violence.

ART. V.

Sec. 1. (1) Upon the demand of any three States, legally assembled in their several Conventions, the Congress shall summon a Convention of all the States, to take into consideration such amendments to the Constitution as the said States shall concur in suggesting at the time when the said demand is made; and should any of the proposed amendments to the Constitution be agreed on by the said Convention—voting by States—and the same be ratified by the Legislatures of two-thirds of the several States, or by conventions in two-thirds thereof—as the one or the other mode of ratification may be proposed by the general convention—they shall thenceforward form a part of this Constitution. But no State shall, without its consent, be deprived of its equal representation in the Senate.

ART. VI.

1.—The Government established by this Constitution is the successor of the Provisional Government of the Confederate States of America, and all the laws passed by the latter shall continue in force until the same shall be repealed or modified; and all the officers appointed by the same shall remain in office until their successors are appointed and qualified, or the offices abolished.

2. All debts contracted and engagements entered into before the adoption of this Constitution shall be as valid against the Confederate States under this Constitution, as under the Provisional Government.

3. This Constitution, and the laws of the Confederate States made in pursuance thereof, and all treaties made, or which shall be made, under the authority of the Confederate States, shall be the supreme law of the land; and the judges in every State shall be bound thereby, any thing in the Constitution or laws of any State to the contrary notwithstanding.

4. The Senators and Representatives before mentioned, and the members of the several State Legislatures, and all executive and judicial offices, both of the Confederate States and of the several States, shall be bound, by oath or affirmation, to support this Constitution; but no religious test shall ever be required as a

qualification to any office or public trust under the Confederate States.

5. The enumeration, in the Constitution, of certain rights, shall not be construed to deny or disparage others retained by the people of the several States.

6. The powers not delegated to the Confederate States by the Constitution, nor prohibited by it to the States, are reserved to the States, respectively, or to the people thereof.

ART. VII.

1. The ratification of the conventions of five States shall be sufficient for the establishment of this Constitution between the States so ratifying the same.

2. When five States shall have ratified this Constitution, in the manner before specified, the Congress under the provisional Constitution shall prescribe the time for holding the election of President and Vice-President; and for the meeting of the electoral college, and for counting the votes, and inaugurating the President. They shall also prescribe the time for holding the first election of members of Congress under this Constitution, and the time for assembling the same. Until the assembling of such Congress, the Congress under the provisional Constitution shall continue to exercise the legislative powers granted them; not extending beyond the time limited by the Constitution of the Provisional Government.

Adopted unanimously by the Congress of the Confederate States of South Carolina, Georgia, Florida, Alabama, Mississippi, Louisiana and Texas, sitting in convention at the capitol, in the city of Montgomery, Ala., on the eleventh day of March, in the year eighteen hundred and sixty-one.

HOWELL COBB,
President of the Congress.

[signatures]

⧈·50·⧈

History of the Southern Confederacy

F. G. DE FONTAINE

This contemporary account of the establishment of the Confederacy appeared first in the *New York Herald*. Part of a longer work which describes the developing conflict between North and South, this portrait of the events surrounding the constitutional convention which formally created the Confederacy offers some insights into the atmosphere in which the break-up of the Union occurred. With his description of the physical environment of the convention, his account of the confederate constitution itself, and his pen-portraits of Jefferson Davis and Alexander Stephens, De Fontaine imparts to his northern readers a sense of the gravity of the occasion, as the seceding states took this historic step.

From *History of the Southern Confederacy*

Chapter IX.
The Six Seceding States and date of their Separation—Organization of the Southern Congress—Names of Members—Election of President and Vice President, and Sketch of their Lives—The New Constitution—The City of Montgomery, c. c.

On Saturday, February 9, 1861, six seceding States of the old Union organized an independent government, adopted a constitution, and elected a President and Vice President. These States passed their respective ordinances of dissolution as follows:—

Source: F. G. De Fontaine, *American Abolitionism, From 1787 to 1861. A Compendium of Historical Fact, Embracing Legislation in Congress and Agitation Without*, New York: D. Appleton Co., 1861. The pamphlet is in the Daniel A. P. Murray Collection in the Library of Congress.

STATE.	DATE.	YEAS.	NAYS.
South Carolina	Dec. 20, 1860	169	0
Mississippi	Jan. 9, 1861	84	15
Alabama	Jan. 11, 1861	61	39
Florida	Jan. 11, 1861	61	0
Georgia	Jan. 19, 1861	208	89
Louisiana	Jan. 25, 1861	113	17

Only two of the seceding States—South Carolina and Georgia—were original members of the confederacy. The others came in in the following order:

Louisiana	April 8, 1812
Mississippi	Dec. 10, 1817
Alabama	Dec. 14, 1819
Florida	Mar. 3, 1845
Texas	Dec. 29, 1845

The Convention which consummated this event assembled on the 4th of February, at Montgomery, Alabama. Hon. R. M. Barnwell, of South Carolina, being appointed temporary chairman, the Divine blessing was invoked by Rev. Dr. Basil Manly.

We give this first impressive prayer in the Congress of the new Confederacy below, and further add, as an illustration of the religious earnestness by which the delegates were one and all animated, that the ministers of Montgomery were invited to open the deliberations each day with invocations to the Throne of Grace:

Oh, Thou God of the Universe, Thou madest all things; Thou madest man upon the earth; Thou hast endowed him with reason and capacity for government. We thank Thee that Thou hast made us at this late period of the world, and in this fair portion of the earth, and hast established a free government and a pure form of religion amongst us. We thank Thee for all the hallowed memories connected with our past history. Thou hast been the God of our fathers; oh, be Thou our God. Let it please Thee to vouchsafe Thy sacred presence to this assembly. Oh, Our Father, we appeal to Thee, the searcher of hearts, for the purity and sincerity of our motives. If we are in violation of any compact still obligatory upon us with those States from which we have separated in order to set up a new government—if we are acting in rebellion to and in contravention of piety towards God and good faith to our fellow man, we cannot hope for Thy presence and blessing. But oh, Thou heart searching God, we trust that Thou seest we are pursuing those rights which were guaranteed to us by the solemn covenants of our fathers and which were cemented by their blood. And now we humbly recognise Thy hand in the Providence which has brought us together. We pray Thee to give the spirit of wisdom to Thy servants, with all necessary grace, that they may act with deliberation and purpose, and that they will wisely adopt such measures in this trying condition of our affairs as shall redound to Thy glory and the good of our country. So direct them that they may merge the lust for spoil and the desire for office into the patriotic desire for the welfare of this great people. Oh God, assist them to preserve our republican form of government and the purity of the forms of religion, without interference with the strongest form of civil government. May God in tender mercy bestow upon the deputies here assembled health and strength of body, together with calmness and soundness of mind; may they aim directly at the glory of God and the welfare of the whole people, and when the hour of trial which may supervene shall come, enable them to stand firm in the exercise of truth, with great prudence and a just regard for the sovereign rights of their constituents. Oh, God grant that the union of these States, and all that may come into this union, may endure as long as the sun and moon shall last, and until the Son of Man shall come a second time to judge the world in righteousness. Preside over this body in its organization and in the distribution of its offices. Let truth and justice, and equal rights be secured to our government. And now, Our Father in Heaven, we acknowledge Thee as Our God—do Thou rule in us, do Thou sway us, do Thou control us, and let the blessings of the Father, Son and Holy Spirit rest upon this assembly now and forever. Amen.

A. R. Lamar, Esq., of Georgia, was then appointed temporary secretary, and the deputies from the several seceding States represented presented their credentials in alphabetical order, and signed their names to the roll of the Convention.
The following is the list:—

ALABAMA
R. W. Walker,
R. H. Smith,
J. L. M. Curry,
W. P. Chiton,
S. F. Hale Colon,
J. McRae,
John Gill Shortor,
David P. Lewis,
Thomas Fearn.

FLORIDA
James B. Owens,
J. Patten Anderson,
Jackson Morton,
(not present)

GEORGIA
Robert Toombs,
Howell Cobb,
F. S. Bartow,
M. J. Crawford,
E. A. Nisbet,
B. H. Hill,
A. R. Wright,
Thomas R. R. Cobb,
A. H. Kenan,
A. H. Stephens

LOUISIANA
John Perkins, Jr.,
A. Declonet,
Charles M. Conrad,
D. F. Kenner,
G. E. Sparrow,
Henry Marshall

MISSISSIPPI
W. P. Harris,
Walter Brooke,
N. S. Wilson,
A. M. Clayton,
W. S. Barry,
J. T. Harrison

SOUTH CAROLINA
R. B. Rhett.
R. W. Barnwell,
L. M. Keitt,
James Chesnut, Jr.
C. G. Memminger,
W. Porcher Miles,
Thomas J. Withers,
W. W. Boyce.

The Hall of the Southern Convention.

The following description is from a Southern paper:—

> On the extreme left, as the visitor enters the Hall, may be seen a list of the names of the gallant corps constituting the Palmetto regiment of South Carolina, so distinguished in the history of the Mexican War; next to that is an impressive representation of Washington delivering his inaugural address; and still farther to the left, a picture of South Carolina's ever memorable statesman, John C. Calhoun; and next to that, an excellent portrait of Albert J. Pickett, "the historian of Alabama." Just to the right of the President's desk is the portrait of Dixon H. Lewis, a representative in Congress from Alabama for a number of years. Immediately over the President's desk is the portrait of the immortal General George Washington, painted by Stuart. There are a few facts connected with the history of this portrait which are, perhaps, deserving of special mention. It was given by Mrs. Curtis to General Benjamin Smith, of North Carolina. At the sale of his estate it was purchased by Mr. Moore, who presented it to Mrs. E. E Clitherall (mother of Judge A. B. Clitherall, of Pickens), in whose possession it has been for forty years. It is one of the three original portraits of General Washington now in existence. A second one, painted by Trumbull, is in the White House at Washington, and is the identical portrait that Mrs. Madison cut out of the frame when the British attacked Washington in 1812. The third is in the possession of a gentleman in Boston, Massachusetts. Next to the portrait of Washington is that of the Old Hero, Andrew Jackson; next in order is an excellent one of Alabama's distinguished son, Honorable W. L. Yancey; and next, a picture of the great orator and statesman, Henry Clay; and next to that, a historical representation of the swamp encampment scene of General Marion, when he invited the British officer to partake of his scanty fare; and on the extreme right of the door, entering into the Hall, is another picture of General Washington, beautifully and artistically wrought upon canvas by some fair hand.

The deputies having handed in their credentials, on motion of Mr. Rhett, of South Carolina, Honorable Howell Cobb, of Georgia, was chosen President of the Convention, and Mr. J. J. Hooper, Secretary. Thus permanently organized, the Convention proceeded with the usual routine of business.

A committee was appointed to report a plan for the Provisional Government upon the basis of the Constitution of the United States, and after remaining in secret session the greater part of the time for five days, the "Congress"—the word "Convention" being entirely ignored on motion of Honorable A. H. Stephens, of Georgia—at half past ten o'clock, on the night of February 8, unanimously adopted a provisional constitution similar in the main to the constitution of the old Union.

The vital points of difference are the following:—

1. The importation of African negroes from any foreign country other than the slaveholding States of the Confederated States is hereby forbidden, and Congress is required to pass such laws as shall effectually prevent the same.

2. Congress shall also have power to prohibit the introduction of slaves from any State not a member of this Confederacy.

The Congress shall have power—

1. To lay and collect taxes, duties, imposts, and excises, for revenue necessary to

pay the debts and carry on the government of the Confederacy, and all duties, imposts, and excises shall be uniform throughout the Confederacy. A slave in one State escaping to another shall be delivered up on the claim of the party to whom said slave may belong by the Executive authority of the State in which such slave may be found; and in any case of any abduction or forcible rescue full compensation, including the value of slave, and all costs and expenses, shall be made to the party by the State in which such abduction or rescue shall take place.

2. The government hereby instituted shall take immediate steps for the settlement of all matters between the States forming it and their late confederates of the United States in relation to the public property and public debt at the time of their withdrawal from them, these States hereby declaring it to be their wish and earnest desire to adjust everything pertaining to the common property, common liabilities, and common obligations of that Union upon principles of right, justice, equity and good faith.

In several other features the new constitution differs from the original. The old one commences with the words—"We the people of the United States," c. The new—"We the deputies of the sovereign and independent States of South Carolina," thus distinctly indicating their sovereign and independent character, and yet their mutual reliance.

Again, the new constitution reverentially invokes "the favor of Almighty God." In the old, the existence of a Supreme Being appears to have been entirely ignored.

In the original, not only was the word "slave" omitted, but even the idea was so studiously avoided as to raise grave questions concerning the intent of the several clauses in which the "institution" is a subject of legislation, while in the new, the word "slaves" is boldly inserted, and the intention of its framers so clearly defined with reference to them that there is hardly a possibility of misapprehension.

Again, contrary to the expectation of the majority of the Northern people, who have persistently urged that the object of the South in establishing a separate government was to re-open the African slave trade, the most stringent measures are to be adopted for its suppression.

All this was done with a unanimity which indicated the harmony of sentiment that prevailed among the people of the seceding States, and among the delegates by whom they were represented in the Southern Congress.

The Election of President and Vice President

The constitution having been adopted, the sixth day's proceedings of the Southern Congress, on Saturday, February 9, were characterized by unusual interest, the galleries being crowded with anxious and enthusiastic spectators.

During the preliminary business several model flags were presented for consideration—one being from the ladies of South Carolina; and a committee was appointed to report on a flag, a seal, a coat of arms and a motto for the Southern confederacy. There were likewise appointed committees on foreign affairs, on finance, on military and naval affairs, on postal affairs, on commerce and on patents.

The Congress then proceeded to the election of a President and Vice President of the Southern confederacy, which resulted, by a unanimous vote, as follows:—

> President—Honorable Jefferson Davis, of Mississippi.
> Vice President—Honorable Alexander H. Stephens, of Georgia.

This announcement was received with the grandest demonstrations of enthusiasm. One hundred guns were fired in the city of Montgomery in honor of the event, and in the evening a serenade was given to the Vice President elect, to which he eloquently responded. Messrs. Chesnut and Keitt, of South Carolina, and Conrad, of Louisiana, likewise made appropriate speeches.

A resolution was adopted in Congress appointing a committee of three Alabama deputies to make arrangements to secure the use of suitable buildings for the use of the several executive departments of the Confederacy.

An ordinance was also passed, continuing in force, until repealed or altered by the Southern Confederacy, all laws of the United States in force or use on the first of November last.

The Committee on Finance were likewise instructed to report promptly a tariff for raising revenue for the support of the government. Under this law a tariff has been laid on all goods brought from the United States. The appointment of a committee was also authorized for the purpose of reporting a constitution for the permanent government of the Confederacy.

These are some of the measures thus far adopted by the new government. The legislation has been prompt, unanimous, and adapted to the exigency of the moment, and there is little doubt that when all the necessary laws have been passed, a strong, healthy, and wealthy confederation will be in the full tide of successful experiment.

The Southern Cabinet is composed of the following gentlemen: —

Secretary of State	Robert Toombs
Secretary of Treasury	C. S. Memminger
Secretary of Interior	Vacancy
Secretary of War	I. P. Walker
Secretary of Navy	John Perkins, Jr.
Postmaster General	H. T. Ebett Attorney
General	J. P. Benjamin

Hon. Jefferson Davis, of Mississippi, President.

Few men have led a life more filled with stirring or eventful incidents than Jefferson Davis. A native of Kentucky, born about 1806, he went in early youth with his father to Mississippi, then a Territory, and was appointed by President Monroe in 1822 to be a cadet at West Point. He graduated with the first honors in 1828 as Brevet Second Lieutenant, and at his own request was placed in active service, being assigned to the command of General (then Colonel) Zachary Taylor, who was stationed in the West. In the frontier wars of the time young Davis distinguished himself in so marked a manner that when a new regiment of dragoons was formed he at once obtained a commission as first lieutenant. During this time a romantic attachment sprang up between him and his prisoner, the famous chief Black Hawk, in which the latter forgot his animosity to the people of the United States in his admiration for Lieutenant Davis, and not until his death was the bond of amity severed between the two brave men.

In 1835 he settled quietly down upon a cotton plantation, devoting himself to a thorough and systematic course of political and scientific education. He was married to a daughter of Gen. Taylor.

In 1843 he took the stump for Polk, and in 1845, having attracted no little attention in his State by his vigor and ability, he was elected to Congress. Ten days after he made his maiden speech. Soon the Mexican war broke out, and a regiment of volunteers having been formed in Mississippi, and himself chosen Colonel, he resigned his post in Congress, and instantly repaired with his command to join the *corps d'armée* under General Taylor. At Monterey and Buena Vista he and his noble regiment achieved the soldiers' highest fame. Twice by his coolness he saved the day at Buena Vista. Wherever fire was hottest or danger to be encountered, there Colonel Davis and the Mississippi Rifles were to be found. He was badly wounded in the early part of the action, but sat his horse steadily till the day was won, and refused to delegate even a portion of his duties to his subordinate officers.

In 1848 he was appointed to fill the vacancy in the Senate of the United States occasioned by the death of General Speight, and in 1850 was elected to that body almost unanimously for the term of six years.

In 1851 he resigned his seat in the Senate to become the State Rights candidate for Governor, but was defeated by Governor Foote.

In 1853 he was called to a seat in the Cabinet of President Pierce, and was Secretary of War during his administration. In 1857 he was elected United States Senator from Mississippi for the term of six years, which office he held until his resignation on the secession of Mississippi from the Union.

Personally, he is the last man who would be selected as a "fire-eater." He is a prim, smooth looking man, with a precise manner, a stiff, soldierly carriage and an austerity that is at first forbidding. He has naturally, however, a genial temper, companionable qualities and a disposition that endears him to all by whom he may be surrounded. As a speaker he is clear, forcible and argumentative; his voice is clear and firm, without tremor, and he is one in every way fitted for the distinguished post to which he has been called.

Hon. Alexander H. Stevens, of Georgia, Vice President.

This gentleman is known throughout the Union as one of the most prominent of Southern politicians and eloquent orators. His father, Andrew B. Stephens, was a planter of moderate means, and his mother (Margaret Grier) was a sister to the famous compiler of Grier's almanacs. She died when he was an infant, leaving him with four brothers and one sister, of whom only one brother survives.

Mr. Stephens was born in Georgia on the 11th of February, 1812. When in his fourteenth year his father died, and the homestead being sold, his share of the entire estate was about five hundred dollars. With a commendable Anglo-Saxon love of his ancestry Mr. Stephens has since repurchased the original estate, which comprised about two hundred and fifty acres, and has added to it about six hundred more. Assisted by friends he entered the University of Georgia in 1828, and in 1832 graduated at the head of his class.

In 1834 he commenced the study of the law, and in less than twelve months was engaged in one of the most important cases in the country. His eloquence has ever had a powerful effect upon juries, enforcing, as it does, arguments of admirable simplicity and legal weight. From 1837 to 1840 he was a member of the Georgia Legislature.

In 1842 he was elected to the State Senate, and in 1843 was elected to Congress. He was a member of the whig party in its palmiest days, but since its dissolution has acted with the men of the South, and such has been the upright, steadfast and patriotic policy he has pursued, that no one in the present era of faction, selfishness or suspicion has whispered an accusation of selfish motives or degrading intrigues against him. In the House he served prominently on the most important committees, and effected the passage of the Kansas–Nebraska bill through the House at a time when its warmest friends despaired of success. He was subsequently appointed chairman of the Committee on Territories, and was also chairman of the special committee to which was referred the Lecompton constitution. By his patriotic course of various measures, he has, from time to time, excited the ire of many of the Southern people, but he has always succeeded in coming out of the contest with flying colors, and his recent elevation is a mark of the profound respect entertained for his qualities as a man and a statesman.

Mr. Stephens is most distinguished as an orator, though he does not look like one who can command the attention of the House at any time or upon any topic. His health from childhood has been very feeble, being afflicted with four abscesses and a continued derangement of the liver, which gives him a consumptive appearance though his lungs are sound. He has never weighed over ninety-six pounds, and to see his attenuated figure bent over his desk, the shoulders contracted and the shape of his slender limbs visible through his garments, a stranger would never select him as the "John Randolph" of our time, more dreaded as an adversary and more prized as an ally in a debate than any other member of the House of Representatives. When speaking he has at first a shrill, sharp voice, but as he warms up with his subject the clear tones and vigorous sentences roll out with a sonorousness that finds its way to every corner of the immense hall. He is witty, rhetorical and solid, and has a dash of keen satire that puts an edge upon every speech. He is a careful student, but so very careful that no trace of study is perceptible as he dashes along in a flow of facts, arguments and language that to common minds is almost bewildering. Possessing hosts of warm friends who are proud of his regard, and enlightened Christian virtue and inflexible integrity, such is Alexander H. Stephens, the Vice President elect of the Southern confederacy.

The New Confederacy.

At this particular juncture it will also be interesting, in view of coming legislation, to note some of the statistics of the several seceding States with reference to their population, State debt, &c. They are as follows:—

	POPULATION IN 1860		STATE DEBT
	FREE	SLAVE	IN 1859
South Carolina	308,186	407,185	$6,192,743
Georgia	615,336	467,400	2,632,722
Alabama	520,444	435,473	5,888,134
Mississippi	407,051	479,607	7,271,707
Louisiana	354,245	312,186	10,703,142
Florida	81,885	63,800	158,000
	2,287,147	2,165,651	

Total 4,452,798

This is a population exceeding by 522,926 that of 1790, at the close of the Revolutionary war of the whole United States.

	1850	1860
Total population of free States	13,454,169	18,950,759
Do. .... Do. ..... Slave States	9,612,969	12,433,409
Do. .... Do. ..... Territories	120,901	262,701
Total population of the United States	23,191,876	31,616,869
Increase in ten years 8,494,993		

The City of Montgomery—The Provisional Capital of the New Confederacy.

The city of Montgomery, the capital of Alabama, has assumed such a sudden importance as the capital of the Southern Confederacy and the seat of the federal operations of the new government, that we give below a brief sketch of its locality and surroundings. It is situated on the left bank of the Alabama River, 331 miles by water from Mobile, and 830 miles from Washington, D.C. It is the second city in the State in respect to trade and population, and is one of the most flourishing inland towns of the Southern States, possessing great facilities for communications with the surrounding country. For steamboat navigation the Alabama River is one of the best in the Union, the largest steamers ascending to this point from Mobile. The city is also the western termination of the Montgomery and West Point Railroad. It contains several extensive iron foundries, mills, factories, large warehouses, numerous elegant stores and private residences. The cotton shipped at this place annually amounts to about one hundred thousand bales. The public records were removed from Tuscaloosa to Montgomery in November, 1847. The State House was destroyed by fire in 1849, and another one was erected on the same site in 1851. The present population of the city is not far from 16,000, and it is probable that, with all its natural advantages, the fact of its present selection as the Southern capital, will soon place it in the first rank of Southern cities.

The Effect of the Southern Congress.

The united front and united action of the six States which have thus formed themselves into the pioneer guard, as it were, of the remaining nine, is an earnest that no one of them, in its sovereign capacity, will undertake a conflict with the old United States without the assent of its brethren. What they have thus far done "in Congress assembled," they have done soberly and after mature consideration; and in their past action we may find assurance that no future movements will be undertaken—especially those of a nature likely to involve them in a civil war — without equal deliberation, calmness, and a just regard for the common welfare. If there should be, it will be the fault of the aggressive policy of some of the Legislatures of the North.

It will be observed that, notwithstanding Texas had already passed the ordinance of secession, as that act had not yet been endorsed by the people, at the time of the sitting of the Convention, she was not regarded as one of the new confederacy, and consequently was unrepresented. North Carolina also sent three Commissioners to deliberate with the delegates of the seceding States—namely, Messrs. D. I. Swain, J. L. Bridgers and M. W. Ransom.

The entire movement bears upon its face all the marks of a well developed, well digested plan of government—a government now as independent as were the old thirteen States after the Fourth of July, 1776, and possessing what our ancestors of that date did not fully have—the wealth, ability and power to meet almost any contingency that may arise. Meanwhile, judging from the disposition of republicans in Congress and throughout the country, the ball thus set in motion will not stop. The States already united will undoubtedly remain so, and form the nucleus around which will gather others. The new Union will grow in strength as it grows in age. According to our recent intelligence from England and France, these two nations will rival each other in endeavoring to first secure the favor of the new Power. With them cotton will be the successful diplomat. Ministers and agents will be appointed, postal facilities will be rearranged, a new navy will spring into existence, prosperity will begin to pour into the newly opened lap, and we shall witness at our very side the success of a people who, by the pertinacity of the selfish political leaders and the political domination of the North, have been driven to measures of defence which are destined to redound to their benefit, but to our cost and national shame. *New York Herald*, Feb. 11, 1861.

⊰·51·⊱

Inaugural Address as Provisional President of the Confederate States

JEFFERSON DAVIS

A bare month after leaving the United States Senate, Jefferson Davis delivered his inaugural message as the provisional president of the Confederacy on 18th February, 1861. Once more, the argument for the constitutional legitimacy of his position was based principally upon an appeal to the political traditions established by the founding fathers of the nation, articulated in the Declaration of Independence and in the federal Constitution itself.

―――――――――――――

Gentlemen of the Congress of the Confederate States of America, Friends and Fellow-Citizens:

Called to the difficult and responsible station of Chief Executive of the Provisional Government which you have instituted, I approach the discharge of the duties assigned to me with an humble distrust of my abilities, but with a sustaining confidence in the wisdom of those who are to guide and to aid me in the administration of public affairs, and an abiding faith in the virtue and patriotism of the people.

Looking forward to the speedy establishment of a permanent government to take the place of this, and which by its greater moral and physical power will be better able to combat with the many difficulties which arise from the conflicting interests of separate nations, I enter upon the duties of the office to which I have been chosen with the hope that the beginning of our career as a Confederacy may not be obstructed by hostile opposition to our enjoyment of the separate existence and independence which we have asserted, and, with the blessing of Providence, intend to maintain. Our present condition, achieved in a manner unprecedented in the history of nations, illustrates the American idea that governments rest upon

Source: Jefferson Davis, Inaugural Address as Provisional President of the Confederate States, 18th February 1861.

the consent of the governed, and that it is the right of the people to alter or abolish governments whenever they become destructive of the ends for which they were established.

The declared purpose of the compact of Union from which we have withdrawn was

> to establish justice, insure domestic tranquillity, provide for the common defense, promote the general welfare, and secure the blessings of liberty to ourselves and our posterity;

and when, in the judgment of the sovereign States now composing this Confederacy, it had been perverted from the purposes for which it was ordained, and had ceased to answer the ends for which it was established, a peaceful appeal to the ballot-box declared that so far as they were concerned, the government created by that compact should cease to exist. In this they merely asserted a right which the Declaration of Independence of 1776 had defined to be inalienable; of the time and occasion for its exercise, they, as sovereigns, were the final judges, each for itself. The impartial and enlightened verdict of mankind will vindicate the rectitude of our conduct, and He who knows the hearts of men will judge of the sincerity with which we labored to preserve the Government of our fathers in its spirit. The right solemnly proclaimed at the birth of the States, and which has been affirmed and reaffirmed in the bills of rights of States subsequently admitted into the Union of 1789, undeniably recognized in the people the power to resume the authority delegated for the purposes of government. Thus the sovereign States here represented proceeded to form this Confederacy, and it is by abuse of language that their act has been denominated a revolution. They formed a new alliance, but within each State its government has remained, the rights of person and property have not been disturbed. The agent through whom they communicated with foreign nations is changed, but this does not necessarily interrupt their international relations.

Sustained by the consciousness that the transition from the former Union to the present Confederacy has not proceeded from a disregard on our part of just obligations, or any failure to perform every constitutional duty, moved by no interest or passion to invade the rights of others, anxious to cultivate peace and commerce with all nations, if we may not hope to avoid war, we may at least expect that posterity will acquit us of having needlessly engaged in it. Doubly justified by the absence of wrong on our part, and by wanton aggression on the part of others, there can be no cause to doubt that the courage and patriotism of the people of the Confederate States will be found equal to any measures of defense which honor and security may require.

An agricultural people, whose chief interest is the export of a commodity required in every manufacturing country, our true policy is peace, and the freest trade which our necessities will permit. It is alike our interest, and that of all those to whom we would sell and from whom we would buy, that there should be the fewest practicable restrictions upon the interchange of commodities. There can be but little rivalry between ours and any manufacturing or navigating community, such as the Northeastern States of the American Union. It must follow, therefore, that a mutual interest would invite good will and kind offices. If, however, passion or the lust of dominion should cloud the judgment or inflame the ambition of those States, we must prepare to meet the emergency and to maintain, by the final arbitrament of the sword, the position which we have assumed among the nations of the earth. We have entered upon the career of independence, and it must be inflexibly pursued. Through many years of controversy with our late associates, the Northern States, we have vainly endeavored to secure tranquillity, and to obtain respect for the rights to which we were entitled. As a necessity, not a choice, we have resorted to the remedy of separation; and henceforth our energies must be directed to the conduct of our own affairs, and the perpetuity of the Confederacy which we have formed. If a just perception of mutual interest shall permit us peaceably to pursue our separate political career, my most earnest desire will have been fulfilled. But, if this be denied to us, and the integrity of our territory and jurisdiction be assailed, it will but remain for us, with firm resolve, to appeal to arms and invoke the blessings of Providence on a just cause.

As a consequence of our new condition and with a view to meet anticipated wants, it will be necessary to provide for the speedy and efficient organization of branches of the executive department, having special charge of foreign intercourse, finance, military affairs, and the postal service.

For purposes of defense, the Confederate States may, under ordinary circumstances, rely mainly upon their militia, but it is deemed advisable, in the present condition of affairs, that there should be a well-instructed and disciplined army, more numerous than would usually be required on a peace establishment. I also suggest that for the protection of our harbors and commerce on the high seas a navy adapted to those objects will be required. These necessities have doubtless engaged the attention of Congress.

With a Constitution differing only from that of our fathers in so far as it is explanatory of their well-known intent, freed from the sectional conflicts which have interfered with the pursuit of the general welfare it is not unreasonable to expect that States from which we have recently parted may seek to unite their fortunes with ours under the government which we have instituted. For this your Constitution makes adequate provision; but beyond this, if I mistake not the judgment and will of the people, a reunion with the States from which we have separated is neither practicable nor desirable. To increase the power, develop the resources, and promote the happiness of a confederacy, it is requisite that there should be so much of homogeneity that the welfare of every portion shall be the aim of the whole. Where this does not exist, antagonisms are engendered which must and should result in separation.

Actuated solely by the desire to preserve our own rights and promote our own welfare, the separation of the Confederate States has been marked by no aggression upon others and followed by no domestic convulsion. Our industrial pursuits have received no check. The cultivation of our fields has progressed as heretofore, and even should we be involved in war there would be no considerable diminution in the production of the staples which have constituted our exports and in which the commercial world has an interest scarcely less than our own. This common interest of the producer and consumer can only be interrupted by an exterior force which should obstruct its transmission to foreign markets—a course of conduct which would be as unjust toward us as it would be detrimental to manufacturing and commercial interests abroad. Should reason guide the action of the Government from which we have separated, a policy so detrimental to the civilized world, the Northern States included, could not be dictated by even the strongest desire to inflict injury upon us; but otherwise a terrible responsibility will rest upon it, and the suffering of millions will bear testimony to the folly and wickedness of our aggressors. In the meantime there will remain to us, besides the ordinary means before suggested, the well-known resources for retaliation upon the commerce of an enemy.

Experience in public stations, of subordinate grade to this which your kindness has conferred, has taught me that care and toil and disappointment are the price of official elevation. You will see many errors to forgive, many deficiencies to tolerate, but you shall not find in me either a want of zeal or fidelity to the cause that is to me highest in hope and of most enduring affection. Your generosity has bestowed upon me an undeserved distinction, one which I neither sought nor desired. Upon the continuance of that sentiment and upon your wisdom and patriotism I rely to direct and support me in the performance of the duty required at my hands.

We have changed the constituent parts, but not the system of our Government. The Constitution formed by our fathers is that of these Confederate States, in their exposition of it, and in the judicial construction it has received, we have a light which reveals its true meaning.

Thus instructed as to the just interpretation of the instrument, and ever remembering that all offices are but trusts held for the people, and that delegated powers are to be strictly construed, I will hope, by due diligence in the performance of my duties, though I may disappoint your expectations, yet to retain, when retiring, something of the good will and confidence which welcome my entrance into office.

It is joyous, in the midst of perilous times, to look around upon a people united in heart, where one purpose of high resolve animates and actuates the whole—where the sacrifices to be made are not weighed in the balance against honor and right and liberty and equality. Obstacles may retard, they cannot long prevent the progress of a movement sanctified by its justice, and sustained by a virtuous people. Reverently let us invoke the God of our fathers to guide and protect us in our efforts to perpetuate the principles which, by his blessing, they were able to vindicate, establish and transmit to their posterity, and with a continuance of His favor, ever gratefully acknowledged, we may hopefully look forward to success, to peace, and to prosperity.

⸭52⸭

Five Proclamations

ABRAHAM LINCOLN

These five proclamations (April–May 1861) by Lincoln as President of the United States effectively set the scene for the onset of Civil War. The first, promulgated on 15th April 1861, begins the military mobilization of North against South by raising a militia. Four days later, Lincoln imposes a blockade against ports in seven Southern states, subsequently extended, in the third proclamation, to include Virginia and North Carolina. On 3rd May, Lincoln calls for a volunteer army of over 40,000 and, in addition, increased the size of the regular army and navy. Finally, on 10th May, the President authorises the suspension of *habeas corpus* in Union fortresses in Florida.

---

1. 15th April 1861

By the President of the United States
A Proclamation

Whereas the laws of the United States have been for some time past and now are opposed and the execution thereof obstructed in the States of South Carolina, Georgia, Alabama, Florida, Mississippi, Louisiana, and Texas by combinations too powerful to be suppressed by the ordinary course of judicial proceedings or by the powers vested in the marshals by law:

Now, therefore, I, Abraham Lincoln, President of the United States, in virtue of the power in me vested by the Constitution and the laws, have thought fit to call forth, and hereby do call forth, the militia of the several States of the Union to the aggregate number of 75,000, in order to suppress said combinations and to cause the laws to be duly executed.

The details for this object will be immediately communicated to the State authorities through the War Department.

I appeal to all loyal citizens to favor, facilitate, and aid this effort to maintain the

Source: James D. Richardson, ed., *A Compilation of the Messages and Papers of the Presidents*, New York: Bureau of National Literature, Inc., 1897, Vol. VII.

honor, the integrity, and the existence of our National Union and the perpetuity of popular government and to redress wrongs already long enough endured.

I deem it proper to say that the first service assigned to the forces hereby called forth will probably be to repossess the forts, places, and property which have been seized from the Union; and in every event the utmost care will be observed, consistently with the objects aforesaid, to avoid any devastation, any destruction of or interference with property, or any disturbance of peaceful citizens in any part of the country.

And I hereby command the persons composing the combinations aforesaid to disperse and retire peaceably to their respective abodes within twenty days from this date.

Deeming that the present condition of public affairs presents an extraordinary occasion, I do hereby, in virtue of the power in me vested by the Constitution, convene both Houses of Congress. Senators and Representatives are therefore summoned to assemble at their respective chambers at 12 o'clock noon on Thursday, the 4th of July next, then and there to consider and determine such measures as, in their wisdom, the public safety and interest may seem to demand.

In witness whereof I have hereunto set my hand and caused the seal of the United States to be affixed.

[SEAL]   Done at the city of Washington, this 15th day of April, A.D. 1861, and of the Independence of the United States the eighty-fifth.

By the President: ABRAHAM LINCOLN.

WILLIAM H. SEWARD, *Secretary of State.*

2. 19th April, 1861

By the President of the United States
A Proclamation

Whereas an insurrection against the Government of the United States has broken out in the States of South Carolina, Georgia, Alabama, Florida, Mississippi, Louisiana, and Texas, and the laws of the United States for the collection of the revenue can not be effectually executed therein conformably to that provision of the Constitution which requires duties to be uniform throughout the United States; and

Whereas a combination of persons engaged in such insurrection have threatened to grant pretended letters of marque to authorize the bearers thereof to commit assaults on the lives, vessels, and property of good citizens of the country lawfully engaged in commerce on the high seas and in waters of the United States; and

Whereas an Executive proclamation has been already issued requiring the persons engaged in these disorderly proceedings to desist therefrom, calling out a militia force for the purpose of repressing the same, and convening Congress in extraordinary session to deliberate and determine thereon:

Now, therefore, I, Abraham Lincoln, President of the United States, with a view to the same purposes before mentioned and to the protection of the public peace and the lives and property of quiet and orderly citizens pursuing their lawful occupations, until Congress shall have assembled and deliberated on the said unlawful proceedings or until the same shall have ceased, have further deemed it advisable to set on foot a blockade of the ports within the States aforesaid, in pursuance of the laws of the United States and of the law of nations in such case provided. For this purpose a competent force will be posted so as to prevent entrance and exit of vessels from the ports aforesaid. If, therefore, with a view to violate such blockade, a vessel shall approach or shall attempt to leave either of the said ports, she will be duly warned by the commander of one of the blockading vessels, who will indorse on her register the fact and date of such warning, and if the same vessel shall again attempt to enter or leave the blockaded port she will be captured and sent to the nearest convenient port for such proceedings against her and her cargo as prize as may be deemed advisable.

And I hereby proclaim and declare that if any person, under the pretended authority of the said States or under any other pretense, shall molest a vessel of the United States or the persons or cargo on board of her, such person will be held amenable to the laws of the United States for the prevention and punishment of piracy.

In witness whereof I have hereunto set my hand and caused the seal of the United States to be affixed.

[SEAL]   Done at the city of Washington, this 19th day of April, A.D. 1861, and of the Independence of the United States the eighty-fifth.

By the President: ABRAHAM LINCOLN.

WILLIAM H. SEWARD, *Secretary of State.*

3. 27th April, 1861

By the President of the United States
A Proclamation

Whereas, for the reasons assigned in my proclamation of the 19th instant, a blockade of the ports of the States of South Carolina, Georgia, Florida, Alabama, Louisiana, Mississippi, and Texas was ordered to be established; and

Whereas since that date public property of the United States has been seized, the collection of the revenue obstructed, and duly commissioned officers of the United States, while engaged in executing the orders or their superiors, have been arrested and held in custody as prisoners or have been impeded in the discharge of their official duties, without due legal process, by persons claiming to act under authorities of the State of Virginia and North Carolina, an efficient blockade of the ports of those States will also be established.

In witness whereof I have hereunto set my hand and caused the seal of the United States to be affixed.

[SEAL]   Done at the city of Washington, this 27th day of April, A.D. 1861, and of the Independence of the United States the eighty-fifth.

By the President: ABRAHAM LINCOLN.

WILLIAM H. SEWARD, *Secretary of State.*

4. 3rd May, 1861

By the President of the United States
A Proclamation

Whereas existing exigencies demand immediate and adequate measures for the protection of the National Constitution and the preservation of the National Union by the suppression of the insurrectionary combinations now existing in several States for opposing the laws of the Union and obstructing the execution thereof, to which end a military force in addition to that called forth by my proclamation of the 15th day of April in the present year appears to be indispensably necessary:

Now, therefore, I, Abraham Lincoln, President of the United States and Commander in Chief of the Army and Navy thereof and of the militia of the several States when called into actual service, do hereby call into the service of the United States 42,034 volunteers to serve for the period of three years, unless sooner discharged, and to be mustered into service as infantry and cavalry. The proportions of each arm and the details of enrollment and organization will be made known through the Department of War.

And I also direct that the Regular Army of the United States be increased by the addition of eight regiments of infantry, one regiment of cavalry, and one regiment of artillery, making altogether a maximum aggregate increase of 22,714 officers and enlisted men, the details of which increase will also be made known through the Department of War.

And I further direct the enlistment for not less than one or more than three years of 18,000 seamen, in addition to the present force, for the naval service of the United States. The details of the enlistment and organization will be made known through the Department of the Navy.

The call for volunteers hereby made and the direction for the increase of the Regular Army and for the enlistment of seamen hereby given, together with the plan of organization adopted for the volunteer and for the regular forces hereby authorized, will be submitted to Congress as soon as assembled.

In the meantime I earnestly invoke the cooperation of all good citizens in the measures hereby adopted for the effectual suppression of unlawful violence, for the impartial enforcement of constitutional laws, and for the speediest possible restoration of peace and order, and with these of happiness and prosperity, throughout our country.

In witness whereof I have hereunto set my hand and caused the seal of the United States to be affixed.

[SEAL]   Done at the city of Washington, this 3rd day of May,
A.D. 1861, and of the Independence of the United States
the eighty-fifth.

By the President: ABRAHAM LINCOLN.

WILLIAM H. SEWARD, *Secretary of State.*

5. 10th May, 1861

By the President of the United States
A Proclamation

Whereas an insurrection exists in the State of Florida by which the lives, liberty, and property of loyal citizens of the United States are endangered; and

Whereas it is deemed proper that all needful measures should be taken for the protection of such citizens and all officers of the United States in the discharge of their public duties in the State aforesaid:

Now, therefore, be it known that I, Abraham Lincoln, President of the United States, do hereby direct the commander of the forces of the United States on the Florida coast to permit no person to exercise any office or authority upon the islands of Key West, the Tortugas, and Santa Rosa which may be inconsistent with the laws and Constitution of the United States, authorizing him at the same time, if he shall find it necessary, to suspend there the writ of *habeas corpus* and to remove from the vicinity of the United States fortresses all dangerous or suspected persons.

In witness whereof I have hereunto set my hand and caused the seal of the United States to be affixed.

[SEAL]   Done at the city of Washington, this 10th day of May,
A.D. 1861, and of the Independence of the United States
the eighty-fifth.

By the President: ABRAHAM LINCOLN.

WILLIAM H. SEWARD, *Secretary of State.*

❧53❧

Cornerstone Speech

ALEXANDER STEPHENS

As Vice-President of the Confederacy, Alexander Stephens delivered this speech in Savannah, Georgia, on 21st March 1861. In it he praises the new constitution of the Confederacy, and justifies the institution of slavery in terms of a simple racist argument. He is adamant that the values of the Confederacy are in accordance with both higher and natural law, and that a recognition of racial differences should form the 'cornerstone' of its *raison d'être*. No official version of this impromptu speech exists, but an account was recorded and published in the *Savannah Republican* and that is the text used here.

At half past seven o'clock on Thursday evening, the largest audience ever assembled at the Athenaeum was in the house, waiting most impatiently for the appearance of the orator of the evening, Hon. A. H. Stephens, Vice-President of the Confederate States of America. The committee, with invited guests, were seated on the stage, when, at the appointed hour, the Hon. C. C. Jones, Mayor, and the speaker, entered, and were greeted by the immense assemblage with deafening rounds of applause.

The Mayor then, in a few pertinent remarks, introduced Mr. Stephens, stating that at the request of a number of the members of the convention, and citizens of Savannah and the State, now here, he had consented to address them upon the present state of public affairs.

Mr. Stephens rose and spoke as follows:

Mr. Mayor, and Gentlemen of the Committee, and Fellow-Citizens: For this reception you will please accept my most profound and sincere thanks. The compliment is doubtless intended as much, or more, perhaps, in honor of the occasion, and my public position, in connection with the great events now crowding upon us, than to me personally and individually. It is however none the less

Source: Alexander H. Stephens, speech as appeared in *Savannah Republican* and reprinted in H. Cleveland, *Alexander H. Stephens, in Public and Private: With Letters and Speeches, before, during, and since the War*, Philadelphia: National Publishing Co., 1866, pp. 717–29.

appreciated by me on that account. We are in the midst of one of the greatest epochs in our history. The last ninety days will mark one of the most memorable eras in the history of modern civilization.

[*There was a general call from the outside of the building for the speaker to go out, that there were more outside than in.*]

The Mayor rose and requested silence at the doors, that Mr. Stephens' health would not permit him to speak in the open air.

Mr. Stephens said he would leave it to the audience whether he should proceed indoors or out. There was a general cry indoors, as the ladies, a large number of whom were present, could not hear outside.

Mr. Stephens said that the accommodation of the ladies would determine the question, and he would proceed where he was.

[*At this point the uproar and clamor outside was greater still for the speaker to go out on the steps. This was quieted by Col. Lawton, Col. Freeman, Judge Jackson, and Mr. J. W. Owens going out and stating the facts of the case to the dense mass of men, women, and children who were outside, and entertaining them in brief speeches—Mr. Stephens all this while quietly sitting down until the furor subsided.*]

Mr. Stephens rose and said: When perfect quiet is restored, I shall proceed. I cannot speak so long as there is any noise or confusion. I shall take my time—I feel quite prepared to spend the night with you if necessary. [*Loud applause*] I very much regret that every one who desires cannot hear what I have to say. Not that I have any display to make, or any thing very entertaining to present, but such views as I have to give, I wish all, not only in this city, but in this State, and throughout our Confederate Republic, could hear, who have a desire to hear them.

I was remarking, that we are passing through one of the greatest revolutions in the annals of the world. Seven States have within the last three months thrown off an old government and formed a new. This revolution has been signally marked, up to this time, by the fact of its having been accomplished without the loss of a single drop of blood. [*Applause*]

This new constitution, or form of government, constitutes the subject to which your attention will be partly invited. In reference to it, I make this first general remark. It amply secures all our ancient rights, franchises, and liberties. All the great principles of Magna Charta are retained in it. No citizen is deprived of life, liberty, or property, but by the judgment of his peers under the laws of the land. The great principle of religious liberty, which was the honor and pride of the old constitution, is still maintained and secured. All the essentials of the old constitution, which have endeared it to the hearts of the American people, have been preserved and perpetuated. [*Applause*] Some changes have been made. Of these I shall speak presently. Some of these I should have preferred not to have seen made; but these, perhaps, meet the cordial approbation of a majority of this audience, if not an overwhelming majority of the people of the Confederacy. Of them, therefore, I will not speak. But other important changes do meet my cordial approbation. They form great improvements upon the old constitution. So, taking the whole new constitution, I have no hesitancy in giving it as my judgment that it is decidedly better than the old. [*Applause*]

Allow me briefly to allude to some of these improvements. The question of building up class interests, or fostering one branch of industry to the prejudice of another under the exercise of the revenue power, which gave us so much trouble under the old constitution, is put at rest forever under the new. We allow the imposition of no duty with a view of giving advantage to one class of persons, in any trade or business, over those of another. All, under our system, stand upon the same broad principles of perfect equality.

Honest labor and enterprise are left free and unrestricted in whatever pursuit they may be engaged. This subject came well nigh causing a rupture of the old Union, under the lead of the gallant Palmetto State, which lies on our border, in 1833. This old thorn of the tariff, which was the cause of so much irritation in the old body politic, is removed forever from the new. [*Applause*]

Again, the subject of internal improvements, under the power of Congress to regulate commerce, is put at rest under our system. The power claimed by construction under the old constitution, was at least a doubtful one—it rested solely upon construction. We of the South, generally apart from considerations of constitutional principles, opposed its exercise upon rounds of its inexpediency and injustice. Notwithstanding this opposition, millions of money, from the common treasury had been drawn for such purposes. Our opposition sprang from no hostility to commerce, or all necessary aids for facilitating it. With us it was simply a question, upon whom the burden should fall. In Georgia, for instance, we have done as much for the cause of internal improvements as any other portion of the country according to population and means. We have stretched out lines of railroads from the seaboard to the mountains; dug down the hills, and filled up the valleys at a cost of not less than twenty-five millions of dollars. All this was done to open an outlet for our products of the interior, and those to the west of us, to reach the marts of the world. No State was in greater need of such facilities than Georgia, but we did not ask that these works should be made by appropriations out of the common treasury. The cost of the grading, the superstructure, and equipments of our roads, was borne by those who entered on the enterprise. Nay, more—not only the cost of the iron, no small item in the aggregate cost, was borne in the same way—but we were compelled to pay into the common treasury several millions of dollars for the privilege of importing the iron, after the price was paid for it abroad. What justice was there in taking this money, which our people paid into the common treasury on the importation of our iron, and applying it to the improvement of rivers and harbors elsewhere?

The true principle is to subject the commerce of every locality, to whatever burdens may be necessary to facilitate it. If Charleston harbor needs improvement, let the commerce of Charleston bear the burden. If the mouth of the Savannah river has to be cleared out, let the sea-going navigation which is benefitted by it, bear the burden. So with the mouths of the Alabama and Mississippi river. Just as the products of the interior, our cotton, wheat, corn, and other articles, have to bear the necessary rates of freight over our railroads to reach the seas. This is again the broad principle of perfect equality and justice. [*Applause*] And it is especially set forth and established in our new constitution.

Another feature to which I will allude, is that the new constitution provides that cabinet ministers and heads of departments may have the privilege of seats upon the floor of the Senate and House of Representatives—may have the right to participate in the debates and discussions upon the various subjects of administration. I should have preferred that this provision should have gone further, and required the President to select his constitutional advisers from the Senate and House of Representatives. That would have conformed entirely to the practice in the British Parliament, which, in my judgment, is one of the wisest provisions in the British constitution. It is the only feature that saves that government. It is that which gives it stability in its facility to change its administration. Ours, as it is, is a great approximation to the right principle.

Under the old constitution, a secretary of the treasury for instance, had no opportunity, save by his annual reports, of presenting any scheme or plan of finance or other matter. He had no opportunity of explaining, expounding, inforcing, or defending his views of policy; his only resort was through the medium of an organ. In the British parliament, the premier brings in his budget and stands before the nation responsible for its every item. If it is indefensible, he falls before the attacks upon it, as he ought to. This will now be the case to a limited extent under our system. In the new constitution, provision has been made by which our heads of departments can speak for themselves and the administration, in behalf of its entire policy, without resorting to the indirect and highly objectionable medium of a newspaper. It is to be greatly hoped that under our system we shall never have what is known as a government organ. [*Rapturous applause*]

[*A noise again arose from the clamor of the crowd outside, who wished to hear Mr. Stephens, and for some moments interrupted him. The mayor rose and called on the police to preserve order. Quiet being restored, Mr. S. proceeded.*]

Another change in the constitution relates to the length of the tenure of the presidential office. In the new constitution it is six years instead of four, and the President rendered ineligible for a re-election. This is certainly a decidedly conservative change. It will remove from the incumbent all temptation to use his office or exert the powers confided to him for any objects of personal ambition. The only incentive to that higher ambition which should move and actuate one holding such high trusts in his hands, will be the good of the people, the advancement, prosperity, happiness, safety, honor, and true glory of the confederacy. [*Applause*]

But not to be tedious in enumerating the numerous changes for the better, allow me to allude to one other—though last, not least. The new constitution has put at rest, forever, all the agitating questions relating to our peculiar institution—African slavery as it exists amongst us—the proper status of the negro in our form of civilization. This was the immediate cause of the late rupture and present revolution.

Jefferson in his forecast, had anticipated this, as the "rock upon which the old Union would split." He was right. What was conjecture with him, is now a realized fact. But whether he fully comprehended the great truth upon which that rock stood and stands, may be doubted. The prevailing ideas entertained by him and most of the leading statesmen at the time of the formation of the old constitution, were that the enslavement of the African was in violation of the laws of nature; that it was wrong in principle, socially, morally, and politically. It was an evil they knew not well how to deal with, but the general opinion of the men of that day was that, somehow or other in the order of Providence, the institution would be evanescent and pass away. This idea, though not incorporated in the constitution, was the prevailing idea at that time. The constitution, it is true, secured every essential guarantee to the institution while it should last, and hence no argument can be justly urged against the constitutional guarantees thus secured, because of the common sentiment of the day. Those ideas, however, were fundamentally wrong. They rested upon the assumption of the equality of races. This was an error. It was a sandy foundation, and the government built upon it fell when the "storm came and the wind blew."

Our new government is founded upon exactly the opposite idea; its foundations are laid, its corner-stone rests upon the great truth, that the negro is not equal to the white man; that slavery—subordination to the superior race—is his natural and normal condition. [*Applause*] This, our new government, is the first, in the history of the world, based upon this great physical, philosophical, and moral truth. This truth has been slow in the process of its development, like all other truths in the various departments of science. It has been so even amongst us. Many who hear me, perhaps, can recollect well, that this truth was not generally admitted, even within their day. The errors of the past generation still clung to many as late as twenty years ago. Those at the North, who still cling to these errors, with a zeal above knowledge, we justly denominate fanatics. All fanaticism springs from an aberration of the mind—from a defect in reasoning. It is a species of insanity. One of the most striking characteristics of insanity, in many instances, is forming correct conclusions from fancied or erroneous premises; so with the anti-slavery fanatics; their conclusions are right if their premises were. They assume that the negro is equal, and hence conclude that he is entitled to equal privileges and rights with the white man. If their premises were correct, their conclusions would be logical and just—but their premise being wrong, their whole argument fails. I recollect once of having heard a gentleman from one of the northern States, of great power and ability, announce in the House of Representatives, with imposing effect, that we of the South would be compelled, ultimately, to yield upon this subject of slavery, that it was as impossible to war successfully against a principle in politics, as it was in physics or mechanics. That the principle would ultimately prevail. That we, in maintaining slavery as it exists with us, were warring against a principle, a principle founded in nature, the principle of the equality of men. The reply I made to him was, that upon his own grounds, we should, ultimately, succeed, and that he and his associates, in this crusade against our institutions, would ultimately fail. The

610

truth announced, that it was as impossible to war successfully against a principle in politics as it was in physics and mechanics, I admitted; but told him that it was he, and those acting with him, who were warring against a principle. They were attempting to make things equal which the Creator had made unequal.

In the conflict thus far, success has been on our side, complete throughout the length and breadth of the Confederate States. It is upon this, as I have stated, our social fabric is firmly planted; and I cannot permit myself to doubt the ultimate success of a full recognition of this principle throughout the civilized and enlightened world.

As I have stated, the truth of this principle may be slow in development, as all truths are and ever have been, in the various branches of science. It was so with the principles announced by Galileo—it was so with Adam Smith and his principles of political economy. It was so with Harvey, and his theory of the circulation of the blood. It is stated that not a single one of the medical profession, living at the time of the announcement of the truths made by him, admitted them. Now, they are universally acknowledged.

May we not, therefore, look with confidence to the ultimate universal acknowledgment of the truths upon which our system rests? It is the first government ever instituted upon the principles in strict conformity to nature, and the ordination of Providence, in furnishing the materials of human society. Many governments have been founded upon the principle of the subordination and serfdom of certain classes of the same race; such were and are in violation of the laws of nature. Our system commits no such violation of nature's laws. With us, all of the white race, however high or low, rich or poor, are equal in the eye of the law. Not so with the negro. Subordination is his place. He, by nature, or by the curse against Canaan, is fitted for that condition which he occupies in our system. The architect, in the construction of buildings, lays the foundation with the proper material—the granite; then comes the brick or the marble. The substratum of our society is made of the material fitted by nature for it, and by experience we know that it is best, not only for the superior, but for the inferior race, that it should be so. It is, indeed, in conformity with the ordinance of the Creator. It is not for us to inquire into the wisdom of his ordinances, or to question them. For his own purposes, he has made one race to differ from another, as he has made "one star to differ from another star in glory."

The great objects of humanity are best attained when there is conformity to his laws and decrees, in the formation of governments as well as in all things else. Our confederacy is founded upon principles in strict conformity with these laws. This stone which was rejected by the first builders "is become the chief of the corner"— the real "corner-stone"—in our new edifice. [Applause]

I have been asked, what of the future? It has been apprehended by some that we would have arrayed against us the civilized world. I care not who or how many they may be against us, when we stand upon the eternal principles of truth, if we are true to ourselves and the principles for which we contend, we are obliged to, and must triumph. [Immense applause]

Thousands of people who begin to understand these truths are not yet completely out of the shell; they do not see them in their length and breadth. We hear much of the civilization and christianization of the barbarous tribes of Africa. In my judgment, those ends will never be attained, but by first teaching them the lesson taught to Adam, that "in the sweat of his brow he should eat his bread," [*Applause*] and teaching them to work, and feed, and clothe themselves.

But to pass on: Some have propounded the inquiry whether it is practicable for us to go on with the confederacy without further accessions? Have we the means and ability to maintain nationality among the powers of the earth? On this point I would barely say, that as anxiously as we all have been, and are, for the border States, with institutions similar to ours, to join us, still we are abundantly able to maintain our position, even if they should ultimately make up their minds not to cast their destiny with us. That they ultimately will join us—be compelled to do it—is my confident belief; but we can get on very well without them, even if they should not.

We have all the essential elements of a high national career. The idea has been given out at the North, and even in the border States, that we are too small and too weak to maintain a separate nationality. This is a great mistake. In extent of territory we embrace five hundred and sixty-four thousand square miles and upward. This is upward of two hundred thousand square miles more than was included within the limits of the original thirteen States. It is an area of country more than double the territory of France or the Austrian empire. France, in round numbers, has but two hundred and twelve thousand square miles. Austria, in round numbers, has two hundred and forty-eight thousand square miles. Ours is greater than both combined. It is greater than all France, Spain, Portugal, and Great Britain, including England, Ireland, and Scotland, together. In population we have upward of five millions, according to the census of 1860; this includes white and black. The entire population, including white and black, of the original thirteen States, was less than four millions in 1790, and still less in '76, when the independence of our fathers was achieved. If they, with a less population, dared maintain their independence against the greatest power on earth, shall we have any apprehension of maintaining ours now?

In point of material wealth and resources, we are greatly in advance of them. The taxable property of the Confederate States cannot be less than twenty-two hundred millions of dollars! This, I think I venture but little in saying, may be considered as five times more than the colonies possessed at the time they achieved their independence. Georgia, alone, possessed last year, according to the report of our comptroller-general, six hundred and seventy-two millions of taxable property. The debts of the seven confederate States sum up in the aggregate less than eighteen millions, while the existing debts of the other of the late United States sum up in the aggregate the enormous amount of one hundred and seventy-four millions of dollars. This is without taking into account the heavy city debts, corporation debts, and railroad debts, which press, and will continue to press, as a heavy incubus upon the resources of those States. These debts, added to others, make a sum total not much under five hundred millions of dollars. With such an area of territory as we have—with such an amount of population—with a climate and soil unsurpassed by any on the face of the earth—with such resources already at our command—with productions which control the commerce of the world-who can entertain any apprehensions as to our ability to succeed, whether others join us or not?

It is true, I believe I state but the common sentiment, when I declare my earnest desire that the border States should join us. The differences of opinion that existed among us anterior to secession, related more to the policy in securing that result by co-operation than from any difference upon the ultimate security we all looked to in common.

These differences of opinion were more in reference to policy than principle, and as Mr. Jefferson said in his inaugural, in 1801, after the heated contest preceding his election, there might be differences of opinion without differences on principle, and that all, to some extent, had been federalists and all republicans; so it may now be said of us, that whatever differences of opinion as to the best policy in having a co-operation with our border sister slave States, if the worst came to the worst, that as we were all co-co-operationists, we are now all for independence, whether they come or not. [*Continued applause*]

In this connection I take this occasion to state, that I was not without grave and serious apprehensions, that if the worst came to the worst, and cutting loose from the old government should be the only remedy for our safety and security, it would be attended with much more serious ills than it has been as yet. Thus far we have seen none of those incidents which usually attend revolutions. No such material as such convulsions usually throw up has been seen. Wisdom, prudence, and patriotism, have marked every step of our progress thus far. This augurs well for the future, and it is a matter of sincere gratification to me, that I am enabled to make the declaration. Of the men I met in the Congress at Montgomery, I may be pardoned for saying this, an abler, wiser, a more conservative, deliberate, determined, resolute, and patriotic body of men, I never met in my life. [*Great applause*]

⟨54⟩

Extracts from the
Staunton Spectator,
April 1861

The *Staunton Spectator*, a Virginia newspaper, offers another insight into the nature of the secession crisis. These extracts, from the critical month of April 1861, reflect an editorial line at the beginning of the month which is clearly anti-secessionist. As the state organised for war, the newspaper stood firmly behind mobilisation. The correspondence reprinted after April 15th shows the prevailing atmosphere of uncertainty and confusion. By the end of the month, however, the newspaper has firmly sided with the cause of the South.

---

1. *The Spectator,* April 2, 1861

Policy of the Border States

Having steadfastly adhered to the doctrine that civil war, or danger of constant collision between the Border, Free and Slave States, could only be averted by a peaceful settlement in the Union of our present troubles, and that it was really the interest of the Border Slave States to maintain their present relations with the Free States on our border, and with the whole Union if possible, we have deduced therefrom a difference between our condition and that of the Gulf States. Nothing that has occurred, therefore, has served to change or even shake the conviction, that we have interests in the Union that are paramount—interests that the Cotton States have not; and that therefore we should not rashly imperil them through any fancied identity of interest with the States that have left us for well or for woe, to work out our own destiny as best we may. We have maintained that it is neither our interest to go with them, nor really essential to our interest that we should. We are glad, therefore, to find so respectable a journal in one of the seceded States, as the *Milledgeville (Geo.) Recorder*, supporting the views we have advocated. In the issue of that journal of the 12th inst., we find the case thus strongly stated, as follows:

Source: The *Staunton Spectator*, April 1861.

"If the line of the Southern Confederacy touched that of the Free States, there being no law or treaty for the rendition of fugitives from labor between foreign Powers, the mischief would be such, practically, that a collision of arms would be unavoidable, unless the Slave States receded altogether from the claims on which they insisted while in the Union, of having their property returned to them under the plain behest of the Constitution and the acts of Congress to carry it into effect. In the simple matter of convenience and expediency, therefore, we believe that the Border States will be of more advantage in their present position to the Southern Confederacy, a wall of defence against Northern aggression, than if they were to become members of it, with all their frontier exposed to fanatical hatred and pillage. We should then have to try an experiment which otherwise we might be under the necessity of making with the Free States, and which no amount of wisdom or valor may contemplate with indifference. If slaves from the Border States are stolen or enticed away by the abolitionists, the game would become vastly interesting in the absence of any stipulations recognizing slaves as property, which we have reason to believe could never be obtained. Outrage would follow outrage in rapid succession, and on a scale of such magnitude that war would be the only mode of redress."

Ought not this candid avowal, from a source entitled to credit, induce the people of the Border Slave States to make every effort compatible with their honor (and we would not have them do more) to avert the catastrophe, before they rush into the vortex of secession? This word, with us, has a deeper signification than it can have in the Gulf States. We trust our people will do nothing rashly.

2. *The Spectator,* April 16, 1861

The Fruits of Secession Agitation.

On the 31st of January last, the Auditor of public Accounts reported that the present rate of taxation, which is forty cents on the hundred dollars' value of property, would yield a surplus of $225,884.57 per annum, which, if applied to the temporary debt created for the defence of the State, would, in less than five years, discharge it. This estimate of that officer was made upon the supposition that the annual increase in the value of property, as a basis and subject of taxation, would, during that period, equal the temporary decrease caused by our national difficulties. But the agitation of the question of secession, and the uncertainty in which the fate of the State has been and is still kept, has had the effect to decrease the value of property, and to increase the expenses of the State to such an extent, that the same officer reported on the 22nd of March that the rate of taxation should be increased the present year to a sum at least equal to sixty cents on every hundred dollars' value of property, and on every subject in the same proportion. This is an increase of fifty per cent. in our taxation. The people may well "groan, groan, GROAN," when they reflect that their taxes are to be increased fifty per cent., whilst their ability to pay has been diminished to an even greater degree. They will not have as much money to pay with, and will have fifty per cent. more to pay. When the people estimate what they have lost by the depreciation in the value of their property, and by the increase of their taxes, they will be able to form some idea of the cost to them of the agitation of the question of secession. They will then begin to realize the truth of what we have frequently told them—that secession, yea, even the contemplation of it, implies increased taxation. If the mere dim prospect and distant probability of secession, which at present exists, causes an increase of fifty per cent. in taxation, what would be the increase of taxation if the hopes of the secessionists should be realized?—"Worm-wood and gall" are sweet when compared with the bitterness of the fruits of secession.

3. *The Spectator,* April 23, 1861

Glorious "Old Augusta."

We feel proud of "Old Augusta"—her noble conduct challenges the admiration of all brave and patriotic citizens. She contains sons as patriotic as ever sacrificed their lives and fortunes for liberty, and as brave soldiers as were ever commanded by Caesar or Napoleon. Her citizens are the sons of brave and patriotic sires, and they have not degenerated. They are ready at all times to respond with alacrity to the call to arms, and are animated with a firm and determined spirit to strike till the last armed foe expires. When their State calls they hesitate not to strike

> For their altars and their fires,
> The green graves of their sires,
> God and their native land.

They in the same patriotic spirit which animated the "Father of his country," cherished a cordial and habitual attachment to the Union, and, with deep and heartfelt devotion, labored with all the earnestness of their natures to preserve it as it had been bequeathed to them by their ancestors. As long as there was a ray of hope, they stood firmly as the friends of the Union and the advocates of a just, honorable and peaceful settlement of all our national difficulties. When others despaired, they still hoped; when others yielded, they still stood firmly. They had the high moral courage to stand firmly where their convictions of patriotic duty commanded, though their motives were impeached and their loyalty distrusted by those who did not appreciate their noble characters.—But as soon as the last ray of hope had been extinguished, as soon as they had seen the President's proclamation, the herald of civil war, and heard the call to arms, they sprang to their feet, donned their military dress, shouldered their guns, bade their fathers and mothers, brothers and sisters a hurried and affectionate farewell, and marched with speed to the place of rendezvous. They did not stop to consider the consequences to themselves individually—they were willing to sacrifice all they possessed—their lives and fortunes—in defence of their native State. Many left their families almost entirely unprovided for—there was no time to consider individual interests when their State called for their services. Some left sick wives and children, and some sick fathers and mothers, brothers and sisters. It was almost enough to melt a heart of adamant to witness such scenes as were present just before the troops left this place. One would call upon his physician and say: "Doctor, my dear wife is sick, I hope you will attend her carefully." Another would say, "Doctor, I have left two sick children, and request you to see them daily." Another would say, "Doctor, my father is old and feeble, I fear I may never see him again, I desire you to keep him alive if you can till I return." Another would say, "Doctor, my dear mother is nearly heart-broken, I hope you will console her as much as possible."

The same patriotic fires which glowed in the bosoms of their noble ancestors, in 1776, burns brightly now upon the altars of the hearts of the brave and chivalric sons of Augusta. This county, we have no doubt, will send more soldiers to the field than any county in the State, though Rockingham and Rockbridge will nobly do their duty. These three adjoining Union counties, we venture to predict, will furnish more soldiers than any other three adjoining counties in the State. We feel convinced that all three of these strong Union counties will do their whole duty. We are sure that the brave and patriotic Union men of these counties will forgive those who, in ignorance of their true characters, charged them with being "submissionists" and "sympathisers with Black Republicanism," and hope that those who did so will have the candor and manliness to acknowledge that they wronged as brave and loyal citizens as ever breathed the air of freedom. Let all feelings of alienation and party spirit be buried, and all stand together in harmony and friendship as a band of affectionate brothers.—"United we stand, divided we fall." In "Union there is strength," in division there is weakness. Let all stand together. We are still for Union—a Union of brave and patriotic men for the defence of our State.

4. *The Spectator,* April 23, 1861

Action of the Town Council

The Town Council on Wednesday, the 17th inst., made an appropriation of $3,000 for the purchase of 100 fire-arms, equipments and ammunition, for the use of the "Home Guard" in Staunton, and $500, to be applied to the wants of the families of the soldiers who have been or will be called into service, and appointed a police of ten for each night till the May Court.

5. *The Spectator*, April 30, 1861

Correspondence.

"Your letter of yesterday . . ."

RICHMOND, April 19th, 1861.

My Dear Sir: Your letter of yesterday has been received. Before this you will have learned through the Press all that has occurred at Norfolk and at this place; but I cannot begin to give you a just conception of the excitement created; not only here, but throughout the whole Southern country, by the proclamation of the 15th, which, in many respects, may be regarded as the most unfortunate document that has ever issued from the Government. In the absence of that paper, this State could never have been carried out of the Union; with it, the Union party, and the Union feeling, has been almost entirely swept out of existence. You cannot meet with one man in a thousand who is not inflamed with a passion for war, and every one seems to regard the proclamation as a declaration of war for the subjugation of the entire South, and for the extermination of slavery; reason (with them on this point) would as soon arrest the motion of the Atlantic, as it would check the current of their passions.

When I saw you in Washington, some ten days since, I had the honor to lay before you and other members of the Cabinet, as well as before Mr. Lincoln himself, a plan for the settlement of our troubles, through the medium of a National Convention, to give to the seceded States leave to withdraw. I thought then, as I do now, that the plan then suggested was the only solution of the dreadful crisis which was upon us. Since that time, matters have assumed a far more frightful aspect, and I now venture to make one more effort to save the unnecessary effusion of brothers' blood; and, in the name of liberty, humanity, and Christianity, I implore you to give it your earnest and solemn deliberation.

I need hardly say that no man in this nation has held in higher appreciation the value of our blessed Union. No man has labored more freely for its loss than mine; [sic] no man can mourn more sorrowfully for its overthrow than I will. No man can condemn more severely the immediate causes that have so unnecessarily led us into this awful and terrible catastrophe than I do. Yet for the first time, after an entire night of sleepless reflection, when I prayed as I never prayed before for wisdom and strength to do my duty, my mind has been brought to the conclusion that a dissolution is an inevitable decree of fate.

I am satisfied that a contest on the part of the General Government, with its perfect military organization, powerful Naval forces, its command of the money, and its credit without limit, backed by eighteen or twenty millions of people, against eight millions without military organization, without naval forces, and without money or credit, is not likely to be of doubtful result in the end—but after that, what then? Can the Union be preserved on such terms, or would it be worth preserving if it could? After the best blood of the country has been shed in war, which has passion, prejudice, and unnatural but mutual hate for its foundation, intensified by the conflict, could the two sections ever be brought together as one people again?—and would it not require large standing armies, in constant active service, to conquer and maintain peace? And would not that end at last in a hateful, loathsome military despotism?

If I am right in all this, would not a peaceful separation, not as a military necessity, but as a triumph of reason, order, law, liberty, morality, and religion, over passion, pride, prejudice, hatred, disorder, and the force of the mob, be a far wiser and more desirable solution of the problem that such scenes as will result from a purely sectional warfare, (result as it may,) and from which the heart sickens, and the soul recoils with horror?

You may cut, maim, kill and destroy; you may sweep down battalions with your artillery; you may block up commerce with your fleets; you may starve out the thousands and tens of thousands of the enemies of the Government. You may overrun, but you cannot subjugate the United South; and if you could do all this, you could not do it without inflicting an equal amount of misery upon those who are its best friends, and who have stood as long as there was a plank to stand upon, by the side of the Union, the Constitution and the laws. Our streets may run red with blood; our dwellings may be leveled with the earth; our fields may be laid waste; our hearthstones may be laid desolate; and then at the last, what end has been gained? Why, the Government has exhibited its power which has never been questioned, but by the idle, the ignorant and the deluded, and for the display of which there will be abundant opportunities, without an effort now, of either side, to cut each other's throats!

So far from its being regarded as a betrayal of weakness by the other powers of the Globe, will it not be looked upon in the present emergency as an act of magnanimity and heroism on the part of the more powerful party to propose terms of peace? Let me, then, as a strong, devoted, unalterable friend of the Union, (if it could be maintained,)—let me as a conscientious and unchangeable opponent of the fatal heresy of secession, urge upon this Administration the policy of of issuing another proclamation, proposing a truce to hostilities, and the immediate assembling of a National Convention to recognize the Independence of such of the States as desire to withdraw from the Union, and make the experiment of separate Government, which it will not, as I think, take them long to discover is the most egregious error that man, in his hour of madness, ever committed.

In five years from this time the remaining United States would be stronger and more powerful than the thirty-four States were six months ago—and you will have a Government permanent and enduring for all time to come, to which all who seek an asylum from oppression may resort hereafter.

I will not undertake to speculate on the experiment of a Southern Republic;—my opinions on that subject are well defined, and too well understood to make it necessary that they should be canvassed here. Let it be tried, and let it work out its own salvation.

If this policy can be adopted, all I shall ask for myself, will be the privilege of retiring to some secluded spot, where I can live in peace, and mourn over the downfall of the best Government—wisely administered—with which man was ever blessed.

I could not willingly take up arms against a Union that I have been taught and accustomed to adore, as indispensable to my own liberties, and I never will raise my hand against my native State, although her arm has ever been against me and mine.

For God's sake, let me implore you to let wisdom, magnanimity, true courage and humanity prevail in your councils, and give peace to a distracted and disssevered country.

I write as one who feels that he is standing on the brink of the grave of all he has cherished on earth; my head is bowed down with grief over the madness that rules the hour, and I pray God to give the wisdom to know, and the strength to perform my duty, my whole duty to my country, my State, and my friends.

I am, with great respect, yours, &c.

Jno. M. Botts.

Hon. EDWARD BATES, Attorney General, &c.

Will you grant me the favor to lay this last effort to serve my country before the Cabinet at its first meeting? I appeal to you as a native son of Virginia to do it.

J. M. B.

Banking Office of A. Nicholas & Co.,
No. 70 Wall Street,
NEW YORK, 15th April, '61.

Col. J. M. McCUE,—Mt. Solon,—Dear Sir:—It is a long time since I had the pleasure of writing you of your health. I have been frequently informed by my friend Sibert who has been kind enough to advise me occasionally respecting Mt. Solon and yourself. We have in this city become highly excited by the news that Fort Sumter was fired into and taken by the troops of the Cotton States. The President's message, calling first for 75,000 troops and then increasing the demand to 175,000, has produced a profound and deep impression that we are about entering into an awful performance, the end of which no man can tell. The only hope now is, that Va. will stand firm by the Union and hold all the border States to the same line of policy—if she does, our misguided South Carolina friends can soon be brought to reason—if she does not, but goes to swell the triumphal car of secession, God knows the end. The universal sentiment here is, that if the Border States do go out, then the war must exterminate the cause which has created this contention. When I heard that South Carolina fired coolly and deliberately and wantonly upon our flag, I cried like a child, that our brothers should fire into us. If the men that did the deed could have seen the eyes that were dimmed, and the stout frames of strong men that shook when the news was received here, they would have wished that the earth had swallowed them up. The newspapers and office seekers have done their best to set the sections against each other. May God forgive them I can't!—My Dear Sir, will

Virginia secede? What is your opinion? Pray let me hear from you soon.

Yours,

A. Nicholas

Mt. Solon, 21st April, '61.

Mr. A. Nicholas,—Dear Sir: Yours of the 15th inst., came to hand a few days ago. Circumstances that have occurred since, have more than answered one of the interrogatories you ask with so much apparent feeling, "Has Virginia seceded?" She has not only seceded, but has on this morning, an army in the field, to defend our rights and institutions, that will carry terror to the hearts of those who vauntingly boast that they will "exterminate the cause," as you are pleased to term it, of all the difficulties between us. Could you, and the myrmidons of abolition, of agrarianism and all that is abominable in a free government, see, as I have had the opportunity within the past few days, the spirit of our people, your craven hearts would collapse within your cowardly carcasses. You who possess means to justify it, will send your hired mercenaries to overpower us, it may be. You may devastate our country, burn our towns, insult and abuse our women, but conquer us you can never do. When our brave and gallant sons are exterminated, if such could be, you will find our wives and daughters more than a match for all the Beechers, and Cheevers and Stowes and that damnable set that you have so long paid Court to, and encouraged, until you have brought this affliction upon the country.

You speak of our "institutions" being the cause of this war, and you will exterminate it forsooth. Let me tell you, sir, that it has been the misguided frenzy and folly and madness of your people, that has been the cause; and that people that has fattened and flourished upon the labor of this institution, and in your pharasaical and puritanical self-righteousness, after hoarding this wealth, would say to us, "stand aside, we are holier than thou," and cannot live under the same government with you. Let me say to you, sir, that the men of New York and New England who, in the war of 1812, could stand by with folded hands and see the flag of their country trailed and trampled in the dust, and convene themselves into a Hartford convention, and refuse to furnish men and means to defend their country and that flag from an insolent foreign foe, can with a very bad grace now shed tears, as you say you did, when you heard that flag was fired upon at Fort Sumter. Your damnable hypocrisy makes my blood boil, and in spite of myself, makes me pray that we may have the earnestly hoped for opportunity of meeting you in sight of the Potomac, and all those who, like you, have been shedding those crocodile tears, and there testing, in the sight of the ashes of the Father of his Country, your sincerity in defending that flag. But permit me to say, sir, that you will not be there. You, and those who think like you, will send as your personal representatives, the miserable mercenary foreigners, that you can gather up in your cities at $10 per month to do your fighting. Would to God it were otherwise, and we could meet you all in person, and your boasted Seventh Regiment besides, who have warmed at our firesides, slept under our roofs, shared our hospitality, and when it was in your interest to do so, have preached up your conservatism. But enough, sir, I have not patience to say more. In the hope I may meet you at Washington, (what I do not expect,)

I am, sir, yours.

J. Marshall McCue.

6. *The Spectator,* April 30, 1861

How Virginia was United.

We have no disposition, says the Lynchburg Virginian, to obtrude old party issues upon the people now, believing that everything of the kind should be deprecated and avoided. Our people are united, as they ought to be, in opposition to Black Republican oppression and tyranny. Yet, we occasionally hear some indiscreet persons reproaching those who were more reluctant to anticipate the issue now forced upon them by others—with being the authors of the mischief we are now suffering. Such persons assume—and it is the merest assumption—that if we had presented a united front in the beginning of the present troubles, there would have been no conflict. They forget that it was simply impossible to bring our people to that point, and that, if even a majority had been found willing to separate from the Union one month ago, a very large minority would have been restless and dissatisfied. The moral force of our action would have been impaired, if no worse consequence had ensued. But, by our patient efforts in behalf of the Union, compromise and peace, we forced Lincoln to a development of his policy, and such a development as has united us to a man. This is the best vindication that could be given of the wisdom of our policy. In confirmation of this view, we submit the following from the Richmond *Examiner*, a journal that lampooned the Convention and the Union men with unwonted severity.—the *Examiner* says:

> The bug-bear of civil war need not frighten no one [sic]. We are not engaged in Virginia civil war, and, thank heaven all danger of that most dreadful of human scourges is past. It almost reconciles us to the delay of the Convention.— That delay has made Virginia a unit—has made the whole South a unit. The natives of the South are leagued and confederated to repel Northern invasion, and establish Southern independence.

And the "delay" of the late Union men brought about this "league" and hearty confederation of Southern men. This shall be our consolation amidst all the sorrows that may await us.

622

ᛤ·55·ᛤ

Message on Constitutional Ratification: 29th April, 1861

JEFFERSON DAVIS

Two weeks after Lincoln's initial proclamation, which was interpreted in the South as a declaration of war, Jefferson Davis was able to announce that the Confederate constitution had been ratified: an important symbolic act that conferred a sense of political and legal legitimacy on the actions of the Southern states. Jefferson Davis's message was optimistic, and at the same time endeavoured to place the event in its historical context, relating it to the enduring issue of the south's position within the old federal union.

Gentlemen of the Congress:

It is my pleasing duty to announce to you that the Constitution framed for the establishment of a permanent Government for the Confederate States has been ratified by conventions in each of those States to which it was referred. To inaugurate the Government in its full proportions and upon its own substantial basis of the popular will, it only remains that it should be held for the designation of the officers to administer it. There is every reason to believe that at no distant day other States, identified in political principles and community of interests with those which you represent, will join this Confederacy, giving to its typical constellation increased splendor, to its Government of free, equal, and sovereign States a wider sphere of usefulness, and to the friends of constitutional liberty a greater security for its harmonious and perpetual existence. It was not, however, for the purpose of making this announcement that I have deemed it my duty to convoke you at an earlier day than that fixed by yourselves for your meeting. The declaration of war made against this Confederacy by Abraham Lincoln, the President of the United States, in his proclamation issued on the 15th day of the present month, rendered it necessary, in my judgment, that you should convene at

Source: Jefferson Davis, "Message on Constitutional Ratification," *Official Records of the Union and Confederate Armies*, Washington D.C.: Government Printing Office, 1880–1901, Series IV, Vol. I.

the earliest practicable moment to devise the measures necessary for the defense of the country. The occasion is indeed an extraordinary one. It justifies me in a brief review of the relations heretofore existing between us and the States which now unite in warfare against us and in a succinct statement of the events which have resulted in this warfare, to the end that mankind may pass intelligent and impartial judgment on its motives and objects. During the war waged against Great Britain by her colonies on this continent a common danger impelled them to a close alliance and to the formation of a Confederation, by the terms of which the colonies, styling themselves States, entered

> *severally* into a firm league of friendship with each other for their common defense, the security of their liberties, and their mutual and general welfare, binding themselves to assist each other against all force offered to or attacks made upon them, or any of them, on account of religion, sovereignty, trade, or any other pretense, whatever.

In order to guard against any misconstruction of their compact the several States made explicit declaration in a distinct article—that

> *each* State *retains* its sovereignty, freedom, and independence, and every power, jurisdiction, and right which is not by this Confederation *expressly delegated* to the United States in Congress assembled.

Under this contract of alliance, the war of the Revolution was successfully waged, and resulted in the treaty of peace with Great Britain in 1783, by the terms of which the several States were each by name recognized to be independent. The Articles of Confederation contained a clause whereby all alterations were prohibited unless confirmed by the Legislatures of every State after being agreed to by the Congress; and in obedience to this provision, under the resolution of Congress of the 21st of February, 1787, the several States appointed delegates who attended a convention

> for the *sole and express purpose* of revising the Articles of Confederation and reporting to Congress and the several Legislatures such alterations and provisions therein as shall, when agreed to in Congress *and confirmed by the States,* render the Federal Constitution adequate to the exigencies of Government and the preservation of the Union.

It was by the delegates chosen by the several States under the resolution just quoted that the Constitution of the United States was framed in 1787 and submitted to the several States for ratification, as shown by the seventh article, which is in these words:

> The ratification of the *conventions of nine States* shall be sufficient for the establishment of this Constitution *between the States* so ratifying the same.

I have italicized certain words in the quotations just for the purpose of attracting attention to the singular and marked caution with which the States endeavored in every possible form to exclude the idea that the separate and independent sovereignty of each State was merged into one common government and nation, and the earnest desire they evinced to impress on the Constitution its true character—that of a compact between independent States. The Constitution of 1787, having, however, omitted the clause already recited from the Articles of Confederation, which provided in explicit terms that each State retained its sovereignty and independence, some alarm was felt in the States, when invited to ratify the Constitution, lest this omission should be construed into an abandonment of their cherished principle, and they refused to be satisfied until amendments were added to the Constitution placing beyond any pretense of doubt the reservation by the States of all their sovereign rights and powers not expressly delegated to the United States by the Constitution.

Strange, indeed, it must appear to the impartial observer, but it is none the less true that all these carefully worded clauses proved unavailing to prevent the rise and growth in the Northern States of a political school which has persistently claimed that the government thus formed was not a compact between States, but was in effect a national government, set up above and over the States. An organization created by the States to secure the blessings of liberty and independence against foreign aggression, has been gradually perverted into a machine for their control of their domestic affairs. The creature has been exalted above its creators; the principals have been made subordinate to the agent appointed by themselves. The people of the Southern States, whose almost exclusive occupation was agriculture, early perceived a tendency in the Northern States to render the common government subservient to their own purposes by imposing burdens on commerce as a protection to their manufacturing and shipping interests. Long and angry controversies grew out of these attempts, often successful, to benefit one section of the country at the expense of the other. And the danger of disruption arising from this cause was enhanced by the fact that the Northern population was increasing, by immigration and other causes, in a greater ratio than the population of the South. By degrees, as the Northern States gained preponderance in the National Congress, self-interest taught their people to yield to ready assent to any plausible advocacy of their right as a majority to govern the minority without control. They learned to listen with impatience to the suggestion of any constitutional impediment to the exercise of their will, and so utterly have the principles of the Constitution been corrupted in the Northern mind that, in the inaugural address delivered by President Lincoln in March last, he asserts as an axiom, which he plainly deems to be undeniable, that the theory of the Constitution requires that in all cases the majority shall govern; and in another memorable instance the same Chief Magistrate did not hesitate to liken the relations between a State and the United States to those which exist between a county and the State in which it is situated and by which it was created. This is the lamentable and fundamental error on which rests the policy that has culminated in his declaration of war against these Confederate States. In addition to the long-continued and deep-seated resentment felt by the Southern States at the persistent abuse of the powers they had delegated to the Congress, for the purpose of enriching the manufacturing and shipping classes of the North at the expense of the South, there has existed for nearly half a century another subject of discord, involving interests of such transcendent magnitude as at all times to create the apprehension in the minds of many devoted lovers of the Union that its permanence was impossible. When the several States delegated certain powers to the United States Congress, a large portion of the laboring population consisted of African slaves imported into the colonies by the mother country. In twelve out of the thirteen States negro slavery existed, and the right of property in slaves was protected by law. This property was recognized in the Constitution, and provision was made against its loss by the escape of the slave. The increase in the number of slaves by further importation from Africa was also secured by a clause forbidding Congress to prohibit the slave-trade anterior to a certain date, and in no clause can there be found any delegation of power to the Congress authorizing it in any manner to legislate to the prejudice, detriment, or discouragement of the owners of that species of property, or excluding it from the protection of the Government.

The climate and soil of the Northern States soon proved unpropitious to the continuance of slave labor, whilst the converse was the case at the South. Under the unrestricted free intercourse between the two sections, the Northern States consulted their own interests by selling their slaves to the South and prohibiting slavery within their limits. The South were willing purchasers of a property suitable to their wants, and paid the price of the acquisition without harboring a suspicion that their quiet possession was to be disturbed by those who were inhibited not only by want of constitutional authority, but by good faith as vendors, from disquieting a title emanating from themselves. As soon, however, as the Northern States that prohibited African slavery within their limits had reached a number sufficient to give their representation a controlling voice in the Congress, a persistent and organized system of hostile measures against the rights of the owners of slaves in the Southern States was inaugurated and gradually extended. A continuous series of measures was devised and prosecuted for the purpose of rendering insecure the tenure of property in slaves. Fanatical organizations, supplied with money by voluntary subscriptions, were assiduously engaged in exciting amongst the slaves a spirit of discontent and revolt; means were furnished for their escape from their owners, and agents secretly employed to entice them to abscond; the constitutional provision for their rendition to their owners was first evaded, then openly denounced as a violation of conscientious obligation and religious duty; men were taught that it was a merit to elude, disobey, and violently oppose the execution of the laws enacted to secure the performance of the promise contained in the constitutional compact; owners of slaves were mobbed and even murdered in open day solely for applying to a magistrate for the arrest of a fugitive slave; the dogmas of these voluntary organizations soon obtained control of the Legislatures of many of the Northern States, and laws were passed providing for the punishment, by ruinous fines and long-continued imprisonment in jails and penitentiaries, of citizens of the Southern States who should dare ask aid of the officers of the law for the recovery of their property. Emboldened by success, the theater of agitation and aggression against the clearly expressed constitutional rights of the Southern States was transferred to the Congress; Senators and Representatives were sent to the common councils of the Nation, whose chief title to this distinction consisted in the display of a spirit of ultra fanaticism, and whose business was not "to promote the general welfare or insure domestic tranquillity," but to awaken the bitterest hatred against the citizens of the sister States by violent denunciation of their institutions; the transaction of public affairs was impeded by repeated efforts to usurp powers not delegated by the Constitution, for the purpose of impairing the security of property in slaves, and reducing those States which held slaves to a condition of inferiority. Finally a great party was organized for the purpose of obtaining the administration of the Government, with the avowed object of using its power for the total exclusion of the slave States from all participation in the benefits of the public domain acquired by all States in common, whether by conquest or purchase; of surrounding them entirely by States in which slavery should be prohibited; of thus rendering the property in slaves so insecure as to be comparatively worthless, and thereby annihilating in effect property worth thousands of millions of dollars. This party, thus organized, succeeded in the month of November last in the election of its candidate for the Presidency of the United States.

In the meantime, under the mild and genial climate of the Southern States and the increasing care and attention for the well-being and comfort of the laboring class, dictated alike by interest and humanity, the African slaves had augmented in number from about 600,000, at the date of the adoption of the constitutional compact, to upward of 4,000,000. In moral and social condition they had been elevated from brutal savages into docile, intelligent, and civilized agricultural laborers, and supplied not only with bodily comforts but with careful religious instruction. Under the supervision of a superior race their labor had been so directed as not only to allow a gradual and marked amelioration of their own condition, but to convert hundreds of thousands of square miles of the wilderness into cultivated lands covered with a prosperous people; towns and cities had sprung into existence, and had rapidly increased in wealth and population under the social system of the South; the white population of the Southern slave-holding States had augmented from about 1,250,000 at the date of the adoption of the Constitution to more than 8,500,000 in 1860; and the productions of the South in cotton, rice, sugar, and tobacco, for the full development and continuance of which the labor of African slaves was and is indispensable, had swollen to an amount which formed nearly three-fourths of the exports of the whole United States and had become absolutely necessary to the wants of civilized man. With interests of such overwhelming magnitude imperiled, the people of the Southern States were driven by the conduct of the North to the adoption of some course of action to avert the danger with which they were openly menaced. With this view the Legislatures of the several States invited the people to select delegates to conventions to be held for the purpose of determining for themselves what measures were best adapted to meet so alarming a crisis in their history. Here it may be proper to observe that from a period as early as 1798 there had existed in all of the States of the Union a party almost uninterruptedly in the majority based upon the creed that each State was, in the last resort, the sole judge as well of its wrongs as of the mode and measure of redress. Indeed, it is obvious that under the law of nations this principle is an axiom as applied to the relations of independent sovereign States, such as those which had united themselves under the constitutional compact. The Democratic party of the United States repeated, in its successful canvass in 1856, the declaration made in numerous previous political contests, that it would

> faithfully abide by and uphold the principles laid down in the Kentucky and Virginia resolutions of 1798, and in the report of Mr. Madison to the Virginia Legislature in 1799; and that it adopts those principles as constituting one of the main foundations of its political creed.

The principles thus emphatically announced embrace that to which I have already adverted—the right of each State to judge of and redress the wrongs of which it complains. These principles were maintained by overwhelming majorities of the people of all the States of the Union at different elections, especially in the elections of Mr. Jefferson in 1805, Mr. Madison in 1809, and Mr. Pierce in 1852. In the exercise of a right so ancient, so well established, and so necessary for self-preservation, the people of the Confederate States, in their conventions, determined that the wrongs which they had suffered and the evils with which they were menaced required that they should revoke the delegation of powers to the Federal Government which they had ratified in their several conventions. They consequently passed ordinances resuming all their rights as sovereign and independent States and dissolved their connection with the other States of the Union.

Having done this, they proceeded to form a new compact amongst themselves by new articles of confederation, which have been also ratified by the conventions of the several States with an approach to unanimity far exceeding that of the conventions which adopted the Constitution of 1787. They have organized their new Government in all its departments; the functions of the executive, legislative, and judicial magistrates are performed in accordance with the will of the people, as displayed not merely in a cheerful acquiescence, but in the enthusiastic support of the Government thus established by themselves; and but for the interference of the Government of the United States in this legitimate exercise of the right of a people to self-government, peace, happiness, and prosperity would now smile on our land. That peace is ardently desired by this Government and people has been manifested in every possible form. Scarce had you assembled in February last when, prior even to the inauguration of the Chief Magistrate you had elected, you passed a resolution expressive of your desire for the appointment of commissioners to be sent to the Government of the United States

> for the purpose of negotiating friendly relations between that Government and the Confederate States of America, and for the settlement of all questions of disagreement between the two Governments upon principles of right, justice, equity, and good faith.

It was my pleasure as well as my duty to co-operate with you in this work of peace. Indeed, in my address to you on taking the oath of office, and before receiving from you the communication of this resolution, I had said as a necessity, not a choice, we have resorted to the remedy of separation, and henceforth our energies must be directed to the conduct of our own affairs and the perpetuity of the Confederacy which we have formed. If a just perception of mutual interests shall permit us peaceably to pursue our separate political career my most earnest desire will have been fulfilled.

It was in furtherance of these accordant views of the Congress and the Executive that I made choice of three discreet, able, and distinguished citizens, who repaired to Washington. Aided by their cordial co-operation and that of the Secretary of State, every effort compatible with self-respect and the dignity of the Confederacy was exhausted before I allowed myself to yield to the conviction that the Government of the United States was determined to attempt the conquest of this people and that our cherished hopes of peace were unattainable.

On the arrival of our commissioners in Washington on the 5th of March they postponed, at the suggestion of a friendly intermediary, doing more than giving in formal notice of their arrival. This was done with a view to afford time to the President, who had just been inaugurated, for the discharge of other pressing official duties in the organization of his Administration before engaging his attention in the object of their mission. It was not until the 12th of the month that they officially addressed the Secretary of State, informing him of the purpose of their arrival, and stating, in the language of their instructions, their wish

to make to the Government of the United States overtures for the opening of negotiations, assuring the Government of the United States that the President, Congress, and people of the Confederate States earnestly desire a peaceful solution of these great questions; that it is neither their interest nor their wish to make any demand which is not founded on strictest justice, nor do any act to injure their late confederates.

To this communication no formal reply was received until the 8th of April. During the interval the commissioners had consented to waive all questions of form. With the firm resolve to avoid war if possible, they went so far even as to hold during that long period unofficial intercourse through an intermediary, whose high position and character inspired the hope of success, and through whom constant assurances were received from the Government of the United States of peaceful intentions; of the determination to evacuate Fort Sumter; and further, that no measure changing the existing status prejudicially to the Confederate States, especially at Fort Pickens, was in contemplation, but that in the event of any change of intention on the subject, notice would be given to the commissioners. The crooked paths of diplomacy can scarcely furnish an example so wanting in courtesy, in candor, and directness as was the course of the United States Government toward our commissioners in Washington. For proof of this I refer to the annexed documents marked ——, taken in connection with further facts, which I now proceed to relate.

Early in April the attention of the whole country, as well as that of our commissioners, was attracted to extraordinary preparations for an extensive naval and military expedition in New York and other Northern ports. These preparations commenced in secrecy, for an expedition whose destination was concealed, only became known when nearly completed, and on the 5th, 6th, and 7th of April, transports and vessels of war with troops, munitions, and military supplies sailed from Northern ports bound southward. Alarmed by so extraordinary a demonstration, the commissioners requested the delivery of an answer to their official communication of the 12th of March, and thereupon received on the 8th of April a reply, dated on the 15th of the previous month, from which it appears that during the whole interval, whilst the commissioners were receiving assurances calculated to inspire hope of the success of their mission, the Secretary of State and the President of the United States had already determined to hold no intercourse with them whatever; to refuse even to listen to any proposals they had to make, and had profited by the delay created by their own assurances in order to prepare secretly the means for effective hostile operations. That these assurances were given has been virtually confessed by the Government of the United States by its sending a messenger to Charleston to give notice of its purpose to use force if opposed in its intention of supplying Fort Sumter. No more striking proof of the absence of good faith in the conduct of the Government of the United States toward this Confederacy can be required than is contained in the circumstances which accompanied this notice. According to the usual course of navigation the vessels composing the expedition designed for the relief of Fort Sumter might be expected to reach Charleston Harbor on the 9th of April. Yet, with our commissioners actually in Washington, detained under assurances that notice should be given of any military movement, the notice was not addressed to them, but a messenger was sent to Charleston to give the notice to the Governor of South Carolina, and the notice was so given at a late hour on the 8th of April, the eve of the very day on which the fleet might be expected to arrive.

That this maneuver failed in its purpose was not the fault of those who contrived it. A heavy tempest delayed the arrival of the expedition and gave time to the commander of our forces at Charleston to ask and receive the instructions of this Government. Even then, under all the provocation incident to the contemptuous refusal to listen to our commissioners, and the tortuous course of the Government of the United States, I was sincerely anxious to avoid the effusion of blood, and directed a proposal to be made to the commander of Fort Sumter, who had avowed himself to be nearly out of provisions, that we would abstain from directing our fire on Fort Sumter if he would promise not to open fire on our forces unless first attacked. This proposal was refused and the conclusion was reached that the design of the United States was to place the besieging force at Charleston between the simultaneous fire of the fleet and the fort. There remained, therefore, no alternative but to direct that the fort should at once be reduced. This order was executed by General Beauregard with the skill and success, which were naturally to be expected from the well-known character of that gallant officer; and although the bombardment lasted but thirty-three hours our flag did not wave over its battered walls until after the appearance of the hostile fleet off Charleston. Fortunately, not a life was lost on our side and we were gratified in being spared the necessity of a useless effusion of blood, by the prudent caution of the officers who commanded the fleet in abstaining from the evidently futile effort to enter the harbor for the relief of Major Anderson.

I refer to the report of the Secretary of War, and the papers which accompany it, for further details of this brilliant affair. In this connection I cannot refrain from a well-deserved tribute to the noble State, the eminent soldierly qualities of whose people were so conspicuously displayed in the port of Charleston. For months they had been irritated by the spectacle of a fortress held within their principal harbor as a standing menace against their peace and independence. Built in part with their own money, its custody confided with their own consent to an agent who held no power over them other than such as they had themselves delegated for their own benefit, intended to be used by that agent for their own protection against foreign attack, they saw it held with persistent tenacity as a means of offense against them by the very Government which they had established for their protection. They had beleaguered it for months, felt entire confidence in their power to capture it, yet yielded to the requirements of discipline, curbed their impatience, submitted without complaint to the unaccustomed hardships, labors, and privations of a protracted siege; and when at length their patience was rewarded by the signal for attack, and success had crowned their steady and gallant conduct, even in the very moment of triumph they evinced a chivalrous regard for the feelings of the brave but unfortunate officer who had been compelled to lower his flag. All manifestations of exultation were checked in his presence. Their commanding general, with their cordial approval and the consent of his Government, refrained from imposing any terms that could wound the sensibilities of the commander of the fort. He was permitted to retire with the honors of war, to salute his flag, to depart freely with all his command, and was escorted to the vessel in which he embarked with the highest marks of respect from those against whom his guns had been so recently directed.

Not only does every event connected with the siege reflect the highest honor on South Carolina, but the forbearance of her people and of this Government from making any harsh use of a victory obtained under circumstances of such peculiar provocation attest to the fullest extent the absence of any purpose beyond securing their own tranquillity and the sincere desire to avoid the calamities of war. Scarcely had the President of the United States received intelligence of the failure of the scheme which he had devised for the re-enforcement of Fort Sumter, when he issued the declaration of war against this Confederacy which has prompted me to convoke you. In this extraordinary production that high functionary affects total ignorance of the existence of an independent Government, which, possessing the entire and enthusiastic devotion of its people, is exercising its functions without question over seven sovereign States, over more than 5,000,000 of people, and over a territory whose area exceeds over half a million of square miles. He terms sovereign States

combinations too powerful to be suppressed by the ordinary course of judicial proceedings or by the powers vested in the marshals by law.

He calls for an army of 75,000 men to act as a posse comitatus in aid of the process of the courts of justice in States where no courts exist whose mandates and decrees are not cheerfully obeyed and respected by a willing people. He avows that "the first service to be assigned to the forces called out" will be not to execute the process of courts, but to capture forts and strongholds situated within the admitted limits of this Confederacy and garrisoned by its troops; and declares that "this effort" is intended "to maintain the perpetuity of popular government." He concludes by commanding "the persons composing the combinations aforesaid," to wit, the 5,000,000 of inhabitants of these States, "to retire peaceably to their respective abodes within twenty days." Apparently contradictory as are the terms of this singular document, one point is unmistakably evident. The President of the United States called for an army of 75,000 men, whose first service was to be to capture our forts. It was a plain declaration of war which I was not at liberty to disregard because of my knowledge that under the Constitution of the United States the President was usurping a power granted exclusively to the Congress. He is the sole organ of communication between that country and foreign powers. The law of nations did not permit me to question the authority of the Executive of a foreign nation to declare war against this Confederacy. Although I might have refrained from taking active measures for our defense, if the States of the Union had all imitated the action of Virginia, North Carolina, Arkansas, Kentucky, Tennessee, and Missouri, by denouncing the call for troops as an unconstitutional usurpation of power to which they refused to respond, I was not at liberty to disregard the fact that many of the States seemed quite content to submit to the exercise of the power assumed by the President of the United States, and were actively engaged in levying troops to be used for the purpose indicated in the proclamation. Deprived of the aid of Congress at the moment I was under the necessity of confining my action to a call on the States for volunteers for the common defense, in accordance with the authority you had confided to me before your adjournment. I deemed it proper, further, to issue proclamation inviting application from persons disposed to aid our defense in private armed vessels on the high seas, to the end that preparations might be made for the immediate issue of letters of marque and reprisal which you alone, under the Constitution, have power to grant. I entertain no doubt you will concur with me in the opinion that in the absence of a fleet of public vessels it will be eminently expedient to supply their place by private armed vessels, so happily styled by the publicists of the United States "the militia of the sea," and so often and justly relied on by them as an efficient and admirable instrument of defense warfare. I earnestly recommend the immediate passage of a law authorizing me to accept the numerous proposals already received. I cannot close this review of the acts of the Government of the United States without referring to a proclamation issued by their President, under date of the 19th instant, in which, after declaring that an insurrection has broken out in this Confederacy against the Government of the United States, he announces a blockade of all the ports of these States, and threatens to punish as pirates all persons who shall molest any vessel of the United States under letters of marque issued by this Government. Notwithstanding the authenticity of this proclamation you will concur with me that it is hard to believe it could have emanated from a President of the United States. Its announcement of a mere paper blockade is so manifestly a violation of the law of nations that it would seem incredible that it could have been issued by authority; but conceding this to be the case so far as the Executive is concerned, it will be difficult to satisfy the people of these States that their late confederates will sanction its declarations—will determine to ignore the usages of civilized nations, and will inaugurate a war of extermination on both sides by treating as pirates open enemies acting under the authority of commissions issued by an organized government. If such proclamation was issued it could only have been published under the sudden influence of passion, and we may rest assured mankind will be spared the horrors of the conflict it seems to invite.

For the details of the administration of the different Departments I refer to the reports of the Secretaries, which accompany this message.

The State Department has furnished the necessary instructions for three commissioners who have been sent to England, France, Russia, and Belgium since your adjournment to ask our recognition as a member of the family of nations, and to make with each of those powers treaties of amity and commerce. Further steps will be taken to enter into like negotiations with the other European powers, in pursuance of your resolutions passed at the last session. Sufficient time has not yet elapsed since the departure of these commissioners for the receipt of any intelligence from them. As I deem it desirable that commissioners or other diplomatic agents should also be sent at an early period to the independent American powers south of our Confederacy, with all of whom it is our interest and earnest wish to maintain the most cordial and friendly relations, I suggest the expediency of making the necessary appropriations for that purpose. Having been officially notified by the public authorities of the State of Virginia that she had withdrawn from the Union and desired to maintain the closest political relations with us which it was possible at this time to establish, I commissioned the Hon. Alexander H. Stephens, Vice-President of the Confederate States, to represent this Government at Richmond. I am happy to inform you that he has concluded a convention with the State of Virginia by which that honored Commonwealth, so long and justly distinguished among her sister States, and so dear to the hearts of thousands of her children in the Confederate States, has united her power and her fortunes with ours and become one of us. This convention, together with the ordinance of Virginia adopting the Provisional Constitution of the Confederacy, will be laid before you for your constitutional action. I have satisfactory assurances from other of our late confederates that they are on the point of adopting similar measures, and I cannot doubt that ere you shall have been many weeks in session the whole of the slave-holding States of the late Union will respond to the call of honor and affection, and by uniting their fortunes with ours promote our common interests and secure our common safety.

In the Treasury Department regulations have been devised and put into execution for carrying out the policy indicated in your legislation on the subject of the navigation of the Mississippi River, as well as for the collection of revenue on the frontier. Free transit has been secured for vessels and merchandise passing through the Confederate States; and delay and inconvenience have been avoided as far as possible, in organizing the revenue service for the various railways entering our territory. As fast as experience shall indicate the possibility of improvement in these regulations no effort will be spared to free commerce from all unnecessary embarrassments and obstructions. Under your act authorizing a loan, proposals were issued inviting subscriptions for $5,000,000 and the call was answered by the prompt subscription of more than $8,000,000 by our own citizens, and not a single bid was made under par. The rapid development of the purpose of the President of the United States to invade our soil, capture our forts, blockade our ports, and wage war against us induced me to direct that the entire subscription should be accepted. It will now become necessary to raise means to a much larger amount to defray the expenses of maintaining our independence and repelling invasion. I invite your special attention to this subject, and the financial condition of the Government, with the suggestion of ways and means for the supply of the Treasury, will be presented to you in a separate communication.

To the Department of Justice you have confided not only the organization and supervision of all matters connected with the courts of justice, but also those connected with patents and with the bureau of public printing. Since your adjournment all the courts, with the exception of those of Mississippi and Texas, have been organized by the appointment of marshals and district attorneys and are now prepared for the exercise of their functions. In the two States just named the gentlemen confirmed as judges declined to accept the appointment and no nominations have yet been made to fill the vacancies. I refer you to the report of the Attorney-General and concur in his recommendation for immediate legislation, especially on the subject of patent rights. Early provision should be made to secure to the subjects of foreign nations the full enjoyment of their property in valuable inventions, and to extend to our own citizens protection, not only for their own inventions, but for such as may have been assigned to them or may hereafter be assigned by persons not alien enemies. The Patent-Office business is much more extensive and important than had been anticipated. The applications for patents, although confined under the law exclusively to citizens of our Confederacy, already average seventy per month, showing the necessity for the prompt organization of a bureau of patents.

The Secretary of War in his report and accompanying documents conveys full information concerning the forces—regular, volunteer, and provisional—raised and called for under the several acts of Congress—their organization and distribution; also an account of the expenditures already made, and the further estimates for the fiscal year ending the 18th of February, 1862, rendered necessary by recent events. I refer to his report also for a full history of the occurrences in Charleston Harbor prior to and including the bombardment and reduction of Fort Sumter, and of the measures subsequently taken for the common defense on receiving the intelligence of the declaration of war against us, made by the President of the United States. There are now in the field at Charleston, Pensacola, Forts Morgan, Jackson, St.

Philip, and Pulaski 19,000 men, and 16,000 are now en route for Virginia. It is proposed to organize and hold in readiness for instant action, in view of the present exigencies of the country, an army of 100,000 men. If further force should be needed, the wisdom and patriotism of Congress will be confidently appealed to for authority to call into the field additional numbers of our noble-spirited volunteers who are constantly tendering service far in excess of our wants.

The operations of the Navy Department have been necessarily restricted by the fact that sufficient time has not yet elapsed for the purchase or construction of more than a limited number of vessels adapted to the public service. Two vessels purchased have been named the Sumter and McRae, and are now being prepared for sea at New Orleans with all possible dispatch. Contracts have also been made at that city with two different establishments for the casting of ordnance—cannon shot and shell—with the view to encourage the manufacture of these articles, so indispensable for our defense, as at many points within our territory as possible. I call your attention to the recommendation of the Secretary for the establishment of a magazine and laboratory for preparation of ordinance stores and the necessary appropriation for that purpose. Hitherto such stores have usually been prepared at the navy-yards, and no appropriation was made at your last session for this object. The Secretary also calls attention to the fact that no provision has been made for the payment of invalid pensions to our own citizens. Many of these persons are advanced in life; they have no means of support, and by the secession of these States have been deprived of their claim against the Government of the United States. I recommend the appropriation of the sum necessary to pay those pensioners, as well as those of the Army, whose claims can scarcely exceed $70,000 per annum.

The Postmaster-General has already succeeded in organizing his Department to such an extent as to be in readiness to assume the direction of our postal affairs on the occurrence of the contingency contemplated by the act of March 15, 1861, or even sooner if desired by Congress. The various books and circulars have been prepared and measures taken to secure supplies of blanks, postage stamps, stamped envelopes, mail bags, locks, keys, &c. He presents a detailed classification and arrangement of his clerical force and asks for its increase. An auditor of the Treasury for this Department is necessary, and a plan is submitted for the organization of his bureau. The great number and magnitude of the accounts of this Department require an increase of the clerical force in the accounting branch in the Treasury. The revenues of this Department are collected and disbursed in modes peculiar to itself, and require a special bureau to secure a proper accountability in the administration of its finances. I call your attention to the additional legislation required for this Department; to the recommendation for changes in the law fixing the rates of postage on newspapers, periodicals, and sealed packages of certain kinds, and specially to the recommendation of the Secretary, in which I concur, that you provide at once for the assumption by him of the control of our entire postal service.

In the military organization of the States provision is made for brigadier and major generals, but in the Army of the Confederate States the highest grade is that of brigadier-general. Hence it will no doubt sometimes occur that where troops of the Confederacy do duty with the militia, the general selected for the command and possessed of the views and purposes of this Government will be superseded by an officer of the militia not having the same advantages. To avoid this contingency in the least objectionable manner I recommend that additional rank be given to the general of the Confederate Army, and concurring in the policy of having but one grade of generals in the Army of the Confederacy, I recommend that the law of its organization be amended so that the grade be that of general. To secure a thorough military education it is deemed essential that officers should enter upon the study of their profession at an early period of life and have elementary instruction in a military school. Until such school shall be established it is recommended that cadets be appointed and attached to companies until they shall have attained the age and have acquired the knowledge to fit them for the duties of lieutenants. I also call your attention to an omission in the law organizing the Army, in relation to military chaplains, and recommend that provision be made for their appointment.

In conclusion, I congratulate you on the fact that in every portion of our country there has been exhibited the most patriotic devotion to our common cause. Transportation companies have freely tendered the use of their lines for troops and supplies. The presidents of the railroads of the Confederacy, in company with others who control lines of communication with States that we hope soon to greet as sisters, assembled in convention in this city, and not only reduced largely the rates heretofore demanded for mail service and conveyance of troops and munitions, but voluntarily proffered to receive their compensation, at these reduced rates, in the bonds of the Confederacy, for the purpose of leaving all the resources of the Government at its disposal for the common defense. Requisitions for troops have been met with such alacrity that the numbers tendering their services have in every instance greatly exceeded the demand. Men of the highest official and social position are serving as volunteers in the ranks. The gravity of age and the zeal of youth rival each other in the desire to be foremost for the public defense; and though at no other point than the one heretofore noticed have they been stimulated by the excitement incident to actual engagement and the hope of distinction for individual achievement, they have borne what for new troops is the most severe ordeal—patient toil and constant vigil, and all the exposure and discomfort of active service, with a resolution and fortitude such as to command approbation and justify the highest expectation of their conduct when active valor shall be required in place of steady endurance. A people thus united and resolved cannot shrink from any sacrifice which they may be called on to make, nor can there be a reasonable doubt of their final success, however long and severe may be the test of their determination to maintain their birthright of freedom and equality as a trust which it is their first duty to transmit undiminished to their posterity. A bounteous Providence cheers us with the promise of abundant crops. The fields of grain which will within a few weeks be ready for the sickle give assurance of the amplest supply of food for man; whilst the corn, cotton, and other staple productions of our soil afford abundant proof that up to this period the season has been propitious. We feel that our cause is just and holy; we protest solemnly in the face of mankind that we desire peace at any sacrifice save that of honor and independence; we seek no conquest, no aggrandizement, no concession of any kind from the States with which we were lately confederated; all we ask is to be let alone; that those who never held power over us shall not now attempt our subjugation by arms. This we will, this we must, resist to the direst extremity. The moment that this pretension is abandoned the sword will drop from our grasp, and we shall be ready to enter into treaties of amity and commerce that cannot but be mutually beneficial. So long as this pretension is maintained, with a firm reliance on that Divine Power which covers with its protection the just cause, we will continue to struggle for our inherent right to freedom, independence, and self-government.

JEFFERSON DAVIS
Montgomery, April 29, 1861

⊰·56·⊱

Special Session Message

ABRAHAM LINCOLN

In this Independence Day message to Congress on 4th July 1861, Lincoln reviews the events of the first four months of his presidential term. He outlines his understanding of the South's position, and, interpreting their action as a rebellion, argues for the over-riding need to preserve the Union.

Fellow Citizens of the Senate and House of Representatives:
Having been convened on an extraordinary occasion, as authorized by the Constitution, your attention is not called to any ordinary subject of legislation.

At the beginning of the present Presidential term, four months ago, the functions of the Federal Government were found to be generally suspended within the several States of South Carolina, Georgia, Alabama, Mississippi, Louisiana, and Florida, excepting only those of the Post-Office Department.

Within these States all the forts, arsenals, dock-yards, custom-houses, and the like, including the movable and stationery property in and about them, had been seized, and were held in open hostility to this Government, excepting only Forts Pickens, Taylor, and Jefferson, on and near the Florida coast, and Fort Sumter, in Charleston Harbor, S.C. The forts thus seized had been put in improved condition; new ones had been built, and armed forces had been organized, and were organizing, all avowedly with the same hostile purpose.

The forts remaining in the possession of the Federal Government in and near these States were either besieged or menaced by warlike preparations, and especially Fort Sumter was nearly surrounded by well-protected hostile batteries, with guns equal in quality to the best of its own and outnumbering the latter as perhaps ten to one. A disproportionate share of the Federal muskets and rifles had somehow found their way into these States and had been seized to be used against the Government. Accumulations of the public revenue lying within them had been seized for the same object. The Navy was scattered in distant seas, leaving but a very small part of it within the immediate reach of the Government. Officers of the

Source: in James D. Richardson, ed., *A Compilation of the Messages and Papers of the Presidents*, New York: Bureau of National Literature, Inc., 1897, Vol. VII.

Federal Army and Navy had resigned in great numbers, and of those resigning a large proportion had taken up arms against the Government. Simultaneously, and in connection with all this, the purpose to sever the Federal Union was openly avowed. In accordance with this purpose an ordinance had been adopted in each of these States declaring the States, respectively, to be separated from the National Union. A formula for instituting a combined government of these States had been promulgated, and this illegal organization, in the character of Confederate States, was already invoking recognition, aid, and intervention from foreign powers.

Finding this condition of things and believing it to be an imperative duty upon the incoming Executive to prevent, if possible, the consummation of such an attempt to destroy the Federal Union, a choice of means to that end became indispensable. This choice was made and was declared in the inaugural address. The policy chosen looked to the exhaustion of all peaceful measures before a resort to any stronger ones. It sought only to hold the public places and property not already wrested from the Government and to collect the revenue, relying for the rest on time, discussion, and the ballot-box. It promised a continuance of the mails, at Government expense, to the very people who were resisting the Government, and it gave repeated pledges against any disturbance, to any of the people or any of their rights. Of all that which a President might constitutionally and justifiably do in such a case, everything was forborne without which it was believed possible to keep the Government on foot.

On the 5th of March (the present incumbent's first full day in office), a letter of Major Anderson, commanding at Fort Sumter, written on the 28th of February, and received at the War Department on the 4th of March, was, by that Department, placed in his hands. This letter expressed the professional opinion of the writer that reenforcements could not be thrown into that fort, within the time for his relief rendered necessary by the limited supply of provisions and with a view of holding possession of the same, with a force of less than 20,000 good and well-disciplined men. This opinion was concurred in by all the officers of his command, and their memoranda on the subject were made inclosures of Major Anderson's letter. The whole was immediately laid before Lieutenant-General Scott, who at once concurred with Major Anderson in opinion. On reflection, however, he took full time, consulting with other officers, both of the Army and the Navy, and at the end of four days came reluctantly, but decidedly, to the same conclusion as before. He also stated at the same time that no such sufficient force was then at the control of the Government or could be raised and brought to the ground within the time when the provisions in the fort would be exhausted. In a purely military point of view this reduced the duty of the Administration in the case to the mere matter of getting the garrison safely out of the fort.

It was believed, however, that to so abandon that position, under the circumstances, would be utterly ruinous; that the *necessity* under which it was to be done would not be fully understood; that by many it would be construed as a part of a *voluntary* policy; that at home it would discourage the friends of the Union, embolden its adversaries, and go far to ensure to the latter a recognition abroad;

that, in fact, it would be our national destruction consummated. This could not be allowed. Starvation was not yet upon the garrison, and ere it would be reached *Fort Pickens* might be reinforced. This last would be a clear indication of *policy* and would better enable the country to accept the evacuation of Fort Sumter as a military *necessity*. An order was at once directed to be sent for the landing of the troops from the steamship *Brooklyn* into Fort Pickens. This order could not go by land but must take the longer and slower route by sea. The first return news from the order was received just one week before the fall of Fort Sumter. The news itself was that the officer commanding the *Sabine*, to which vessel the troops had been transferred from the *Brooklyn*, acting upon some *quasi* armistice of the late Administration (and of the existence of which the present Administration, up to the time the order was dispatched, had only too vague and uncertain rumors to fix attention), had refused to land the troops. To now reinforce Fort Pickens before a crisis would be reached at Fort Sumter was impossible—rendered so by the near exhaustion of provisions in the latter-named fort. In precaution against such a conjuncture, the Government had a few days before commenced preparing a expedition, as well adapted as might be, to relieve Fort Sumter, which expedition was intended to be ultimately used or not, according to circumstances. The strongest anticipated case for using it was now presented, and it was resolved to send it forward. As had been intended, in this contingency, it was also resolved to notify the Governor of South Carolina that he might expect an attempt would be made to provision the fort, and that if the attempt should not be resisted there would be no effort to throw in men, arms, or ammunition, without further notice, or in case of an attack upon the fort. This notice was accordingly given, whereupon the fort was attacked and bombarded to its fall without even awaiting the arrival of the provisioning expedition.

It is thus seen that the assault upon and reduction of Fort Sumter was in no sense a matter of self-defense on the part of the assailants. They well knew that the garrison in the fort could by no possibility commit aggression upon them. They knew—they were expressly notified—that the giving of bread to the few brave and hungry men of the garrison was all which would on that occasion be attempted unless themselves, by resisting so much, should provoke more. They knew that this Government desired to keep the garrison in the fort, not to assail them, but merely to maintain visible possession, and thus to preserve the Union from actual and immediate dissolution, trusting, as herein-before stated, to time, discussion, and the ballot-box for final adjustment; and they assailed and reduced the fort for precisely the reverse object—to drive out the visible authority of the Federal Union and thus force it to immediate dissolution. That this was their object the Executive well understood, and having said to them in the inaugural address, "You can have no conflict without being yourselves the aggressors," he took pains not only to keep this declaration good, but also to keep the case so free from the power of ingenious sophistry as that the world should not be able to misunderstand it. By the affair at Fort Sumter, with its surrounding circumstances, that point was reached. Then and thereby the assailants of the Government began the conflict of arms, without a gun in sight or in expectancy to return their fire, save only the few in the fort sent to that harbor years before for their own protection and still ready to give that protection in whatever was lawful. In this act, discarding all else, they have forced upon the country the distinct issue, "Immediate dissolution or blood."

And this issue embraces more than the fate of these United States. It presents to the whole family of man the question whether a constitutional republic or democracy—a Government of the people, by the same people—can or cannot maintain its territorial integrity against its own domestic foes. It presents the question whether discontented individuals, too few in numbers to control administration, according to organic law, in any case, can always, upon the pretenses made in this case, or on any other pretenses, or arbitrarily without any pretense, break up their Government and thus practically put an end to free government upon the earth. It forces us to ask: "Is there, in all republics, this inherent and fatal weakness?" "Must a government, of necessity, be too *strong* for the liberties of its own people, or too *weak* to maintain its own existence?"

So viewing the issue, no choice was left but to call out the war power of the Government; and so to resist force employed for its destruction by force for its preservation.

The call was made, and the response of the country was most gratifying, surpassing in unanimity and spirit the most sanguine expectation. Yet none of the States commonly called slave States, except Delaware, gave a regiment through regular State organization. A few regiments have been organized within some others of those States by individual enterprise and received into the Government service. Of course the seceded States, so called (and to which Texas had been joined about the time of the inauguration), gave no troops to the cause of the Union. The border States, so called, were not uniform in their action, some of them being almost *for* the Union, while in others—as Virginia, North Carolina, Tennessee, and Arkansas— the Union sentiment was nearly repressed and silenced. The course taken in Virginia was the most remarkable, perhaps the most important. A convention elected by the people of that State to consider this very question of disrupting the Federal Union was in session at the capital of Virginia when Fort Sumter fell. To this body the people had chosen a large majority of *professed* Union men. Almost immediately after the fall of Sumter many members of that majority went over to the original disunion minority and with them adopted an ordinance for withdrawing the State from the Union. Whether this change was wrought by their great approval of the assault upon Sumter or their great resentment at the Government's resistance to that assault is not definitely known. Although they submitted the ordinance for ratification to a vote of the people to be taken on a day then somewhat more than a month distant, the convention and the Legislature (which was also in session at the same time and place), with leading men of the State not members of either, immediately commenced acting as if the State were already out of the Union. They pushed military preparations vigorously forward all over the State. They seized the U.S. Armory at Harper's Ferry and the navy-yard at Gosport, near Norfolk. They received—perhaps invited—into their State large bodies of troops with their warlike appointments from the so-called seceded States. They formally entered into a treaty of temporary alliance and co-operation with the so-called "Confederate States," and sent members to their Congress at Montgomery. And finally, they permitted the insurrectionary Government to be transferred to their capital at Richmond.

The people of Virginia have thus allowed this giant insurrection to make its nest within her borders, and this Government has no choice left but to deal with it *where* it finds it; And it has the less regret, as the loyal citizens have in due form claimed its protection. Those loyal citizens this Government is bound to recognize and protect as being Virginia.

In the border States, so-called—in fact, the middle States—there are those who favor a policy which they call "armed neutrality;" that is, an arming of those States to prevent the Union forces passing one way or the disunion the other over their soil. This would be disunion completed. Figuratively speaking, it would be the building of an impassable wall along the line of separation—and yet, not quite an impassable one, for under the guise of neutrality it would tie the hands of the Union men, and freely pass supplies from among them to the insurrectionists, which it could not do as an open enemy. At a stroke it would take all the trouble off the hands of secession, except only what proceeds from the external blockade. It would do for the disunionists that which of all things they most desire—feed them well and give them disunion without a struggle of their own. It recognizes no fidelity to the Constitution, no obligation to maintain the Union, and while very many who have favored it are doubtless loyal citizens it is nevertheless very injurious in effect.

Recurring to the action of the Government, it may be stated that at first a call was made for 75,000 militia, and rapidly following this a proclamation was issued for closing the ports of the insurrectionary districts by proceedings in the nature of blockade. So far all was believed to be strictly legal. At this point the insurrectionists announced their purpose to enter upon the practice of privateering.

Other calls were made for volunteers to serve for three years, unless sooner discharged, and also for large additions to the Regular Army and Navy. These measures, whether strictly legal or not, were ventured upon under what appeared to be a popular demand and a public necessity, trusting then, as now, that Congress would readily ratify them. It is believed that nothing has been done beyond the constitutional competency of Congress.

Soon after the first call for militia it was considered a duty to authorize the commanding general in proper cases according to his discretion, to suspend the privilege of the writ of *habeas corpus,* or in other words to arrest and detain, without resort to the ordinary processes and forms of law, such individuals as he might deem dangerous to the public safety. This authority has purposely been exercised but very sparingly. Nevertheless the legality and propriety of what has been done under it are questioned and the attention of the country has been called to the proposition that one who is sworn to "take care that the laws be faithfully executed" should not himself violate them. Of course some consideration was given to the questions of power and propriety before this matter was acted upon. The whole of the laws which were required to be faithfully executed were being resisted and failing of execution in nearly one-third of the States. Must they be allowed to finally fail of execution, even had it been perfectly clear that by the use of the means necessary to their execution some single law, made in such extreme tenderness of the citizen's liberty that practically it relieves more of the guilty than of the innocent, should to a very limited extent be violated? To state the question more directly, are all the laws *but one* to go unexecuted and the Government itself go to pieces lest that one be violated? Even in such a case would not the official oath be broken if the Government should be overthrown, when it was believed that disregarding the single law would tend to preserve it? But it was not believed that this question was presented. It was not believed that any law was violated. The provision of the Constitution that "the privilege of the writ of *habeas corpus* shall not be suspended unless when in cases of rebellion or invasion the public safety may require it," is equivalent to a provision— is a provision—that such privilege may be suspended when in cases of rebellion or invasion the public safety does require it. It was decided that we have a case of rebellion, and that the public safety *does* require the qualified suspension of the privilege of the writ which was authorized to be made. Now, it is insisted that Congress and not the Executive is vested with this power. But the Constitution itself is silent as to which, or who, is to exercise the power; and as the provision was plainly made for a dangerous emergency, it cannot be believed the framers of the instrument intended that in every case the danger should run its course until Congress could be called together, the very assembling of which might be prevented, as was intended in this case, by the rebellion.

No more extended argument is now offered, as an opinion at some length will probably be presented by the Attorney-General. Whether there shall be any legislation upon the subject, and if any, what, is submitted entirely to the better judgment of Congress.

The forbearance of this Government had been so extraordinary and so long continued as to lead some foreign nations to shape their action as if they supposed the early destruction of our national Union was probable. While this, on discovery, gave the Executive some concern, he is now happy to say that the sovereignty and rights of the United States are now everywhere practically respected by foreign powers, and a general sympathy with the country is manifested throughout the world.

The reports of the Secretaries of the Treasury, War, and the Navy will give the information in detail deemed necessary and convenient for your deliberation and action, while the Executive and all the Departments will stand ready to supply omissions or to communicate new facts considered important for you to know.

It is now recommended that you give the legal means for making this contest a short and a decisive one; that you place at the control of the Government for the work at least 400,000 men and $400,000,000. That number of men is about one-tenth of those of proper ages within the regions where apparently *all* are willing to engage, and the sum is less than a twenty-third part of the money value owned by the men who seem ready to devote the whole. A debt of $600,000,000 *now* is a less sum per head than was the debt of our Revolution when we came out of that struggle, and the money value in the country now bears even a greater proportion to what it was *then* than does the population. Surely each man has as strong a motive *now* to *preserve* our liberties as each had *then* to *establish* them.

A right result now will be worth more to the world than ten times the men and ten times the money. The evidence reaching us from the country leaves no doubt that the material for the work is abundant, and that it needs only the hand of legislation to give it legal sanction and the hand of the Executive to give it practical shape and efficiency. One of the greatest perplexities of the Government is to avoid receiving troops faster than it can provide for them. In a word, the people will save their Government if the Government itself will do its part only indifferently well.

It might seem at first thought to be of little difference whether the present movement at the South be called "secession" or "rebellion." The movers, however, well understand the difference. At the beginning they knew they could never raise their treason to any respectable magnitude by any name which implies *violation* of law. They knew their people possessed as much of moral sense, as much of devotion to law and order, and as much pride in and reverence for the history and Government of their common country as any other civilized and patriotic people. They knew they could make no advancement directly in the teeth of these strong and noble sentiments. Accordingly they commenced by an insidious debauching of the public mind. They invented an ingenious sophism, which, if conceded, was followed by perfectly logical steps through all the incidents to the complete destruction of the Union. The sophism itself is, that any State of the Union may, *consistently* with the national Constitution, and therefore *lawfully* and *peacefully*, withdraw from the Union without the consent of the Union or of any other State. The little disguise that the supposed right is to be exercised only for just cause, themselves to be the sole judge of its justice, is too thin to merit any notice.

With rebellion thus sugar coated, they have been drugging the public mind of their section for more than thirty years, and until at length they have brought many good men to a willingness to take up arms against the Government the day *after* some assemblage of men have enacted the farcical pretense of taking their State out of the Union, who could have been brought to no such thing the day *before.*

This sophism derives much, perhaps the whole, of its currency from the assumption that there is some omnipotent and sacred supremacy pertaining to a *State*—to each State of our Federal Union. Our States have neither more nor less power than that reserved to them in the Union by the Constitution—no one of them ever having been a State *out* of the Union. The original ones passed into the Union even *before* they cast off their British colonial dependence, and the new ones each came into the Union from a condition of dependence, excepting Texas; and even Texas in its temporary independence was never designated a State. The new ones only took the designation of States on coming into the Union, while that name was first adopted for the old ones in and by the Declaration of Independence. Therein the "United Colonies" were declared to be "free and independent States;" but even then the object plainly was not to declare their independence of *one another* or of the *Union,* but directly the contrary, as their mutual pledge and their mutual action before, at the time, and afterward, abundantly show. The express plighting of faith by each and all of the original thirteen in the Articles of Confederation, two years later, that the Union shall be perpetual is most conclusive. Having never been States, either in substance or in name, *outside* of the Union, whence this magical omnipotence of "State rights," asserting a claim of power to lawfully destroy the Union itself? Much is said about the "sovereignty" of the States, but the word even is not in the national Constitution, nor, as is believed, in any of the State constitutions. What is a "sovereignty" in the political sense of the term? Would it be far wrong to define it "a political community without a political superior?" Tested by this, no one of our States, except Texas, ever was a sovereignty; and even Texas gave up the character on coming into the Union, by which act she acknowledged the Constitution of the United States and the laws and treaties of the United States made in pursuance of the Constitution to be for her the supreme law of the land. The States have their status in the Union, and they have no other legal status. If they break from this they can only do so against law and by revolution. The Union, and not themselves separately, procured their independence and their liberty. By conquest or purchase the Union gave each of them whatever of independence and liberty it has. The Union is older than any of the States, and in fact it created them as States. Originally some dependent colonies made the Union, and in turn the Union threw off their old dependence for them and made them States, such as they are. Not one of them ever had a State constitution independent of the Union. Of course it is not forgotten that all the new States framed their constitutions before they entered the Union, nevertheless dependent upon and preparatory to coming into the Union.

Unquestionably the States have the powers and rights reserved to them in and by the national Constitution; but among these, surely, are not included all conceivable powers, however mischievous or destructive; but, at most, such only as were known in the world, at the time, as governmental powers; and certainly a power to destroy the Government itself had never been known as a governmental—as a merely administrative power. This relative matter of national power and State rights, as a principle, is no other than the principle of *generality* and *locality*. Whatever concerns the whole should be confined to the whole—to the General Government; while whatever concerns *only* the State should be left exclusively to the State. This is all there is of original principle about it. Whether the national Constitution, in defining boundaries between the two, has applied the principle with exact accuracy is not to be questioned. We are all bound by that defining, without question.

What is now combatted is the principle that secession is *consistent* with the Constitution—is *lawful* and *peaceful*. It is not contended that there is any express law for it; and nothing should ever be implied as law which leads to unjust or absurd consequences. The nation purchased, with money, the countries out of which several of these States were formed. Is it just that they shall go off without leave and without refunding? The nation paid very large sums (in the aggregate, I believe, nearly a hundred millions) to relieve Florida of the aboriginal tribes. Is it just that she shall now be off without consent, or without making any return? The nation is now in debt for money applied to the benefit of these so-called seceding States, in common with the rest. Is it just either that creditors shall go unpaid, or the remaining States pay the whole? A part of the present national debt was contracted to pay the old debts of Texas. Is it just that she shall leave and pay no part of this herself? Again, if one State may secede, so may another; and when all shall have seceded none is left to pay the debts. Is this quite just to creditors? Did we notify them of this sage view of ours when we borrowed their money? If we now recognize this doctrine by allowing the seceders to go in peace, it is difficult to see what we can do if others choose to go, or to extort terms upon which they will promise to remain.

The seceders insist that our Constitution admits of secession. They have assumed to make a national constitution of their own, in which, of necessity, they have either *discarded* or *retained* the right of secession, as, they insist, it exists in ours. If they have discarded it, they thereby admit that on principle it ought not to be in ours. If they have retained it by their own construction of ours, they show that to be consistent they must secede from one another whenever they shall find it the easiest way of settling their debts or effecting any other selfish or unjust object. The principle itself is one of disintegration and upon which no Government can possibly endure.

If all the States save one should assert the power to *drive* that one out of the Union, it is presumed the whole class of seceder politicians would at once deny the power and denounce the act as the greatest outrage upon States rights. But suppose that precisely the same act, instead of being called "driving the one out," should be called "the seceding of the others from that one," it would be exactly what the seceders claim to do; unless, indeed, they make the point that the one, because it is a minority, may rightfully do what the others, because they are a majority, may not rightfully do. These politicians are subtle and profound on the rights of minorities. They are not partial to the power which made the Constitution, and speaks from the preamble, calling itself "we, the people."

It may well be questioned whether there is to-day a majority of the legally qualified voters of any State, except, perhaps, South Carolina, in favor of disunion. There is much reason to believe that the Union men are the majority in many, if not in every other one, of the so-called seceded States. The contrary has not been demonstrated in any one of them. It is ventured to affirm this, even of Virginia and Tennessee; for the result of an election, held in military camps, where the bayonets are all on one side of the question voted upon, can scarcely be considered as demonstrating popular sentiment. At such an election all that large class who are, at once, *for* the Union and *against* coercion would be coerced to vote against the Union.

It may be affirmed, without extravagance, that the free institutions we enjoy have developed the powers and improved the condition of our whole people beyond any example in the world. Of this we now have a striking and an impressive illustration. So large an army as the Government has now on foot was never before known without a soldier in it but who had taken his place there of his own free choice. But more than this; there are many single regiments whose members, one and another, possess full practical knowledge of all the arts, sciences, professions, and whatever else, whether useful or elegant, is known in the world; and there is scarcely one from which there could not be selected a President, a Cabinet, a Congress, and perhaps a court abundantly competent to administer the Government itself. Nor do I say this is not true, also in the army of our late friends, now adversaries, in this contest; but if it is, so much better the reason why the Government which has conferred such benefits on them and us should not be broken up. Whoever, in any section, proposes to abandon such a Government would do well to consider in deference to what principle it is that he does it—what better he is likely to get in its stead—whether the substitute will give, or be intended to give, so much of good to the people. There are some foreshadowings on this subject. Our adversaries have adopted some declarations of independence, in which, unlike the good old one, penned by Jefferson, they omit the words "all men are created equal." Why? They have adopted a temporary national constitution, in the preamble of which, unlike our good old one, signed by Washington, they omit "We, the people," and substitute "We, the deputies of the sovereign and independent States." Why? Why this deliberate pressing out of view the rights of men and the authority of the people?

This is essentially a people's contest. On the side of the Union it is a struggle for maintaining in the world that form and substance of government whose leading object is to elevate the condition of men—to lift artificial weights from all shoulders; to clear the paths of laudable pursuit for all; to afford all an unfettered start and a fair chance in the race of life. Yielding to partial and temporary departures, from necessity, this is the leading object of the Government for whose existence we contend.

I am most happy to believe that the plain people understand and appreciate this. It is worthy of note that while in this, the Government's hour of trial, large numbers of those in the Army and Navy who have been favored with the offices have resigned and proved false to the hand which had pampered them, not one common soldier or common sailor deserted his flag,

Great honor is due to those officers who remained true, despite the example of their treacherous associates; but the greatest honor, and most important fact of all, is the unanimous firmness of the common soldiers and common sailors. To the last man, so far as known, they have successfully resisted the traitorous efforts of those whose commands but an hour before they obeyed as absolute law. This is the patriotic instinct of plain people. They understand, without an argument, that destroying the Government which was made by Washington means no good to them.

Our popular Government has often been called an experiment. Two points in it our people have already settled—the successful *establishing* and the successful *administering* of it. One still remains—its successful *maintenance* against a formidable internal attempt to overthrow it. It is now for them to demonstrate to the world that those who can fairly carry an election can also suppress a rebellion; that ballots are the rightful and peaceful successors of bullets; and that when ballots have fairly and constitutionally decided there can be no successful appeal back to bullets; that there can be no successful appeal except to ballots themselves, at succeeding elections. Such will be a great lesson of peace; teaching men that what they cannot take by an election, neither can they take it by a war; teaching all the folly of being the beginners of a war.

Lest there might be some uneasiness in the minds of candid men as to what is to be the course of the Government toward the Southern States after the rebellion shall have been suppressed, the Executive deems it proper to say, it will be his purpose then, as ever, to be guided by the Constitution and the laws; and that he probably will have no different understanding of the powers and duties of the Federal Government relatively to the rights of the States and the people, under the Constitution, than that expressed in the inaugural address.

He desires to preserve the Government, that it may be administered for all, as it was administered by the men who made it. Loyal citizens everywhere have the right to claim this of their Government; and the Government has no right to withhold or neglect it. It is not perceived that, in giving it, there is any coercion, any conquest, or any subjugation, in any just sense of those terms.

The Constitution provides, and all States have accepted the provision, that, "The United States shall guarantee to every State in this Union a republican form of government." But if a State may lawfully go out of the Union, having done so, it may also discard the republican form of government; so that to prevent its going out is an indispensable *means* to the *end* of maintaining the guaranty mentioned; and when an end is lawful and obligatory the indispensable means to it are also lawful and obligatory.

It was with the deepest regret that the Executive found the duty of employing the war power, in defense of the Government, forced upon him. He could but perform this duty or surrender the existence of the Government. No compromise by public servants could, in this case, be a cure; not that compromises are not often proper, but that no popular Government can long survive a marked precedent, that those who carry an election can only save the Government from immediate destruction by giving up the main point upon which the people gave the election. The people themselves, and not their servants, can safely reverse their own deliberate decisions.

As a private citizen the Executive could not have consented that these institutions shall perish; much less could he in betrayal of so vast and so sacred a trust as these free people had confided to him. He felt that he had no moral right to shrink, nor even to count the chances of his own life, in what might follow. In full view of his great responsibility he has, so far, done what he has deemed his duty. You will now, according to your own judgment, perform yours. He sincerely hopes that your views and your action may so accord with his as to assure all faithful citizens who have been disturbed in their rights of a certain and speedy restoration to them, under the Constitution and the laws.

And having thus chosen our course, without guile and with pure purpose, let us renew our trust in God, and go forward without fear and with manly hearts.

ABRAHAM LINCOLN
4th July, 1861